"The authors of *Core J2EE Patterns* have harvested a really useful set of patterns. They show you how to apply these patterns and how to refactor your system to take advantage of them. It's just like having a team of experts sitting at your side."

—Grady Booch, Chief Scientist, Rational Software Corporation, excerpted from Foreword

"This book is an excellent collection of patterns. [It] captures vital experience for J2EE development. Don't build an enterprise bean without it. [Additionally,] refactoring is increasingly the approach of choice for making changes to an existing system. The authors are the first group to extend my work on refactoring into a new direction—into the world of J2EE design. Not just am I grateful that someone has built on my earlier work, I'm glad they've used their experience to outline how to do these transformations."

–Martin Fowler, Chief Scientist, ThoughtWorks, excerpted from Foreword

"*Core J2EE Patterns* is the gospel that should accompany every J2EE application server. The book delivers a definitive, battle-tested pattern language, along with refactoring strategies, for designing, implementing, and maintaining healthy real-world J2EE applications. Built upon the in-the-trenches expertise of its veteran architect authors, this volume unites the platform's many technologies and APIs in a way that application architects can use, and provides insightful answers to the why's, when's, and how's of the J2EE platform."

—Sean Neville, JRun Enterprise Architect, Macromedia

"The authors do a great job describing useful patterns for application architectures. The section on refactoring is worth the price of the entire book!"

—Craig McClanahan, Struts Lead Architect

"With the maturity of J2EE, it is more important than ever to apply sound engineering principles to application design. *Core J2EE Patterns* is an invaluable guide for architects and analysts trying to decide their strategy for implementing enterprise applications on the J2EE platform. Common patterns for best practice are explored in detail, as well as ways to avoid bad designs."

—Craig Russell, JDO Architect

core J2EE™ PATTERNS

Best Practices and Design Strategies

Second Edition

DEEPAK ALUR
JOHN CRUPI
DAN MALKS

PEARSON
Education

ISBN 978-81-7758-671-8

First Impression, 2006
Second Impression, 2007
Third Impression, 2007
Fourth Impression, 2008
Fifth Impression, 2009

Published by Dorling Kindersley (India) Pvt. Ltd., licensees of Pearson Education in South Asia.

Head Office: 482, F.I.E., Patparganj, Delhi 110 092, India.
Registered Office: 14 Local Shopping Centre, Panchsheel Park, New Delhi 110 017, India.

Printed in India by Sheel Print N Pack.

To **Kavya, Shivaba, and Samiksha** –
For your endless support, love and inspiration.
– D.A.

To **Ellen and Rachel** –
For your support, understanding and love.
– J.C.

To **Beth, Sarah, and Jonathan** -
For your support and for bringing special meaning to everything in my life.
– D.M.

Contents

Foreword

In the world of software, a pattern is a tangible manifestation of an organization's tribal memory. A pattern provides a common solution to a common problem and so, within the culture of one specific organization or within one domain, naming and then specifying a pattern represents the codification of a common solution, drawn from proven, prior experience. Having a good language of patterns at your disposal is like having an extended team of experts sitting at your side during development: by applying one of their patterns, you in effect take the benefit of their hard-won knowledge. As such, the best patterns are not so much invented as they are discovered and then harvested from existing, successful systems. Thus, at its most mature state, a pattern is full of things that work, absent of things that don't work, and revealing of the wisdom and rationale of its designers.

Deep, really useful, patterns are typically ancient: you see one and will often remark, "Hey, I've done that before." However, the very naming of the pattern gives you a vocabulary that you didn't have previously and so helps you apply that pattern in ways you otherwise might have not have realized. Ultimately, the effect of such a pattern will be to make your system simpler.

Patterns not only help you build simpler systems that work, but they also help you build beautiful programs. In a culture of time starvation, writing beautiful software is often impossible. That's sad, for as professionals, we strive to build things of quality. By applying a good set of patterns, it is possible to bring a degree of elegance in to your systems that might otherwise have been lacking.

The authors of *Core J2EE Patterns* have harvested a really useful set of patterns. Don't get me wrong: J2EE is certainly an important platform, enabling teams to build some very powerful systems. However, reality is, there is still a wide semantic gap between the abstractions and services that J2EE provides and the final application that a team must build. Patterns such as specified in this book represent solutions that appear again and again in filling that gap. By applying these patterns, you thus carry out the primary means of reducing software risk: you write less software. Rather than discovering these solutions on your own, apply these patterns, which have already proven their utility in existing systems.

More than just naming a set of patterns, the authors make them approachable by specifying their semantics using the UML. Additionally, they show you how to apply these patterns and how to refactor your system to take advantage of them. Again, it's just like having a team of experts sitting at your side.

Grady Booch
Chief Scientist
Rational Software Corporation

Foreword

ThoughtWorks started to work with J2EE in late 1998. At that time, we found a lot of cool (if somewhat immature) technology, but with little guidance on how to use it well. We coped, partly because we had a lot of experience in other OO server environments. But we've seen many clients who've struggled, not because of problems in the technology—but due to not knowing how to use it well.

For many years, I've been a big fan of patterns as a way to capture design expertise—to catalog practical solutions to recurring problems. Over the last couple of years, various pioneers have been working with J2EE and uncovering the patterns that make for an effective J2EE solution. This book is an excellent collection of those patterns, capturing many of the techniques that we had to discover by trial and error.

That's why this book is important. Knowing the APIs backwards is one thing; knowing how to design good software is something else. This book is the first book I've seen that's really concentrated on capturing this design knowledge, and I'm relieved to see they've done a damned fine job of doing it. If you're working with J2EE you need to be aware of these patterns.

Furthermore, this book recognizes that design doesn't end when you start writing code. People make decisions that don't turn out that way. In this situation, you need to fix your design and you need to fix it in a disciplined way. Refactoring is increasingly the approach of choice for making changes to an existing system. The authors are the first group to extend my work on refactoring into a new direction—into the world of J2EE design. Not just am I grateful that someone has built on my earlier work, I'm glad they've used their experience to outline how to do these transformations.

In the end, it's that experience that counts. Capturing design experience in books is one of the hardest things to do, yet is so necessary for our profession to grow. This book captures vital experience for J2EE development. Don't build an enterprise bean without it.

Martin Fowler
Chief Scientist
ThoughtWorks

Preface

Since the time the first edition was published, we have received a tremendous amount of feedback on the original 15 patterns. The J2EE pattern community list server [JPCLS] has been very active and successful over the last few years with many brisk exchanges daily. During this time, we have also been involved in a number of significant large-scale J2EE architecture and development projects with our customers. The process of cultivating this experience and feedback into updating the original patterns and documenting the new ones has been laborious. We have specifically focused on the most requested elements of the feedback: support for recent versions of the J2EE technology specifications and web services.

The original 15 patterns have been completely revised and updated, and now cover J2EE 1.4. We have added many new strategies for the original patterns. We have also documented six new patterns that aim to improve the pattern language and provide you with abstractions you can use to build, understand, and use J2EE frameworks. While each of these patterns is itself immensely useful, we also believe that the patterns can be more powerful when combined to solve larger problems. In this edition, we introduce a new area we are pursuing called **micro-architectures**.

Micro-architectures are building blocks for building applications and systems. They represent a higher level of abstraction than the individual patterns described in the catalog, and are expressed by a combination of patterns linked to solve a problem that commonly recurs in application architectures.

We consider a micro-architecture to be a prescriptive solution put together as a network of related patterns, to solve a larger problem, such as designing a subsystem.

We have included a micro-architecture in this edition called *Web Worker. Web Worker* solves the problem of how to integrate a J2EE application with a workflow system. Specifically, it discusses the integration patterns involved in having a workflow system direct the users to interact with a J2EE application.

This book is about patterns for the Java 2 Platform, Enterprise Edition (J2EE). The J2EE patterns documented in this edition provide solutions for problems typically encountered by designers of software applications for the J2EE platform. All the patterns documented in the catalog have been discovered in the field, where they have been used to create successful J2EE applications for our customers.

This book describes proven solutions for the J2EE platform with a particular emphasis on such key J2EE technologies as: JavaServer Pages (JSP), servlets, Enterprise JavaBeans (EJB) components, Java Message Service (JMS), JDBC, and Java Naming and Directory Interface (JNDI). We offer solutions for recurring problems for the J2EE platform through the J2EE Pattern Catalog and J2EE refactorings. You can apply these ideas when developing new systems or when improving the design of existing systems. The patterns in this book will help you quickly gain the proficiency and skills to build robust, efficient enterprise applications.

Today, as in the past, many of us naively assume that **learning a technology** is synonymous with **learning to design** with the technology. Certainly learning the technology is an important part to being successful in designing with the technology. Many existing Java books are excellent at explaining technology details, such as API specifics and so forth, but at the same time they give no insight on applying the technology. Learning to design comes from experience and from sharing knowledge on best practices and bad practices.

The experiences we have conveyed in this book are derived from the work we have done in the field. We are part of Sun Microsystems, Inc.'s Sun Java Center (SJC) consulting organization. In our work, we often encounter situations where, because technology is moving so quickly, designers and developers are still struggling to understand the technology, let alone how to design with the technology.

It is not good enough to tell designers and developers to write good code, nor is it sufficient to suggest using servlets and JSP for developing the presentation tier and EJB components for developing the business tier.

So, given this scenario, where does an aspiring J2EE architect learn not only what to do, but what not to do? What are the best practices? What are the bad practices? How do you go from problem to design to implementation?

Sun Java Center and the J2EE Pattern Catalog

Since its inception, SJC architects have been working with clients all over the world to successfully design, architect, build, and deploy various types of systems based on Java and J2EE. The SJC is a rapidly growing consulting organization constantly adding new hires to its ranks of experienced architects.

Recognizing the need to capture and share proven designs and architectures, we started to document our work on the J2EE platform in the form of patterns in 1999. Although we looked in the existing literature, we could not find a catalog of patterns that dealt specifically with the J2EE platform. We found many books dealing with one or more of the J2EE technologies, and these books do an excellent job of explaining the technology and unraveling the nuances of the specifications. Some books offered extra help by providing some design considerations.

Since we first publicly presented our ideas on J2EE patterns at the JavaOne Conference in June 2000, we have received an overwhelming response from architects and developers. While some individuals expressed great interest in learning more about the patterns, others confirmed that they had applied the patterns, but had never named or documented them. This interest in patterns for the J2EE platform further motivated us to continue our work.

Thus, we put together the J2EE Pattern Catalog, which was initially made available to the entire J2EE community in beta form via the Java Developer Connection in March, 2001. Based largely on community feedback, the beta documentation evolved into the release you see in this book.

We hope these patterns, best practices, strategies, bad practices, and refactorings for the J2EE Platform provide the same benefits to you as they do for us.

What This Book Is About

This book is about:

- *Using patterns for the J2EE Platform.*
  Based on our collective J2EE platform experience, we have assembled the pattern catalog in this book. The J2EE Pattern Catalog describes various best practices related to architecting and designing applications for the J2EE platform. This book focuses on the following four J2EE technologies: servlets, JSP, EJB components, and JMS.
- *Using best practices to design applications that use JSP, Servlet, EJB components, and JMS technologies.*
  It is not sufficient to merely learn the technology and the APIs. It is equally important to learn to design with the technology. We have documented what we have experienced to be the best practices for these technologies.
- *Preventing re-inventing-the-wheel when it comes to design and architecture for the J2EE platform.*
  Patterns promote design reuse. Reusing known solutions reduces the cycle time for designing and developing applications, including J2EE applications.
- *Identifying bad practices in existing designs and refactoring these designs to move to a better solution using the J2EE patterns.*
  Knowing what works well is good. Knowing what does not work is equally important. We have documented some of the bad practices we have experienced when designing applications for the J2EE platform.

What This Book Is Not

This book is not about:

- *How to program with Java or J2EE technologies*
  This book is not about programming. While this book is heavily based on the J2EE technologies, we do not describe the specific APIs. If you wish to learn about programming using Java or using any of the J2EE technologies, there are a number of excellent books and online resources from which to learn. The online tutorials on the official Java home page

at http://java.sun.com are highly recommended if you wish to learn about individual technologies. The official specifications for J2EE technologies are also available from the Java home page.

- *What process and methodology to use*

  We do not suggest any type of process or methodology to use since the material presented in this book is not related to either. Hence, this book does not teach you about a process or methodology to follow in your projects. If you would like to learn more about processes and methodologies, there are a good number of books that deal with various object-oriented methodologies and new books on lightweight processes, such as Extreme Programming.

- *How to use Unified Modeling Language (UML)*

  This book is not going to teach you about UML. We use UML extensively (specifically class and sequence diagrams) to document the patterns and describe the static and dynamic interactions. If you want to learn more about UML, please refer to the "UML User Guide" [Booch] and the "UML Reference Manual" [Rumbaugh] by Grady Booch, Ivar Jacobson and James Rumbaugh.

Who Should Read this Book

This book is for all J2EE enthusiasts, programmers, architects, developers, and technical managers. In short, anyone who is remotely interested in designing, architecting and developing applications for the J2EE platform.

We have attempted to distinguish this book as a training guide for J2EE architects and designers. We all recognize the importance of good designs and well-architected projects, and that we need good architects to get there.

The use of well-documented patterns, best practices, and bad practices to share and transfer knowledge and experience can prove invaluable for teams with varied experience levels, and we hope that this book answers some of these needs.

How This Book Is Organized

This book is organized two parts.

Part 1

Part 1, "Patterns and J2EE" covers an introduction to J2EE and patterns. It deals with design considerations for JSP, servlets, and enterprise beans. This part also includes bad practices and refactorings for the J2EE platform.

Chapter 1: "Introduction" on page 6 is a brief discussion on various topics, including patterns, J2EE platform, defining a pattern, and pattern categorization. It ends by introducing the J2EE Pattern Catalog.

Chapter 2: "Presentation Tier Design Considerations and Bad Practices" on page 18 and Chapter 3 "Business Tier Design Considerations and Bad Practices" on page 44 discuss the design considerations and bad practices for the presentation tier and business/integration tiers respectively. The design considerations are issues that a J2EE developer/designer/architect needs to consider while working with the J2EE platform. The topics presented in these chapters point the reader to other sources (such as official specifications and well written books on these topics) for more detailed information on these issues.

Chapter 4: "J2EE Refactorings" on page 62 includes some of the refactorings we have experienced in our work in the field that has enabled us to move our design from a less optimal solution to a better solution. The refactorings provide another way to think about the material in the rest of the book, providing what we believe to be valuable companion material to the pattern catalog. This chapter shows how we have been influenced by Martin Fowler and his book "Refactoring" [Fowler]. For those readers who are familiar with the Refactoring book, the format of this chapter will be very familiar. However, the content of this chapter is entirely in the context of J2EE technologies, whereas Martin Fowler addresses refactoring at a different level.

Part 2

Part 2, "J2EE Pattern Catalog" presents the J2EE pattern catalog. The catalog contains the patterns that form the core of this book.

Chapter 5, "J2EE Patterns Overview" on page 117 provides an overview of the J2EE pattern catalog. This chapter begins with a high level discussion of the pattern ideas and explains the way the patterns are categorized into tiers. It also explains the J2EE pattern template, which is used to present all patterns in this book. The chapter discusses all the J2EE patterns and uses a diagram to show their inter-relationships. It also provides what we have termed a roadmap to the pattern catalog. This roadmap presents common J2EE design and architecture-related questions with references to patterns or refactorings that provide solutions to these questions. Understanding the pattern relationships and the roadmap is key to using these patterns.

Chapter 6, "Presentation Tier Patterns" on page 143 presents eight patterns that pertain to using servlets, JSP, JavaBeans, and custom tags to design web-based applications for the J2EE platform. The patterns describe numerous implementation strategies, and address common problems such as request handling, application partitioning, and generating composite displays.

Chapter 7, "Business Tier Patterns" on page 301 presents nine patterns that pertain to using EJB technology to design business components for the J2EE platform. The patterns in this chapter provide the best practices for using the EJB and JMS technologies. Where relevant, these patterns include discussion on other technologies, such as JNDI and JDBC.

Chapter 8, "Integration Tier Patterns" on page 461 presents four patterns that pertain to integrating J2EE applications with the resource tier and external systems. The patterns deal with using JDBC and JMS to enable integration between business tier and resource tier components.

"Web Worker Micro-Architecture" on page 581 discusses an advance topic of using multiple patterns to solve a larger problem. It specifically discusses the Web Worker micro-architecture which illustrates how to combine multiple patterns to integrate a J2EE application and a workflow system.

Companion Web Site and Contact Information

The official companion web site where we will provide updates and other material is:

http://www.corej2eepatterns.com

We are also listed under the Sun Java Blueprints site:

http://java.sun.com/blueprints/corej2eepatterns

You can email your comments, suggestions and feedback to the authors at:

j2eepatterns-feedback@sun.com

The J2EE Pattern community list server, j2eepatterns-interest@java.sun.com is available for public subscription and participation. To subscribe to the interest group and review the discussion archives, please visit:

http://archives.java.sun.com/archives/j2eepatterns-interest.html

Acknowledgments

We wish to thank Cheryln Chin, Vice President of Global Sun Software Services and James Baty, Distinguished Engineer and Sun Services Chief Architect, without whose support, vision, and belief in our work this effort would never have been realized.

We give our most thanks and gratitude to Rajmohan "Raj" Krishnamurthy. Without Raj, we wouldn't have many of our code samples or all his excellent review comments. He has been indispensible in helping us plan, develop, and review this edition.

We wish to express our thanks and gratitude to our expert reviewers for their insights, review comments, and feedback which contributed to making these patterns more clear and useful than they would have been otherwise: Martin Fowler, Chief Scientist, ThoughtWorks, Inc; Sean Brydon and Inderjeet Singh from the Sun J2EE BluePrints team; Craig Russel, Java Data Objects (JDO) Specification Lead/Product Architect, Sun Microsystems, Inc.; David Jordan, JDO Expert, ObjectIdentity, Inc.; Mark Roth, JSP Specification Lead, Sun Microsystems, Inc.; Eric Evans, Domain Language; Mario Kosmiskas, Solutions Architect, BEA Systems, Inc.; Brent Carlson, VP of Technology, LogicLibrary; Sean Neville, Macromedia, Inc.; Sameer Tyagi, Java Architect, Sun Java Center; Chris Steel; Bill Dudney; Gary Bollinger; and Gregor Hohpe, ThoughtWorks, Inc.

With a book like this, there are always countless contributions that make it possible and we couldn't possibly do justice to everyone.

We wish to thank the Sun Jackpot team led by James Gosling and Michael Van de Vanter for adopting and progressing *Core J2EE Patterns* into new arenas.

We also wish to thank eBay.com V3 team led by Chuck Geiger, and Ford Financials ATD Frameworks team led by Terry Bone, for adopting patterns into their organizations to build their next generation architecture and platforms.

We thank our colleagues from the Sun Java Center: Murali Kaundinya, Ashok Mollin, Ramesh Nagappan, and Heidi Schuster.

We wish to thank JetBrains, Inc. for providing IntelliJ IDEA which we enjoyed using to code the samples in this book.

We also wish to thank the many members of J2EE Pattern community list server (j2eepatterns-interest@sun.com) for the various discussions and feedback over the years.

A very special thank you to Solveig Haugland, our technical editor. She has been a vital part of this team. Her technical editing has contributed greatly to improving the final manuscript of this book.

We wish to thank Greg Doench and Debby Van Dijk from Prentice Hall for believing in us and promoting us.

Special thanks to sugar-free Red Bull for providing us the added lift to write 16 hours a day.

Acknowledgments – First Edition

We wish to thank Stu Stern, Director of Global Sun Java Center and Mark Bauhaus, VP of .COM Consulting without whose support, vision, and belief in our work this effort would never have been realized.

We wish to thank Ann Betser, without whose support, encouragement and skilled advice, we would have been lost.

We wish to express our sincere thanks to the PSA/iWorkflow reference implementation team of SJC architects: Fred Bloom, Narayan Chintalapati, Anders Eliasson, Kartik Ganeshan, Murali Kalyanakrishnan, Kamran Khan, Rita El Khoury, Rajmohan Krishnamurty, Ragu Sivaraman, Robert Skoczylas, Minnie Tanglao, and Basant Verma.

We wish to thank the Sun Java Center J2EE Patterns Working Group members: Mohammed Akif, Thorbiörn Fritzon, Beniot Garbinato, Paul Jatkowski, Karim Mazouni, Nick Wilde, and Andrew X. Yang.

We wish to thank Brendan McCarthy, SJC Chief Methodologist for keeping us in balance and for all the advice.

We wish to thank Jennifer Helms and John Kapson for introducing the patterns to customers.

We wish to express our gratitude to the following SJC architects from around the world for their support, feedback, and advice: Mark Cade, Mark Cao, Torbjörn Dahlén, Peter Gratzer, Bernard Van Haecke, Patricia de las Heras, Scott Herndon, Grant Holland, Girish Ippadi, Murali Kaundinya, Denys Kim, Stephen Kirkham, Todd Lasseigne, Sunil Mathew, Fred Muhlenberg, Vivek Pande, John Prentice, Alexis Roos, Gero Vermaas, Miguel Vidal.

We wish to thank our management Hank Harris, Dan Hushon, Jeff Johnson, Nimish Radia, Chris Steel, and Alex Wong for their support and encouragement.

We wish to thank the following Sun colleagues for their collaboration:

Bruce Delagi from Software Systems group; Mark Hapner, Vlada Matena from Java Software Engineering; Paul Butterworth and Jim Dibble from Forte Products Group; Deepak Balakrishna from iPlanet Products Group; Larry Freeman, Cori Kaylor, Rick Saletta, and Inderjeet Singh from the J2EE Blueprints Team; Heidi Dailey; Dana Nourie, Laureen Hudson, Edward Ort, Margaret Ong, and Jenny Pratt from Java Developer Connection.

We wish to thank the following for their feedback, advice, and support:

Martin Fowler and Josh Mackenzie from ThoughtWorks, Inc.; Richard Monson-Haefel; Phil Nosonowitz and Carl Reed from Goldman Sachs; Jack Greenfield, Wojtek Kozaczynski, and Jon Lawrence from Rational Software; Alexander Aptus from TogetherSoft; Kent Mitchell from Zaplets.com; Bill Dudney; David Geary; Hans Bergsten; Members of the J2EE Patterns Interest group (j2eepatterns-interest@java.sun.com).

We wish to express our special thanks and gratitude to our lead technical editor Beth Stearns, transforming our manuscripts and making them readable, at the same time keeping us on track, and working with us all the way with a heavily demanding schedule.

We wish to thank the technical editors Daniel S. Barclay, Steven J. Halter, Spencer Roberts, and Chris Taylor for their expertise, meticulous review and feedback.

We wish to thank Greg Doench, Lisa Iarkowski, Mary Sudul, and Debby Van Dijk from Prentice Hall; Michael Alread and Rachel Borden from Sun Microsystems Press, for doing everything it took to produce this book.

core J2EE™ PATTERNS

Best Practices and Design Strategies

Part 1

Patterns and J2EE

Part 1 includes the following chapters:

- Chapter 1—Introduction
- Chapter 2—Presentation Tier Design Considerations and Bad Practices
- Chapter 3—Business Tier Design Considerations and Bad Practices
- Chapter 4—J2EE Refactorings

When applying the patterns from the catalog, developers will need to consider numerous adjunct design issues, such as the ones discussed in these chapters. These include issues affecting numerous aspects of the system, including security, data integrity, manageability, and scalability.

Many of these design issues could be captured in pattern form, as well, although they primarily focus on issues at a lower level of abstraction than those described in the J2EE Pattern Catalog. Instead of documenting each as a pattern, we have chosen to document them more informally, simply describing each as a design issue to be considered when implementing systems based on the pattern catalog. While a complete discussion of each issue is outside the scope of this book, we wanted to mention these concerns, and encourage the reader to investigate these issues.

Chapter 1 presents a high-level discussion of patterns and J2EE. The chapter presents numerous pattern definitions, information on pattern categorization, and some benefits of using patterns. This chapter sets the context for our J2EE patterns work and provides the rationale and motivation behind the J2EE Pattern Catalog.

Chapters 2 and 3 highlight less than optimal ways to solve certain problems—solutions that we term **bad practices**. Each bad practice provides a brief problem summary accompanied by a list of solution references. The solution references are a list of pointers to other sections of the book with related material, suggesting preferred ways to solve these problems. Typically, these references are to a pattern in the catalog, to a refactoring, or to a combination of the two.

Chapter 4 presents refactorings for the J2EE Platform. The presentation format of this chapter is based on that in Martin Fowler's book Refactoring [Fowler], an excellent guide for those wishing to learn more about software design. Each refactoring identifies a simple problem and solution statement, offers motivations for improving the problem, and suggests mechanics for doing so.

Introduction

Topics in This Chapter

- What Is J2EE?
- What Are Patterns?
- J2EE Pattern Catalog
- Patterns, Frameworks, and Reuse

Chapter 1

The last five years have been extraordinary with respect to the changing landscape of enterprise software development. At the center of this change is the Java 2 Platform, Enterprise Edition (J2EE), which provides a unified platform for developing distributed, server-centric applications. The widespread adoption of the strategic, enabling technologies of J2EE have provided the development community with open standards on which to build service-based architectures for the enterprise.

At the same time, **learning** J2EE technologies is too often confused with learning to **design** with J2EE technologies. Many existing Java books do an excellent job of explaining specific aspects of the technology, but are not always clear on how to apply it.

J2EE architects need to understand more than just the relevant APIs. They need to understand issues like the following:

- What are the best practices?
- What are the bad practices?
- What are the common recurring problems and proven solutions to these problems?
- How is code refactored from a less optimal scenario, or bad practice, to a better one typically described by a pattern?

That is what this book is all about. Communicating these patterns using a standard pattern template makes them a powerful mechanism for communication exchange and reuse, and we can leverage them to improve the way we design and build software.

What Is J2EE?

J2EE is a platform for developing distributed enterprise software applications. Since the inception of the Java language, it has undergone tremendous adoption and growth. More and more technologies have become part of the Java platform, and new APIs and standards have been developed to address various needs. Eventually, Sun and a group of industry leaders, under the auspices of the open Java Community Process (JCP), unified all these enterprise-related standards and APIs in the J2EE Platform.

The J2EE Platform offers numerous advantages to the enterprise:

- J2EE establishes standards for areas of enterprise computing needs such as database connectivity, enterprise business components, message-oriented middleware (MOM), Web-related components, communication protocols, and interoperability.
- J2EE promotes best-of-breed implementations based on open standards, protecting technological investment.
- J2EE provides a standard platform for building software components that are portable across vendor implementations, avoiding vendor lock-in.
- J2EE decreases time to market because much of the infrastructure and plumbing is provided by the vendors' products, which are implemented according to the standard J2EE specification. IT organizations can now get out of the middleware business and concentrate on building applications for their business.
- J2EE increases programmer productivity, because Java programmers can relatively easily learn J2EE technologies based on the Java language. All enterprise software development can be accomplished under the J2EE platform, using Java as the programming language.
- J2EE promotes interoperability within existing heterogeneous environments.

What Is a Pattern?

Historical References

In the 1970s, Christopher Alexander [Alex, Alex2] wrote a number of books documenting patterns in civil engineering and architecture. The software community subsequently adopted the idea of patterns based on his work, though there was burgeoning interest in the software community in these ideas already.

Patterns in software were popularized by the book *Design Patterns: Elements of Reusable Object-Oriented Software* by Erich Gamma, Richard Helm, Ralph Johnson, and John Vlissides (also known as the Gang of Four, or GoF). Of course, while the Gang of Four work resulted in patterns becoming a common discussion topic in software development teams around the world, the important point to remember is that the patterns they describe were not invented by these authors. Instead, having recognized recurring designs in numerous projects, the authors identified and documented this collection.

Many software pattern books have been published since the GoF book, covering patterns for various domains and purposes. We provide references to a selected list of these titles and encourage you to investigate the other types of patterns described in these books.

Defining a Pattern

Patterns are about communicating problems and solutions. Simply put, patterns enable us to document a known recurring problem and its solution in a particular context, and to communicate this knowledge to others. One of the key elements in the previous statement is the word *recurring,* since the goal of the pattern is to foster conceptual reuse over time.

We explore this in more detail in Chapter 5, in the section "What Is a Pattern?" on page 118.

This well-known pattern definition comes from Christopher Alexander in *A Pattern Language* [Alex2]:

> Each pattern is a three-part rule, which expresses a relation between a certain context, a problem, and a solution.
>
> —*Christopher Alexander*

Alexander expands his definition further, and noted patterns figure Richard Gabriel [Gabriel] discusses this definition in more detail [Hillside]. Gabriel offers his own version of Alexander's definition as applied to software:

> Each pattern is a three-part rule, which expresses a relation between a certain context, a certain system of forces which occurs repeatedly in that context, and a certain software configuration which allows these forces to resolve themselves. [See A Timeless Way of Hacking.]
>
> —*Richard Gabriel*

This is a fairly rigorous definition, but there are also much looser ones. For example, Martin Fowler offers the following definition in *Analysis Patterns* [Fowler2]:

> A pattern is an idea that has been useful in one practical context and will probably be useful in others.
>
> —*Martin Fowler*

As you can see, there are many definitions for a pattern, but all these definitions have a common theme relating to the recurrence of a problem/solution pair in a particular context.

Some of the common characteristics of patterns are as follows:

- Patterns are observed through experience.
- Patterns are typically written in a structured format (see "Pattern Template" on page 129).
- Patterns prevent reinventing the wheel.
- Patterns exist at different levels of abstraction.
- Patterns undergo continuous improvement.
- Patterns are reusable artifacts.
- Patterns communicate designs and best practices.
- Patterns can be used together to solve a larger problem.

Many great minds have spent a significant amount of time attempting to define and refine the notion of a software pattern. Suffice it to say, we do not presume to be great minds, nor do we wish to spend time expanding these discussions. Instead, we attempt to be true to aspects of these various definitions, focusing on the most simple and recurring theme in each.

Categorizing Patterns

Patterns, then, represent expert solutions to recurring problems in a context and thus have been captured at many levels of abstraction and in numerous domains. Numerous categories have been suggested for classifying software patterns, with some of the most common being:

- Design patterns
- Architectural patterns
- Analysis patterns
- Creational patterns
- Structural patterns
- Behavioral patterns

Even this brief list of categories has numerous levels of abstraction and orthogonal classification schemes. Many taxonomies have been suggested, but there is no one right way to document these ideas.

We refer to the patterns in the catalog simply as **J2EE patterns**. Each pattern hovers somewhere between a design pattern and an architectural pattern, while the strategies document portions of each pattern at a lower level of abstraction. The only scheme we have introduced is to classify each pattern within one of the following three logical architectural tiers:

- Presentation tier
- Business tier
- Integration tier

At some point in the evolution of the pattern catalog, perhaps it will grow to a size that will warrant its being classified using a more sophisticated scheme. Currently, however, we prefer to keep things simple and not to introduce any new terms unnecessarily.

J2EE Pattern Catalog

Continuous Evolution

The J2EE patterns described in this book are based on our collective experience of working on the J2EE platform with Sun Services Java Center clients around the world. The Sun Services Java Center, a part of Sun Professional Services, is a consulting organization focused on building Java technology-based solutions for customers. We have been creating solutions for the J2EE platform since the platform's inception, focusing on achieving Quality of Service goals such as scalability, availability, and performance.

During the early days, as we designed, developed, and implemented various systems on the J2EE platform, we started documenting our experiences in an informal way as design considerations, ideas, and notes. As the knowledge base grew, we recognized a need for a slightly more formal documentation to capture and communicate this knowledge. We transitioned to documenting these ideas as patterns, since patterns are ideally suited to capturing and communicating knowledge related to recurring problems and solutions.

The first order of business was to sort out the level of abstraction with which the patterns were to be documented. Some problems and solutions overlapped others in that the core of the problem was the same, but the solution was implemented in a different manner. To address this overlap, we had to tackle the issue of the level of abstraction and the granularity with which we defined each pattern. As you will see in the J2EE pattern catalog, we eventually settled on a level of abstraction that hovers somewhere between design pattern and architectural pattern. The details related to the solutions that deal with implementation at a lower level of abstraction are addressed in the *Strategies* sections in our pattern template (see "Pattern Template" on page 129). This allows us to describe each pattern at a higher level of abstraction and at the same time discuss the implementation details.

Each pattern has been named and renamed many times. Additionally, each pattern has been rewritten many times, based on community feedback. Needless to say, these patterns, like all patterns, are subject to continuous improvement and will certainly evolve as the technology and specifications change.

The J2EE pattern catalog currently includes 21 patterns and is presented in Chapter 6, "Presentation Tier Patterns", Chapter 7, "Business Tier Patterns", and Chapter 8, "Integration Tier Patterns". Each pattern is documented in our pattern template.

Table 1-1 on page 13 lists the patterns included in the catalog.

Table 1-1 Patterns in the J2EE Pattern Catalog

Tier	*Pattern Name*
Presentation Tiers	*Intercepting Filter* (144) *Front Controller* (166) *Context Object* (181) *Application Controller* (205) *View Helper* (240) *Composite View* (262) *Service to Worker* (276) *Dispatcher View* (288)
Business Tier	*Business Delegate* (302) *Service Locator* (315) *Session Façade* (341) *Application Service* (357) *Business Object* (374) *Composite Entity* (391) *Transfer Object* (415) *Transfer Object Assembler* (433) *Value List Handler* (444)
Integration Tier	*Data Access Object (462)* *Service Activator (496)* *Domain Store (516)* *Web Service Broker (557)*

How to Use the J2EE Pattern Catalog

One of the challenges when using any set of patterns is understanding how to best use the patterns in combination. As Christopher Alexander says in his book, *A Pattern Language* [Alex2]:

> In short, no pattern is an isolated entity. Each pattern can exist in the world, only to the extent that is supported by other patterns: the larger patterns in which it is embedded, and the patterns of the same size that surround it, and the smaller patterns which are embedded in it.
>
> —Christopher Alexander

The patterns in the J2EE pattern catalog are no exception to this rule. The pattern relationships diagram, explained in Chapter 5, "J2EE Patterns Overview" describes how each pattern is supported by other patterns in the catalog. Chapter 5 also provides a roadmap to the J2EE pattern catalog, presented in tabular form, with common J2EE design and architecture-related questions paired with pattern or refactoring references, providing solutions to each question. To gain the maximum benefit from using these patterns, it is recommended that the pattern relationships and the pattern roadmap be well understood.

As you study each pattern in detail, you will see the patterns and strategies that are embedded within it, in which it is contained, and which it supports. Sometimes the pattern builds on other patterns from the J2EE pattern catalog or from other patterns described in well-known literature such as *Design Patterns: Elements of Reusable Object-Oriented Software* [GoF] or *Patterns of Software Architecture* [POSA1, POSA2].

In an attempt to aid you in further understanding the patterns, their interrelationships, pattern selection, and pattern usage, we have provided supporting chapters in Part 1. We present bad practices and refactorings for the J2EE platform. For each bad practice that has been listed in these chapters, we provide links to refactorings or patterns that offer solutions to alleviate the problems created by that bad practice. In the "J2EE Refactorings" chapter we present refactorings that describe the steps involved in moving from a less optimal solution to a preferred one. The mechanics section of each refactoring provides references to patterns and design considerations that influence the direction of the refactoring.

Finally, in the Epilogue we discuss new directions we are investigating in the area of **micro-architecture**. Micro-architectures are building blocks upon which we build applications and systems, representing a higher level of abstraction than the individuals patterns described in the catalog. We consider a micro-architecture to be a prescriptive solution put together as a network of related patterns, to solve a larger problem, such as designing a subsystem.

We selected the "Web Worker Micro-Architecture" on page 581 to demonstrate how to use a combination of J2EE patterns to integrate a J2EE application with a workflow system.

Benefits of Using Patterns

You can use the J2EE patterns in this book to improve your system design, and you can apply them at any point in a project life cycle. The patterns in the catalog are documented at a relatively high level of abstraction and will provide great benefit when applied early in a project. Alternatively, if you apply a pattern during the implementation phase, you might have to rework existing code. In this case, the refactorings in Chapter 4, "J2EE Refactorings" might prove quite useful.

What are the benefits of using patterns? We describe in the following sections some of the benefits of using and applying patterns in a project. In brief, patterns:

- Leverage a proven solution.
- Provide a common vocabulary.
- Constrain solution space.

Leverage a Proven Solution

The solution a pattern offers has been used over and over again to solve similar problems at different times in different projects. Thus, patterns provide a powerful mechanism for reuse, helping developers and architects to avoid reinventing the wheel.

Common Vocabulary

Patterns provide software designers with a common vocabulary. As designers, we use patterns not only to help us leverage and duplicate successful designs, but also to help us convey ideas to developers using a common vocabulary and format.

A designer who does not rely on patterns needs to expend more effort to communicate his design to other designers or developers. Software designers use the pattern vocabulary to communicate effectively. This is similar to the real world, where we use a common vocabulary to communicate and exchange ideas. Just as in the real world, developers can build their vocabulary by learning and understanding patterns, increasing their design vocabulary as new patterns are documented.

Once you start to use these patterns, you'll notice that you'll quickly begin to incorporate the pattern names into your vocabulary—and that you use the names of the patterns to replace lengthy descriptions. For example, suppose your problem solution entails use of a *Transfer Object* (415)pattern. At first, you might describe the problem without putting a label on it. You might describe the need for your application to exchange data with enterprise beans, the need to maximize performance given the network overhead with remote invocations, and so forth. Later, once you've learned how to apply the *Transfer Object* (415) pattern to the problem, you might refer to a similar situation in terms of a *Transfer Object* (415) solution and build from there.

To understand the impact of the pattern vocabulary, consider this exercise after you and another team member are familiar with the pattern catalog. Without using pattern names, try to explain what can be conveyed by simple sentences such as the following, in which the pattern names from the J2EE pattern catalog are italicized:

- We should use *Data Access Objects* (462) in our servlets and session beans.
- How about using *Transfer Object* (415) for transferring data to and from enterprise beans, and encapsulating all access to business services with *Business Delegate* (302)?
- Let's use a *Front Controller* (166) and *Service to Worker* (276). We might have to use *Composite View* (262) for some complex pages.

Constrains Solution Space

Pattern application introduces a major design component—constraints. Using a pattern constrains or creates boundaries within a solution space to which a design and implementation can be applied. Thus, a pattern strongly suggests to a developer boundaries to which an implementation might adhere. Going outside of these boundaries breaks the adherence to the pattern and design, and can lead to the unwanted introduction of an anti-pattern.

However, patterns do not stifle creativity. Instead, they describe a structure or shape at some level of abstraction. Designers and developers still have many options implementing the patterns within these boundaries.

Patterns, Frameworks, and Reuse

We have been chasing the illustrious software reuse goal for years now and have only had moderate success. In fact, most of the commercial reuse success has been in the user interface area, not in business components, which is our focus. As business system architects, we strive to promote reuse, but have really been concentrating on reuse at the design and architecture levels. The pattern catalog has proven a powerful way to promote this level of reuse.

There are numerous relationships among the patterns in the catalog, and these relationships are sometimes referred to as being part of a **pattern language**. We provide a diagram of these relationships in Figure 5.2 on page 132. Another way to describe these relationships is in terms of a **pattern framework**, or a collection of patterns in a united scenario. This concept is key to identifying end-to-end solutions and wiring components together at the pattern level. Micro-architecture leverages this idea and provides a broader basis for building solutions using a set of patterns.

Developers must understand more than discrete patterns in isolation, and have been asking for best practices as to how to link patterns together to form larger solutions. Combining the patterns from the catalog in this manner is what we refer to as **leveraging a J2EE pattern framework**. A framework, in this context, is about linking patterns together to form a solution to address a set of requirements. We think that this type of usage will drive the next generation of tools in J2EE development. Such automation of a pattern-driven process requires

- Identifying scenarios and offering patterns that apply to each tier.
- Identifying pattern combinations, or motifs, to provide pattern frameworks.
- Selecting implementation strategies for each role.

We provide a bit more information on this evolving area of development in the Epilogue on micro-architecture.

Summary

By now you should have a good understanding of what constitutes a pattern and what this book is all about. The next chapter discusses presentation tier design considerations and bad practices.

Presentation Tier Design Considerations and Bad Practices

Topics in This Chapter

- Presentation Tier Design Considerations
- Presentation Tier Bad Practices

Chapter 2

Presentation Tier Design Considerations

When developers apply the presentation patterns that appear in the catalog in this book, there will be adjunct design issues to consider. These issues relate to designing with patterns at a variety of levels, and they can affect numerous aspects of a system, including security, data integrity, manageability, and scalability. We discuss these issues in this chapter.

Although many of these design issues could be captured in pattern form, we chose not to do so because they focus on issues at a lower level of abstraction than the presentation patterns in the catalog. Rather than documenting each issue as a pattern, we have chosen to document them more informally: We simply describe each issue as one that you should consider when implementing systems based on the pattern catalog.

Session Management

The term **user session** describes a conversation that spans multiple requests between a client and a server. We rely on the concept of user session in the discussion in the following sections.

Session State on the Client

Saving session state on the client involves serializing and embedding the session state within the view markup HTML page that is returned to the client.

There are benefits to persisting session state on the client:

- It is relatively easy to implement.
- It works well when saving minimal amounts of state.

Additionally, this strategy virtually eliminates the problem of replicating state across servers in those situations that implement load balancing across physical machines.

There are two common strategies for saving session state on the client—HTML hidden fields and HTTP cookies—and we describe these strategies next. A third strategy entails embedding the session state directly into the URIs referenced in each page. The following line shows an example.

```
<form action=someServlet?var1=x&var2=y method=GET>
```

Although this third strategy is less common, it shares many of the limitations of the following two methods.

HTML Hidden Fields

Although it is relatively easy to implement this strategy, there are numerous drawbacks to using HTML hidden fields to save session state on the client. These drawbacks are especially apparent when saving large amounts of state. Saving large amounts of state negatively affects performance. Since all view markup now embeds or contains the state, it must traverse the network with each request and response.

Additionally, when you utilize hidden fields to save session state, the persisted state is limited to string values, so any object references must be "stringified". It is also exposed in clear text in the generated HTML source, unless specifically encrypted.

HTTP Cookies

As with the hidden fields strategy, it is relatively easy to implement the HTTP cookies strategy. This strategy unfortunately shares many of the same drawbacks. In particular, saving large amounts of state causes performance to suffer, because all the session state must traverse the network for each request and response.

We also run into size and type limitations when saving session state on the client. There are limitations on the size of cookie headers, and this limits the amount of data that can be persisted. Moreover, as with hidden fields, when you use cookies to save session state, the persisted state is limited to "stringified" values.

Security Concerns of Client-Side Session State

When you save session state on the client, security issues are introduced that you must consider. If you do not want your data exposed to the client, then you need to employ some method of encryption to secure the data.

Although saving session state on the client is relatively easy to implement initially, it has numerous drawbacks that take time and thought to overcome. For projects that deal with large amounts of data, as is typical with enterprise systems, these drawbacks far outweigh the benefits.

Session State in the Presentation Tier

When session state is maintained on the server, it is retrieved using a session ID and typically persists until one of the following occurs:

- A predefined session timeout is exceeded.

- The session is manually invalidated.
- The state is removed from the session.

Note: After a server shutdown, some in-memory session management mechanisms might not be recoverable.

It is clearly preferable for applications with large amounts of session state to save their session state on the server. When state is saved on the server, you are not constrained by the size or type limitations of client-side session management. Additionally, you avoid raising the security issues associated with exposing session state to the client, and you do not have the performance impact of passing the session state across the network on each request.

You also benefit from the flexibility offered by this strategy. By persisting your session state on the server, you have the flexibility to trade off simplicity versus complexity and to address scalability and performance.

If you save session state on the server, you must decide how to make this state available to each server from which you run the application. This issue is one that requires you to deal with the replication of session state among clustered software instances across load-balanced hardware, and it is a multidimensional problem. However, numerous application servers now provide a variety of out-of-the-box solutions. There are solutions available that are above the application server level. One such solution is to maintain a "sticky" user experience, where you use traffic management software, such as that available from Resonate [Resonate], to route users to the same server to handle each request in their session. This is also referred to as **server affinity**.

Another alternative is to store session state in either the business tier or the resource tier. Enterprise JavaBeans components can be used to hold session state in the business tier, and a relational database can be used in the resource tier. For more information on the business-tier option, please refer to "Using Session Beans" on page 46.

Controlling Client Access

There are numerous reasons to restrict or control client access to certain application resources. In this section, we examine two of these scenarios.

One reason to restrict or control client access is to guard a view, or portions of a view, from direct access by a client. This issue might occur, for example, when only registered or logged-in users should be allowed access to a particular view, or if access to portions of a view should be restricted to users based on role.

After describing this issue, we discuss a secondary scenario relating to controlling the flow of a user through the application. The latter discussion points out concerns relating to duplicate form submissions, since multiple submissions could result in unwanted duplicate transactions.

Guarding a View

In some cases, a resource is restricted in its entirety from being accessed by certain users. There are several strategies that accomplish this goal. One is including application logic that executes when the controller or view is processed, disallowing access. A second strategy is to configure the runtime system to allow access to certain resources only via an internal invocation from another application resource. In this case, access to these resources must be routed through another presentation-tier application resource, such as a servlet controller. Access to these restricted resources is not available via a direct browser invocation.

One common way of dealing with this issue is to use a controller as a delegation point for this type of access control. Another common variation involves embedding a guard directly within a view. We cover controller-based resource protection in "Presentation Tier Refactorings" on page 64 and in the pattern catalog, so we will focus here on view-based control strategies. We describe these strategies first, before considering the alternative strategy of controlling access through configuration.

Embedding Guard Within View

There are two common variations for embedding a guard within a view's processing logic. One variation blocks access to an entire resource, while the other blocks access to portions of that resource.

Including an All-or-Nothing Guard per View

In some cases, the logic embedded within the view processing code allows or denies access on an all-or-nothing basis. In other words, this logic prevents a particular user from accessing a particular view in its entirety. Typically, this type of guard is better encapsulated within a centralized controller, so that the logic is not sprinkled throughout the code. This strategy is reasonable to use when only a small fraction of pages need a guard. Typically, this scenario occurs when a nontechnical individual needs to rotate a small number of static pages onto a site. If the client must still be logged into the site to view these pages, then add a custom tag helper to the top of each page to complete the access check, as shown in Example 2.1.

Example 2.1 Including an All-or-Nothing Guard per View

```
<%@ taglib uri="/WEB-INF/corej2eetaglibrary.tld"
prefix="corePatterns" %>

<corePatterns:guard/>
<HTML>
.
.
.
</HTML>
```

Including a Guard for Portions of a View

In other cases, the logic embedded within the view processing code simply denies access to portions of a view. This secondary strategy can be used in combination with the previously mentioned all-or-nothing strategy. To clarify this discussion, let's use an analogy of controlling access to a room in a building. The all-or-nothing guard tells users whether they can walk into the room or not, while the secondary guard logic tells users what they are allowed to see once they are in the room. Following are some examples of why you might want to utilize this strategy.

Portions of View Not Displayed Based on User Role

A portion of the view might not be displayed based on the user's role. For example, when viewing her organizational information, a manager has access to a subview dealing with administering review materials for her employees. An employee might only see his own organizational information, and be restricted from the portions of the user interface that allow access to any review-related information, as shown in Example 2.2.

Example 2.2 Portions of View Not Displayed Based on User Role

```
<%@ taglib uri="/WEB-INF/corej2eetaglibrary.tld"
    prefix="corePatterns" %>

<HTML>
.
.
.
<corePatterns:guard role="manager">
<b>This should be seen only by managers!</b>
```

```
<corePatterns:guard/>
.
.
.
</HTML>
```

Portions of View Not Displayed Based on System State or Error Conditions

Depending on the system environment, the display layout can be modified. For example, if a user interface for administering hardware CPUs is used with a single-CPU hardware device, portions of the display that relate solely to multiple CPU devices might not be shown.

Guarding by Configuration

To restrict the client from directly accessing particular views, you can configure the presentation engine to allow access to these resources only via other internal resources, such as a servlet controller using a RequestDispatcher. Additionally, you can leverage the security mechanisms that are built into the Web container, based on the servlet specification, version 2.2 and later. Security constraints are defined in the deployment descriptor, called web.xml.

The **basic** and **form-based** authentication methods, also described in the Servlet specification, rely on this security information. Rather than repeat the specification here, we refer you to the current specification for details on these methods. (See http://java.sun.com/ products/servlet/index.html.)

So that you understand what to expect when adding declarative security constraints to your environment, we present a brief discussion of this topic and how it relates to all-or-nothing guarding by configuration. Finally, we describe one simple and generic alternative for all-or-nothing protection of a resource.

Resource Guards via Standard Security Constraints

You can configure applications with a security constraint, and you can use this declarative security programmatically to control access based on user roles. You can make resources available to certain roles of users and disallowed to others. Moreover, as described in "Embedding Guard Within View" on page 23, portions of a view can be restricted based on these user roles as well. If there are certain resources that should be disallowed in their entirety for all direct browser requests, as in the all-or-nothing scenario described in the previous section, then those resources can be constrained to a security role that is not assigned to any users. Resources configured in this manner remain inaccessible to all direct browser requests, as long as the security role remains unassigned. See Example 2.3 for an excerpt of a web.xml configuration file that defines a security role to restrict direct browser access.

The role name is "sensitive" and the restricted resources are named sensitive1.jsp, sensitive2.jsp, and sensitive3.jsp. Unless a user or group is assigned the "sensitive" role, then clients will not be able to directly access these JavaServer Pages (JSPs). At the same time, since internally dispatched requests are not restricted by these security constraints, a request that is handled initially by a servlet controller and then forwarded to one of these three resources will indeed receive access to these JSPs.

Finally, note that there is some inconsistency in the implementation of this aspect of the servlet specification version 2.2 across vendor products. Servers supporting the servlet specification version 2.3 should all be consistent on this issue.

Example 2.3 Unassigned Security Role Provides All-or-Nothing Control

```
<security-constraint>
      <web-resource-collection>
      <web-resource-name>SensitiveResources </web-resource-name>
      <description>A Collection of Sensitive Resources
      </description>
      <url-pattern>/trade/jsp/internalaccess/sensitive1.jsp
      </url-pattern>
      <url-pattern>
           /trade/jsp/internalaccess/sensitive2.jsp
      </url-pattern>
      <url-pattern>
      /trade/jsp/internalaccess/sensitive3.jsp
      </url-pattern>
     <http-method>GET</http-method>
     <http-method>POST</http-method>
    </web-resource-collection>
    <auth-constraint>
      <role-name>sensitive</role-name>
    </auth-constraint>
  </security-constraint>
```

Resource Guards via Simple and Generic Configuration

There is a simple and generic way to restrict a client from directly accessing a certain resource, such as a JSP. This method requires no configuration file modifications, such as those shown in Example 2.3. This method simply involves placing the resource under the /WEB-INF/ directory of the Web application. For example, to block direct browser access to a view called info.jsp in the securityissues Web application, we could place the JSP source file in the following subdirectory:

```
/securityissues/WEB-INF/internalaccessonly/info.jsp.
```

Direct public access is disallowed to the /WEB-INF/ directory, its subdirectories, and consequently to info.jsp. On the other hand, a controller servlet can still forward to this resource, if desired. This is an all-or-nothing method of control, since resources configured in this manner are disallowed in their entirety to direct browser access.

For an example, please refer to "Hide Resources From a Client" on page 88.

Duplicate Form Submissions

Users working in a browser client environment can use the Back button and inadvertently resubmit the same form they had previously submitted, possibly invoking a duplicate transaction. Similarly, a user might click the Stop button on the browser before receiving a confirmation page, and subsequently resubmit the same form. In most cases, we want to trap and disallow these duplicate submissions, and using a controlling servlet provides a control point for addressing this problem.

Synchronizer (or Déjà vu) Token

This strategy addresses the problem of duplicate form submissions. A synchronizer token is set in a user's session and included with each form returned to the client. When that form is submitted, the synchronizer token in the form is compared to the synchronizer token in the session. The tokens should match the first time the form is submitted. If the tokens do not match, then the form submission can be disallowed and an error returned to the user. Token mismatch might occur when the user submits a form, then clicks the Back button in the browser and attempts to resubmit the same form.

On the other hand, if the two token values match, then we are confident that the flow of control is exactly as expected. At this point, the token value in the session is modified to a new value and the form submission is accepted.

You can also use this strategy to control direct browser access to certain pages, as described in the sections on resource guards. For example, assume a user bookmarks page A of an application, where page A should only be accessed from pages B and C. When the user selects page A via the bookmark, the page is accessed out of order and the synchronizer token will be in an unsynchronized state, or it might not exist at all. Either way, the access can be disallowed if desired.

Please refer to page 67 in the *Introduce Synchronizer Token* presentation tier refactoring section, for an example of this strategy.

Validation

It is often desirable to perform validation both on the client and on the server. Although client validation processing is typically less sophisticated than server validation, it provides high-level checks, such as whether a form field is empty. Server-side validation is often much more comprehensive. While both types of processing are appropriate in an application, it is not recommended to include only client-side validation. One major reason not to rely solely on client-side validation is that client-side scripting languages are user-configurable and thus can be disabled at any time.

Detailed discussion of validation strategies is outside the scope of this book. At the same time, we want to mention these issues as ones to consider while designing your systems, and hope you will refer to the existing literature in order to investigate further.

Validation on Client

Input validation is performed on the client. Typically, this involves embedding scripting code, such as JavaScript, within the client view. As stated, client-side validation is a fine complement for server-side validation, but should not be used alone.

Validation on Server

Input validation is performed on the server. There are several typical strategies for doing server validation. These strategies are form-centric validation and validation based on abstract types.

Form-Centric Validation

The form-centric validation strategy forces an application to include lots of methods that validate various pieces of state for each form submitted. Typically, these methods overlap with respect to the logic they include, such that reuse and modularity suffer. Since there is a validation method that is specific to each Web form that is posted, there is no central code to handle required fields or numeric-only fields. In this case, although there might be a field on multiple different forms that is considered a required field, each is handled separately and redundantly in numerous places in the application. This strategy is relatively easy to implement and is effective, but it leads to duplication of code as an application grows.

To provide a more flexible, reusable, and maintainable solution, the model data can be considered at a different level of abstraction. This approach is considered in the following alternative strategy, Example 2.5 on page 30. An example of form-centric validation is shown in the listing in Example 2.4.

Example 2.4 Form-Centric Validation

```
/**If the first name or last name fields were left blank, then an error will
        be returned to client. With this strategy, these checks for the
        existence of a requirod field are duplicated. If this validation
        logic were abstracted into a separate component, it could be
        reused across forms (see Validation Based on Abstract Types
        strategy)**/
public Vector validate()
{
Vector errorCollection = new Vector();
     if ((firstname == null) ||
  (firstname.trim().length() < 1))
      errorCollection.addElement("firstname required");
     if ((lastname == null) || (lastname.trim().length() < 1))
      errorCollection.addElement("lastname required");
return errorCollection;
}
```

Validation Based on Abstract Types

You could use this strategy on either the client or server, but it is preferred on the server in a browser-based or thin-client environment.

The typing and constraints information is abstracted out of the model state and into a generic framework. This separates the validation of the model from the application logic in which the model is being used, thus reducing their coupling.

Model validation is performed by comparing the metadata and constraints to the model state. The metadata and constraints about the model are typically accessible from some sort of simple data store, such as a properties file. A benefit of this approach is that the system becomes more generic, because it factors the state typing and constraint information out of the application logic.

An example is to have a component or subsystem that encapsulates validation logic, such as deciding whether a string is empty, whether a certain number is within a valid range, whether a string is formatted in a particular way, and so on. When various disparate application components want to validate different aspects of a model, each component does not write its own validation code. Rather, the centralized validation mechanism is used. The centralized validation mechanism will typically be configured either programmatically, through some sort of factory, or declaratively, using configuration files.

Thus, the validation mechanism is more generic, focusing on the model state and its requirements, independent of the other parts of the application. A drawback to using this strategy is the potential reduction in efficiency and performance. Also, more generic solutions, although often powerful, are sometimes less easily understood and maintained.

An example scenario follows. An XML-based configuration file describes a variety of validations, such as "required field," "all-numeric field," and so on. Additionally, handler classes can be designated for each of these validations. Finally, a mapping links HTML form values to a specific type of validation. The code for validating a particular form field simply becomes something similar to the code snippet shown in Example 2.5.

Example 2.5 Validation Based on Abstract Types

```
//firstNameString="Dan"
//formFieldName="form1.firstname"
Validator.getInstance().validate(firstNameString, formFieldName);
```

Helper Properties—Integrity and Consistency

JavaBean helper classes are typically used to hold intermediate state when it is passed in with a client request. JSP runtime engines provide a mechanism for automatically copying parameter values from a servlet request object into properties of these JavaBean helpers. The JSP syntax is as follows:

```
<jsp:setProperty name="helper" property="*"/>
```

This tells the JSP engine to copy all **matching** parameter values into the corresponding properties in a JavaBean called "helper," shown in Example 2.6:

Example 2.6 Helper Properties – A Simple JavaBean Helper

```
public class Helper
{
   private String first;
   private String last;

   public String getFirst() {
```

```
        return first;
    }

    public void setFirst(String aString) {
        first=aString;
    }

    public String getLast() {
        return last;
    }

    public void setLast(String aString) {
        last=aString;
    }

}
```

How is a match determined, though? If a request parameter exists with the same name and same type as the helper bean property, then it is considered a match. Practically, then, each parameter is compared to each bean property name and the type of the bean property setter method.

Although this mechanism is simple, it can produce some confusing and unwanted side effects. First of all, it is important to note what happens when a request parameter has an empty value. Many developers assume that a request parameter with an empty string value should, if matched to a bean property, cause that bean property to take on the value of an empty string, or null. The spec-compliant behavior is actually to make no changes to the matching bean property in this case, though. Furthermore, since JavaBean helper instances are typically reused across requests, such confusion can lead to data values being inconsistent and incorrect.

Figure 2.1 on page 32 shows the sort of problem that this might cause.

Request 1 includes values for the parameter named "first" and the one named "last," and each of the corresponding bean properties is set. Request 2 includes a value only for the "last" parameter, causing only that one property to be set in the bean. The value for the "first" parameter is unchanged. It is not reset to an empty string, or null, simply because there is no value in the request parameter. As you can see in Figure 2.1, this might lead to inconsistencies if the bean values are not reset manually between requests.

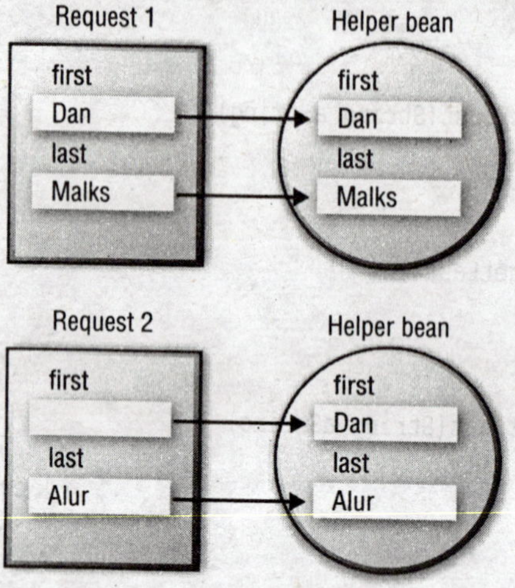

Figure 2.1 Helper Properties

Another related issue to consider when designing your application is the behavior of HTML form interfaces when controls of the form are not selected. For example, if a form has multiple checkboxes, it is not unreasonable to expect that *un*checking every checkbox would result in clearing out these values on the server. In the case of the request object created based on this interface, however, there would simply not be a parameter included in this request object for any of the checkbox values. Thus, no parameter values relating to these checkboxes are sent to the server (see http://www.w3.org for full HTML specification).

Since there is no parameter passed to the server, the matching bean property will remain unchanged when using the <jsp:setProperty> action, as described. So, in this case, unless the developer manually modifies these values, there is the potential for inconsistent and incorrect data values to exist in the application. As stated, a simple design solution to this problem is to reset all state in the JavaBean between requests.

Presentation Tier Bad Practices

Bad practices are less than optimal solutions that conflict with many of the patterns' recommendations. When we documented the patterns and best practices, we naturally discarded those practices that were less than optimal.

In this part of the book, we highlight what we consider to be bad practices in the presentation tier.

In each section, we briefly describe the bad practice and provide numerous references to design issues, refactorings, and patterns that provide further information and preferable alternatives. We do not provide an in-depth discussion of each bad practice, but rather present a brief synopsis as a starting point for further investigation.

The "Problem Summary" section provides a quick description of a less than optimal situation, while the "Solution Reference" section includes references to:

- **Patterns** Provide information on context and trade-offs;
- **Design considerations** Provide related details;
- **Refactorings** Describe the journey from the less than optimal situation (**Bad Practice**) to a more optimal one, a best practice, or pattern.

Consider this part of the book as a roadmap, using the references to locate further detail and description in other parts of the book.

Control Code in Multiple Views

Problem Summary

Custom tag helpers can be included at the top of a JSP View to perform access control and other types of checks. If a large number of views include similar helper references, maintaining this code becomes difficult, since changes must be made in multiple places.

Solution Reference

Consolidate control code, introducing a controller and associated Command helpers.

- **Refactoring** See "Introduce a Controller" on page 64.
- **Refactoring** See "Localize Disparate Logic" on page 72.

- **Pattern** See Front Controller – "Command and Controller Strategy" on page 174.

When there is a need to include similar control code in multiple places, such as when only a portion of a JSP View is to be restricted from a particular user, delegate the work to a reusable helper class.

- **Pattern** See *View Helper* (240)
- **Design** See "Guarding a View" on page 23.

Exposing Presentation-Tier Data Structures to Business Tier

Problem Summary

Presentation-tier data structures, such as HttpServletRequest, should be confined to the presentation tier. Sharing these details with the business tier, or any other tier, increases coupling between these tiers, dramatically reducing the reusability of the available services. If the method signature in the business service accepts a parameter of type HttpServletRequest, then any other clients to this service (even those outside of the Web space) must wrap their request state in an HttpServletRequest object. Additionally, in this case the business-tier services need to understand how to interact with these presentation tier-specific data structures, increasing the complexity of the business-tier code and increasing the coupling between the tiers.

Solution Reference

Instead of sharing data structures specific to the presentation tier with the business tier, copy the relevant state into more generic data structures and share those. Alternatively, extract and share the relevant state from the presentation tier-specific data structure as individual parameters.

- **Refactoring** See "Hide Presentation Tier-Specific Details From the Business Tier" on page 80.

Exposing Presentation-Tier Data Structures to Domain Objects

Problem Summary

Sharing request handling data structures, such as HttpServletRequest, with domain objects needlessly increases the coupling between these two distinct aspects of the application. Domain objects should be reusable components, and if their implementation relies on protocol or tier-specific details, their potential for reuse is reduced. Furthermore, maintaining and debugging tightly coupled applications is more difficult.

Solution Reference

Instead of passing an HttpServletRequest object as a parameter, copy the state from the request object into a more generic data structure and share this object with the domain object. Alternatively, extract the relevant state from the HttpServletRequest object and provide each piece of state as an individual parameter to the domain object.

- **Refactoring** See "Hide Presentation Tier-Specific Details From the Business Tier" on page 80.

Allowing Duplicate Form Submissions

Problem Summary

One of the limitations of the browser-client environment is the lack of control an application has over client navigation. A user might submit an order form that results in a transaction that debits a credit card account and initiates shipment of a product to a residence. If, after receiving the confirmation page, the user clicks the Back button, then the same form could be resubmitted.

Solution Reference

To address these issues, monitor and control the request flow.

- **Refactoring** See "Introduce Synchronizer Token" on page 67.
- **Refactoring** See "Controlling Client Access" on page 22.
- **Design** See "Synchronizer (or Déjà vu) Token" on page 27.

Exposing Sensitive Resources to Direct Client Access

Problem Summary

Security is one of the most important issues in enterprise environments. If there is no need for a client to have direct access to certain information, then this information must be protected. If specific configuration files, property files, JSPs, and class files are not secured appropriately, then clients might inadvertently or maliciously retrieve sensitive information.

Solution Reference

Protect sensitive resources, disallowing direct client access

- **Refactoring** See "Hide Resources From a Client" on page 88.
- **Refactoring** See "Controlling Client Access" on page 22.

Assuming <jsp:setProperty> Will Reset Bean Properties

Problem Summary

While the expected behavior of the <jsp:setProperty> standard tag is to copy request parameter values into JavaBean helper properties of the same name, its behavior when dealing with parameters that have empty values is often confusing. For example, a parameter with an empty value is ignored, although many developers incorrectly assume that the matching JavaBean property will be assigned a null or empty string value.

Solution Reference

Take into account the less than intuitive nature of how properties are set when using the <jsp:setProperty> tag, and initialize bean properties before use.

- **Design** See "Helper Properties—Integrity and Consistency" on page 30.

Creating Fat Controllers

Problem Summary

Control code that is duplicated in multiple JSP views should, in many cases, be refactored into a controller. If too much code is added to a controller, though, it becomes too heavyweight and cumbersome to maintain, test, and debug. For example, unit testing a servlet controller, particularly a "fat controller," is more complicated than unit testing individual helper classes that are independent of the HTTP protocol.

Solution Reference

A controller is typically the initial contact point for handling a request, but it should also be a delegation point, working in coordination with other control classes. Command objects are used to encapsulate control code to which the controller delegates. It is much easier to unit test these JavaBean command objects, independent of the servlet engine, than it is to test less modular code.

- **Refactoring** See "Introduce a Controller" on page 64.
- **Pattern** See Front Controller–"Command and Controller Strategy" on page 174.
- **Refactoring** See "Localize Disparate Logic" on page 72.
- **Pattern** See *View Helper* (240).

Using Helpers as Scriplets

Problem Summary

Using helpers minimizes the amount of Java scriptlet code that is embedded within a view. However, if helpers merely expose the same abstraction level as the Java code, then by using helpers you simply continue to expose the code's implementation, as you do with scriptlets, instead of its intent.

Solution Reference

This section shows four ways to approach the same piece of code, starting with mingling HTML with scriptlet code, and continuing on with an improvement in each subsequent example. Consider these tradeoffs as you decide how to structure your application.

Java scriptlet code exposes too many of the implementation details of formatting processing logic within a view, as shown in Example 2.7. Use helpers to replace this Java scriptlet code and hide the implementation details of the formatting processing logic. While it is acceptable for helpers to expose **some** of the implementation details, try to minimize this exposure by having the helpers expose a higher-level abstraction.

Example 2.7 Java Scriptlet in View

```
<html>
<head><title>Member Ratings</title></head>
<body>

<jsp:useBean id="memberlist" type="java.util.List" scope="request"/>

<div align="center">
<h3> 10 Most Credit-Risk Members</h3>
<table border="1" >
    <tr>
        <th> Name </th>
        <th> Phone </th>
        <th> Email </th>
        <th> City </th>
        <th> Balance </th>
    </tr>
<%
Iterator members = memberlist.listIterator();
int maxrows = 0;
while ( members.hasNext()) {
    MemberTO member = (MemberTO)members.next();
    // Biz Rule: Do not include Platinum members in this report
    if ( ( member.getPrivilege().equalsIgnoreCase("Gold") ||
           member.getPrivilege().equalsIgnoreCase("Silver")) &&
          (member.getCreditBalance() > 5000) && (maxrows < 10)) {
%>
    <tr>
        <td><%= member.getName()%></td>
        <td><%= member.getPhone()%></td>
        <td><%= member.getEmail()%></td>
        <td><%= member.getCity()%></td>
        <td><%= member.getCreditBalance()%></td>
    </tr>
<%
        maxrows++;
    }
}
%>
</table>

</div>
```

```

</body>

</html>
```

Example 2.8 shows the use of JSTL [JSTL] helpers in a way that continues to expose similar implementation details as were exposed with the Java scriptlet code in Example 2.7. Using helpers in this way is an improvement but doesn't give maximum readability, modularity, and reusability benefits.

Example 2.8 Using JSTL Helpers

```
<%@ taglib prefix="c" uri="http://java.sun.com/jstl/core" %>

<html>
<head><title>Member Ratings</title></head>
<body>

<jsp:useBean id="memberlist" type="java.util.List" scope="request"/>

<div align="center">
<h3> 10 Most Credit-Risk Members</h3>
<table border="1" >
    <tr>
        <th> Name </th>
        <th> Phone </th>
        <th> Email </th>
        <th> City </th>
        <th> Balance </th>
    </tr>
<c:set value="0" var="RowCount"/>
<c:forEach var="member" items="${memberlist}">
<c:if test="${(member.privilege == 'Gold' or member.privilege=='Silver')
                and (member.creditBalance > 5000) and (RowCount < 10 )}">
    <tr>
        <td><B><c:out value="${member.name}"/></B></td>
        <td><c:out value="${member.phone}"/></td>
        <td><c:out value="${member.email}"/></td>
        <td><c:out value="${member.city}"/></td>
        <td><c:out value="${member.creditBalance}"/></td>
    </tr>
    <c:set value="${RowCount+1}" var="RowCount"/>
</c:if>
```

```
</c:forEach>
</table>
</div>
</body>
</html>
```

Example 2.9 shows helpers that provide a higher-level abstraction, so that when you read the code you can quickly understand its **intent**, namely to build a member table. Example 2.9 mingles some HTML markup in the Java code of the buildMemberTable tag, but provides a modular, reusable piece of code.

Example 2.9 Using Custom Tags

```
<%@ taglib uri='/WEB-INF/corej2eetaglibrary.tld' prefix='cjp' %>

<html>
<head><title>Member Ratings</title></head>
<body>

<jsp:useBean id="memberlist" type="java.util.List" scope="request"/>

<div align="center">
<h3> 10 Credit-Risk Members</h3>
<cjp:buildMemberTable privilege="Gold,Silver" credit="5000" rows="10"/>
</div>
</body>
</html>
```

Finally, Example 2.10 shows tag files, supported in JSP 2.0+, which provide the readability and abstraction level of custom tags, combined with the ease of the JSTL example.

Example 2.10 Tag File Helpers

```
<%@ taglib prefix="tags" tagdir="/WEB-INF/tags" %>

<html>
<head><title>Member Ratings</title></head>
<body>

<div align="center">
<h3> 10 Most Credit-Risk Members</h3>

```

```
    <tags:memberList privilege="Gold" credit="5000" rows="10">
       <jsp:attribute name="nameStyle">
      <B>${name}</B>
       </jsp:attribute>
    </tags:memberList>

    <br>

    <tags:memberList privilege="Silver" credit="4000" rows="7">
       <jsp:attribute name="nameStyle">
      <font color="red"><B>${name}</B></font>
       </jsp:attribute>
    </tags:memberList>

</body>
</html>
```

Example 2.11 Tag File Helper

```
<%@tag import="java.util.*"%>
<%@tag import="util.*"%>
<%@ taglib prefix="c" uri="http://java.sun.com/jstl/core_rt" %>
<%@ attribute name="nameStyle" fragment="true" %>
<%@ attribute name="privilege"%>
<%@ attribute name="credit"%>
<%@ attribute name="rows"%>

<%@ variable name-given="name" %>

<jsp:useBean id="memberlist" type="java.util.List" scope="request"/>

<table border="1" >
   <tr>
        <th> Name </th>
        <th> Phone </th>
        <th> Email </th>
        <th> City </th>
        <th> Balance </th>
   </tr>
<c:set value="0" var="RowCount"/>
<c:forEach var="member" items="${memberlist}">
<c:if test="${(member.privilege == privilege)
        and (member.creditBalance > credit) and (RowCount < rows )}">
```

```
    <tr>
        <td>
            <c:set var="name" value="${member.name}"/>
            <jsp:invoke fragment="nameStyle"/>
        </td>
        <td><c:out value="${member.phone}"/></td>
        <td><c:out value="${member.email}"/></td>
        <td><c:out value="${member.city}"/></td>
        <td><c:out value="${member.creditBalance}"/></td>
    </tr>
    <c:set value="${RowCount+1}" var="RowCount"/>
</c:if>
</c:forEach>
</table>
```

Business Tier Design Considerations and Bad Practices

Topics in This Chapter

- Business Tier Design Considerations
- Business and Integration Tiers Bad Practices

Chapter 3

Business Tier Design Considerations

When you apply the business tier and integration tier patterns in this book, you'll need to know about related design issues, which we cover in this chapter. These issues cover a variety of topics, and can affect many aspects of a system.

The discussions in this chapter simply describe each issue as a design issue that you should consider when implementing systems based on the J2EE pattern catalog.

Using Session Beans

Session beans are distributed business components with the following characteristics, per the EJB specification:

- A session bean is dedicated to a single client or user.
- A session bean lives only for the duration of the client's session.
- A session bean does not survive container crashes.
- A session bean is not a persistent object.
- A session bean can time out.
- A session bean can be transaction aware.
- A session bean can be used to model stateful or stateless conversations between the client and the business tier-components.

Note: In this section, we use the term **workflow** in the context of EJB to represent the logic associated with the enterprise beans communication. For example, workflow encompasses how session bean A calls session bean B, then entity bean C.

Session Bean—Stateless Versus Stateful

Session beans come in two flavors—stateless and stateful. A stateless session bean does not hold any conversational state. Hence, once a client's method invocation on a stateless session beans is completed, the container is free to reuse that session bean instance for another client. This allows the container to maintain a pool of session beans and to reuse session beans among multiple clients. The container pools stateless session beans so that it can reuse them more efficiently by sharing them with multiple clients. The container returns a stateless session bean to the pool after the client completes its invocation. The container may allocate a different instance from the pool to subsequent client invocations.

A stateful session bean holds conversational state. A stateful session bean may be pooled, but since the session bean is holding state on behalf of a client, the bean cannot simultaneously be shared with and handle requests from another client.

The container does not pool stateful session beans in the same manner as it pools stateless session beans because stateful session beans hold client session state. Stateful session beans are allocated to a client and remain allocated to the client as long as the client session is active. Thus, stateful session beans need more resource overhead than stateless session beans, for the added advantage of maintaining conversational state.

Many designers believe that using stateless session beans is a more viable session bean design strategy for scalable systems. This belief stems from building distributed object systems with older technologies, because without an inherent infrastructure to manage component life cycle, such systems rapidly lost scalability characteristics as resource demands increased. Scalability loss was due to the lack of component life cycle, causing the service to continue to consume resources as the number of clients and objects increased.

An EJB container manages the life cycle of enterprise beans and is responsible for monitoring system resources to best manage enterprise bean instances. The container manages a pool of enterprise beans and brings enterprise beans in and out of memory (called **activation** and **passivation**, respectively) to optimize invocation and resource consumption.

Scalability problems are typically due to the misapplication of stateful and stateless session beans. The choice of using stateful or stateless session beans must depend upon the business process being implemented. A business process that needs only one method call to complete the service is a non-conversational business process. Such processes are suitably implemented using a stateless session bean. A business process that needs multiple method calls to complete the service is a conversational business process. It is suitably implemented using a stateful session bean.

However, some designers choose stateless session beans, hoping to increase scalability, and they may wrongly decide to model all business processes as stateless session beans. When using stateless session beans for conversational business processes, every method invocation requires the state to be passed by the client to the bean, reconstructed at the business tier, or retrieved from a persistent store. These techniques could result in reduced scalability due to the associated overheads in network traffic, reconstruction time, or access time respectively.

Storing State on the Business Tier

Some design considerations for storing state on the Web server are discussed in "Session State in the Presentation Tier" on page 21. Here we continue that discussion to explore when it is appropriate to store state in a stateful session bean instead of in an HttpSession.

One of the considerations is to determine what types of clients access the business services in your system. If the architecture is solely a Web-based application, where all the clients come through a Web server either via a servlet or a JSP, then conversational state may be maintained in an HttpSession in the web tier. This scenario is shown in Figure 3.1.

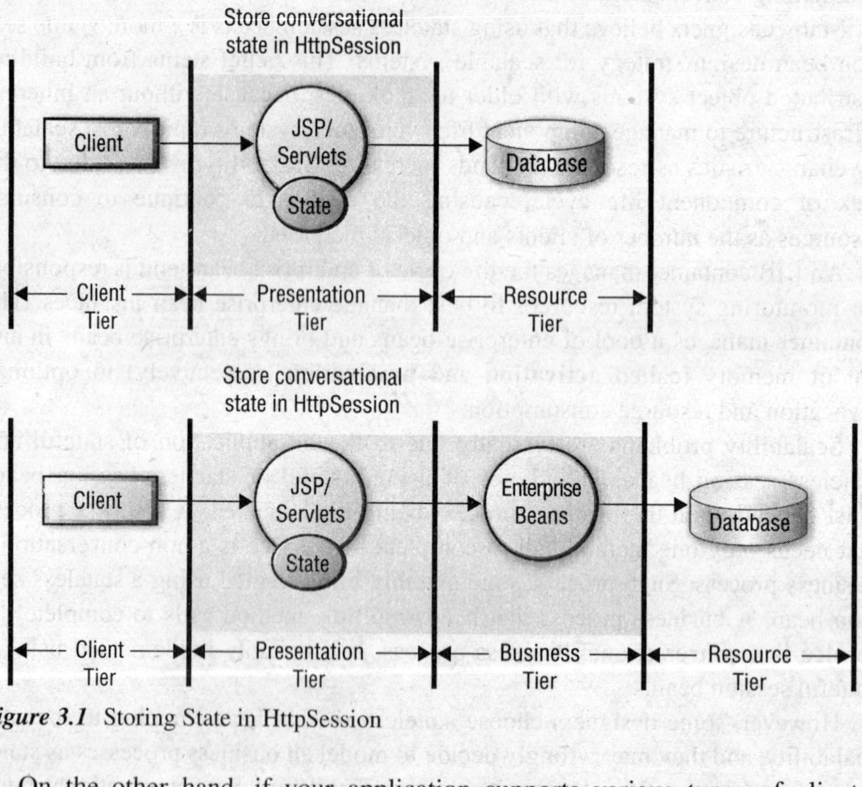

Figure 3.1 Storing State in HttpSession

On the other hand, if your application supports various types of clients, including Web clients, Java applications, other applications, and even other enterprise beans, then conversational state can be maintained in the EJB layer using stateful session beans. This is shown in Figure 3.2.

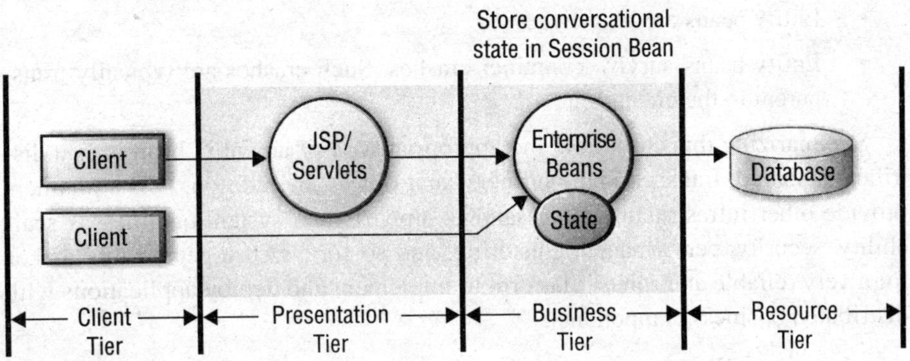

Figure 3.2 Storing State in Session Beans

We have presented some basic discussion on the subject of state management here and in the previous chapter (see "Session State on the Client" on page 20). A full-scale discussion is outside the scope of this book, since the problem is multi-dimensional and depends very much on the deployment environment, including:

- Hardware
- Traffic management
- Clustering of Web container
- Clustering of EJB container
- Server affinity
- Session replication
- Session persistence

We touch on this issue because it is one that should be considered during development and deployment.

Using Entity Beans

Using entity beans appropriately is a question of design heuristics, experience, need, and technology. Entity beans are best suited as coarse-grained business components. Entity beans are distributed objects and have the following characteristics, per the EJB specification:

- Entity beans provide an object view of persistent data.
- Entity beans are transactional.

- Entity beans are multiuser.
- Entity beans are long-lived.
- Entity beans survive container crashes. Such crashes are typically transparent to the clients.

Summarizing this definition, the appropriate use of an entity bean is as a distributed, shared, transactional, and persistent object. In addition, EJB containers provide other infrastructure necessary to support such system qualities as scalability, security, performance, clustering, and so forth. All together, this makes for a very reliable and robust platform to implement and deploy applications with distributed business components.

Entity Bean Primary Keys

Entity beans are uniquely identified by their primary keys. A primary key can be a simple key, made up of a single attribute, or it can be a composite key, made up of a group of attributes from the entity bean. For entity beans with a single-field primary key, where the primary key is a primitive type, it is possible to implement the entity bean without defining an explicit primary key class. The deployer can specify the primary key field in the deployment descriptor for the entity bean. However, when the primary key is a composite key, a separate class for the primary key must be specified. This class must be a simple Java class that implements the serializable interface with the attributes that define the composite key for the entity bean. The attribute names and types in the primary key class must match those in the entity bean, and also must be declared public in both the bean implementation class and primary key class.

As a suggested best practice, the primary key class must implement the optional `java.lang.Object` methods, such as `equals` and `hashCode`.

- Override the `equals()` method to properly evaluate the equality of two primary keys by comparing values for each part of the composite key.
- Override the `Object.hashCode()` method to return a unique number representing the hash code for the primary key instance. Ensure that the hash code is indeed unique when you use your primary key attribute values to compute the hash code.

Business Logic in Entity Beans

A common question in entity bean design is what kind of business logic it should contain. Some designers feel that entity beans should contain only persistence logic and simple methods to get and set data values. They feel that entity beans should not contain business logic, which is often misunderstood to mean that only code related to getting and setting data must be included in the entity bean.

Business logic generally includes any logic associated with providing some service. For this discussion, consider business logic to include all logic related to processing, workflow, business rules, data, and so forth. The following is a list of sample questions to explore the possible results of adding business logic into an entity:

- Will the business logic introduce entity-entity relationships?
- Will the entity bean become responsible for managing workflow of user interaction?
- Will the entity bean take on the responsibilities that should belong in some other business component?

A "yes" answer to any of these questions helps identify whether introducing business logic into the entity bean can have an adverse impact, especially if you use remote entity beans. It is desirable to investigate the design to avoid inter-entity-bean dependencies as much as possible, since such dependences create overheads that may impede overall application performance.

In general, the entity bean should contain business logic that is self-contained to manage its data and its dependent objects' data. Thus, it may be necessary to identify, extract, and move business logic that introduces entity-bean-to-entity-bean interaction from the entity bean into a session bean by applying the *Session Façade* pattern. The *Composite Entity* (391) pattern and some of the refactorings discuss the issues related to entity bean design.

If any workflow associated with multiple entity beans is identified, then you can implement the workflow in a session bean instead of in an entity bean. Use a *Session Façade* (341) or *Application Service* (357).

- See "Merge Session Beans" on page 96.
- See "Reduce Inter-Entity Bean Communication" on page 98.
- See "Move Business Logic to Session" on page 100.
- See *Session Façade* (341)
- See *Business Object* (374)
- See *Composite Entity* (391)
- See *Application Service* (357)

For bean-managed persistence in entity beans, data access code is best implemented outside entity beans.

- See "Separate Data Access Code" on page 102.
- See *Data Access Object* (462).

Caching Enterprise Bean Remote References and Handles

When clients use an enterprise bean, they might need to cache some reference to an enterprise bean for future use. You will encounter this when using business delegates (see *Business Delegate* (302)), where a delegate connects to a session bean and invokes the necessary business methods on the bean on behalf of the client.

When the client uses the business delegate for the first time, the delegate needs to perform a lookup using the EJB Home object to obtain a remote reference to the session bean. For subsequent requests, the business delegate can avoid lookups by caching a remote reference or its handle as necessary.

The EJB Home handle can also be cached to avoid an additional Java Naming and Directory Interface (JNDI) lookup for the enterprise bean home. For more details on using an EJB Handle or the EJB Home Handle, please refer to the current EJB specification.

Business and Integration Tiers Bad Practices

Mapping the Object Model Directly to the Entity Bean Model

Problem Summary

One of the common practices in designing an EJB application is to map the object model directly into entity beans; that is, each class in the object model is transformed into an entity bean. This results in a large number of fine-grained entity beans.

The container and network overhead increases as the number of enterprise beans increases. Such mapping also transforms object relationships into entity-bean-to-entity-bean relationships. This is best avoided, since entity-bean-to-entity-bean relationships introduce severe performance implications for remote entity beans.

Solution Reference

Identify the parent-dependent object relationships in the object model and design them as coarse-grained entity beans. This results in fewer entity beans, where each entity bean composes a group of related objects from the object model.

- **Refactoring** See "Reduce Inter-Entity Bean Communication" on page 98.
- **Pattern** See *Composite Entity* (391)

Consolidate related workflow operations into session beans to provide a uniform coarse-grained service access layer.

- **Refactoring** See "Merge Session Beans" on page 96.
- **Pattern** See *Session Façade* (341)

Mapping the Relational Model Directly to the Entity Bean Model

Problem Summary

When designing an EJB model, it is bad practice to model each row in a table as an entity bean. While entity beans are best designed as coarse-grained objects, this mapping results in a large number of fine-grained entity beans, and it affects scalability.

Such mapping also implements inter-table relationships that is, primary key/foreign key relationships) as entity-bean-to-entity-bean relationships.

Solution Reference

Design your enterprise bean application using an object-oriented approach instead of relying on the preexisting relational database design to produce the EJB model.

- **Bad Practice** See solution reference for "Mapping the Object Model Directly to the Entity Bean Model" on page 53.

Avoid inter-entity relationships by designing coarse-grained business objects by identifying parent-dependent objects.

- **Refactoring** See "Reduce Inter-Entity Bean Communication" on page 98.
- **Refactoring** See "Move Business Logic to Session" on page 100.
- **Pattern** See *Composite Entity* (391)

Mapping Each Use Case to a Session Bean

Problem Summary

Some designers implement each use case with its own unique session bean. This creates fine-grained controllers responsible for servicing only one type of interaction. The drawback of this approach is that it can result in a large number of session beans and significantly increase the complexity of the application.

Solution Reference

Apply the *Session Façade* pattern to aggregate a group of the related interactions into a single session bean. This results in fewer session beans for the application, and leverages the advantages of applying the *Session Façade* pattern.

- **Refactoring** See "Merge Session Beans" on page 96.
- **Pattern** See *Session Façade* (341)

Exposing All Enterprise Bean Attributes via Getter/Setter Methods

Problem Summary

Exposing each enterprise bean attribute using getter/setter methods is a bad practice. This forces the client to invoke numerous fine-grained remote invocations and creates the potential to introduce a significant amount of network chattiness across the tiers. Each method call is potentially remote and carries with it a certain network overhead that impacts performance and scalability.

Solution Reference

Use a value object to transfer aggregate data to and from the client instead of exposing the getters and setters for each attribute.

- **Pattern** See *Transfer Object* (415).

Embedding Service Lookup in Clients

Problem Summary

Clients and presentation-tier objects frequently need to look up the enterprise beans. In an EJB environment, the container uses JNDI to provide this service.

Putting the burden of locating services on the application client can introduce a proliferation of lookup code in the application code. Any change to the lookup code propagates to all clients that look up the services. Also, embedding lookup code in clients exposes them to the complexity of the underlying implementation and introduces dependency on the lookup code.

Solution Reference

Encapsulate implementation details of the lookup mechanisms using a *Service Locator* (315).

- **Pattern** See *Service Locator* (315)

Encapsulate the implementation details of business tier-components, such as session and entity beans, using *Business Delegate* (302). This simplifies client code since they no longer deal with enterprise beans and services. *Business Delegate* (302) can in turn use the *Service Locator* (315).

- **Refactoring** See "Introduce Business Delegate" on page 94.
- **Pattern** See *Business Delegate* (302).

Using Entity Beans as Read-Only Objects

Problem Summary

Any entity bean method is subject to transaction semantics based on its transaction isolation levels specified in the deployment descriptor. Using an entity bean as a read-only object simply wastes expensive resources and results in unnecessary update transactions to the persistent store. This is due to the invocation of the ejbStore() methods by the container during the entity bean's life cycle. Since the container has no way of knowing if the data was changed during a method invocation, it must assume that it has and invoke the ejbStore() operation. Thus, the container makes no distinction between read-only and read-write entity beans. However, some containers may provide read-only entity beans, but these are vendor proprietary implementations.

Solution Reference

Encapsulate all access to the data source using *Data Access Object* (462) pattern. This provides a centralized layer of data access code and also simplifies entity bean code.

- **Pattern** See *Data Access Object* (462).

Implement access to read-only functionality using a session bean, typically as a Session Façade that uses a DAO.

- **Pattern** See *Session Façade* (341)

You can implement *Value List Handler* (444) to obtain a list of *Transfer Objects* (415).

- **Pattern** See *Value List Handler* (444).

You can implement *Transfer Objects* (415) to obtain a complex data model from the business tier.

- **Pattern** See *Transfer Object Assembler* (433).

Using Entity Beans as Fine-Grained Objects

Problem Summary

Entity beans are meant to represent coarse-grained transactional persistent business components. Using a remote entity bean to represent fine-grained objects increases the overall network communication and container overhead. This impacts application performance and scalability.

Think of a fine-grained object as an object that has little meaning without its association to another object (typically a coarse-grained parent object). For example, an item object can be thought of as a fined-grained object because it has little value until it is associated with an order object. In this example, the order object is the coarse-grained object and the item object is the fine-grained (dependent) object.

Solution Reference

When designing enterprise beans based on a preexisting RDBMS schema,

- **Bad Practice** See "Mapping the Relational Model Directly to the Entity Bean Model" on page 53.

When designing enterprise beans using an object model,

- **Bad Practice** See "Mapping the Object Model Directly to the Entity Bean Model" on page 53.

Design coarse-grained entity beans and session beans. Apply the following patterns and refactorings that promote coarse-grained enterprise beans design.

- **Pattern** See *Composite Entity* (391).
- **Pattern** See *Session Façade* (341).
- **Refactoring** See "Reduce Inter-Entity Bean Communication" on page 98.
- **Refactoring** See "Move Business Logic to Session" on page 100.
- **Refactoring** See "Business Logic in Entity Beans" on page 50.
- **Refactoring** See "Merge Session Beans" on page 96.

Storing Entire Entity Bean-Dependent Object Graph

Problem Summary

When a complex tree structure of dependent objects is used in an entity bean, performance can degrade rapidly when loading and storing an entire tree of dependent objects. When the container invokes the entity bean's ejbLoad() method, either for the initial load or for reloads to synchronize with the persistent store, loading the entire tree of dependent objects can prove wasteful. Similarly, when the container invokes the entity bean's ejbStore() method at any time, storing the entire tree of objects can be quite expensive and unnecessary.

Solution Reference

Identify the dependent objects that have changed since the previous store operation and store only those objects to the persistent store.

- **Pattern** See *Composite Entity* (391) and *Store Optimization (Dirty Marker) Strategy* (397).

Implement a strategy to load only data that is most accessed and required. Load the remaining dependent objects on demand.

- **Pattern** See *Composite Entity* (391) and *Lazy Loading Strategy* on page 396.

By applying these strategies, it is possible to prevent loading and storing an entire tree of dependent objects.

Exposing EJB-related Exceptions to Non-EJB Clients

Problem Summary

Enterprise beans can throw business application exceptions to clients. When an application throws an application exception, the container simply throws the exception to the client. This allows the client to gracefully handle the exception and possibly take another action. It is reasonable to expect the application developer to understand and handle such application-level exceptions.

However, despite employing such good programming practices as designing and using application exceptions, the clients may still receive EJB-related exceptions, such as a java.rmi.RemoteException. This can happen if the enterprise bean or the container encounters a system failure related to the enterprise bean.

The burden is on the application developer, who may not even be aware of or knowledgeable about EJB exceptions and semantics, to understand the implementation details of the non-application exceptions that may be thrown by business tier-components. In addition, non-application exceptions may not provide relevant information to help the user rectify the problem.

Solution Reference

Decouple the clients from the business tier and hide the business-tier implementation details from clients, using business delegates. Business delegates intercept all service exceptions and may throw an application exception. Business delegates are plain Java objects that are local to the client. Typically, business delegates are developed by the EJB developers and provided to the client developers.

- **Refactoring** See "Introduce Business Delegate" on page 94.
- **Pattern** See *Business Delegate* (302).

Using Entity Bean Finder Methods to Return a Large Results Set

Problem Summary

Frequently, applications require the ability to search and obtain a list of values. Using an EJB finder method to look up a large collection of entity beans will return a collection of remote references. Consequently, the client has to invoke a method on each remote reference to get the data. This is a remote call and can become very expensive, especially impacting performance, when the caller invokes remote calls on each entity bean reference in the collection.

Solution Reference

Implement queries using session beans and DAOs to obtain a list of *Transfer Objects* (415) instead of remote references. Use a DAO to perform searches instead of EJB finder methods.

- **Pattern** See *Value List Handler* (444).
- **Pattern** See "Data Access Object" on page 462.

Client Aggregates Data from Business Components

Problem Summary

The application clients (in the client or presentation tier) typically need the data model for the application from the business tier. Since the model is implemented by business components—such as entity beans, session beans, and arbitrary objects in the business tier—the client must locate, interact with, and extract the necessary data from various business components to construct the data model.

These client actions introduce network overhead due to multiple invocations from the client into the business tier. In addition, the client becomes tightly coupled with the application model. In applications where there are various types of clients, this coupling problem multiplies: A change to the model requires changes to all clients that contain code to interact with those model elements comprised of business components.

Solution Reference

Decouple the client from model construction. Implement a business-tier component that is responsible for the construction of the required application model.

- **Pattern** See *Transfer Object Assembler* (433).

Using Enterprise Beans for Long-Lived Transactions

Problem Summary

Enterprise beans (pre-EJB 2.0) are suitable for synchronous processing. Furthermore, enterprise beans do well if each method implemented in a bean produces an outcome within a predictable and acceptable time period.

If an enterprise bean method takes a significant amount of time to process a client request, or if it blocks while processing, this also blocks the container resources, such as memory and threads, used by the bean. This can severely impact performance and deplete system resources.

An enterprise bean transaction that takes a long time to complete potentially locks out resources from other enterprise bean instances that need those resources, resulting in performance bottlenecks.

Solution Reference

Implement asynchronous processing service using a message-oriented middleware (MOM) with a Java Message Service (JMS) API to facilitate long-lived transactions.

- **Pattern** See "Service Activator" on page 496.

Stateless Session Bean Reconstructs Conversational State for Each Invocation

Problem Summary

Some designers choose stateless session beans to increase scalability. They may inadvertently decide to model all business processes as stateless session beans even though the session beans require conversational state. But, since the session bean is stateless, it must rebuild conversational state in every method invocation. The state may have to be rebuilt by retrieving data from a database. This completely defeats the purpose of using stateless session beans to improve performance and scalability and can severely degrade performance.

Solution Reference

Analyze the interaction model before choosing the stateless session bean mode. The choice of stateful or stateless session bean depends on the need for maintaining conversational state across method invocations in stateful session bean versus the cost of rebuilding the state during each invocation in stateless session bean.

- **Pattern** See *Transfer Object Assembler* (433), *Stateless Session Façade Strategy* on page 345, and *Stateful Session Façade Strategy* on page 345.
- **Design** See "Session Bean—Stateless Versus Stateful" on page 46 and "Storing State on the Business Tier" on page 48.

J2EE Refactorings

Topics in This Chapter

- Presentation Tier Refactorings
- Business and Integration Tier Refactorings
- General Refactorings

Chapter 4

Presentation Tier Refactorings

The refactorings in this section apply to the presentation tier.

Introduce a Controller

Control logic is scattered throughout the application, typically duplicated in multiple JavaServer Pages (JSP) views.

Extract control logic into one or more controller classes that serve as the initial contact point for handling a client request.

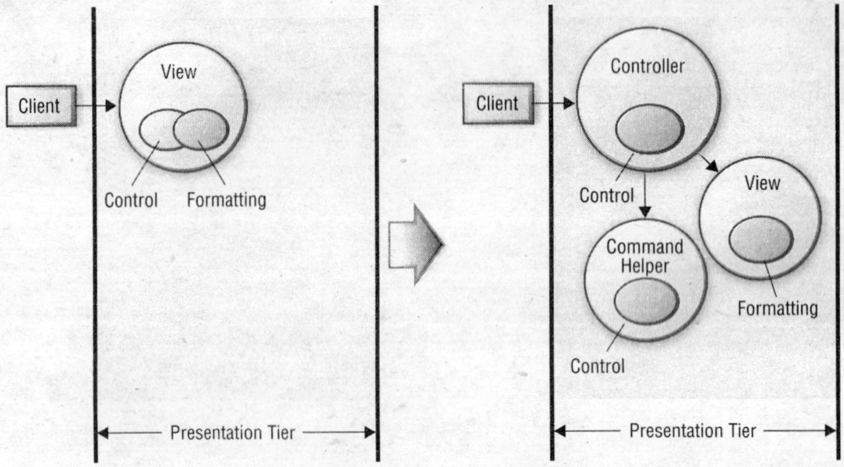

Figure 4.1 Introduce a Controller

Motivation

Control code that is duplicated in multiple JSP also needs to be maintained in each JSP. Extracting this code into one or more centralized controller class improves the modularity, reusability, and maintainability of the application.

Mechanics

- ❑ Use the *Front Controller* (166) pattern as a guide for applying *Extract Class* [Fowler] to create a controller class, moving duplicate control logic from individual JSP into this controller.

- ⇨ *See Front Controller (166).*
- ⇨ *Remember that the controller is a delegation point for controlling the request handling. Partition the code with an eye toward modularity and reuse. Do not necessarily embed all the control code directly within a single controller, but rather consider creating helper components to which it may delegate. See "Creating Fat Controllers" on page 36.*

- ❑ Control code may also be encapsulated in command objects that work in coordination with the controller, utilizing the *Command* pattern [GoF].
  - ⇨ *See Front Controller (166), Command and Controller strategy.*
  - ⇨ *See Application Controller (205), Command and Controller strategy.*

Example

Assume we have the structure shown in Example 4.1 in many of our JSP.

Example 4.1 Introduce a Controller – JSP Structure

```
<HTML>
<BODY>
<control:grant_access/>
.
.
.


</BODY>
</HTML>
```

The three vertical dots represent the body of each JSP, which is not being shown in this example. While this body portion differs for each JSP, the helper at the top of the page, implemented as a custom tag, is the same. This helper is responsible for controlling access to this page. It is an "all-or-nothing" type of control, meaning that a client is either granted access to the whole page or is denied access entirely.

If we change the design and introduce a controller, as described in the mechanics, then each of our JSP will no longer include the <control:grant_access/> tag, as seen in Example 4.1.

Instead, we have a centralized controller that manages this behavior, handling the access control check that we removed from each JSP. Example 4.2 is a snippet of code from the controller, which is implemented as a servlet.

Example 4.2 Introduce a Controller - Controller Structure

```

if (grantAccess())
{
    dispatchToNextView();
}
else
{
    dispatchToAccessDeniedView();
}
```

Of course, helpers are suitable for control code in some cases. For example, if only a small fraction of our JSP need this type of access control, then it is not unreasonable to include a custom tag helper in each of these few pages to accomplish this goal. Another reason we might use custom tags in individual JSP is to control access to specific subviews of a composite view (see *CompositeView* (264)).

If we are already using a controller, then we still might want to add this behavior in this centralized place, since the number of pages we want to protect might grow over time. To handle the case of an existing controller, we simply extract control code from our views and add it to the existing controller. In effect, we are moving methods (using *Move Method* [Fowler]) instead of extracting a new class.

Introduce Synchronizer Token

Clients make duplicate resource requests that should be monitored and controlled, or clients access certain views out of order by returning to previously bookmarked pages.

Use a shared token to monitor and control the request flow and client access to certain resources.

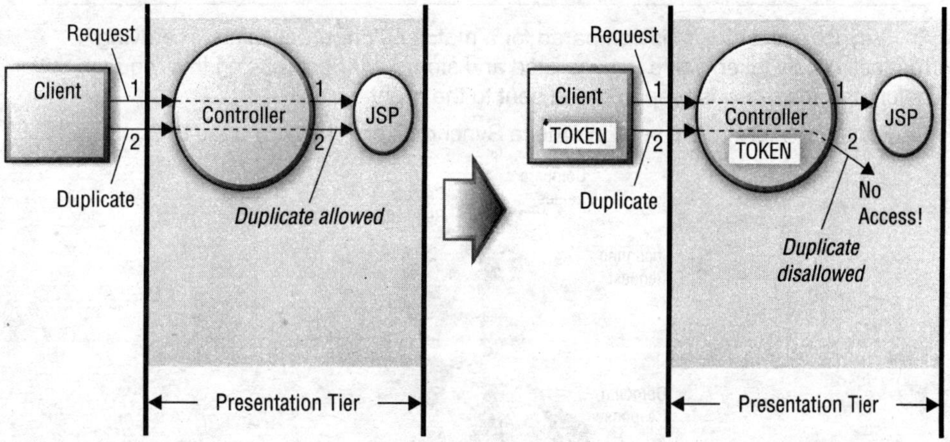

Figure 4.2 Introduce Synchronizer Token

Motivation

There are a number of scenarios in which control of an incoming request is desired. One of the most common reasons is the desire to control duplicate request submissions from a client. Such duplicate submissions may occur when the user clicks the Back or Stop browser buttons and resubmits a form.

While this issue is mainly one of controlling the order or flow of the requests, there is also the issue of controlling access based on permissions. For introducing permission-based control, see "Hide Resources From a Client" on page 88.

Mechanics

- ❑ Create one or more helper classes responsible for generating and comparing one-time-use, unique tokens.
- ❑ Alternatively, this logic may be added to already existing control components.

- ❑ The component managing this activity (typically a controller, but possibly a JSP) delegates to these helpers, managing the temporary storage of a fresh token for each client submission.

  A copy of the token is stored per user on the server and on the client browser. The token is typically stored on the client browser as a hidden field and on the server in a user session.

Design Note: When Is a Token Generated and Stored? When Is a Token Checked?

A synchronizer token is compared for a match before processing an arriving request. A new token value is generated and stored after processing this request, but before the response is prepared and sent to the client.

For more information, see "Introduce Synchronizer Token" on page 67.

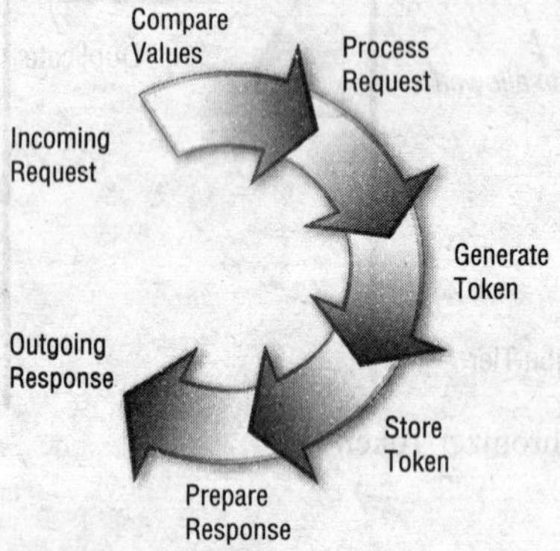

Synchronizer Token Life Cycle

- ❑ Add logic to check whether the token arriving with the client request matches the token in the user session.

  ⇨ *The token arriving from the client in the current request should be the same token that the server sent to the client with its last response. Thus a match of these two values confirms that this is not a duplicate submission, while a mismatch suggests this possibility.*

  ⇨ *As stated, a mismatch might also occur for other reasons, such as a user navigating directly to a bookmarked page, but a duplicate request submission is the most common reason. (See Presentation Tier Design Considerations, Controlling Client Access" on page 22 for more information.)*

- ❑ A controller typically manages token generation and comparison. Consider introducing a controller, if one does not already exist.
  - ⇨ *See "Introduce a Controller" on page 64.*
  - ⇨ *Without a controller to centralize management of token generation and comparison, this behavior must be referenced from each JSP.*
  - ⇨ *Typically, the JSP delegates to a helper component, implemented as either a JavaBean or custom tag (see Application Controller (205)), which encapsulates the responsibilities token management.*

The source code excerpts in Introduce Synchronizer Token are reprinted with permission under the Apache Software License, Version 1.1. See page 625 to view the terms of this license.

Example

The Struts presentation framework applies several of the *J2EE* patterns and refactorings. It introduces this exact type of request flow control, and we use excerpts from this open source framework in our example. Instead of creating a separate utility class to encapsulate the token generation and matching logic, Struts simply adds this functionality to a preexisting class that is part of its control mechanism. The class is called *Action*, and it is a common superclass for all actions. Actions are Command objects that extend the controller functionality. This is an application of the *Front Controller* (166) pattern, *Command and Controller* strategy. As shown in Example 4.3, the saveToken() method, which is part of the Action class, generates and stores token values.

Example 4.3 Generate and Store Token

```

/**
 * Save a new transaction token in the
 * user's current session, creating
 * a new session if necessary.
 *
 * @param request The servlet request we are processing
 */
protected void saveToken(HttpServletRequest request) {

HttpSession session = request.getSession();
String token = generateToken(request);
if (token != null)
  session.setAttribute(TRANSACTION_TOKEN_KEY, token);
}
```

This method generates a unique token, calculated using the session ID and the current time, and stores this value into the user session.

At some point (usually immediately) prior to generating the HTML display for the client responsible for submitting a request that we do not want to duplicate (this display typically includes a form to be posted back to the server), a one-time token value is set, as previously described, by making the following method invocation:

```
saveToken(request);
```

Additionally, the JSP responsible for generating this HTML display also includes logic that delegates to a helper class to generate a hidden field that includes this token value. Thus, the page sent to the client, which typically includes a form that will be submitted back to the server, includes a hidden field of the following form:

```
<input type="hidden" name="org.apache.struts.taglib.html.TOKEN"
value="8d2c392e93a39d299ec45a22">
```

The value attribute of this hidden field is the value of the token that was generated by the saveToken() method.

When the client submits the page that includes this hidden field, the controller delegates to a Command object (again, a subclass of the Action class) that compares the token value in the user session with the value in the request object parameter that came from the hidden field in the page. The Command object uses the method shown in Example 4.4, also excerpted from its superclass (the Action class again), to compare the values.

Example 4.4 Check For a Valid Token

```

/**
* Return <code>true</code> if there is a transaction
* token stored in the user's current session, and
* the value submitted as a request request parameter
* with this action matches it.
*
* Returns <code>false</code>
* under any of the following circumstances:
* <ul>
* <li>No session associated with this request</li>
* <li>No transaction token saved in the session</li>
```

```
* <li>No transaction token included as a request
* parameter</li>
* <li>The included transaction token value does not
*     match the transaction token in the user's
*     session</li>
* </ul>
*
* @param request The servlet request we are processing
*/

protected boolean isTokenValid(HttpServletRequest request) {

    // Retrieve the saved transaction token from our
    // session
    HttpSession session = request.getSession(false);
    if (session == null)
        return (false);
    String saved = (String)
        session.getAttribute(TRANSACTION_TOKEN_KEY);
    if (saved == null)
        return (false);
    // Retrieve the transaction token included in this
    // request

    String token = (String)
        request.getParameter(Constants.TOKEN_KEY);
    if (token == null)
        return (false);

    // Do the values match?
    return (saved.equals(token));

}
```


If there is a match, then we are certain that this request submission is not a duplicate. If the tokens do not match, then we are able to take appropriate action to deal with this potentially duplicate form submission.

Localize Disparate Logic

Business logic and presentation formatting are intermingled within a JSP view.

Extract business logic into one or more helper classes that can be used by the JSP or by a controller.

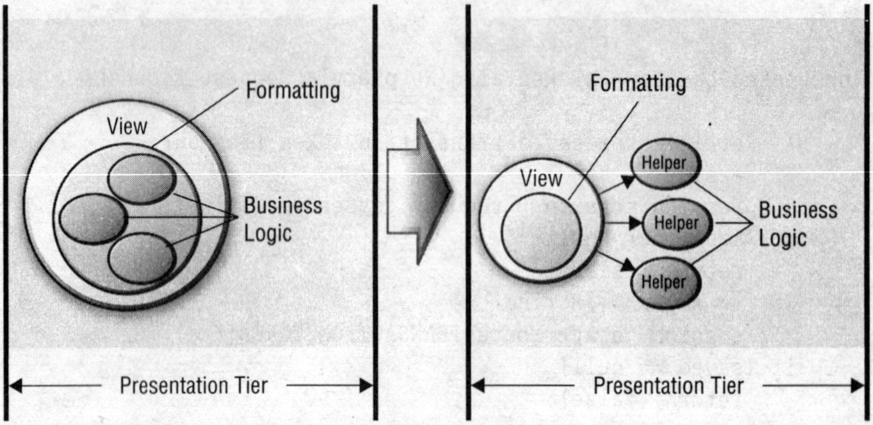

Figure 4.3 Localize Disparate Logic: Factor Back

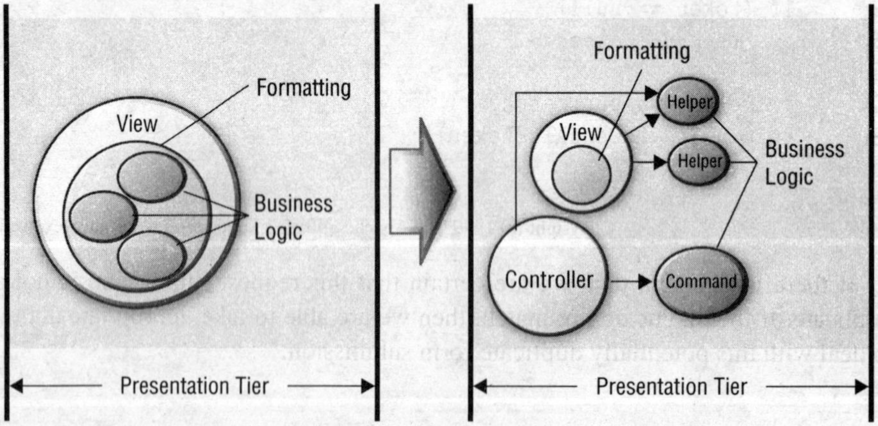

Figure 4.4 Localize Disparate Logic: Factor Forward

Motivation

To create cleaner abstractions, increase cohesion and reduce coupling, which improves modularity and reusability. Well-partitioned, modular applications also provide better separation of developer roles, since Web developers own formatting code, while software developers own business logic.

Mechanics

- ❑ Use the *View Helper* (240) pattern as a guide for applying *Extract Class* [Fowler] to create new helper classes, moving business logic from the JSP into these helpers.
- ❑ Delegate to these helper classes from the JSP.
  - ➪ *See View Helper (240).*
  - ➪ *The initial contact point for handling the client request could be the view, as shown in the Factor Back diagram in Figure 4.3. See Dispatcher View (288).*
- ❑ Consider introducing a controller, if one does not already exist.
  - ➪ *See "Introduce a Controller" on page 64.*
  - ➪ *As shown in Figure 4.4, the controller can use a command helper.*
  - ➪ *The initial contact point for handling the client request could be the controller, as shown in the Factor Forward diagram. See Service to Worker (276).*

Example

We start with the sample code listed in Example 4.5. It is a JSP that includes lots of scriptlet code, mingling business logic with the view.

Example 4.5 JSP with Scriptlet Code

```

<html>
<head><title>Employee List</title></head>
<body>
<%-- Display All employees belonging to a department and earning
at most the given salary --%>

<%

    // Get the department for which the employees are
```

```
    // to be listed
    String deptidStr = request.getParameter(
        Constants.REQ_DEPTID);

    // Get the max salary constraint
    String salaryStr = request.getParameter(
        Constants.REQ_SALARY);

    // validate parameters

    // if salary or department not specified, go to
    // error page
    if ( (deptidStr == null) || (salaryStr == null ) )
    {
       request.setAttribute(Constants.ATTR_MESSAGE,
        "Insufficient query parameters specified" +
        "(Department and Salary)");
       request.getRequestDispatcher("/error.jsp").
         forward(request, response);
    }

    // convert to numerics
    int deptid = 0;
    float salary = 0;
    try
    {
        deptid = Integer.parseInt(deptidStr);
        salary = Float.parseFloat(salaryStr);
    }
    catch(NumberFormatException e)
    {
       request.setAttribute(Constants.ATTR_MESSAGE,
          "Invalid Search Values" +
          "(department id and salary )");
       request.getRequestDispatcher("/error.jsp").
          forward(request, response);

    }

    // check if they within legal limits
    if ( salary < 0  )
    {
      request.setAttribute(Constants.ATTR_MESSAGE,
```

```
        "Invalid Search Values" +
        "(department id and salary )");
      request.getRequestDispatcher("/error.jsp").
        forward(request, response);
    }

%>

<h3><center> List of employees in department # <%=deptid%>
    earning at most <%= salary %>. </h3>

<%
    Iterator employees = new EmployeeDelegate().
         getEmployees(deptid);
%>

<table border="1" >
    <tr>
        <th> First Name </th>
        <th> Last Name </th>
        <th> Designation </th>
        <th> Employee Id </th>
        <th> Tax Deductibles </th>
        <th> Performance Remarks </th>
        <th> Yearly Salary</th>
    </tr>
<%
    while ( employees.hasNext() )
    {
        EmployeeVO employee = (EmployeeVO)
              employees.next();

        // display only if search criteria is met
        if ( employee.getYearlySalary() <= salary )
        {
%>
        <tr>
          <td> <%=employee.getFirstName()%></td>

          <td> <%=employee.getLastName()%></td>
          <td> <%=employee.getDesignation()%></td>
          <td> <%=employee.getId()%></td>
          <td> <%=employee.getNoOfDeductibles()%></td>
```

```
            <td> <%=employee.getPerformanceRemarks()%>
                 </td>
            <td> <%=employee.getYearlySalary()%></td>
          </tr>
<%
          }
     }
%>
</table>

<%@ include file="/jsp/trace.jsp" %>
<P> <B>Business logic and presentation formatting are
              intermingled within this JSP view. </B>

</body>
</html>
```

This JSP generates an HTML table that lists employees at a certain salary level. The JSP encapsulates formatting and business logic, as shown in Figure 4.5.

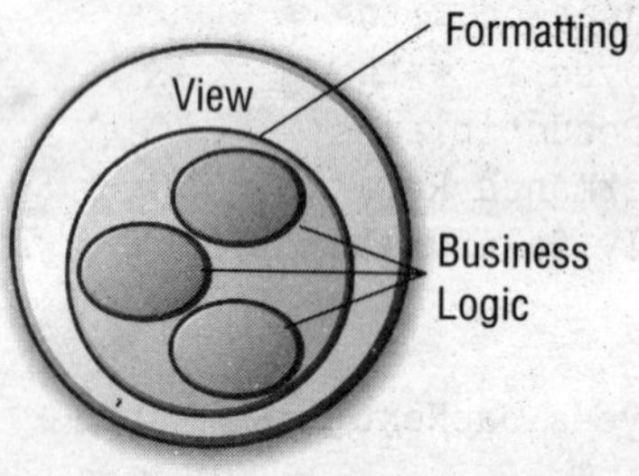

Figure 4.5 View With Mingled Business Logic and Formatting Code

As Example 4.6 shows, we apply the *View Helper* (240) pattern, changing the design and extracting scriptlet code from the JSP view.

Example 4.6 JSP with Scriptlet Code Extracted

```

<%@ taglib uri="/WEB-INF/corepatternstaglibrary.tld"
    prefix="corepatterns" %>
<html>
<head><title>Employee List</title></head>
<body>

```

```
<corepatterns:employeeAdapter />

<h3><center>List of employees in
  <corepatterns:department attribute="id"/>
  department - Using Custom Tag Helper Strategy </h3>

<table border="1" >
    <tr>
        <th> First Name </th>
        <th> Last Name </th>
        <th> Designation </th>
        <th> Employee Id </th>
        <th> Tax Deductibles </th>
        <th> Performance Remarks </th>
        <th> Yearly Salary</th>
    </tr>
    <corepatterns:employeelist id="employeelist_key">
    <tr>
      <td><corepatterns:employee
            attribute="FirstName"/></td>
      <td><corepatterns:employee
            attribute="LastName"/></td>
      <td><corepatterns:employee
            attribute="Designation"/> </td>
        <td><corepatterns:employee
            attribute="Id"/></td>
        <td><corepatterns:employee
            attribute="NoOfDeductibles"/></td>
        <td><corepatterns:employee
            attribute="PerformanceRemarks"/></td>
        <td><corepatterns:employee
            attribute="YearlySalary"/></td>
        <td>
     </tr>
    </corepatterns:employeelist>
</table>

</body>
</html>
```

Additionally, we have written two custom tag helpers to encapsulate our business and presentation formatting processing logic by adapting the data model into the rows and columns of our HTML table.

The two helpers are the <corepatterns:employeelist> tag and the <corepatterns:employee> tag.

Figure 4.6 shows that we have moved from the design represented by the left side of the arrow to the one represented on the right side.

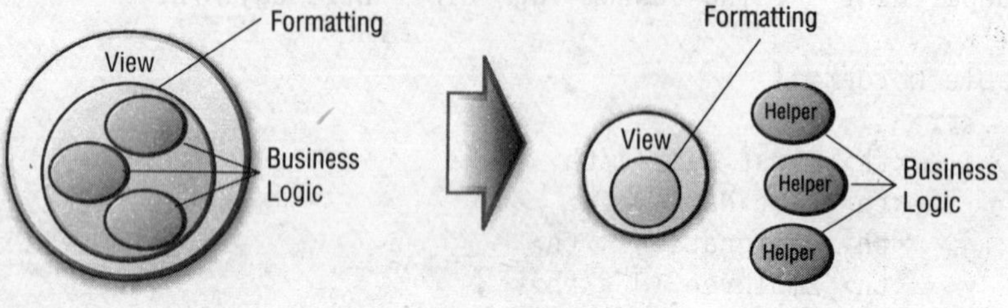

Figure 4.6 Extracting Business Logic Into Helper Classes

Business logic has been extracted into helper classes instead of being embedded directly within the JSP. These helpers handle a variety of tasks, including content retrieval, access control, and adapting model state for display. In the second case, the helper actually encapsulates some of the presentation processing logic, such as formatting a result set into an HTML table. See also "Remove Conversions from View" on page 84. This helps us meet our goal of extracting as much programming logic from the view as possible, thus using the JSP to ask the helper for the completed table, instead of including scriptlet code in the JSP to generate the table.

Helper components may be implemented as JavaBeans or custom tags (see *Application Controller* (205)). JavaBean helpers are well suited to encapsulating content retrieval logic and storing the results, while custom tag helpers are well suited to the aforementioned task of converting the model for display, such as creating a table from a result set. There is quite a bit of overlap, though, so other factors, such as developer experience and manageability issues, may affect the decision about how to implement a helper.

Applying the second bullet of the mechanics, we simply delegate the work to the helpers, as shown in Figure 4.7.

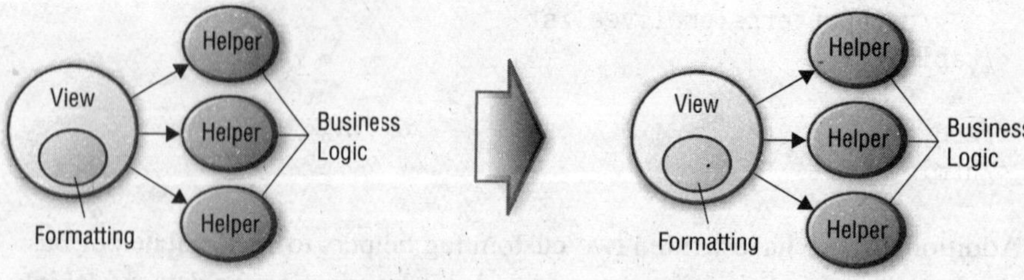

Figure 4.7 Delegate Work to Helpers

The JSP view uses the helper classes to perform the view processing and generation. Typically, a controller is used in front of the JSP as the initial contact point for client requests (see *Front Controller* (166) and *Introduce a Controller* on page 64). The controller dispatches to the view, but prior to doing so, the controller may also delegate work to the helper components (see *Service to Worker* (276)).

Having introduced a controller, we have made the transition in Figure 4.8.

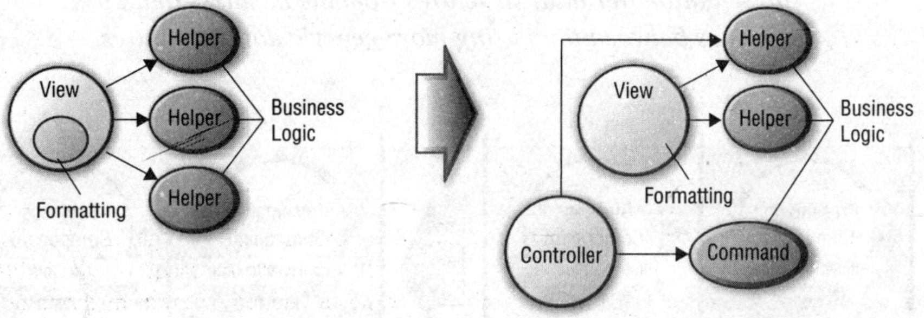

Figure 4.8 Introducing a Controller

Hide Presentation Tier-Specific Details From the Business Tier

Request handling and/or protocol-related data structures are exposed from the presentation tier to the business tier.

Remove all references to request handling and protocol-related presentation tier data structures from the business tier. Pass values between tiers using more generic data structures.

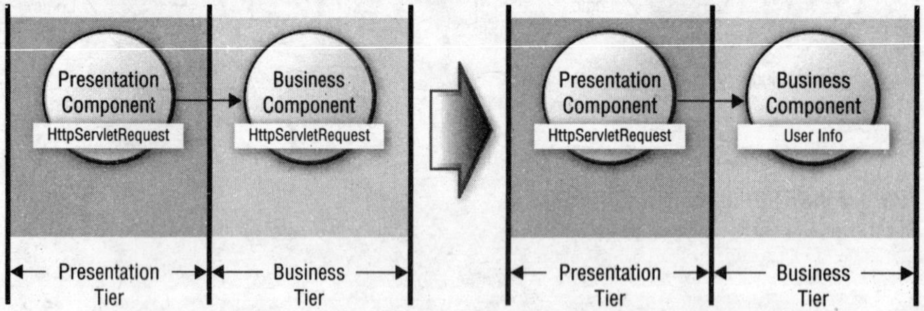

Figure 4.9 Hide Presentation Tier-Specific Details From the Business Tier

Motivation

Implementation details specific to one tier should not be introduced in another tier. The service API exposed by the business tier to the presentation tier will likely be used by other clients as well. If the service API accepts parameters with types, such as HttpServletRequest, then every client to the service is forced to package its data in a servlet request data structure. This drastically reduces the service's reusability.

Mechanics

- ❑ Replace all references to presentation-tier data structures in the business tier with references to more generic data structures and types.
  - ⇨ *These are typically business-tier methods accepting parameters with types such as* HttpServletRequest *that might be replaced with parameters of more generic types, such as String, int, or UserInfo.*
- ❑ Modify client code in the presentation tier that invokes these methods.

- ⇨ *Pieces of the presentation tier data structure may be passed to the business tier methods as individual arguments. For example, if the* HttpServletRequest *has parameters x, y, and z, a method in the business tier, instead of accepting the* HttpServletRequest *as a parameter, might accept these three arguments individually as* Strings. *One drawback of passing fine-grained, individual arguments is that this strategy more tightly couples the details of the presentation tier with the business service API. Thus, if the state required by the service changes, then the service API must change.*
- ⇨ *A slightly more flexible alternative is to copy the relevant state from the presentation tier data structure into a more generic data structure, such as a Transfer Object (415), which is passed into the business tier. In this case the service API continues to accept this object, even if its implementation details change.*

❑ Alternatively, implement a strategy of overlaying interface types, if a presentation-tier framework, such as the popular Struts project [Struts], is used.

- ⇨ *When handling a request, frameworks typically create numerous data structures. For example, typically a framework will transparently complete the step of copying the relevant state from the* HttpServletRequest *data structure to a more generic data structure, massaging request parameters into a framework-specific data type. While this data type may fulfill the same basic role as a Transfer Object (415), it is a framework-specific data type. Thus, passing this data structure into the business tier introduces coupling between the request-handling framework and the business services.*
- ⇨ *In this case, one could still take the approach just described and copy the framework-specific data structure into a generic structure before passing it to the business tier. Instead, a more efficient solution is to simply create a generic type of interface that mirrors the methods of the framework-specific type. If this interface type is overlaid onto the framework-specific object, then this object can be shared with the business tier without any coupling to the specific framework.*
- ⇨ *For example, if the framework instantiates a subclass of* a.framework.StateBean *called* my.stuff.MyStateBean, *it will be of type* StateBean.

Note: Instance creation is typically done via a factory. Parameters are not shown, for simplicity.

```
a.framework.StateBean bean = new my.stuff.MyStateBean(...);
```

⇨ *If the business tier accepted this bean as a parameter, the type would be* StateBean*:*

```
public void aRemoteBizTierMethod(a.framework.StateBean bean)
```

⇨ *Instead of passing the bean of type* StateBean *into the business tier, introduce a new Interface called* my.stuff.MyStateVO*, implemented by* my.stuff.MyStateBean*:*

```
public class MyStateBean extends a.framework.StateBean implements MyStateVO
```

⇨ *Now the business tier can include the following method signature:*

```
public void aRemoteBizTierMethod(my.stuff.MyStateVO bean)
```

⇨ *There is no need to copy parameters into a more generic Transfer Object (415), and the framework type is no longer exposed across tiers.*

❑ Finally, on a separate note, remember that you can further reduce the coupling among the logically unrelated parts of the application by applying this refactoring to presentation-tier domain objects, as well.

Visually, we are describing something similar to Figure 4.10.

Figure 4.10 Hiding Presentation Tier-Specific Details From Domain Objects

⇨ *The same motivation and mechanics apply to this situation, since we don't want to reduce the reusability of our basic domain objects, such as* Customer *objects.*

⇨ *This localizes all references to protocol-related data structures in and around the request handling components, such as the controller. An example of decoupling the HttpServletRequest from a domain object is shown in Example 4.7 and Example 4.8 in the "Example" section.*

Example

The Customer class in Example 4.7 accepts an HttpServletRequest instance as a parameter, which greatly reduces the generic nature of this domain object. If a non-web client wanted to use this Customer class, it would somehow need to first generate an HttpServletRequest object, which is inappropriate.

Example 4.7 Tight Coupling Between a Domain Object and HttpServletRequest Object

```
/** The following excerpt shows a domain object that is too
tightly coupled with HttpServletRequest **/
public class Customer
{
  public Customer ( HttpServletRequest request )
  {
       firstName = request.getParameter("firstname");
       lastName = request.getParameter("lastname ");
  }
}
```

Instead of exposing the HttpServletRequest object to a general Customer object, simply decouple the two, as shown in Example 4.8:

Example 4.8 Reduced Coupling Between a Domain Object and HttpServletRequest object

```
// Domain Object not coupled with HttpServletRequest
public class Customer
{
  public Customer ( String first, String last )
  {
    firstName = first;
    lastName = last;
  }
}
```

Remove Conversions from View

Portions of the model are converted for display within a view component.

Extract all conversion code from view and encapsulate it in one or more helper classes.

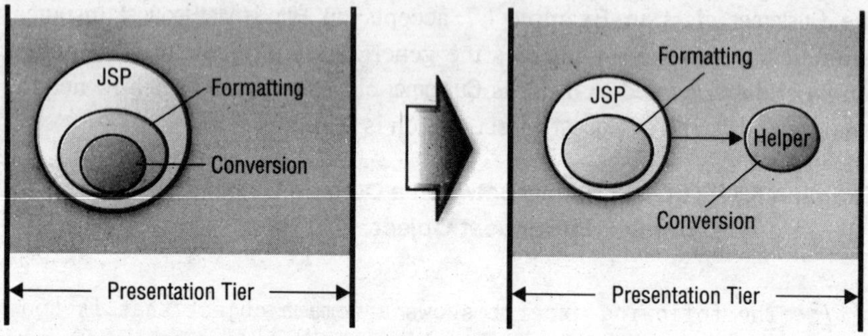

Figure 4.11 Remove Conversions From View

Motivation

Directly embedding logic that converts the model for display in the JSP view reduces the application's modularity and reusability. Since such conversions might occur in multiple JSP, the code would need to be duplicated, creating a copy-and-paste type of reuse that is a maintenance headache.

Mechanics

- ❑ Apply *Extract Class* [Fowler] to move the converting and adapting logic from individual JSP into helper classes.
  - ⇨ *An example is adapting a database result set into an HTML table via some application code.*
- ❑ Invoke these helpers from the JSP to process the conversions and adaptations as desired.
  - ⇨ *The conversion is performed by the helper class to which the JSP delegates.*

Example

In this example, we examine logic that converts a collection of items, such as a result set, into an HTML table.

While this is indeed formatting logic in one sense, it is also conversion code, generating a table of results from an intermediate model. The implementation of this dynamic conversion is reusable if it is encapsulated in a custom tag instead of being embedded directly within a JSP.

Example 4.9 is an example of a JSP that includes this type of conversion logic embedded directly in its source.

Example 4.9 Conversion Logic Embedded Within View

```

<html>
<head><title>Employee List</title></head>
<body>

<h3><head><center> List of employees</h3>

<%
     String firstName =
       (String)request.getParameter("firstName");
     String lastName  =
       (String)request.getParameter("lastName");
     if ( firstName == null )
       // if none specific, fetch all
       firstName = "";
     if ( lastName == null )
       lastName = "";

     EmployeeDelegate empDelegate = new
             EmployeeDelegate();
     Iterator employees =
         empDelegate.getEmployees(
           EmployeeDelegate.ALL_DEPARTMENTS);
%>

<table border="1" >
     <tr>
         <th> First Name </th>
         <th> Last Name </th>
         <th> Designation </th>
     </tr>
<%
     while ( employees.hasNext() )
     {
```

```

            EmployeeVO employee = (EmployeeVO)
                                    employees.next();

            if ( employee.getFirstName().
                       startsWith(firstName) &&
                     employee.getLastName().
                       startsWith(lastName) ) {
%>
  <tr>
    <td><%=employee.getFirstName().toUpperCase() %></td>
    <td> <%=employee.getLastName().toUpperCase() %></td>
    <td> <%=employee.getDesignation()%></td>
  </tr>
<%
            }
        }
%>
</table>
```

The first step is to extract this logic into helper classes. Custom tag helpers make the most sense in this case, since we want to remove as much scriptlet code from the JSP as possible. The JSP is then modified to delegate to these helpers to complete the processing. Example 4.10 shows the JSP after these steps.

Example 4.10 Logic Extracted Into Helper Classes

```

<html>
<head><title>Employee List - Refactored </title>
</head>
<body>

<h3> <center>List of employees</h3>

<corepatterns:employeeAdapter />

<table border="1" >
    <tr>
        <th> First Name </th>
        <th> Last Name </th>
        <th> Designation </th>
    </tr>
```

```

<corepatterns:employeelist id="employeelist"
    match="FirstName, LastName">
<tr>

    <td><corepatterns:employee attribute= "FirstName"
        case="Upper" /> </td>
    <td><corepatterns:employee attribute= "LastName"
        case="Upper" /></td>
    <td><corepatterns:employee attribute= "Designation" />
       </td>
    <td>
 </tr>
</corepatterns:employeelist>
</table>
```

Now let's examine another type of conversion. In some cases, portions of the model are converted to HTML via XSL transformations. This can also be accomplished using custom tag helpers. Once again, this allows us to extract the logic from the JSP itself, providing us with more modular and reusable components. Here is an example of a JSP that uses custom tag helpers to perform its conversions, instead of performing such conversions inline:

```
<%@taglib uri="http://jakarta.apache.org/taglibs/xsl-1.0"
prefix="xsl" %>
<xsl:apply nameXml="model" propertyXml="xml"
xsl="/stylesheet/transform.xsl"/>
```

The Jakarta taglibs [JakartaTaglibs] XSL apply tag is used to generate the entire output of this page. It could be used to simply generate component pieces of the page in the same manner. The tag invocation relies on the fact that a bean exists in a page scope called "model," with a property named "xml." In other words, there is an instance of a bean in a page scope that has a method with the following signature:

```
public String getXml()
```

It's worth noting that these types of conversions can be performed entirely independent of JSP. Depending on numerous factors, such as the storage format of the content and existence of various legacy technologies, one might choose this route.

Hide Resources From a Client

Certain resources, such as JSP views, are directly accessible to clients, though access should be restricted.

Hide certain resources via container configuration or by using a control component.

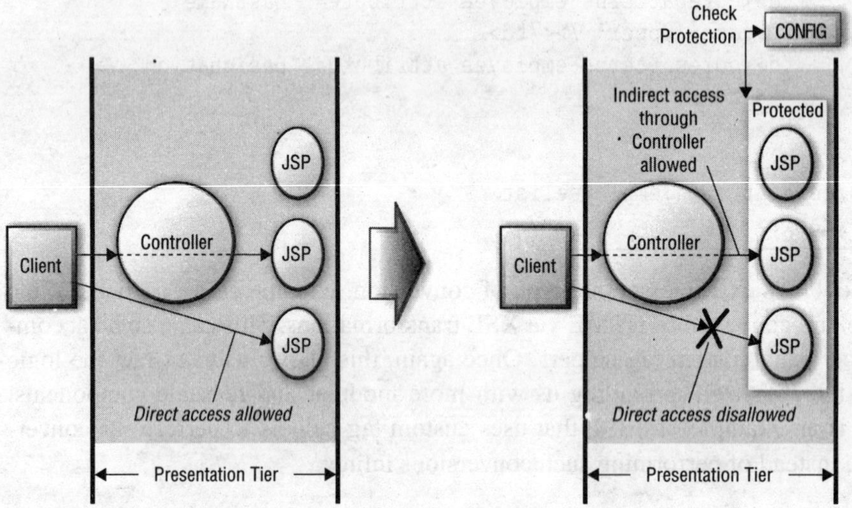

Figure 4.12 Restricted via Container Configuration

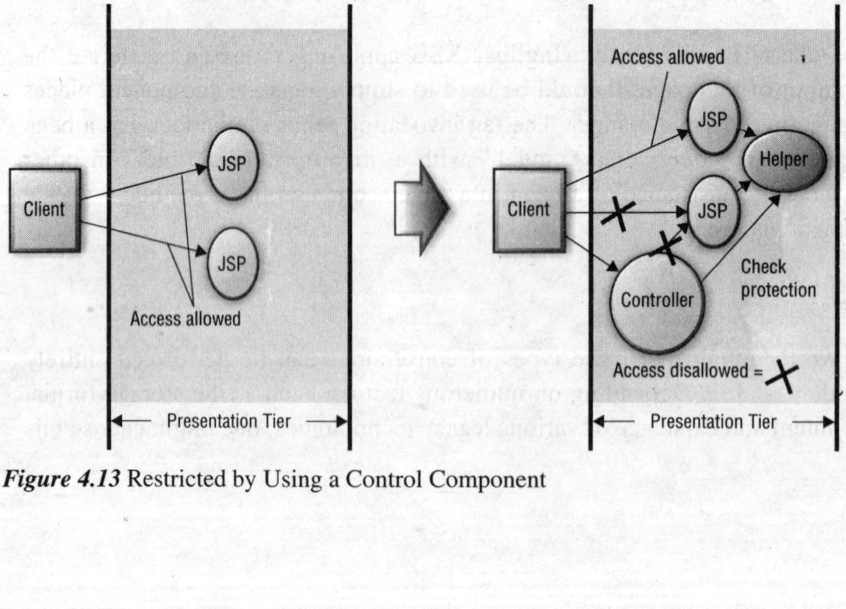

Figure 4.13 Restricted by Using a Control Component

Motivation

You frequently want to be able to control an incoming request. This refactoring describes permission-based control and protection.

If the order or flow of the client requests must be controlled, then apply Introduce Synchronizer Token (see "Introduce Synchronizer Token" on page 67).

Mechanics

- ❑ Restrict access to certain resources (such as Web resources, servlets, among others) via configuration, by moving these resources into a subdirectory of the /WEB-INF/ subdirectory of the Web application.
  - ⇨ *For example, to block direct browser access to a view called* info.jsp, *in the* securityissues *Web application, we could place the JSP source file in the following subdirectory:* */securityissues/WEB-INF/internalaccessonly/ info.jsp.*
- ❑ Restrict access using a control component.
  - ⇨ *Introduce a controller (see "Introduce a Controller" on page 64) may be applied and the controller can manage access to protected resources.*
  - ⇨ *Additionally, each resource to be protected can manage its own access control, meaning it would delegate to a helper class to perform this processing.*
- ❑ Create one or more helper classes.
  - ⇨ *Depending on the implementation, either the controller or each JSP itself delegates to these helper classes to check whether the resource should be served.*

Example

Restricted by Container Configuration

We can make a JSP called info.jsp inaccessible to our client, except via a controller, by moving the JSP under the /WEB-INF/ directory.

If we have a web application called corepatterns, then we might start with the following configuration under our server root directory:

```
/corepatterns/secure_page.jsp
```

By default, this allows direct client access to this resource, as shown in the following URL:

```
http://localhost:8080/corepatterns/secure_page.jsp
```

To restrict direct access, we can simply move the JSP file to a subdirectory of the /WEB-INF/ directory, giving us the following under our server root:

```
/corepatterns/WEB-INF/privateaccess/secure_page.jsp
```

The /WEB-INF/ directory hierarchy is accessible only indirectly via internal requests, such as those coming through a controller and a RequestDispatcher. Thus, a browser client can only access this file now using a URL similar to the following:

```
http://localhost:8080/corepatterns/controller?view=
     /corepatterns/WEB-INF/privateaccess/secure_page.jsp
```

Note: The previous URL is for example purposes only and is *not* a recommended way to pass path information to the server. The view query parameter should not expose the server's directory structure. It does so in this example only to clarify the example's intent.

If this request is handled by a servlet controller, then it can forward the request to secure_page.jsp, using the RequestDispatcher.

On the other hand, if an attempt is made to access the resource directly, as shown in the following code snipped, the server responds that the requested resource is not available, as shown in Figure 4.14.

```
http://localhost:8080/corepatterns/WEB-INF/privateaccess/secure_page.jsp
```

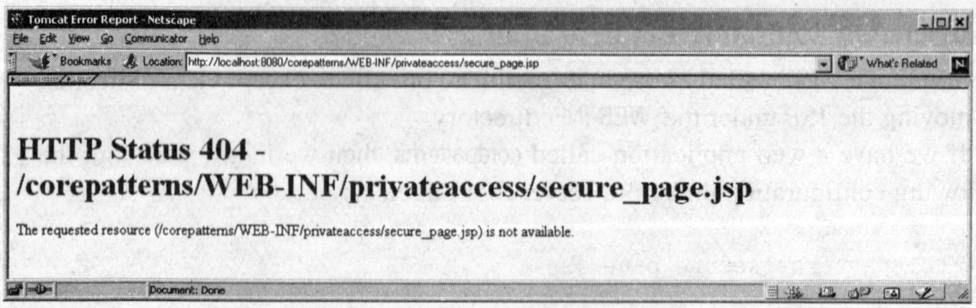

Figure 4.14 Restricting Direct Browser Access via Simple File Configuration

Restricted by Using a Control Component

Another option for restricting access is to delegate to a control component, as shown in Figure 4.13 and Example 4.11.

Example 4.11 Controlling Access Using a Control Component

```

<%@ taglib uri="/WEB-INF/corepatternstaglibrary.tld"
prefix="corepatterns" %>
<corepatterns:guard/>
<html>
<head><title>Hide Resource from Client</title></head>
<body>

<h2>This view is shown to the client only if the
control component allows access. The view delegates
the control check to the guard tag at the top of the
page.</h2>
</body>
</html>
```

Business and Integration Tier Refactorings

Wrap Entities With Session

Entity beans from the business tier are exposed to clients in another tier.

Use a Session Façade (341) to encapsulate the entity beans.

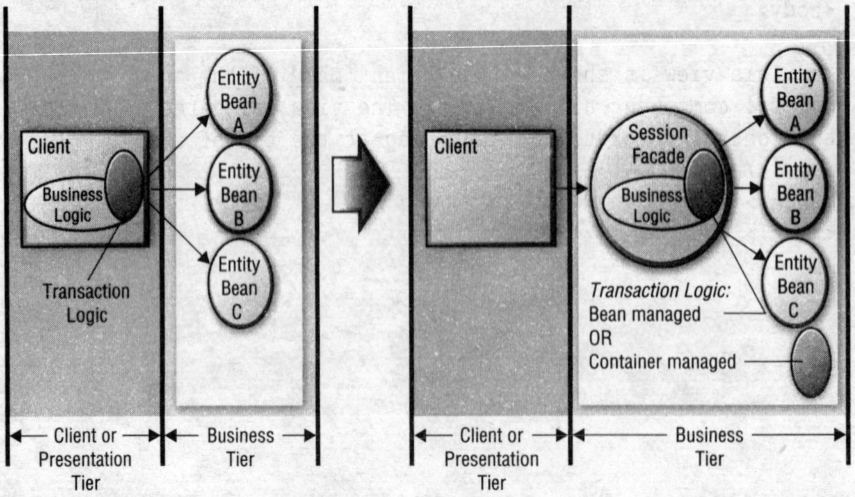

Figure 4.15 Wrap Entities with Session

Motivation

Entity beans are coarse-grained distributed persistent objects. Exposing the entity bean to clients in a different tier results in network overhead and performance degradation. Each client invocation on the entity bean is a remote network method call, which is expensive.

Entity beans mandate container-managed transaction. Exposing the entity bean to the clients may put the burden on the client developer to understand, design, and demarcate transactions when dealing with multiple entity beans. The client developer has to obtain a user transaction from the transaction manager and code the interaction with entity beans to occur within the context of that transaction. Since the client implements the transaction management, it is not possible to use the benefits of container-managed transaction demarcation.

Mechanics

- ❑ Move the business logic to interact with the entity beans out of the application client.
  - ➪ *Use Extract Class [Fowler] to extract the logic from the client.*
- ❑ Use a session bean as a façade to the entity beans.
  - ➪ *This session bean can contain the entity bean interaction logic and associated workflow logic.*
  - ➪ *See Session Façade (341).*
- ❑ Implement session beans to provide a consolidated uniform access layer to the entity beans by applying the *Session Façade* (341).
  - ➪ *The number of interactions between the client and the entity beans is now moved into the Session Façade (341) in the business tier.*
  - ➪ *Thus, the number of remote method invocations from the client is reduced.*
- ❑ Implement transaction logic in session beans if using bean-managed transactions. For container-managed transactions, specify the transaction attributes for the session bean in the deployment descriptor.
  - ➪ *Since the session bean interacts with the entity beans, the client is no longer responsible for demarcating transactions.*
  - ➪ *Thus, all transaction demarcation is now delegated to either the session bean or the container, depending on whether the designer has chosen user-managed or container-managed transactions.*

Introduce Business Delegate

Session beans in the business tier are exposed to clients in other tiers.

Use a Business Delegate (302) to decouple the tiers and to hide the implementation details.

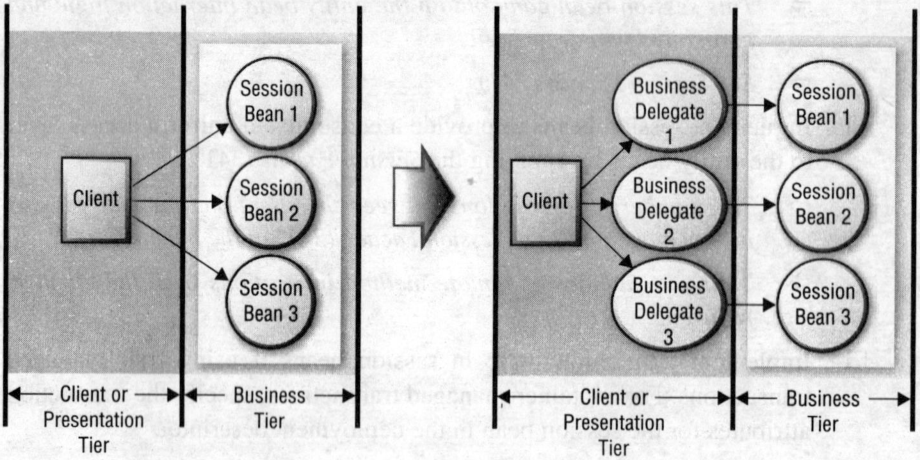

Figure 4.16 Introduce Business Delegate

Motivation

Session beans are used to implement façades for entity beans, as discussed in "Wrap Entities With Session" on page 92. Session beans provide coarse-grained interfaces to business services. But, exposing the session bean directly to the application client creates a tight coupling between the application client code and the session bean.

Exposing the session bean to the application client increases the prevalence of session bean calls throughout the client code. Thus, any change to the session bean interface impacts every point in the application client code where the session bean is called, and thus creates highly brittle code. The clients also are exposed to service-level exceptions encountered when dealing with enterprise beans. This effect is further exaggerated if you consider applications with different types of clients, where each such client uses the session bean interface to obtain some service.

Mechanics

- ❑ For each session bean that is directly exposed to clients across the tier, introduce a *Business Delegate* (302).
  - ➪ *Business Delegate (302) implementations are POJOs that encapsulate the business tier details and intercept service level exceptions on behalf of the client.*
  - ➪ *See Business Delegate (302).*
- ❑ Implement each *Business Delegate* (302) to deal with its session bean, typically as a façade. A *Business Delegate* (302) is designed with a one-to-one relationship with its *Session Façade* (341).
  - ➪ *Business Delegate (302) reduces the coupling between the client tier and the business services (session beans) by hiding the implementation details.*
  - ➪ *The clients deal with the business delegates by invoking methods on them locally.*
- ❑ Encapsulate code related to lookup services and caching in *Business Delegate* (302).
  - ➪ *Business Delegate (302) can use a Service Locator (315) to look up business services.*
  - ➪ *See Service Locator (315).*

Merge Session Beans

There is a one-to-one mapping between session beans and entity beans.

Maps business services to session beans. Eliminate or combine session beans that act solely as entity bean proxies into session beans that represent coarse-grained business services.

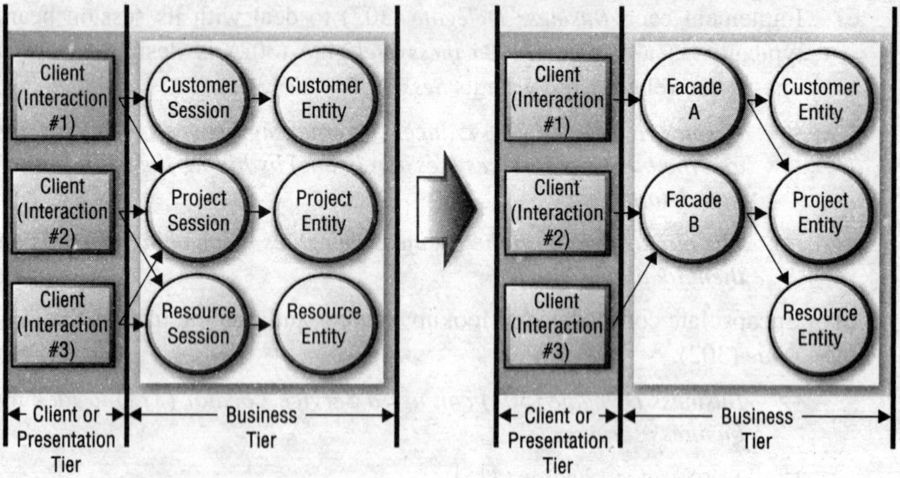

Figure 4.17 Merge Session Beans

Motivation

A one-to-one mapping of a session bean to an entity bean does not yield any benefits. Such mapping only introduces a layer of session beans acting as proxies. Typically this happens when developers create session beans to front entity beans, rather than to represent coarse-grained services.

Some designers interpret "Wrap Entities With Session" to mean that every entity bean should be protected by its own session bean. This is not a correct interpretation, since it results in design of session beans as proxies rather than as façades. The drawbacks of exposing the entity beans to clients is discussed in "Wrap Entities With Session" on page 92.

In Figure 4.17, different clients are servicing different interactions. Each interaction involves one or more entity beans. With a one-to-one mapping of a session bean to an entity bean, the client has to interact with each session bean fronting an entity bean. Since the session bean is essentially a proxy to the entity, this scenario is similar to exposing the entity bean directly to the client.

Mechanics

- ❑ Implement session beans as façades to entity beans. Thus, each session bean provides a coarse-grained business service interface to the clients.
- ❑ Consolidate fine-grained session beans or a set of session beans that are proxies to entity beans into a single session bean.
  - ⇨ *Session beans represent coarse-grained business service.*
  - ⇨ *Entity beans represent coarse-grained, transactional persistent data.*
  - ⇨ *See Session Façade (341)*
- ❑ Consolidate a set of related interactions that involve one or more entity beans into a single *Session Façade* (341) instead of implementing each interaction using a unique session bean.
  - ⇨ *This results in a fewer number of session beans that provide a uniform coarse-grained business service access to entity beans.*
  - ⇨ *The number of Session Façade (341) implementations is related to the grouping of interactions and not to the number of entity beans.*

Reduce Inter-Entity Bean Communication

Inter-entity bean relationships introduce overhead in the model.

Reduce the inter-entity bean relationships by using coarse-grained entity bean (Composite Entity) with dependent objects.

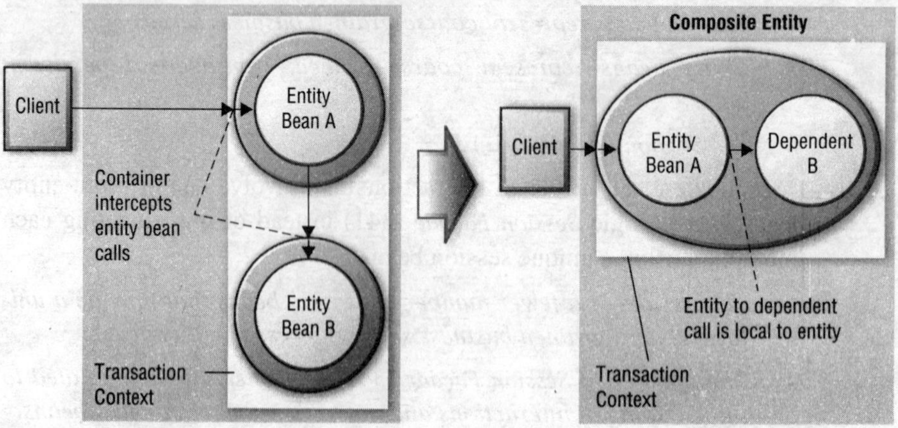

Figure 4.18 Reduce Inter-Entity Bean Communication

Motivation

Entity beans have significantly more overhead than plain Java objects. Calls to entity bean methods are remote and incur network overhead. Also, entity beans must interact with an external data source.

Even if two entity beans are in the same container, remote method invocation semantics apply (the container is involved in the communication) when one entity bean calls the other bean. Some container implementations may optimize such calls, because they recognize that the call comes from an object within the same container, but this is vendor-specific and cannot be relied upon.

Another issue is the inability for the entity bean to demarcate a transaction. When using entity beans, you are only allowed to have container-managed transactions. This means that, depending on the transaction attribute of the entity bean method, the container may start a new transaction, participate in the current transaction, or do neither. When a client invokes a method on an entity bean, the transaction includes the chain of dependent entity beans and binds them into the transaction's context. This reduces the performance throughput of the entity beans as a whole, because any transaction may lock multiple entity beans and possibly introduce deadlock situations.

Mechanics

- ❑ Design and implement entity beans as coarse-grained objects with root and dependent objects.
  - ⇨ *Transform an entity-bean-to-entity-bean relationship into an entity-bean-to-dependent-object relationship.*
  - ⇨ *Dependent objects are not entity beans. Rather, they are objects contained within an entity bean. A relationship between an entity bean and its dependent objects is a local relationship with no network overhead.*
  - ⇨ *Optimize load and store operations for Composite Entity (391) using the Lazy Loading Strategy (396) and Store Optimization (Dirty Marker) Strategy (397) respectively.*
  - ⇨ *See Composite Entity (391)*
- ❑ Extract and move business logic related to working with other entities from the entity bean into a session bean.
  - ⇨ *Use Extract Method [Fowler] and/or Move Method [Fowler] to move such business logic into a session bean, applying the Session Façade (341) pattern.*
  - ⇨ *See Session Façade (341).*

Move Business Logic to Session

Inter-entity bean relationships introduce overhead in the model.

Encapsulate the workflow related to inter-entity bean relationships in a session bean (Session façade).

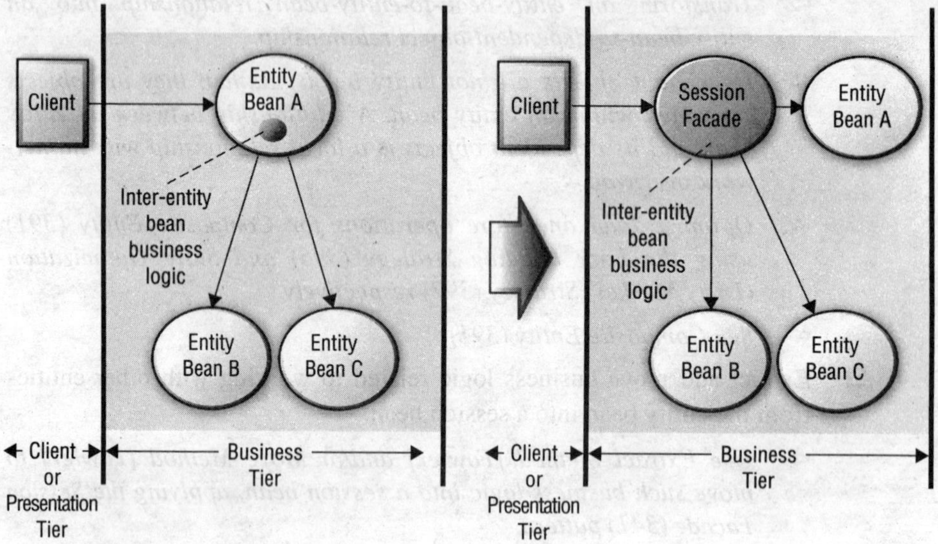

Figure 4.19 Move Business Logic to Session

Motivation

In "Reduce Inter-Entity Bean Communication" on page 98, we discussed the problems associated with direct inter-entity-bean dependencies. The problem is that an entity may contain business logic that deals with other entity beans. This creates a direct or indirect dependency on another entity bean. The same problems discussed in "Reduce Inter-Entity Bean Communication" apply to this scenario too.

Mechanics

- ❑ Extract and move business logic related to working with other entities from the entity bean into a session bean.

- ⇨ *Use Extract Method [Fowler] and/or Move Method [Fowler] to move such business logic into a session bean applying the Session Façade (341) pattern.*
- ⇨ *See Session Façade (341).*
- ⇨ *See "Wrap Entities With Session" on page 92.*

General Refactorings

Separate Data Access Code

Data access code is embedded directly within a class that has other unrelated responsibilities.

Extract the data access code into a new class and move the new class logically and/or physically closer to the data source.

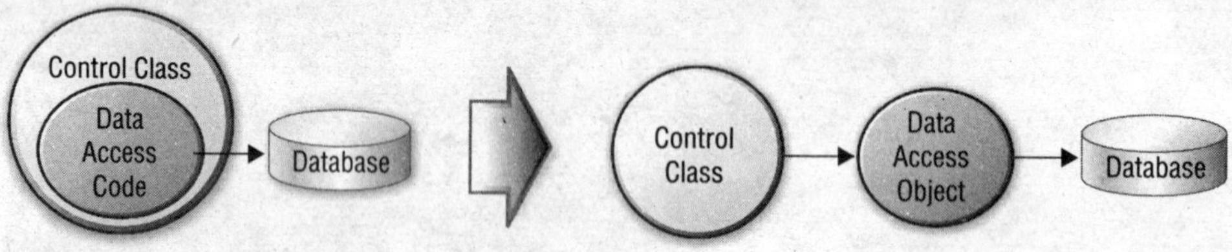

Figure 4.20 Separate Data Access Code

Motivation

Create cleaner abstractions, increase cohesion, and reduce coupling, thus improving modularity and reusability.

Mechanics

- ❑ Identify and extract the data access logic from the controller object.
  - ⇨ *Use Extract Class [Fowler] to create a new class and move data access code from the original class into the new Data Access Object (DAO) class.*
  - ⇨ *Consider including the DAO as part of the name of the new class in order to flag its role as a Data Access Object.*
  - ⇨ *See Data Access Object (462).*
- ❑ Use the new DAO from the controller to access data.
- ❑ For related information on application partitioning, see *Refactor Architecture by Tiers* on page 105.

Example

Consider an example where a servlet has embedded data access code to access some user information. Applying the first two bullets, assume we change the design, as shown in Figure 4.21.

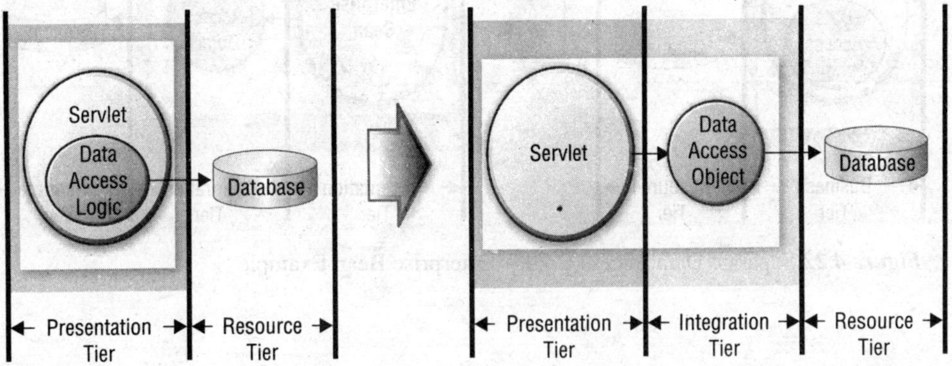

Figure 4.21 Separate Data Access Code – Servlet Example

We now have two classes: one for the servlet, which acts as a controller, and the other a new object called UserDAO, which acts as a data access object to access user information. The UserDAO encapsulates all Java Database Connectivity (JDBC) code and decouples the servlet from the implementation details. The servlet code is much simpler as a result.

Consider another example where the persistence logic is embedded in an enterprise bean using bean-managed persistence. Combining the persistence code with the enterprise bean code creates brittle, tightly coupled code. When the persistence code is part of the enterprise bean, any change to the persistence store requires changing the bean's persistence code. Such coupling has a negative impact on enterprise bean code maintenance. This is another example of how this refactoring can help.

Applying this refactoring, we change the design as in Figure 4.22 on page 104.

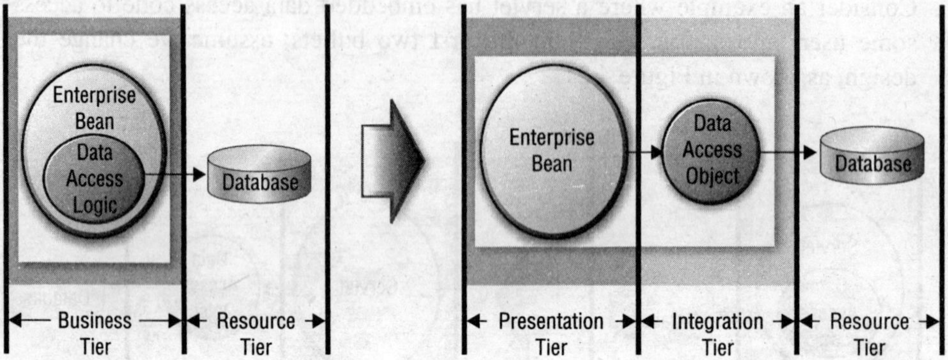

Figure 4.22 Separate Data Access Code – Enterprise Bean Example

Refactor Architecture by Tiers

Increasing architectural sophistication requires changing the localization of data access logic and processing logic.

Move data access code logically and/or physically closer to actual data source. Move processing logic out of client and presentation tiers into business tier.

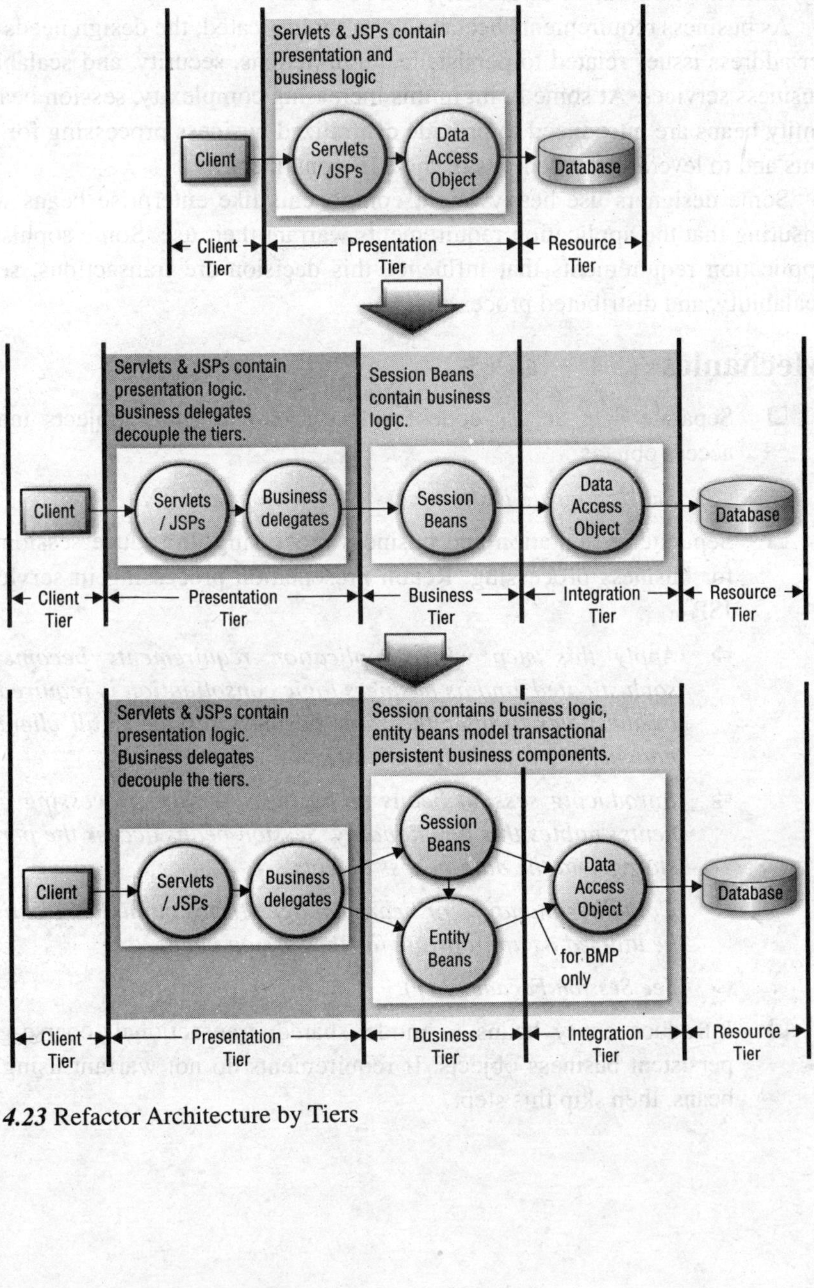

Figure 4.23 Refactor Architecture by Tiers

Motivation

"Separate Data Access Code" on page 102 demonstrates refactoring data access logic, while this refactoring discusses other types of business logic in an application.

The J2EE platform offers clear separation of concerns into the roles of servlets, JSP, and EJB components to provide maximum benefits in terms of scalability, flexibility, transactions, security, and so forth.

As business requirements become more sophisticated, the design needs to better address issues related to persistence, transactions, security, and scalability of business services. At some point in this increasing complexity, session beans and entity beans are introduced to provide centralized business processing for all clients and to leverage the benefits of the EJB container.

Some designers use heavyweight components like enterprise beans without ensuring that the application requirements warrant their use. Some sophisticated application requirements that influence this decision are transactions, security, scalability, and distributed processing.

Mechanics

- ❑ Separate data access code from control and entity objects into data access objects.
  - ⇨ *See "Separate Data Access Code" on page 102.*
- ❑ Separate presentation and business processing. Introduce session beans for business processing. Retain presentation processing in servlets and JSP.
  - ⇨ *Apply this step when application requirements become more sophisticated, and as business logic consolidation is required at the business tier to offer the same business service to all clients (i.e., not only to presentation clients).*
  - ⇨ *Introducing session beans as business service processing components enables this functionality. Session beans access the persistent storage via the data access objects.*
  - ⇨ *Container-managed or bean-managed transaction demarcation can be utilized as appropriate for the session beans.*
  - ⇨ *See Session Facade (341).*
- ❑ Introduce entity beans to model-shared, transactional, coarse-grained persistent business objects. If requirements do not warrant using entity beans, then skip this step.

- ➪ *Apply this step when the persistent business components become increasingly complex and you wish to leverage the entity bean benefits, including container-managed transactions and container-managed persistence (CMP).*
- ➪ *Entity beans offer container-managed transaction for transaction demarcation. This allows declarative programming for transaction demarcation without hardcoding the transaction logic into the enterprise beans.*
- ➪ *See Transfer Object (415) and Composite Entity (391)*

- ❑ Decouple presentation tier and business tier components, using business delegates.
  - ➪ *Business Delegate (302) decouples the presentation-tier components from business-tier components and hides the complexity of lookup and other implementation details.*
  - ➪ *See Business Delegate (302).*

Use A Connection Pool

Database connections are not shared. Instead, clients manage their own connections for making database invocations.

Use a Connection Pool to pre-initialize multiple Connections, improving scalability and performance.

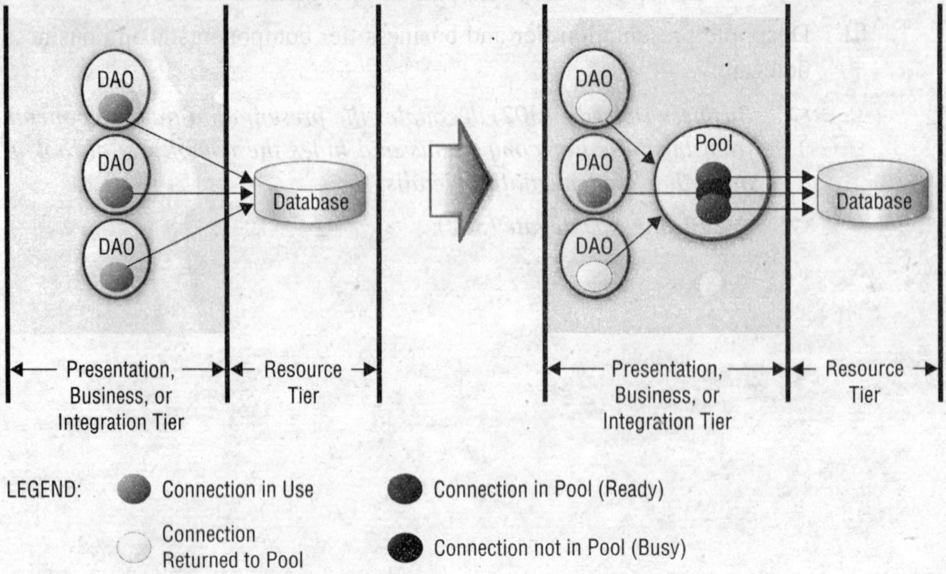

Figure 4.24 Use a Connection Pool

Motivation

Opening a connection to a database is a fairly expensive operation that takes time and resources to perform. Both performance and scalability are affected. Since database connections are limited, if each client manages its own connection, the total number of connections will likely be exhausted far sooner than desired.

This issue arises in the presentation tier on projects that use a phased approach to introducing EJB technology. In this case, components in the presentation tier initially interact directly with a database, and the data access code is later moved into the business tier and encapsulated in an EJB layer. See "Separate Data Access Code" on page 102 and "Refactor Architecture by Tiers" on page 105.

Mechanics

- ❑ Create an interface for connection management, including methods for retrieving and returning a connection.
  - ⇨ *Apply Extract Class [Fowler] and/or Move Method [Fowler], moving the existing connection retrieval code into a class that implements the connection management interface.*
  - ⇨ *At the points from which the connection code was extracted, substitute invocations to an instance of this new class; that is,* `connectionMgr.getConnection()` *and* `connectionMgr.returnConnection(conn)`.
  - ⇨ *Note that the JDBC specification, version 2, includes a standard mechanism for introducing connection pooling. This mechanism, if available, is the recommended way to introduce connection pooling. In the JDBC specification version 2, the management interface is named* `javax.sql.DataSource` *and it provides a factory for pooled Connection objects.*
  - ⇨ *At this point, only the structure and interface has been standardized, but the functionality is the same.*
  - ⇨ *Still no pooling is implemented, unless the JDBC 2.0 DataSource factory is utilized, which is recommended.*

- ❑ Modify the implementation of the connection retrieval methods within the connection manager implementation to pre-initialize some Connection instances and share them among users, thus introducing pooling.
  - ⇨ *There are numerous publicly available implementations from which to choose.*
  - ⇨ *Clients of these connection manager instances are typically DAOs. See "Separate Data Access Code" on page 102.*
  - ⇨ *Data access code typically migrates logically closer to the database as a project evolves. See "Refactor Architecture by Tiers" on page 105.*

Part 2

J2EE Pattern Catalog

Part 2 includes the following chapters:

- Chapter 5, “J2EE Patterns Overview
- Chapter 6, “Presentation Tier Patterns
- Chapter 7, “Business Tier Patterns
- Chapter 8, “Integration Tier Patterns
- Epilogue, “Web Worker Micro-Architecture”

Chapter 5, “J2EE Patterns Overview,” provides an overview of the J2EE Pattern Catalog with a discussion on our tiered approach. The chapter provides a guide to the pattern catalog and describes the terminology and UML Stereotypes used to describe each pattern. The template used to document each pattern is also defined and discussed. One of the important aspects of the chapter is the discussion of the relationships among various patterns in the catalog—both with each other, as well as with patterns in other literature, such as “Design Patterns” [GoF], “Patterns of Software Architecture,” Volume 1 [POSA1] and Volume 2 [POSA2]. Another useful artifact in this chapter is the J2EE Patterns roadmap, which presents a table of common requirements mapped to various patterns and refactorings.

The subsequent chapters describe the patterns in the J2EE Pattern Catalog.

Chapter 6, "Presentation Tier Patterns," providese patterns for the presentation tier. These patterns describe the best practices for using servlets and JavaServer Pages (JSP) technologies.

Chapter 7, "Business Tier Patterns," provides patterns for the business tier. These patterns describe the best practices for designing your business tier using Enterprise JavaBeans (EJBs) and POJOs (plain old Java objects).

Chapter 8, "Integration Tier Patterns," provides patterns for the integration tier. These patterns describe the best practices for Web services, Java Database Connectivity (JDBC), and Java Messaging Service (JMS),

The Epilogue describes Web Worker, a micro-architecture for J2EE workflow integration.

J2EE Patterns Overview

Topics in This Chapter

- What Is a Pattern?
- The Tiered Approach
- J2EE Patterns
- Guide to the Catalog
- J2EE Pattern Relationships
- Relationship to Known Patterns
- Patterns Roadmap
- Summary

Chapter 5

The J2EE patterns are a collection of J2EE-based solutions to common problems. They reflect the collective expertise and experience of Java architects at the Sun Java Center, gained from successfully executing numerous J2EE engagements. The Sun Java Center is Sun's consulting organization, focused on architecting Java technology-based solutions for customers. The Sun Java Center has been architecting solutions for the J2EE platform since its early days, focusing on achieving Quality of Service (QoS) qualities, such as scalability, availability, performance, securability, reliability, and flexibility.

These J2EE patterns describe typical problems encountered by enterprise application developers and provide solutions for these problems. We have formulated these solutions based on our ongoing work with numerous J2EE customers and on exchanges with other Java architects experiencing similar problems. The patterns capture the essence of these solutions, and they represent the solution refinement that takes place over the course of time and from collective experience. To put it another way, they extract the core issues of each problem, offering solutions that represent an applicable distillation of theory and practice.

Our work has focused on the J2EE area, especially regarding such J2EE components as Enterprise Java Beans (EJB), JavaServer Pages (JSP), and servlets. During our work with J2EE customers implementing the various components, we have come to recognize the common problems and difficult areas that may impede a good implementation. We've also developed effective best practices and approaches for using the J2EE components in combination.

The patterns presented here extract these "best practice" approaches and present them to you in a way that enables you to apply the patterns to your own particular application and to accommodate your own needs. The patterns clearly and simply express proven techniques. They make it easier for you to reuse successful designs and architectures. Simply put, you can use the patterns to design your J2EE system successfully and quickly.

What Is a Pattern?

In Chapter 1, we discussed how different experts define a pattern. We also discussed some of the peripheral issues around patterns including the benefits of using patterns. Here, we revisit this discussion in the context of the J2EE Pattern Catalog.

As discussed in Chapter 1, some experts define a pattern as a recurring **solution** to a **problem** in a **context**.

These terms—context, problem, and solution—deserve a bit of explanation. First, what is a context? A context is the environment, surroundings, situation, or interrelated conditions within which something exists. Second, what is a problem? A problem is an unsettled question, something that needs to be investigated and solved. Typically, the problem is constrained by the context in which it occurs. Finally, the solution refers to the answer to the problem in a context that helps resolve the issues.

So, if we have a solution to a problem in a context, is it a pattern? Not necessarily. The characteristic of recurrence also needs to be associated with the definition of a pattern. That is, a pattern is only useful if it can be applied repeatedly. Is that all? Perhaps not. As you can see, while the concept of a pattern is fairly simple, actually defining the term is more complex.

We point you to the references so that you can dig more deeply into the pattern history and learn about patterns in other areas. In our catalog, a pattern is described according to its main characteristics: **problem**, and **solution**, along with other important aspects, such as **forces** and **consequences**. The section describing the pattern template (see "Pattern Template" on page 129) explains these characteristics in more detail.

Identifying a Pattern

We have handled many J2EE projects at the Sun Java Center, and over time we have noticed that similar problems recur across these projects. We have also seen similar solutions emerge for these problems. While the implementation strategies varied, the overall solutions were quite similar. Let us discuss, in brief, our pattern identification process.

When we see a problem and solution recur, we try to identify and document its characteristics using the pattern template. At first, we consider these initial documents to be candidate patterns. However, we do not add candidate patterns to the pattern catalog until we are able to observe and document their usage multiple times on different projects. We also undertake the process of pattern mining by looking for patterns in implemented solutions.

As part of the pattern validation process, we use the **Rule of Three**, as it is known in the pattern community. This rule is a guide for transitioning a candidate pattern into the pattern catalog. According to this rule, a solution remains a candidate pattern until it has been verified in at least three different systems. Certainly, there is much room for interpretation with rules such as this, but they help provide a context for pattern identification.

Often, similar solutions may represent a single pattern. When deciding how to form the pattern, it is important to consider how to best communicate the solution. Sometimes, a separate name improves communication among developers. If so, then consider documenting two similar solutions as two different patterns. On the other hand, it might be better to communicate the solution by distilling the similar ideas into a pattern/strategy combination.

Patterns Versus Strategies

When we started documenting the J2EE patterns, we made the decision to document them at a relatively high level of abstraction. At the same time, each pattern includes various strategies that provide lower level implementation details. Through the strategies, each pattern documents a solution at multiple levels of abstraction. We could have documented some of these strategies as patterns in their own right; however, we feel that our current template structure most clearly communicates the relationship of the strategies to the higher level pattern structure in which they are included.

While we continue to have lively debates about converting these strategies to patterns, we have deferred these decisions for now, believing the current documentation to be clear. We have noted some of the issues with respect to the relationship of the strategies to the patterns:

- The patterns exist at a higher level of abstraction than the strategies.
- The patterns include the most recommended or most common implementations as strategies.

- Strategies provide an extensibility point for each pattern. Developers discover and invent new ways to implement the patterns, producing new strategies for well-known patterns.
- Strategies promote better communication by providing names for lower level aspects of a particular solution.

The Tiered Approach

Since this catalog describes patterns that help you build applications that run on the J2EE platform, and since a J2EE platform (and application) is a multitiered system, we view the system in terms of **tiers**. A tier is a logical partition of the separation of concerns in the system. Each tier is assigned its unique responsibility in the system. We view each tier as logically separated from one another. Each tier is loosely coupled with the adjacent tier. We represent the whole system as a stack of tiers. See Figure 5.1.

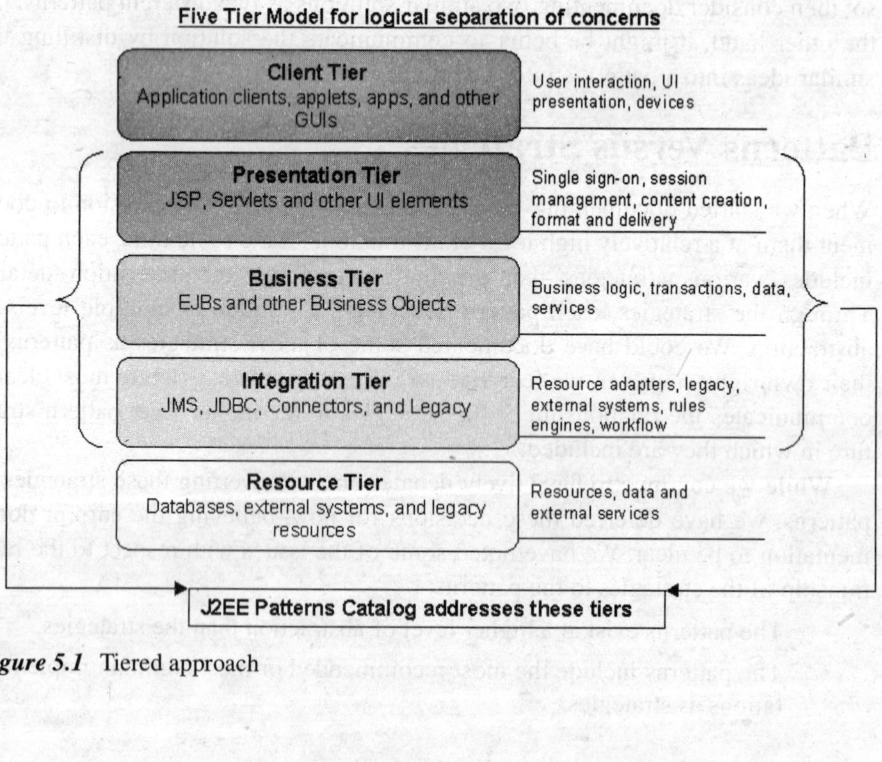

Figure 5.1 Tiered approach

Client Tier

This tier represents all device or system clients accessing the system or the application. A client can be a Web browser, a Java or other application, a Java applet, a WAP phone, a network application, or some device introduced in the future. It could even be a batch process.

Presentation Tier

This tier encapsulates all presentation logic required to service the clients that access the system. The presentation tier intercepts the client requests, provides single sign-on, conducts session management, controls access to business services, constructs the responses, and delivers the responses to the client. Servlets and JSP reside in this tier. Note that servlets and JSP are not themselves UI elements, but they produce UI elements.

Business Tier

This tier provides the business services required by the application clients. The tier contains the business data and business logic. Typically, most business processing for the application is centralized into this tier. It is possible that, due to legacy systems, some business processing may occur in the resource tier. Enterprise bean components are the usual and preferred solution for implementing the business objects in the business tier.

Integration Tier

This tier is responsible for communicating with external resources and systems such as data stores and legacy applications. The business tier is coupled with the integration tier whenever the business objects require data or services that reside in the resource tier. The components in this tier can use JDBC, J2EE connector technology, or some proprietary middleware to work with the resource tier.

Resource Tier

This is the tier that contains the business data and external resources such as mainframes and legacy systems, business-to-business (B2B) integration systems, and services such as credit card authorization.

J2EE Patterns

We used the tiered approach to divide the J2EE patterns according to functionality, and our pattern catalog follows this approach. The presentation tier patterns contain the patterns related to servlets and JSP technology. The business tier patterns contain the patterns related to the EJB technology. The integration tier patterns contain the patterns related to JMS and JDBC. See Figure 5.2 on page 132.

Presentation Tier Patterns

Table 5-1 lists the presentation tier patterns, along with a brief description of each pattern.

Table 5-1 Presentation Tier Patterns

Pattern Name	*Synopsis*
Intercepting Filter (144)	Facilitates preprocessing and post-processing of a request.
Front Controller (166)	Provides a centralized controller for managing the handling of a request.
Context Object (181)	Encapsulates state in a protocol-independent way to be shared throughout your application.
Application Controller (205)	Centralizes and modularizes action and view management.
View Helper (240)	Encapsulates logic that is not related to presentation formatting into Helper components.
Composite View (262)	Creates an aggregate View from atomic subcomponents.
Service to Worker (276)	Combines a Dispatcher component with the *Front Controller* (166) and *View Helper* (240) patterns.
Dispatcher View (288)	Combines a Dispatcher component with the *Front Controller* (166) and *View Helper* (240) patterns, deferring many activities to View processing.

Business Tier Patterns

Table 5-2 lists the business tier patterns, along with a brief synopsis of each pattern.

Table 5-2 Business Tier Patterns

Pattern Name	*Synopsis*
Business Delegate (302)	Encapsulates access to a business service.
Service Locator (315)	Encapsulates service and component lookups.
Session Façade (341)	Encapsulates business-tier components and exposes a coarse-grained service to remote clients.
Application Service (357)	Centralizes and aggregates behavior to provide a uniform service layer.
Business Object (374)	Separates business data and logic using an object model.
Composite Entity (391)	Implements persistent *Business Objects* (374) using local entity beans and POJOs.
Transfer Object (415)	Carries data across a tier.
Transfer Object Assembler (433)	Assembles a composite transfer object from multiple data sources.
Value List Handler (444)	Handles the search, caches the results, and provide the ability to traverse and select items from the results.

Integration Tier Patterns

Table 5-3 lists the integration tier patterns and a brief description of each pattern.

Table 5-3 Integration Tier Patterns

Pattern Name	*Synopsis*
Data Access Object (462)	Abstracts and encapsulates access to persistent store.

Table 5-3 Integration Tier Patterns (continued)

Pattern Name	*Synopsis*
Service Activator (496)	Receives messages and invokes processing asynchronously.
Domain Store (516)	Provides a transparent persistence mechanism for business objects.
Web Service Broker (557)	Exposes one or more services using XML and web protocols

Guide to the Catalog

To help you effectively understand and use the J2EE patterns in the catalog, we suggest that you familiarize yourself with this section before reading the individual patterns. Here we introduce the pattern terminology and explain our use of the Unified Modeling Language (UML), stereotypes, and the pattern template. In short, we explain how to use these patterns. We also provide a high-level roadmap to the patterns in the catalog.

Terminology

Players in the enterprise computing area, and particularly establishments using Java-based systems, have incorporated a number of terms and acronyms into their language. While many readers are familiar with these terms, sometimes their use varies from one setting to another. To avoid misunderstandings and to keep things consistent, we define in Table 5-4 how we use these terms and acronyms.

Table 5-4 Terminology

Term	*Description/Definition*	*Used In*
BMP	Bean-managed persistence: a strategy for entity beans where the bean developer implements the persistence logic for entity beans.	Business tier patterns

Table 5-4 Terminology (continued)

Term	*Description/Definition*	*Used In*
CMP	Container-managed persistence: a strategy for entity beans where the container services transparently manage the persistence of entity beans.	Business tier patterns
Composite	A complex object that holds other objects. Also related to the Composite pattern described in the GoF book. (See GoF later in this table.)	*Composite View* (262), *Composite Entity* (391)
Controller	Interacts with a client, controlling and managing the handling of each request.	Presentation and business tier patterns
Data Access Object	An object that encapsulates and abstracts access to data from a persistent store or an external system.	Business and integration tier patterns
Delegate	A stand-in, or surrogate, object for another component; an intermediate layer. A Delegate has qualities of a proxy and façade.	*Business Delegate* (302) and many other patterns
Dependent Object	An object that does not exist by itself and whose lifecycle is managed by another object.	*Business Objects* (374) and *Composite Entity* (391)
Dispatcher	Some of the responsibilities of a Controller include managing the choice of and dispatching to an appropriate View. This behavior may be partitioned into a separate component, referred to as a Dispatcher.	*Dispatcher View* (288), *Service to Worker* (276)

Table 5-4 Terminology (continued)

Term	*Description/Definition*	*Used In*
Enterprise Bean	Refers to an Enterprise JavaBean component; can be a session or entity bean instance. When this term is used, it means that the bean instance can be either an entity or a session bean.	Many places in this literature
Façade	A pattern for hiding underlying complexities; described in the GoF book.	*Session Façade* pattern
Factory (Abstract Factory or Factory Method)	Patterns described in the GoF book for creating objects or families of objects.	Business tier patterns: *Data Access Object* (462)
Iterator	A pattern to provide accessors to underlying collection facilities; described in the GoF book.	*Value List Handler (444)*
GoF	Gang of Four—refers to the authors of the popular design patterns book, *Design Patterns: Elements of Reusable Object-Oriented Software,* by Erich Gamma, Richard Helm, Ralph Johnson, and John Vlissides. [GoF]	Many places in this literature
Helper	Responsible for helping the Controller and/or View. For example, the Controller and View may delegate the following to a Helper: content retrieval, validation, storing the model or adapting it for use by the display.	Presentation tier patterns, *Business Delegate* (302)
Independent Object	An object that can exist by itself and may manage the lifecycles of its dependent objects.	*Composite Entity* (391) pattern

Table 5-4 Terminology (continued)

Term	*Description/Definition*	*Used In*
Model	A physical or logical representation of the system or its subsystem.	Presentation and business tier patterns
Persistent Store	Represents persistent storage systems such as RDBMSs, ODBMSs, file systems, and so forth.	Business and integration tier patterns
Proxy	A pattern to provide a placeholder for another object to control access to it; described in the GoF book.	Many places in this literature
Scriptlet	Application logic embedded directly within a JSP.	Presentation tier patterns
Session Bean	Refers to a stateless or stateful session bean. May also refer collectively to the session bean's home, remote object, and bean implementation.	Business tier patterns
Singleton	A pattern that provides a single instance of an object, as described in the GoF book.	Many places in this literature
Template	Template text refers to the literal text encapsulated within a JSP View. Additionally, a template may refer to a specific layout of components in a display.	Presentation tier patterns
Transfer Object	A serializable POJO that is used to carry data from one object/tier to another. It does not contain any business methods.	Business tier patterns

Table 5-4 Terminology (continued)

Term	*Description/Definition*	*Used In*
View	The View manages the graphics and text that make up the display. It interacts with Helpers to get data values with which to populate the display. Additionally, it may delegate activities, such as content retrieval, to its Helpers.	Presentation tier patterns

Use of UML

We have used UML extensively in the pattern catalog, particularly as follows:

- **Class diagrams** – We use the class diagrams to show the structure of the pattern solution and the structure of the implementation strategies. This provides the static view of the solution.
- **Sequence (or Interaction) diagrams** – We use these diagrams to show the interactions between different participants in a solution or a strategy. This provides the dynamic view of the solution.
- **Stereotypes** – We use stereotypes to indicate different types of objects and roles in the class and interaction diagrams. The list of stereotypes and their meanings is included in Table 5-5.

Each pattern in the pattern catalog includes a class diagram that shows the structure of the solution and a sequence diagram that shows the interactions for the pattern. In addition, patterns with multiple strategies use class and sequence diagrams to explain each strategy.

To learn more about UML, please see the Bibliography.

UML Stereotypes

While reading the patterns and their diagrams, you will encounter certain stereotypes. Stereotypes are terms coined or used by designers and architects. We created and used these stereotypes to present the diagrams in a concise and easy to understand manner. Note that some of the stereotypes relate to the terminology explained in the previous section. In addition to these stereotypes, we also use pattern names and the main roles of a pattern as the stereotypes when it helps in explaining a pattern and its strategies.

Table 5-5 UML Stereotypes

Stereotype	*Meaning*
EJB	Represents an enterprise bean component; associated with a business object. This is a role that is usually fulfilled by a session or entity bean.
SessionEJB	Represents a session bean as a whole without specifying the session bean remote interface, home interface, or the bean implementation.
EntityEJB	Represents an entity bean as a whole without specifying the entity bean remote interface, home interface, the bean implementation, or the primary key.
View	A View represents and displays information to the client.
JSP	A JavaServer Page; a View is typically implemented as a JSP.
Servlet	A Java servlet; a Controller is typically implemented as a servlet.
Singleton	A class that has a single instance in accordance with the Singleton pattern.
Custom Tag	JSP custom tags are used to implement Helper objects, as are JavaBeans. A Helper is responsible for such activities as gathering data required by the View and for adapting this data model for use by the View. Helpers can service requests for data from the View by simply providing access to the raw data or by formatting the data as Web content.

Pattern Template

The J2EE patterns are all structured according to a defined pattern template. The pattern template consists of sections presenting various attributes for a given pattern. You'll also notice that we've tried to give each J2EE pattern a descriptive pattern name. While it is difficult to fully encompass a single pattern in its name, the pattern names are intended to provide sufficient insight into the function of the pattern. Just as with names in real life, those assigned to patterns affect how the reader will interpret and eventually use that pattern.

We have adopted a pattern template that consists of the following sections:

- *Problem:* Describes the design issues faced by the developer.
- *Forces:* Lists the reasons and motivations that affect the problem and the solution. The list of forces highlights the reasons why one might choose to use the pattern and provides a justification for using the pattern.
- *Solution:* Describes the solution approach briefly and the solution elements in detail. The solution section contains two subsections:
    - *Structure:* Uses UML class diagrams to show the basic structure of the solution. The UML Sequence diagrams in this section present the dynamic mechanisms of the solution. There is a detailed explanation of the participants and collaborations.
    - *Strategies:* Describes different ways a pattern may be implemented. Please see "Patterns Versus Strategies" on page 119 to gain a better understanding of strategies. Where a strategy can be demonstated using code, we include a code snippet in this section. If the code is more elaborate and lengthier than a snippet, we include it in the "Sample Code" section of the pattern template.
- *Consequences:* Here we describe the pattern trade-offs. Generally, this section focuses on the results of using a particular pattern or its strategy, and notes the pros and cons that may result from the application of the pattern.
- *Sample Code:* This section includes example implementations and code listings for the patterns and the strategies. This section is rendered optional if code samples can be adequately included with the discussion in the "Strategies" section.
- *Related Patterns:* This section lists other relevant patterns in the J2EE Pattern Catalog or from other external resources, such as the GoF design patterns. For each related pattern, there is a brief description of its relationship to the pattern being described.

J2EE Pattern Relationships

A recent focus group of architects and designers raised a major concern: There seems to be a lack of understanding of how to apply patterns in combination to form larger solutions. We address this problem with a high-level visual of the patterns and their relationships. This diagram is called the J2EE Pattern Relationships Diagram and is shown in Figure 5.2. In the Epilogue, "Web Worker

Micro-Architecture", we explore example use cases to demonstrate how many patterns come together to form a patterns framework to realize a use case.

Individual patterns offer their context, problem, and solution when addressing a particular need. However, it is important to step back and grasp the big picture to put the patterns to their best use. This grasping the big picture results in better application of the patterns in a J2EE application.

Reiterating Christopher Alexander's quote from Chapter 1, a pattern does not exist in isolation and needs the support of other patterns to bring meaning and usefulness. Virtually every pattern in the catalog has a relationship to other patterns. Understanding these relationships when designing and architecting a solution helps in the following ways:

- Enables you to consider what other new problems may be introduced when you consider applying a pattern to solve your problem. This is the domino effect: What new problems are introduced when a particular pattern is introduced into the architecture? It is critical to identify these conflicts before coding begins.
- Enables you to revisit the pattern relationships to determine alternate solutions. After possible problems are identified, revisit the pattern relationships and collect alternate solutions. Perhaps the new problems can be addressed by selecting a different pattern or by using another pattern in combination with the one you have already chosen.

Figure 5.2 on page 132 shows the relationships among the patterns.

Intercepting Filter (144) intercepts incoming requests and outgoing responses and applies a filter. These filters may be added and removed in a declarative manner, allowing them to be applied unobtrusively in a variety of combinations. After this preprocessing and/or post-processing is complete, the final filter in the group vectors control to the original target object. For an incoming request, this is often a *Front Controller* (166), but may be a *View* (240).

Front Controller (166) is a container to hold the common processing logic that occurs within the presentation tier and that may otherwise be erroneously placed in a View. A controller handles requests and manages content retrieval, security, view management, and navigation, delegating to a Dispatcher component to dispatch to a View.

Application Controller (205) centralizes control, retrieval, and invocation of view and command processing. While a *Front Controller* (166) acts as a centralized access point and controller for incoming requests, the *Application Controller* (205) is responsible for identifying and invoking commands, and for identifying and dispatching to views.

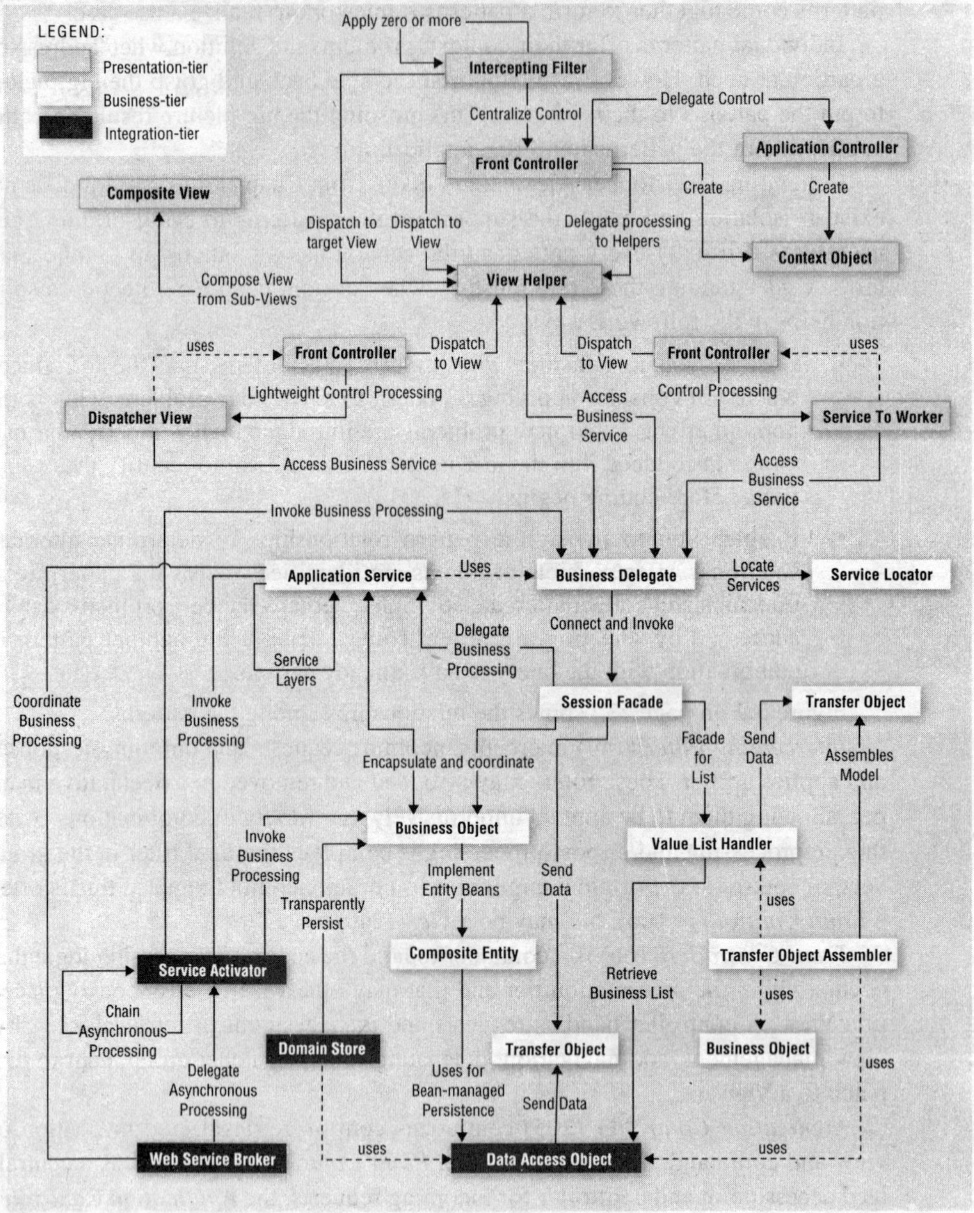

Figure 5.2 J2EE Pattern Relationships

Context Object (181) encapsulates state in a protocol-independent way to be shared throughout your application. Using *Context Object* (181) makes testing easier, facilitating a more generic test environment with reduced dependence upon a specific container.

View Helper (240) encourages the separation of formatting-related code from other business logic. It suggests using Helper components to encapsulate logic relating to initiating content retrieval, validation, and adapting and formatting the model. The View component is then left to encapsulate the presentation formatting. Helper components typically delegate to the business services via a *Business Delegate* (302) or an *Application Service* (357), while a View may be composed of multiple subcomponents to create its template.

Composite View (262) suggests composing a View from numerous atomic pieces. Multiple smaller views, both static and dynamic, are pieced together to create a single template. The *Service to Worker* (276) and *Dispatcher View* (288) patterns represent a common combination of other patterns from the catalog. The two patterns share a common structure, consisting of a controller working with a Dispatcher, Views, and Helpers. *Service to Worker* (276) and *Dispatcher View* (288) have similar participant roles, but differ in the division of labor among those roles. Unlike *Service to Worker* (276), *Dispatcher View* (288) defers business processing until view processing has been performed.

Business Delegate (302) reduces coupling between remote tiers and provides an entry point for accessing remote services in the business tier. A *Business Delegate* (302) might also cache data as necessary to improve performance. A *Business Delegate* (302) encapsulates a *Session Façade* (341) and maintains a one-to-one relationship with that *Session Façade* (341). An *Application Service* (357) uses a *Business Delegate* (302) to invoke a *Session Façade* (341).

Service Locator (315) encapsulates the implementation mechanisms for looking up business service components. A *Business Delegate* (302) uses a *Service Locator* (315) to connect to a *Session Façade* (341). Other clients that need to locate and connect to *Session Façade* (341), other business-tier services, and web services can use a *Service Locator* (315).

Session Façade (341) provides coarse-grained services to the clients by hiding the complexities of the business service interactions. A *Session Façade* (341) might invoke several *Application Service* (357) implementations or *Business Objects* (374). A *Session Façade* (341) can also encapsulate a *Value List Handler* (444).

Application Service (357) centralizes and aggregates behavior to provide a uniform service layer to the business tier services. An *Application Service* (357) might interact with other services or *Business Objects* (374). An *Application Ser-*

vice (357) can invoke other *Application Services* (357) and thus create a layer of services in your application.

Business Object (374) implements your conceptual domain model using an object model. *Business Objects* (374) separate business data and logic into a separate layer in your application. *Business Objects* (374) typically represent persistent objects and can be transparently persisted using *Domain Store* (516).

Composite Entity (391) implements a *Business Object* (374) using local entity beans and POJOs. When implemented with bean-managed persistence, a *Composite Entity* (391) uses *Data Access Objects* (462) to facilitate persistence.

The *Transfer Object* (415) pattern provides the best techniques and strategies to exchange data across tiers (that is, across system boundaries) to reduce the network overhead by minimizing the number of calls to get data from another tier.

The *Transfer Object Assembler* constructs a composite *Transfer Object* (415) from various sources. These sources could be EJB components, *Data Access Objects* (462), or other arbitrary Java objects. This pattern is most useful when the client needs to obtain data for the application model or part of the model.

The *Value List Handler* (444) uses the GoF iterator pattern to provide query execution and processing services. The *Value List Handler* (444) caches the results of the query execution and return subsets of the result to the clients as requested. By using this pattern, it is possible to avoid overheads associated with finding large numbers of entity beans. The *Value List Handler* (444) uses a *Data Access Object* (462) to execute a query and fetch the results from a persistent store.

Data Access Object (462) enables loose coupling between the business and resource tiers. *Data Access Object* (462) encapsulates all the data access logic to create, retrieve, delete, and update data from a persistent store. *Data Access Object* (462) uses *Transfer Object* (415) to send and receive data.

Service Activator (496) enables asynchronous processing in your enterprise applications using JMS. A *Service Activator* (496) can invoke *Application Service* (357), *Session Façade* (341) or *Business Objects* (374). You can also use several *Service Activators* (496) to provide parallel asynchronous processing for long running tasks.

Domain Store (516) provides a powerful mechanism to implement transparent persistence for your object model. It combines and links several other patterns including *Data Access Objects* (462). *Web Service Broker* (557) exposes and brokers one or more services in your application to external clients as a web service using XML and standard web protocols. A *Web Service Broker* (557) can interact with *Application Service* (357) and *Session Façade* (341). A *Web Service Broker* (557) uses one or more *Service Activators* (496) to perform asynchronous processing of a request.

Relationship to Known Patterns

There is a wealth of software pattern documentation available today. The patterns in these different books are at various levels of abstraction. There are architecture patterns, design patterns, analysis patterns, and programming patterns. The most popular and influential of these books is *Design Patterns: Elements of Reusable Object-Oriented Software,* [GoF] better known as the Gang of Four, or GoF book. The patterns in the GoF book describe expert solutions for object design. We also reference patterns from *Patterns of Enterprise Application Architecture* [PEAA], by Martin Fowler.

Our pattern catalog includes patterns that describe the structure of an application and others that describe design elements. The unifying theme of the pattern catalog is its support of the J2EE platform. In some cases, the patterns in the catalog are based on or related to an existing pattern in the literature. In these cases, we communicate this relationship by referencing the existing pattern in the name of the J2EE pattern and/or including a reference and citation in the *Related Patterns* section at the end of each pattern description. For example, some patterns are based on GoF patterns but are considered in a J2EE context. In those cases, the J2EE pattern name includes the GoF pattern name as well as a reference to the GoF pattern in the related patterns section.

Patterns Roadmap

Here we present a list of common requirements that architects encounter when creating solutions with the J2EE. We present the requirement or motivation in a brief statement, followed by a list of one or more patterns addressing that requirement. While this requirements list is not exhaustive, we hope that it helps you to quickly identify the relevant patterns based on your needs.

Table 5-1 shows the functions typically handled by the presentation tier patterns and indicates which pattern provides a solution.

Table 5-1 Presentation Tier Patterns

If you are looking for this	*Find it here*
Preprocessing or postprocessing of your requests	**Pattern** *Intercepting Filter* (144)
Adding logging, debugging, or some other behavior to be completed for each request	**Pattern** *Front Controller* (166) **Pattern** *Intercepting Filter* (144)

Table 5-1 Presentation Tier Patterns (continued)

If you are looking for this	*Find it here*
Centralizing control for request handling	**Pattern** *Front Controller* (166) **Pattern** *Intercepting Filter* (144) **Pattern** *Application Controller* (205)
Creating a generic command interface or context object for reducing coupling between control components and helper components	**Pattern** *Front Controller* (166) **Pattern** *Application Controller* (205) **Pattern** *Context Object* (181)
Whether to implement your Controller as a servlet or JSP	**Pattern** *Front Controller* (166)
Creating a View from numerous sub-Views	**Pattern** *Composite View* (262)
Whether to implement your View as a servlet or JSP	**Pattern** *View Helper* (240)
How to partition your View and Model	**Pattern** *View Helper* (240)
Where to encapsulate your presentation-related data formatting logic	**Pattern** *View Helper* (240)
Whether to implement your Helper components as JavaBeans or Custom tags	**Pattern** *View Helper* (240)
Combining multiple presentation patterns	**Pattern** *Intercepting Filter* (144) **Pattern** *Dispatcher View* (288)
Where to encapsulate View Management and Navigation logic, which involves choosing a View and dispatching to it	**Pattern** *Service to Worker* (276) **Pattern** *Dispatcher View* (288)
Where to store session state	**Design** "Session State on the Client" (20) **Design** "Session State in the Presentation Tier" (21) **Design** "Storing State on the Business Tier" (48)

Table 5-1 Presentation Tier Patterns (continued)

If you are looking for this	*Find it here*
Controlling client access to a certain View or sub-View	**Design** "Controlling Client Access" (22) **Refactoring** "Hide Resources From a Client" (88)
Controlling the flow of requests into the application	**Design** "Duplicate Form Submissions" (27) **Design** "Introduce Synchronizer Token" (67)
Controlling duplicate form submissions	**Design** "Duplicate Form Submissions" (27) **Refactoring** "Introduce Synchronizer Token" (67)
Design issues using JSP standard property auto-population mechanism via <jsp:setProperty>	**Design** "Helper Properties—Integrity and Consistency" (30)
Reducing coupling between presentation tier and business tier	**Refactoring** "Hide Presentation Tier-Specific Details From the Business Tier" (80) **Refactoring** "Introduce Business Delegate" (94)
Partitioning data access code	**Refactoring** "Separate Data Access Code" (102)

Table 5-2 shows the functions handled by the business tier patterns and indicates where you can find the particular pattern or patterns that may provide solutions.

Table 5-2 Business Tier Patterns

If you are looking for this	*Find it here*
Minimize coupling between presentation and business tiers	**Pattern** *Business Delegate* (302)
Cache business services for clients	**Pattern** *Business Delegate* (302)

Table 5-2 Business Tier Patterns (continued)

If you are looking for this	*Find it here*
Hide implementation details of business service lookup/creation/access	**Pattern** *Business Delegate* (302) **Pattern** *Service Locator* (315)
Isolate vendor and technology dependencies for services lookup	**Pattern** *Service Locator* (315)
Provide uniform method for business service lookup and creation	**Pattern** *Service Locator* (315)
Hide the complexity and dependencies for enterprise bean and JMS component lookup	**Pattern** *Service Locator* (315)
Transfer data between business objects and clients across tiers	**Pattern** *Transfer Object* (415)
Provide simpler uniform interface to remote clients	**Pattern** *Business Delegate* (302) **Pattern** *Session Façade* (341) **Pattern** *Application Service* (357)
Reduce remote method invocations by providing coarse-grained method access to business tier components	**Pattern** *Session Façade* (341)
Manage relationships between enterprise bean components and hide the complexity of interactions	**Pattern** *Session Façade* (341)
Protect the business tier components from direct exposure to clients	**Pattern** *Session Façade* (341) **Pattern** *Application Service* (357)
Provide uniform boundary access to business tier components	**Pattern** *Session Façade* (341) **Pattern** *Application Service* (357)
Implement complex conceptual domain model using objects	**Pattern** *Business Object* (374)

Table 5-2 Business Tier Patterns (continued)

If you are looking for this	*Find it here*
Identify coarse-grained objects and dependent objects for business objects and entity bean design	**Pattern** *Business Object* (374) **Pattern** *Composite Entity* (391)
Design for coarse-grained entity beans	**Pattern** *Composite Entity* (391)
Reduce or eliminate the entity bean clients' dependency on the database schema	**Pattern** *Composite Entity* (391)
Reduce or eliminate entity bean to entity bean remote relationships	**Pattern** *Composite Entity* (391)
Reduce number of entity beans and improve manageability	**Pattern** *Composite Entity* (391)
Obtain the application data model for the application from various business tier components	**Pattern** *Transfer Object Assembler* (433)
On the fly construction of the application data model	**Pattern** *Transfer Object Assembler* (433)
Hide the complexity of data model construction from the clients	**Pattern** *Transfer Object Assembler* (433)
Provide business tier query and results list processing facility	**Pattern** *Value List Handler* (444)
Minimize the overhead of using enterprise bean finder methods	**Pattern** *Value List Handler* (444)
Provide query-results caching for clients on the server side with forward and backward navigation	**Pattern** *Value List Handler* (444)
Trade-offs between using stateful and stateless session beans	**Design** "Session Bean—Stateless Versus Stateful" (46)
Provide protection to entity beans from direct client access	**Refactoring** "Wrap Entities With Session" (92)
Encapsulate business services to hide the implementation details of the business tier	**Refactoring** "Introduce Business Delegate" (94)

Table 5-2 Business Tier Patterns (continued)

If you are looking for this	*Find it here*
Coding business logic in entity beans	**Design** "Business Logic in Entity Beans" (50) **Refactoring** "Move Business Logic to Session" (100)
Provide session beans as coarse-grained business services	**Refactoring** "Merge Session Beans" (96) **Refactoring** "Wrap Entities With Session" (92)
Minimize and/or eliminate network and container overhead due to entity-bean-to-entity-bean communication	**Refactoring** "Reduce Inter-Entity Bean Communication" (98)
Partition data access code	**Refactoring** "Separate Data Access Code" (102)

Table 5-3 shows the functions typically handled by the presentation tier patterns and indicates which pattern provides a solution.

Table 5-3 Integration Tier Patterns

If you are looking for this	*Find it here*
Minimize coupling between business and resource tiers	**Pattern** *Data Access Object* (462)
Centralize access to resource tiers	**Pattern** *Data Access Object* (462)
Minimize complexity of resource access in business tier components	**Pattern** *Data Access Object* (462)
Provide asynchronous processing for enterprise applications	**Pattern** *Service Activator* (496)
Send an asynchronous request to a business service	**Pattern** *Service Activator* (496)
Asynchronously process a request as a set of parallel tasks	**Pattern** *Service Activator* (496)
Transparently persist an object model	**Pattern** *Domain Store* (516)

Table 5-3 Integration Tier Patterns (continued)

If you are looking for this	*Find it here*
Implement a custom persistence framework	**Pattern** *Domain Store* (516)
Expose a web service using XML and standard Internet protocol	**Pattern** *Web Service Broker* (557)
Aggregate and broker existing services as web services	**Pattern** *Web Service Broker* (557)

Summary

So far, we have seen the basic concepts behind the J2EE patterns, understood the tiers for pattern categorization, explored the relationships between different patterns, and taken a look at the roadmap to help guide you to a particular pattern. In the following chapters, we present the patterns individually.

There are three chapters, for presentation, business, and integration tiers. Refer to the appropriate chapter to find the pattern you're interested in.

Presentation Tier Patterns

Topics in This Chapter

- Intercepting Filter
- Front Controller
- Context Object
- Application Controller
- View Helper
- Composite View
- Service to Worker
- Dispatcher View

Chapter 6

Intercepting Filter

Problem

You want to intercept and manipulate a request and a response before and after the request is processed.

Preprocessing and **postprocessing** of a request refer to actions taken before and after the core **processing** of that request. Some of these actions determine whether processing will continue, while others manipulate the incoming or outgoing data stream into a form suitable for further processing. For example:

- Does the client have a valid session?
- Does the request path violate any constraints?
- Do you support the browser type of the client?
- What encoding does the client use to send the data?
- Is the request stream encrypted or compressed?

A common approach to handling these and other types of processing requests is to implement a series of conditional checks, typically with nested if/then/else statements to control the flow of execution. However, since you do similar types of things in each of these processing statements, you have a great deal of duplicated code. Handling preprocessing and postprocessing in this way leads to code fragility and a copy-and-paste style of programming because the flow of the control and the specific processing behavior is compiled into the application.

Additionally, this approach leads to increased coupling between the pre and postprocessing components and the core application processing code.

Forces

- You want centralized, common processing across requests, such as checking the data-encoding scheme of each request, logging information about each request, or compressing an outgoing response.
- You want pre and postprocessing components loosely coupled with core request-handling services to facilitate unobtrusive addition and removal.
- You want pre and postprocessing components independent of each other and self contained to facilitate reuse.

Solution

Use an *Intercepting Filter* as a pluggable filter to pre and postprocess requests and responses. A filter manager combines loosely coupled filters in a chain, delegating control to the appropriate filter. In this way, you can add, remove, and combine these filters in various ways without changing existing code.

As with other systems where there is a significant number of duplicated tasks, it's a good idea to take that duplicated processing, factor it out, and make it coarse grained enough to apply broadly. This is what pluggable filters accomplish.

In effect, you are able to decorate the main processing with a variety of common services, such as logging and debugging. Filters are independent of the main application code, and you can add or remove them declaratively.

Filters are controlled declaratively using a deployment descriptor, as described in the "Servlet Specification," version 2.3. The "Servlet 2.3 Specification" includes a standard mechanism for building filter chains and unobtrusively adding and removing filters from those chains. A deployment configuration file sets up a chain of filters and can include a mapping of specific URLs to this filter chain. When a client requests a resource that matches the configured URL mapping, the filters in the chain are invoked before (preprocessing) and/or after (postprocessing) the invocation of the requested target resource.

Structure

Figure 6.1 represents the *Intercepting Filter* class diagram.

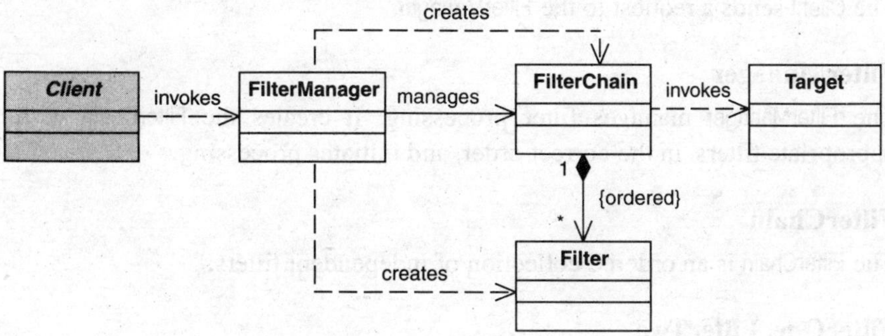

Figure 6.1 *Intercepting Filter* Class Diagram

Participants and Responsibilities

Figure 6.2 represents the *Intercepting Filter* sequence diagram.

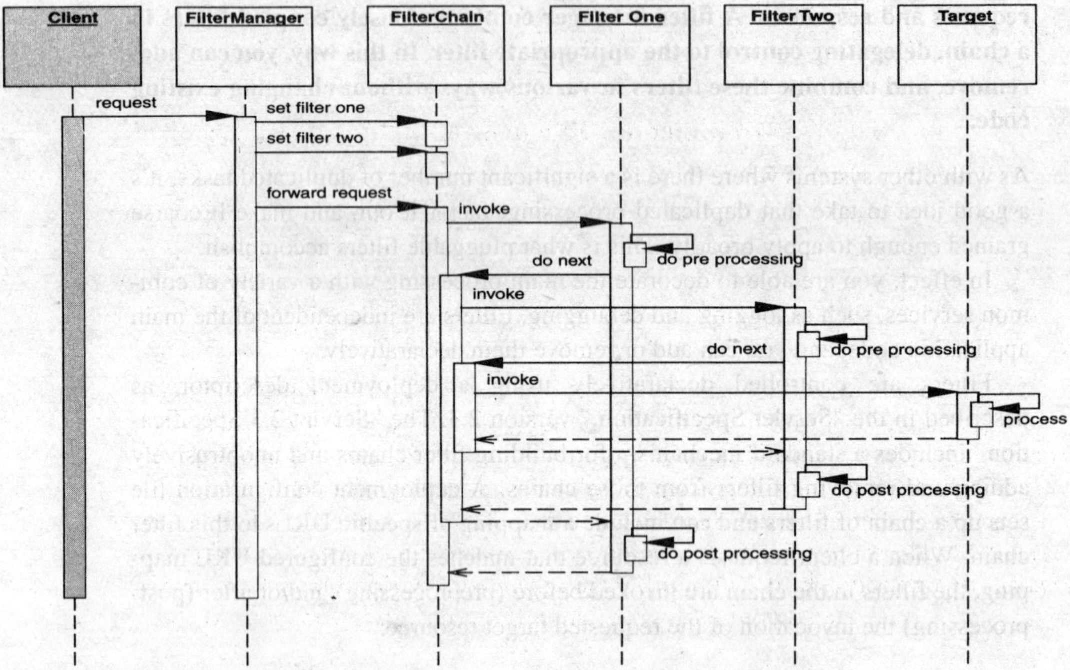

Figure 6.2 *Intercepting Filter* Sequence Diagram

Client

The Client sends a request to the FilterManager.

FilterManager

The FilterManager manages filter processing. It creates the FilterChain with the appropriate filters, in the correct order, and initiates processing.

FilterChain

The FilterChain is an ordered collection of independent filters.

FilterOne, FilterTwo

FilterOne and FilterTwo represent individual filters that are mapped to a Target. The FilterChain coordinates the processing of filters.

Target

The Target is the resource requested by the client.

Strategies

Standard Filter Strategy

Filters are controlled declaratively using a deployment descriptor, as described in the servlet specification, version 2.3. The Servlet 2.3 Specification includes a standard mechanism for building filter chains and unobtrusively adding and removing filters from those chains. Filters are based upon a standard interface, and are loosely coupled to each other, as well as to the target resources for which they perform pre or postprocessing. Configure each filter declaratively by modifying the deployment descriptor for a web application.

The example for this strategy is a filter that preprocesses requests of any encoding type such that the core request-handling code can handle each request.

Why might this be necessary? An example is HTML forms that include a file upload use a different encoding type than that of basic forms. As a result, form data that accompanies the upload is not available via simple getParameter() invocations. In order to get at this form data, the example includes two filters that preprocess requests, translating all encoding types into a single consistent format. The format has all form data available as request attributes.

Each filter handles a different encoding type:

- One filter handles the standard form encoding of type application/x-www-form-urlencoded
- The other handles the less common encoding type multipart/form-data, which is used for forms that include file uploads.

The filters translate all form data into request attributes, so the core request handling mechanism can work with every request in the same manner, instead of with special casing for different encodings.

Example 6.1 through Example 6.4 provide code for this example, and Figure 6.3 on page 152 shows the sequence diagram.

The base filter, shown in Example 6.1, provides default behavior for the *Standard Filter* callback methods.

Example 6.1 Base Filter – Standard Filter Strategy

```
public class BaseEncodeFilter implements javax.servlet.Filter {

  private javax.servlet.FilterConfig filterConfig;

```

```
  public void doFilter(
      javax.servlet.ServletRequest servletRequest,
          javax.servlet.ServletResponse servletResponse,
          javax.servlet.FilterChain filterChain)
          throws java.io.IOException,
          javax.servlet.ServletException {

    filterChain.doFilter(servletRequest, servletResponse);
  }

  protected javax.servlet.FilterConfig getFilterConfig() {
    return filterConfig;
  }

  public void destroy() { }

  public void init(javax.servlet.FilterConfig filterConfig)
      throws javax.servlet.ServletException {
    this.filterConfig = filterConfig;
  }

}
```

Example 6.2 shows a filter that translates requests using the common application form encoding scheme.

Example 6.2 StandardEncodeFilter – Standard Filter Strategy

```
public class StandardEncodeFilter extends BaseEncodeFilter {
  // Creates new StandardEncodeFilter
  public StandardEncodeFilter() {  }

  public void doFilter(javax.servlet.ServletRequest
      servletRequest,javax.servlet.ServletResponse
          servletResponse,javax.servlet.FilterChain filterChain)
          throws java.io.IOException,
          javax.servlet.ServletException {

    String contentType = servletRequest.getContentType();
    if ((contentType == null) || contentType.equalsIgnoreCase(
        "application/x-www-form-urlencoded")) {
      translateParamsToAttributes(servletRequest, servletResponse);
    }
```

```

    filterChain.doFilter(servletRequest, servletResponse);
  }

  private void translateParamsToAttributes(
      ServletRequest request, ServletResponse response) {
    Enumeration paramNames = request.getParameterNames();

    while (paramNames.hasMoreElements()) {
      String paramName = (String) paramNames.nextElement();
      String [] values;
      values = request.getParameterValues(paramName);
      if (values.length == 1)
        request.setAttribute(paramName, values[0]);
      else
        request.setAttribute(paramName, values);
    }
  }
}
```

Example 6.3 shows the filter that handles the translation of requests. The requests use the multipart form encoding scheme. The code for these filters is based on the final draft of the servlet specification, version 2.3. Both filters inherit from a base filter (see *Base Filter Strategy* on page 158).

Example 6.3 MultipartEncodeFilter – Standard Filter Strategy

```
public class MultipartEncodeFilter extends BaseEncodeFilter {
  public MultipartEncodeFilter() { }
  public void doFilter(
      javax.servlet.ServletRequest servletRequest,
          javax.servlet.ServletResponse servletResponse,
          javax.servlet.FilterChain filterChain)
          throws java.io.IOException,
          javax.servlet.ServletException {

    String contentType = servletRequest.getContentType();
    // Only filter this request if it is multipart
    // encoding
    if (contentType.startsWith("multipart/form-data")) {
      try {
        String uploadFolder = getFilterConfig().
            getInitParameter("UploadFolder");
```

```
        if (uploadFolder == null)
          uploadFolder = ".";
        /** The MultipartRequest class is:
          * Copyright (C) 2001 by Jason Hunter
          * <jhunter@servlets.com>. All rights reserved.
        **/
        MultipartRequest multi = new MultipartRequest(
            servletRequest, uploadFolder, 1 * 1024 * 1024 );
        Enumeration params = multi.getParameterNames();
        while (params.hasMoreElements()) {
          String name = (String)params.nextElement();
          String value = multi.getParameter(name);
          servletRequest.setAttribute(name, value);
        }
        Enumeration files = multi.getFileNames();
        while (files.hasMoreElements()) {
          String name = (String)files.nextElement();
          String filename = multi.getFilesystemName(name);
          String type = multi.getContentType(name);
          File f = multi.getFile(name);
          // At this point, do something with the
          // file, as necessary
        }
      } catch (IOException e) {
        LogManager.logMessage("error reading or saving file"+ e);
      }
    } // end if
    filterChain.doFilter(servletRequest, servletResponse);
  } // end method doFilter()
}
```

The excerpt in Example 6.4 is from the deployment descriptor for the web application containing this example. It shows how these two filters are registered and then mapped to a resource; in this case it's a simple test servlet.

Example 6.4 Deployment Descriptor – Standard Filter Strategy

```
.
.
.
<filter>
  <filter-name>StandardEncodeFilter</filter-name>
  <display-name>StandardEncodeFilter</display-name>
  <description></description>
```

```
    <filter-class> corepatterns.filters.encodefilter.
        StandardEncodeFilter</filter-class>
  </filter>
  <filter>
    <filter-name>MultipartEncodeFilter</filter-name>
    <display-name>MultipartEncodeFilter</display-name>
    <description></description>
    <filter-class>corepatterns.filters.encodefilter.
        MultipartEncodeFilter</filter-class>
    <init-param>
      <param-name>UploadFolder</param-name>
      <param-value>/home/files</param-value>
    </init-param>
  </filter>
  .
  .
  .
  <filter-mapping>
    <filter-name>StandardEncodeFilter</filter-name>
    <url-pattern>/EncodeTestServlet</url-pattern>
  </filter-mapping>
  <filter-mapping>
    <filter-name>MultipartEncodeFilter</filter-name>
    <url-pattern>/EncodeTestServlet</url-pattern>
  </filter-mapping>
  .
  .
  .
```

The sequence diagram for this example is shown in Figure 6.3.

The StandardEncodeFilter and the MultiPartEncodeFilter intercept control when a client makes a request to the controller servlet. The container fulfills the role of filter manager, and directs control to these filters by invoking their doFilter methods. After completing its processing, each filter passes control to its containing FilterChain. The filter instructs its FilterChain to execute the next filter. Once both filters have received and subsequently relinquished control, the next component to receive control is the actual target resource, in this case the controller servlet.

Filters, as supported in version 2.3 of the servlet specification, also support wrapping the request and response objects. This feature lets you build a much more powerful mechanism than could be built using the custom implementation suggested by the *Custom Filter* strategy. Of course, you can custom build a hybrid approach combining the two strategies but this approach would still lack the power of the *Standard Filter* strategy, as supported by the servlet specification.

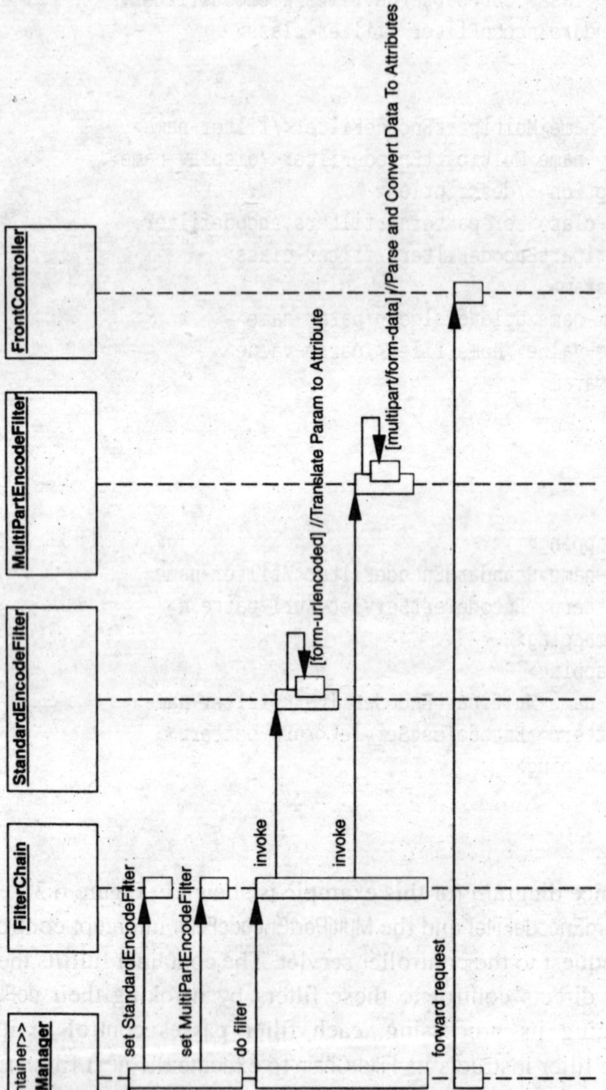

Figure 6.3 *Intercepting Filter, Standard Filter* Strategy – Encoding Conversion Example

Custom Filter Strategy

Implement the Filter with your own custom strategy. This is less flexible and less powerful than the preferred *Standard Filter* strategy that is available in containers supporting the 2.3 servlet specification and later. This *Custom Filter* strategy is less powerful because it doesn't support wrapping request and response objects in a standard and portable way. Additionally, the request object cannot be modified, and you must introduce some sort of buffering mechanism if filters are to control the output stream.

To implement the *Custom Filter* strategy, you could use the *Decorator* pattern [GoF] to wrap filters around the core request-processing logic. For example, apply a debugging filter that wraps an authentication filter.

Example 6.5 and Example 6.6 show how you could create this mechanism programmatically.

Example 6.5 Implementing a Filter – Debugging Filter

```
public class DebuggingFilter implements Processor {
  private Processor nextProcessor;

  public DebuggingFilter(Processor nextProcessor) {
    this.nextProcessor = nextProcessor;
  }

  public void execute(ServletRequest request,
      ServletResponse response)
      throws IOException, ServletException {
    // Do some filter processing here, such as
    // displaying request parameters

    nextProcessor.execute(request, response);
  }
}
```

Example 6.6 Handling Requests

```
public void processRequest(ServletRequest req, ServletResponse res)
    throws IOException, ServletException {
  Processor processors = new DebuggingFilter(
      new AuthenticationFilter(new CoreProcessor()));
  processors.execute(req, res);

  //Then dispatch to next resource, which is probably
  // the View to display
```

```
    dispatcher.dispatch(req, res);
}

```

In the servlet controller, delegate to a method called ProcessRequest to handle incoming requests, as shown in Example 6.7.

Example 6.7 Implementing a Filter – Core Processor

```
public class CoreProcessor implements Processor {

  public CoreProcessor() { }

  public void execute(ServletRequest req, ServletResponse res)
      throws IOException, ServletException {
    //Do core processing here
  }
}
```

For example purposes only, imagine that each processing component writes to standard output when it is executed. Example 6.8 shows the possible execution output.

Example 6.8 Messages Written to Standard Output

```
Debugging filter preprocessing completed...
Authentication filter processing completed...
Core processing completed...
Debugging filter post-processing completed...
```

Example 6.8 shows standard output when a chain of processors is executed in order. Each processor, except for the last one in the chain, is considered a filter. The final processor component is where you encapsulate the core processing you want to complete for each request. Given this design, you will need to change the code in the CoreProcessor class, as well as in any filter classes, when you want to modify how you handle requests.

Figure 6.4 is a sequence diagram describing the flow of control for the filter code of Example 6.5, Example 6.6, and Example 6.8.

Notice that with a *Decorator* implementation, each filter invokes on the next filter directly, though using a generic interface. You could implement this strategy a different way using a FilterManager and FilterChain. In this case, these two components coordinate and manage filter processing, and the individual filters do not communicate with one another directly.

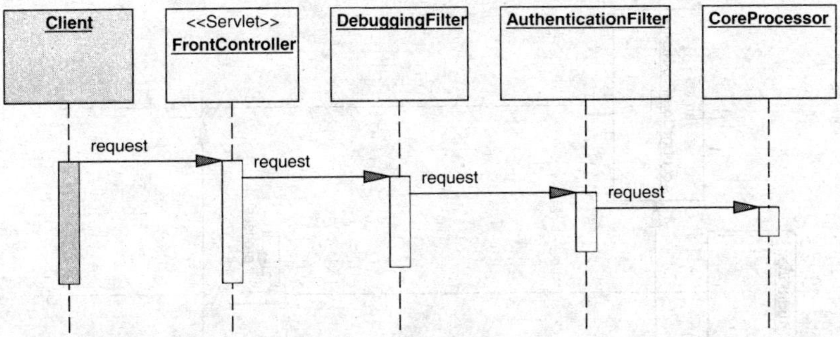

Figure 6.4 Sequence Diagram for *Custom Filter* Strategy, *Decorator* Implementation

This design approximates a servlet 2.3-compliant implementation, though it is still a custom strategy. Example 6.9 is just such a FilterManager class, which creates a FilterChain; the FilterChain is shown in Example 6.10. The FilterChain adds filters to the chain in the appropriate order, processes the filters, and finally processes the target resource. (For the sake of brevity, adding filters to the chain is done in the FilterChain constructor, but would normally be done in place of the comment.)

Figure 6.5 on page 156 is a sequence diagram for this code.

Example 6.9 FilterManager – Custom Filter Strategy

```
public class FilterManager {
  public void processFilter(Filter target,
      javax.servlet.http.HttpServletRequest request,
          javax.servlet.http.HttpServletResponse response)
              throws javax.servlet.ServletException,
                  java.io.IOException {

    FilterChain filterChain = new FilterChain();
    // The filter manager builds the filter chain here if necessary
    // Pipe request through Filter Chain
    filterChain.processFilter(request, response);

    //process target resource
    target.execute(request, response);
  }
}
```

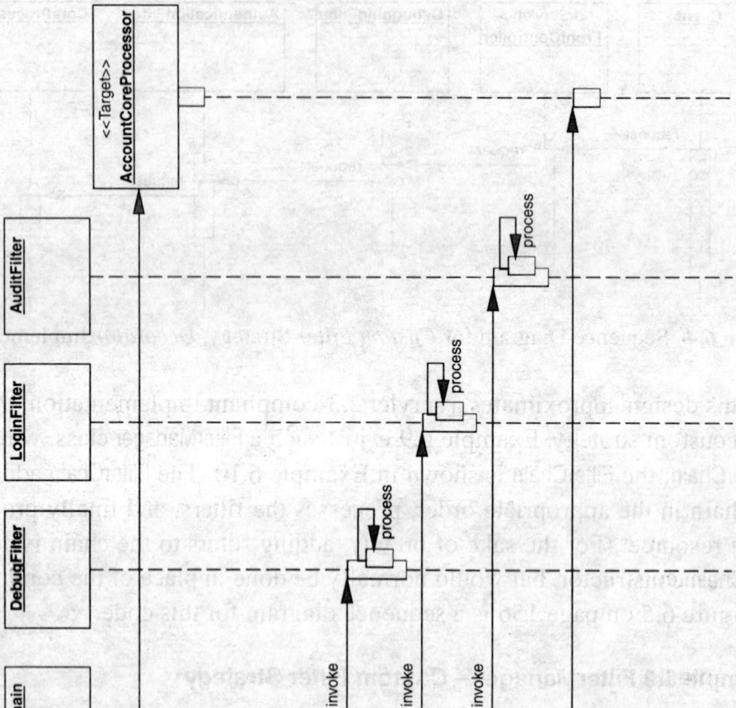

Figure 6.5 Sequence Diagram for *Custom Filter* Strategy, Nondecorator Implementation

Example 6.10 FilterChain – Custom Filter Strategy

```
public class FilterChain {
  // filter chain
  private List myFilters = new ArrayList();

  // Creates new FilterChain
  public FilterChain() {
    // plug-in default filter services for example
    // only. This would typically be done in the
    // FilterManager, but is done here for example
    // purposes
    addFilter(new DebugFilter());
    addFilter(new LoginFilter());
    addFilter(new AuditFilter());
  }

  public void processFilter(
      javax.servlet.http.HttpServletRequest request,
        javax.servlet.http.HttpServletResponse response)
          throws javax.servlet.ServletException,
            java.io.IOException {

    Filter filter;
    // apply filters
    Iterator filters = myFilters.iterator();
    while (filters.hasNext()) {
      filter = (Filter)filters.next();
      // pass request & response through various
      // filters
      filter.execute(request, response);
    }
  }

  public void addFilter(Filter filter) {
    myFilters.add(filter);
  }
}
```

You can't create very flexible or powerful filters with this strategy. Instead, use the *Standard Filter* strategy where possible. Filters are added and removed programmatically. While you could write a proprietary mechanism for handling adding and removing filters via a configuration file, you still would have no way of wrapping the request and response objects. Additionally, without a sophisticated buffering mechanism, this strategy does not provide flexible postprocessing.

The *Standard Filter* strategy provides solutions to these issues, leveraging features of the 2.3 servlet specification

Base Filter Strategy

A base filter serves as a common superclass for all filters. Common features can be encapsulated in the base filter and shared among all filters. For example, a base filter is a good place to include default behavior for the container callback methods in the *Standard Filter* strategy. Example 6.11 shows one way to do this.

Example 6.11 Base Filter Strategy

```
public class BaseEncodeFilter implements javax.servlet.Filter {
  private javax.servlet.FilterConfig filterConfig;

  public BaseEncodeFilter() { }

  public void init(javax.servlet.FilterConfig filterConfig) {
    this.filterConfig = filterConfig;
  }

  public void doFilter(javax.servlet.ServletRequest servletRequest,
      javax.servlet.ServletResponse servletResponse,
      javax.servlet.FilterChain filterChain)
      throws java.io.IOException,
      javax.servlet.ServletException {

    filterChain.doFilter(servletRequest, servletResponse);
  }

  protected javax.servlet.FilterConfig getFilterConfig() {
    return filterConfig;
  }
}
```

Template Filter Strategy

A key benefit of using this strategy is that it abstracts away the details of the underlying servlet API and focuses on implementing preprocessing and postprocessing logic. This means you no longer need to deal with the semantics of method invocations such as chain.doFilter(req, res), but rather simply with method invocations such as doPreProcessing(req, res), which are much more intuitive.

This strategy builds on the *Base Filter* strategy, which simply describes using a base class to encapsulate all the details of the filter API (see *Base Filter Strategy* on page 158). The *Template Filter* strategy uses this base class to provide *Template Method* [Gof] functionality. In this case, the base filter dictates the general steps that every filter must perform, while leaving the specifics of **how** to complete that step to each filter subclass. This approach provides the inversion of control that is common in frameworks, meaning that the superclass (or base class) dictates the flow of control to its subclasses. Typically, the methods of the superclass are coarsely defined, basic methods that simply impose a limited structure on each template.

You can combine this strategy with any other filter strategy. Example 6.12 and Example 6.13 show how to use this strategy with the *Declared Filter* strategy.

Example 6.12 shows a base filter called TemplateFilter, as follows.

Example 6.12 Using a Template Filter Strategy

```
public abstract class TemplateFilter implements javax.servlet.Filter {
  private FilterConfig filterConfig;
  public void init(FilterConfig filterConfig) throws ServletException {
    this.filterConfig = filterConfig;
  }

  protected FilterConfig getFilterConfig() {
    return filterConfig;
  }

  public void doFilter(ServletRequest request,
      ServletResponse response, FilterChain chain)
      throws IOException, ServletException {

    // Preprocessing for each filter
    doPreProcessing(request, response);

    // Pass control to the next filter in the chain or
    // to the target resource. This method invocation is what logically
    // demarcates preprocessing from postprocessing.
    chain.doFilter(request, response);

    // Post-processing for each filter
    doPostProcessing(request, response);
```

```
}
  public abstract void doPreProcessing(ServletRequest request,
      ServletResponse response) { }

  public abstract void doPostProcessing(ServletRequest request,
      ServletResponse response) { }

  public void destroy() { }
}
```

Given this class definition for TemplateFilter, each filter is implemented as a subclass that implements only the doPreProcessing and doPostProcessing methods. These subclasses have the option, though, of implementing all three methods. Example 6.13 is an example of a filter subclass that implements the two mandatory methods (dictated by the superclass template filter).

Example 6.13 Logging Filter

```
public class LoggingFilter extends TemplateFilter {
  public void doPreProcessing(ServletRequest req, ServletResponse res) {
    //do some preprocessing here, such as logging some information about
    // the request before it's been handled.
  }

  public void doPostProcessing(ServletRequest req, ServletResponse res){
    // do some post-processing here, such as logging some information
    // about the request and response after the request has been handled
    // and the response generated.
  }
}
```

In the sequence diagram in Figure 6.6 on page 161, filter subclasses, such as LoggingFilter, define specific processing by overriding the abstract doPreProcessing and doPostProcessing methods. As a result, the template filter imposes a flow of control upon each filter and focuses filter developers on the semantics of writing pre and postprocessing logic. Finally, since it is a **base filter**, it also provides a place for encapsulating code that is common to every filter.

A sequence diagram for this strategy is shown in Figure 6.6.

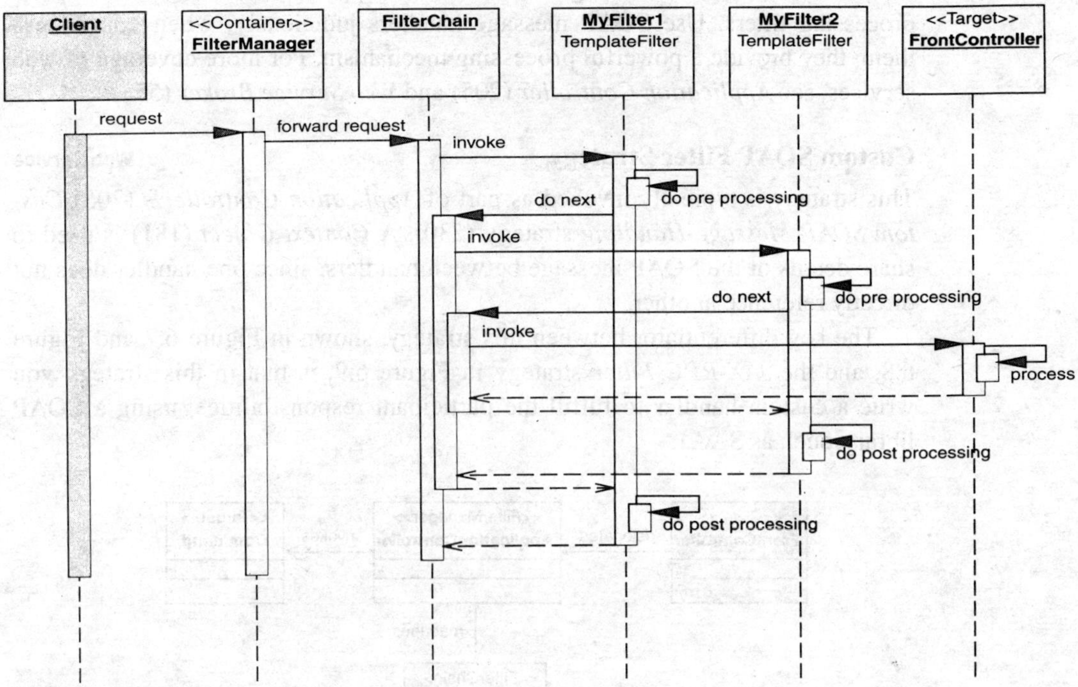

Figure 6.6 *Intercepting Filter, Template Filter* Strategy Sequence Diagram

Web Service Message-Handling Strategies

While using *Intercepting Filter* is common in the presentation tier, certain *Intercepting Filter* strategies are relevant in other tiers, as well. The *Custom SOAP Filter* and *JAX-RPC Filter* message-handling strategies are examples of filters used in the client, presentation, and integration tiers to handle pre and postprocessing of web service requests.

When loosely coupled, these chained filters are used to handle and manipulate web service requests and are often referred to as **message handlers**. These filters intercept incoming messages and perform pre and postprocessing on information in the message.

Similarly, the filters act on outgoing responses. For example, a message handler might validate a digital signature, sign a message, or log information about a message. Messages must be serialized from XML to Java and vice versa, as each message enters and leaves the handler mechanism.

The SOAP With Attachments API for Java, or SAAJ [SAAJ], allows developers to work with SOAP messages and provides support for building pre and post-processing filters. Use SOAP message handlers judiciously; when you do use them, they provide a powerful processing mechanism. For more coverage of web services, see *Application Controller* (205) and *Web Service Broker* (557).

Custom SOAP Filter Strategy **Web Service**

This strategy is typically invoked as part of *Application Controller's* (205) *Custom SOAP Message-Handling* strategy (230). A *Context Object* (181) is used to share details of the SOAP message between handlers, since one handler does not directly reference another.

The key differentiator between this strategy, shown in Figure 6.7 and Figure 6.8, and the *JAX-RPC Filter* strategy in Figure 6.9, is that in this strategy you write a custom handler to fulfill the participant responsibilities, using a SOAP library, such as SAAJ.

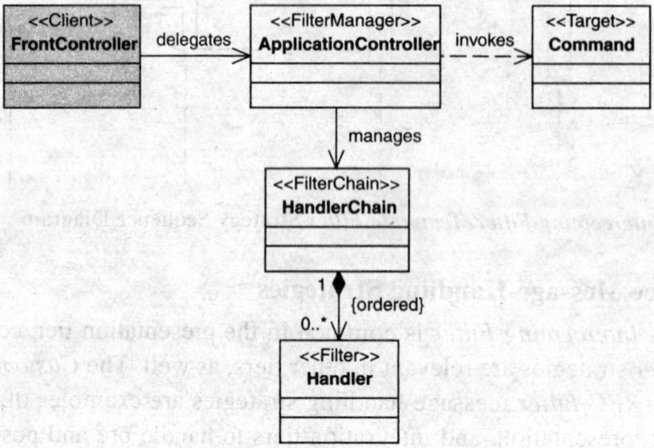

Figure 6.7 *Custom SOAP Filter* Strategy Class Diagram

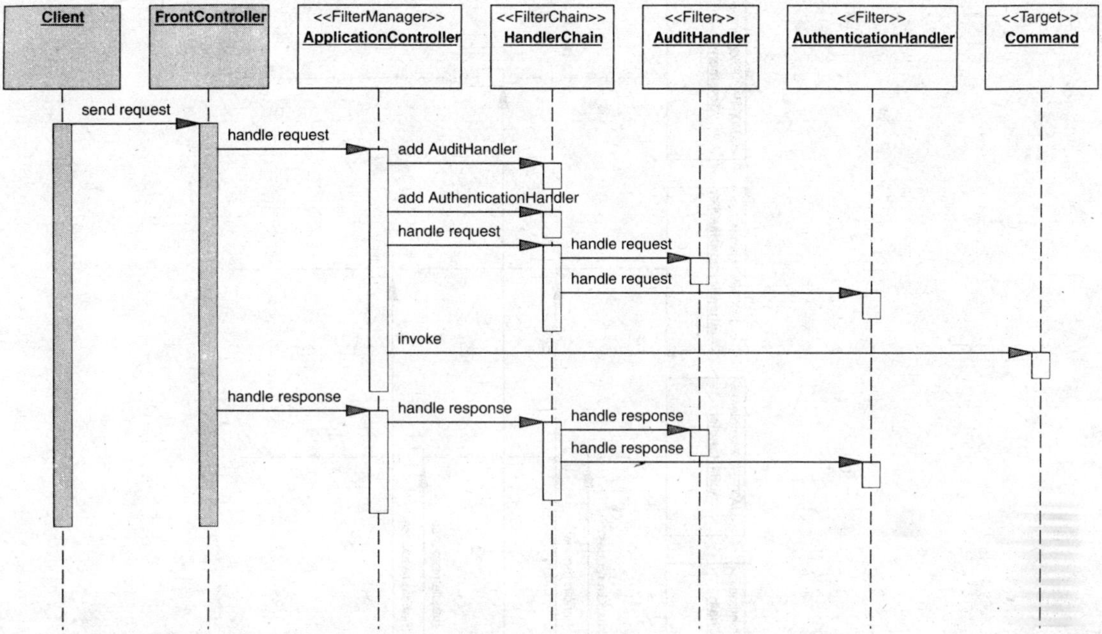

Figure 6.8 Custom SOAP Filter Strategy Sequence Diagram

JAX-RPC Filter Strategy

Web Service

This strategy is typically invoked as part of *Application Controller's* (205) *JAX-RPC Message-Handling* strategy (235). A *Context Object* (181) is used to share details of the SOAP message between handlers, since one handler does not directly reference another.

The key differentiator between this strategy and the *Custom SOAP Filter* strategy is that in this strategy most of the participant responsibilities are performed by the JAX-RPC runtime engine. The handlers are implemented either on the client side of the RPC invocation, on the server side of the RPC invocation, or on both sides. Thus, you can insert handlers on either side of the network connection. You build message handlers with JAX-RPC using SAAJ, which offers powerful processing capabilities when used judiciously.

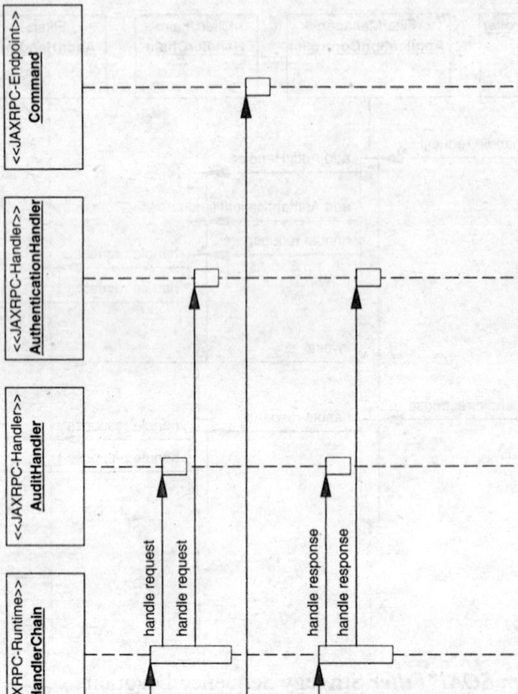

Figure 6.9 *JAX-RPC Filter* Strategy Sequence Diagram

Consequences

- ***Centralizes control with loosely coupled handlers***
  Filters provide a central place for handling processing across multiple requests, as does a controller. Filters are better suited to massaging requests and responses for ultimate handling by a target resource, such as a controller. Additionally, a controller often ties together the management of numerous unrelated common services, such as authentication, logging, encryption, and so forth. Filtering allows for much more loosely coupled handlers, which can be combined in various permutations.
- ***Improves reusability***
  Filters promote cleaner application partitioning and encourage reuse. You can transparently add or remove these pluggable interceptors from existing code, and due to their standard interface, they work in any permutations and are reusable for varying presentations.
- ***Declarative and flexible configuration***
  Numerous services are combined in varying permutations without a single recompile of the core code base.
- ***Information sharing is inefficient***
  Sharing information between filters can be inefficient, since by definition each filter is loosely coupled. If large amounts of information must be shared between filters, then this approach might prove to be costly.

Related Patterns

- ***Front Controller (166)***
  The controller solves some similar problems, but is better suited to handling core processing.
- ***Decorator [GoF]***
  The *Intercepting Filter* is related to the *Decorator*, which provides for dynamically pluggable wrappers.
- ***Template Method [GoF]***
  The *Template Method* is used to implement the *Template Filter* strategy.
- ***Interceptor [POSA2]***
  The *Intercepting Filter* is related to the *Interceptor*, which allows services to be added transparently and triggered automatically.
- ***Pipes and Filters [POSA1]***
  The *Intercepting Filter* is related to *Pipes and Filters*.

Front Controller

Problem

You want a centralized access point for presentation-tier request handling.

The system requires a centralized access point for request handling. Without a central access point, control code that is common across multiple requests is duplicated in numerous places, such as within multiple views. When control code is intermingled with view-creation code, the application is less modular and cohesive. Additionally, having control code in numerous places is difficult to maintain and a single code change might require changes be made in numerous places.

Forces

- You want to avoid duplicate control logic.
- You want to apply common logic to multiple requests.
- You want to separate system processing logic from the view.
- You want to centralize controlled access points into your system.

Solution

Use a *Front Controller* as the initial point of contact for handling all related requests. The *Front Controller* centralizes control logic that might otherwise be duplicated, and manages the key request handling activities.

The *Front Controller* provides a centralized entry point for handling requests. By centralizing control logic, the *Front Controller* also helps reduce the amount of programming logic embedded directly in the views. For a JSP view, for instance. this reduces the temptation to use large amounts of Java code, called **scriptlet code**, embedded within the JSP.

This pattern is similar to the *Intercepting Filter* (144), because they both factor out and consolidate common presentation-tier control logic. A key difference is that *Intercepting Filter* (144) provides a loosely-coupled set of chained processors and powerful strategies for specifically performing pre and post processing. Centralizing control in a *Front Controller* and reducing business and processing logic in the view promotes code reuse across requests, reducing duplication. Unless the control logic is trivial, using a *Front Controller* is preferable to embedding code in multiple views, because the latter approach leads to a reuse-by-copy-and-paste environment, which is more error-prone.

This approach can also mean each developer on a team approaches the same coding task differently when that task should be done consistently, enforced and controlled in a more centralized manner. For example, if individual developers are responsible for adding a <tag:checkLogin/> guard to specific pages to enforce access control, ensuring consistency is difficult, since a developer might forget to do it.

A *Front Controller* typically uses an *Application Controller* (205), which is responsible for action and view management.

- **Action management** refers to locating and routing to the specific actions that will service a request.
- **View management** refers to finding and dispatching to the appropriate view. While this behavior can be folded into the *Front Controller*, partitioning it into separate classes as part of an *Application Controller* (205) improves modularity, maintainability, and reusability.

Though handling related requests is centralized, this does not imply any specific limitation on the number of handlers in the system. The most common usage is to have a single *Front Controller* handling all requests, but an application can certainly use multiple controllers instead, with each mapped to a set of distinct services.

In the former, more typical case of using a single controller, server administration tasks are reduced, since only a single component is registered with the web server. This means that adding a new type of service does not require registering that service with the web server. This reduces the administration burden and facilitates hot deployment.

In the latter case, where several controllers are employed, each must be registered with the web server. Adding a new type of service means registering that service with the web server.

Design Note: Processing a Request

Processing a request involves two types of activities: request handling and view processing. During the request handling process, several activities must be performed in the presentation tier:

- Protocol handling and context transformation
- Navigation and routing
- Core processing
- Dispatch

Protocol handling involves handling a protocol-specific request, and **context transformation** involves the transfer of protocol-specific state into a more general form. An example of this is retrieving parameters from an HttpServletRequest instance and populating a MyRequest object that can be used independent of any servlet-related artifacts.

Navigation and routing mean choosing the routing for handling a particular request, such as what objects will perform the core processing for this request, and what view will be used to display the results.

Core processing is the actual servicing of the request.

Dispatch involves transferring control from one part of the application to another, such as from the request-handling mechanism to the view-processing components.

Structure

Figure 6.10 represents the *Front Controller* class diagram.

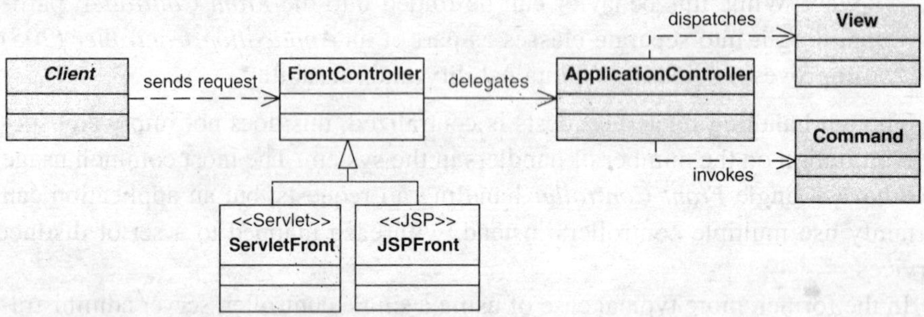

Figure 6.10 *Front Controller* Class Diagram

The most common usage of *Front Controller* is in combination with an *Application Controller* (205) and commands using *Command and Controller* strategy (174). However, it is certainly possible to invoke a helper object with strongly typed methods directly from the controller, in effect bypassing the *Application Controller* (205). For instance, if there is a non-remote business tier, the controller might directly invoke a *Business Object* (374), an *Application Service* (357), or a POJO façade, each of which fulfills the role of helper. Alternately, if there is a remote business tier, then the controller could invoke a *Business Delegate* (302), which also fulfills the role of a helper in this scenario. Invoking a helper directly from a *Front Controller* is shown in the alternate class diagram, Figure 6.11 on page 169.

In both cases, though, the controller would use conditional logic, which is reasonable only in limited use, to resolve the incoming request to the correct helper object. One way to reduce the amount of conditional logic in any one controller is to provide multiple *Front Controllers*, each used for a set of use cases, such as having an AccountController or OrderController. This groups the conditional logic, making it more maintainable, though this approach means introducing numerous servlet controllers. Doing so adds some complexity in the areas of administration, deployment, and maintenance.

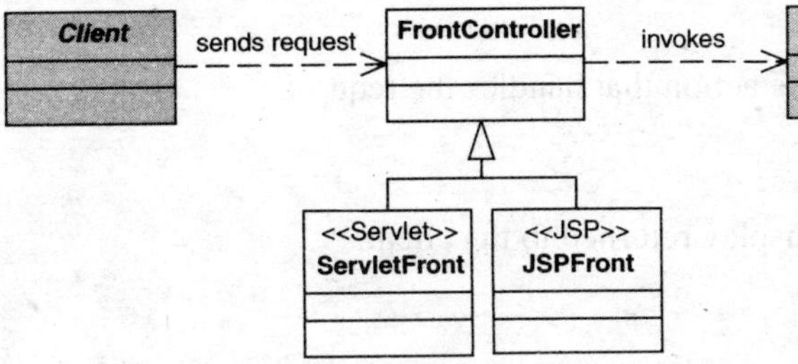

Figure 6.11 Front Controller Class Diagram Using Helpers

Participants and Responsibilities

Figure 6.12 shows the *Front Controller* sequence diagram.

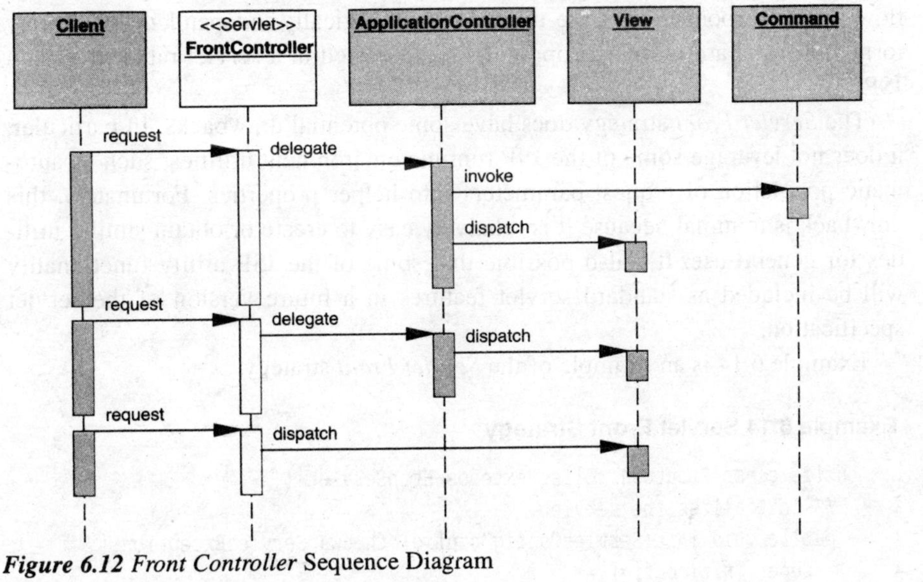

Figure 6.12 Front Controller Sequence Diagram

FrontController

The FrontController is the initial contact point for handling requests in the system. It delegates to an ApplicationController to perform action and view management.

ApplicationController

An ApplicationController is responsible for action and view management, including locating and routing to the specific actions that will service a request, and finding and dispatching to the appropriate view.

Command

A Command performs the action that handles the request.

View

A View represents the display returned to the client.

Strategies

There are several strategies for implementing a controller.

Servlet Front Strategy

This strategy suggests implementing the controller as a servlet. Though semantically equivalent, it is preferred to the *JSP Front* strategy. The controller manages the aspects of request handling that are related to business processing and control flow. These responsibilities are related to, but logically independent of, display formatting, and are more appropriately encapsulated in a servlet rather than in a JSP.

The *Servlet Front* strategy does have some potential drawbacks. In particular, it does not leverage some of the JSP runtime environment utilities, such as automatic population of request parameters into helper properties. Fortunately, this drawback is minimal because it is relatively easy to create or obtain similar utilities for general use. It's also possible that some of the JSP utility functionality will be included as standard servlet features in a future version of the servlet specification.

Example 6.14 is an example of the *Servlet Front* strategy.

Example 6.14 Servlet Front Strategy

```
public class FrontController extends HttpServlet {
  // Initializes the servlet.
  public void init(ServletConfig config) throws ServletException {
    super.init(config);
  }

  // Destroys the servlet.
  public void destroy() { }
```

```
/** Processes requests for both HTTP
  * <code>GET</code> and <code>POST</code> methods.
  * @param request servlet request
  * @param response servlet response
  */
protected void processRequest(HttpServletRequest request,
    HttpServletResponse response) throws ServletException,
    java.io.IOException {

  String page;
  /**ApplicationResources provides a simple API
   * for retrieving constants and other
   * preconfigured values**/
  ApplicationResources resource = ApplicationResources.getInstance();
  try {
    // create Context Object
    RequestContext requestContext =
        new RequestContext(request, response);

    // invoke request-processing components to handle
    // incoming request
    ApplicationController applicationController = new
        ApplicationControllerImpl();
    ResponseContext responseContext =
        applicationController.handleRequest(requestContext);

     // invoke response-processing components to
     // handle response logic
     applicationController.handleResponse(
         requestContext, responseContext);
  } catch (Exception e) {
    LogManager.logMessage("FrontController:exception : " +
        e.getMessage());
    request.setAttribute(resource.getMessageAttr(),
        "Exception occurred : " + e.getMessage());
    page = resource.getErrorPage(e);
    // dispatch control to site-unavailable view
    dispatch(request, response, page);
  }
}

/** Handles the HTTP <code>GET</code> method.
```

```
   * @param request servlet request
   * @param response servlet response
   */
  protected void doGet(HttpServletRequest request,
      HttpServletResponse response) throws ServletException,
      java.io.IOException {

    processRequest(request, response);
  }

  /** Handles the HTTP <code>POST</code> method.
   * @param request servlet request
   * @param response servlet response
   */
  protected void doPost(HttpServletRequest request,
      HttpServletResponse response)
      throws ServletException, java.io.IOException {

    processRequest(request, response);
  }

  protected void dispatch(HttpServletRequest request,
      HttpServletResponse response, String page)
      throws javax.servlet.ServletException, java.io.IOException {

    RequestDispatcher dispatcher = this.getServletContext().
        getRequestDispatcher(page);
    dispatcher.forward(request, response);
  }

  /** Returns a short description of the servlet */
  public String getServletInfo() {
    return "Front Controller Pattern" +
    " Servlet Front Strategy Example";
  }
}
```

JSP Front Strategy

A controller handles processing that is not specifically related to display formatting, so it is a mismatch to implement this component as a JSP. The *Servlet Front* strategy is preferred to the *JSP Front* strategy.

Implementing the controller as a JSP is clearly not preferred for another reason: It requires a software developer to work with a page of markup to modify request-handling logic. A software developer will typically find the *JSP Front* strategy more cumbersome when completing the cycle of coding, compilation, testing, and debugging.

Example 6.15 is an example of the *JSP Front* strategy.

Example 6.15 JSP Front Strategy

```
<%@page contentType="text/html"%>
<%@ page import="corepatterns.util.*" %>
<%@ taglib prefix="c" uri="http://java.sun.com/jstl/core" %>

<html>
<head><title>JSP Front Controller</title></head>
<body>

<h3><center> Employee Profile </h3>

<%
  /** Control logic goes here...
    * At some point in code block we retrieve employee information,
    * encapsulate it within a value object and place this bean in
    * request scope with the key "employee". This code was omitted.
    * We either dispatch to another JSP at this point or simply allow
    * the remaining portions of scriptlet code to execute
   **/
%>
<jsp:useBean id="employee" scope="request"
    class="corepatterns.util.EmployeeTO"/>
<FORM method=POST >
<table width="60%">
<tr>
  <td> First Name : </td>
  <td> <input type="text" name="<%=Constants.FLD_FIRSTNAME%>"
      value="<c:out value='${employee.firstName}'/>">
  </td>
</tr>

<tr>
  <td>  Last Name : </td>
  <td> <input type="text" name="<%=Constants.FLD_LASTNAME%>"
      value="<c:out value='${employee.lastName}'/>">
```

```
  </td>
 </tr>
 <tr>
  <td> Employee ID : </td>
  <td> <input type="text" name="<%=Constants.FLD_EMPID%>"
      value="<c:out value='${employee.id}'/>">
  </td>
 </tr>
 <tr>
  <td> <input type="submit" name="employee_profile"> </td>
  <td> </td>
 </tr>
 </table>
 </FORM>

 </body>
 </html>
```

Command and Controller Strategy

Application Controller (205) describes the general use of commands to perform action management as part of its *Command Handler* strategy (209). Using a command handler along with a *Front Controller* is called *The Command and Controller* strategy.

Using the *Command* pattern [GoF] provides a generic interface to the helper objects that service a request. This minimizes the coupling between these components. This provides a flexible and easily extensible mechanism for developers to add request-handling behaviors.

Because the command processing is not coupled with the command invocation, the command processing mechanism can be reused with various types of clients, not just browsers. This strategy also facilitates the creation of composite commands (see *Composite* pattern [GoF]). See Example 6.16 for sample code and Figure 6.13 on page 176 for a sequence diagram.

Example 6.16 Command and Controller Strategy

```
/** This processRequest method is invoked from both
* the servlet doGet and doPost methods **/
protected void processRequest(HttpServletRequest request,
    HttpServletResponse response) throws ServletException,
    java.io.IOException {

  String resultPage;
```

```
    try {
      RequestHelper helper = new RequestHelper(request);

      /** the getCommand() method internally uses a
        * factory to retrieve command objects as follows:
        * Command command = CommandFactory.create(
        * request.getParameter(op));
       **/
      Command command =  helper.getCommand();
      // delegate request to a command object helper
      resultPage = command.execute(request, response);
    } catch (Exception e) {
      LogManager.logMessage("FrontController", e.getMessage());
      resultPage = ApplicationResources.getInstance().getErrorPage(e);
    }
    dispatch(request, response, resultPage);
  }
```

Figure 6.13 on page 176 shows the sequence diagram for this strategy.

Physical Resource Mapping Strategy

In this strategy, all requests are made to specific physical resource names rather than logical names. An example is http://some.server.com/resource1.jsp. In the case of a controller, an example URL might be http://some.server.com/servlet/Controller.

The *Logical Resource Mapping* strategy is typically preferred over this strategy because logical mapping provides much greater flexibility.

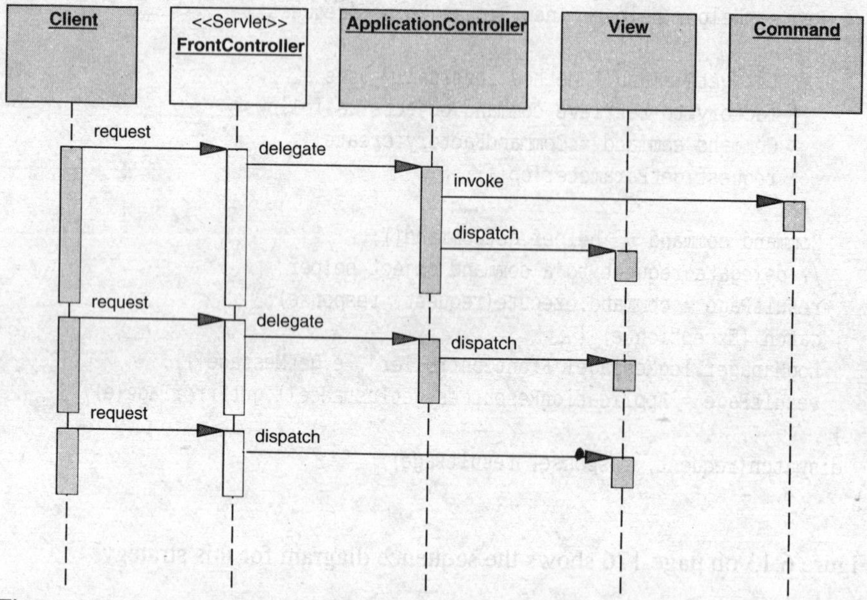

Figure 6.13 Command and Controller Strategy Sequence Diagram

Logical Resource Mapping Strategy

In this strategy, requests are made to logical resource names rather than to specific physical names. You can then declaratively modify the physical resources to which these logical names refer.

For example, the URL http://some.server.com/process could be mapped as follows:

process=resource1.jsp
or
process=resource2.jsp
or
process=servletController

The *Logical Resource Mapping* strategy is much more flexible than the *Physical Resource Mapping* strategy, which requires that you make changes to each resource.

Multiplexed Resource Mapping Strategy

This is actually a substrategy of the *Logical Resource Naming* strategy. This strategy maps not just a single logical name, but an entire set of logical names, to a single physical resource. For example, a wildcard mapping might map all requests that end with .ctrl to a specific handler.

A possible request and mapping are shown in Table 6-1.

Table 6-1 Request and Mapping

Request	*Mapping*
http://some.server.com/action.ctrl	*.ctrl = servletController

This is the strategy JSP engines use to ensure that requests for JSP resources (resources whose names end in .jsp) are processed by a specific handler.

You can add information to a request, providing further details to leverage for this logical mapping. See Table 6-2.

Table 6-2 Request and Mapping With Additional Information.

Request	*Mapping*
http://some.server.com/profile.ctrl?usecase= create	*.ctrl = servletController

A key benefit of using this strategy is that it provides great flexibility when you're designing your request-handling components. When combined with other strategies, such as the *Command and Controller* strategy, you can create a powerful request-handling framework.

Consider a controller that handles all requests ending in .ctrl, as described previously. In addition, assume the left side of this dot-delimited resource name (Profile in the previous example) to be one part of the name of a use case. Now combine this name with the query parameter value (Create in the previous example). This means signaling the request handler to process a use case called **create profile**. The multiplexed resource mapping sends the request to servletController, which is part of the mapping shown in Table 6-2. The controller creates the appropriate command object, as described in the *Command and Controller* strategy.

How does the controller know the command object to which it should delegate? Leveraging the additional information in the request URI, the controller delegates to the command object that handles profile creation. This might be a ProfileCommand object that services requests for Profile creation and modification, or it might be a more specific ProfileCreationCommand object.

Dispatcher in Controller Strategy

When view management and associated dispatcher functionality are minimal, both can be folded into the controller, as shown in Figure 6.14. and Figure 6.15.

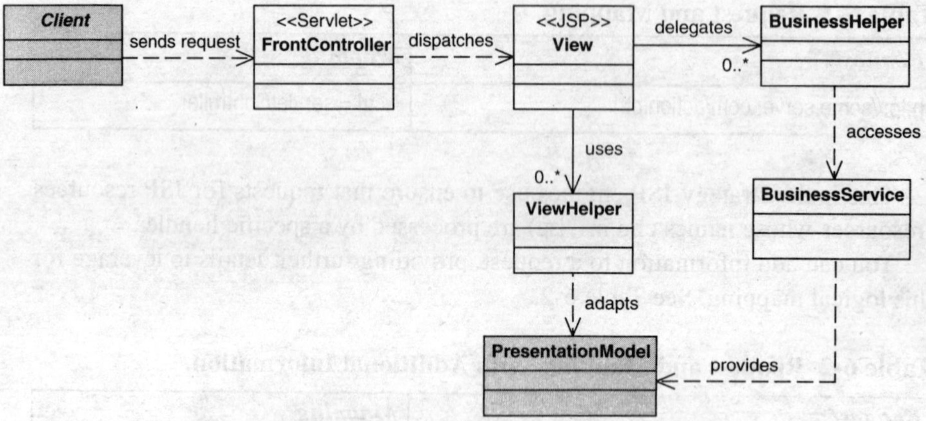

Figure 6.14 Dispatcher in the *Controller* Class Diagram

In effect, view management functionality, usually performed by an *Application Controller* (205), is handled inline within the *Front Controller.* Basic view management is best accomplished in this manner. The *View* uses a *Business Helper* to help perform limited action management and a *ViewHelper* to help generate the *View.* This approach to request handling is referred to as *Dispatcher View* (288).

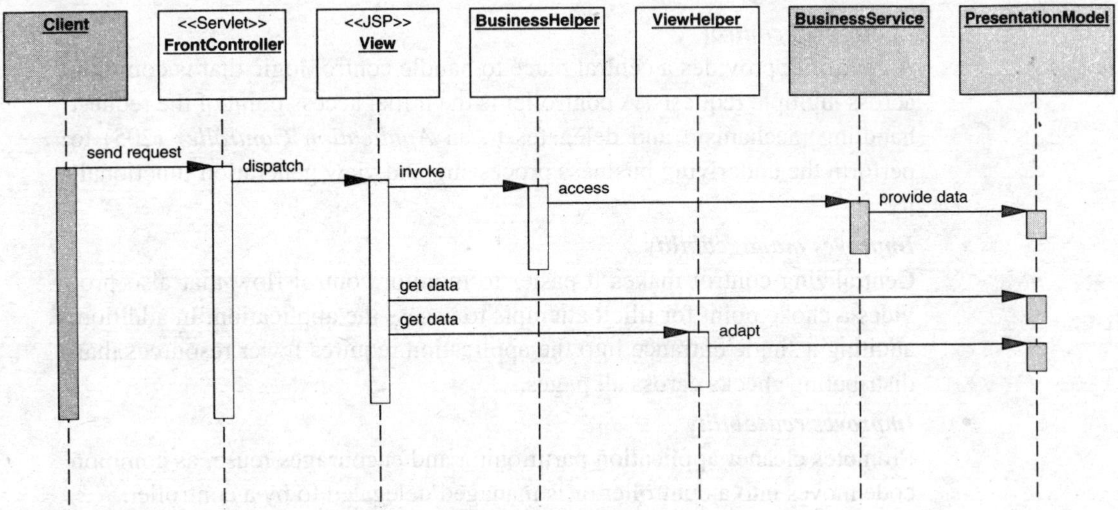

Figure 6.15 Dispatcher in the *Controller* Sequence Diagram

Base Front Strategy

Used in combination with the *Servlet Front* strategy, this strategy implements a controller base class, whose implementation other controllers can extend. The *Base Front* can contain common and default implementations, while each subclass can override these implementations. The drawback of this strategy is that any shared superclass, while promoting reuse and sharing, raises the issue of creating a fragile hierarchy, where changes necessary for one subclass affect all subclasses.

Filter Controller Strategy

Intercepting Filter (144) provides similar support for centralizing request-processing control. This means that aspects of a controller can reasonably be implemented as a filter. While filters primarily focus on request interception and decoration using chaining, *Front Controller* acts as a central access point for related requests and a delegation point to *Application Controller* (205). While control logic, like logging or debugging, can be managed via filters or a *Front Controller*, each component complements the other and can be used cooperatively.

Consequences

- ***Centralizes control***
  A controller provides a central place to handle control logic that is common across multiple requests. A controller is the initial access point of the request handling mechanism and delegates to an *Application Controller* (205) to perform the underlying business processing and view generation functionality.
- ***Improves manageability***
  Centralizing control makes it easier to monitor control flow that also provides a choke point for illicit attempts to access the application. In addition, auditing a single entrance into the application requires fewer resources than distributing checks across all pages.
- ***Improves reusability***
  Promotes cleaner application partitioning and encourages reuse, as common code moves into a controller or is managed/delegated to by a controller.
- ***Improves role separation***
  A controller promotes cleaner separation of team roles, since one role (software developer) can more easily maintain programming logic while another (web production) maintains markup for view generation.

Related Patterns

- ***Intercepting Filter (144)***
  Both *Intercepting Filter* (144) and *Front Controller* describe ways to centralize control of certain aspects of request processing.
- ***Application Controller (205)***
  Application Controller (205) encapsulates the action and view management code to which the controller delegates.
- ***View Helper (240)***
  View Helper (240) describes factoring business and processing logic out of the view and into helper objects and a central point of control and dispatch. Control-flow logic is factored **forward** into the controller and formatting-related code moves **back** into the helpers.
- ***Dispatcher View (288) and Service to Worker (276)***
  Dispatcher View (288) and *Service to Worker* (276) represent different usage patterns. *Service to Worker* (276) is a controller-centric architecture, highlighting the *Front Controller*, while *Dispatcher View* (288) is a view-centric architecture.

Context Object

Problem

You want to avoid using protocol-specific system information outside of its relevant context.

An application typically uses system information, such as request, configuration, and security data, throughout the lifecycle of a request and response. Aspects of this system information are accessed based on their relevance to a certain processing context. When application-specific components and services are exposed to system information that is outside their context, flexibility and reusability of these components are reduced. Using a protocol-specific API outside its relevant context means exposing all the components that use this API to specific interface and parsing details. Each client component is then tightly coupled with that specific protocol.

For example, web components receive protocol-specific HTTP requests. Sharing HTTP requests with other components both within and outside the presentation tier exposes these components to protocol specifics. When that protocol or its details change; for example, if certain elements or field names of a form change; the client code must change. Configuration and security data are two more common examples of system data that is used throughout an application, while remaining loosely coupled with the application-specific services.

Forces

- You have components and services that need access to system information.
- You want to decouple application components and services from the protocol specifics of system information.
- You want to expose only the relevant APIs within a context.

Solution

Use a *Context Object* to encapsulate state in a protocol-independent way to be shared throughout your application.

Encapsulating system data in a *Context Object* allows it to be shared with other parts of the application without coupling the application to a specific protocol.

For example, an HTTP request parameter exists for each field of an HTML form and a *Context Object* can store this data in a protocol-independent manner while facilitating its conversion and validation. Then other parts of the application simply access the information in the *Context Object*, without any knowledge of the HTTP protocol. Any changes in the protocol are handled by the *Context Object*, and no other parts of the application need to change.

The reduced dependency on protocol-specific objects also eases testing, facilitating a more generic test environment with reduced dependence upon a specific container. For example, an HttpServletRequest could be wrapped in a *Context Object* and this same *Context Object* could then easily be used for testing outside of a web container. For testing purposes the *Context Object* could simply hold dummy data, instead of holding the container-specific HttpServletRequest class or its attributes. Using a *Context Object* also helps hide presentation tier-specific details from the business tier by abstracting state so that it can be shared between tiers. The *Context Object* is protocol neutral and the loose coupling that it provides improves the reusability and maintainability of the application.

This aspect of using a *Context Object* raises the question about its relationship to a *Transfer Object* (415). *Transfer Object*s carry state across remote tiers. While a *Context Object* acts as a *Transfer Object* (415) when it is used for this purpose, a *Context Object*'s main goal is to share system information in a protocol-independent way, improving the reusability and maintainability of an application.

A *Context Object* reduces the coupling between unrelated system and application components in this way. On the other hand, a *Transfer Object* (415) main goal is to reduce remote network communication, improving performance. Additionally, *Transfer Objects* often have relationships with other *Transfer Objects*, mirroring the business data they represent, while *Context Object*s represent infrastructure state.

Structure

Figure 6.16 shows the class diagram for *Context Object*.

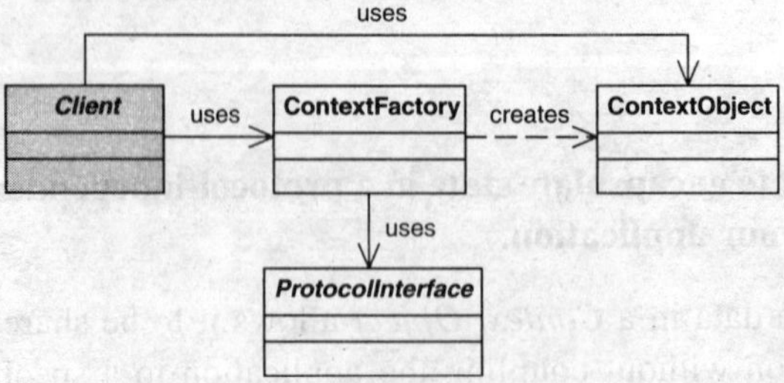

Figure 6.16 Class Diagram for *Context Object*

Participants and Responsibilities

Figure 6.17 shows the sequence diagram for *Context Object*.

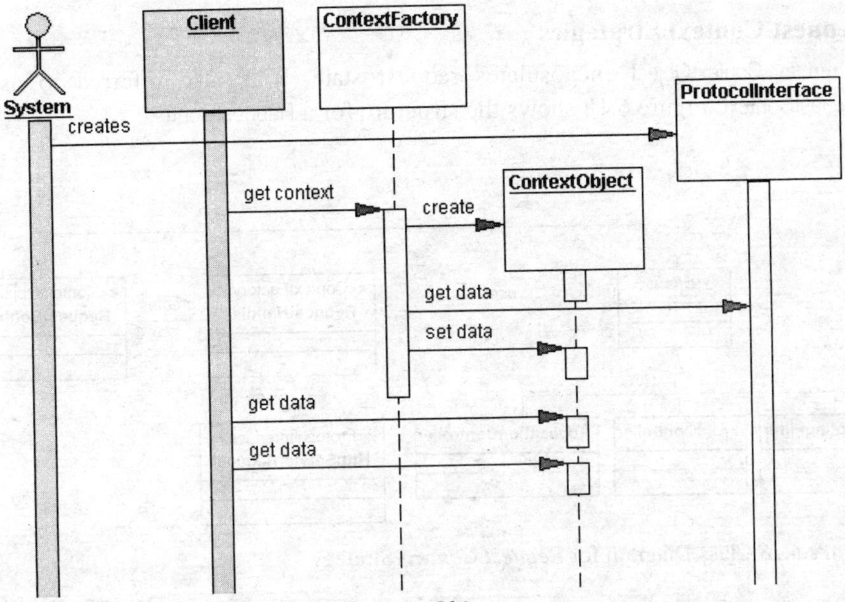

Figure 6.17 Sequence Diagram for *Context Object*

A Client uses a ContextFactory to create a ContextObject using a ProtocolInterface. The ContextObject shields the surrounding application components and services from the underlying details of the ProtocolInterface.

Client

Creates an object with ProtocolInterface.

ProtocolInterface

An object that exposes protocol or tier-specific details.

ContextFactory

A ContextFactory creates a protocol- and tier-independent ContextObject.

ContextObject

ContextObject is a generic object used to share domain-neutral state throughout an application.

Strategies

There are numerous strategies to implement a Context Object, so these strategies are grouped based on the type of *Context Object* being created.

Request Context Strategies

When a ContextObject encapsulates request state, it is also referred to as a RequestContext. Figure 6.18 shows the structure for a RequestContext:

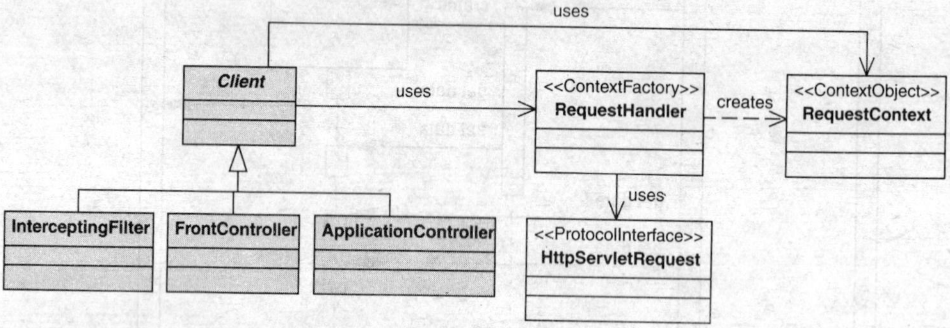

Figure 6.18 Class Diagram for *Request Context* Strategy

An HttpServletRequest is a protocol-specific Request object and should have limited exposure within an application. The ContextFactory creates a ContextObject and transfers state into it from the HttpServletRequest. The Client role is typically filled by an *Intercepting Filter* (144), *Front Controller* (166), or *Application Controller* (205).

The data in the RequestContext typically goes through an initial form-level validation at this point; for example, a check for empty fields or a check for a credit card number having the correct number of digits. As business processing is performed, the ContextObject state will typically go through a second round of validation that is **business-related**, such as whether a value is within an appropriate range.

There are several approaches to implementing a RequestContext, as follows.

Request Context Map Strategy

This is the most basic of the adapter strategies. The relevant request state is transferred into a standard Map implementation, which is passed around. The benefit to this approach is its simplicity.

There are tradeoffs for this simplicity, though. Using a standard Map-based implementation provides a loosely typed ContextObject. Doing so means foregoing the leverage you would have from writing your own custom class, including custom helper methods and stronger typing.

Example 6.17 shows the request context map strategy.

Example 6.17 Request Context Map Strategy

```
public class FrontController extends HttpServlet {
. . .
  private void processRequest(HttpServletRequest request,
      HttpServletResponse response) throws ServletException,
          java.io.IOException {

    // create RequestContext object using Map Strategy
    Map requestContextMap = new HashMap(request.getParameterMap());
    Dispatcher dispatcher = new Dispatcher(request, response);
    requestContextMap.put("dispatcher", dispatcher);

    // Create ApplicationController instance
    ApplicationController applicationController =
        new ApplicationControllerImpl();

    // Request processing
    ResponseContext responseContext =
        applicationController.handleRequest(requestContextMap);

    // Response processing
    applicationController.handleResponse(requestContextMap,
        responseContext);
  }
  . . .
}
```

Request Context POJO Strategy

Another approach is to use a POJO to encapsulate the request. Depending on your application, this approach will introduce certain benefits and some drawbacks, as well. Using a POJO means that you can introduce stronger typing and can add helper methods to create more complex properties, based on existing ones. In other words, all the properties that the bean exposes need not actually exist as attributes of the bean.

Example 6.18 through Example 6.21 show the code for this strategy.

Example 6.18 Front Controller

```
public class FrontController extends HttpServlet {
  private ApplicationController applicationController;

  public void init(ServletConfig servletConfig) throws
      ServletException{

    super.init(servletConfig);

    // Initialize Request Processing(Stateless) Components
    applicationController = new ApplicationControllerImpl();
    applicationController.initialize();
  }

  // called from doGet and doPost
  protected void process(HttpServletRequest request,
      HttpServletResponse response) throws java.io.IOException {

    // Create RequestContext based on request type
    RequestContextFactory requestContextFactory =
        RequestContextFactory.getInstance();
    RequestContext requestContext =
        requestContextFactory.createRequestContext(request);

    // Request Processing
    ResponseContext responseContext =
        applicationController.handleRequest(requestContext);

    // View Management - Navigate and Dispatch to appropriate view
    Dispatcher dispatcher = new Dispatcher(request, response);
    responseContext.setDispatcher(dispatcher);
    applicationController.handleResponse(requestContext,
        responseContext);
  }
  . . .
}
```

Example 6.19 ApplicationControllerImpl

```
public class ApplicationControllerImpl implements
    ApplicationController {

  public void initialize() {
```

```
    commandMapper = CommandMapper.getInstance();
  }

  public ResponseContext handleRequest(RequestContext requestContext) {
    ResponseContext responseContext = null;
    try {
      // validate request parameters
      requestContext.validate();

      // Translate command name into Command abstraction
      String commandName = requestContext.getCommandName();
      Command command = commandMapper.getCommand(commandName);

      // Invoke Command
      responseContext = command.execute(requestContext);

      // Identify View Name
      CommandMap  mapEntry = commandMapper.getCommandMap(commandName);
      String viewName = mapEntry.getViewName();
      responseContext.setLogicalViewName(viewName);
    } catch (ValidatorException e1) {
      // Handle Exception
    }
    return responseContext;
  }
. . .
```

Example 6.20 RequestContextFactory

```
// POJO ContextObject Factory
public class RequestContextFactory {
  public RequestContext createRequestContext(ServletRequest request) {

    RequestContext requestContext = null;
    try {
      // Identify command string from request object
      String commandId = getCommandId(request);
      // Identify POJO RequestContext Class for the given Command,
      // using CommandMap
      CommandMapper commandMapper = CommandMapper.getInstance();
      CommandMap  mapEntry = commandMapper.getCommandMap(commandId);
      Class requestContextClass = mapEntry.getContextObjectClass();

```

```
      // Instantiate POJO
      requestContext  = (RequestContext)
          requestContextClass.newInstance();

      // Set Protcol-specific Request object
      requestContext.initialize(request);
    } catch(java.lang.InstantiationException e) {
      // Handle Exception
    } catch(java.lang.IllegalAccessException e) { }
    return requestContext;
  }

  private String getCommandId(ServletRequest request) {
    String commandId = null;
    if ( request instanceof HttpServletRequest) {
      String pathInfo = ((HttpServletRequest)request).getPathInfo();
      commandId =  pathInfo.substring(1);   // skip the leading '/'
    }
    return commandId;
  }
}
```

Example 6.21 ProjectRegistrationRequestContext

```
// Specialized POJO Request Context - instances of these get created by
// the RequestContextFactory class.
public class ProjectRegistrationRequestContext extends
    HttpRequestContext {

  public ProjectRegistrationRequestContext(HttpServletRequest request){
    super(request);
    initialize(request);
  }

  public ProjectRegistrationRequestContext() { }

  public void initialize(ServletRequest request) {
    setRequest(request);
    setProjectName(request.getParameter("projectName"));
    setProjectDescription(request.getParameter("projectdescription"));
    setProjectManager(request.getParameter("projectmanager"));
  }

```

```
  public String getProjectDescription() {
    return projectDescription;
  }

  public void setProjectDescription(String projectDescription) {
    this.projectDescription = projectDescription;
  }

  public String getProjectManager() {
    return projectManager;
  }

  public void setProjectManager(String projectManager) {
    this.projectManager = projectManager;
  }

  public String getProjectName() {
    return projectName;
  }

  public void setProjectName(String projectName) {
    this.projectName = projectName;
  }

  public boolean validate() {
    // Validation Rules
    return true;
  }
  . . .
}
```

A major drawback of this approach is the fact that you must define accessor methods for each property, if you have an application with many properties, you must create one or more accessor methods for each of these properties. This is a potentially daunting task from a development and maintenance standpoint.

A hybrid approach to this strategy offers the benefits of the POJO strategy and the ease of development and maintenance that comes with a Map-based approach. This hybrid approach is to use a code generation facility to generate your ContextObjects. One common industry example of the POJO strategy is the Struts [Struts] framework ActionForm class.

An example of the hybrid approach to the strategy is the Struts framework DynaActionForm. Another example of this hybrid approach is using a code generation facility, such as xDoclet [xDoclet].

Example 6.22 shows an example of each approach.

Example 6.22 POJO Request Context Creation Using DynaActionForm

```
<struts-config>
  <form-beans>
    <form-bean  name="projectRegistrationForm"
        type="org.apache.struts.action.DynaActionForm">
      <form-property name="projectName" type="java.lang.String"/>
      <form-property name="projectDescription"
          type="java.lang.String"/>
      <form-property name="idCustomer" type="java.lang.String"/>
      <form-property name="projectManager" type="java.lang.String"/>
      <form-property name="startDate" type="java.util.Date"/>
      <form-property name="endDate" type="java.util.Date"/>
      <form-property name="emailAlias" type="java.lang.String"/>
    </form-bean>
  ...
</struts-config>
```

Example 6.23 Context Object POJO Generation Using XDoclet

```
/**
  * It is an example of how to use the XDoclet tags to generate POJO
  * Context Object  from
  * Entity Class definition.
  *
  * @ejb.finder
  *    role-name="Manager"
  *    signature="Collection findAll()'
  *    transaction-type="NotSupported"
  *
  * @ejb.transaction
  *    type="Required"
  *
  * @ejb.pk
  *    generate="true"
  *
  * @ejb.data-object
  *    name="{0}TO"
  *    equals="true"
```

```
   *
   * @ejb.persistence
   *     table-name="employee"
   *
   * @struts.form
   *     name="Context"
   *     include-all="true"
   *
   */
// Entity Bean class
public abstract class EmployeeBean  implements EntityBean {
  private EntityContext ctx;
  . . .
}
```

Running the previous EmployeeBeanEntity class using xdoclet generates the following:

Example 6.24 Xdoclet Output

```
/**
 * Generated by XDoclet/ejbdoclet/strutsform.
 * This class can be further processed with
 * XDoclet/webdoclet/strutsconfigxml.
 *
 * @struts.form name="corej2eepatterns.ejb.Employee.Context"
 */
public class EmployeeContextForm extends
    org.apache.struts.action.ActionForm implements java.io.Serializable{

  protected java.lang.String id;
  protected java.lang.String lastName;
  protected java.lang.String firstName;
  protected java.lang.String phone;
  protected java.lang.String fax;
  protected java.util.Date creationDate;

  /** Default empty constructor. */
  public EmployeeContextForm() { }

  . . .
}
```

Request Context Validation Strategy

Validations in the presentation tier are often performed in coordination with a RequestContext since a RequestContext encapsulates incoming request state. Once the server accepts a request, the request state is usually validated before it is shared with other parts of the application. The RequestContext stores the state in case it must be returned to the client "as-is" with an appropriate error message upon validation.

Two levels of validation are typical as part of a web application.

- The first type is **form-level validation**, which validates that input has been entered in an acceptable format, such as a credit card number having the correct number of digits.
- The second type is **business validation**, including credit card authorization.

Each of these validations has some business aspect to it, and in fact there is some uncertainty about whether certain validations are form level or business level. Consider, for example, a credit card expiration date. While dealing with this value is clearly part of business-level validation, you might also do a preliminary form-level check of the expiration date to make sure that it has not already passed, before passing this information along to the business tier. Another example is a preliminary character-length check of a username and password, and for their usage of the appropriate combination of alpha and/or numeric characters, with a follow-on validation authenticating the username/password combination.

Separating these validation rules from the programming logic improves the reusability of the validation mechanism as a whole, since the rules can be updated independent of the code. Moreover, given the potential interdependence of multiple tiers upon the validation rules, separating the rules from tier-specific code reduces the coupling between tiers.

The aforementioned aspects of validation design are closely aligned with the motivations and design of a *Context Object*, which explains why the two implementations are often interrelated to a degree. The following example implementation of this strategy uses the Jakarta Commons Validator [Jakarta-Valid].

Example 6.25 Validation support in Request Context Object

```
// Base RequestContext class provides validation scaffolding
public class RequestContext {
  public RequestContext (ServletRequest request) {
    setRequest(request);
  }

```

```
  public ValidatorResults validate() throws ValidatorException {
    try {
      InputStream inputStream =
          Thread.currentThread().getContextClassLoader().
          getResourceAsStream(getValidationResourceName());
      // Create an instance of ValidatorResources to initialize from an
      // xml file
      ValidatorResources resources = new ValidatorResources();
      ValidatorResourcesInitializer.initialize(resources, inputStream);

      // Construct validator based onloaded resources and form name
      Validator validator = new Validator(resources,
          getValidationFormName());

      // add the name bean to the validator as a resource
      // for the validations to be performed on.
      validator.addResource(Validator.BEAN_KEY, this);

      // Validation
      ValidatorResults validatorResultsAggregate = null;
      validatorResultsAggregate = validator.validate();

      // Perform generic validation error handling, if any
      return validatorResultsAggregate;
    } catch (IOException e) {
      // Handle Exception
    }
    return null;
  }

  . . .

  public void setRequest(ServletRequest request) {
    this.request = request;
  }

  private ServletRequest request;
}
```

Example 6.26 Specialized Request Context Provide Specialized Context Validations

```
public class ProjectRegistrationRequestContext extends RequestContext {

  public ProjectRegistrationRequestContext(HttpServletRequest request) {
    super(request);
    initialize(request);
  }
  public ProjectRegistrationRequestContext() { }

  public void initialize(ServletRequest request) {
    setRequest(request);
    setProjectName(request.getParameter("projectName"));
    setProjectDescription(request.getParameter("projectdescription"));
    setIdCustomer(request.getParameter("customerid"));
    setProjectManager(request.getParameter("projectmanager"));
    setStartDate(request.getParameter("startdate"));
    setStartDate(request.getParameter("enddate"));
    setEmailAlias(request.getParameter("emailalias"));
  }

  . . .

  // Specialized Context Validation
  public ValidatorResults validate() {
    ValidatorResults validatorResultsAggregate = null;
    try {
      validatorResultsAggregate = super.validate();
      ValidatorResult validatorResult = validatorResultsAggregate.
          getValidatorResult("projectName");
      if ( validatorResult.isValid("required") == false ) {
        // handle Missing Project Name
      }

      validatorResult = validatorResultsAggregate.
          getValidatorResult("projectDescription");
      if ( validatorResult.isValid("required") == false ) {
        // handle missing Project Description
      }

      validatorResult = validatorResultsAggregate.
          getValidatorResult("emailAlias");
```

```
        if ( validatorResult.isValid("email") == false ) {
          // handle Invalid email id error
        }
      } catch (ValidatorException e) {
        // Handle Exception
      }
      return validatorResults;
    }

    public String getValidationFormName() {
      return "ProjectRegistrationForm";
    }
}
```

Example 6.27 Form-validators.xml

```
Form-validators.xml

<form-validation>
  <global>
    <validator name="required" classname=
        "corepatterns.ContextObject.adapterpojo.RequestValidator"
         method="validateRequired" methodParams=
         "java.lang.Object,org.apache.commons.validator.Field"/>

    <validator name="email" classname=
        "corepatterns.ContextObject.adapterpojo.RequestValidator"
         method="validateEmail" methodParams=
         "java.lang.Object,org.apache.commons.validator.Field"/>

  </global>
  <formset>
    <form name="ProjectRegistrationForm">
      <field property="projectName" depends="required">
        <arg0 key="ProjectRegistrationForm.projectname.displayname"/>
      </field>
      <field property="projectDescription" depends="required">
        <arg0 key=
            "ProjectRegistrationForm.projectdescription.displayname"/>
      </field>
      <field property="emailAlias" depends ="required">
        <arg0 key="ProjectRegistrationForm.emailalias.displayname"/>
      </field>
```

```
    </form>
  </formset>
</form-validation>
```

Configuration Context Strategies

When a ContextObject encapsulates configuration state, it is also referred to as a ConfigurationContext.

JSTL Configuration Strategy

It is common for applications to group configuration-specific data in order to share it across several contexts. For example, the JSP Standard Tag Library Specification (JSTL) [JSTL], version 1.0, which specifies standard tags for JSP, includes a configuration class that provides just such functionality. The class allows components in various contexts, including different JSP scopes, to share configuration data. The class is javax.servlet.jsp.jstl.core.Config and provides methods for getting and setting configuration data, such as the relevant locale for a particular user. Here is an example of how the Config class facilitates data sharing throughout the web tier.

Example 6.28 JSTL Configuration Strategy

```
<!--
  The JSTL Config encapsulates data for use across several contexts.
-->
<corej2eepatterns:Announcements>

  <b>Announcements:</b><br>

  <!-- Display Request-specific Announcements, if any  -->
  <c_rt:out value='<%= Config.get(request,
      Constants.ANNOUNCEMENTS)%>'/> <br>

  <!-- Display User-specific Announements, if any -->
  <c_rt:out value='<%= Config.get(session,
      Constants.ANNOUNCEMENTS)%>'/><br>

  <!-- Display Global Announements, if any -->
  <c_rt:out value='<%=
      Config.get(application,Constants.ANNOUNCEMENTS)%>'/> <br>

</corej2eepatterns:Announcements>
```

Example 6.29 Tag Handler Using JSTL Config

```
public class AnnouncementsTag extends TagSupport implements Tag {
  public int doStartTag() throws JspException {

    String announcements = (String)Config.find(pageContext,
        Constants.DISPLAY_ANNOUNCEMENT);
    if ( "true".equalsIgnoreCase(announcements)) {
      . . .

      return EVAL_BODY_INCLUDE;
    }
    return SKIP_BODY;
  }
}
```

Security Context Strategy

When a ContextObject encapsulates security state, it is also referred to as a SecurityContext. Figure 6.19 shows the use of a SecurityContext for authentication.

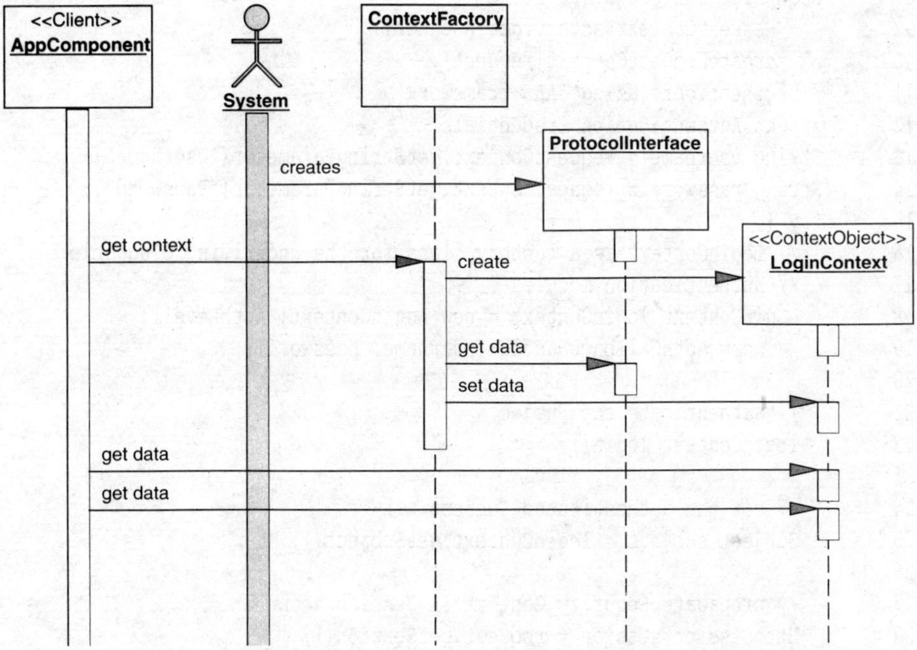

Figure 6.19 Using SecurityContext for Authentication

The Java Authentication and Authorization Service (JAAS) [JAAS] is part of Java 2 Platform, Standard Edition version 1.4 [J2SE1.4]. JAAS uses a ContextObject called LoginContext to provide authentication services. A JAAS LoginContext shields its clients from the implementation details of the underlying authentication mechanism and provides a modular, pluggable, callback mechanism for interaction with the user.

A LoginContext uses a configuration file that includes details about the linkage to the mechanism that will be used to authenticate the user. The ContextObject hides these implementation details from its clients.

Example 6.30 Security Context Propagation Using LoginContext

```
public class FrontController extends HttpServlet {

  . . .
  protected void process(HttpServletRequest request,
      HttpServletResponse response) throws java.io.IOException {

    // create Context Object from request
    RequestContext requestContext =
        RequestContextFactory.getInstance().
        createRequestContext(request);
    // Authenticate using JAAS framework
    // Get Authentication Credentials
    String username = requestContext.getStringParameter("UserName");
    String password = requestContext.getStringParameter("Password");
    try {
      // LoginContext is a factory class for the underlying pluggable
      // authentication modules
      LoginContext loginContext = new LoginContext("AuthLevel1",
          new AuthCallbackHandler(username, password));

      // authenticate the Subject
      loginContext.login();

      // get the authenticated Subject
      Subject subject = loginContext.getSubject();

      // propagate Security Context in session scope
      HttpSession session = request.getSession();
      session.setAttribute("SecurityContext", subject);
    } catch (LoginException le) {
      // handle exception
```

```
        }
        . . .
    }
}
```

General Context Object Strategies

Context Object Factory Strategy

A *Context Object Factory* is used to obtain varying types of *Context Objects*, each with a similar but slightly different use. Using a factory for obtaining *Context Objects* allows the factory to control object creation and population, as well as pooling, if necessary.

Example 6.31 Context Object Factory

```
public class FrontController extends HttpServlet {

  protected void processRequest(HttpServletRequest request,
      HttpServletResponse response)
      throws ServletException, java.io.IOException {
    . . .
    // Identify incoming Request Type
    String requestType = getRequestType(request);

    // Instantialte Specialized RequestContext based on incoming
    // request type
    RequestContextFactory requestContextFactory =
        RequestContextFactory.getInstance();

    RequestContext requestContext =
        requestContextFactory.getRequestContext(requestType,  request);
    . . .
  }
}
```

Example 6.32 RequestContextFactory

```
public class RequestContextFactory {
  static RequestContextFactory factory = new RequestContextFactory();

  static public RequestContextFactory getInstance() {
    return factory;
  }
```

```

    public RequestContext getRequestContext(String requestType,
        ServletRequest request) {

      RequestContext requestContext;
      if (Constants.SOAP_PROTOCOL.equalsIgnoreCase(requestType) == true) {
        requestContext = new SOAPRequestContextImpl(
            (HttpServletRequest) request);
      } else {
        requestContext = new HttpRequestContext(
            (HttpServletRequest) request);
      }
      return requestContext;
    }
}
```

Context Object Auto-Population Strategy

The underlying mechanics of implementing this pattern involve moving state from one object to another. You can use reflection to automate this process in the case where you have relatively simple mappings, such as moving similarly named properties from one object to another. Instead of manually moving each piece of state, use a utility class to automatically move bean properties around. For example, you can automatically transfer the parameters of an HttpRequest into a JavaBean using a utility that matches the parameter names to bean properties and copies the parameter values accordingly. In fact, the built-in "wildcarding" facility of the JSP container provides this functionality. This wildcard bean auto-population facility is limited to use within a JSP invocation, so it is not as useful as a decoupled utility class, which can be used directly from a *Front Controller* (166) or other control code.

The open source community has several utilities that facilitate implementing this strategy, most notably the Jakarta Commons subproject BeanUtils package, which provides a variety of bean introspection utilities (See http://jakarta.apache.org/commons/beanutils/api/index.html). An example is shown in Example 6.33.

Example 6.33 Auto-populating ContextObject: RequestContextFactory

```
// Context Object Factory
public class RequestContextFactory {

  . . .

```

```
  public RequestContext createRequestContext(Class contextClass,
      ServletRequest request) {
    RequestContext requestContext = null;
    try  {
      // Instantiate ContextObject Class
      requestContext = (RequestContext) contextClass.newInstance();

      // Using Introspection, populate the values of ContextObject from
      // request instance
      AutoPopulateRequestContext.populateBean(requestContext, request);
    } catch(java.lang.InstantiationException e) {
      // Handle Exception
    } catch(java.lang.IllegalAccessException e) {
      // Handle Exception
    }
    return requestContext;
  }
}
```

Example 6.34 Auto-populating ContextObject: AutoPopulateRequestContext

```
// Context Object helper
public class AutoPopulateRequestContext {

  public static void populateBean(Object bean, ServletRequest request) {

    Enumeration enum = request.getParameterNames();

    while ( enum.hasMoreElements()) {
      String parameterName = (String)enum.nextElement();
      if ( PropertyUtils.isWriteable(bean, parameterName)) {

        String values[] = request.getParameterValues(parameterName);
        try {
          if ( values.length == 1 ) {
            PropertyUtils.setSimpleProperty(
            bean, parameterName, values[0]);
          } else {
            for ( int iValue=0; iValue < values.length; iValue++)
              PropertyUtils.setIndexedProperty(
              bean, parameterName, iValue, values[iValue]);
          }
        } catch (IllegalAccessException e) {
```

```
          // handle exception
        } catch (InvocationTargetException e) {
          // handle exception
        } catch (NoSuchMethodException e) {
          // handle exception
        }
      }
    }
  }
}
```

Example 6.35 Auto-populating ContextObject: ProjectRegistrationRequestContext

```
// Specialized Context Object
public class ProjectRegistrationRequestContext extends RequestContext {
  public String getProjectDescription() {
    return projectDescription;
  }

  public void setProjectDescription(String projectDescription) {
    this.projectDescription = projectDescription;
  }

  public String getProjectManager() {
    return projectManager;
  }

  public void setProjectManager(String projectManager) {
    this.projectManager = projectManager;
  }

  public String getProjectName() {
    return projectName;
  }

  public void setProjectName(String projectName) {
    this.projectName = projectName;
  }

  public boolean validate() {
    return true;
  }
```

```

    private String projectName;
    private String projectDescription;
    private String projectManager;
}
```

Consequences

- ***Improves reusability and maintainability***
  Application components and subsystems are more generic and can be reused for various types of clients, since the application interfaces are not polluted with protocol-specific data types.
- ***Improves testability***
  Using *Context Objects* helps remove dependencies on protocol-specific code that might tie a runtime environment to a container, such as a web server or an application server. Testing is easier when such dependencies are limited or removed, since automated testing tools, such as JUnit [Junit] can work directly with *Context Objects*.
- ***Reduces constraints on evolution of interfaces***
  Interfaces that accept a *Context Object*, instead of the numerous objects that the *Context Object* encapsulates, are less tied to these specific details that might constrain later changes. This is important when developing frameworks, but is also valuable in general.
- ***Reduces performance***
  There is a modest performance hit, because state is transferred from one object to another. This reduction in performance is usually far outweighed by the benefits of improved reusability and maintainability of the application subcomponents.

Related Patterns

- ***Intercepting Filter (144)***
  An *Intercepting Filter* (144) can use a ContextFactory to create a *Context Object* during web request handling.
- ***Front Controller (166)***
  A *Front Controller* (166) can use a ContextFactory to create a *Context Object* during web request handling.

- ***Application Controller (205)***

  An *Application Controller* (205) can use a ContextFactory to create a *Context Object* during web request handling.

- ***Transfer Object (415)***

  A *Transfer Object* (415) is used specifically to transfer state across remote tiers to reduce network communication, while a *Context Object* is used to hide implementation details, improving reuse and maintainability.

Application Controller

Problem

You want to centralize and modularize action and view management.

In the presentation tier, there are typically two decisions to be made upon the arrival of each request:

- First, the incoming request must be resolved to an action that services the request. This is called **action management**.
- Second, the appropriate view is located and dispatched. This is called **view management**.

You can encapsulate action management and view management in different parts of the application. Embedding this behavior within a *Front Controller* (166) centralizes the functionality, but as the application grows and the code becomes more complex, it's a good idea to move this behavior into a separate set of classes, improving the code's modularity, reusability, and extensibility.

Forces

- You want to reuse action and view-management code.
- You want to improve request-handling extensibility, such as adding use case functionality to an application incrementally.
- You want to improve code modularity and maintainability, making it easier to extend the application and easier to test discrete parts of your request-handling code independent of a web container.

Solution

Use an *Application Controller* to centralize retrieval and invocation of request-processing components, such as commands and views.

In the presentation tier, you map incoming request parameters to specific request-processing classes, and to view components that handle each request. **Action management** refers to locating and invoking actions to handle specific requests, while **view management** refers to navigating and dispatching to the appropriate view or view-generation mechanism. While a *Front Controller* (166) acts as a centralized access point and controller for incoming requests, the mechanism for identifying and invoking commands and for identifying and dispatching to views can be broken out into its own set of components.

Separating this code from the *Front Controller* (166) provides several benefits. First, it separates this basic request management behavior from the protocol-specific code of the *Front Controller* (166). This improves the modularity of the system, while enhancing its reusability. Certain *Application Controller* components can be reused to handle requests from numerous channels, such as from a web application or a web service.

Note: Key aspects of request handling, such as validation, error handling, authentication, and access control can easily be plugged into a request-handling mechanism that is centralized and modularized in this way.

Additionally, separating these aspects of request management from a servlet-based *Front Controller* (166) makes it easier to test outside of a web container, simplifying testing. As you consider the action management and view management-related implementation strategies on the following pages, remember that view management activities are often nested within command management activities (See the design note "Nested Command and View Management" on page 215). Each strategy is documented individually, though, since they are logically separate aspects of *Application Controller.*

This pattern is used in combination with other patterns in the catalog. A *Context* Object (181) facilitates communication between a *Front Controller* (166) and the *Application Controller*, shielding it from some of the protocol-specific parts of the application, such as an HttpServletRequest. A *Context Object* (181) is often created using a *Context Object Factory* (199) and a single class can serve the dual role of *Application Controller* and *Context Object Factory.* The *Application Controller* often coordinates with a *Context Object* (181) in order to perform validation.

You might use this pattern if your application requires that users traverse screens in a specific order. This approach is covered in more detail in the *Navigation and Flow Control Strategy* section.

Finally, this pattern is realized as part of the Struts Framework [Struts], which uses declarative mappings to facilitate both action and view management. For more on how Struts uses this pattern, see the Design Note "Nested Command and View Management" on page 215.

Structure

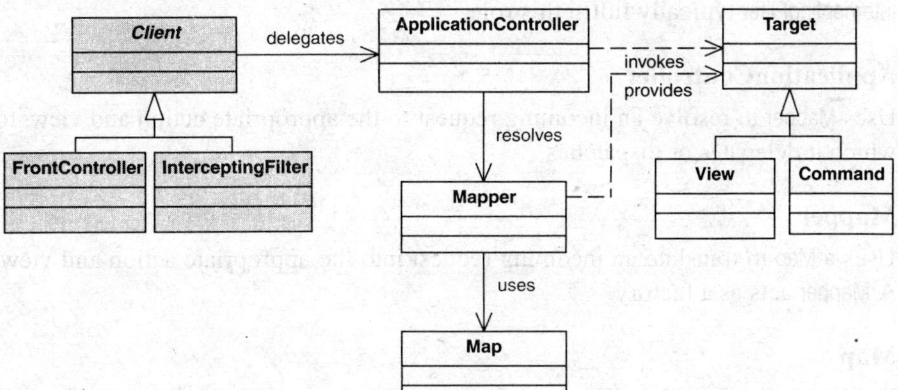

Figure 6.20 Class Diagram for *Application Controller*

Participants and Responsibilities

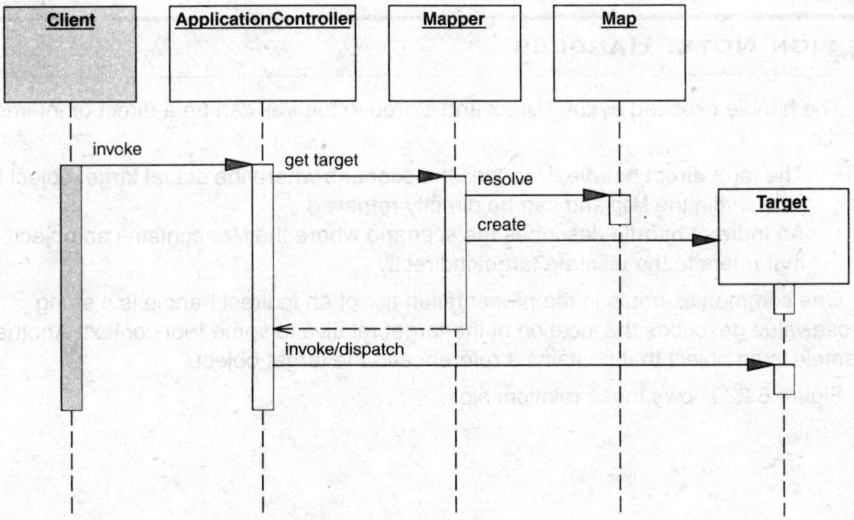

Figure 6.21 Sequence Diagram for *Application Controller*

Client

Invokes the Application Controller. In the presentation tier, a FrontController or an InterceptingFilter typically fulfill this role.

ApplicationController

Uses Mapper to resolve an incoming request to the appropriate action and view, to which it delegates or dispatches.

Mapper

Uses a Map to translate an incoming request into the appropriate action and view. A Mapper acts as a factory.

Map

Holds references to handles that represent target resources. Maps might be realized as a class or a registry. (See the Design Note "Handles".)

Target

A resource that helps fulfill a particular request, including commands, views, and style sheets.

DESIGN NOTE: HANDLES

The handle exposed by the Mapper and stored in the Map can be a direct or indirect handle.

- The term **direct handle** describes the scenario where the actual target object is held within the Map and can be directly retrieved.
- An **indirect handle** describes the scenario where the Map contains an object that refers to the ultimate target indirectly.

One common example in the presentation tier of an indirect handle is a string whose value describes the location of the target relative to some root context. Another example is an object that contains a reference to the target object.

Figure 6.22 shows these relationships.

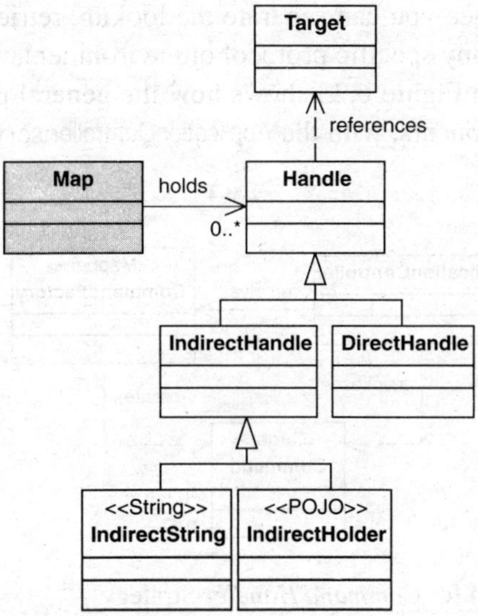

Figure 6.22 Handle Class Diagram

Strategies

Command Handler Strategy

An *Application Controller* that obtains and invokes *Command Objects* [GoF] is also referred to as a *Command Handler.* A *Command Handler* manages the life-cycle of these command objects, which support an application's use cases and function within the scope of a single request rather than across multiple requests. Retrieved via a *Command Factory Method* [GoF], commands encapsulate use case-specific processing logic and are only loosely coupled with the object that invokes them. By encapsulating various use case-related actions as command objects that share a common interface, you make your application more extensible and modular and simplify adding new behavior.

Since the commands are invoked via a common interface, such as execute(), you can build a simple, reusable request-handling framework. You can aggregate commands to create *Composite* [GoF] commands, and the *Application Controller* can provide a mechanism for compensating activities, such as "undoing" a particular request.

You can also reuse the *Application Controller* and its underlying commands in multiple contexts, since you can separate the lookup, retrieval, and invocation of the commands from any specific protocol or environment.

The class diagram in Figure 6.23 shows how the general pattern roles map to command-related components, with the ApplicationController serving as a *Command Handler.*

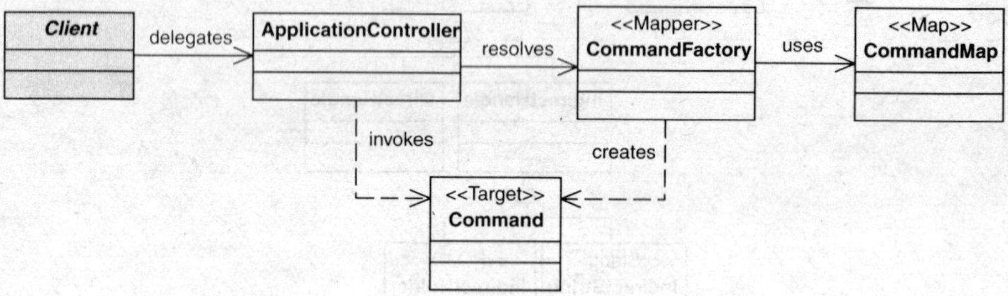

Figure 6.23 Class Diagram for *Command Handler* Strategy

Alternatively, the command can be handed to a *Command Processor* [POSA] for execution, as shown in Figure 6.24. A *Command Processor* manages command objects, providing for invocation scheduling, logging, and caching for subsequent undo. The ApplicationController itself can also handle many of the responsibilities of the CommandProcessor, so a physically separate class is not necessary.

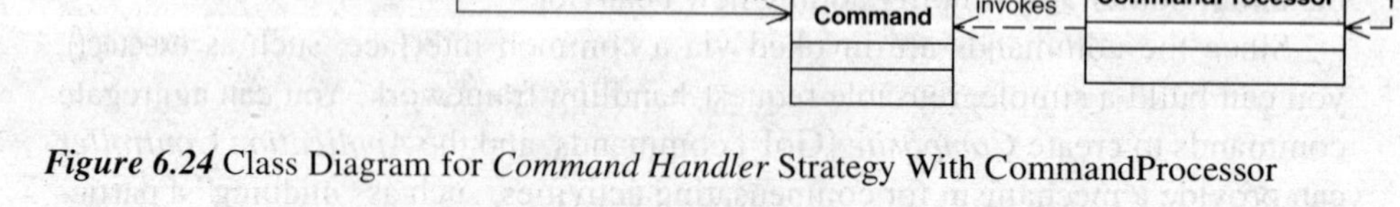

Figure 6.24 Class Diagram for *Command Handler* Strategy With CommandProcessor

In the presentation tier, delegating to a *Command Handler* from a *Front Controller* (166) is a common approach and this canonical usage is referred to in the *Front Controller* (166) pattern as *Command and Controller* strategy (174). This combination is shown in the sequence diagram in Figure 6.25 where the Client role is a *Front Controller* (166).

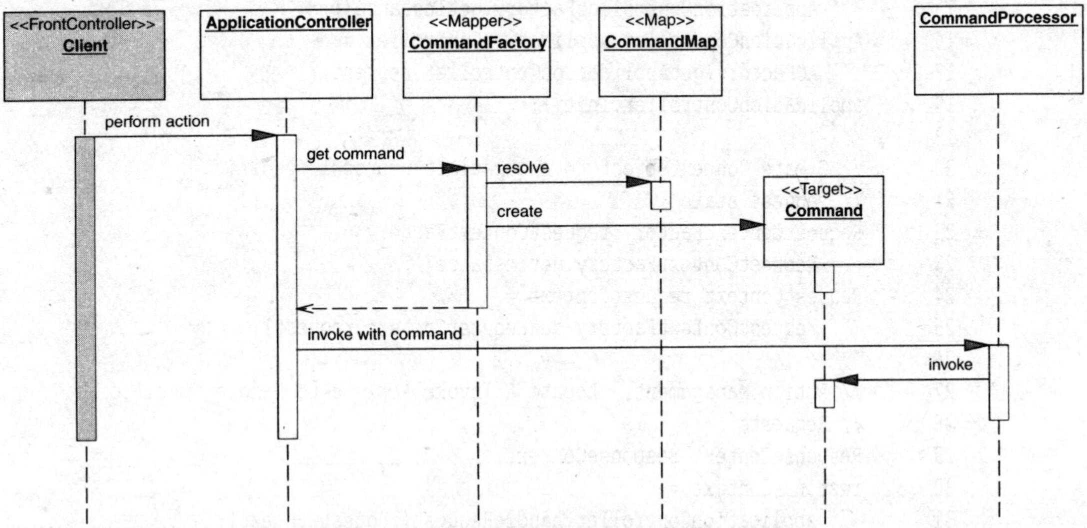

Figure 6.25 Sequence Diagram for *Command Handler* Strategy

In lieu of using commands, the ApplicationController could directly invoke strongly typed methods of a target object. In this case, the ApplicationController would directly invoke a *Business Delegate* (302); in the case of a remote business tier or a *Business Object* (374), it would invoke an *Application Service* (357); or a POJO service façade in the case of a non-remote business tier.

Example 6.36 demonstrates implementing the *Command Handler* strategy with FrontController.

Example 6.36 Implementing Command Handler strategy: FrontController

```
public class FrontController extends HttpServlet {
  . . .

  /** Processes requests for both HTTP <code>GET</code> and
    * <code>POST</code> methods.
    * @param request servlet request
    * @param response servlet response
    */
  protected void processRequest(HttpServletRequest request,
      HttpServletResponse response)
          throws ServletException, java.io.IOException {
```

```

    // Create ApplicationController for handling incoming request
    ApplicationControllerFactory ACFactory =
        ApplicationControllerFactory.getInstance();
    ApplicationController applicationController =
        ACFactory.getApplicationController(request);
    applicationController.init();

    // Create ContextObject to encapsulate protocol-specific
    // request state
    RequestContextFactory requestContextFactory =
        RequestContextFactory.getInstance();
    RequestContext requestContext =
        requestContextFactory.getRequestContext(request);

    // Action Management - Locate & Invoke Actions to handle specific
    // Requests
    ResponseContext responseContext;
    responseContext =
        applicationController.handleRequest(requestContext);
    responseContext.setResponse(response);

    // View Management - Navigate and Dispatch to appropriate View
    applicationController.handleResponse(requestContext,
        responseContext);
    applicationController.destroy();
  }

}
```

Example 6.37 ApplicationController interface

```
interface ApplicationController {
  void init();
  ResponseContext handleRequest(RequestContext requestContext);
  void  handleResponse(RequestContext requestContext, ResponseContext
     responseContext);
  void destroy();
}
```

Example 6.38 WebApplicationController Implementation

```
// Application Controller implementation responsible for handling
// Web application requests
class WebApplicationController implements ApplicationController {

  public void init() { }

  public ResponseContext handleRequest(RequestContext requestContext) {
    ResponseContext responseContext = null;
    try {
      // Identify command name
      String commandName = requestContext.getCommandName();

      // resolve command name to Command Object
      CommandFactory commandFactory = CommandFactory.getInstance();
      Command command = commandFactory.getCommand(commandName);

      // Execute Command using CommandProcessor
      CommandProcessor commandProcessor = new CommandProcessor();
      responseContext = commandProcessor.invoke(command,
          requestContext);
    } catch (java.lang.InstantiationException e) {
      // Handle Exception
    } catch (java.lang.IllegalAccessException e) {
      // Handle Exception
    }
    return responseContext;
  }
  . . .
}
```

View Handler Strategy

An *Application Controller* that obtains and invokes view-related objects is referred to as a *View Handler*. The *Application Controller* resolves and dispatches to the appropriate view, an activity referred to more generally as **view management**. **Action management**, as described in the *Command Handler* strategy (209) and **view management**, described here, are logically distinct activities. In practice, though, the two activities are typically combined. For more on this, see the Design Note "Nested Command and View Management" on page 215. The value of centralized view management is improved modularity, extensibility, maintainability, and reusability.

An XSLT-based view generation mechanism is alternatively referred to as a *Transform Handler* (221). Figure 6.26 shows how the general roles map to view related components. The ApplicationController delegates to a Mapper, which is a ViewFactory, and the Target is a View.

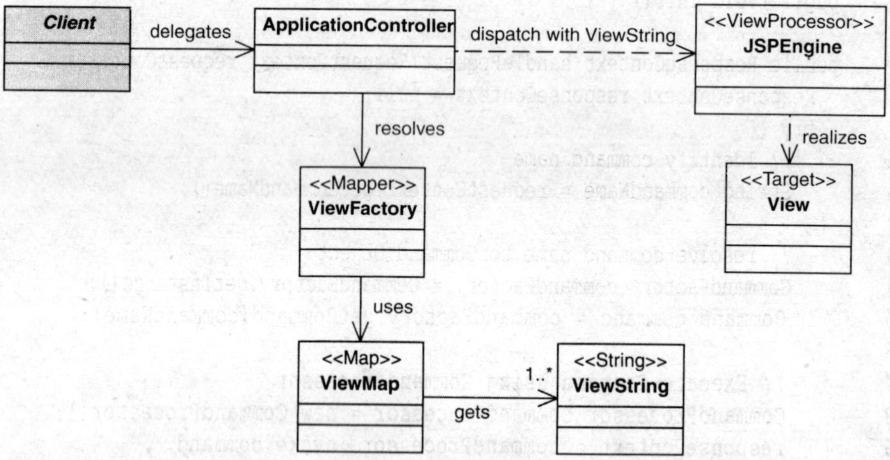

Figure 6.26 Class Diagram for *View Handler* Strategy

Figure 6.27 shows the interaction of these roles.

The ViewString participant represents an indirect handle to the View participant. It is similar to the ViewHandle participant in *Nested Command and View Management* (215).

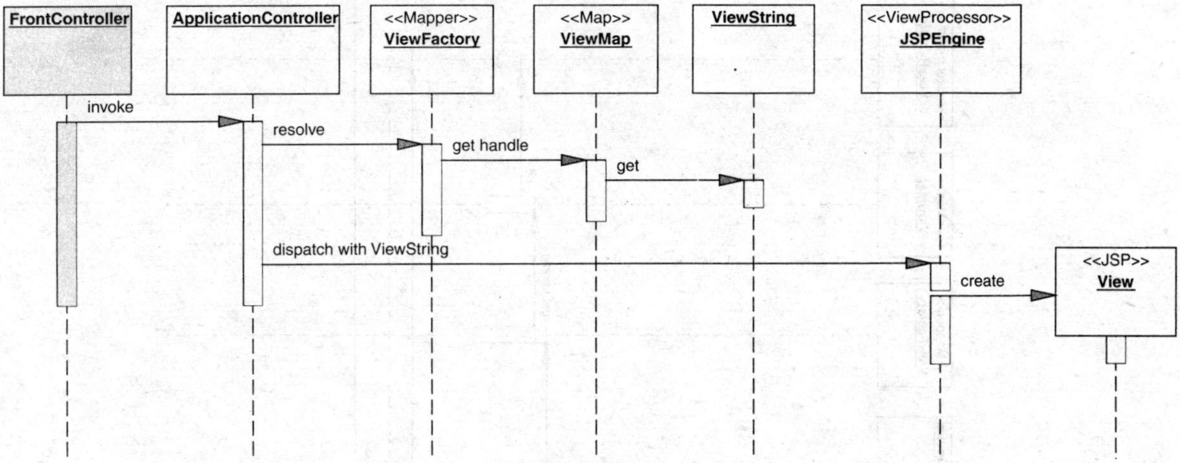

Figure 6.27 Sequence Diagram for *View Handler* Strategy

Design Note: Nested Command and View Management

While action and view management are treated as logically separate activities for the sake of documenting the *Application Controller* pattern implementation strategies, these two activities are often intermingled or nested.

A common scenario is described in Figure 6.28 on page 216, where a *Front Controller* (166) client delegates to an *Application Controller* to resolve an incoming request to the appropriate command, invoke that command, and dispatch to the view. This sort of scenario is realized within the Struts [Struts] framework. The command prepares and returns an indirect view handle (see the Design Note "Handles" on page 208), based upon the result of the command invocation.

Thus, the command shares some of the responsibility for view management with the ApplicationController participant.

Application Controller and Struts

The *Application Controller* pattern is applied within the Struts framework [Struts]. The ActionServlet class in Struts is a *Front Controller* (166) that delegates request-handling responsibilities to a RequestProcessor, which is an *Application Controller*.

The RequestProcessor class acts as a *Command Handler* and a *View Handler*, performing both action and view management. The RequestProcessor uses a CommandMapper (shown in this section as CommandFactory), realized in Struts by the ModuleConfig component and the struts-config.xml, to locate an indirect command handle for the incoming request using the Struts ActionConfig as a CommandMap.

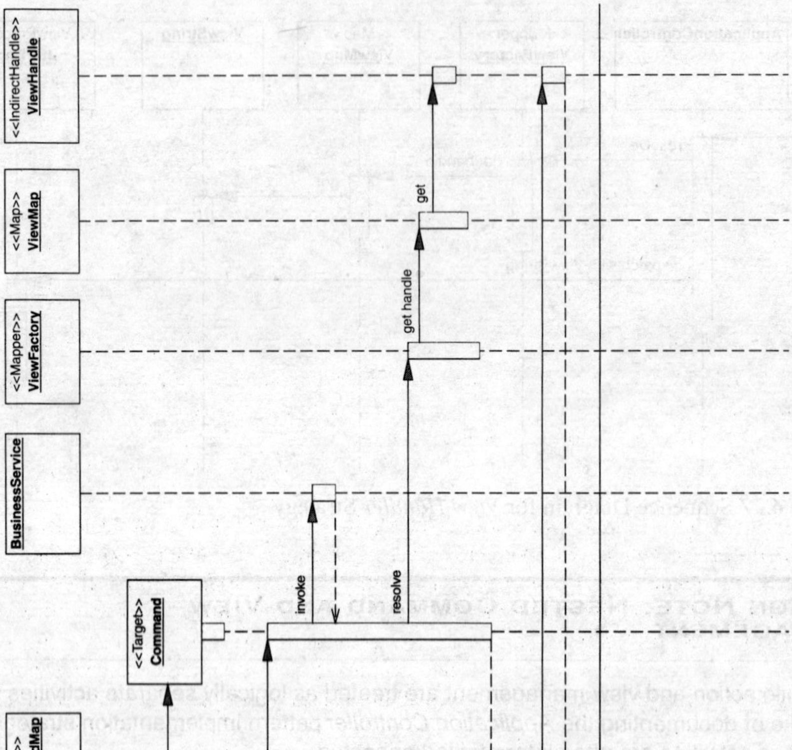

Figure 6.28 Nested Command and View Management

The RequestProcessor uses the command handle to instantiate and execute a command, which subsequently invokes a business service. An ActionMapping fulfills the role of a ViewMapper (shown in Figure 6.28 as ViewFactory), retrieving the appropriate indirect POJO view handle, realized as a Struts ActionForward class and using the handle to dispatch to the appropriate view.

Example 6.39 ActionServlet Code Example

```
// Front Controller
public class ActionServlet extends HttpServlet {

  protected void process(HttpServletRequest request,
      HttpServletResponse response) {

    // Invoke ApplicationController for command & view management
    getRequestProcessor(getModuleConfig(request)).
        process(request,response);
  }

}
```

Example 6.40 ApplicationController Implementation

```
public class RequestProcessor {
  public void process(HttpServletRequest request,
      HttpServletResponse response)
      throws IOException, ServletException {

    // Identify Command Id (path) from request object
    String path = processPath(request, response);
    . . .
    // Identify Command Map based on Command Id
    ActionMapping mapping = processMapping(request, response, path);
    if (mapping == null) {
      return;
    }

    // Authorize user based on Command-Map security settings
    if (!processRoles(request, response, mapping)) {
      return;
    }

    // Identify Command Context Object from CommandMap
    ActionForm form = processActionForm(request, response, mapping);
```

```

    // Auto-populate Context Object from request
    processPopulate(request, response, form, mapping);

    // Validate Context Object request state
    if (!processValidate(request, response, form, mapping)) {
      return;
    }
    // Create or acquire the Command instance to process this request
    Action action = processActionCreate(request, response, mapping);
    if (action == null) {
      return;
    }
    . . .

    // Execute Command and get ViewHandle
    ActionForward forward =  action.execute(mapping, form, request,
        response);

    // Dispatch to appropriate View using ViewHandle
    processActionForward(request, response, forward);

  }


  // Handle Response
  protected void processActionForward(HttpServletRequest request,
      HttpServletResponse response, ActionForward forward)
      throws IOException, ServletException {
    . . .
    // Dispatch to View
    RequestDispatcher rd =
        getServletContext().getRequestDispatcher(uri);
    rd.forward(request, response);
    . . .

  }
}
```

Example 6.41 Command and View Map Entry

```
<action-mappings>
<!-- Edit mail subscription -->
```

```
  <action path="/editSubscription" type=
      "corepatterns.EditSubscriptionAction" attribute=
      "subscriptionForm" scope="request" validate="false">
    <forward name="failure" path="/jsp/mainMenu.jsp"/>
    <forward name="success" path="/jsp/subscription.jsp"/>
  </action>

</action-mappings>
```

Example 6.42 Sample Command (Action) Implementation

```
public final class EditRegistrationAction extends Action {
  public ActionForward execute(ActionMapping mapping, ActionForm form,
      HttpServletRequest request, HttpServletResponse response)
      throws Exception {
    // Execute business logic
    . . .
    // Use ViewMapper to identify and retreive appropriate ViewHandle
    return (mapping.findForward("success"));
  }
}
```

Example 6.43 Implementing View Handler Strategy: WebApplicationController

```
// Application Controller Implementation to handle Web
// Application Requests
class WebApplicationController implements ApplicationController {

  . . .
  // Handle View Navigation and Dispatching to appropriate View
  public void handleResponse(RequestContext requestContext,
      ResponseContext responseContext) {
    ViewFactory viewFactory = ViewFactory.getInstance();

    // Identify view template based on logical view name, user agent,
    // locale, etc
    String viewTemplate = viewFactory.getViewTemplate(
        requestContext, responseContext.getLogicalViewName());

    // dispatch to view processor
    dispatch(requestContext.getRequest(), responseContext.getResponse(),
        viewTemplate);
```

```
  }

  public void destroy() { }

  // dispatcher method
  private void dispatch(HttpServletRequest request,
      HttpServletResponse response, String page) {

    try {
      RequestDispatcher dispatcher = request.getRequestDispatcher(page);
      dispatcher.forward(request, response);
    } catch(Exception e) {
      // Handle Exception
    }
  }
}
```

Example 6.44 View Factory

```
public class ViewFactory {
  private static ViewFactory ourInstance;

  public synchronized static ViewFactory getInstance() {
    if (ourInstance == null) {
      ourInstance = new ViewFactory();
    }
    return ourInstance;
  }

  public String getViewTemplate(RequestContext requestContext,
      String logicalViewName) {

    String viewHandle;
    Locale locale = requestContext.getUserLocale();
    String userAgent = requestContext.getUserAgent();

    // Identify ViewHandle from View Map
    viewHandle = getViewHandle(logicalViewName, userAgent, locale);
    return viewHandle;
  }

  private String getViewHandle(String logicalViewName,
      String userAgent, Locale locale) {
```

```

    // select the View template to be displayed based on
    // logical view name, user locale, device type
    ViewMapKey viewKey = new ViewMapKey(
        logicalViewName, userAgent, locale);
    return (String) viewMap.get(viewKey);
  }

  private ViewFactory() {
    initializeViewMap();
  }

  private void initializeViewMap() {
    // initialization stub - This information would typically be
    // loaded from a ViewRegistry
    // viewMap.put ( logicalViewName, viewTemplateName);
  }

  private Map viewMap = new HashMap();
}
```

Transform Handler Strategy

An ApplicationController that obtains and invokes view-related objects for use with a transformation engine is referred to as a TransformHandler. Figure 6.29 shows how the general roles map to view related components.

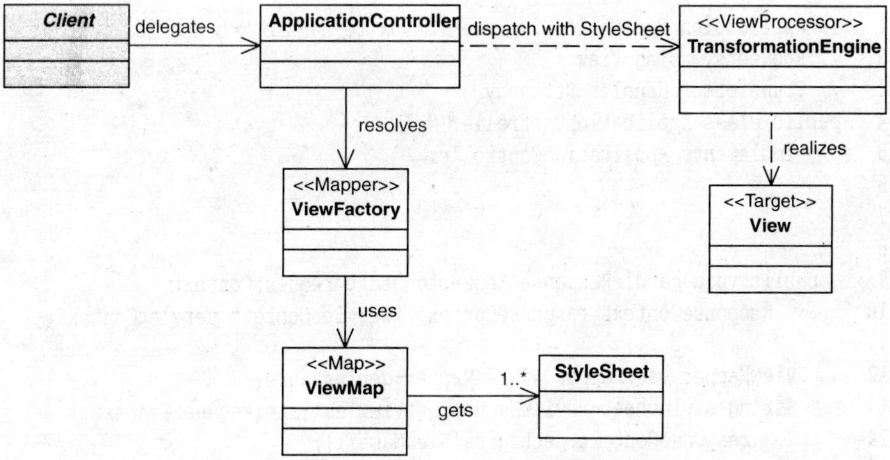

Figure 6.29 Class Diagram for *Transformer Handler* Strategy

The ApplicationController collaborates with a Mapper, which is a ViewFactory, and the Target is a View, generated from a StyleSheet.

Figure 6.30 on page 222 shows the interaction of these components.

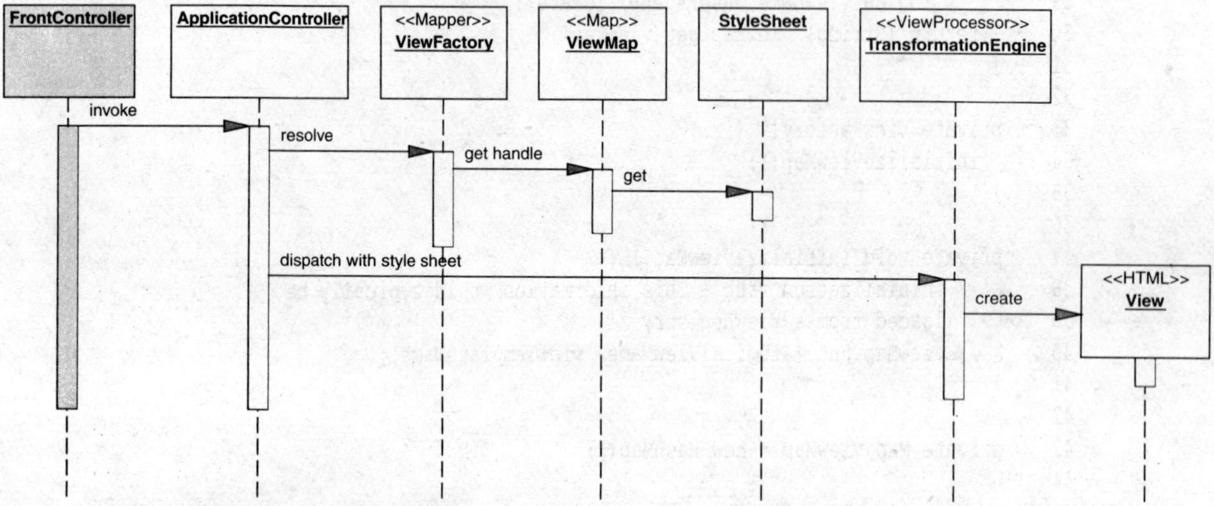

Figure 6.30 Sequence Diagram for *Transformer Handler* Strategy

A transform handler is used in *Performing a View Transform* (246) and is a specific type of view handler. See Example 6.45.

Example 6.45 Transformer Handler Strategy: ApplicationControllerImpl

```
// Application Controller implementation to handle Web Application
// Requests, using View
// Transformer Handler Strategy
public class ApplicationControllerImpl
    implements ApplicationController {

  . . .

  public void handleResponse(RequestContext requestContext,
      ResponseContext responseContext, ServletContext servletContext) {

    ViewMapper viewMapper = ViewMapper.getInstance();
    String stylesheet = viewMapper.getViewTemplate(requestContext,
        responseContext.getLogicalViewName());

    TransformHelper helper;
```

```
    helper = new TransformHelper();

    Reader xmlReader  = new StringReader(
        (String)responseContext.getData());
    InputStream xslStream =
        servletContext.getResourceAsStream(stylesheet);
    helper.transform(requestContext.getRequest(),
        responseContext.getResponse(), xmlReader, xslStream);
  }
}
```

Example 6.46 TransformerHelper

```
class TransformHelper {

  public void transform(ServletRequest request,
      ServletResponse response, Reader xmlReader,
      InputStream xslStream) {

    try {
      // SAXParserFactory
      SAXParserFactory parserFactory = SAXParserFactory.newInstance();
      SAXParser parser = parserFactory.newSAXParser();
      Source xmlSource = new StreamSource(xmlReader);
      Source xslSource = new StreamSource(xslStream);
      Result outputTarget = new StreamResult(response.getWriter());

      Transformer transformer = TransformerFactory.newInstance().
          newTransformer(xslSource);

      transformer.transform(xmlSource, outputTarget);
    } catch(Exception e) {
      // Handle Exception
    }
  }
}
```

Navigation and Flow Control Strategy

Users typically need to move through application screens in a particular order. You can control this flow through the application in several ways.

- The most basic way is simply to check whether a particular precondition has been satisfied before allowing access to a certain page. For example, check if users have logged in before allowing them to view their account information. This approach can be characterized as a simple **policy-based strategy**, and it does not address sophisticated, multi-screen navigation requirements such as guiding a user through a specific group of screens in a particular order.

- If you have requirements about the flow order of the screens and this order depends on the current state of parts of the application, then the flow control can leverage a simple state-machine. You can easily make these rules declarative, so this strategy can also help reduce the coupling between your code and the navigation/flow control constraints.
- Finally, for limiting duplicate requests, another common flow-control requirement, see *Introduce Synchronizer Token*. It works with *Application Controller* and *Front Controller* (166) to help control duplicate requests.

Example 6.47 Navigation and Flow Control strategy

```
// Application Controller with flow control

public class ApplicationControllerImpl
    implements ApplicationController {

  public ResponseContext handleRequest(Map requestContextMap) {
    ResponseContext responseContext = null;
    try {

      // Identify requested Order-processing operation
      // from ContextObject
      String orderEvent =  getOrderEvent(requestContextMap);
      String orderState =  getOrderStatus(requestContextMap);

      // Create Command based on business Event and current State
      CommandAndViewFactory factory =
          CommandAndViewFactory.getInstance();
      CommandViewHandle result = factory.getCommand(
          orderEvent, orderState);

      // Instantiate Command from Indirect Handle
      Command command =
          (Command)result.getCommandHandle().newInstance();

      // Execute Business-tier Service
      responseContext = command.execute(requestContextMap);
```

```
      // set view name
      responseContext.setLogicalViewName(result.getViewName());
    } catch(Exception e) {
      // Handle Exception
    }
    return responseContext;
  }
  . . .
  private String getOrderStatus(Map requestContext) {
    String id = ((String[])requestContext.
        get(OrderStatus.STATUS_PARAM))[0];
    return id;
  }

  private String getOrderEvent(Map requestContext) {
    String orderEvent = ((String[])requestContext.
        get(Constants.REQ_OPCODE))[0];
    return orderEvent;
  }
}
```

Example 6.48 CommandAndViewFactory

```
// Command and View Dual-Factory creates Command and View
// instances based on current application state and requested operation
public class CommandAndViewFactory {
  private static CommandAndViewFactory ourInstance;

  public synchronized static CommandAndViewFactory getInstance() {
    if (ourInstance == null) {
      ourInstance = new CommandAndViewFactory();
    }
    return ourInstance;
  }

  private CommandAndViewFactory() {
    commandviewMap = CommandViewMap.getInstance();
  }

  public CommandViewHandle getCommand(String event, String state) {
    CommandViewHandle handle =
        commandviewMap.getCommandViewHandle(event, state);
```

```
    return handle;
  }

  public String getView(String event, String state) {
    return commandviewMap.
        getCommandViewHandle(event, state).getViewName();
  }

  CommandViewMap commandviewMap;
}

class CommandViewMap {

  private static CommandViewMap ourInstance;

    public synchronized static CommandViewMap getInstance() {
      if (ourInstance == null) {
        ourInstance = new CommandViewMap();
      }
      return ourInstance;
    }

  private CommandViewMap() {
    initialize();
  }

  // Initialize map for all valid state and event combinations
  private void initialize() {
    addEventStateEntry(
        OrderEvents.EnterOrder, OrderStatus.ORDER_NEW,
        PlaceOrderCommand.class,
        "/jsp/ApplicationController/OrderPlaced");

    addEventStateEntry(OrderEvents.ApproveOrder,
        OrderStatus.ORDER_PLACED, ApproveOrderCommand.class,
        "/jsp/ApplicationController/OrderApproved");

    addEventStateEntry(OrderEvents.DeclineOrder,
        OrderStatus.ORDER_PLACED,
        DeclineOrderCommand.class,
        "/jsp/ApplicationController/OrderDeclined");

    addEventStateEntry(OrderEvents.TerminateOrder,
```

```
        OrderStatus.ORDER_PLACED, TerminateOrderCommand.class,
        "/jsp/ApplicationController/OrderTerminated");

    addEventStateEntry(OrderEvents.ShipOrder,
        OrderStatus.ORDER_APPROVED, TerminateOrderCommand.class,
        "/jsp/ApplicationController/OrderShipped");

    addEventStateEntry(OrderEvents.TerminateOrder,
        OrderStatus.ORDER_APPROVED,  TerminateOrderCommand.class,
        "/jsp/ApplicationController/OrderTerminated");

    addEventStateEntry(OrderEvents.TerminateOrder,
        OrderStatus.ORDER_DECLINED, TerminateOrderCommand.class,
        "/jsp/ApplicationController/OrderTerminated");
    . . .
  }

  void addEventStateEntry(String event, Object state,
      Class domainCommand, String viewName) {
    CommandViewHandle newResponse =
        new CommandViewHandle(domainCommand, viewName);
    if ( !events.containsKey(event))
      events.put(event, new HashMap());
    getEventMap(event).put(state, newResponse);
  }

  private Map getEventMap(String key ) {
    return (Map)events.get(key);
  }

  public CommandViewHandle getCommandViewHandle(
      String operation, String state) {
    return (CommandViewHandle)getEventMap(operation).get(state);
  }
  private Map events = new HashMap();
}

class CommandViewHandle {
  public CommandViewHandle(Class domainCommand, String viewName) {
    this.domainCommand = domainCommand;
    this.viewName = viewName;
  }

```

```
  public Class getCommandHandle() {
    return domainCommand;
  }

  public String getViewName() {
    return viewName;
  }

  private Class domainCommand;
  private String viewName;
}
```

Design Note: Event Listeners – ServletContext, HttpSession, and Custom Event Listeners

Some aspects of request handling might depend on application life-cycle events or attribute-based events, such as those summarized in Table 6-1, that are related to ServletContext or HttpSession. Additionally, you can use custom events and event-handling mechanisms to trigger specific aspects of the request handling.

- For the **Lifecycle**, the container is signaling that the servlet context is ready to service the first request. Alternately, the servlet context is on the verge of being destroyed.
- For **Changes to Attributes**, the servlet context has had attributes added, replaced, or removed.
- For **Lifecycle**, the container is signaling that an HttpSession has been created. Alternately the HttpSession has timed out, or it has been invalidated.
- For **Changes to Attributes**, an HttpSession object has had attributes added, replaced, or removed.

Table 6-1 Supported Event Types

Event Type	***Description***	***Listener Interface***
Servlet context events		
Lifecycle	The servlet context is available and has just been created. It is ready to service its first request. Alternately the servlet context is about to be shut down.	javax.Servlet.ServletContextListener

Table 6-1 Supported Event Types

Event Type	*Description*	*Listener Interface*
Changes to Attributes	On the servlet context, there are attributes that have been added, removed, or replaced.	javax.Servlet.ServletContextAttributesListener
HttpSession Events		
Lifecycle	An HttpSession just been created. It's also possible that it has been invalidated or timed out.	javax.Servlet.http.HttpSessionListener
Changes to Attributes	In an HttpSession object, there are attributes that have been added, removed, or replaced.	javax.Servlet.http.HttpSessionAttributesListener

Message Handling Strategies

Web Service

An *Application Controller* is commonly used in the presentation tier to perform action and view management along with a *Front Controller* (166). However, an *Application Controller* can also be used in other tiers and in other contexts. For example, an *Application Controller* might also support web service requests that require routing and action management. Thus, while the most common usage of an *Application Controller* is in the presentation tier, you can use it in a variety of ways in other tiers, as well.

The SOAP with Attachments API for Java, or SAAJ, [SAAJ] allows developers to work with SOAP messages and provides support for building message handlers, which are a type of filter. One should use SOAP message handlers judiciously and when doing so, they provide a powerful processing mechanism.

Custom SOAP Message Handling Strategy

Web Service

For a web service request, the *Application Controller* manages the message handling, including invoking a chain of message handlers to do pre and/or postprocessing. These loosely coupled handlers are *Intercepting Filter* (144) and are also described in *Intercepting Filter's Custom SOAP Filter* strategy.

Figure 6.31 and Figure 6.32 show the participants and how they interact.

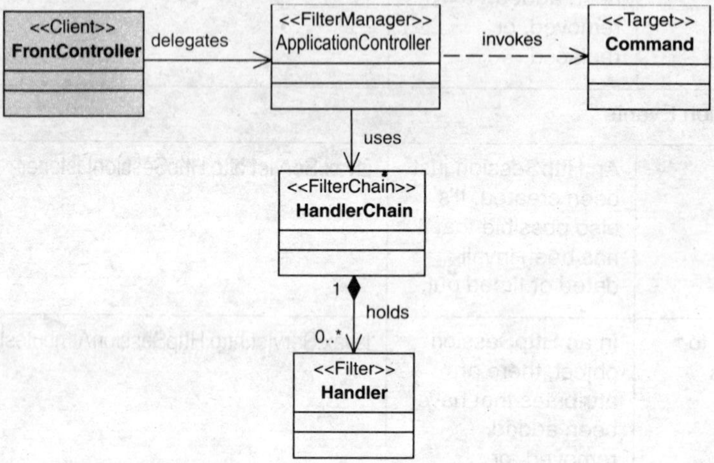

Figure 6.31 Custom SOAP Handler strategy

A *Front Controller* (166) typically acts as the central access point for SOAP requests. In this strategy, the controller delegates to an *Application Controller*, which uses a *Custom SOAP Filter* (162) to perform the pre and postprocessing of the message. The *Application Controller* then performs action and view management, including the appropriate validation and error handling. The "view" is, in effect, simply the response that is prepared for return to the client.

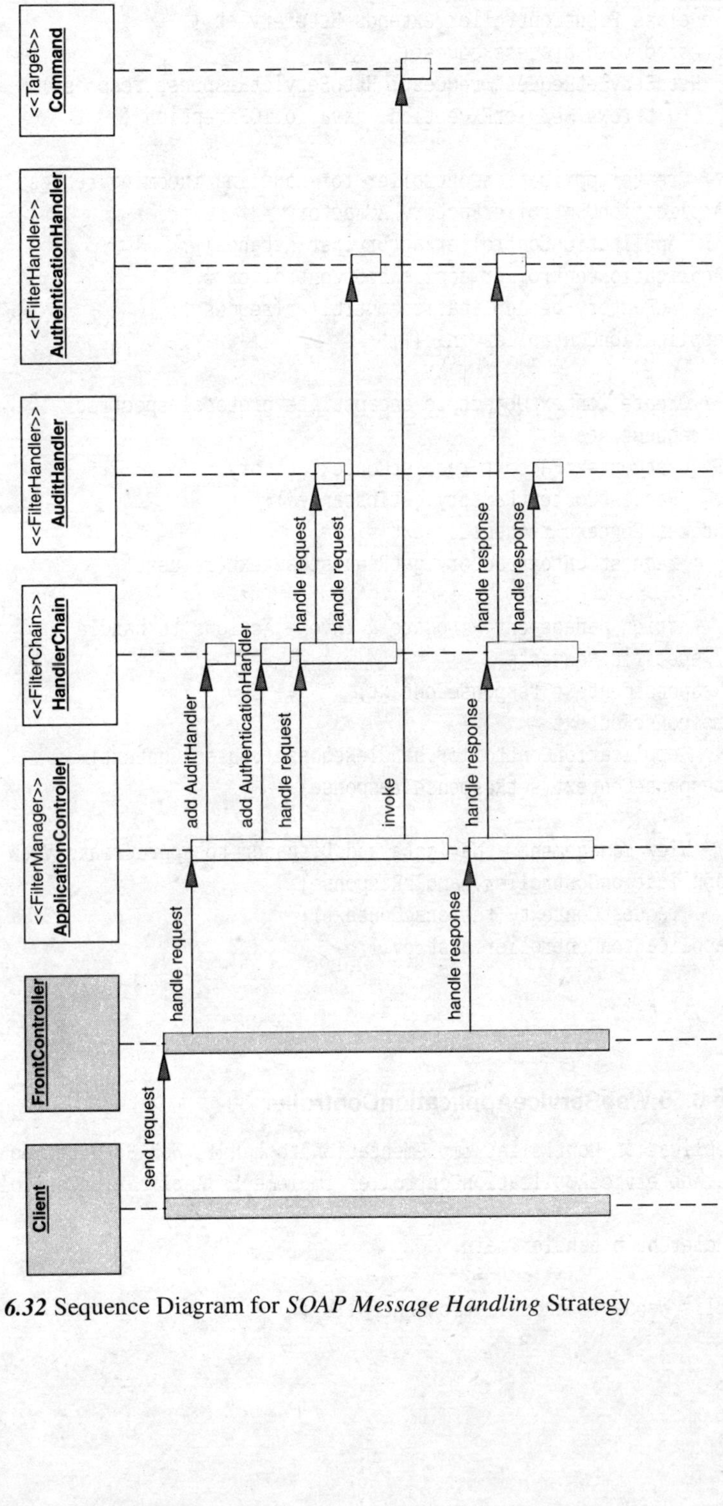

Figure 6.32 Sequence Diagram for *SOAP Message Handling* Strategy

Example 6.49 SOAP Message Handling Strategy

```
public class FrontController extends HttpServlet {
  protected void processRequest(
      HttpServletRequest request, HttpServletResponse response)
          throws ServletException, java.io.IOException {

    // Create ApplicationController for handling incoming request
    ApplicationControllerFactory ACFactory =
        ApplicationControllerFactory.getInstance();
    ApplicationController applicationController =
        ACFactory.getApplicationController(request);
    applicationController.init();

    // Create ContextObject to encapsulate protocol-specific
    //request state
    RequestContextFactory requestContextFactory =
        RequestContextFactory.getInstance();
    RequestContext requestContext =
        requestContextFactory.getRequestContext(request);

    // Action Management - Locate & Invoke Actions to handle
    //specific Requests
    ResponseContext responseContext;
    responseContext =
        applicationController.handleRequest(requestContext);
    responseContext.setResponse(response);

    // View Management - Navigate and Dispatch to appropriate View
    applicationController.handleResponse(
        requestContext, responseContext);
    applicationController.destroy();
  }
  . . .
}
```

Example 6.50 WebServiceApplicationController

```
// Application Controller implementation to handle Web Service Request
class WebServiceApplicationController implements ApplicationController {

  HandlerChain handlerChain;

  public WebServiceApplicationController() {}
```

```
  public void init() {
    handlerChain = new HandlerChain();
    handlerChain.addHandler(new AuditHandler());
    handlerChain.addHandler(new AuthenticationHandler());
  }

  public ResponseContext handleRequest(RequestContext requestContext) {
    ResponseContext responseContext = null;
    try {
      SOAPRequestContext soapRequestContext =
          (SOAPRequestContext)requestContext;

      // create a SOAPMessage from incoming HTTP stream
      SOAPMessage soapMessage = soapRequestContext.getSOAPMessage();

      // pre-process SOAPMessage by Message Handlers
      handlerChain.handleRequest(soapMessage);

      // Identify Command Name from protocol-specific request
      String commandName = soapRequestContext.getCommandName();

      // resolve command name to Command Object
      CommandFactory commandFactory = CommandFactory.getInstance();
      Command command = commandFactory.getCommand(commandName);

      // Invoke Command using a CommandProcessor
      CommandProcessor commandProcessor = new CommandProcessor();
      Object result = commandProcessor.invoke(command, requestContext);

      // Create Response context based on Command results
      responseContext = ResponseContextFactory.getInstance().
          createResponseContext(result, null);
    } catch(java.lang.InstantiationException e) {
      // Handle Exception
    } catch(java.lang.IllegalAccessException e ) {
      // Handle Exception
    }
    return responseContext;
  }

  public void handleResponse(
    RequestContext requestContext, ResponseContext responseContext) {
```

```
    try {

      // create response SOAPResponse message from
      // previously-obtained Command result
      SOAPMessage soapMessage = null;
      Object payload = responseContext.getData();

      soapMessage = SOAPHttpFacade.createSOAPMessage(payload);
      if (soapMessage != null) {
        // post-process Response Message by SOAP Message Handlers
        handlerChain.handleResponse(soapMessage);

        // Need to saveChanges because we're going to use the
        // MimeHeaders to set HTTP response information. These
        // MimeHeaders are generated as part of the save.

        if (soapMessage.saveRequired()) {
          soapMessage.saveChanges();
        }

        HttpServletResponse response = (HttpServletResponse)
        responseContext.getResponse();
        response.setStatus(HttpServletResponse.SC_OK);

        SOAPHttpFacade.putHeaders(
            soapMessage.getMimeHeaders(), response);
        writeResponse(
            (HttpServletResponse)responseContext.
                getResponse(), soapMessage);
      }
    } catch (SOAPException e) {
      // Handle Exception
    }
  }

  public void destroy() { }

  private void writeResponse(
      HttpServletResponse response, SOAPMessage soapResponse) {
    try {
      // Write out the message on the response stream.
      response.setContentType("text/xml"); // SOAP 1.1 Message
      OutputStream outputStream = response.getOutputStream();
```

```
        soapResponse.writeTo(outputStream);
        outputStream.flush();
      } catch(SOAPException e) {
        // Handle Exception
        response.setStatus(HttpServletResponse.SC_NO_CONTENT);
      } catch(java.io.IOException e) {
        // Handle Exception
        response.setStatus(HttpServletResponse.SC_NO_CONTENT);
      }
    }
    . . .
}
```

Figure 6.33 on page 236 shows the *JAX-RPC Message-Handler* strategy.

JAX-RPC Message Handling Strategy

Web Service

For a web service request, the *Application Controller* manages aspects of the request handling, including invoking a chain of message handlers to do pre and/or postprocessing. These handlers are implemented in the web service's client tier if they perform client-specific logic. Handlers are implemented in the presentation tier or integration tier if they contain code that is common across requests and responses on the receiving side. These loosely coupled handlers are *Intercepting Filter* (144) and are also described in the *Intercepting Filter JAX-RPC Filter* strategy (163).

A *Front Controller* (166) typically acts as the central access point for SOAP requests. In this strategy, the controller delegates to an *Application Controller*, which uses a *JAX-RPC Filter* strategy (163) to perform the pre and postprocessing of the message. The *Application Controller* then performs action and view management, including the appropriate validation and error handling. The "view" is, in effect, simply the response that is prepared for return to the client. These message handlers are built using SAAJ.

The major difference between this strategy and the *Custom SOAP Message-Handling* strategy covered previously is that in this strategy the JAX-RPC runtime engine handles most of the participant responsibilities of the pattern.

See Example 6.51 on page 237.

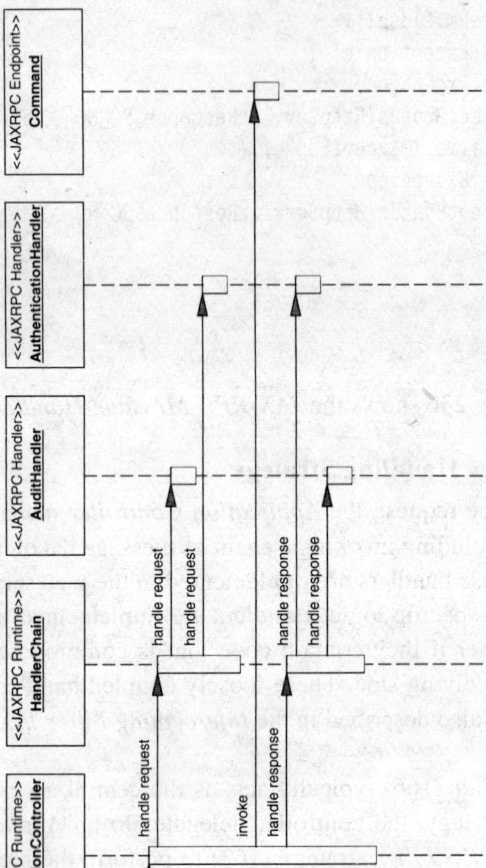

Figure 6.33 Sequence Diagram for *JAX-RPC Message-Handler* Strategy

Example 6.51 JAX-RPC Message-Handler Strategy

```
import javax.xml.rpc.handler.Handler;
import javax.xml.rpc.handler.soap.SOAPMessageContext;
import javax.xml.soap.SOAPMessage;
. . .
import org.apache.xml.security.signature.XMLSignature;
import org.apache.xpath.CachedXPathAPI;
import org.apache.xml.security.utils.Constants;

public class AuthenticationHandler extends GenericHandler
    implements Handler {

  private String DSIG_NS = "xmlns:ds";
  private String DSIG_SIGNATURE_SEARCH_EXPR = "//ds:Signature";
  String BaseURI = "http://xml-security";

  public AuthenticationHandler() { }

  public void init(HandlerInfo config) {
    org.apache.xml.security.Init.init();
  }

  public boolean handleRequest (MessageContext context) {
    try {
      SOAPMessageContext soapMessageContext =
          (SOAPMessageContext) context;
      SOAPMessage soapMessage = soapMessageContext.getMessage();
      Source source = soapMessage.getSOAPPart().getContent();

      // get Document from Source
      Document signedDoc = getDocument(source);

      // XPath expression evaluator
      CachedXPathAPI xPath = new CachedXPathAPI();

      // namespace Node is used for resolving namespace prefixes
      // in the following xpath search
      Element nsctx = signedDoc.createElement("nsctx");
      nsctx.setAttribute(DSIG_NS, Constants.SignatureSpecNS);

      // Use XPath expression to find the Signature Element
      Element signatureElem =
```

```
            (Element)xPath.selectSingleNode(
            signedDoc, DSIG_SIGNATURE_SEARCH_EXPR, nsctx);

        // check to make sure that the document claims to have been signed
        if (signatureElem == null) {
          // Handle Missing Signature scenario
          System.out.println("The document is not signed");
          return false;
        }

        // Verify Signature
        XMLSignature signature = new XMLSignature(signatureElem, BaseURI);
        boolean verify = signature.checkSignatureValue(
            signature.getKeyInfo().getPublicKey());

        // Audit Verification Message
        System.out.println("The signature is" + (verify ? " ": " not ") +
            "valid");

        return verify;
      } catch(Exception e) {
        // Handle Exception
      }
      return false;
    }

    public boolean handleResponse(MessageContext context) {
      return true;
    }
    . . .
}
```

Consequences

- ***Improves modularity***
  Separating common action and view management code, into its own set of classes makes the application more modular. This modularity might also ease testing, since aspects of the *Application Controller* functionality will not be tied to a web container.
- ***Improves reusability***
  You can reuse the common, modular components.

- ***Improves extensibility***
  Functionality can be added to the request handling mechanism in a predictable way, and independent of protocol-specific or network access code. Declarative flow control reduces coupling between code and navigation/flow control rules, allowing these rules to be modified without recompiling or modifying code.

Related Patterns

- ***Front Controller (166)***
  A *Front Controller* (166) uses an *Application Controller* to perform action and view management.
- ***Service Locator (315)***
  A *Service Locator* (315) performs service location and retrieval. A *Service Locator* (315) is a coarser object, often uses sophisticated infrastructure for lookup, and doesn't manage routing. It also doesn't address view management.
- ***Command Processor [POSA]***
  A *Command Processor* manages command invocations, providing invocation scheduling, logging, and undo/redo functionality.
- ***Command Pattern [GoF]***
  A *Command* encapsulates a request in an object, separating the request from its invocation.
- ***Composite Pattern [GoF]***
  A *Composite* represents objects as part-whole hierarchies, treating individual objects and compositions of objects uniformly.
- ***Application Controller [PEAA]***
  Martin Fowler's description of *Application Controller* [PEAA] seems to focus on controlling a user's navigation through an application using a state machine, as described in the *Navigation and Flow Control* strategy. However, the *Application Controller* [PEAA] and our documentation of *Application Controller* have the same core intent.

View Helper

Problem

You want to separate a view from its processing logic.

Mingling control logic, data access logic and formatting logic within view components leads to problems with modularity, reuse, maintenance, and role separation. Mingling logic this way violates the higher-level design goal of separating a model from its view and control code.

Separating the model, view, and control components in the presentation tier is an important design goal. A *Front Controller* (166) can encapsulate control logic, but you still must consider the important separation of model and display-related components.

Processing a request involves two types of activities: request handling and view processing. Within the view processing activity category, **view preparation** and **view creation** are two distinct processing phases within the web tier, and each phase involves processing logic that is wholly unrelated to the other phase.

- The view preparation phase involves request handling, action management, and view management. A request is resolved to a specific action, that action is invoked and the appropriate view is identified, with the request then being dispatched to that view.
- Subsequently, during view creation, the view retrieves content from its model, using helpers to retrieve and adapt the model state. Often extracted and adapted from *Transfer Object* (415), this content is inserted, formatted, and converted into the static template text of the view to generate a dynamic response.

Using JSP and other template-based views for view creation means you have the opportunity to embed Java scriptlet code in the view. If you use scriptlet code this way, you can't reuse that logic easily and the application is less flexible.

Moreover, embedded programming logic within a view often acts as control code or performs view preparation activities, such as content retrieval. As the sophistication of an application increases, mingling control logic, data access logic and presentation formatting logic within view components leads to problems with modularity, reuse, maintenance, and role separation. This mingling violates the higher-level design goal of separating a model from its view and control code.

Forces

- You want to use template-based views, such as JSP.
- You want to avoid embedding program logic in the view.
- You want to separate programming logic from the view to facilitate division of labor between software developers and web page designers.

Solution

Use *Views* to encapsulate formatting code and *Helpers* to encapsulate view-processing logic. A View delegates its processing responsibilities to its helper classes, implemented as POJOs, custom tags, or tag files. Helpers serve as adapters between the view and the model, and perform processing related to formatting logic, such as generating an HTML table.

This pattern helps tease apart the responsibilities of a view and its helpers. This pattern might well be referred to as ***View and Helper***, since it establishes these two components as key abstractions with unique responsibilities.

This pattern applies primarily to template-based views like JSP. Static template text and markup tags define the overall template view, and hooks to programming logic are encapsulated in helpers and embedded in the template.

Encapsulating processing logic in a helper instead of a view makes applications more modular and facilitates component reuse. A common approach for reusing logic that is embedded in a template-based view is to copy and paste it elsewhere. This sort of duplication makes a system harder to maintain, since the same bug potentially needs to be corrected in multiple places. Therefore, if scriptlet code dominates a JSP view, apply this pattern in order to **localize disparate logic** (72).

The overriding goal when applying this pattern is partitioning processing logic, such as control, formatting, business, and data access logic outside of the view.

- Business logic will typically map to a model object, such as a *Transfer Object* (415) or *Business Object* (374).
- Data access logic is encapsulated within *Data Access Objects* (462).
- Control logic maps to a *Front Controller* (166) along with commands and helpers, and formatting logic to helpers.

There is some perceived overlap in the role of a helper object and the role of the model, since one of the model's primary responsibilities is managing the business logic that fulfills a related request, and this activity is often initiated and facilitated by a helper object in the web tier. In actuality, the model is encapsulated within *Business Object* (374) to which the helpers delegate. The main responsibility of *View Helper* objects is to format and adapt the model to a particular view.

The JavaServer Pages Standard Tag Library [JSTL] provides a standard set of tags that support common needs, such as iteration and conditional logic. Using these tags lets you avoid embedding processing logic in the form of scriptlet code in the JSP.

Another aspect of JSTL is the data access tags that provide database access from within a view. In simple applications, you can use the JSTL data access without considering consequences,. However, within enterprise applications of any size, using the data access tags violates the design principle of separating data access logic from the view. A better choice in this case is to use a *Data Access Object* (462), which encapsulates data access code and provides a more maintainable and reusable solution.

Finally, JSTL and JSP 2.0 integrate a powerful Expression Language (EL), which provides another alternative to using Java scriptlet code within JSP. The following examples show how powerful the EL is. Instead of accessing a JavaBean helper from within a JSP, as follows:

```
<% bean.getVar1(); %> or
<% var1 = bean.getVar1(); var1.getVar2(); %>
```

You can use the EL, as follows:

```
${bean.var1} or ${bean.var1.var2}
```

Developing your own helpers, either as custom tags or tag files, will provide benefits too, offering higher-level abstractions that more clearly communicate the intent of your code.

Whether you use JSTL or create custom tags, however, the goal is to avoid using helpers as scriptlets.

For more about JSTL and the EL, see "Implementation versus Intent" on page 253, the *Tag File Helper* strategy (*254*), and http://java.sun.com/jsp.

If you don't use a *Front Controller* (166) and/or *Intercepting Filters* (144) as a central control mechanism, then the view becomes the initial contact point for handling a request, as described in *Service to Worker* (276). This is fine in some cases but a different approach is preferred in others.

For simpler cases, which involve little or no action management or business-service invocations, this works fine. One example is requests for static content or requests to view information that already exists in memory, and so must merely be formatted for display. These sorts of use cases do view creation but not view preparation.

For more dynamic requests, those requiring view preparation and view creation, use a controller-centric approach, such as *Service to Worker* (276).

Remember that both approaches are typically combined within the same application to handle the appropriate use cases.

There are multiple strategies within this pattern for implementing the view component. The preferred strategy, *Template-Based View* strategy (248), suggests using a template-based mechanism, such as JSP as the view component. The other principle strategy is the *Controller-Based View* strategy (249), which uses a control component, such as a servlet, as the view or as the view-managing component. Using a controller to manage view creation with XSLT is discussed in *View Transform*.

DESIGN NOTE: VIEW PROCESSING

As previously stated, request processing can be subdivided into two key areas: request handling and view processing. Several activities must be performed in the presentation tier during the latter, view processing. These activities can be broken down into two main categories, **view preparation** and **view creation**:

- View preparation – Involves populating model objects and identifying and/or generating an appropriate view component. View preparation occurs as part of the core processing of a request, as model objects initiate content retrieval and store state retrieved from a data source. Typically, the data will be retrieved via *Transfer Object* (415) and can be encapsulated within *Business Object s* (374).
- View creation – Involves transforming state from the model into dynamic content that is embedded within the view component.

Structure

Example 6.35 is the *View Helper* class diagram.

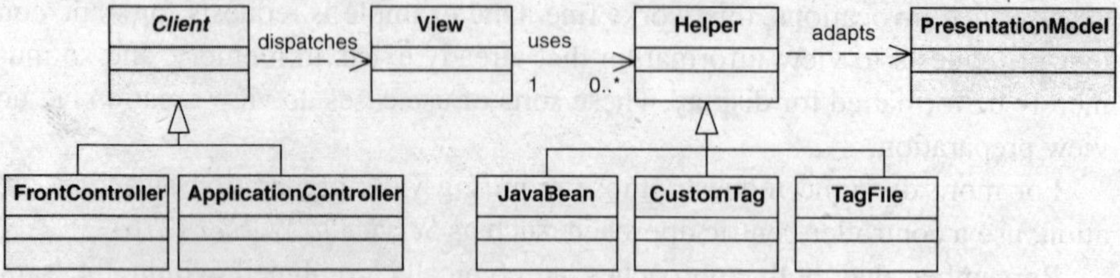

Figure 6.34 View Helper Class Diagram

Participants and Responsibilities

Example 6.36 is a *View Helper* sequence diagram. A centralized *Front Controller* (166) typically mediates between the requesting client and the view, in which case this controller fulfills the role of Client in the diagram. In some cases, though, particularly when a response is mostly or entirely static, a centralized controller is not used and the client invokes the view directly. This usage pattern is referred to as *Dispatcher View* (288).

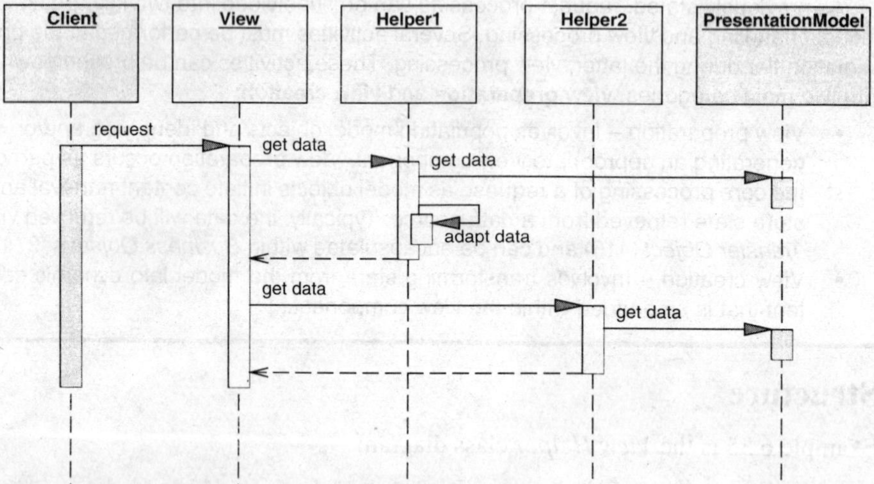

Figure 6.35 View Helper Sequence Diagram

As noted in the class diagram, there might not be helpers associated with a view. In this simple case, the page can be entirely static or include very small amounts of inline scriptlet code.

Client

A Client dispatches to the View.

View

A View represents and displays information to the Client. The information that is used in a dynamic display is retrieved and converted from a presentation model by helpers.

Helper1, Helper2

A helper encapsulates processing logic for generating and formatting a View. A helper typically adapts a PresentationModel for a view or provides access to the raw data of the PresentationModel.

A view works with any number of helpers, typically implemented as JavaBeans, custom tags, or tag files.

PresentationModel

The PresentationModel holds the data retrieved from the business service, used to generate the View.

DESIGN NOTE: VIEW TRANSFORM USING XSLT

There are two main approaches to generating a view from a presentation model. The **functional approach** is commonly used when your presentation model is XML based, and the **imperative approach** is most often used when your presentation model is object based.

- Functional Approach – When your presentation model is XML, the most common approach for view generation is to perform a *View Transform* using the extensible stylesheet language (XSL). XSL is a language consisting of three major components, two of which are dedicated to accessing and transforming XML. These two components are XSL Transformations (XSLT) and XML Path Language (XPath), a robust expression language used by XSLT [XSL].

  How is this approach different from the typical JSP approach? XML is fed into a transforming engine along with a style sheet that describes how each part of the XML model should look in the view. The style sheet's formatting rules are matched to portions of the XML, triggering transformations that result in a different set of XML, adapted for the view. The style sheet encapsulates formatting-related code only, reducing its coupling to the XML content, which serves as the model.
- Imperative Approach – If your presentation model is object-based rather than XML-based, the imperative approach to view creation, using JSP and *View Helpers (240),* is a good fit. This approach is well-suited to a development process that involves using many of the popular HTML page authoring tools, since

a page is generated and then tags are embedded within the page to handle dynamic substitution and runtime.

If your business data is already in XML, you need to decide whether to convert that data to objects or transform it directly to a view with no intermediate conversion. Any conversion from one form to another takes time and reduces efficiency, so consider the reusability of the various formats in order to gauge the overall value of the conversion.

Deciding on an Approach

Advantages of the XML/XSLT Functional Approach

If a business has a pre-existing, strong investment in XML, then it makes sense to embrace that foundation and build from it. In this sort of environment, the business tier might return XML to its clients in the web tier and thus a functional approach to view creation is more appropriate, using a transformation engine and style sheets.

Benefits of the XML/XSLT approach are language independence and platform independence. An XML model can be generated from code running on one platform, while the subsequent *View Transform* can be performed on another platform. *Web Service Broker* (557) deals with this issue in the broader context of handling a web service request.

Issues Regarding the XML/XSLT Functional Approach

While an often-stated benefit of the XML/XSLT approach is that it provides **more** protection against the bad practice of mingling nonformatting-related processing logic with your formatting markup, this claim is not entirely accurate. In fact, XSL's expression language, Xpath, makes it quite easy and common to embed processing logic, such as conditionals and flow control, within the formatting code. This situation is quite similar to what occurs when mingling Java scriptlet code and HTML formatting in JSP.

Keep in mind that expertise in XSLT, currently the most typical approach for XML transformation, is often a niche skill in a typical, OO-centric software development organization. Another consideration when using XSLT is that testing and debugging can be challenging, especially for those more accustomed to an OO development cycle. If you're planning to use XSLT extensively, be sure you have enough skilled people.

Performing a View Transform

You can perform a *View Transform* in the client tier or the presentation tier. It is most common in the presentation tier, and performing it there also reduces the risks associated with exposing certain security and data access information to the client tier. A *View Transform* is performed as part of the *Application Controller* (205) *Transform Handler* strategy (221).

You can perform a *View Transform* using interpretation or compilation, in the client tier or in the presentation tier.

- Transformations can be interpreted at runtime with a style sheet, as shown in Example 6.37.

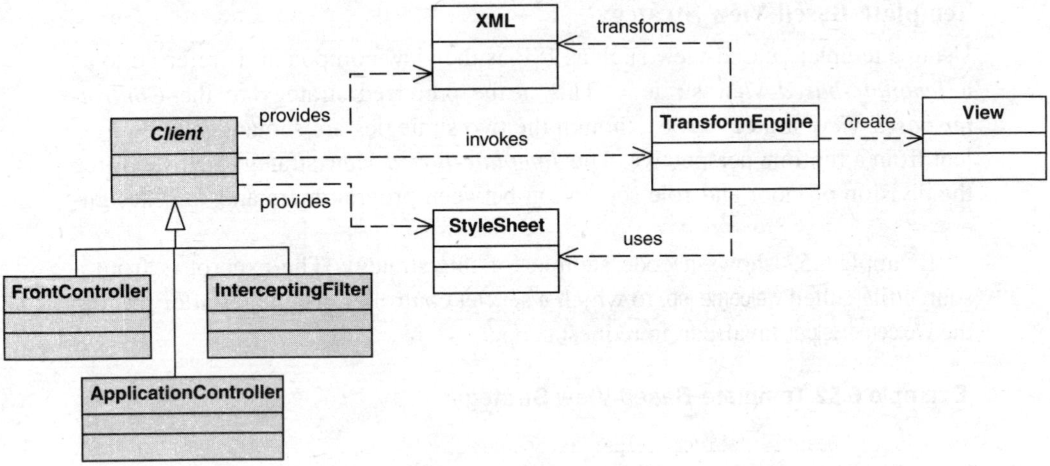

Figure 6.36 Using Style Sheets

- Another approach is to compile style sheets into transformation engines called translets to which XML is fed, as shown in Figure 6.37. The Java API for XML Processing (JAXP) version 1.2 offers standard support for compiled transformations, using an XSLT compiler (XSLTC) [JAXP]. Compiled style sheets offer a performance boost for scenarios with repeated transformations. Additionally, compiled transformation engines are usually lighter weight than their interpretive counterparts, since the compiler need only generate code for the XSLT behavior that is explicitly referenced in the style sheet.

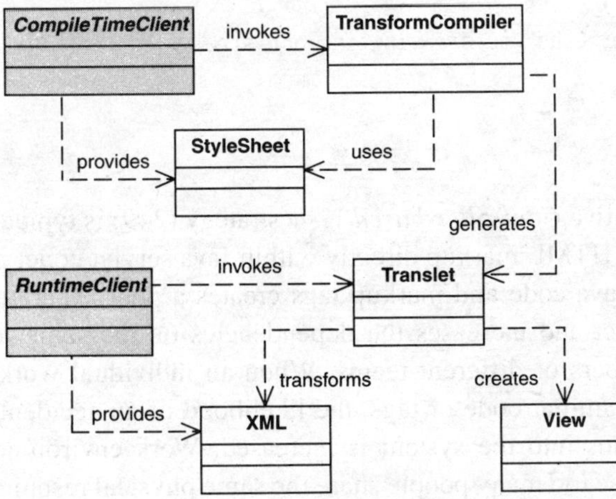

Figure 6.37 Using Translets

Strategies

Template-Based View Strategy

Using a template-based view such as JSP as the view component is referred to as a *Template-based View* strategy. This is the preferred strategy to the *Controller-based View* strategy (166), though the two strategies are semantically equivalent from a runtime perspective. The *Template-Based View* strategy helps enforce the division of labor and role separation between programmers and web designers.

Example 6.52 shows a code sample for this strategy. The excerpt is from a source file called welcome.jsp, to which a servlet controller dispatches after placing the WelcomeHelper JavaBean in request scope.

Example 6.52 Template-Based View Strategy

```
<jsp:useBean id="welcomeHelper" scope="request"
 class="corepatterns.util.WelcomeHelper" />

<HTML>
<BODY bgcolor="FFFFFF">
<c:if test = "${welcomeHelper.nameExists == true}">
<center><H3> Welcome <b>
<c:out value='${welcomeHelper.name}'/>
</b><br><br> </H3></center>
</c:if>


<H4><center>Glad you are visiting our site!</center></H4>

</BODY>
</HTML>
```

The alternative *Controller-based View* strategy (249) is typically implemented by embedding HTML markup directly within Java servlet code.

Mingling Java code and markup tags creates a poor separation of user roles within a project and increases the dependencies on the same resources among multiple members of different teams. When an individual works on a template containing unfamiliar code or tags, the likelihood of an accidental change introducing problems into the system is increased. Work environment efficiency is reduced because too many people share the same physical resource source control and management complexity increases.

These problems are more likely to occur in larger enterprise environments that have more complicated system requirements and that use teams of developers. They are less likely to occur with small systems that have simple business requirements and use few developers, because the same individual might fill the roles mentioned previously. However, keep in mind that projects often start small—with simple requirements and few developers—but can ultimately evolve to become sophisticated enough to benefit from these suggestions.

Controller-Based View Strategy

The *Controller-based View* strategy uses a servlet as the view. This strategy is semantically equivalent at runtime to the preferred template-based view strategy when using JSP, since JSP are translated to servlets by runtime. However, at development time, the controller-based view strategy is often more cumbersome for the software development and web production teams because it embeds markup tags directly within the Java code. When HTML tags are embedded within the Java code, the view template is more difficult to update and modify.

A similar approach, though not what is described within this strategy, is using a controller to **manage** view creation. This alternate approach has the controller coordinating a transformation engine with style sheets and an XML model to perform a *View Transform*.

Example 6.53 shows the *Controller-based View* manager strategy.

Example 6.53 Controller-Based View Manager Strategy

```
public class EmployeeListServlet extends HttpServlet {
  public void init(ServletConfig config) throws ServletException {
    super.init(config);
  }

  public void destroy() { }

  /** Processes requests for both HTTP
   * <code>GET</code> and <code>POST</code> methods.
   * @param request servlet request
   * @param response servlet response
   */
  protected void processRequest(
      HttpServletRequest request, HttpServletResponse response)
      throws ServletException, java.io.IOException {
    String title = "Controller-based View Strategy";
    try {
      response.setContentType("text/html");
```

```
      java.io.PrintWriter out = response.getWriter();
      out.println("<html><title>"+title+"</title>");
      out.println("<body>");
      out.println("<h2><center>Employees List</h2>");
      EmployeeDelegate delegate = new EmployeeDelegate();
      /** ApplicationResources provides a simple API for
       *  retrieving constants and other preconfigured values **/
      Iterator employees = delegate.getEmployees(
         ApplicationResources.getInstance().getAllDepartments());
      out.println("<table border=2>");
      out.println("<tr><th>First Name</th>" +
         "<th>Last Name</th>" +
         "<th>Designation</th><th>Id</th></tr>");
      while (employees.hasNext()) {
         out.println("<tr>");
         EmployeeTO emp = (EmployeeTO)employees.next();
         out.println("<td>" + emp.getFirstName() + "</td>");
         out.println("<td>" + emp.getLastName() + "</td>");
         out.println("<td>" + emp.getDesignation() + "</td>");
         out.println("<td>" + emp.getId() + "</td>");
         out.println("</tr>");
      }
      out.println("</table>");
      out.println("<br><br>");
      out.println("</body>");
      out.println("</html>");
      out.close();
    }
    catch (Exception e) {
      LogManager.logMessage("Handle this exception",
        e.getMessage() );
    }
  }

  /** Handles the HTTP <code>GET</code> method.
   *  @param request servlet request
   *  @param response servlet response
   */
  protected void doGet(HttpServletRequest request,
      HttpServletResponse response)
      throws ServletException, java.io.IOException {
       processRequest(request, response);
  }
```

```
    /** Handles the HTTP <code>POST</code> method.
      * @param request servlet request
      * @param response servlet response
      */
    protected void doPost(HttpServletRequest request,
        HttpServletResponse response)
        throws ServletException, java.io.IOException {
      processRequest(request, response);
    }

    /** Returns a short description of the servlet. */
    public String getServletInfo() {
      return "Example of Servlet View. " + "JSP View is preferable.";
    }

    /** dispatcher method **/
    protected void dispatch(HttpServletRequest request,
        HttpServletResponse response, String page)
        throws javax.servlet.ServletException, java.io.IOException {
      RequestDispatcher dispatcher =
        getServletContext().getRequestDispatcher(page);
      dispatcher.forward(request, response);
    }
}
```

JavaBean Helper Strategy

The helper is implemented as a JavaBean. Using helpers results in a cleaner separation of the view from the business, processing, and formatting logic in an application, since this logic is factored out of the view and into the helper components.

Using the *JavaBean Helper* strategy requires less upfront work than the *Custom Tag Helper* strategy, since JavaBeans are more easily constructed and integrated into a JSP environment. Additionally, even novice developers understand JavaBeans. This strategy is also easier to manage since the only resulting artifacts are the completed JavaBeans. An example of this strategy is shown in Example 6.54.

Example 6.54 JavaBean Helper Strategy

```
<jsp:useBean id="welcomeHelper" scope="request"
 class="corepatterns.util.WelcomeHelper" />

```

```
<HTML>
<BODY bgcolor="FFFFFF">
<c:if test = "${welcomeHelper.nameExists == true}">
<center><H3> Welcome <b>
<c:out value='${welcomeHelper.name}'/>
</b><br><br> </H3></center>
</c:if>
<H4><center>Glad you are visiting our site!</center></H4>
</BODY>
</HTML>
```

The problem with this strategy is that it is difficult to effectively extract implementation details from the view.

Custom Tag Helper Strategy

The helper is implemented as a custom tag, which adapts the model for use by the view.

Using the *Custom Tag Helper* strategy requires more upfront work than the *JavaBean Helper* strategy, since custom tag development is moderately complicated. Writing custom tags instead of writing JavaBeans not only adds complexity to the development process, but also to the task of integrating and managing the completed code. The benefit of using custom tags is their flexibility and extensibility.

To use this strategy, you need to configure the environment with numerous artifacts, including the tag itself, a tag library descriptor, and configuration files. An excerpt of a JSP view using this strategy is shown in Example 6.55.

Example 6.55 Custom Tag Helper Strategy

```
<%@ taglib uri="/web-INF/corepatternstaglibrary.tld"
 prefix="corepatterns" %>
<html>
<head><title>Employee List</title></head>
<body>
<div align="center">
<h3> List of employees in <corepatterns:department attribute="id"/>
 department - Using Custom Tag Helper Strategy. </h3>
<table border="1" >
```

```
    <tr>
        <th> First Name </th>
        <th> Last Name </th>
        <th> Designation </th>
        <th> Employee Id </th>
        <th> Tax Deductibles </th>
        <th> Performance Remarks </th>
        <th> Yearly Salary</th>
    </tr>
    <corepatterns:employeelist id="employeelist_key">
    <tr>
        <td><corepatterns:employee attribute="FirstName"/> </td>
        <td><corepatterns:employee attribute="LastName"/></td>
        <td><corepatterns:employee attribute="Designation"/> </td>
        <td><corepatterns:employee attribute="Id"/></td>
        <td><corepatterns:employee attribute="NoOfDeductibles"/></td>
        <td><corepatterns:employee attribute="PerformanceRemarks"/></td>
        <td><corepatterns:employee attribute="YearlySalary"/></td>
        <td>
     </tr>
    </corepatterns:employeelist>
</table>
</div>
</body>
</html>
```

Design Note: Implementation versus Intent

Starting with version 2.0, JSP offers some powerful features that directly address the design goal of separating control code, business logic, and formatting processing logic from the view. Two important aspects of the specification that support this goal are tag files and the Expression Language (EL). (See http://java.sun.com/jsp.)

These features support several of the implementation strategies described in the patterns. One of the main benefits of using helpers to extract programming code and processing logic from template markup is to provide improved separation of control and model logic from the view. An important way to assess the effectiveness of this separation is to ask how well the remaining helper code, embedded within the template, exposes its **intent** versus its **implementation**.

For example, assume you have scriptlet code that performs some conditional checks, and then loops through a collection of results and generates an HTML table. You could extract that code into a custom tag helper that performs the same processing, but hides the details within the tag itself.

On the other hand, it is not unusual for that scriptlet code to be replaced with semantically equivalent tags, such as an <IF> tag or a <ForEach> tag. In this case, while the resulting markup is cleaner since it no longer mingles scriptlet code with markup, the substituted tags are semantically equivalent and therefore expose the same implementation details.

In effect, one programming language was simply replaced with another and the same implementation details are exposed. Using helpers as scriptlets is poor form but is acceptable in limited usage. A powerful strategy to avoid this problem is to use a tag file helper.

Tag File Helper Strategy

If most or all the tags that are used within a JSP view are semantically equivalent to the Java scriptlets that they are replacing, then, in effect, one programming language is being replaced with another and the implementation details of the code continue to be exposed within the view. Tag files offer a solution to this problem of exposing too many implementation details within your markup by allowing reusable code to be extracted into a handler without your having to write a custom tag. Tag files are also much easier to configure and deploy than custom tags, since there are fewer artifacts to maintain.

However, make sure non-technical team members know that while creating a tag file is quite easy, understanding the key abstractions and the best ways to implement those abstractions is not. Continue to preserve the appropriate role separation within the team.

For instance, Example 6.56, extracted from a JSP, uses JSTL tags. It is an improvement over using scriptlet code, but still exposes the implementation details of the HTML table creation.

Example 6.56 Using JSTL, example.jsp

```
<%-- example.jsp --%>
<%-- note: this example uses JSTL (URL ref) --%>

<table>
<c:forEach var="product" items="${products}" varStatus="status">
<tr>
  <td><c:out value="${status.count}"/></td>
  <td><c:out value="${product.name}"/></td>
</tr>
</c:forEach>
</table>

```

Introducing a tag file and using the Expression Language (EL), which is integrated into JSP 2.0 and beyond, improves the code in the JSP. Doing so more clearly exposes the intent of the code and hides the implementation, as shown in Example 6.57.

Example 6.57 Using Tag File and EL, example.jsp

```
<%-- example.jsp --%>
<%-- Using a tag file with the EL--%>

  <%@ taglib prefix="tag" tagdir="/web-INF/tags/" %>

  <tag:buildtable products="${products}"/>

```

The tag file, buildtable.tag, is placed in the /web-INF/tags directory and the container automatically generates a tag handler to produce the expected output. The buildtable.tag file is shown in Example 6.58.

Example 6.58 Tag File, buildtable.tag

```
<%-- /web-INF/tags/buildtable.tag --%>
<%@ attribute name="products" type="java.util.Collection" %>
<%@ taglib prefix="c" uri="http://java.sun.com/jstl/core" %>
<table>
  <c:forEach var="product" items="${products}" varStatus="status">
    <tr>
      <td><c:out value="${status.count}"/></td>
      <td><c:out value="${product.name}"/></td>
    </tr>
  </c:forEach>
</table>
```

Business Delegate as Helper Strategy

Helper components often make invocations to a remote business tier. Use a *Business Delegate* (302) to hide the underlying implementation details of this request. The helper simply invokes a business service without knowing the details about its physical implementation and distribution.

One could combine the notion of the helper component and the *Business Delegate* (302), since both are implemented as POJOs, and you might not need to add yet another layer to your application. One major distinction between a helper and a *Business Delegate* (302), though, is as follows: A helper component is written by a developer working in the presentation tier, while the delegate is typically written by a developer working on the services in the business tier. The delegate might also be provided as part of a framework. This means that this strategy is as much about who actually writes the delegate as it is about the implementation.

If there is some overlap in developer roles, then consider using the *Business Delegate as Helper Strategy* (255).

Design Note: Helpers

JavaBean helpers are used as command objects (see *Front Controller, Command and Controller Strategy* on page 174), for storing an intermediate model (see *Transfer Object* (415)), and for adapting this model for the view (see *Application Controller* on page 205).

Like JavaBean helpers, custom tag helpers can fulfill each of these roles, except for acting as a command object. Unlike JavaBean helpers, custom tag helpers are well suited to control flow and iteration within a view. Custom tag helpers used in this way encapsulate logic that would otherwise be embedded directly within the JSP as scriptlet code.

Tag files (JSP 2.0+) are another way to achieve the same goal as using custom tags, but without having to go through the programming effort associated with developing a tag (see *Tag File Helper Strategy* on page 254). Custom tag helpers and tag file helpers are collectively referred to as **tag helpers**.

Another area where tag helpers are preferred is adapting and formatting raw data for display. For example, a tag can iterate over a collection of results, format those results into an HTML table, and embed the table within a JSP view without requiring any Java scriptlet code.

Consider an example in which a web client is requesting account information from a system, as shown in Figure 6.38.

There are two JavaBean helpers shown in this diagram; the AccountCommand object and the AccountBO object. The TableFormatter object is a custom tag helper.

The *Front Controller* (166) handles the request and delegates to a *Application Controller* (205). The *Application Controller* (205) obtains the appropriate command object, using its *Command Handler* strategy (209). In this case, the command object processes requests for account information. The controller invokes the command object, which asks a *Business Object* (374) for information about the account. The *Business Object* (374) uses its persistence mechanism to request these details from a database. Once the data has been retrieved, the *Application Controller* (205) resolves and dispatches to the appropriate view, using its *View Handler* strategy (213).

So how do the helpers and command objects interact with a *Business Object* (374) and how does the *Business Object* (374) interact with the database? Let's take a look at two cases, one simpler and the other more sophisticated.

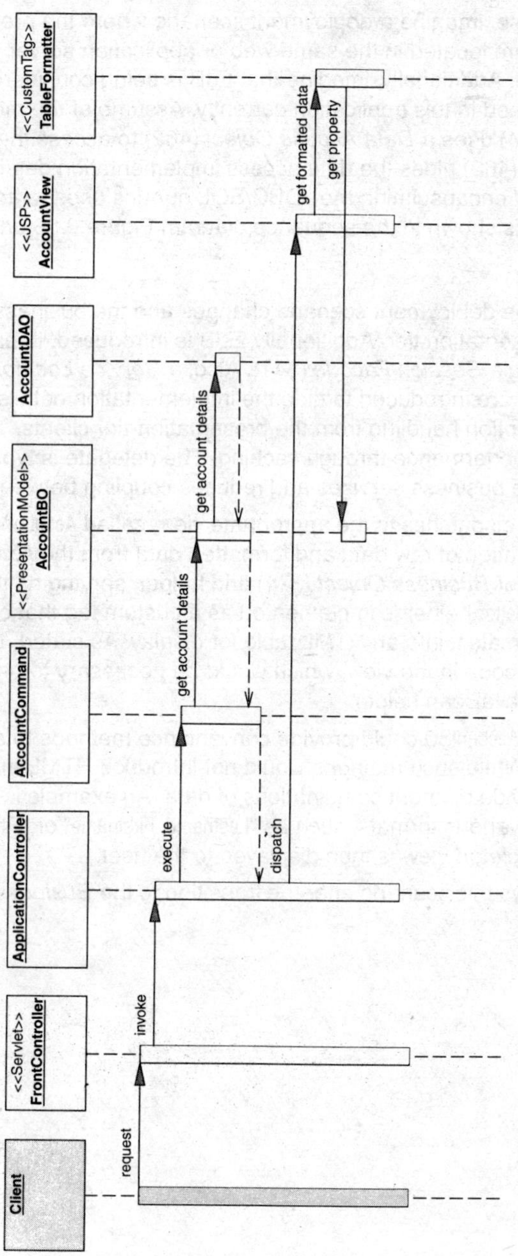

Figure 6.38 Using Helpers – Non-Remote Business Tier

Simple Case

In the simpler case, imagine a deployment scenario where the presentation tier and a business tier are located in the same web or application server and share the same process space. Additionally, imagine that EJB is being considered for future projects, but is not used in this application currently. Assume at the moment that the *Business Object* (374) uses a *Data Access Object* (462) to access the database. The *Data Access Object* (462) hides the data access implementation details from the *Business Object* (374) by encapsulating the JDBC/SQL queries used to access the database. This scenario is shown in the sequence diagram Figure 6.36 on page 247.

More Complex Case

At some point, the deployment scenario changes and the business tier is now remote from the presentation tier. Additionally, EJB is introduced, in part to bridge the distributed tiers using a *Session Façade* (341). Also, a *Service Locator* (315) and *Business Delegate* (302) are introduced to hide the implementation details of EJB lookup, invocation, and exception handling from the presentation-tier clients. The delegate might also improve performance through caching. The delegate is typically written by the developers of the business services and reduces coupling between tiers.

The FrontController dispatches to the appropriate view, called AccountView.jsp. The view then grabs a combination of raw data and formatted data from the AccountBO, which serves the dual role of *Business Object* (374) and helper, serving as the presentation model. The TableFormatter helper is implemented as a custom tag that cycles through the raw data and formats it into an HTML table for display. As stated, this conversion requires no scriptlet code in the view, which would be necessary to perform the same functionality with a JavaBean helper.

Additionally, the AccountBO could provide convenience methods to adapt the raw data in other ways. While such methods would not introduce HTML markup into the data, they might provide different combinations of data. An example is to return the full name of the user in various formats, such as "Lastname, Firstname" or "Firstname Lastname", and so on. The completed view is then displayed to the user.

Figure 6.39 shows this scenario after the transition to the *Business Delegate* (302).

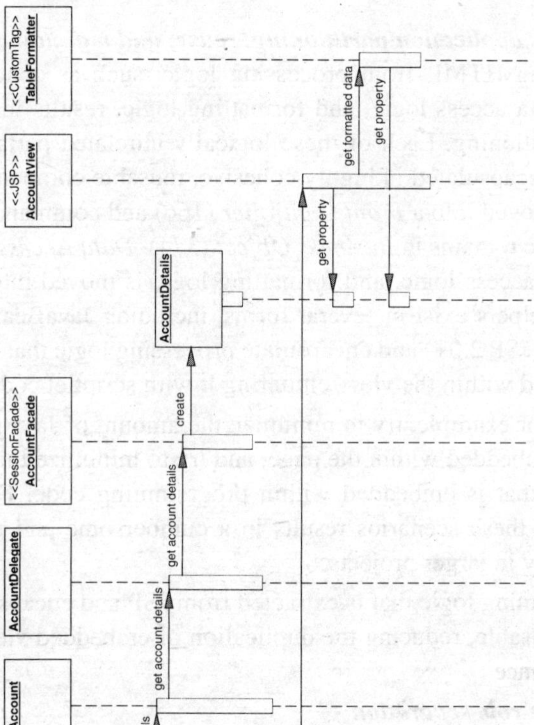

Figure 6.39 Using helpers – Remote Business Tier

Consequences

- ***Improves application partitioning, reuse, and maintainability***
  Separating HTML from processing logic, such as control logic, business logic, data access logic, and formatting logic, results in improved application partitioning. Each of these logically unrelated parts of the application can be encapsulated in highly cohesive, reusable components. Control logic can be moved into a *Front Controller* (166) and command helpers, and business logic remains in *Business Object* (374). *Data Access ObjectS.* (462) get the data access logic, and formatting logic is moved into tag helpers. As a result, helpers exist in several forms, including JavaBeans, custom tags, or tag files (JSP 2.0+) and encapsulate processing logic that might otherwise be embedded within the view, cluttering it with scriptlet code.

  In JSP, for example, try to minimize the amount of Java programming logic that is embedded within the page, and try to minimize the amount of HTML markup that is embedded within programming code. Failing to minimize either of these scenarios results in a cumbersome and unwieldy situation, especially in larger projects.

  Programming logic that is extracted from JSP and encapsulated within helpers is reusable, reducing the duplication of embedded view code and easing maintenance.

- ***Improves role separation***
  Using helpers to separate processing logic from views also reduces the potential dependencies that individuals fulfilling different roles might have on the same resources. For example, if processing logic is embedded within a view, then a software developer is tasked with maintaining code that is embedded within HTML markup. Then, a web production team member would need to modify page layout and design components that are mingled with Java code. Neither individual fulfilling these roles is likely to be familiar with the implementation specifics of the other individual's work, raising the likelihood of accidental modifications introducing bugs into the system.

- ***Eases testing***
  As processing logic is extracted into separate helper components, testing individual pieces of code becomes much easier. Testing a piece of code that is embedded within a JSP is much more difficult than testing code that is encapsulated within a separate class.

- ***Helper usage mirrors scriptlets***
  One important reason for extracting processing logic from a page is to reduce the implementation details that are embedded directly within the page. It is important to keep in mind, though, that it is not a panacea to simply use JavaBeans or custom tags within your JSP. The use of certain generic helpers only replaces the embedded Java code with a references to helpers that, in effect, produce the same problem of exposing the **implementation details**, as opposed to the **intent** of the code.

  An example is the use of a conditional helper, such as a custom tag that models the conditional logic of an 'if' statement. Heavy usage of this sort of helper tag may simply mirror the scriptlet code that it is intended to replace. As a result, the resulting fragment continues to look like programming logic embedded within the page. Using helpers as scriptlets is a bad practice, although it is often done in an attempt to apply *View Helper.*

Related Patterns

- ***Front Controller (166)***
  A *Front Controller* (166) typically delegates to an *Application Controller* (205), to perform action and view management.
- ***Application Controller (205)***
  An *Application Controller* (205) manages view preparation and view creation, delegating to views and helpers.
- ***View Transform (246)***
  An alternative approach to view creation is to perform a *View Transform*.
- ***Business Delegate (302)***
  A *Business Delegate* (302) reduces the coupling between a helper object and a remote business service, upon which the helper object can invoke.

Composite View

Problem

You want to build a view from modular, atomic component parts that are combined to create a composite whole, while managing the content and the layout independently.

Developing and maintaining dynamic views is challenging, since there are often aspects of both the view content and the view layout that are common across multiple views. When content and layout are intertwined, it is harder to maintain and extend the views. Reuse and modularity also suffer when common code is duplicated across views.

Forces

- You want common subviews, such as headers, footers and tables reused in multiple views, which may appear in different locations within each page layout.
- You have content in subviews which might which frequently change or might be subject to certain access controls, such as limiting access to users in certain roles.
- You want to avoid directly embedding and duplicating subviews in multiple views which makes layout changes difficult to manage and maintain.

Solution

Use *Composite Views* that are composed of multiple atomic subviews. Each subview of the overall template can be included dynamically in the whole, and the layout of the page can be managed independently of the content.

Composite Views are based on the inclusion and substitution of modular dynamic and static template fragments. *Composite Views* promote the reuse of atomic portions of the view by encouraging modular design. It is appropriate to use a *Composite View* to generate pages containing display components that can be combined in a variety of ways.

This scenario occurs, for example, with portal sites that include numerous independent subviews, such as news feeds, weather information, and stock quotes on a single page. The layout of the page is managed and modified independently of the subview content.

Another benefit of this pattern is that web designers can prototype the layout of a site, plugging static content into each of the template regions. As site development progresses, the actual content is substituted for these placeholders. This approach provides improved modularity and reusability, as well as improved maintainability.

Figure 6.40 shows Sun's Java home page, java.sun.com. Four regions are identified: Navigation, Search, Feature Story, and Headlines. While the content for each of these component subviews might originate from different data sources, they are laid out seamlessly to create a single composite page.

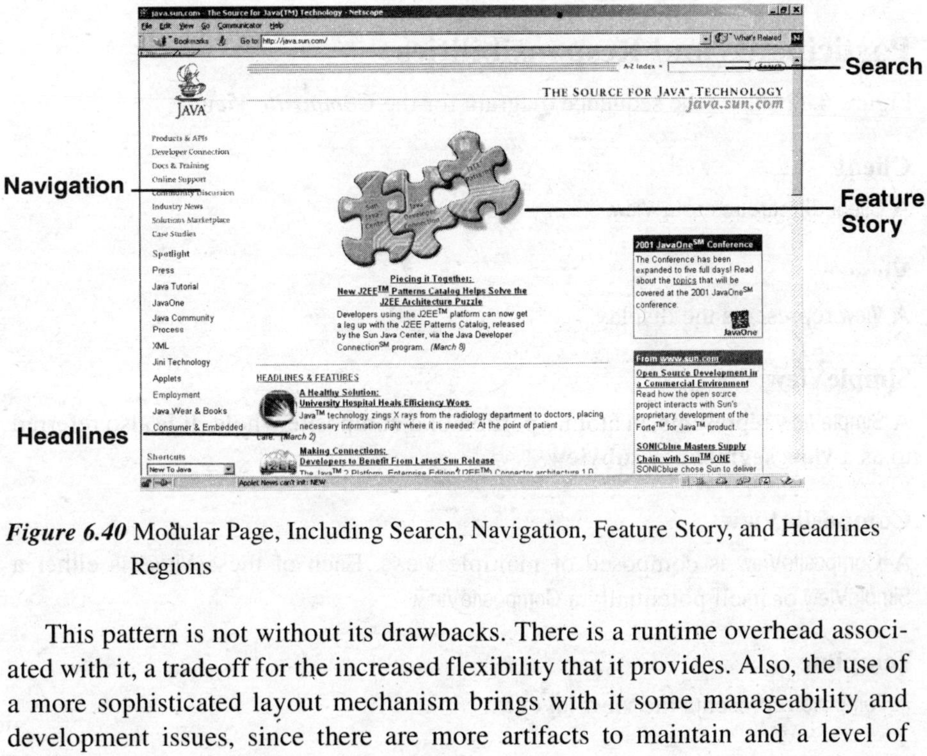

Figure 6.40 Modular Page, Including Search, Navigation, Feature Story, and Headlines Regions

This pattern is not without its drawbacks. There is a runtime overhead associated with it, a tradeoff for the increased flexibility that it provides. Also, the use of a more sophisticated layout mechanism brings with it some manageability and development issues, since there are more artifacts to maintain and a level of implementation indirection to understand.

Structure

Figure 6.41 shows the class diagram that represents the *Composite View*.

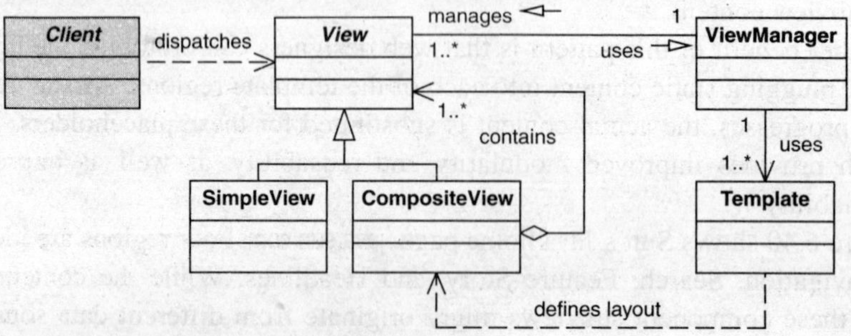

Figure 6.41 Composite View Class Diagram

Participants and Responsibilities

Figure 6.42 shows the sequence diagram for the *Composite View.*

Client

A Client dispatches to a View.

View

A View represents the display.

SimpleView

A SimpleView represents an atomic portion of a composite whole. It is also referred to as a **view segment** or **subview.**

CompositeView

A CompositeView is composed of multiple Views. Each of these Views is either a SimpleView or itself potentially a CompositeView.

Template

A Template represents the view layout.

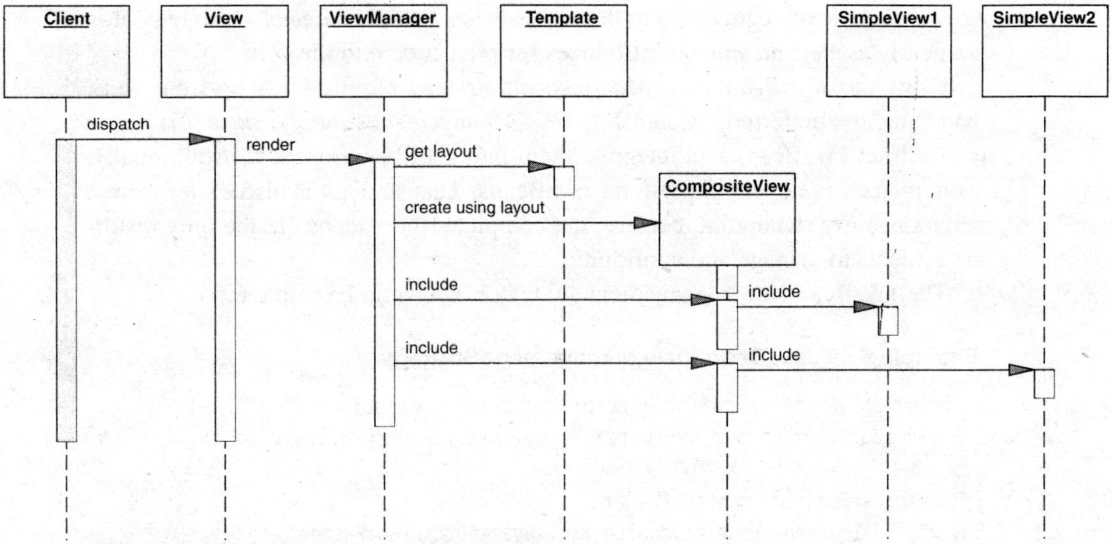

Figure 6.42 *Composite View* Sequence Diagram

ViewManager

A ViewManager uses a Template to enforce a layout into which it places the appropriate content, allowing a ViewManager to manage content and layout independently.

A simple ViewManager might use the standard JSP include tag (<jsp:include>) to include SimpleView segments into a Template.

Alternatively, a more sophisticated ViewManager might use POJOs or custom tag helpers to provide content and layout management in a more comprehensive and robust manner. Using POJOs or custom tags makes conditional inclusion easier to accomplish. For example, certain view segments may be included only if the user maps to a particular role or certain system conditions are satisfied. Furthermore, using helper components for view management allows for more sophisticated control of the page structure as a whole, which is useful for creating reusable page layouts.

Strategies

JavaBean View Management Strategy

Content and layout management is implemented using JavaBeans and JSP standard tags, as shown in Example 6.60. The view delegates to a JavaBean, which implements the custom logic to control view layout and composition. The decisions on page layout can be based on user roles or security policies, making it much more powerful than the standard JSP include functionality. While this strategy is semantically equivalent to the *Custom Tag View Management* strategy, it is not nearly as elegant, since it introduces scriptlet code into the view.

Using the *JavaBean View Management* strategy requires less up-front work than using the preferred *Custom Tag View Management* strategy, since it is easier to construct JavaBeans and integrate them into a JSP environment. Additionally, even novice developers understand JavaBeans. This strategy is also easier from a maintainability standpoint, because the completed JavaBeans are the only resulting artifacts to manage and configure.

The JavaBean view management strategy is shown in Example 6.60.

Example 6.59 JavaBean View Management Strategy

```
<%@ taglib prefix="c" uri="http://java.sun.com/jstl/core" %>
<%@ taglib uri="/web-INF/corej2eetaglibrary.tld" prefix="cjp" %>

<jsp:useBean id="contentFeeder"
 class="corepatterns.compositeview.javabean.ContentFeeder"
 scope="request" />

<table valign="top" cellpadding="30%"  width="100%">

    <cjp:personalizer interest='global'>
        <tr>
            <td><B><c:out value="${contentFeeder.worldNews}"/></B></td>
        </tr>
    </cjp:personalizer>

    <cjp:personalizer interest='technology'>
        <tr>
            <td>
                <U><c:out value="${contentFeeder.technologyNews}"/></U>
            </td>
        </tr>
    </cjp:personalizer>

    <cjp:personalizer interest='weird'>
        <tr>
            <td><I><c:out value="${contentFeeder.weirdNews}"/></I></td>
        </tr>
    </cjp:personalizer>
```

```
       <cjp:personalizer interest='astronomy'>
           <tr>
               <td><c:out value="${contentFeeder.astronomyNews}"/></td>
           </tr>
       </cjp:personalizer>
   </table>
```

With the introduction of the JSTL [JSTL] and Expression Language (EL) [JSTL, JSP], the flow control within the view is performed by the JSTL tags and the EL, while the JavaBean becomes a stateholder. When using this strategy, it is important to avoid overly *Using Helpers as Scriptlets*.

Standard Tag View Management Strategy

View management is implemented using standard JSP tags, such as the <jsp:include> tag. Using standard tags for managing the layout and composition of views is an easy strategy to implement. However, it does not provide the power and flexibility of the preferred *Custom Tag View Management* strategy, since the layout for individual pages remains embedded within that page. This means that while this strategy allows the underlying content to vary dynamically, any site-wide layout changes would require individual modifications to numerous JSP.

This strategy is shown in Example 6.60.

Example 6.60 Standard Tag View Management Strategy

```
<html>
<body>
<jsp:include
  page="/jsp/CompositeView/javabean/banner.seg" flush="true"/>
<table width="100%">
  <tr align="left" valign="middle">
    <td width="20%">
      <jsp:include page="/jsp/CompositeView/javabean/ProfilePane.jsp"
           flush="true"/>
    </td>
    <td width="70%" align="center">
      <jsp:include page="/jsp/CompositeView/javabean/mainpanel.jsp"
           lush="true"/>
    </td>
  </tr>
</table>
```

```
<jsp:include page="/jsp/CompositeView/javabean/footer.seg"
      flush="true"/>
</body>
</html>
```

When you create a composite display using standard tags, you can include both static content, such as an HTML file, and dynamic content, such as a JSP. Additionally, the content can be included at translation time or at runtime.

If the content is included at translation time, then the page display will remain unchanged until the JSP is recompiled, at which point any modifications to included content will be visible. In other words, the page is laid out and generated once, each time the JSP is recompiled.

Example 6.61 shows an excerpt of a JSP that generates a composite page in this way, using the standard JSP include directive <%@ include %>, which includes content at translation time.

Runtime inclusion of content means that changes to underlying subviews are visible in the composite page the next time a client accesses the page. This is much more dynamic and can be accomplished using the standard JSP include tag <jsp:include>, as shown in Example 6.62. There is of course some runtime overhead associated with this type of view generation, but it is the tradeoff for the increased flexibility of on-the-fly content modifications.

Example 6.61 Composite View with Translation-Time Content inclusion

```
<table border=1 valign="top" cellpadding="2%" width="100%">
    <tr>
      <td><%@ include file="news/worldnews.html" %> </td>
    </tr>
    <tr>
      <td><%@ include file="news/countrynews.html" %> </td>
    </tr>
    <tr>
      <td><%@ include file="news/customnews.html" %> </td>
    </tr>
    <tr>
      <td><%@ include file="news/astronomy.html" %> </td>
    </tr>
</table>
```

Example 6.62 Composite View With Runtime Content Inclusion

```
<table border=1 valign="top" cellpadding="2%" width="100%">
    <tr>
        <td><jsp:include page="news/worldnews.jsp" flush="true"/> </td>
    </tr>
    <tr>
        <td><jsp:include page="news/countrynews.jsp" flush="true"/></td>
    </tr>
    <tr>
        <td><jsp:include page="news/customnews.jsp" flush="true"/> </td>
    </tr>
    <tr>
        <td><jsp:include page="news/astronomy.jsp" flush="true"/> </td>
    </tr>
</table>
```

Custom Tag View Management Strategy

A *View Manager*, which performs content and layout management, is implemented using custom tags. This is the preferred strategy for implementing *Composite View.* Tags handle page content and layout in a more powerful and flexible manner than can be achieved using the standard JSP include tag, but also require a higher level of effort. Using this strategy, you can easily base page layout on such things as user roles or security policies.

Using this strategy requires more upfront work than the other view management strategies, since custom tag development is more complicated than simply using JavaBeans or standard tags. Not only is there more complexity in the development process, but there is much more complexity with respect to integrating and managing the completed tags. Using this strategy requires creating numerous artifacts, including the tag itself, a tag library descriptor, configuration files, and configuring the environment with these artifacts. However, using this strategy is much less complex if you use an existing third-party tag library.

The JSP excerpt in Example 6.63 shows a possible implementation using a third-party library. Please refer to that code sample for more detail. The region tag acts as a view manager, using a template to provide a specific layout and populating the logical sections of that template with the appropriate content.

Example 6.63 JSP Excerpt Using Third-Party Library

```
<region:render template='/jsp/CompositeView/templates/portal.jsp'>

    <region:put section='banner'
     content='/jsp/CompositeView/templates/banner.jsp' />

    <region:put section='controlpanel'
     content='/jsp/CompositeView/templates/ProfilePane.jsp' />

    <region:put section='mainpanel'
     content='/jsp/CompositeView/templates/mainpanel.jsp' />

    <region:put section='footer'
     content='/jsp/CompositeView/templates/footer.jsp' />

</region:render>
```

Transformer View Management Strategy

View management is implemented using an XSL transformer. This strategy would typically be combined with the *Custom Tag View Management* strategy, using custom tags to implement and delegate to the appropriate components. In effect, one or more *View Transforms* are embedded within the page to help create the composite whole. The following excerpt shows the use of a custom tag from within a JSP to convert a model using a stylesheet and transformer:

```
<xsl:transform model="portfolioHelper"
      stylesheet="/transform/styles/generalPortfolio.xsl"/>
```

Of course, the transformation could be abstracted behind a helper that would more clearly communicate the intent of the transformation, as opposed to exposing its implementation directly within the view, as follows:

```
<finance:renderPortfolio type="General" model="portfolioHelper" />
```

Early-Binding Resource Strategy

This is another name for translation-time content inclusion, as described in the *Standard Tag View Management* strategy and shown in Example 6.62 on page 269. It is appropriate for maintaining and updating a relatively static template and is recommended if a view includes headers and footers that change infrequently.

Late-Binding Resource Strategy

This is another name for runtime-content inclusion, as described in the *Standard Tag View Management* strategy and shown in Example 6.63 on page 270. It is appropriate for composite pages whose content might change frequently.

DESIGN NOTE: DYNAMIC RESOURCE SUBVIEWS

If the subview included at runtime is a dynamic resource, such as a JSP, then this subview might also be a *Composite View*, including more runtime content. Weigh the flexibility offered by such nested composite structures against their runtime overhead and consider it in light of specific project requirements.

Consequences

- ***Improves modularity and reuse***
  The pattern promotes modular design. It is possible to reuse atomic portions of a template, such as a table of stock quotes, in numerous views, and to decorate these reused portions with different information. This pattern permits the table to be moved into its own module and simply included where necessary. This type of dynamic layout and composition reduces duplication, fosters reuse, and improves maintainability.
- ***Adds role-based or policy-based control***
  A *Composite View* might conditionally include view template fragments based on runtime decisions, such as user role or security policy.
- ***Enhances maintainability***
  Managing changes to portions of a template is much more efficient when the template is not hardcoded directly into the view markup. When the template content is kept separate from the view, you can modify modular portions of template content independently of the template layout. Additionally, these changes are available to the client immediately, depending on the implementation strategy. You can more easily manage modifications to page layout as well, since changes are centralized.
- ***Reduces maintainability***
  Aggregating atomic pieces of the display to create a single view introduces the potential for display errors, since subviews are page fragments. This is a limitation that can become a maintainability issue. For example, if a JSP is generating an HTML page using a main page that includes three subviews, and the subviews each include the HTML open and close tag (that is, <HTML> and </HTML>), then the composed page will be invalid. When you use this

pattern, be aware that subviews must not be complete views. You must account for tag usage quite strictly in order to create valid *Composite Views*, and this can become a maintainability issue.

- ***Reduces performance***
  Generating a display that includes numerous subviews might slow performance. Runtime inclusion of subviews will result in a delay each time the page is served to the client. In environments that have specific response times requirements, such performance slowdowns, though typically extremely minimal, might not be acceptable. An alternative is to move the subview inclusion to translation time, though this limits the subview to changing only when the page is retranslated.

Sample Code

The most powerful implementation strategy for *Composite View* is the *Custom Tag View Management* strategy. In fact, several custom tag libraries are currently available for implementing *Composite Views* in this way. These libraries provide view management that separates layout from content and provides for modular, pluggable subviews.

This sample uses a template library written by David Geary and featured in detail in “Advanced JavaServer Pages” [Geary].

The template library describes three basic components: **sections**, **regions**, and **templates**.

- A section is a reusable component that renders HTML or JSP.
- A region describes content by defining sections.
- A template controls the layout of regions and sections in a rendered page.

Example 6.64 shows one way to define and render a region.

Example 6.64 A Region and Sections

```
<region:render template='portal.jsp'>
    <region:put section='banner'       content='banner.jsp' />
    <region:put section='controlpanel' content='ProfilePane.jsp' />
    <region:put section='mainpanel'    content='mainpanel.jsp' />
    <region:put section='footer'       content='footer.jsp' />
</region:render>
```

A region defines its content by matching logical section names with a portion of content, such as banner.jsp.

The layout for the region and its sections is defined by a template, to which each region is associated. In this case, the template is named portal.jsp, as defined in Example 6.65.

Example 6.65 Template Definition

```
<region:render section='banner'/>
<table width="100%">
    <tr align="left" valign="middle">
        <td width="20%">
            <!-- menu region -->
            <region:render section='controlpanel' />
        </td>
        <td width="70%" align="center">
            <!-- contents -->
            <region:render section='mainpanel' />
        </td>
    </tr>
</table>
</region:render>
```

A site with numerous views and a single consistent layout has one JSP containing code that looks similar to the template definition in Example 6.66, and many JSP that look similar to Example 6.65, defining alternate regions and sections. Sections are JSP fragments that are used as subviews to build a composite whole as defined by a template. The banner.jsp section is shown in Example 6.66.

Example 6.66 Section Subview – banner.jsp

```
<table width="100%" bgcolor="#C0C0C0">
<tr align="left" valign="middle">
  <td width="100%">

    <TABLE ALIGN="left" BORDER=1 WIDTH="100%">
    <TR ALIGN="left" VALIGN="middle">
      <TD>Logo</TD>
      <TD><center>Sun Java Center</TD>
    </TR>
    </TABLE>

  </td>
</tr>
</table>
```

The *Custom Tag View Management* strategy is arguably the most powerful strategy for the *Composite View* design pattern, because—like the *Transformer View Management* strategy—it encapsulates page layout. Encapsulating layout makes it easy to modify and reuse. However, encapsulating layout is just the beginning. Because the *Custom Tag View Management* strategy uses JSP custom tags, you can easily add desirable features, such as:

- Conditionally including content based on a user's role
- Nesting one region inside another
- Defining regions that inherit from other regions

The Regions Tag Library discussed in this section provides the features listed previously, as Example 6.67, through Example 6.69 illustrate.

Example 6.67 Role-based Content

```
<region:render template='portal.jsp'>
  <region:put section='banner' content='banner.jsp' role='customer'/>
</region:render>
```

In Example 6.68, the portal shows its banner to customers.

Example 6.68 Nested Regions

```
<region:define id='BANNER' template='twoColumns.jsp'>
    <region:put section='logo' content='logo.jsp'/>

    <region:put section='advertisement' content='advertisement.jsp'/>
</region:define>
...
<region:define id="PORTAL" template='portal.jsp'>
    <region:put section='banner' content='BANNER'/>
  ...
    <region:put section='footer' content='footer.jsp'/>
</region:render>
```

In Example 6.69, two regions are defined: a portal and a banner. The PORTAL region puts the BANNER region in its banner section. (The Regions library lets you define regions with <region:define>.)

Example 6.69 Extending Regions

```
<region:define id='PORTAL' template='portal.jsp'>
    <region:put section='banner' content='BANNER'/>
  ...
    <region:put section='footer' content='footer.jsp'/>
</region:render>

<region:define id='PORTAL_WITH_SPECIAL_FOOTER' region='PORTAL'>
    <region:put section='footer' content='specialfooter.jsp'/>
</region:define>
```

Example 6.69 also defines two regions: a portal, and a portal with a special footer. All of the regions defined in the PORTAL region are inherited by the PORTAL_WITH_SPECIAL_FOOTER region except for the footer region, which PORTAL_WITH_SPECIAL_FOOTER overrides.

Composite Views are a modular, flexible, and extensible way to build JSP views for your J2EE application.

Related Patterns

- ***View Helper (240)***
  A *Composite View* can fulfill the role of View in *View Helper* (240).
- ***Composite [GoF]***
  A *Composite View* is based on *Composite* [GoF], which describes part-whole hierarchies where a composite object is composed of numerous subparts.

Service to Worker

Problem

You want to perform core request handling and invoke business logic before control is passed to the view.

In certain use cases, business and the data services are invoked before the view is rendered. For any particular request, the answers to the following questions provide insight into how much work needs to be done during the **view preparation** phase of request processing.

- How sophisticated is the control logic?
- How dynamic is the response content?
- How sophisticated is the business logic and model?

Forces

- You want specific business logic executed to service a request in order to retrieve content that will be used to generate a dynamic response.
- You have view selections which may depend on responses from business service invocations.
- You may have to use a framework or library in the application.

Solution

Use *Service to Worker* to centralize control and request handling to retrieve a presentation model before turning control over to the view. The view generates a dynamic response based on the presentation model.

Service to Worker is composed of several other patterns. Centralized control, request handling, and view creation are accomplished using *Front Controller* (166), *Application Controller* (205), and *View Helper* (240) respectively.

Service to Worker and *Dispatcher View* (288) represent the two most common presentation usage scenarios. While *Service to Worker* is a controller-centric architecture, *Dispatcher View* (288) is a view-centric architecture. Unlike *Service to Worker*, *Dispatcher View* (288) defers business processing until view processing is performed.

Here's an example of a typical *Service to Worker* use case. A client submits a request to a controller with a query parameter that describes an action to be completed:

```
http://some.server.com/Controller?action=login
```

A *Front Controller* (166) deals with the network-specific protocol elements of the request. The controller then delegates to an *Application Controller* (205), passing along a newly created *Context Object* (181). The *Application Controller* (205) acts as a *Command Handler* (209), mapping the logical name login to the appropriate command, such as LoginCmd, and invoking that command.

DESIGN NOTE: FRONT CONTROLLER

A *Front Controller* (166) typically creates a *Context Object* (181) to encapsulate aspects of the request state in a protocol-independent way before passing control to an *Application Controller* (205).

Based on the outcome of invoking the business services that will be initiated from executing this command, the application controller acts as a *View Handler* (213), determining the appropriate view and dispatching to that view.

Finally, whether an application uses *Service to Worker* or *Dispatcher View* (288) might also be driven by the use of specific frameworks or libraries, since those frameworks or libraries might implicitly support a specific combination of patterns. If your development team is required to use the Struts framework [Struts] for example, the application would strongly support *Service to Worker*, while allowing for *Dispatcher View* (288) in specific cases.

Structure

Example 6.47 represents the *Service to Worker*, with command.

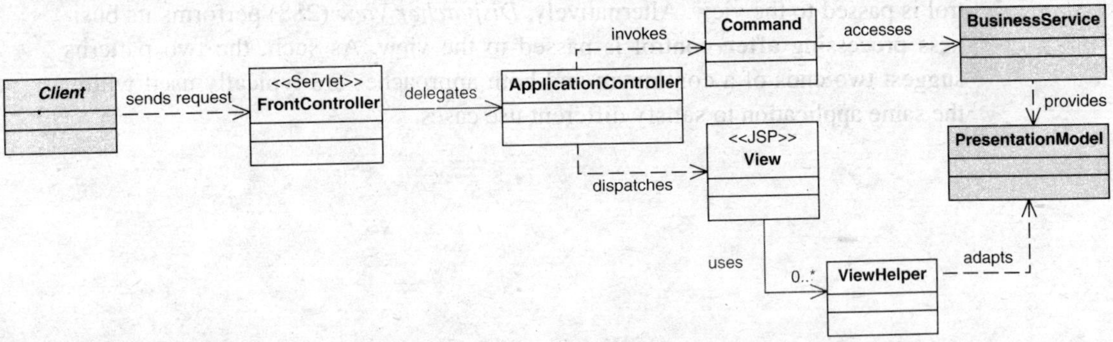

Figure 6.43 *Service to Worker* Class Diagram – With Command

The class diagram in Example 6.48 represents the *Service to Worker*, with helper.

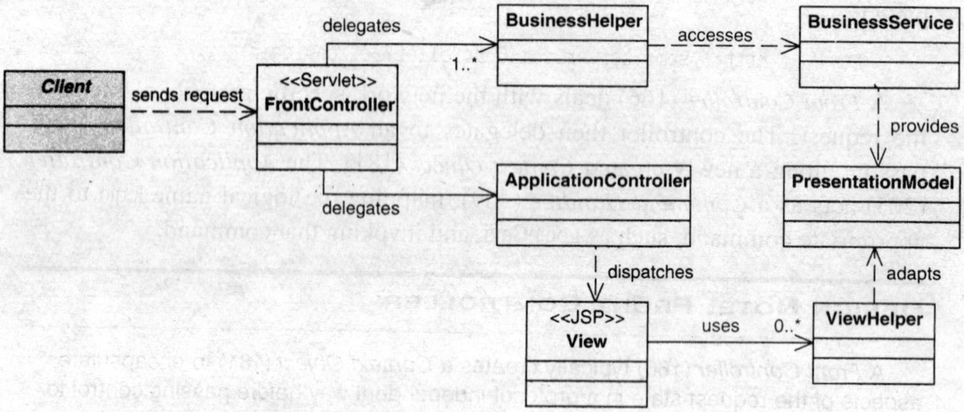

Figure 6.44 *Service to Worker* Class Diagram – With Helper

Participants and Responsibilities

Example 6.49 shows the sequence diagram that represents the *Service to Worker*.

A *Front Controller* (166) receives the request and delegates to an *Application Controller* (205), which performs action management, resolving the incoming request to the appropriate command and invoking that command. The command invokes a business service, which returns a presentation model. At this point, the *Application Controller* (205) performs view management, identifying the view and dispatching to it. Finally, *View Helper* (240) adapt and transform the presentation model for the view. The view can be a *Composite View* (262), though this is not central to the pattern.

As shown in this scenario, business processing logic is completed before control is passed to the view. Alternatively, *Dispatcher View* (288) performs its business processing **after** control is passed to the view. As such, the two patterns suggest two ends of a continuum and both approaches are typically used within the same application to satisfy different use cases.

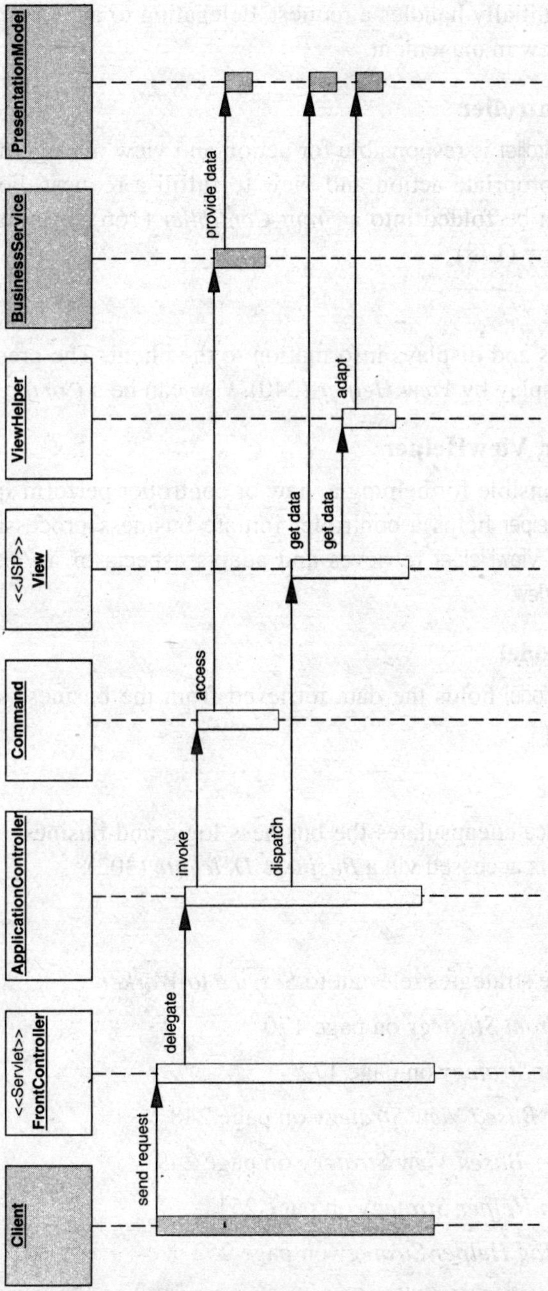

Figure 6.45 *Service to Worker* Sequence Diagram

FrontController

A FrontController initially handles a request, delegating to an application controller for action and view management.

ApplicationController

An ApplicationController is responsible for action and view management. It manages choosing the appropriate action and view to fulfill a request. For simple cases, this behavior can be folded into a *Front Controller* (166), using a *Dispatcher in Controller* strategy (178).

View

A View represents and displays information to the client. The presentation model is adapted for display by *View Helper* (240). View can be a *Composite View* (262).

BusinessHelper, ViewHelper

A helper is responsible for helping a view or controller perform specific processing. A BusinessHelper helps a controller initiate business processing to handle a request, while a ViewHelper retrieves and adapts aspects of a PresentationModel to help generate a View.

PresentationModel

The PresentationModel holds the data retrieved from the business service, used to generate the View.

BusinessService

The BusinessService encapsulates the business logic and business state. A remote business service is accessed via a *Business Delegate* (302).

Strategies

Following are the strategies relevant to *Service to Worker*.

- *Servlet Front Strategy* on page 170
- *JSP Front Strategy* on page 172
- *Template-Based View Strategy* on page 248
- *Controller-Based View Strategy* on page 249
- *JavaBean Helper Strategy* on page 251
- *Custom Tag Helper Strategy* on page 252
- *Dispatcher in Controller Strategy* on page 178

Consequences

- ***Centralizes control and improves modularity, reusability, and maintainability***
  Centralizing control and request-handling logic improves the system's modularity and reusability. Common request processing code can be reused, reducing the sort of duplication that occurs if processing logic is embedded within views. Less duplication means improved maintainability, since changes are made in a single location.
- ***Improves role separation***
  Centralizing control and request-handling logic separates it from view creation code and allows for a cleaner separation of team roles. Software developers can focus on maintaining programming logic while page authors can focus on the view.

Sample Code

The code samples in Example 6.70 through Example 6.74 show an implementation of *Service to Worker* using a controller servlet, an *Application Controller* (205) using a *Command Handler* (209), and a *View Handler* (213) to dispatch to a view. The implementation includes the *Servlet Front* strategy (170), *Command and Controller* strategy (174), *Template-based View* strategy (248), and *JavaBean Helper* strategy (251).

The view is a very basic form of *Composite View* (262). A screen shot of the resulting display is shown in Figure 6.50 on page 298.

Example 6.70 shows the controller servlet delegating to an *Application Controller* (205). The controller uses a command object that maps to the appropriate action to service this request. Using the *Application Controller* (205) command handler with a *Front Controller* (166) in this way is also referred to as the *Command and Controller* strategy (174). The command object is retrieved via a factory invocation, which returns a generic command type, an interface shown in Example 6.71 on page 284 The sample code uses a LogManager to log messages.

The screen shots in Figure 6.50 on page 298 and Figure 6.51 on page 299 show these messages displayed at the bottom of the page, for the purposes of this example.

Example 6.70 Controller Servlet with Command and Controller Strategy

```
public class Controller extends HttpServlet {
  /** Processes requests for both HTTP
   * <code>GET</code> and <code>POST</code> methods.
```

```
    * @param request servlet request
    * @param response servlet response
    */
  protected void processRequest(HttpServletRequest request,
      HttpServletResponse response)
      throws ServletException, java.io.IOException {
    String next;

    try {
      // create Context Object
      RequestContext requestContext =
        new RequestContext(request, response);

      // invoke request-processing components to
      // handle incoming request
      ApplicationController applicationController =
        new ApplicationControllerImpl();
      ResponseContext responseContext =
        applicationController.handleRequest(requestContext);

      // invoke response-processing components to
      // handle response logic
      applicationController.handleResponse(requestContext,
        responseContext);
    }
    catch (Exception e) {
      LogManager.logMessage(
        "FrontController(CommandStrategy)",
        e.getMessage() );

      /** ApplicationResources provides a simple API
        * for retrieving constants and other
        * preconfigured values **/
      next = ApplicationResources.getInstance().getErrorPage(e);
    }

    dispatch(request, response, next);

  }

  /** Handles the HTTP <code>GET</code> method.
   * @param request servlet request
   * @param response servlet response
```

```
  */
  protected void doGet(HttpServletRequest request,
      HttpServletResponse response)
      throws ServletException, java.io.IOException {
    processRequest(request, response);
  }

  /** Handles the HTTP <code>POST</code> method.
   * @param request servlet request
   * @param response servlet response
   */
  protected void doPost(HttpServletRequest request,
      HttpServletResponse response)
      throws ServletException, java.io.IOException {
    processRequest(request, response);
  }

  /** Returns a short description of the servlet. */
  public String getServletInfo() {
    return getSignature();
  }

  /** dispatcher method */
  protected void dispatch(HttpServletRequest request,
      HttpServletResponse response, String page)
      throws javax.servlet.ServletException, java.io.IOException {
    RequestDispatcher dispatcher =
      getServletContext().getRequestDispatcher(page);
    dispatcher.forward(request, response);
  }

  public void init(ServletConfig config) throws ServletException {
    super.init(config);
  }

  public void destroy() { }

  private String getSignature() {
    return "ServiceToWorker-Controller";
  }
}
```

Example 6.71 Command Interface

```
public interface Command {
   ResponseContext execute(RequestContext requestContext);
}
```

Each *Command Object* [Gof] implements this generic interface and the command object in this case is an instance of the ViewAccountDetails class, which is shown in Example 6.72 on page 284. The command instance uses a *Business Delegate* (302) to invoke the remote business tier. It then uses a *View Helper* (240) to determine the next view to which control should be dispatched and to dispatch to this view.

Example 6.72 ViewAccountDetailsCommand

```
public class AccountCommand implements Command {
   public AccountCommand() { }

   // view account details operation
   public ResponseContext execute(RequestContext requestContext) {

      String accountId =
         requestContext.getStringParameter("AccountId");

      /** Use an business delegate to retrieve data
       * from application service, and store result
       * in a response object.
       * Note: Object creation could be avoided via
       * factory, but for example purposes object
       * instantiation is shown **/

      AccountDelegate delegate = new AccountDelegate();
      AccountTO accountTO;
      accountTO= delegate.getAccountProfile(accountId);

      // This info could come from biz-tier components
      String logicalViewName = "AccountProfile";

      ResponseContextFactory factory =
         ResponseContextFactory.getInstance();

      ResponseContext responseContext =
         factory.createResponseContext(accountTO, logicalViewName);
```

```

        return responseContext;

    }
}
```

Example 6.73 AccountDelegate

```
public class AccountDelegate {
    public AccountProfileTO getAccountProfile(String accountId) {
        AccountProfileTO accountProfile = null;
        try {
            AccountSessionHome home =
                (AccountSessionHome) ServiceLocator.getInstance().
                 getEJBHome("Account", AccountSessionHome.class);
            AccountSession session = home.create();

            // Invoke Account Session Façade to get Account Profile
            accountProfile = session.getAccountDetails(accountId);
        }
        catch(CreateException ex) {
            // Translate the Session create exception into
            // application exception
        }
        catch(RemoteException ex) {
            // Translate the Remote exception into
            // application exception
        }
        return accountProfile;
    }
}
```

The invocation on the business service via the delegate yields an *Account Transfer Object* (415) which acts as an intermediate model for the view. Example 6.74 shows accountdetails.jsp, the JSP to which the request is dispatched. The *Transfer Object* is imported via the standard <jsp:useBean> tag and its properties accessed with the standard <jsp:getProperty> tag. Also, the view uses a very simple composite strategy, doing a translation-time inclusion of the trace.jsp subview, which is responsible for displaying log information on the display solely for example purposes. These basic view management strategies are used simply for example purposes.

Example 6.74 View – accountdetails.jsp

```
<html>
<head><title>AccountDetails</title></head>
<body>

<jsp:useBean id="account" scope="request"
  class="corepatterns.util.AccountTO" />

<h2>
  <center> Account Detail for <c:out value='${account.accountHolder}'/>
</h2> <br><br>
<table border=3>
<tr>
<td>
Account Number :
</td>
<td>
<c:out value='${account.number}'/>
</td>
</tr>

<tr>
<td>
Account Type:
</td>
<td>
<c:out value='${account.type}'/>
</td>
</tr>

<tr>
<td>
Account Balance:
</td>

<td>
<c:out value='${account.balance}'/>
</td>
</tr>

<tr>
<td>
```

```
OverDraft Limit:
</td>
<td>
<c:out value='${account.overdraftLimit}'/>
</td>
</tr>

</table>

<br>
<br>

</center>
<%@ include file="/jsp/trace.seg" %>
</body>
</html>
```

Related Patterns

- ***Front Controller (166), Application Controller (205), and View Helper (240)***

  Service to Worker is a controller-centric architecture, highlighting a *Front Controller* (166). The *Front Controller* (166) delegates to an *Application Controller* (205) for navigation and dispatch, then to a view and helpers.

- ***Composite View (262)***

  The view can be a *Composite View* (262).

- ***Business Delegate (302)***

  A *Business Delegate* (302) is used to hide any remote semantics of the business service.

- ***Dispatcher View (288)***

  Dispatcher View (288) is a view-centric architecture, where business processing is done after control is passed to the view.

Dispatcher View

Problem

You want a view to handle a request and generate a response, while managing limited amounts of business processing.

In certain use cases, there is little or no business processing performed before rendering the view. This is the case when the view is static or is generated from an existing presentation model. The view requests limited business or data access services.

Forces

- You have static views.
- You have views generated from an existing presentation model.
- You have views which are independent of any business service response.
- You have limited business processing.

Solution

Use *Dispatcher View* with views as the initial access point for a request. Business processing, if necessary in limited form, is managed by the views.

Use this approach when response generation requires little or no dynamic content, via a business service or data access call. Here are the two most common uses of *Dispatcher View*:

1) The response is entirely static
   Example: The response is a static page of HTML.
2) The response is dynamic, but is generated from an existing presentation model

Example: A request retrieves a presentation model for use by a view. This intermediate model is placed in a temporary store, such as the HttpSession. A later request is handled directly by a view, which simply uses the existing presentation model to generate a dynamic response.

Alternately, use *Service to Worker* (276) if there is a large dynamic component to the response and the presentation model must be retrieved via business service invocations.

Also note that in more limited applications, one might consider using this approach. For example, it is quite common for developers to write "one-off" testing or reporting tools for limited use that will use a *Dispatcher View* approach, embedding data access queries directly into a JSP. For simple applications with limited use, this is often done to save time, but keep in mind the obvious tradeoffs in maintainability and reusability.

A *Front Controller* (166) can be used as part of *Dispatcher View*, but the controller typically does nothing more than forward to a view. Such cases are examples of a *Dispatcher in Controller* strategy (178). A client might submit a request that includes a query parameter describing an action to be performed. For example:

```
http://some.server.com/Controller?action=showaccount.jsp
```

The sole responsibility of the controller in this case is to dispatch to the view showaccount.jsp.

An *Application Controller* (205) can also be used in a very limited form as part of *Dispatcher View*, performing basic view management. If a client submits a request that includes a logical reference to an action, then the *Application Controller* (205) resolves that logical name to a concrete view. For example, consider the following request:

```
http://some.server.com/Controller?action=showaccount
```

The *Application Controller* (205) acts as a *View Handler* (213), resolving the logical name showaccount to an actual view name, which might be showaccount.jsp. The *Application Controller* (205) then dispatches to that view.

Structure

Figure 6.46 shows the class diagram that represents the *Dispatcher View*.

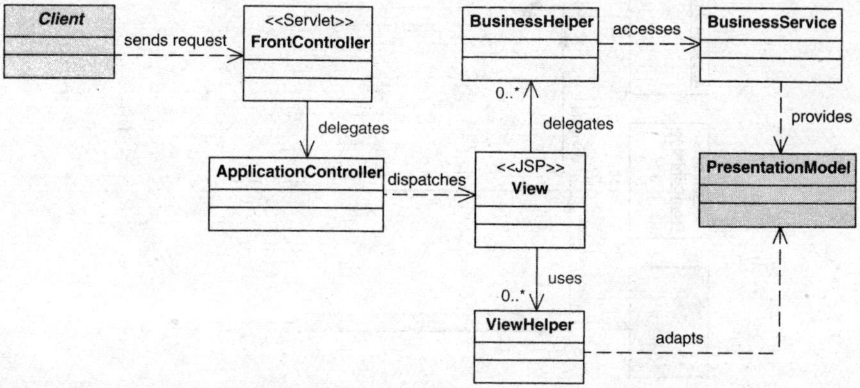

Figure 6.46 *Dispatcher View* Class Diagram

Participants and Responsibilities

Figure 6.47 shows the *Dispatcher View* sequence diagram.

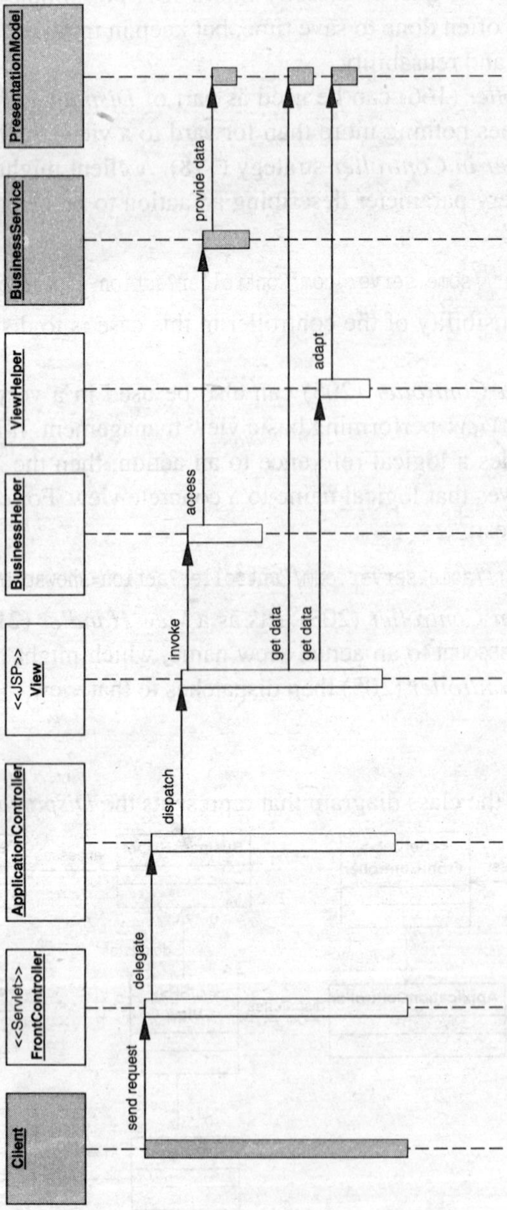

Figure 6.47 *Dispatcher View* Sequence Diagram

Notice that unlike *Service to Worker* (276), business service invocations, if they occur at all, are deferred until control is passed to the view.

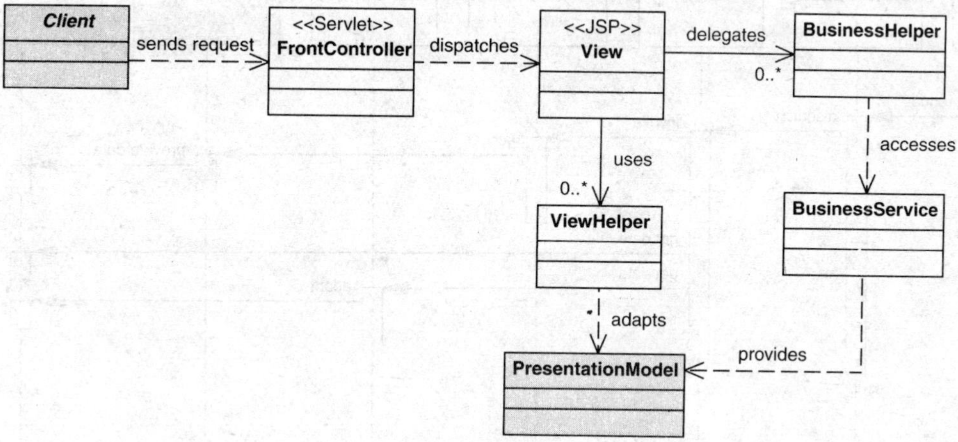

Figure 6.48 *Dispatcher in Controller* Strategy Class Diagram

While *Application Controller* (205) typically handles view management, this functionality is limited in *Dispatcher View* and can be encapsulated directly within the controller (see "Dispatcher in Controller Strategy" on page 178) or the view. The *Dispatcher in Controller* strategy is common when there is limited or no action management to be performed.

See Figure 6.48 and Figure 6.49 on page 292.

In fact, in the *Dispatcher View* approach, view management is most often performed by the container, since there is often no application-level logic required. An example is a view called main.jsp that is given the alias name first. The container processes the following request, translating the alias name to the physical resource name, and dispatching to that view:

```
http://some.server.com/first --> /mywebapp/main.jsp
```

Notice how the *Application Controller* (205) roles are fulfilled by the container mechanism in this case.

As shown in this scenario, if there is any business processing to be done, it is deferred until after control is passed to the view. Alternately, *Service to Worker* (276) performs its business processing **before** control is passed to the view. As such, the two patterns suggest two ends of a continuum and both approaches are typically used within the same application to satisfy different use cases.

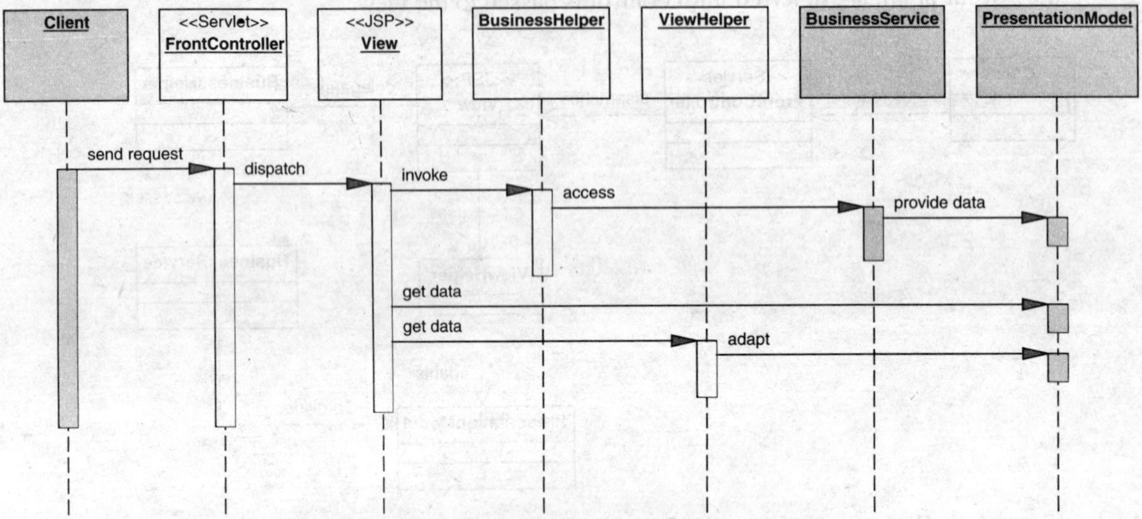

Figure 6.49 Dispatcher in Controller Strategy Sequence Diagram

FrontController

A FrontController can be used to initially handle the request, though its responsibilities are limited.

ApplicationController

An ApplicationController can be used to perform limited view management, but no action management. The application controller roles and responsibilities may be fulfilled directly by the container.

View

A View represents and displays information to the client. The PresentationModel is adapted for display by *View Helpers* (240). The view can be a *Composite View* (262).

BusinessHelper, ViewHelper

A helper is responsible for helping a view or controller perform specific processing. A BusinessHelper helps a controller initiate business processing to handle a request, while a ViewHelper retrieves and adapts aspects of a PresentationModel to help generate a View.

PresentationModel

The PresentationModel holds the data retrieved from the business service, used to generate the View.

BusinessService

The BusinessService encapsulates the business logic and business state. A remote business service is accessed via a *Business Delegate* (302).

Strategies

Following are the strategies relevant to *Dispatcher View.*

- "Servlet Front Strategy" on page 170
- "JSP Front Strategy" on page 172
- "Template-Based View Strategy" on page 248
- "Controller-Based View Strategy" on page 249
- "JavaBean Helper Strategy" on page 251
- "Custom Tag Helper Strategy" on page 252
- "Dispatcher in Controller Strategy" on page 178.

Consequences

- ***Leverages frameworks and libraries***
  Frameworks and libraries realize and support specific patterns. The *Dispatcher View* approach is supported in standard and custom libraries that provide view adapters and transformers and, for **limited** use, data access tags. An example of one standard library is JSTL [JSTL].
- ***Introduces potential for poor separation of the view from the model and control logic***
  Since business processing is managed by the view, the *Dispatcher View* approach is inappropriate for handling requests that rely upon heavy business processing or data access. Embedding processing logic of any form within a view should be minimized, as discussed in *Front Controller* (166) and *View Helper* (240). The overriding goal is to separate control and business logic from the view (see "Design Note on MVC") and to localize disparate logic.

- ***Separates processing logic from view and improves reusability***
  View Helpers (240) adapt and convert the presentation model for the view. Processing logic that might otherwise be embedded within the view is extracted into reusable helpers, exposing less of the code's implementation details and more of its intent.

Sample Code

The following sample code shows an implementation of the *Dispatcher View* pattern, including the *Servlet Front* strategy, *Dispatcher in Controller* strategy, *Template-based View* strategy, and *Custom Tag* and *JavaBean Helper* strategies. A very basic *Composite View* (262) is used as well. A screen shot of the resulting display is shown in Figure 6.51.

Example 6.75 shows the controller servlet, which simply performs an authentication check and passes control to the appropriate view. Notice that the controller does not directly delegate to any helper components to invoke the business tier. If handling this request requires business processing, that processing is deferred until control is passed to the view, which is called accountdetails.jsp and is shown in Example 6.76.

The sample code uses a LogManager to log messages. These messages are displayed at the bottom of the output page, for the purposes of this example, and are shown in Figure 6.50 on page 298 and Figure 6.51 on page 299.

Example 6.75 Dispatcher View Controller Servlet

```
public class Controller extends HttpServlet {

   /** Processes requests for both HTTP
    * <code>GET</code> and <code>POST</code> methods.
    * @param request servlet request
    * @param response servlet response
    */
   protected void processRequest(HttpServletRequest request,
         HttpServletResponse response)
         throws ServletException, java.io.IOException {
      String nextview;
      try {
         LogManager.recordStrategy(request, "Dispatcher View",
            " Servlet Front Strategy;" +
            " Template-Based View Strategy;" +
            " Custom tag helper Strategy");
         LogManager.logMessage(request, getSignature(),
```

```
          "Process incoming request. ");

      // Use a helper object to gather parameter
      // specific information.
      RequestHelper helper = new
         RequestHelper(request, response);
      LogManager.logMessage(request, getSignature(),
         " Authenticate user");

      Authenticator auth = new BasicAuthenticator();
      auth.authenticate(helper);

      // This is an oversimplification for the sake of
      // simplicity. Typically, there will be a
      // mapping from logical name to resource name at
      // this point
      LogManager.logMessage(request, getSignature(),
         "Getting nextview");
      nextview = request.getParameter("nextview");

      LogManager.logMessage(request, getSignature(),
         "Dispatching to view: " + nextview);
    }
    catch (Exception e) {
      LogManager.logMessage("Handle exception appropriately",
         e.getMessage() );


      /** ApplicationResources provides a simple API
       * for retrieving constants and other
       * preconfigured values**/
      nextview = ApplicationResources.getInstance().
         getErrorPage(e);
    }
    dispatch(request, response, nextview);
  }

  /** Handles the HTTP <code>GET</code> method.
   * @param request servlet request
   * @param response servlet response
   */
  protected void doGet(HttpServletRequest request,
      HttpServletResponse response)
```

```
      throws ServletException, java.io.IOException {
    processRequest(request, response);
  }

  /** Handles the HTTP <code>POST</code> method.
   * @param request servlet request
   * @param response servlet response
   */
  protected void doPost(HttpServletRequest request,
      HttpServletResponse response)
      throws ServletException, java.io.IOException {
    processRequest(request, response);
  }

  /** Returns a short description of the servlet. */
  public String getServletInfo() {
    return getSignature();
  }

  public void init(ServletConfig config) throws ServletException {
    super.init(config);
  }

  public void destroy() { }

  /**
   * dispatcher method
   */
  protected void dispatch(HttpServletRequest request,
      HttpServletResponse response, String page)
      throws javax.servlet.ServletException, java.io.IOException {
    RequestDispatcher dispatcher =
      getServletContext().getRequestDispatcher(page);
    dispatcher.forward(request, response);
  }

  private String getSignature() {
    return "DispatcherView-Controller";
  }
}
```

Notice that the view uses custom tag helpers to manage the invocation of business services in order to retrieve the presentation model. When custom tags are used in this manner, they should delegate to standalone components that perform the work. This way, the general processing logic is loosely coupled to the tag implementation. If tag helpers are not used with *Dispatcher View*, then too much processing logic might mingle with the view, a situation to avoid.

Example 6.76 View – accountdetails.jsp

```
<%@ taglib uri="/web-INF/corepatternstaglibrary.tld"
    prefix="corepatterns" %>

<html>
<head><title>AccountDetails</title></head>
<body>

<corepatterns:AccountQuery queryParams="custid,acctkey" scope="request" />

<h2>
<center> Account Detail for <corepatterns:Account attribute="owner" />
</h2>
<br><br>

<tr>
    <td>Account Number :</td>
    <td><corepatterns:Account attribute="number" /></td>
</tr>


<tr>
    <td>Account Type:</td>
    <td><corepatterns:Account attribute="type" /></td>
</tr>

<tr>
    <td>Account Balance:</td>
    <td><corepatterns:Account attribute="balance" /></td>
</tr>

<tr>
    <td>OverDraft Limit:</td>
    <td><corepatterns:Account attribute="overdraftLimit" /></td>
</tr>
```

```
<table border=3>
</table>
</corepatterns:AccountQuery>

<br>
<br>

</center>
<%@ include file="/jsp/trace.seg" %>
</body>
</html>
```

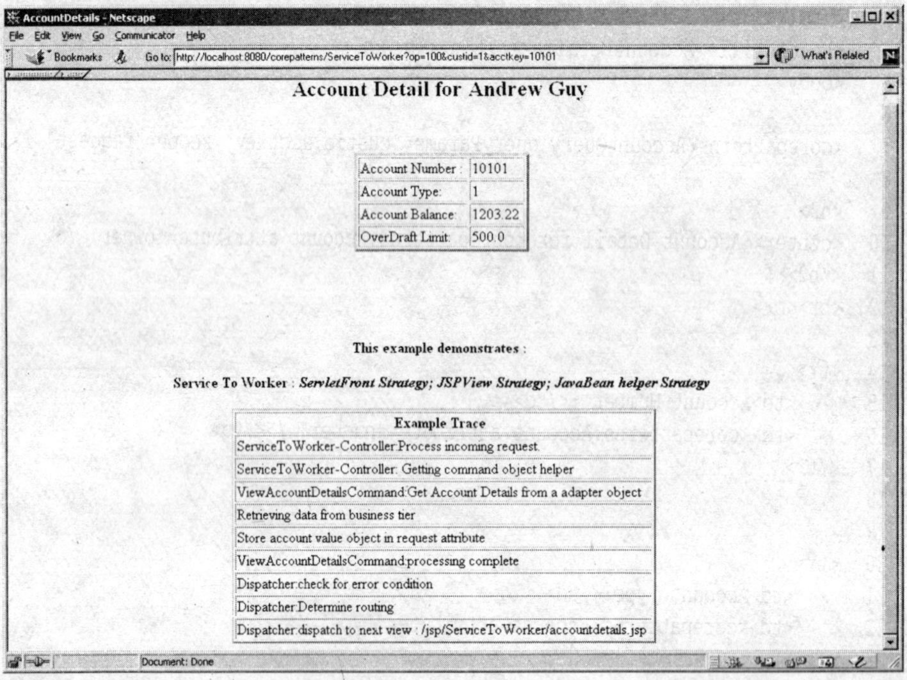

Figure 6.50 *Service to Worker* Sample Screen Shot

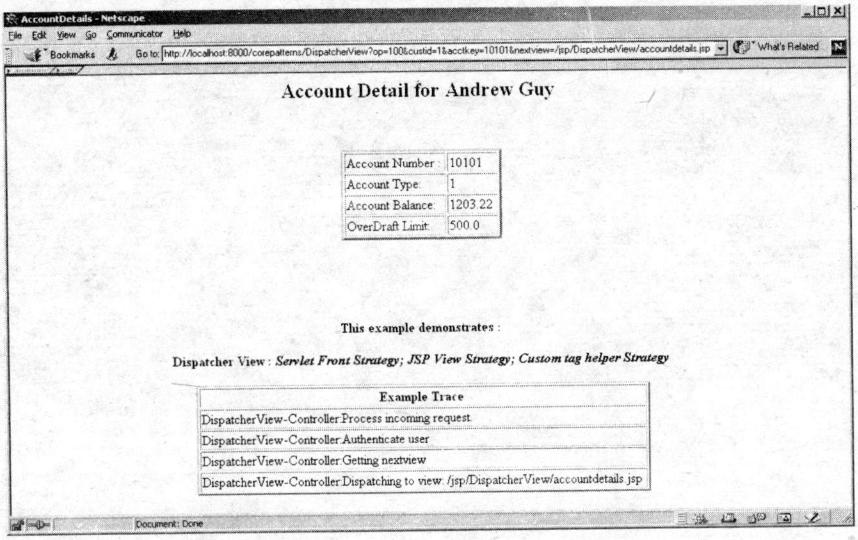

Figure 6.51 *Dispatcher View* Sample Screen Shot

Related Patterns

- ***Front Controller (166)***
  In a *Dispatcher View* approach, a *Front Controller* (166) can handle the request or the request may be handled initially by the view.
- ***Application Controller (205)***
  An *Application Controller* (205) will often not be used with *Dispatcher View*. An *Application Controller* (205) is used in those cases where limited view management is required to resolve an incoming request to the actual view.
- ***View Helper (240)***
  Helpers mainly adapt and transform the presentation model for the view, but also help with any limited business processing that is initiated from the view.
- ***Composite View (262)***
  The view can be a *Composite View* (262)
- ***Service to Worker (276)***
  The *Service to Worker* (276) approach centralizes control, request handling, and business processing before control is passed to the view. *Dispatcher View*, defers this behavior, if needed, to the time of view processing.

Business Tier Patterns

Topics in This Chapter

- Business Delegate
- Service Locator
- Session Façade
- Application Service
- Business Object
- Composite Entity
- Transfer Object
- Transfer Object Assembler
- Value List Handler

Chapter 7

Business Delegate

Problem

You want to hide clients from the complexity of remote communication with business service components.

When clients access remote business service components directly, the following problems can occur.

Clients interact directly with the business service interface. This means that when the business service code changes, the client code might need to be changed, as well. This increases the amount of maintenance you need to do and decreases the system's flexibility.

Another problem relates to network performance. When clients interact directly with the business services API, a single action in the client can require many complex fine-grained interactions with the business services. This leads to embedding business logic into the clients without any client-side caching or aggregation of services, thus reducing maintainability. Since this takes place over a network, it also decreases network performance.

A third problem is that interacting so closely with the business service API can mean the client code needs infrastructure code to interact with a remote distributed middle tier. This infrastructure code deals with naming services, such as JNDI, handling network failures, and retry logic.

Forces

- You want to access the business-tier components from your presentation-tier components and clients, such as devices, web services, and rich clients.
- You want to minimize coupling between clients and the business services, thus hiding the underlying implementation details of the service, such as lookup and access.
- You want to avoid unnecessary invocation of remote services.
- You want to translate network exceptions into application or user exceptions.
- You want to hide the details of service creation, reconfiguration, and invocation retries from the clients.

Solution

Use a *Business Delegate* to encapsulate access to a business service. The *Business Delegate* hides the implementation details of the business service, such as lookup and access mechanisms.

A *Business Delegate* acts as a client-side business abstraction: it abstracts and hides the implementation details of the business services. Using a *Business Delegate* reduces the coupling between the client and the system's business services. Depending on the implementation strategy, the *Business Delegate* might shield clients from possible volatility in the implementation of the business service API. Potentially, this reduces the number of changes that must be made to the client code when the business service API or its underlying implementation changes.

However, interface methods in the *Business Delegate* might still require modification if the underlying business service API changes. Admittedly, though, it is more likely that changes will be made to the business service than to the *Business Delegate*.

Developers are sometimes skeptical when a design goal, such as abstracting the business layer causes additional up front work in return for future gains. However, using a *Business Delegate* has the following benefits:

- The main benefit is hiding the details of the underlying service. For example, by using the *Business Delegate*, the client becomes transparent to naming and lookup services.
- A *Business Delegate* also handles the exceptions from the business services, such as java.rmi.Remote exceptions, JMS exceptions, and so on. The *Business Delegate* might intercept such service-level exceptions and generate application-level exceptions instead. Application-level exceptions are easier to handle by the clients, and are more likely to be user friendly.
- A *Business Delegate* can also transparently perform any retry or recovery operations necessary in the event of a service failure, without exposing the client to the problem, unless it is determined that the problem is not resolvable. These gains present a compelling reason to use the pattern.
- The *Business Delegate* (302) can cache results and references to remote business services. Caching can significantly improve performance, because it limits unnecessary and potentially costly round trips over the network.

A *Business Delegate* (302) uses a *Service Locator* (315) to locate the business service. The *Service Locator* (315) is responsible for hiding the underlying implementation details of the business service lookup code.

When a *Business Delegate* (302) is used with a *Session Façade* (341), typically there is a one-to-one relationship. This one-to-one relationship exists because logic that might have been encapsulated in a *Business Delegate* (302) relating to its interaction with multiple business services (creating a one-to-many relationship) will often be factored back into a *Session Façade* (341).

The *Business Delegate* (302) pattern is categorized as a business-tier pattern and not a presentation-tier pattern because the *Business Delegate* is a **logical** abstraction, not a **physical** one. When used with a presentation tier, the actual *Business Delegate* components live in the presentation tier. However, they are a logical extension of the business tier. Because of this, and because of the pattern's close association with business components such as *Session Façade* (341), we recommend that business service developers implement *Business Delegates*.

Structure

Figure 7.1 shows the class diagram for the *Business Delegate* pattern. The client asks the BusinessDelegate component to provide access to the underlying business service. The BusinessDelegate uses a ServiceLocator to locate the required BusinessService component.

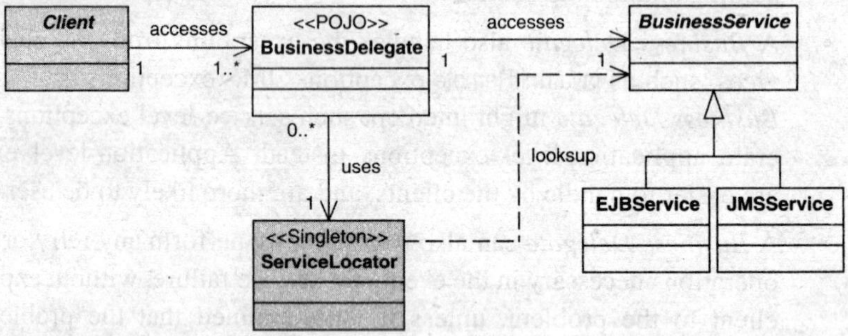

Figure 7.1 *Business Delegate* Class Diagram

Participants and Responsibilities

Figure 7.2 on page 305 and Figure 7.3 show sequence diagrams that illustrate typical interactions for the *Business Delegate* pattern.

The get ID message in the sequence diagram shows that the BusinessDelegate can obtain a String representation of the Handle (such as the EJBHandle object) for the

BusinessService. The client can use the ID string to reconnect to the same BusinessService it was using previously.

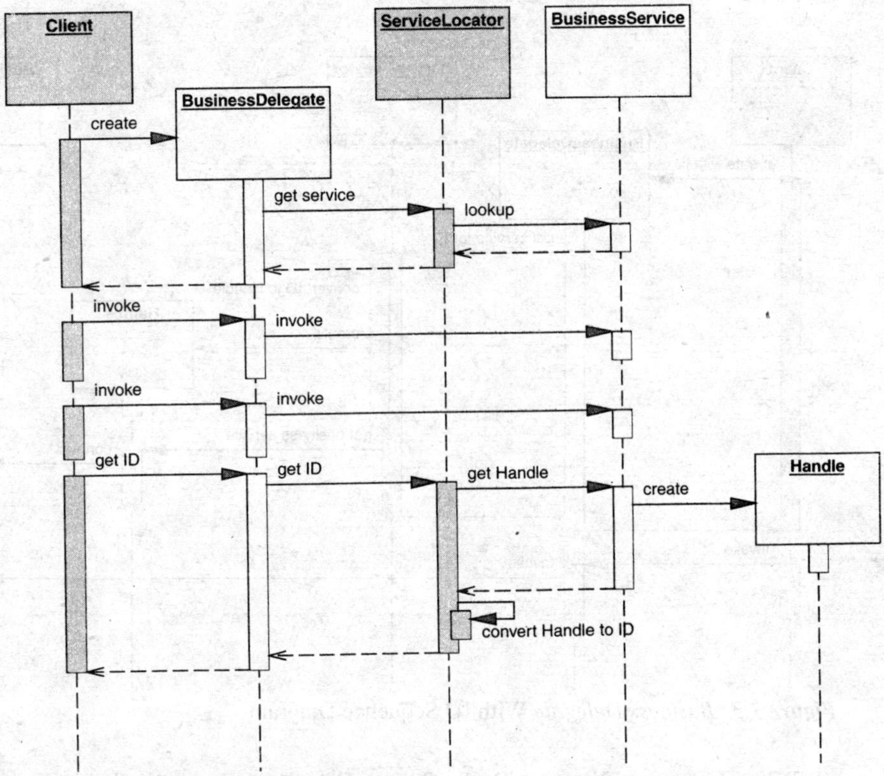

Figure 7.2 Business Delegate Sequence Diagram

This technique avoids new lookups, because a Handle can reconnect to its BusinessService instance. Note that Handle objects are implemented by the container provider and might not be portable across containers from different vendors.

The sequence diagram in Figure 7.3 on page 306 shows the Client obtaining a reference to a previously used BusinessService, such as a session or an entity bean, using its Handle.

BusinessDelegate

The BusinessDelegate's role is to provide control and protection for the business service. The BusinessDelegate can expose two types of constructors to clients:

- A default constructor to instantiate the BusinessDelegate.

- A constructor to instantiate the BusinessDelegate with an ID as an argument, where ID is a string representation of the reference to a remote object, such as EJBHome or EJBObject.

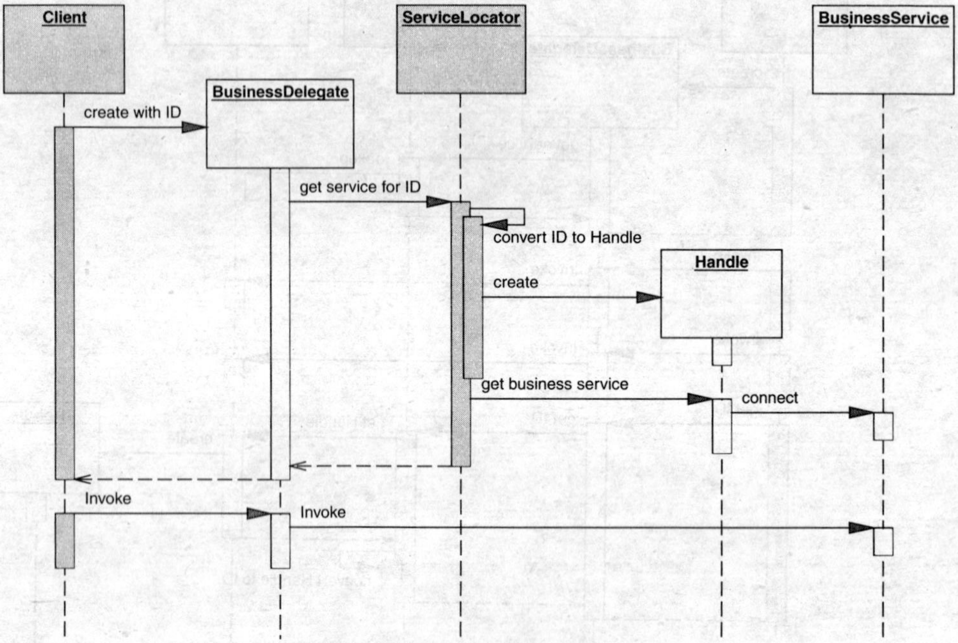

Figure 7.3 *Business Delegate* With ID Sequence Diagram

When created without an ID, the BusinessDelegate requests the business service from the ServiceLocator, typically implemented as a *Service Locator* (315), which returns a service factory object, such as an EJBHome. The BusinessDelegate uses the service factory to locate, create, or remove a BusinessService, such as an enterprise bean.

When initialized with an ID string, the BusinessDelegate uses the ID string to reconnect to the BusinessService, shielding the client from the underlying implementation details of BusinessService naming and lookup. The client never directly makes a remote invocation on a BusinessService; instead, the client uses the BusinessDelegate.

ServiceLocator

The ServiceLocator is a role fulfilled by a *Service Locator* (315) implementation. The ServiceLocator encapsulates the implementation details of locating a BusinessService component.

BusinessService

The BusinessService is a business-tier component, such as an enterprise bean, that is being accessed by the client. The component is typically implemented as a *Session Façade* (341) or a JMS component.

Strategies

Business Delegate offers a simple but powerful abstraction to decouple the business service components in the business tier from the rest of the application. This makes it easier for application developers to use these business services. The following are some of the common implementation strategies for the *Business Delegate* pattern.

Delegates Strategy

A *Business Delegate* exposes an interface that provides clients access to the underlying functionality of the business service API.

In the *Delegate Proxy* strategy, a *Business Delegate* acts as a proxy for a remote business service, passing client method calls to the service object for which it is acting as a proxy. Because you implement this delegate proxy as a business-tier developer, you can add behavior such as some types of validation and caching business data and references. Caching can include the remote references to a session bean's home or remote objects to improve performance by reducing the number of lookups. The *Business Delegate* can also convert, such references to String representations (IDs) and vice versa, using a *Service Locator* (315).

Delegate Adapter Strategy

If you're running a B2B environment, you must assume that the systems interacting with yours might not be running on J2EE. You must provide a solution for integrating these external systems so they can interact with your system, and using XML is a common approach. The *Delegate Adapter* is a good strategy for doing this. Figure 7.4 gives an example.

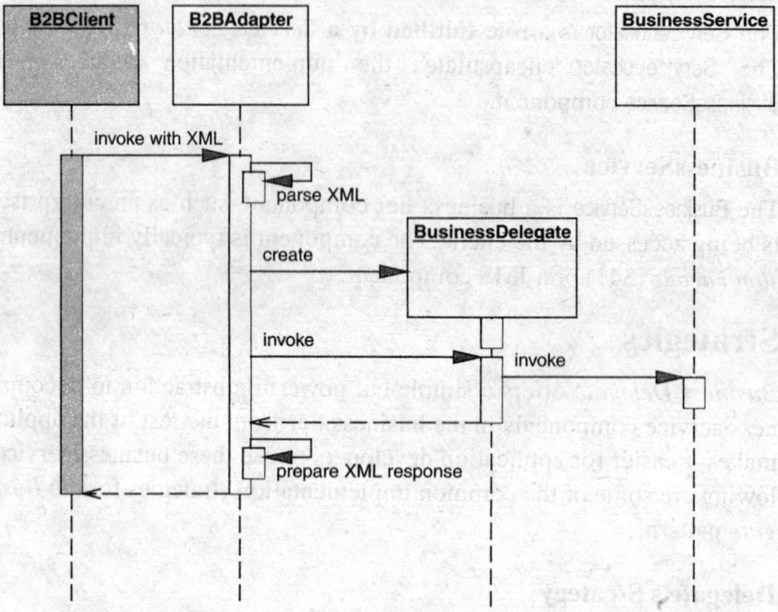

Figure 7.4 Using the *Business Delegate* Pattern With an *Adapter* Strategy

Consequences

- ***Reduces coupling, improves maintainability***
  The *Business Delegate* reduces coupling between the presentation tier and the business tier by hiding all business-tier implementation details. Managing changes is easier because they are centralized in the *Business Delegate*.
- ***Translates business service exceptions***
  The *Business Delegate* translates network or infrastructure-related exceptions into business exceptions, shielding clients from the knowledge of the underlying implementation specifics.
- ***Improves availability***
  When a *Business Delegate* encounters a business service failure, the delegate can implement automatic recovery features without exposing the problem to the client. If the recovery succeeds, the client doesn't need to know about the failure. If the recovery attempt fails, then the *Business Delegate* needs to inform the client of the failure. Additionally, the *Business Delegate* methods can be synchronized, if necessary.

- ***Exposes a simpler, uniform interface to the business tier***
  The *Business Delegate* is implemented as a simple Java object, making it easier for application developers to use business-tier components without dealing with the complexities of the business-service implementations.
- ***Improves performance***
  The *Business Delegate* can cache information on behalf of the presentation-tier components to improve performance for common service requests.
- ***Introduces an additional layer***
  The *Business Delegate* adds a layer that might be seen as increasing complexity and decreasing flexibility. However, the benefits of the pattern outweigh such drawbacks.
- ***Hides remoteness***
  Location transparency is a benefit of this pattern, but it can lead to problems if you don't keep in mind where the *Business Delegate* resides. A *Business Delegate* is a **client-side proxy** to a **remote service**. Even though a *Business Delegate* is implemented as a local POJO, when you call a method on a *Business Delegate*, the *Business Delegate* typically has to make a call across the network to the underlying business service to fulfill this request. Therefore, try to keep calls to the *Business Delegate* to a minimum to prevent excess network traffic.

Sample Code

Implementing the Business Delegate Pattern

Consider a professional services application (PSA), which has resources (consultants) assigned to projects (engagements). The presentation-tier component must access a *Session Façade* (341). Apply the *Business Delegate* pattern to implement a ResourceDelegate object, which encapsulates the details of dealing with the ResourceSession *Session Façade* (341).

The ResourceDelegate implementation for this example is shown in Example 7.1, and the corresponding remote interface for the ResourceSession *Session Façade* (341) is shown in Example 7.2.

Example 7.1 Implementing Business Delegate pattern – ResourceDelegate

```

// imports
...

public class ResourceDelegate {
```

```java

  // Remote reference for Session Facade
  private ResourceSession session;

  // Class for Session Facade's Home object
  private static final Class homeClazz =
    corepatterns.apps.psa.ejb.ResourceSessionHome.class;

  // Default Constructor. Looks up home and connects to
  // session by creating a new one.
  public ResourceDelegate() throws ResourceException {
    try {
      ResourceSessionHome home =
        (ResourceSessionHome) ServiceLocator.getInstance().
          getRemoteHome("Resource", homeClazz);
      session = home.create();
    } catch (ServiceLocatorException ex) {
      // Translate Service Locator exception into
      // application exception
      throw new ResourceException(...);
    } catch (CreateException ex) {
      // Translate the Session create exception into
      // application exception
      throw new ResourceException(...);
    } catch (RemoteException ex) {
      // Translate the Remote exception into application
      // exception
      throw new ResourceException(...);
    }
  }

  // Constructor that accepts an ID (Handle id) and
  // reconnects to the prior session bean instead of creating
  // a new one
  public ResourceDelegate(String id)
  throws ResourceException {
    // reconnect to the session bean for the given id
    reconnect(id);
  }

  // Returns a String ID the client can use at a later time
  // to reconnect to the session bean
  public String getID() {
```

```
    try {
      return ServiceLocator.getId(session);
    } catch (Exception e) {
      // Throw an application exception
    }
  }

  // method to reconnect using String ID
  public void reconnect(String id) throws ResourceException {
    try {
      session =
        (ResourceSession) ServiceLocator.getService(id);
    } catch (RemoteException ex) {
      // Translate the Remote exception into application
      // exception
      throw new ResourceException(...);
    }
  }

  // The following are the business methods proxied to the
  // Session Facade. If any service exception is encountered,
  // these methods convert them into application exceptions
  // such as ResourceException, SkillSetException, and so on.
  public ResourceTO setCurrentResource(String resourceId)
  throws ResourceException {
    try {
      return session.setCurrentResource(resourceId);
    } catch (RemoteException ex) {
      // Translate the service exception into
      // application exception
      throw new ResourceException(...);
    }
  }

  public ResourceTO getResourceDetails()
  throws ResourceException {

    try {
      return session.getResourceDetails();
    } catch (RemoteException ex) {
      // Translate the service exception into application
      // exception
      throw new ResourceException(...);
```

```
    }
  }

  public void setResourceDetails(ResourceTO to)
  throws ResourceException {
    try {
      session.setResourceDetails(to);
    } catch (RemoteException ex) {
      throw new ResourceException(...);
    }
  }

  public void addNewResource(ResourceTO to)
  throws ResourceException {
    try {
      session.addResource(to);
    } catch (RemoteException ex) {
      throw new ResourceException(...);
    }
  }

  // all other proxy method to session bean
  ...
}
```

Example 7.2 Remote Interface for ResourceSession

```
// imports
...
public interface ResourceSession extends EJBObject {

  public ResourceTO setCurrentResource(String resourceId)
  throws RemoteException, ResourceException;

  public ResourceTO getResourceDetails()
  throws RemoteException, ResourceException;

  public void setResourceDetails(ResourceTO resource)
  throws RemoteException, ResourceException;

  public void addResource(ResourceTO resource)
  throws RemoteException, ResourceException;

```

```
    public void removeResource()
    throws RemoteException, ResourceException;

    // methods for managing blockout time by the resource
    public void addBlockoutTime(Collection blockoutTime)
    throws RemoteException, BlockoutTimeException;

    public void updateBlockoutTime(Collection blockoutTime)
    throws RemoteException, BlockoutTimeException;

    public void removeBlockoutTime(Collection blockoutTime)
    throws RemoteException, BlockoutTimeException;

    public void removeAllBlockoutTime()
    throws RemoteException, BlockoutTimeException;

    // methods for resource skillsets time by the resource
    public void addSkillSets(Collection skillSet)
    throws RemoteException, SkillSetException;

    public void updateSkillSets(Collection skillSet)
    throws RemoteException, SkillSetException;

    public void removeSkillSet(Collection skillSet)
    throws RemoteException, SkillSetException;

    ...
}

```

Related Patterns

- ***Service Locator (315)***
  The *Business Delegate* (302) typically uses a *Service Locator* (315) to encapsulate the implementation details of business service lookup. When the *Business Delegate* needs to look up a business service, it delegates the lookup functionality to the *Service Locator* (315).
- ***Session Façade (341)***
  For most EJB applications, the *Business Delegate* communicates with a *Session Façade* (341) and maintains a one-to-one relationship with that facade. Typically, the developer who implements a *Session Façade* (341) also provides corresponding *Business Delegate* implementations.

- ***Proxy [GoF]***
  A *Business Delegate* can act as a proxy, providing a stand-in for objects in the business tier. The *Delegate Proxy* strategy provides this functionality.
- ***Adapter [GoF]***
  A *Business Delegate* can use the *Adapter* design pattern to provide integration for otherwise incompatible systems.
- ***Broker [POSA1]***
  A *Business Delegate* acts as a *Broker* to decouple the business-tier objects from the clients in other tiers.

Service Locator

Problem

You want to transparently locate business components and services in a uniform manner.

J2EE applications clients need to locate and access business-tier components and services. For example, when a *Business Delegate* (302) in the presentation tier needs to access a *Session Façade* (341) in the business tier, the *Business Delegate* (302) needs to first look up the EJB Home for the *Session Façade* (341) and invoke the home's create method to obtain a *Session Façade* (341) instance. Similarly, when a JMS client needs to obtain a JMS Connection or a JMS Session, it must first look up a JMS ConnectionFactory object and then obtain the connection or session from the factory.

In J2EE applications, the business-tier components, such as EJB components; and integration-tier components such as JDBC data sources and JMS components; are typically registered in a central registry. The clients use the JNDI (Java Naming and Directory Interface) API to interact with this registry and obtain an InitialContext object that holds the component name to object bindings. When you implement a lookup mechanism in your clients, you deal with several problems related to complexity, duplication of code, performance degradation, and vendor dependency.

Dealing with the JNDI API and InitialContexts can be complex because doing this involves repeated usage of the InitialContext objects, lookup operations, class cast operations, and handling low-level exceptions and timeouts. The application clients need to be isolated from this complexity. JNDI code might get duplicated in different clients because all clients that need to access a JNDI-administered service or component needed to perform the lookup. Creating a JNDI initial context object and performing a lookup on an EJB home object is potentially an expensive operation, and if performed repeatedly will degrade application performance.

Another problem is that the InitialContext and other context factories registered in the JNDI registry are vendor-supplied implementations. If application clients directly access specific implementations of such objects, doing so introduces vendor or product dependency in the application and makes your code non-portable.

Forces

- You want to use the JNDI API to look up and use business components, such as enterprise beans and JMS components, and services such as data sources.
- You want to centralize and reuse the implementation of lookup mechanisms for J2EE application clients.
- You want to encapsulate vendor dependencies for registry implementations, and hide the dependency and complexity from the clients.
- You want to avoid performance overhead related to initial context creation and service lookups.
- You want to reestablish a connection to a previously accessed enterprise bean instance, using its Handle object.

Solution

Use a *Service Locator* to implement and encapsulate service and component lookup. A *Service Locator* hides the implementation details of the lookup mechanism and encapsulates related dependencies.

Application clients can reuse the *Service Locator* to reduce code complexity, provide a single point of control, and improve performance by providing a caching facility. You typically need a single *Service Locator* for the entire application. However, it is not uncommon to see two *Service Locator* implementations in an application, one for the presentation tier and one for business tier. A *Service Locator* reduces the client's dependency on the underlying lookup infrastructure, and optimizes resource-intensive lookup and creation operations.

A *Service Locator* is typically implemented as a *Singleton*. However, J2EE applications run in a J2EE container that typically uses multiple class loaders and JVMs, making it impossible to have a true *Singleton* with only one instance. Therefore, you might need multiple instances of the *Service Locator* in a distributed environment. However, since the *Service Locator* does not cache any data that needs to be concurrently accessed, you don't need to replicate and synchronize changes across these multiple instances.

Structure

Figure 7.5 shows the class diagram representing the relationships for the *Service Locator* pattern.

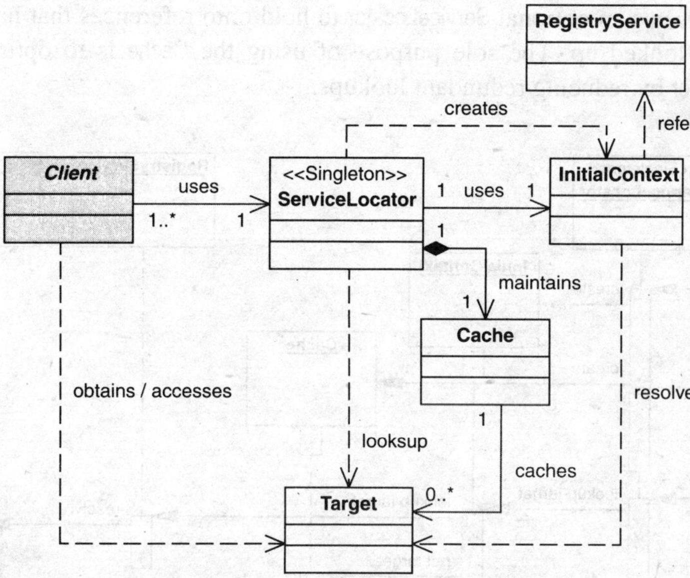

Figure 7.5 Service Locator Class Diagram

Participants and Responsibilities

Figure 7.6 contains the sequence diagram that shows the interaction between the various participants of the *Service Locator* pattern.

Client

Client represents a client of the *Service Locator* that needs to locate and access a component or service in the business or integration tier. For example, a *Business Delegate* (302) performs the role of a client of the *Service Locator* when it locates and accesses its *Session Façade* (341). Similarly, a *Data Access Object* (462) fulfills the Client role when it uses a ServiceLocator to obtain a JDBC DataSource instance.

ServiceLocator

The ServiceLocator encapsulates the API lookup (naming) services, vendor dependencies, lookup complexities, and business object creation, and provides a simple interface to clients. This reduces the client's complexity and increases reuse.

Cache

Cache represents an optional ServiceLocator to hold onto references that have been previously looked up. The sole purpose of using the Cache is to optimize the ServiceLocator by reducing redundant lookups.

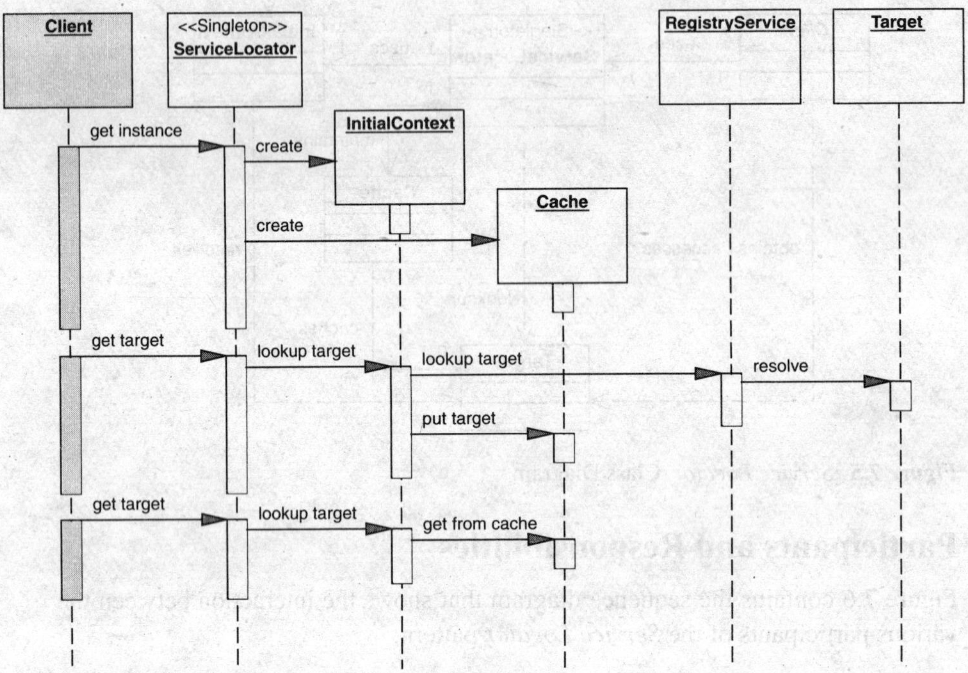

Figure 7.6 *Service Locator* Sequence Diagram

InitialContext

The InitialContext object is the starting point in the lookup and creation process. Service providers provide the context object, which varies depending on the type of Target looked up by the ServiceLocator. A ServiceLocator that provides services for different types of Target components (such as enterprise beans, JMS components, and so on) uses corresponding types of context objects, each obtained from a different provider. For example, the context provider for an EJB application server might be different from the context provider for a JMS service.

Target

Target represents the service or component, in the business or integration tiers, that the Client is looking up using the ServiceLocator. For example, when a Client looks up an EJB component, the Target is fulfilled by an EJB Home object. Other components that fill the role of the Target (depending on what is being looked up) are: a JDBC DataSource instance, JMS ConnectionFactory object, such as a TopicConnectionFactory (for publish/subscribe messaging model), or a QueueConnectionFactory (for point-to-point messaging model).

RegistryService

RegistryService represents the registry implementation that holds the references to the services or components that are registered as service providers for Clients. The RegistryService is a publish and lookup service, such as the JNDI registry, UDDI registry, and eBXML RegRep.

Strategies

The following strategies describe *Service Locator* for EJB and JMS components. You can combine the *EJB Service Locator* strategy and the *JMS Service Locator* strategies in a single *Service Locator* implementation to cater to all lookups.

EJB Service Locator Strategy

The class diagram for the *EJB Service Locator* strategy is shown in Figure 7.7. EJB Clients in a J2EE application can use a *Service Locator* to look up EJB components. The JNDI environment is set up (location, authentication credentials, and so on.) so that it connects to the naming and directory service used by the application. The Client uses an InitialContext to locate the JNDI registry service and looks up the requested EJB Home object (Target) using a registered JNDI name.

Once the EJB Home object is obtained, it can be cached in the ServiceLocator for future use to avoid another JNDI lookup when the client needs the same home object again. When the Client obtains the EJBHome object, it can create, remove, or find (for entity beans) the enterprise bean instances. An EJB *Service Locator* can look up both local and remote home objects.

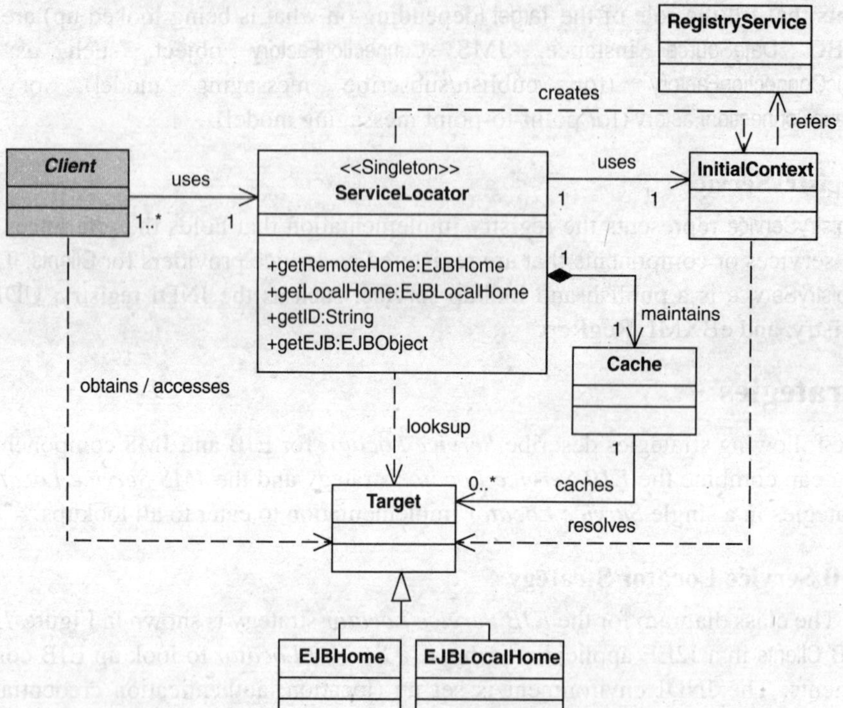

Figure 7.7 EJB Service Locator Strategy Class Diagram

When looking up a remote home object, the EJB *Service Locator* uses the PortableRemoteObject.narrow() method to narrow the search for the looked-up object to the correct EJB Home class. When looking up local EJB home objects, a class cast is sufficient without using the PortableRemoteObject.narrow() operation.

The interaction among the participants in a *Service Locator* for an enterprise bean is shown in Figure 7.8.

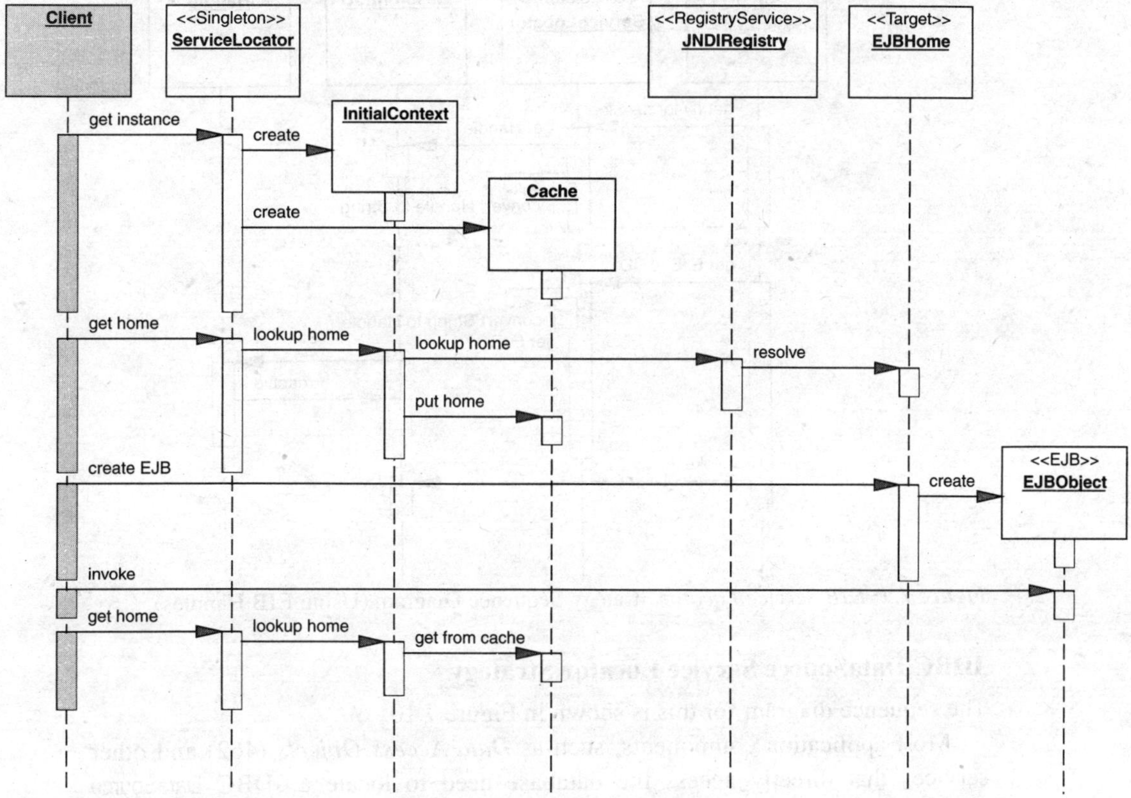

Figure 7.8 EJB Service Locator Strategy Sequence Diagram

You can further extend the *EJB Service Locator* strategy to provide a serialized version of the EJB handler to the Client. The Client can use this handle to subsequently connect back to the EJB component it was previously connected to, provided that EJB component still exists. The sequence diagram in Figure 7.9 shows an example of this strategy where the Client obtains a String representation of the EJB Handle for a session bean. At a later point, it provides that String ID to the *Service Locator* to reconnect to the same session bean. The *Service Locator* converts this ID into the EJB Handle and reconnects to the session bean, provided it has not been removed or timed out.

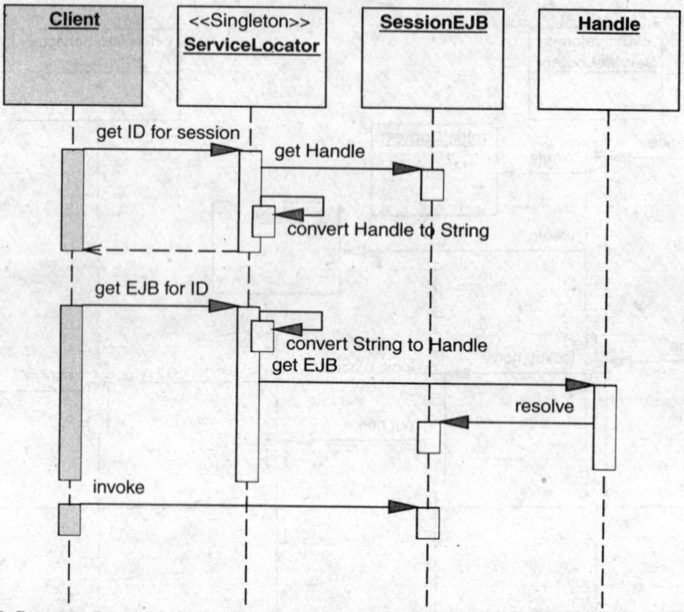

Figure 7.9 *EJB Service Locator* Strategy Sequence Diagram (Using EJB Handles)

JDBC DataSource Service Locator Strategy

The sequence diagram for this is shown in Figure 7.10.

Most application components, such as *Data Access Objects* (462) and other services that directly access the database need to locate a JDBC DataSource instance.

The *Service Locator* can implement JDBC data source lookup functionality to cater to this requirement. The role of the Target in Figure 7.5 is fulfilled by a JDBC DataSource instance.

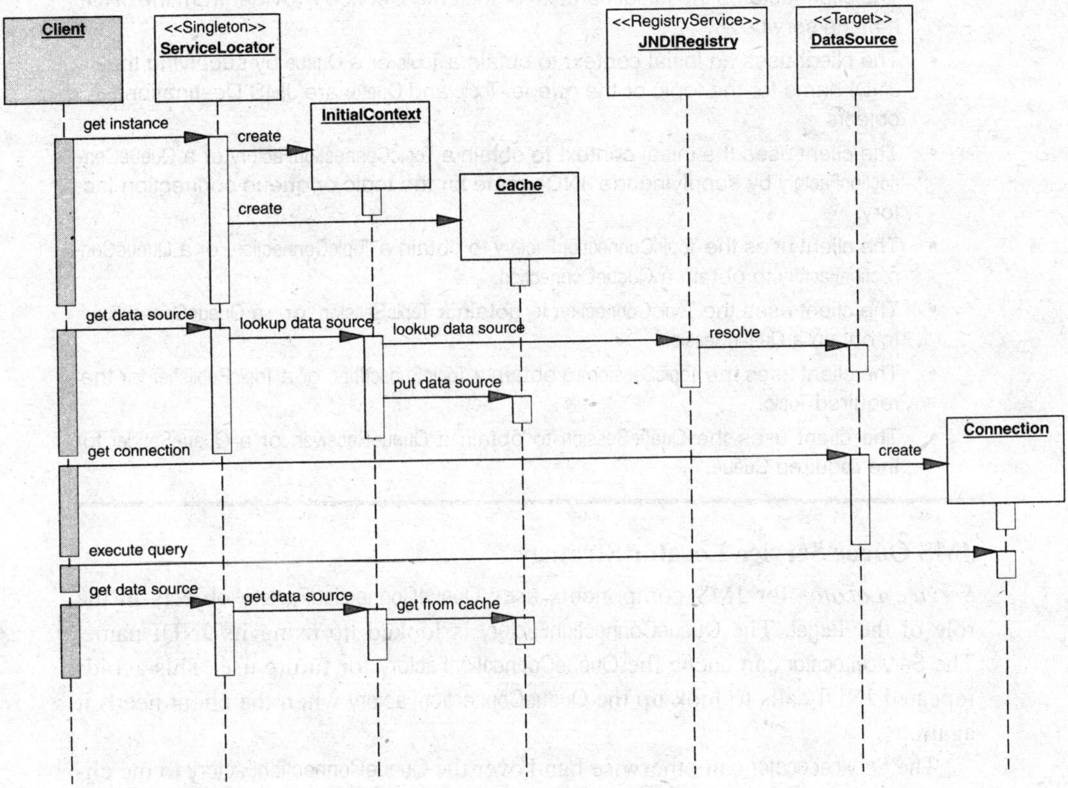

Figure 7.10 JDBC Service Locator Strategy Sequence Diagram

JMS Service Locator Strategies

JMS clients in the application need to look up various JMS components, such as Topic, TopicConnectionFactory, Queue, and QueueConnectionFactory objects. The following two strategies, *JMS Queue Service Locator* strategy and *JMS Topic Service Locator* strategy, are used by JMS clients.

Design Note: Clients and JMS Components

Looking up and creating JMS components—Topic, Queue, QueueConnection, QueueSession, TopicConnection, and TopicSession—involves the following steps. Note that in these steps, Topic is used for the publish/subscribe messaging model and Queue is used for the point-to-point messaging model.

- The JNDI environment is set up (location, authentication credentials, etc.) so that it connects to the naming and directory service used by the application.

- The client obtains the initial context for the JMS Service Provider from the JNDI naming service.
- The client uses an initial context to obtain a Topic or a Queue by supplying the JNDI name for the topic or the queue. Topic and Queue are JMS Destination objects.
- The client uses the initial context to obtain a TopicConnectionFactory or a QueueConnectionFactory by supplying the JNDI name for the topic or queue connection factory.
- The client uses the TopicConnectionFactory to obtain a TopicConnection, or a QueueConnectionFactory to obtain a QueueConnection.
- The client uses the TopicConnection to obtain a TopicSession, or a QueueConnection to obtain a QueueSession.
- The client uses the TopicSession to obtain a TopicSubscriber, or a TopicPublisher for the required Topic.
- The client uses the QueueSession to obtain a QueueReceiver, or a QueueSender for the required Queue.

JMS Queue Service Locator Strategy

Service Locator for JMS components uses QueueConnectionFactory objects in the role of the Target. The QueueConnectionFactory is looked up using its JNDI name. The ServiceLocator can cache the QueueConnectionFactory for future use. This avoids repeated JNDI calls to look up the QueueConnectionFactory when the client needs it again.

The ServiceLocator can otherwise hand over the QueueConnectionFactory to the client. The Client can then use it to create a QueueConnection. You need a QueueConnection to obtain a QueueSession or to create a Message, a QueueSender (to send messages to the queue), or a QueueReceiver (to receive messages from a queue).

The class diagram for the *JMS Queue Service Locator* strategy is shown in Figure 7.11. In this diagram, the Queue is a JMS Destination object registered as a JNDI-administered object representing the queue. You can obtain the Queue object from the context by looking it up using its JNDI name.

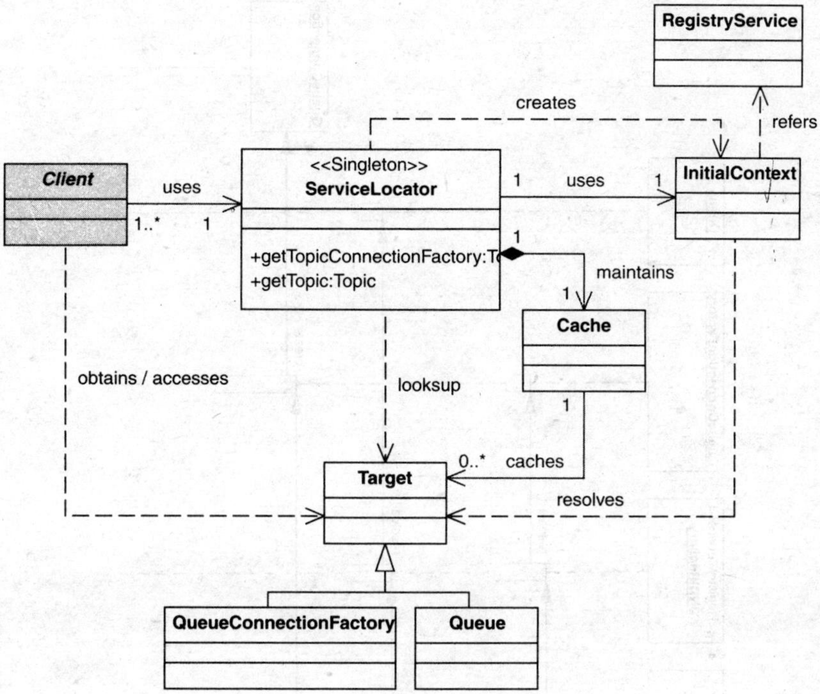

Figure 7.11 *JMS Queue Service Locator* Strategy Class Diagram

The interaction among the participants in a *Service Locator* for point-to-point messaging using JMS Queues is shown in Figure 7.12.

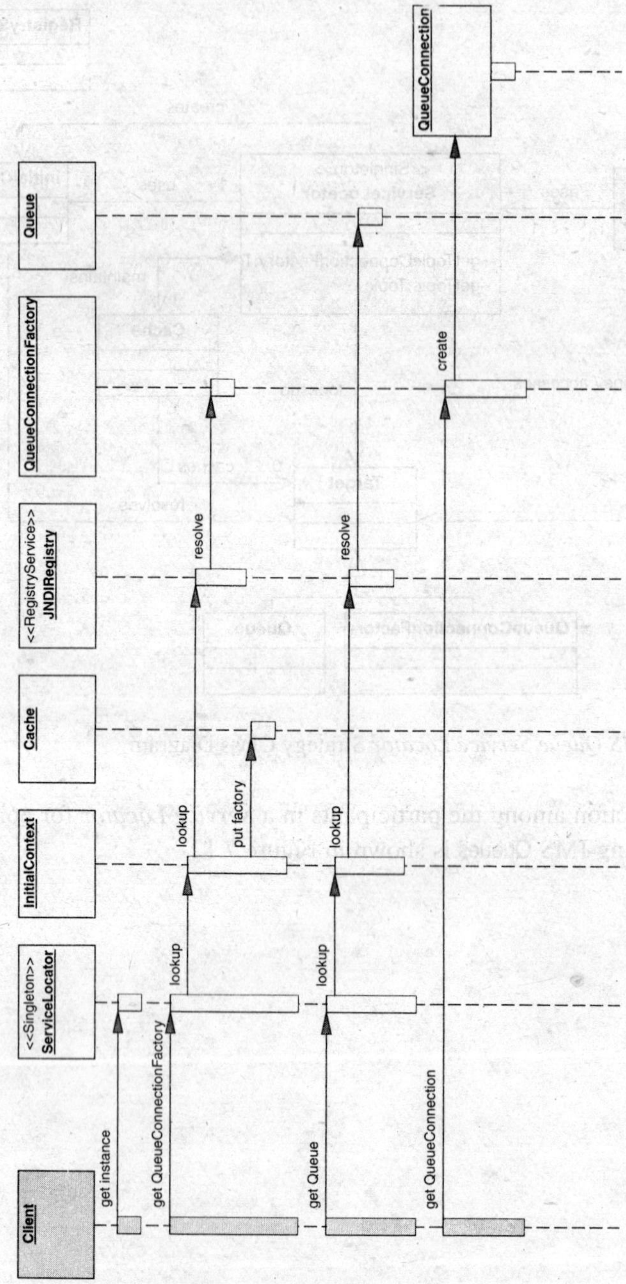

Figure 7.12 *JMS Queue Service Locator* Strategy Sequence Diagram

JMS Topic Service Locator Strategy

The *Service Locator* for JMS components uses TopicConnectionFactory objects in the role of the Target. The TopicConnectionFactory is looked up using its JNDI name. The ServiceLocator can cache the TopicConnectionFactory for future use.

This avoids repeated JNDI calls to look up the TopicConnectionFactory when the client needs it again. The ServiceLocator can otherwise hand over the TopicConnectionFactory to the client.

The Client can then use the TopicConnectionFactory to create a TopicConnection. You need a TopicConnection to obtain a TopicSession or to create a Message, a TopicPublisher (to publish messages to a topic), or a TopicSubscriber (to subscribe to a topic).

The class diagram for the *JMS Topic Service Locator* strategy is shown in Figure 7.13. In this diagram, the Topic is a JMS Destination object registered as a JNDI-administered object representing the topic. You can obtain the Topic object from the context by looking it up using its JNDI name.

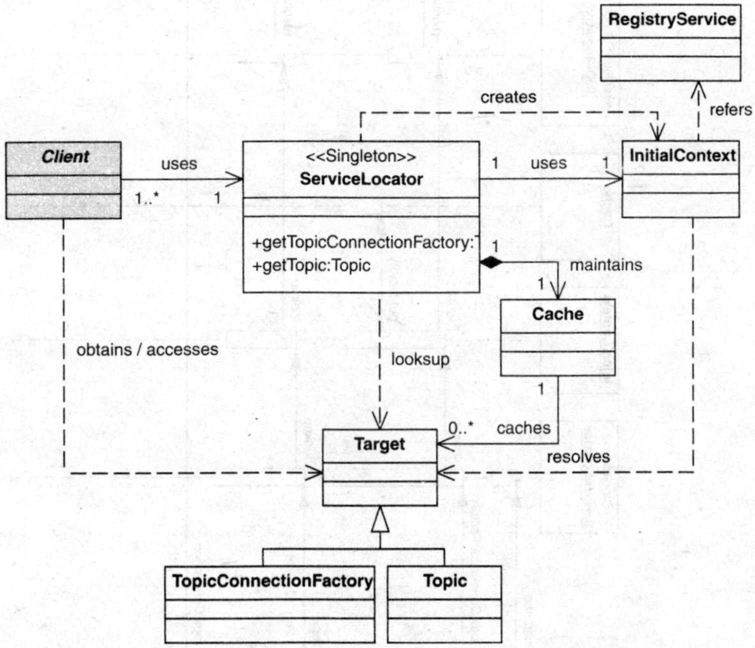

Figure 7.13 *JMS Topic Service Locator* Strategy Class Diagram

The interaction among the participants in a *Service Locator* for publish/subscribe messaging using JMS Topics is shown in Figure 7.14 on page 328.

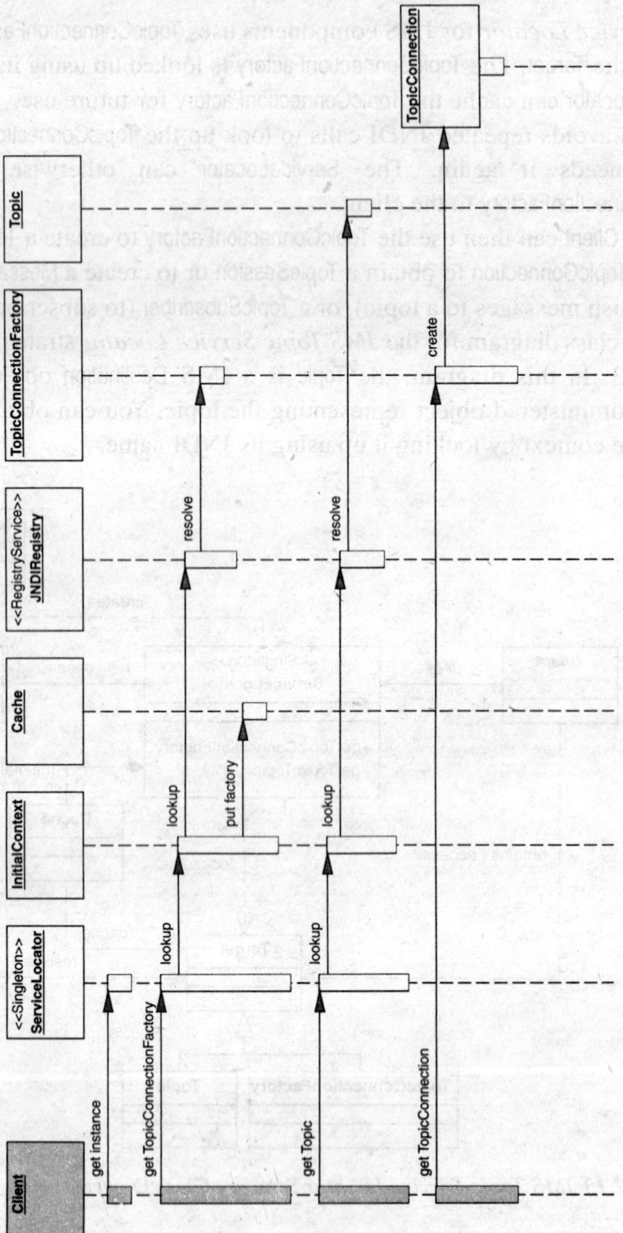

***Figure 7.14** JMS Topic Service Locator* **Strategy Sequence Diagram**

Web Service Locator Strategy

If your application needs to locate a web service published in a UDDI registry or ebXML registry/repository, you can use the *Web Service Locator* strategy. The *Web Service Locator* can look up and obtain a connection to the registry/repository and provide other methods to search for different services in that registry/repository. The sample code in Example 7.9 on page 337 shows a sample implementation of this strategy.

Consequences

- ***Abstracts complexity***
  The *Service Locator* encapsulates the complexity of the service lookup and creation process (described in the problem) and keeps it hidden from the client.
- ***Provides uniform service access to clients***
  The *Service Locator* provides a useful and precise interface that all clients can use. The interface ensures that all types of clients in the application uniformly access business objects, in terms of lookup and creation. This uniformity reduces development and maintenance overhead.
- ***Facilitates adding EJB business components***
  Because clients of enterprise beans are not aware of the EJB Home objects, you can add new EJB Home objects for enterprise beans developed and deployed at a later time without impacting the clients. JMS clients are not directly aware of the JMS connection factories, so you can add new connection factories without impacting the clients.
- ***Improves network performance***
  The clients are not involved in lookup and object creation. Because the *Service Locator* performs this work, it can aggregate the network calls required to look up and create business objects.
- ***Improves client performance by caching***
  The *Service Locator* can cache the initial context objects and references to the factory objects (EJBHome, JMS connection factories). Also, when accessing web services, the *Service Locator* can cache WSDL definitions and endpoints.

Sample Code

Implementing Service Locator

Example 7.3 shows a sample *Service Locator* implementation that is implemented as a *Singleton* [GoF] and caches service objects.

Example 7.3 ServiceLocator.java: Implementing a Service Locator

```
package com.corej2eepatterns.servicelocator;

// imports
public class ServiceLocator {

    private InitialContext initialContext;
    private Map cache;

    private static ServiceLocator _instance;

    static {
        try {
            _instance = new ServiceLocator();
        } catch (ServiceLocatorException se) {
            System.err.println(se);
            se.printStackTrace(System.err);
        }
    }

    private ServiceLocator() throws ServiceLocatorException {
        try {
            initialContext = new InitialContext();
            cache = Collections.
                synchronizedMap(new HashMap());
        } catch (NamingException ne) {
            throw new ServiceLocatorException(ne);
        } catch (Exception e) {
            throw new ServiceLocatorException(e);
        }
    }

    static public ServiceLocator getInstance() {
        return _instance;
    }
```

```

    // implement lookup methods here
    . . .
}
```

Implementing EJB Service Locator

Example 7.4 shows the *Service Locator* implementing the *EJB Service Locator* strategy to look up local and remote EJBHome objects. Additionally, the sample code in Example 7.5 implements the convenience methods to obtain String representations of EJB Handles and to reconnect to a previously used EJB component using a String handle.

Example 7.4 ServiceLocator.java: Implementing EJB Service Locator Strategy

```
package com.corej2eepatterns.servicelocator;

// imports
public class ServiceLocator {
    . . .
    // look up a local home given the JNDI name for the
    // local home
    public EJBLocalHome getLocalHome(String jndiHomeName)
    throws ServiceLocatorException {
        EJBLocalHome localHome = null;
        try {
            if (cache.containsKey(jndiHomeName)) {
                localHome = (EJBLocalHome)
                    cache.get(jndiHomeName);
            } else {
                localHome = (EJBLocalHome)
                    initialContext.lookup(jndiHomeName);
                cache.put(jndiHomeName, localHome);
            }
        } catch (NamingException nex) {
            throw new ServiceLocatorException(nex);
        } catch (Exception ex) {
            throw new ServiceLocatorException(ex);
        }
        return localHome;
    }

```

```
    // lookup a remote home given the JNDI name for the
    // remote home
    public EJBHome getRemoteHome(
        String jndiHomeName, Class homeClassName)
    throws ServiceLocatorException {
        EJBHome remoteHome = null;
        try {
            if (cache.containsKey(jndiHomeName)) {
                remoteHome =
                    (EJBHome) cache.get(jndiHomeName);
            } else {
                Object objref =
                    initialContext.lookup(jndiHomeName);
                Object obj = PortableRemoteObject.
                    narrow(objref, homeClassName);
                remoteHome = (EJBHome)obj;
                cache.put(jndiHomeName, remoteHome);
            }
        } catch (NamingException nex) {
            throw new ServiceLocatorException(nex);
        } catch (Exception ex) {
            throw new ServiceLocatorException(ex);
        }
        return remoteHome;
    }

    . . .
}
```

Example 7.5 ServiceLocator.java: Implementing EJB Service Locator Strategy – Using a Handle

```
package com.corej2eepatterns.servicelocator;

// imports
public class ServiceLocator {
    . . .

    public EJBObject getService(String id)
    throws ServiceLocatorException {
        if (id == null) {
            throw new ServiceLocatorException(
            "Invalid ID: Cannot create Handle");
```

```
        }
        try {
            byte[] bytes = new String(id).getBytes();
            InputStream io = new ByteArrayInputStream(bytes);
            ObjectInputStream os = new ObjectInputStream(io);
            javax.ejb.Handle handle =
                (javax.ejb.Handle) os.readObject();
            return handle.getEJBObject();
        } catch (Exception ex) {
            throw new ServiceLocatorException(ex);
        }
    }

    // Returns the String that represents the given
    // EJBObject's handle in serialized format.
    public String getId(EJBObject session)
    throws ServiceLocatorException {
        String id=null;
        try {
            javax.ejb.Handle handle = session.getHandle();
            ByteArrayOutputStream fo =
                new ByteArrayOutputStream();
            ObjectOutputStream so =
                new ObjectOutputStream(fo);
            so.writeObject(handle);
            so.flush();
            so.close();
            id = new String(fo.toByteArray());
        } catch (RemoteException rex) {
            throw new ServiceLocatorException(rex);
        } catch (IOException ioex) {
            throw new ServiceLocatorException(ioex);
        }

        return id;
    }
    . . .
}
```

Implementing JMS Service Locator

Example 7.6 and Example 7.7 show the *JMS Service Locator* strategies to obtain Topic, TopicConnectionFactory, Queue, and QueueConnectionFactory.

Example 7.6 ServiceLocator.java: Implementing JMS Topic Service Locator Strategy

```
package com.corej2eepatterns.servicelocator;

// imports
public class ServiceLocator {
    . . .

    // lookup and return a TopicConnectionFactory
    public TopicConnectionFactory getTopicConnectionFactory(
        String topicConnectionFactoryName)
    throws ServiceLocatorException {
        TopicConnectionFactory topicFactory = null;
        try {
          if (cache.containsKey(topicConnectionFactoryName)) {
              topicFactory = (TopicConnectionFactory)
                  cache.get(topicConnectionFactoryName);
          } else {
              topicFactory = (TopicConnectionFactory)
                initialContext.
                    lookup(topicConnectionFactoryName);
              cache.put(topicConnectionFactoryName,
                  topicFactory);
          }
        } catch (NamingException nex) {
            throw new ServiceLocatorException(nex);
        } catch (Exception ex) {
            throw new ServiceLocatorException(ex);
        }
        return topicFactory;
    }

    // lookup and return a TopicConnectionFactory
    public  Topic getTopic(String topicName)
    throws ServiceLocatorException {
        Topic topic = null;
        try {
```

```
            if (cache.containsKey(topicName)) {
                topic = (Topic) cache.get(topicName);
            } else {
                topic =
                    (Topic)initialContext.lookup(topicName);
                cache.put(topicName, topic);
            }
        } catch (NamingException nex) {
            throw new ServiceLocatorException(nex);
        } catch (Exception ex) {
            throw new ServiceLocatorException(ex);
        }
        return topic;
    }

    . . .
}
```

Example 7.7 ServiceLocator.java: Implementing JMS Queue Service Locator Strategy

```
package com.corej2eepatterns.servicelocator;

// imports
public class ServiceLocator {
    . . .

    public QueueConnectionFactory getQueueConnectionFactory(
        String queueConnectionFactoryName)
    throws ServiceLocatorException {
        QueueConnectionFactory queueFactory = null;
        try {
          if (cache.containsKey(queueConnectionFactoryName)) {
              queueFactory = (QueueConnectionFactory)
                  cache.get(queueConnectionFactoryName);
          } else {
              queueFactory = (QueueConnectionFactory)
                  initialContext.lookup(
                      queueConnectionFactoryName);
              cache.put(queueConnectionFactoryName,
                  queueFactory);
          }
        } catch (NamingException nex) {
```

```
            throw new ServiceLocatorException(nex);
        } catch (Exception ex) {
            throw new ServiceLocatorException(ex);
        }

        return queueFactory;
    }

    public Queue getQueue(String queueName)
    throws ServiceLocatorException {
        Queue queue = null;
        try {
            if (cache.containsKey(queueName)) {
                queue = (Queue) cache.get(queueName);
            } else {
                queue =
                    (Queue)initialContext.lookup(queueName);
                cache.put(queueName, queue);
            }
        } catch (NamingException nex) {
            throw new ServiceLocatorException(nex);
        } catch (Exception ex) {
            throw new ServiceLocatorException(ex);
        }

        return queue;
    }
    . . .
}
```

Implementing JDBC DataSource Service Locator

Example 7.8 shows a sample implementation for the JDBC *DataSource Service Locator* strategy.

Example 7.8 ServiceLocator.java: Implementing JDBC DataSource Service Locator Strategy

```
package com.corej2eepatterns.servicelocator;

// imports
public class ServiceLocator {
    . . .

```

```
    public DataSource getDataSource(String dataSourceName)
    throws ServiceLocatorException {
        DataSource dataSource = null;
        try {
            if (cache.containsKey(dataSourceName)) {
                dataSource =
                    (DataSource) cache.get(dataSourceName);
            } else {
                dataSource = (DataSource)
                    initialContext.lookup(dataSourceName);
                cache.put(dataSourceName, dataSource );
            }
        } catch (NamingException nex) {
            throw new ServiceLocatorException(nex);
        } catch (Exception ex) {
            throw new ServiceLocatorException(ex);
        }
        return dataSource;
    }
    . . .
}
```

Implementing Web Service Locator

Example 7.9 shows a sample implementation for the *Web Service Locator* strategy.

Example 7.9 ServiceLocator.java: Implementing Web Service Locator Strategy

```
package com.corej2eepatterns.servicelocator;
// imports
public class ServiceLocator {
    . . .

  // returns a Connection to a UDDI registry
  public Connection getRegistryConnection(String registryURL)
  {
    javax.xml.registry.Connection
      registryConnection = null;
    try {
      if (cache.containsKey(registryURL)) {
        registryConnection =
          (Connection) cache.get(registryURL);
```

```
      } else {
         // Create a Connection to the registry
         // after setting standard JAXR properties such as
         // javax.xml.registry.queryManagerURL

         javax.xml.registry.ConnectionFactory factory =
            ConnectionFactory.newInstance();

         // Define connection configuration properties
         Properties props = new Properties();
         props.setProperty(
            "javax.xml.registry.queryManagerURL",
            registryURL);
         props.setProperty(
            "javax.xml.registry.factoryClass",
        "com.sun.xml.registry.uddi.ConnectionFactoryImpl");
         factory.setProperties(props);

         registryConnection = factory.createConnection();
         cache.put(registryURL, registryConnection);
      }
    } catch (Exception e) {
      throw new ServiceLocatorException(e);
    } catch (JAXRException je) {
      throw new ServiceLocatorException(je);
    }
   return registryConnection;
  }

  // Searches a Registry for a Service URI Endpoint using a
  // tModelKey of a published Service.
  // registryURL - is the URL of the UDDI provider
  // tModelKey   - is the search string specific to
  //      Published Businesses
  public String getServiceAccessURI(
    String registryURL, String tModelKey) {

    javax.xml.registry.Connection regCon = null;
    javax.xml.registry.RegistryService regSvc = null;
    javax.xml.registry.BusinessQueryManager
      queryManager = null;
    javax.xml.registry.BusinessLifeCycleManager
      lifeCycleManager = null;
```

```
String serviceAccessURI = null;
try {
  if (cache.containsKey(tModelKey)) {
    serviceAccessURI = (String) cache.get(tModelKey);
  } else {
    regCon = getRegistryConnection(registryURL);
    regSvc = regCon.getRegistryService();
    queryManager = regSvc.getBusinessQueryManager();
    javax.xml.registry.infomodel.RegistryObject
      regob = businessQueryManager.
        getRegistryObject(tModelKey,
          BusinessLifeCycleManager.CONCEPT);
    Collection coll = new ArrayList();
    coll.add(regob);

    //Find organizations
    BulkResponse results =
      businessQueryManager.findOrganizations(
        null, null, null, coll, null, null);

    Collection co = results.getCollection();
    Iterator it = co.iterator();

    while (it.hasNext()) {
      Organization org = (Organization)it.next();
      String orgName = org.getName().getValue();
      Collection cc = org.getServices();
      for (Iterator iterator=cc.iterator();
        iterator.hasNext();) {
        Service service = (Service) iterator.next();
        Collection cb = service.getServiceBindings();
        for (Iterator ito = cb.iterator();
          ito.hasNext();) {
          ServiceBinding serviceBinding =
            (ServiceBinding) ito.next();
          if (serviceBinding != null ||
            serviceBinding.getAccessURI() != null) {
              serviceBinding.getAccessURI());
              serviceAccessURI =
                serviceBinding.getAccessURI();
              cache.put(tModelKey,
                serviceBinding.getAccessURI());
          }
```

```
                }
            }
        }
    }
  } catch (JAXRException e) {
    throw new ServiceLocatorException(e);
  }

  return serviceAccessURI;
}

. . .
}

```

Related Patterns

- ***Business Delegate (302)***
  Business Delegate (302) uses a *Service Locator* (315) to locate and obtain references to the business service objects, such as EJB objects, JMS topics, and JMS queues. This separates the complexity of service location from the *Business Delegate* (302), leading to loose coupling and increased manageability.
- ***Session Façade (341)***
  Session Façade (341) uses a *Service Locator* (315) to locate and obtain home and remote references to the session beans and entity beans, as well as to locate a data source.
- ***Transfer Object Assembler (433)***
  Transfer Object Assembler **(433)** uses a *Service Locator* (315) to locate references to session beans and entity beans that it needs to access data and build a composite transfer object.
- ***Data Access Object (462)***
  A *Data Access Object* (462) uses a *Service Locator* (315) to look up and obtain a reference to a data source.

Session Façade

Problem

You want to expose business components and services to remote clients.

Session Façade addresses two issues: controlling client access to business objects, and limiting network traffic between remote clients and fine-grained business components and services.

Client access to business components Typically, multi-tiered J2EE applications have server-side components that are implemented as *Business Objects* (374), as POJOs, or as entity beans. However, exposing these components and allowing clients to directly access them can cause the following problems:

- Tight coupling between the client and the business components leads to direct dependency, so when you change a business component interface, it affects the clients directly.
- Direct access also might require the client to have complex logic to coordinate and interact with many business components, and to be aware of the potentially complex relationships among those business components. Thus, the client must have the complex logic to do lookups, demarcate transactions, manage security, and do business processing. This increases the complexity and responsibility of the client.
- When you have different types of clients, direct access to business components leads to inconsistent use of the common business components because each type of client embeds this interaction independent of other types of clients. This might also lead to duplication of code in the various clients. This decreases the maintainability and flexibility of the implementation.

Remote client access to fine-grained components Applications might have fine-grained business-tier components and services that must be accessed by remote clients. When clients access the business components directly, they might remotely access numerous fine-grained components repeatedly. This increases the chattiness of the application and leads to network performance degradation due to many remote network calls.

Forces

- You want to avoid giving clients direct access to business-tier components, to prevent tight coupling with the clients.
- You want to provide a remote access layer to your *Business Objects* (374) and other business-tier components.
- You want to aggregate and expose your *Application Services* (357) and other services to remote clients.
- You want to centralize and aggregate all business logic that needs to be exposed to remote clients.
- You want to hide the complex interactions and interdependencies between business components and services to improve manageability, centralize logic, increase flexibility, and improve ability to cope with changes.

Solution

Use a *Session Façade* to encapsulate business-tier components and expose a coarse-grained service to remote clients. Clients access *a Session Façade* instead of accessing business components directly.

A *Session Façade* is implemented as a session bean and interacts with business components, such as *Business Objects* (374) and *Application Services* (357). A *Session Façade* provides a remote service layer that exposes only the required interfaces used by the clients.

A *Session Façade* works best when it contains little or no business logic. When business logic is present, it should be placed in the *Application Service* (357), which is invoked by the *Session Façade*.

DESIGN NOTE: USE CASES AND *SESSION FAÇADES*

So, how do you identify the *Session Façade* through studying use cases? Mapping every use case to a *Session Façade* results in too many facades. This defeats the intention of having fewer coarse-grained session beans, and is not recommended.

Instead, as you identify different use cases during the modeling process and design the services they need, you should identify related services. Then group and partition these services so that they are implemented as coarse-grained *Session Façades*. Alternatively, you might choose to design and implement these services as a layer of *Application Services* (357) and remotely expose them using a layer of *Session Façades*. Grouping related services in this manner results in fewer *Session Façades* in your application.

For example, for a banking application, you might group the interactions related to managing an **Account** into a single *Session Façade*. The use cases related to managing an **Account**, such as **Create New Account**, **Change Account Information**, **View Account information**, and so on, all deal with **Account** business objects.

Structure

Figure 7.15 shows the class diagram representing the *Session Façade* pattern.

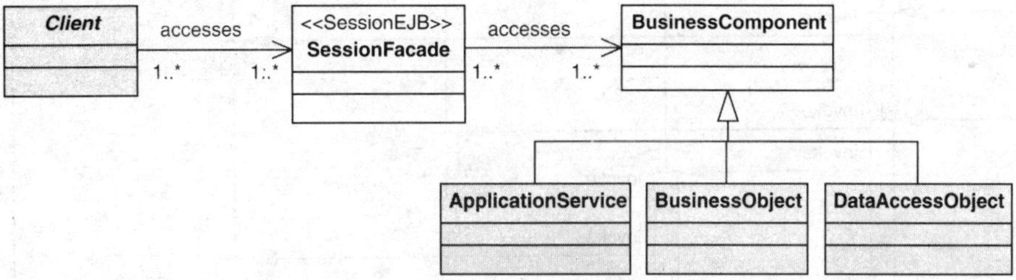

Figure 7.15 *Session Façade* Class Diagram

Participants and Collaborations

Figure 7.16 on page 344 contains the sequence diagram that shows the interactions of a *Session Façade* with *Business Objects* (374) implemented as entity beans, and a POJO *Application Service* (357), all acting as participants in fulfilling the requests from the Client.

Client

The Client represents the client of the *Session Façade* that needs access to the business service. This client is typically a *Business Delegate* (302) in another tier.

SessionFacade

The SessionFacade is the main role of this pattern. The SessionFacade is implemented as a session bean, stateful or stateless as needed to support the use cases it services. The SessionFacade hides the complexity of dealing with several BusinessComponents that participate in a use case and thereby provides a higher-level, coarse-grained remote service abstraction to the Clients.

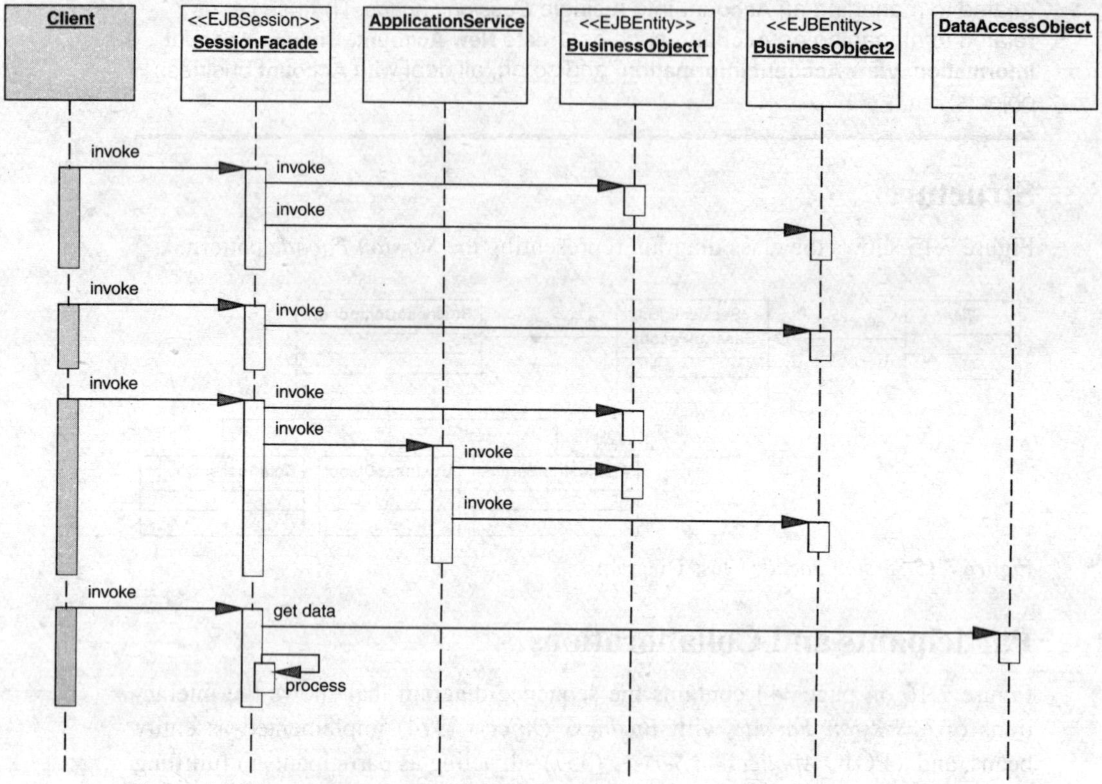

Figure 7.16 Session Façade Sequence Diagram

BusinessComponent

BusinessComponent participates in fulfilling the client's request. A BusinessComponent can be implemented as a *Business Object* (374) that models business data and behavior, or as an *Application Service* (357). For example, in the sequence diagram, the *Business Object* (374) participants are implemented as entity beans, as shown in BusinessObject1 and BusinessObject2.The ApplicationService participant is implemented as a POJO.

ApplicationService

ApplicationService encapsulates the BusinessObjects and implements the business logic that is executed to provide the required service. The SessionFacade can interact with several ApplicationService objects to fulfill a single request from the client.

DataAccessObject

DataAccessObject represents a role when you use *Data Access Objects* (462) with a *Session Façade*. In some applications, a *Session Façade* can directly use one or more *Data Access Objects* (462) to obtain business data. Typically, this is done in simple applications that do not require a layer of *Business Objects* (374) in the business tier.

Session Façade Strategies

Stateless *Session Façade* Strategy

When implementing the *Session Façade*, you must first decide whether the facade session bean is a stateful or stateless session bean. You base this decision on the business process implemented by the *Session Façade* to service a use case request.

A business process that needs only one method call to complete the service is a **non-conversational business process**. Such processes are suitably implemented using a stateless session bean.

Study the use cases and scenarios to determine the *Session Façade* definitions. If the use case is nonconversational, then the client initiates the use case, using a single method in the *Session Façade*. When the method completes, the use case completes also. There is no need to save the conversational state between one method invocation and the next. In this scenario, the *Session Façade* can be implemented as a stateless session bean.

Stateful *Session Façade* Strategy

A business process that needs multiple method calls to complete the service is a **conversational business process**. The conversational state must be saved between each client method invocation. In this scenario, a stateful session bean might be a more suitable approach for implementing the *Session Façade*.

Consequences

- ***Introduces a layer that provides services to remote clients***
  Session Façades introduce a layer between clients and the business tier to provide coarse-grained remote services. For some applications, this might be unnecessary overhead, especially if the business tier is implemented without using EJB components. However, *Session Façades* have almost become a necessity in J2EE applications because they provide remote services and leverage the benefits of an EJB container, such as transactions, security, and lifecycle management.

- ***Exposes a uniform coarse-grained interface***
  A *Session Façade* encapsulates the complexity of the underlying business component interactions and presents the client with a simpler coarse-grained service-layer interface to the system that is easy to understand and use. In addition, by providing a *Business Delegate* (302) for each *Session Façade*, you can make it easier for client-side developers to leverage the power of *Session Façades.*
- ***Reduces coupling between the tiers***
  Using a *Session Façade* decouples the business components from the clients, and reduces tight coupling and dependency between the presentation and business tiers. You can additionally implement *Application Services* (357) to encapsulate the complex business logic that acts on several *Business Objects* (374). Instead of implementing the business logic, the *Session Façades* can delegate the business logic to *Application Service* (357) to implement.
- ***Promotes layering, increases flexibility and maintainability***
  When using *Session Façades* with *Application Services* (357), you increase the flexibility of the system by layering and centralizing interactions. This provides a greater ability to cope with changes due to reduced coupling. Although changes to the business logic might require changes in the *Application Services* (357)or even the *Session Façades*, the layering makes such changes more manageable.
- ***Reduces complexity***
  Using *Application Services (*357), you reduce the complexity of *Session Façades*. Using *Business Delegate* (302) for accessing *Session Façades* reduces the complexity of client code. This helps make the system more maintainable and flexible.
- ***Improves performance, reduces fine-grained remote methods***
  The *Session Façade* can also improve performance because it reduces the number of remote network invocations by aggregating various fine-grained interactions into a coarse-grained method. Furthermore, the *Session Façades* are typically located in the same process space as the participating business components, enabling faster communication between the two.
- ***Centralizes security management***
  You can manage security policies for the application at the *Session Façade* level, since this is the tier presented to the clients. Because of the *Session Façade*'s coarse-grained access, it is easier and more manageable to define security policies at this level rather than implementing security policies for each participating fine-grained business component.

- ***Centralizes transaction control***
  The *Session Façade* represents the coarse-grained remote access point to business-tier services, so centralizing and applying transaction management at the *Session Façade* layer is easier. The *Session Façade* offers a central place for managing and defining transaction control in a coarse-grained fashion. This is simpler than managing transactions in finer-grained business components or at the client side.
- ***Exposes fewer remote interfaces to clients***
  The *Session Façade* presents a coarse-grained access mechanism to the business components, which greatly reduces the number of business components exposed to the client. This reduces the scope for application performance degradation because the number of interactions between the clients and the *Session Façade* is lower than the number of direct interactions between the client and the individual business components.

Sample Code

Implementing the *Session Façade*

Consider a professional services application (PSA). The workflow related to entity beans (such as Project and Resource) is encapsulated in ProjectResourceManagerSession, which is implemented using the *Session Façade* pattern. Example 7.10 shows the interaction with Resource and Project entity beans, as well as other business components, such as *Value List Handler* (444) and *Transfer Object Assemblers* (433).

Example 7.10 Implementing *Session Façade* – Session Bean

```

package corepatterns.apps.psa.ejb;

import java.util.*;
import java.rmi.RemoteException;
import javax.ejb.*;
import javax.naming.*;
import corepatterns.apps.psa.core.*;
import corepatterns.util.ServiceLocator;
import corepatterns.util.ServiceLocatorException;

// Note: all try/catch details not shown for brevity.

public class ProjectResourceManagerSession
```

```
    implements SessionBean {

  private SessionContext context;

  // Remote references for the entity Beans
  // encapsulated by this facade
  private Resource resourceEntity = null;
  private Project projectEntity = null;
  ...

  // default create
  public void ejbCreate() throws CreateException { }

  // create method to create this facade and to establish
  // connections to the required entity beans using primary
  // key values
  public void ejbCreate(String resourceId, String projectId,
      ...)
  throws CreateException, ResourceException {

    try {
      // locate and connect to entity beans
      connectToEntities(resourceId, projectId, ...);
    } catch (...) {
      // Handle exceptions
    }
  }

  // method to connect the session facade to its
  // entity beans using the primary key values
  private void connectToEntities (String resourceId,
    String projectId)
  throws ResourceException {
    resourceEntity = getResourceEntity(resourceId);
    projectEntity = getProjectEntity(projectId);
    ...
  }

  // method to reconnect the session facade to a different
  // set of entity beans using primary key values
  public resetEntities(String resourceId, String projectId,
      ...)
  throws PSAException {
```

```

    connectToEntities(resourceId, projectId, ...);
  }

  // private method to get Home for Resource
  private ResourceHome getResourceHome()
  throws ServiceLocatorException {
    return ServiceLocator.getInstance().getLocalHome(
      "ResourceEntity", ResourceHome.class);
  }

  // private method to get Home for Project
  private ProjectHome getProjectHome()
  throws ServiceLocatorException {
    return ServiceLocator.getInstance().getLocalHome(
      "ProjectEntity", ProjectHome.class);
  }

  // private method to get Resource entity
  private Resource getResourceEntity(String resourceId)
  throws ResourceException {
    try {
      ResourceHome home = getResourceHome();
      return (Resource) home.findByPrimaryKey(resourceId);
    } catch (...) {
      // Handle exceptions
    }
  }

  // private method to get Project entity
  private Project getProjectEntity(String projectId)
  throws ProjectException {
    // similar to getResourceEntity
    ...
  }

  // Method to encapsulate workflow related to assigning a
  // resource to a project. It deals with Project and
  // Resource Entity beans
  public void assignResourceToProject(int numHours)
  throws PSAException {

    try {
```

```
        if ((projectEntity == null) ||
            (resourceEntity == null)) {
          // SessionFacade not connected to entities
          throw new PSAException(...);
        }

        // Get Resource data
        ResourceTO resourceTO =
          resourceEntity.getResourceData();

        // Get Project data
        ProjectTO projectTO =projectEntity.getProjectData();

        // first add Resource to Project
        projectEntity.addResource(resourceTO);

        // Create a new Commitment for the Project
        CommitmentTO commitment = new CommitmentTO(...);

        // add the commitment to the Resource
        projectEntity.addCommitment(commitment);

      } catch (...) {
        // Handle exceptions
      }
    }

    // Similarly implement other business methods to
    // facilitate various use cases/interactions
    public void unassignResourceFromProject()
    throws PSAException {
      ...
    }

    // Methods working with ResourceEntity
    public ResourceTO getResourceData()
    throws ResourceException {
      ...
    }

    // Update Resource Entity Bean
    public void setResourceData(ResourceTO resource)
    throws ResourceException {
```

```
    ...
}

// Create new Resource Entity bean
public ResourceTO createNewResource(ResourceTO resource)
throws ResourceException {
    ...
}

// Methods for managing resource's blockout time
public void addBlockoutTime(Collection blockoutTime)
throws RemoteException,BlockoutTimeException {
    ...
}

public void updateBlockoutTime(Collection blockoutTime)
throws RemoteException, BlockoutTimeException {
    ...
}

public Collection getResourceCommitments()
throws RemoteException, ResourceException {
    ...
}

// Methods working with ProjectEntity
public ProjectTO getProjectData()
throws ProjectException {
    ...
}

// Update Project Entity Bean
public void setProjectData(ProjectTO project)
throws ProjectException {
    ...
}

// Create new Project Entity bean
public ProjectTO createNewProject(ProjectTO project)
throws ProjectException {
    ...
}
```

```
...

// Other session facade method examples

// This proxies a call to a Transfer Object Assembler
// to obtain a composite transfer object.
// See Transfer Object Assembler pattern.
public ProjectCTO getProjectDetailsData()
throws PSAException {
   try {
      ProjectTOAHome projectTOAHome = (ProjectTOAHome)
         ServiceLocator.getInstance().getRemoteHome(
            "ProjectTOA", ProjectTOAHome.class);

      // Transfer Object Assembler session bean
      ProjectTOA projectTOA =  projectTOAHome.create(...);
      return projectTOA.getData(...);
   } catch (...) {

         // Handle / throw exceptions
   }
}

// These method proxies a call to a ValueListHandler to get
// a list of projects. See Value List Handler pattern.
public Collection getProjectsList(Date start, Date end)
throws PSAException {
   try {
      ProjectListHandlerHome projectVLHHome =
         (ProjectVLHHome)
            ServiceLocator.getInstance().getRemoteHome(
               "ProjectListHandler", ProjectVLHHome.class);

      // Value List Handler session bean
      ProjectListHandler projectListHandler =
         projectVLHHome.create();
      return projectListHandler.getProjects(start, end);
   } catch (...) {
         // Handle / throw exceptions
   }
}

...
```

```
    public void ejbActivate() {
      ...
    }

    public void ejbPassivate() {
      context = null;
    }

    public void setSessionContext(SessionContext ctx) {
          this.context = ctx;
    }

    public void ejbRemove() {
      ...
    }
}
```

The remote interface for the *Session Façade* is listed in Example 7.11.

Example 7.11 Implementing *Session Façade* – Remote Interface

```

package corepatterns.apps.psa.ejb;

import java.rmi.RemoteException;
import javax.ejb.*;
import corepatterns.apps.psa.core.*;

// Note: all try/catch details not shown for brevity.

public interface ProjectResourceManager extends EJBObject {

   public resetEntities(String resourceId, String projectId,
     ...)
   throws RemoteException, ResourceException ;

   public void assignResourceToProject(int numHours)
   throws RemoteException, ResourceException ;

   public void unassignResourceFromProject()
   throws RemoteException, ResourceException ;

```

```
    ...

    public ResourceTO getResourceData()
    throws RemoteException, ResourceException ;

    public void setResourceData(ResourceTO resource)
    throws RemoteException, ResourceException ;

    public ResourceTO createNewResource(ResourceTO resource)
    throws ResourceException ;

    public void addBlockoutTime(Collection blockoutTime)
    throws RemoteException,BlockoutTimeException ;

    public void updateBlockoutTime(Collection blockoutTime)
    throws RemoteException,BlockoutTimeException ;

    public Collection getResourceCommitments()
    throws RemoteException, ResourceException;

    public ProjectTO getProjectData()
    throws RemoteException, ProjectException ;

    public void setProjectData(ProjectTO project)
    throws RemoteException, ProjectException ;

    public ProjectTO createNewProject(ProjectTO project)
    throws RemoteException, ProjectException ;

    ...

    public ProjectCTO getProjectDetailsData()
    throws RemoteException, PSAException ;

    public Collection getProjectsList(Date start, Date end)
    throws RemoteException, PSAException ;

    ...
}
```

The Home interface for the *Session Façade* is shown in Example 7.12.

Example 7.12 Implementing *Session Façade* – Home Interface

```

package corepatterns.apps.psa.ejb;

import javax.ejb.EJBHome;
import java.rmi.RemoteException;
import corepatterns.apps.psa.core.ResourceException;
import javax.ejb.*;

public interface ProjectResourceManagerHome
extends EJBHome {

    public ProjectResourceManager create()
    throws RemoteException,CreateException;

    public ProjectResourceManager create(String resourceId,
        String projectId, ...)
    throws RemoteException,CreateException;
}
```

Related Patterns

- ***Business Delegate (302)***
  The *Business Delegate* (302) is the client-side abstraction for a *Session Façade*. The *Business Delegate* (302) proxies or adapts the client request to a *Session Façade* that provides the requested service.
- ***Business Object (374)***
  The *Session Façade* encapsulates complex interactions of *Business Objects* (374) that participate in processing a use case request.
- ***Application Service (357)***
  In some applications, *Application Services* (357) are used to encapsulate complex business logic and business rules. In these applications, the *Session Façade* implementations become simpler because they mostly delegate to *Application Services* (357) and *Business Objects* (374).

- ***Data Access Object (462)***
  The *Session Façade* might sometimes access a *Data Access Object* (462) directly to obtain and store data. This is typical in simpler applications that do not use *Business Objects* (374). The *Session Façades* encapsulate trivial business logic and use *Data Access Objects* (462) to facilitate persistence.
- ***Service Locator*** (315)
  The *Session Façade* can use a *Service Locator* (315) to look up other business components, such as entity beans and session beans. This reduces the code complexity in the facade and leverages the benefits of the *Service Locator* (315) pattern.
- ***Broker [POSA1]***
  The *Session Façade* performs the role of a *Broker* to decouple the *Business Objects* (374) and fine-grained services from their client tier.
- ***Facade [GoF]***
  The *Session Façade* is based on the *Facade* design pattern.

Application Service

Problem

You want to centralize business logic across several business-tier components and services.

Service facades, such as *Session Façade* (341) or POJO Facades, contain little or no business logic and expose a simple, coarse-grained interface. *Business ObjectS.* (374) expose an interface by encapsulating cohesive behavior that is specific to a set of related business operations.

Applications implement use cases that coordinate multiple *Business Objects* (374) and services. However, you shouldn't implement use case-coordinating behavior specifically within *Business Objects* (374), because it increases coupling and reduces cohesion between these *Business Objects* (374). Likewise, you don't want to add this business logic to a service facade, because the business logic potentially gets duplicated among different facades, reducing the reusability and maintainability of common code.

In J2EE applications that do not use EJB components, the business-tier components such as *Business Objects* (374) and other services are implemented as POJOs. Though these objects are local objects, you still want to avoid exposing them directly to the clients because that exposure introduces coupling and dependencies between the clients and these business tier components. Even in applications that do not use *Business Objects* (374), you still want to encapsulate business logic in the business tier instead of embedding it in facades or clients.

Forces

- You want to minimize business logic in **service facades**.
- You have business logic acting on multiple *Business Objects* (374) or services.
- You want to provide a coarser-grained service API over existing business-tier components and services.
- You want to encapsulate use case-specific logic outside of individual *Business Objects* (374).

Solution

Use an *Application Service* to centralize and aggregate behavior to provide a uniform service layer.

Application Service provides a central location to implement business logic that encapsulates *Business Object* (374) and services. Implementing the business logic this way, extrinsically to the *Business Object* (374), is a one way to reduce coupling among *Business Objects* (374). With an *Application Service*, you encapsulate this higher-level business logic in a separate component that uses the underlying *Business Objects* (374) and services.

Application Service is also used to provide a central business logic implementation layer even if you are not using *Business Objects* (374) in your application. In this scenario, *Application Services* can include all the procedural business logic required to implement different services in your application and can use *Data Access Objects* (462) when necessary to deal with persistent data.

In non-EJB applications, where you need to reduce coupling between the presentation-tier components and business-tier components such as *Business Objects* (374) and other services, *Application Services* provide that intermediary function between the two tiers. An *Application Service* exposes a finer-grained interface than a service facade and a coarser-grained interface than the underlying *Business Objects* (374) and other services.

Application Services provide the background infrastructure for **service facades** (see *Design Note: Service Facade* on page 360). These facades become simpler to implement and contain less code because they can delegate the business processing to *Application Services. Application Services* contain business logic and service facades typically do not contain business logic. Instead, service facades use *Application Services* and *Business Objects* (374) that contain business logic.

For example, consider the case when you implement your service facade using *Session Façade* (341). For those applications where the business logic becomes complex, the *Session Façade* (341) and its methods become lengthy and bloated. This can be avoided by using *Application Service* that the *Session Façade* (341) can use to delegate to process a request.

When you embed business logic into a remote *Session Façade* (341), you also reduce the reusability of that logic. If different use cases need to re-use that logic, it becomes cumbersome because it is embedded in a remote *Session Façade* (341) and might promote a cut-and-paste practice to reuse code, making it harder to maintain the facades. If the business logic needs to be reusable across different facades, the *Application Service* becomes a better home for such reusable logic and results in simpler and more elegant and maintainable *Session Façade* (341) implementations.

Application Service is also useful for applications with interactions that depend on external factors. In some applications, interactions with a *Business Object* (374) can vary from one use case to another. The application might also need to have different kinds of clients (or channels). If each kind of client or use case imposes a certain behavior on a particular *Business Object* (374), that *Business Object* (374) becomes more and more complex because it has to handle all possible special cases. While common processing logic across **all** request types is best encapsulated within the *Business Objects* (374) to facilitate reuse, specific processing logic for **each** request type, as with different interactions per use case or per client type, is best encapsulated within an *Application Service*.

With these types of variations in interactions, you might use the *Application Service Layer* strategy. This strategy layers several *Application Services* on top of each other, starting with those that encapsulate common extrinsic business logic, then adding another for use-case specific business logic, and another at the top for application services that might contain client-type specific business processing.

An *Application Service* can be used to implement logic to coordinate with external services. If your application needs to access an external service, such as an email system, legacy system or a web service, implementing this access logic in an *Application Service* provides a reusable service component.

Design Note: Business Logic

As you implement business logic in *Application Services* and *Business Objects* (374), you might want to consider where you want to draw the line to put the business logic. Some designers tend to ignore the fact that *Business Objects* (374) can have business logic, and might choose not to implement any business logic in the *Business Objects* (374).

Instead, they might implement business logic as a separate layer using *Application Services*. On the other hand, implementing all the business logic in *Business Objects* (374) without a service layer would make the *Business Objects* (374) bloated and less reusable.

Design Note: Service Facade

In enterprise applications that use EJB components, *Session Façades (341)* provide the *Facade* [GoF] implementation in the business tier using session beans. These facades are meant to encapsulate and expose business behavior in a coarse-grained manner to the application clients and hide the complexities of business components and their interactions. However, when you design enterprise applications that do not use EJB components, you still need to provide a behavior similar to the *Session Façades (341)*. But, instead of using session beans, we use POJOs to implement the facades, hence the term *POJO Facades*.

In order to provide a common vocabulary to discuss both *POJO Facades* and *Session Façades (341)*, we introduce the term **service facades**. Service facades are business-tier facades that are implemented either as POJOs or session beans. Thus when you see the term "service facade," we use it to indicate either a POJO Facade or a *Session Façade (341)*. Figure 7.17 illustrates these relationships.

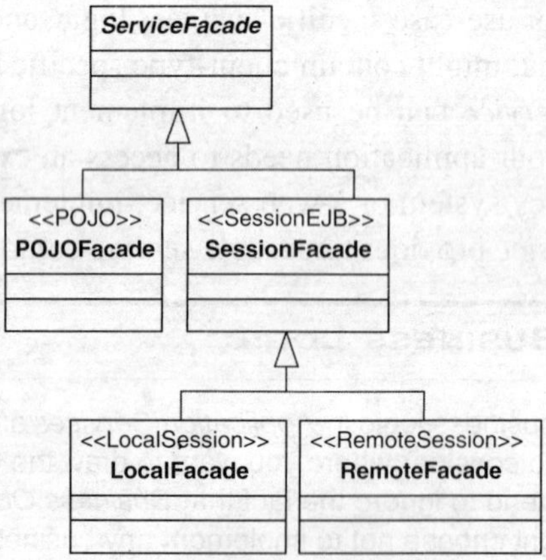

Figure 7.17 *Service Facade* Class Diagram

Structure

Figure 7.18 shows the structure of the *Application Service*. The client accesses an *Application Service* to invoke a business method. Each business method in an *Application Service* implementation can in turn use several business objects, data access objects, or other *Application Services*.

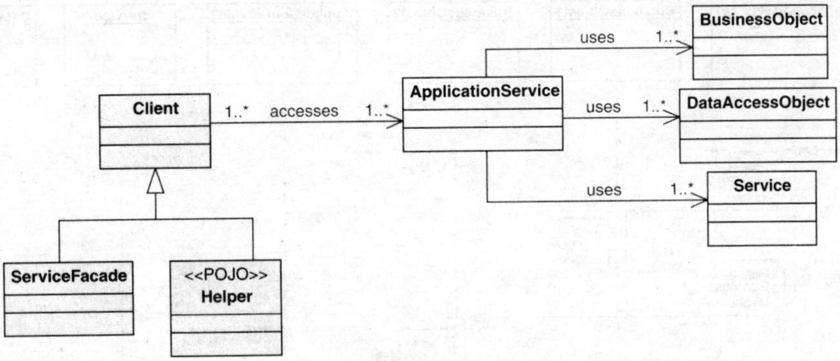

Figure 7.18 *Application Service* Class Diagram

Participants and Responsibilities

Figure 7.19 illustrates the interaction of various participants in the *Application Service* pattern. The client invokes the business method in an ApplicationService object. The business method performs the necessary business processing including initialization, invoking *Business Objects* (374), invoking other ApplicationService instances, accessing *Data Access Objects* (462), and executing business logic to provide the invoked service.

The process messages for ApplicationService and BusinessObjects in the sequence diagrams represent the business logic execution. An ApplicationService encapsulates business logic that is extrinsic to business objects. A BusinessObject encapsulates intrinsic business logic. In other words, an ApplicationService encapsulates business logic that acts upon multiple BusinessObjects, whereas a BusinessObject encapsulates business logic that acts upon the business data contained within and managed by the BusinessObject.

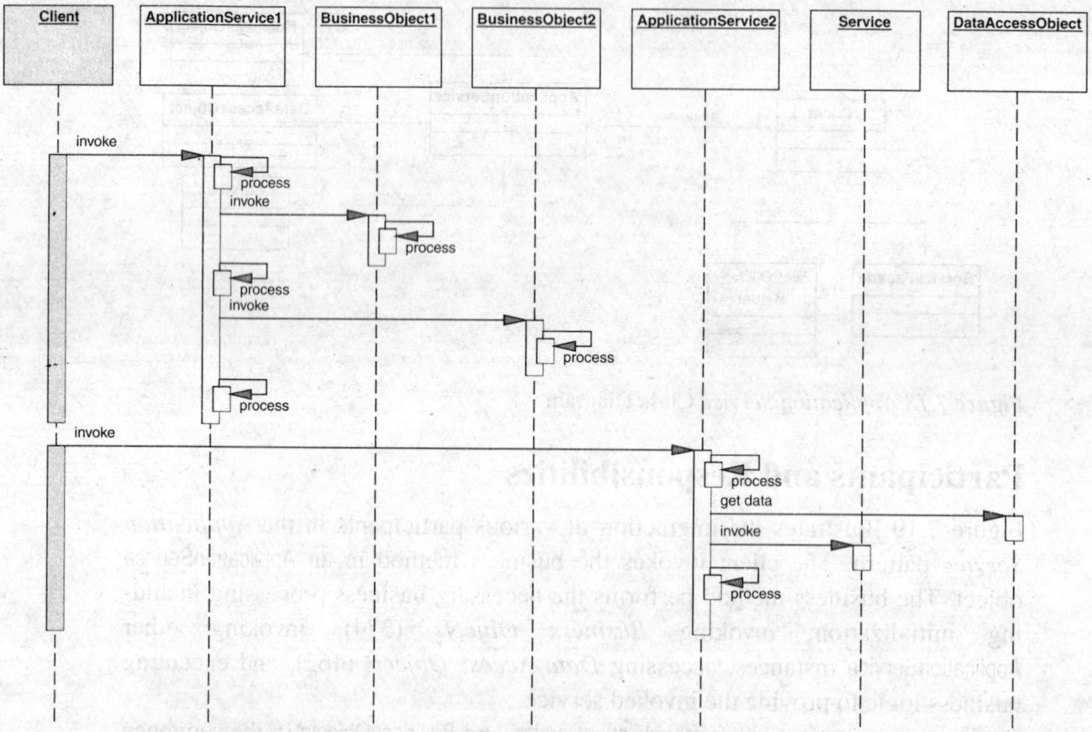

Figure 7.19 Application Service Sequence Diagram

Client

Client is a role that is typically fulfilled by a service facade, implemented as a POJO or a *Session Façades* (341) . The Client can also be another *Application Service* or a POJO helper object.

ApplicationService

ApplicationService represents the main role in this pattern and encapsulates the business logic required to provide a specific service. It can encapsulate a variety of business logic types, such as common logic acting on several BusinessObjects, use case-specific business logic, or logic specific to a particular kind of client or channel type. An ApplicationService can invoke a business method in a BusinessObject or another ApplicationService. Implementing *Application Services* as POJOs is more common because it enhances reusability of the control logic across different clients and facilitates easy layering of *Application Services*.

BusinessObject

BusinessObject represents instances of *Business Objects* (374) that the ApplicationService can access to perform a service. Typically, an ApplicationService accesses multiple BusinessObjects in order to fulfill a service request.

Service

Service represents an arbitrary component that provides any service in the applications. These can be common functions or utilities that are frequently used to aid the processing of a business-tier service request.

DataAccessObject

DataAccessObject represents instances of *Data Access Objects* (462) for those scenarios where the ApplicationService directly accesses the business data without using a BusinessObject.

Strategies

Application Service Command Strategy

Application Services can be implemented using the *Command* pattern [GoF]. You can use an *Application Controller* (205) to provide the request processing mechanism.

In Figure 7.20, the Command is shown separately from an ApplicationService.

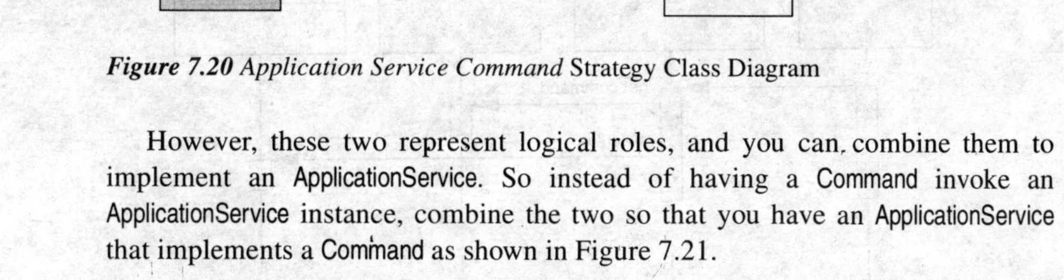

Figure 7.20 *Application Service Command* Strategy Class Diagram

However, these two represent logical roles, and you can combine them to implement an ApplicationService. So instead of having a Command invoke an ApplicationService instance, combine the two so that you have an ApplicationService that implements a Command as shown in Figure 7.21.

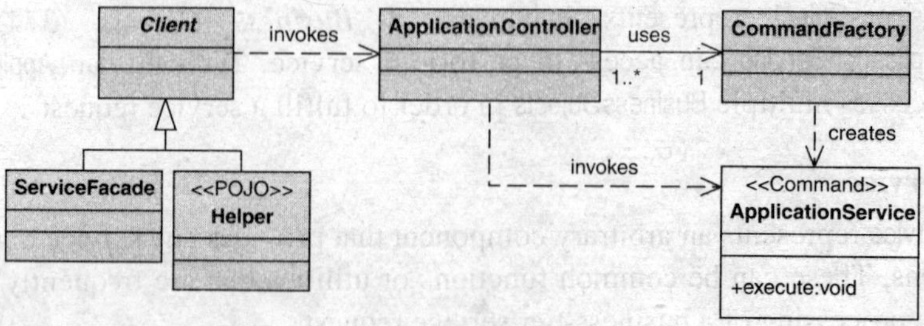

Figure 7.21 Alternative Class Diagram for *Application Service Command* Strategy

The sequence diagram in Figure 7.22 illustrates the interaction of the *Application Service Command* strategy.

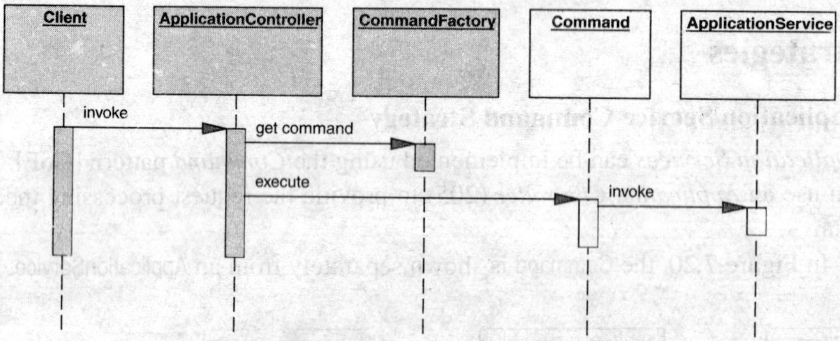

Figure 7.22 *Application Service Command* Strategy Sequence Diagram

The alternate sequence diagram for the *Application Service Command* strategy is shown in Figure 7.23.

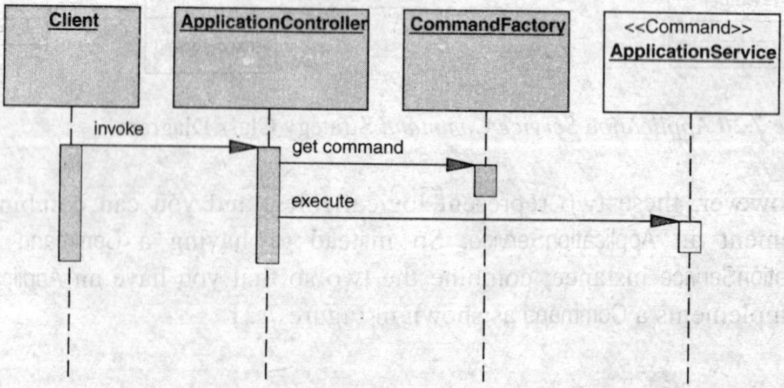

Figure 7.23 Alternate Sequence Diagram for *Application Service Command* Strategy

GoF Strategy for Application Service Strategy

You can implement *Application Services* using the *Strategy* pattern [GoF]. Since *Application Service* primarily implements processing logic, implementing it using the *Strategy* pattern is ideal, when there are multiple variations of the same service.

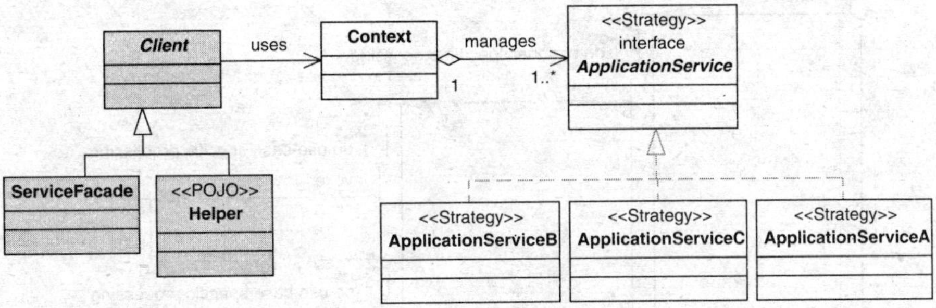

Figure 7.24 GoF *Strategy Application Service* Strategy Class Diagram

Application Service Layer Strategy

Application Services can be categorized based on their function and reusability.

- At the bottom are those application services that encapsulate common extrinsic business logic that is not use case-specific or client specific.
- The next layer has application services that contain use case-specific business logic and use the services of the generic application services below them.
- The top layer has application services that can contain client type-specific business processing.

Figure 7.25 illustrates the structure of the *Application Service Layer* strategy.

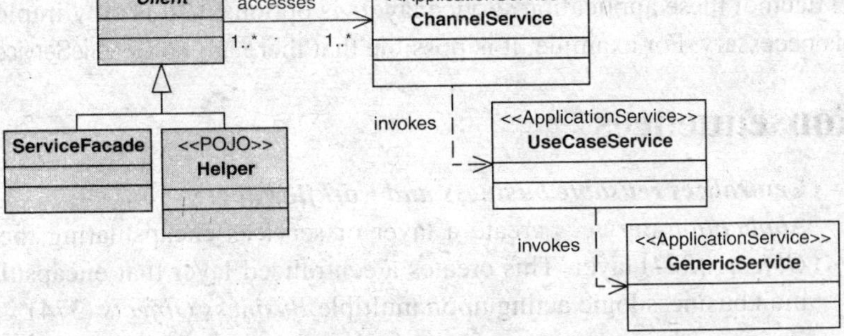

Figure 7.25 *Application Service Layer* Strategy Class Diagram

The sequence diagram shown in Figure 7.26 illustrates the interactions of the *Application Services Layer* strategy.

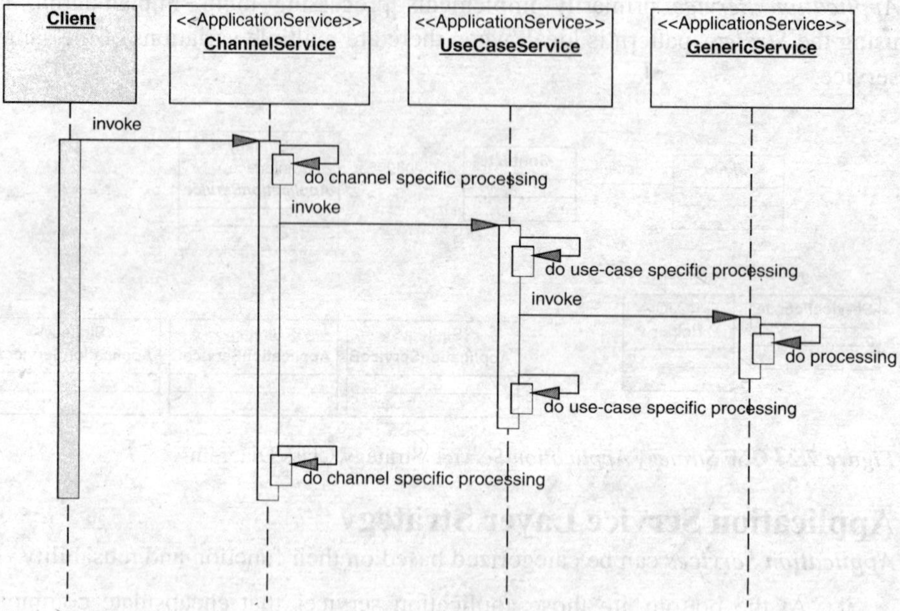

Figure 7.26 *Application Service Layer* Strategy Sequence Diagram

The client invokes the ChannelService, which is an ApplicationService implementation that encapsulates channel specific pre and postprocessing. After performing the preprocessing, it in turn invokes the UseCaseService, which is another ApplicationService implementation that encapsulates use case-specific pre and postprocessing. The UseCaseService then performs the preprocessing and invokes the GenericService, which is an ApplicationService implementation that encapsulates the common business processing logic for all channels and use cases.

Each of these application service layers is optional and is only implemented if it is necessary. For example, it is possible that there are no GenericServices.

Consequences

- ***Centralizes reusable business and workflow logic***
  Application Services create a layer of services encapsulating the *Business Objects (374)* layer. This creates a centralized layer that encapsulates common business logic acting upon multiple *Business Objects* (374).

- ***Improves reusability of business logic***
  Application Services create a set of reusable components that can be reused across various use case implementations. *Application Services* encapsulate inter-*Business Object* (374) operations.
- ***Avoids duplication of code***
  By creating a centralized reusable layer of business logic, the *Application Services* avoid duplication of code in the clients, such as facades and helpers, and in other *Application Services.*
- ***Simplifies facade implementations***
  Business logic is moved away from the service facades, whether they are implemented as *Session Façades* (341) or POJO facades. The facades become simpler because they are only responsible for aggregating *Application Services* interaction and delegating to one or more *Application Services* to fulfill the requested service.
- ***Introduces additional layer in the business tier***
  The *Application Service* creates an additional layer in the business tier. which you might consider an unnecessary overhead for some applications. However, the additional layer provides for a powerful abstraction in the application to encapsulate reusable common business logic.

Sample Code

The class diagram in Figure 7.27 shows an example for *Application Service* implemented in an order processing system. The components and their responsibilities in this example are:

- OrderSystemFacade is a *Session Façade* (341) for the order system. It communicates with the *Application Service* components: CompanyAppService and OrderAppService.
- CompanyAppService is an *Application Service* component responsible for the business logic and interactions with several business objects: Company, Account and AccountManager.
- OrderAppService is an *Application Service* component responsible for the for the business logic and interactions with the business objects Order and Account.
- EmailAppService is an *Application Service* component responsible for implementing email service. EmailAppService is used by CompanyAppService and OrderAppService.

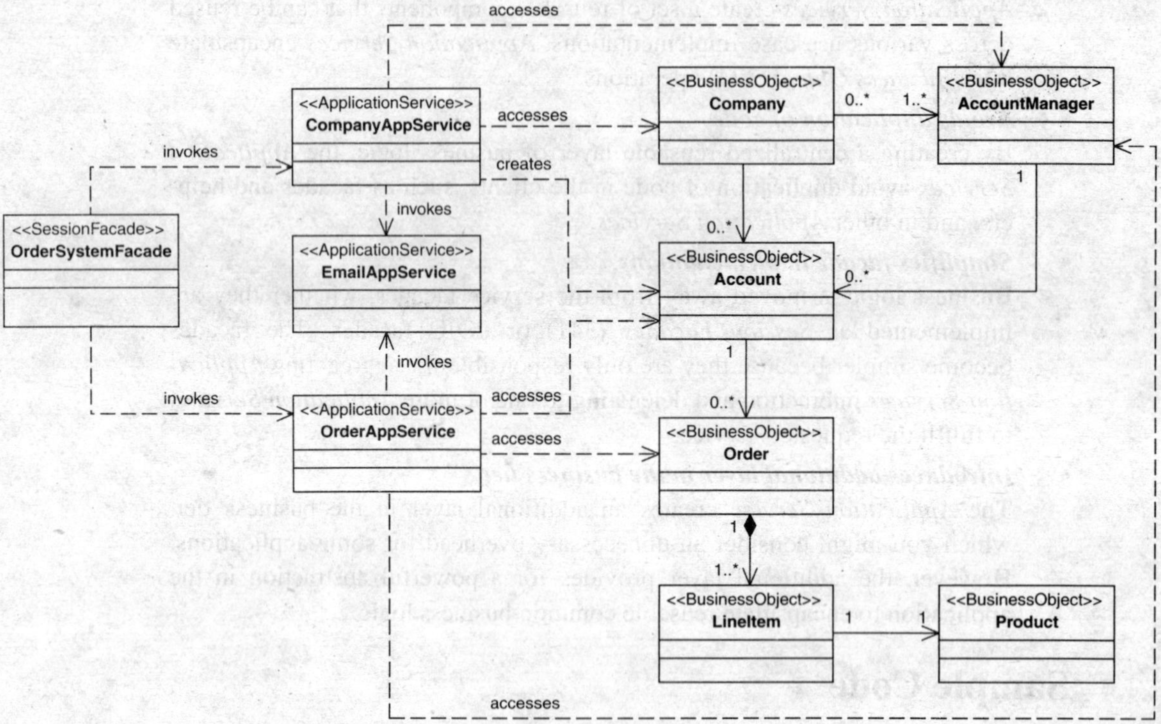

Figure 7.27 Application Service: Order System Example Class Diagram

Example 7.13 OrderServiceFacadeSession

```

import javax.ejb.SessionContext;
import javax.ejb.EJBException;
import java.rmi.RemoteException;
import java.util.Date;

public class OrderSystemFacade
implements javax.ejb.SessionBean, OrderSystemClient {

    public void setSessionContext(
        SessionContext sessionContext)
    throws EJBException, RemoteException {
    }

```

```
    public void ejbRemove()
    throws EJBException, RemoteException {
    }

    public void ejbActivate()
    throws EJBException, RemoteException {
    }

    public void ejbPassivate()
    throws EJBException, RemoteException {
    }

    public void placeOrder( OrderTO order ) {
        OrderAppService pas = new OrderAppService();
        pas.placeOrder( order );
    }

    public void addAccount(AccountTO account) {
        CompanyAppService cas = new CompanyAppService();
        cas.addAccount(account);
    }

    public void createCompany( CompanyTO company) {
        CompanyAppService cas = new CompanyAppService();
        cas.addCompany(company);
    }
}
```

Example 7.14 CustomerAppService

```

public class CompanyAppService {

    public void addCompany(CompanyTO companyTO) {
        Company customer = new Company(companyTO);
        // Persist customer
    }

    public void addAccount(String companyId,
        AccountTO accountTO) {
    throws AccountException {

        Company company = null;
```

```
        // Get Company
        // company = findCompany(companyId);

        if (company == null)
            throw new AccountException(
               "Company Id: " + companyId + " doesn't exist");

        Account account = new Account(accountTO);
        company.addAccount(account);

        AccountManager accountManager = null;
        accountManager = getAccountManager(company.getZip());
        account.addAccountManager(accountManager);

        // Send email to Account Manager notifying the
        // new account
        EmailAppService emailAppService =
            new EmailAppService();
        emailAppService.notifyAccountManager(accountManager,
            account);
    }
}
```

Example 7.15 OrderAppService

```

public class OrderAppService {

    public OrderAppService() {
    }

    public void placeOrder(OrderTO orderTO)
    throws AccountException {
        Company company = null;
        Account account = null;

        String companyId = orderTO.companyId;
        String accountId = orderTO.accountId;

        // Lookup Company
        company = getCompany(companyId);

        // Lookup account
        account = company.getAccount(accountId);
```

```
        // add the order to the account
        Order order = new Order(orderTO);

        // calculate discount
        calculateDiscount(company, account, order);

        account.addOrder(order);
        AccountManager accountManager =
            account.getAccountManager();

        // Send email to Account Manager notifying the
        // new order
        EmailAppService emailAppService =
            new EmailAppService();
        emailAppService.notifyAccountManager(accountManager,
            order);
    }

    public void calculateDiscount(Company company,
        Account account, Order order) {
    }

}
```

Example 7.16 EmailAppService

```
// import

public EmailAppService {

    public void notifyAccountManager(
        AccountManager accountManager, Order order) {
        // integrate with the Email API to send an email
        // notification
    }

    public void notifyAccountManager(
        AccountManager accountManager, Account account) {
        // integrate with the Email API to send an email
        // notification
    }
}
```

Example 7.17 Order

```

import java.util.Collection;

public class Order {
    String orderId;
    Collection lineItems;

    . . .

    public void addLineItems( LineItem[] lines ) {
        for( int i = 0; i < lines.length; i++ ) {
            lineItems.add( lines[ i ] );
        }
    }
}
```

Example 7.18 OrderTO

```

import java.util.Date;

public class OrderTO implements java.io.Serializable {
    public String companyId;
    public String accountId;
    public String orderId;
    public LineItemTO[] lineItems;
    public Date   orderDate;
}
```

Example 7.19 LineItem

```

import java.util.Date;

public class LineItem {
    String  productId;
    float   price;
    int     quantity;
    Date    deliveryDate;

    public LineItem(LineItemTO lineItem) {
        this.productId = lineItem.getProductId();
        this.price = lineItem.getPrice();
```

```
        this.quantity = lineItem.getQuantity();
        this.deliveryDate = lineItem.getDeliveryDate();
    }
}
```

Example 7.20 LineItemTO

```

import java.util.Date;

public class LineItemTO implements java.io.Serializable {
    public String productId;
    public float  price;
    public int    quantity;
    public Date   deliveryDate;
}
```

Related Patterns

- ***Session Façade (341***
  Application Services provide the background infrastructure for *Session Façades* (341, which become simpler to implement and contain less code because they can delegate the business processing to *Application Services.*
- ***Business Object (374)***
  In applications that use *Business Objects* (374), *Application Services* encapsulate cross-*Business Objects* (374) logic and interact with several *Business Objects* (374).
- ***Data Access Object (462)***
  In some applications, an *Application Service* can use a *Data Access Object* (462) directly to access data in a data store.
- ***Service Layer [PEAA]***
  Application Service is similar to *Service Layer* pattern in that both aim to promote a service layer in your application. *Service Layer* explains how a set of services can be used to create a boundary layer for your application.
- ***Transaction Script [PEAA]***
  When an *Application Service* is used without *Business Objects* (374), it becomes a service object where you can implement your procedural logic. *Transaction Script* describes the use of procedural approach to implementing business logic in your application.

Business Object

Problem

You have a conceptual domain model with business logic and relationship.

When there is little or no business logic in a business operation, applications will typically let clients directly access business data in the data store. For example, a presentation tier component such as a command helper or JSP view, or a business-tier component can directly access a *Data Access Object* (462). In this scenario, there is no notion of an object model in the business tier. Instead, the application requirements are fulfilled by a procedural implementation. This approach is acceptable for some applications when the data model closely represents the conceptual domain model.

However, if you have a conceptual model that exhibits a variety of business behavior and relationships, implementing such applications using a procedural approach causes the following problems:

- Reusability is reduced and business logic code gets duplicated.
- Bloated procedure implementations that become lengthy and complex.
- Poor maintainability due to duplication and because business logic is spread over different modules.

Design Note: Terminology – Business Model, Business Object Model, Domain Model, Object Model, Data Model

For understanding these terms, we turn to the definitions in *The Unified Software Development Process* [Jacobson, et al].

- A **business model** comprises two models: a **business use-case model** to describe the business actors and the business processes, and a **business object model** to describe business entities used by the business use cases.
- A **domain model** is defined as an abstract model that captures the most important types of objects in the context of the system. The domain objects represent the "things" that exist or events that transpire in the environment in which the system works.

Further, Jacobson et al state that the domain model is a simplified variant of the business model and the two terms are used interchangeably. This is exactly what we see in practice when analysts, designers and developers use the several terms interchangeably - business model, business object model, domain model, and domain object model. This usage dilutes these terms and renders them somewhat ambiguous.

In our discussion in this book, we use the term **conceptual model** to mean the abstract model, which mainly describes domain entities, their relationships and business rules. To describe a concrete object-oriented implementation model of a conceptual model, we use the term **object model**, which describes the classes and relationships used to realize a conceptual model. We use another term, **data model**, to mean the data implementation model, such as an Entity-Relationship (ER) model for an RDBMS database.

Forces

- You have a conceptual model containing structured, interrelated composite objects.
- You have a conceptual model with sophisticated business logic, validation and business rules.
- You want to separate the business state and related behavior from the rest of the application, improving cohesion and reusability.
- You want to centralize business logic and state in an application.
- You want to increase reusability of business logic and avoid duplication of code.

Solution

Use *Business Objects* to separate business data and logic using an object model.

Business Objects encapsulate and manage business data, behavior and persistence. *Business Objects* help separate persistence logic from business logic. *Business Objects* maintain the core business data, and implement the behavior that is common to the entire application or domain.

In an application that uses *Business Objects*, the client interacts with the *Business Objects*, which manage their own persistence using one of the several persistence strategies. *Business Objects* implement a reusable layer of business entities that describe the business domain. A *Business Object* implements a well-defined business domain concept and includes intrinsic business logic and business rules that apply to that domain concept. Higher-level or extrinsic business logic that operates on several *Business Objects* is implemented in a service layer, using *Application Service* (357)) and *Session Façades* (341), to insulate the object model from clients, preventing direct access.

There are primarily two strategies for implementing *Business Objects.* For each you choose the type of object to create and the persistence mechanism.

- The first strategy is to use POJOs and choose a persistence mechanism that meets your needs. Choose from the following: custom *Data Access Objects* (462), JDO-like custom persistence framework implementation using *Domain Store* (516), JDO standard compliant implementation.
- The second strategy is to use entity beans as shown in *Composite Entity* (391). With this strategy, you have to decide whether to use BMP or CMP for persistence.

Additionally, for both strategies, you also need to consider the requirements for security, transaction management, pooling, caching, and concurrency when implementing *Business Objects.*

Some simpler applications might expose *Business Objects* to all clients. Accessing the *Business Objects* directly leads to fine-grained interactions. This might work fine for POJO applications where the clients and the *Business Objects* are located in the same JVM process space, but can result in an inconsistent and inefficient implementation for remote applications. For more sophisticated applications, instead of directly exposing *Business Objects* to all clients, encapsulate those using *Service Facades* and POJO *Application Services* (357)).

For remote applications, use *Session Façades* (341), to form a remote service facade layer through which the *Business Objects* are exposed to its clients. Thus, *Business Objects* are not returned to clients outside of the business layer. Instead, use *Transfer Objects* (415) to exchange data between clients and *Business Objects* for remote applications.

Identifying, designing and persisting *Business Objects* is a complex task that often takes considerable time and resources. The following topics discuss how to identity business objects and how to select the appropriate persistence mechanism.

DESIGN NOTE: BUSINESS OBJECTS IN A NON-BUSINESS SPACE

The term **Business Object** works in a majority of problem spaces we deal with, we have chosen it as the pattern name. However, in some "non-business" problem domain, the term **Business Object** might not be well accepted. Some examples of such problem spaces are health care, government organizations, the military, and charitable organizations, where these organizations do not consider themselves to be in a business. Other examples are for high-tech applications, statistical applications, mathematical modeling, analytical modeling, etc., where there is no "business".

In such cases, don't use the term Business Object. The term **Domain Object** typically reflects the same concepts documented here as Business Object.

Identifying Candidate Business Objects

Conceptual domain model's entities are the objects that users create, access and manipulate in a use case. Entities represent business data in a system that is typically stateful, persistent and long-lived. Entities are reused in various use cases for different purposes and are identified as nouns in those use cases. For example, entities in an Order Processing System might be Order, Item, Invoice, and Account. These entities are user-facing or business-facing and as such, users of your system will be able to identify and describe them.

In addition to these entities, look for association entities that represent a meaningful business association between any two entities. For example, in an order processing system, you might recognize Order and Item as two separate entities, and in addition also identify an Order-Item association entity. So, when a user wishes to create a new order for an item, the create order use case will have to create a corresponding Order-Item entity. These entities are typically designer/architect-facing, not user-facing, since developers usually create the entities to support the implementation of user-facing entities.

After you have identified all entities, you must implement them as stateful, persistent, long-lived *Business Objects*. The *Business Objects* typically have identity and map to a physical data representation within a data store, such as a relational database.

Note: Identifying business objects is a complex topic. You can find a wide variety of literature regarding modeling and identifying your business object entities. You might want to refer to the following resources:

- *Object-Oriented Software Engineering: A Use Case Driven Approach* by Ivar Jacobson [OOSE]
- *Software Reuse: Architecture Process and Organization for Business Success by Jacobson*, et al [SR]
- *Domain-Driven Design*, by Eric Evans [DDD]

Business Objects and Persistence

Now that you've found the Business Objects, you need to determine how you'll store their data. *Business Objects* help separate persistence logic from business logic. Since *Business Objects* are almost always persistent, you need to map the object's state to a data store using some persistence mechanism. One option is to use a *Domain Store* (516) offers a framework to implement custom transparent persistence for your *Business Objects*.

While it is possible to code persistence logic into the *Business Objects*, we strongly recommend against it, as doing so clutters the *Business Objects* with persistence logic and results in a tight coupling across tiers between business-tier and persistence-tier components. Combining two logically unrelated aspects of the system in this way reduces object cohesion, modularity and maintainability. Moreover, the primary purpose of the *Business Object* is to model business state and behavior. As this object model becomes more complex, embedding persistence logic leads to unmanageable code and tightly couples the object model to the data model.

Design Note: Implementing Business Object Persistence

One of the core characteristics of a *Business Object* is that it represents persistent business information. Persistence can be achieved in different ways.

- Using entity beans persistence
- Using custom *Data Access Objects* (462)
- Using Java Data Objects (JDO)
- Using a *Domain Store* (516)

Using Entity Beans Persistence

You can use entity beans a *Business Objects* as described in *Composite Entity* (391). With entity beans, you can choose to implement persistence either as bean-managed persistence or container-managed persistence. If you use bean-managed persistence, you typically use *Data Access Objects* (462).

Using Custom Data Access Objects

You can use *Data Access Objects* (462) to provide your persistence mechanisms for your *Business Objects*. To do this, create a *Business Object* that delegates the storing and retrieving of the business data to the custom *Data Access Objects* (462). *Business Object* creation is no different than creating any other object. However, when you want to persist a *Business Object* to the data store, you delegate to a *Data Access Object* (462) rather than embedding persistence logic in the *Business Object*. You can also use *Data Access Objects* (462) to retrieve the state for existing *Business Objects*. While this separates the data access logic from business logic, it is still not a transparent way to implement *Business Object* persistence, because they have to have knowledge of *Data Access Objects* (462). A better alternative to use *Data Access Objects* (462) transparently is to use them via a *Domain Store* (516).

Using Java Data Objects

Java Data Objects offer another way to persist your *Business Object.* This option is appealing because the persistence mechanism becomes completely transparent to the *Business Objects.* The JDO technology uses a mechanism called "enhancers", where the *Business Object* class is enhanced at the class or byte code level with persistence capabilities. A number of off-the-shelf persistence solutions are based on JDO, so this strategy lets you choose the best suitable JDO solution for your needs.

Using Domain Store

Domain Store (516) describes transparent persistence for the object model. It describes a custom persistence mechanism and a JDO style persistence mechanism. For more details on how you can implement persistence for your *Business Objects*, please refer to *Domain Store* (516).

Structure

The class diagram for the *Business Object* pattern is shown in Figure 7.28.

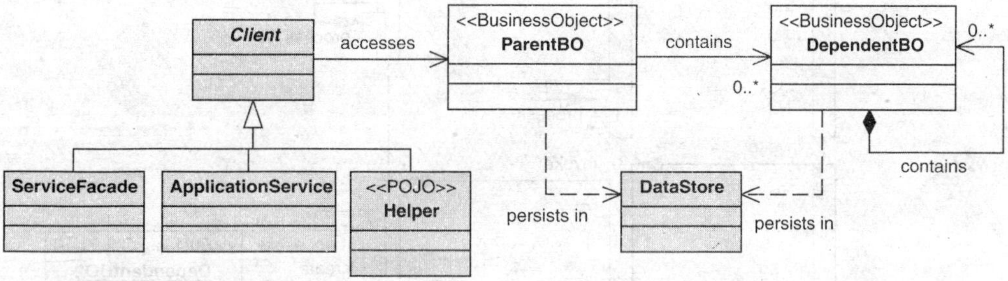

Figure 7.28 *Business Object* Class Diagram

Participants and Responsibilities

Figure 7.29 on page 380 explains the interaction of the various participants for the *Business Object* pattern.

The client invokes a business method in ParentObject, which loads its data from the data store. The ParentObject executes its intrinsic business logic acting upon its data. The ParentObject stores its data if any changes need to be persisted to the data store. The ParentObject can invoke methods of its dependent BusinessObjects (DependentBO1 and DependentBO2) to fulfill the client's request. Each of these dependent objects executes its own (intrinsic) business logic and rules and also interacts with the data store as needed.

Client

The Client represents a client of the BusinessObject. The Client is typically a *Session Façade* (341), a helper object (see *View Helper* (240)), or an *Application Service* (357) that needs to access the BusinessObject.

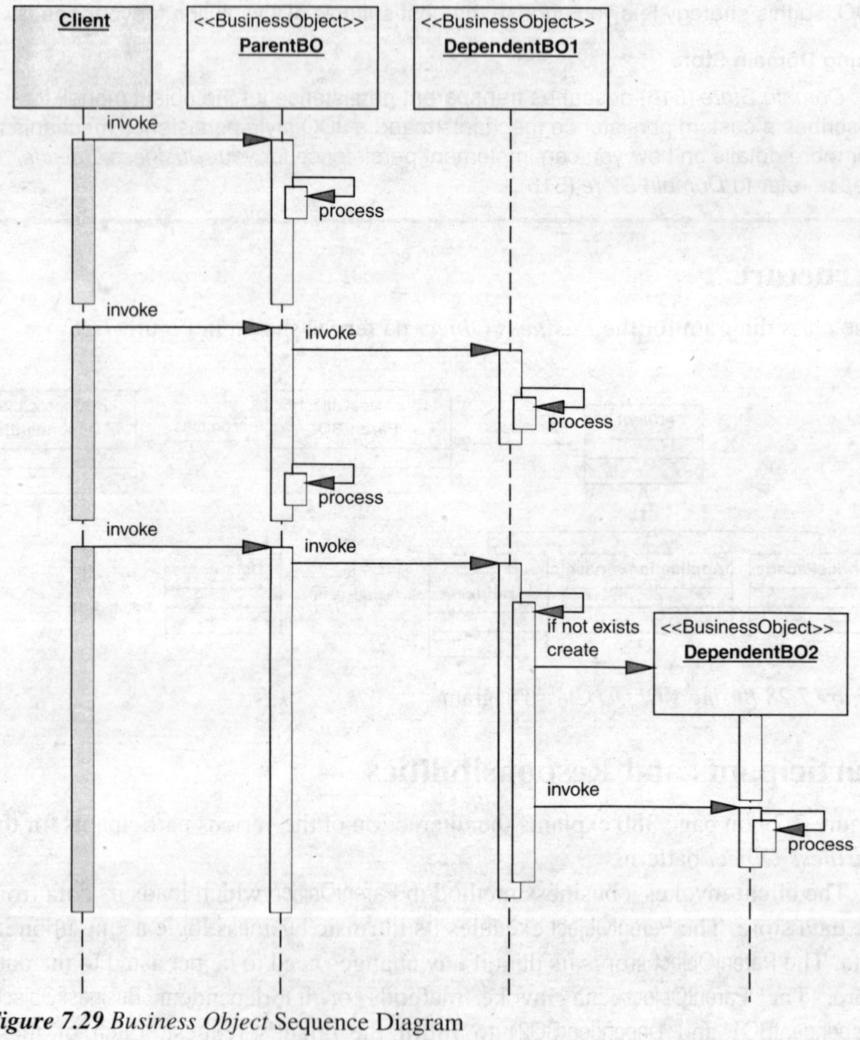

Figure 7.29 *Business Object* Sequence Diagram

ParentBO

ParentBO is the top-level BusinessObject that represents the parent object in the composite BusinessObject model. The parent object encapsulates dependent objects and implements its own intrinsic business logic and business rules.

DependentBO

These are dependent BusinessObjects that are managed by the ParentBO. Dependent BusinessObjects are tightly coupled to their parents and rely on their parents for their lifecycle management. Dependent objects do not exist without their parent objects. Each dependent object implements its own intrinsic business logic and rules to fulfill its responsibilities.

DESIGN NOTE: BUSINESS OBJECTS AND VALIDATIONS

Business Objects act as the guardians of data and are responsible for maintaining the integrity of data. To accomplish this, the *Business Objects* have to perform validations on all the data supplied to them by the clients.

In a multi-tier application, the validation can be performed in multiple locations. For example, when you are submitting new data to an application, the presentation tier might perform validations on the form input to ensure that the required fields are filled in and to ensure that integrity and data type checks are performed on all the fields in the form. It might also perform other validations that help the application prevent an unnecessary invocation to the business tier. Thus, it is possible to have validations performed in the *Front Controller* (166), *Application Controller* (205), and Command Objects in the presentation tier.

Once the presentation tier is satisfied that the data is valid, it allows the request to invoke the business tier, which performs its own sets of validations. Some of these validations can be duplicates of those performed in the presentation tier.

However, this duplicate validation might be necessary because the business tier cannot simply rely on another tier ensuring the integrity of the data. Some of the clients invoking the business objects might not be in the presentation tier. They might be in the integration tier, which would warrant a validation in the business tier anyway. The touch points in the business tier that include validation logic are *Session Façades* (341), *Application Services* (357) and *Business Objects* (374).

Strategies

POJO Business Object Strategy

You can implement *Business Objects* as POJOs even if you are using an EJB container. For example, you can have an EJB application that uses *Session Façades* (341) without implementing entity beans. You can also have a J2EE application that uses JSP and servlet technologies, but does not use EJB technology. In this case, you can implement *Business Objects* as POJOs. When implementing them this way, consider how doing so affects the various aspects of the architecture, such as security, transactions, caching, pooling, concurrency, and persistence.

As an optimization technique, some applications implement a caching mechanism to load and hold on to the *Business Object*. While this works relatively easily in POJO applications in a single process space, it becomes a tough problem in a distributed multi-tier application where a *Business Object* might end up getting instantiated in multiple VMs or containers. Maintaining consistency and integrity of the business data across these multiple instances is a very complex problem to solve. This requires synchronization of state among the instances, and between the instances and the data store, to guarantee the integrity of the business data and avoid stale data.

You need to choose your persistence mechanism for this strategy. It has different degrees of transparency, depending on the persistence mechanism you choose. The following is a summary of options based on *Implementing Business Object Persistence* on page 378.

- When you implement your own custom JDBC persistence mechanism using *Data Access Objects* (462), the persistence mechanism is tightly integrated with the *Business Objects*. The *Business Objects* are responsible for persisting themselves.
- For a more transparent persistence, try using the *Domain Store* (516), which is still a custom solution, but decouples the persistence mechanism from the *Business Objects* implementation.
- Similarly, you can use JDO to realize the benefits as the *Domain Store* (516), but with an industry standard approach and API for object persistence.
- Finally, you can use one of the off-the-shelf object-relational mapping solutions, which come with a wide variety of features and levels of transparency.

Composite Entity Business Object Strategy

You can implement *Business Objects* as entity beans in an EJB application and is explained in detail in *Composite Entity* (391). Prior to the EJB 2.x specification, the entity beans were always implemented as remote objects leading to poor performance.

EJB version 2.x specification introduced the concept of **local entity beans**. We recommend that when you implement *Business Objects* as entity beans, use local entity beans. This lets you avoid the overhead of remote objects and still leverage the other powerful features of EJB technology, such as security, transactions and container managed persistence (CMP). Furthermore, you must provide *Session Façades* (341) to encapsulate the entity bean *Business Objects*.

Regardless of how you manage persistence, entity beans offer other benefits such as transaction and security management. While EJB transactions and security might not address every application requirement, entity beans are still suitable for many applications that use role-based security, container-managed transactions, and so forth. For further details on implementing *Business Objects* as entity beans, please see *Composite Entity* (391).

Design Note: POJOs or Entity Beans for Business Objects

While using POJO *Business Objects* might appear to be simple and straightforward, this impression exists only while we overlook the infrastructure and container support required to make it work. It is a common mistake to underestimate what it takes to implement a fully functional *Business Object* infrastructure. Business objects have complex lifecycle management requirements and might need supporting services for persistence, security, transaction management, caching, object pooling and concurrency control, to name a few. Some applications might delegate most of these requirements to the persistent store and use a procedural approach or a light-weight *Business Object* wrapper approach.

You need to evaluate these requirements when you choose between using POJOs or entity beans to implement your *Business Objects*. If you are not careful, you will end up implementing a home-grown system that resembles an EJB container, instead of using a proven off-the-shelf implementation. Table 7-1 offers a comparison of POJO and Entity Bean approaches to help you understand the trade-offs of choosing POJOs or entity beans to implement your *Business Objects*.

Table 7-1 Comparison of POJO and Entity Bean Business Objects

Feature	POJO	Entity Beans
Security	If the *Session Façades* (341) manage all accesses to the POJO *Business Objects*, then the EJB security model is provided by the EJB container and can be leveraged in the *Session Façades* (341). If EJB technology is not used, then you will have to provide and manage your own application security using custom framework or using the Java API provided by Java Authentication and Authorization Service [JAAS].	If the *Session Façades* (341) manage all accesses to the *Business Objects*, the EJB container provides the EJB security model. The security model can be leveraged in the *Session Façades* (341) as well as entity beans that implement the *Business Objects*.

Transaction	Similar to security. If you're using *Session Façades* (341), then the session beans can leverage the transaction services provided by the EJB container. If you're not using EJB technologies, the transaction services will most likely depend on the persistence strategies used.	Similar to security. If you're using *Session Façades* (341), then the session beans can leverage the transaction services provided by the EJB container. In addition, entity beans come with default container managed transactions.
Caching	POJO *Business Objects* are not cached unless you implement specific caching mechanisms in your application. Caching yields significant performance benefits for POJOs, but increases the complexity of your application.	The EJB container manages the lifecycle of the entity beans. Entity beans are typically not cached. When a transaction begins, the container activates an instance from a pool of available instances or creates if an instance does not exist.
Pooling	POJO *Business Objects* are not explicitly pooled. If you want pooling, you have to implement your own mechanisms, though that might not yield any significant benefits.	Since the container manages the lifecycle of entity beans, pooling of entity beans is delegated to the container and you don't implement any mechanisms to pool entity bean *Business Objects*.
Concurrency	It is your responsibility to ensure that concurrent access to the same *Business Object* instance is properly handled and that it guarantees data integrity at all times. You might have to use a locking scheme, such as optimistic or pessimistic locking. Martin Fowler offers a good discussion on concurrency problems in his book [PEAA] under *Concurrency* and *Offline Concurrency Patterns*, with these patterns - *Optimistic Lock*, *Pessimistic Lock*, *Coarse-grained Lock* and *Implicit Lock*.	The container will ensure that concurrent access to the entity bean is serialized and that the integrity of the entity bean is maintained at all times.

Data Synchronization	In a multi-tier application, it is possible to end up with multiple instances of a *Business Object* in different JVMs or containers. It is your responsibility to make sure that the implementation will enforce proper data synchronization to propagate changes in one instance of a *Business Object* to all other existing instances.	If multiple instances of the same entity bean are required in different JVMs or containers, it is the EJB container's responsibility to ensure that all instances are synchronized with the same business data and that changes are propagated across container boundaries, ensuring integrity of the data.
Persistence	Since the *Business Objects* are implemented as POJOs, they are unable to use the CMP strategies that entity beans can use. Instead, you can make use of other powerful options to facilitate persistence of POJO *Business Objects*, such as DAOs, *Domain Store* (516), JDO or a commercial O-R mapping tool (see *Implementing Business Object Persistence* on page 378).	Business Objects implemented as entity beans can leverage the power or CMP and can model the relationships between related Business Object entity beans using CMR. You also have the option of implementing custom persistence mechanisms using BMP and implementing relationships in the code as CMR is only applicable for CMP entity beans.

Consequences

- ***Promotes object-oriented approach to the business model implementation***
  Business Objects create a logical layer of responsibility that reflects object model implementation of the business model. For OO multi-tier applications, this is a natural approach to implementing the business tier using objects.
- ***Centralizes business behavior and state, and promotes reuse***
  Business objects provide a centralized and modular approach to multi-tier architecture by abstracting and implementing the business logic, rules and behavior in a separate set of components. Such centralization provides for and promotes reuse of the abstractions in the business tier across use cases and different kinds of clients.

- ***Avoids duplication of and improves maintainability of code***
  Due to centralization of business state and behavior, clients avoid embedding business logic and thereby avoid duplication of code. Using *Business Objects* improves the maintainability of the system as a whole because they promote reusability and centralization of code.
- ***Separates persistence logic from business logic***
  Persistence mechanism can be hidden and separated from the *Business Objects*. You can use various persistence strategies such as JDO, custom JDBC, object-relational mapping tools, or entity beans to facilitate persistence of *Business Objects*.
- ***Promotes service-oriented architecture***
  Business objects act as a centralized object model to all clients in an application. You can build various services on top of *Business Object*, which can also use other services such as persistence, business rules, integration, and so forth. This facilitates separation of concerns in a multi-tiered application and facilitates service-oriented architecture.
- ***POJO implementations can induce, and are susceptible to, stale data***
  When you implement *Business Objects* as POJOs in a distributed multi-tier application, a *Business Object* might end up instantiated in multiple VMs or containers. The application is responsible for ensuring that these multiple instances maintain consistency and integrity of the business data. This might require synchronization of state among the instances, and between the instances and the data store, to guarantee the integrity of the business data and avoid stale data. On the other hand, when you implement the *Business Objects* as entity beans, the container handles the creation, synchronization, and other lifecycle management of all instances so you don't need to address this issue of data integrity.
- ***Adds extra layer of indirection***
  In some applications, such strict separation of concerns might be considered a formality rather than a necessity. This is especially true for applications with a trivial business model and business logic, or if the data model is a sufficient representation of the business model and letting presentation components access the data in the resource tier directly using *Data Access Objects* (462) is simpler. However, many designers might start out with the assumption that the data model is sufficient and then later realize that such an assumption was premature due to insufficient analysis. Fixing this problem later in the development stage can be expensive.

- ***Can result in bloated objects***
  Certain use cases may only require the intrinsic behavior encapsulated within a *Business Object*. A *Business Object* tends to get bloated as more and more use case-specific behavior is implemented in it. To avoid bloating the *Business Objects*, implement any extrinsic business behavior specific to a particular use case or client **and** business behavior that acts on multiple *Business Objects* in the form of an *Application Service* (357), rather than including it in the *Business Object*.

Sample Code

The following example demonstrates the *Business Object* pattern.

Implementing POJO Business Object

This example illustrates the *POJO Business Object* strategy. The sample code for CustomerBO and ContactInfoBO is shown in Example 7.21 and Example 7.22 respectively.

Example 7.21 Business Object: CustomerBO.java

```

public class CustomerBO {
    // CustomerData is a Data Object
    private CustomerData customerData;

    // ContactInfoBO is a dependent Business Object
    private ContactInfoBO contactInfoBO;

    public CustomerBO(CustomerData customerData) {
        // validate CustomerData values
        . . .
        // copy customer data to this object
        this.customerData = customerData;
    }

    public ContactInfoBO getContactInfoBO () {
        // if ContactInfoBO is not created, get data from
        // customer data and wrap it with the
        // ContactInfoBO wrapper
        if (contactInfoBO == null)
            contactInfoBO = new ContactInfoBO(
            customerData.getContactInfoData());
```

```
        return contactInfoBO;
    }

    // business methods for CustomerBO
    . . .
}
```

Example 7.22 Business Object: ContactInfoBO.java

```

public class ContactInfoBO {
    // ContactInfoData is a Data Object
    private ContactInfoData contactInfoData;

    public ContactInfoBO(ContactInfoData contactInfoData) {
        // validate ContactInfoData values
        . . .
        // copy contact info data to this object
        this.contactInfoData = contactInfoData;
    }

    // Method to return address data
    public AddressData getAddressData () {
        return contactInfoData.getAddressData();
    }

    // business methods for ContactInfoBO
    . . .
}
```

Implementing Entity Bean Business Object

The *Composite Entity* (391) describes the implementation of *Business Objects* using entity beans. Please refer to the *Sample Code* section of the *Composite Entity* (391) pattern.

Related Patterns

- ***Composite Entity (391)***
  You can implement *Business Objects* using local entity beans in EJB 2.x. Local entity beans are recommended over remote entity beans to implement *Business Objects*. *Composite Entity* (391) discusses the details of implementing *Business Objects* with entity beans.

- ***Application Service (357)***
  Atomic business logic and rules related to a single *Business Object* are typically implemented within that *Business Object*. However, in most applications, you also have business logic that acts on multiple *Business Objects*. You might also need to provide business behavior specific to use cases, client types, or channels on top of what the *Business Objects* inherently implement. Using *Application Service* (357) is an excellent way to implement business logic that acts upon several *Business Objects* and thereby provides a service encapsulation layer for the *Business Objects*

- ***Transfer Object (415)***
  You can use *Transfer Objects* to carry data to and from the *Business Objects*. Some developers are tempted to use *Transfer Objects* (415) as the internal state representation for *Business Objects*. However, a *Business Object* wrapping a *Transfer Object* (415) is not recommended because it violates the intention of the *Transfer Object* (415) pattern and tightly couples the two types of objects. (See *Business Object Wraps Transfer Object* (390)).

- ***Data Access Object (462)***
  You can use *Data Access Objects* (462) to facilitate *Business Objects* persistence, in implementations that use custom JDBC mechanisms.

- ***Domain Store (516)***
  You can use *Domain Store* (516) to provide *Business Objects* persistence to leverage the power of custom implementation of transparent persistence mechanisms, similar to standard JDO implementations.

- ***Transaction Script and Domain Model [PEAA]***
  Transaction Script discusses a procedural implementation of business logic and *Domain Model* discusses the object-oriented implementation. While the *Domain Model* and *Business Object* pattern are very similar, the term **business object** is more commonly used by developers and architects in the field and is more precise. We have seen extensive use of the term **business object** in numerous projects that fall in line with the concepts outlined in this pattern.

Design Note: Business Object Wraps Transfer Object

Some developers have a tendency to wrap *Transfer Objects* (415) with *Business Objects* because the state information required maintained is similar to the state information represented by the *Transfer Object* (415). Another reason why developers tend to wrap the *Transfer Object* (415) with a *Business Object* is because they feel that *Transfer Objects* (415) are proliferating the system and by reusing them somehow, it is possible to limit the proliferation and to make the *Transfer Objects* (415) more useful in other ways. This logic is flawed due to the following reasons:

- **What about the intent of the Transfer Object?**
  The intent of the *Transfer Object* (415) is to carry data across the tier and not model the state of a *Business Object*. This intention is violated by this strategy as it lends additional meaning to the transfer object. If the *Transfer Object* (415) reuse is more important than keeping them true to their intention, then you might want to use this strategy. A *Transfer Object* (415) is intended to facilitate a use-case's specific data transfer needs and reflects that use-case's requirement very closely.
- **What happens if you add or remove a field in the Transfer Object?**
  Changing a *Transfer Object* may require a change to the *Business Object* if that change needs to be reflected to the *Business Object*'s clients. For example, if you remove a field, then the *Business Object* might need to be modified to reflect to this change. Such changes can have wide repercussions in the business objects layer and beyond.
- **What happens if you add or remove a field in the Business Object?**
  If you add a new field to the *Business Object*, or remove one that existed, then the *Transfer Object* (415) will have to make the corresponding change to keep up. Such a change can have a cascading effect and affect a change in all the clients that use the *Business Object* and the *Transfer Object* (415).
- **What if the Business Object needs to send a different Transfer Object (415) to the client than the one it wraps?**
  The *Business Object* has to create a different *Transfer Object* (415) as required by its clients, regardless of the one it wraps. This only contributes to more proliferation of *Transfer Object* (415) than to limit it.
- **What happens if the Business Object needs derived fields that are then sent to the clients?**
  This implies that the *Business Object* has to create another *Transfer Object* (415) to send the derived data anyway. Or you can change the existing *Transfer Object* (415) to accommodate the additional fields to carry derived data. This has the same effect as described previously when you change a *Transfer Object* (415).

Composite Entity

Problem

You want to use entity beans to implement your conceptual domain model

Business Objects (374) are objects containing business logic and business state. In J2EE applications, you can implement *Business Objects* (374) using entity beans; however, problems can arise when using entity beans to implement *Business Objects* (374).

The first problem is deciding whether to use remote or local entity beans. Remote entity beans are associated with network overhead and can degrade the performance of the application when not used appropriately. Local entity beans were introduced in the EJB 2.0 specification, and might not be available in implementations supporting only EJB version 1.1. Some EJB 1.1 containers optimize the inter-entity bean; however, such optimization is vendor-specific and not standard. Local entities in EJB 2.x containers are co-located with their clients, allowing you more control over performance and network overhead. However, note that such co-location might be somewhat less efficient than working with POJO *Business Objects* (374), as the container does a lot of this optimization transparently and also provides other services such as security and transaction management to each entity bean method invocation.

The second problem is deciding how to implement persistence of your *Business Objects* (374) as entity beans. You can implement transparent persistence using container-managed persistence and not write your own persistence code. However, if you have a legacy persistence implementation or need to implement unique requirements based on your persistence mechanism, CMP might not be suitable. You must implement bean-managed persistence (BMP) to persist your business objects to the data store.

Finally, you have to solve the problem of implementing your *Business Object* (374) relationships using a container-managed relationship (CMR) or bean-managed relationships. CMR can be used only if you are implementing CMP and requires that all the related entity beans be implemented as local entities.

Forces

- You want to avoid the drawbacks of remote entity beans, such as network overhead and remote inter-entity bean relationships.
- You want to leverage bean-managed persistence (BMP) using custom or legacy persistence implementations.
- You want to implement parent-child relationships efficiently when implementing *Business Objects* (374) as entity beans.
- You want to encapsulate and aggregate existing POJO *Business Objects* (374) with entity beans.
- You want to leverage EJB container transaction management and security features.
- You want to encapsulate the physical database design from the clients.

Solution

Use a *Composite Entity* to implement persistent *Business Objects* (374) using local entity beans and POJOs. *Composite Entity* aggregates a set of related *Business Objects* into coarse-grained entity bean implementations.

In a J2EE application, *Business Objects* (374) are implemented as **parent objects** and **dependent objects**.

- A **parent object** is reusable, independently deployable, manages its own life cycle, and manages its relationships to other objects. Each parent object might contain and manage the lifecycles of one or more objects called **dependent objects**.
- A **dependent object** can be a simple self-contained object or might contain other dependent objects. The lifecycle of a dependent object is tightly coupled to the lifecycle of its parent object. Dependent objects are not directly exposed to clients and a client can access them only through their parent object. Dependent objects don't exist by themselves and rely on their parent for identity and management.

A *Composite Entity* bean can implement a parent object and all its related dependent objects. Aggregation of *Business Objects* (374) combines interrelated persistent objects, such as Order and LineItems, into a coarse-grained implementation, potentially reducing the number of different entity beans in the application.

With the EJB 1.1 specification, you can implement entity beans only as **remote** objects. This means you encounter the common problems of distributed components, primarily network overhead and object granularity. In this scenario, implement the parent object as a remote entity bean and all the dependent objects as POJOs. Implementing dependent objects as entity beans is not a good idea because they degrade your application performance. This is due to network overhead caused by inter-communication, which is related to managing the inter-entity bean parent-dependent relationships.

With EJB 2.x, you can implement entity beans as remote **or** local objects. When implementing entity beans in EJB 2.x, use local entity beans to implement your parent *Business Objects* (374). You can then choose to implement your dependent objects as POJOs (as you do under the EJB 1.1 specification) or local entity beans. The relationships between the parent and dependent *Business Objects* (374) can be implemented using bean-managed relationships (when using BMP) or CMR (when using CMP). To implement CMR, the dependent objects must be implemented as local entity beans instead of POJOs.

To implement persistence of your *Business Objects* (374), you must choose between container-managed persistence (CMP) or bean-managed persistence (BMP). CMP is gaining popularity with newer applications using EJB 2.x compliant containers. Even though CMP in EJB 2.x is much more sophisticated than it was in EJB 1.x, it might not always meet performance requirements. Or you might have unique or legacy persistence requirements that are not fulfilled by using CMP. In these cases, you must use BMP to implement your persistence.

Composite Entity enables you to leverage the benefits of using entity beans in your application and allows you to exploit the powerful features of the EJB architecture, such as container-managed transactions, security, and persistence.

Regardless of whether you implement *Composite Entity* using local or remote entity beans, do not expose the entity beans to the application clients directly. Instead, encapsulate all entity beans behind a *Session Façade* (341) and allow all clients to access the *Session Façade* (341), which can interact with the required *Composite Entities* (391) behind the scenes.

Some applications might have little business logic interaction and trivial business logic, in which case you might expose your *Composite Entities* (391) to the application clients. However, exercise caution if you do this, because you'll encounter problems, such as maintainability as your application becomes more sophisticated.

Structure

The class diagram in Figure 7.30 shows the structure of the *Composite Entity* pattern.

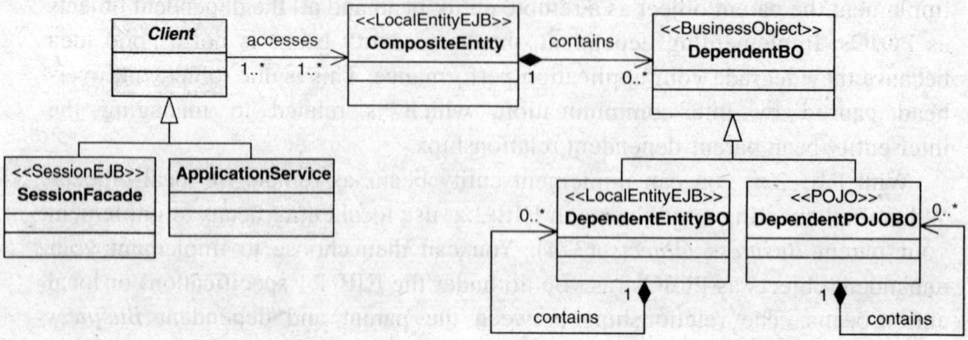

Figure 7.30 Composite Entity Class Diagram

The sequence diagram in Figure 7.31 shows the interactions in the *Composite Entity* pattern.

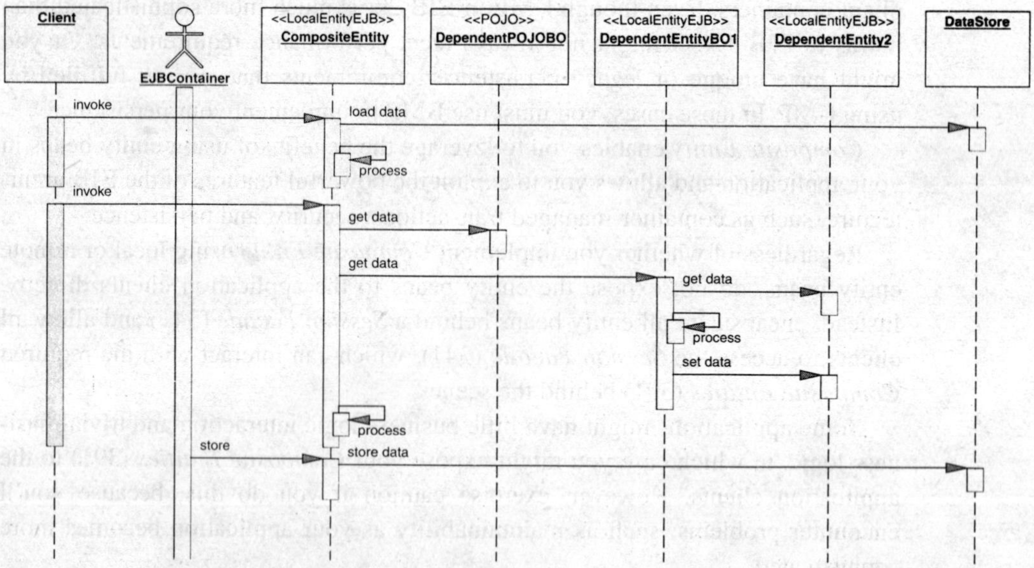

Figure 7.31 Composite Entity Sequence Diagram

Participants and Responsibilities

CompositeEntity

CompositeEntity is the coarse-grained entity bean that contains dependent objects.

DependentBO, DependentEntityBO, and DependentPOJOBO

A dependent object depends on the parent object that manages its lifecycle. A dependent object can contain other dependent objects; thus there might be a tree of objects within the *Composite Entity.* You can implement dependent objects as local entity beans (e.g. DependentEntity1 and DependentEntity2) or POJOs (e.g. DependentPOJO).

DataStore

DataStore represents the persistent store to which the business data gets persisted.

EJBContainer

EJBContainer invokes the load and store operations. The EJB Specification contains detailed object interaction diagrams, which can help you understand how the EJB container interacts with entity beans to load, store, activate, and passivate.

Strategies

This section explains different strategies for implementing a *Composite Entity.*

Composite Entity Remote Facade Strategy

In applications that have trivial or no business logic, the *Business Objects* (374) can implement all the necessary business logic and rules for the application. For such applications, using *Session Façade* (341) to encapsulate *Business Object Composite Entity* beans might seem to introduce an unnecessary layer of session beans. The *Session Façade* (341) ends up being proxy to the *Composite Entities* (391) and does not add much value.

In this case,, your remote clients might directly access *Composite Entities* (391). The parent object in the *Composite Entity* is implemented as a remote entity bean and the dependent objects are implemented as local entity beans or POJOs. The *Composite Entity* (remote entity parent object) performs the role of a *Facade* [GoF] by encapsulating the parent and the dependent objects and exposing a simpler interface to the clients. As your application becomes more sophisticated, this approach leads to many problems. Developers might inappropriately implement newer *Business Objects* (374) as remote entity beans without using the recommended *Session Façade* (341) approach to encapsulating entity beans.

It is important to note that this strategy is used very rarely. Even in the simplest of applications, it is likely to have a service layer composed of *Application Services* (357) and *Session Façade* (341).

Design Note: Entity Facade

A *Business Object* (374) implements complex relationships and encapsulates dependent business objects. In effect, it acts as a Facade [GoF] to all the objects it encapsulates. In J2EE applications that do not use entity beans, the *Business Objects* (374) are implemented as POJOs.

In J2EE applications that use entity beans, *Business Objects* (374) are implemented as *Composite Entities* (391), typically using local entity beans and POJOs. However, if the *Composite Entity Remote Facade* strategy meets your needs, you can implement a *Composite Entity* using a remote entity bean for the parent object and local entity beans or POJOs for its dependent objects.

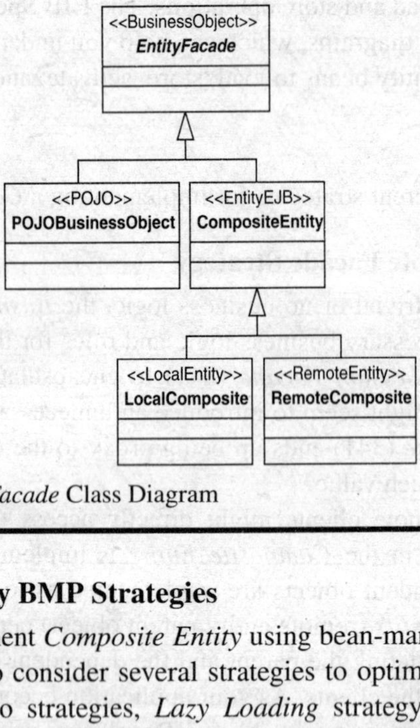

Figure 7.32 *Entity Facade* Class Diagram

Composite Entity BMP Strategies

When you implement *Composite Entity* using bean-managed persistence (BMP), you might want to consider several strategies to optimize your implementation. The following two strategies, *Lazy Loading* strategy and *Store Optimization (Dirty Marker)* strategy, relate to BMP *Composite Entity* implementations.

Lazy Loading Strategy

A *Composite Entity* can be composed of many levels of dependent objects in its tree of objects. However, loading all the dependent objects when the composite entity's ejbLoad() method is called by the EJB Container might take considerable time and resources.

One way to optimize this is by using a lazy loading strategy for loading the dependent objects. When the ejbLoad() method is called, at first load only those dependent objects that are most crucial to the *Composite Entity* clients. Subsequently, when the clients access a dependent object that has not yet been loaded from the database, the *Composite Entity* can perform a load on demand.

Thus, if some dependent objects are not used, they are not loaded on initialization. However, when the clients subsequently need those dependent objects, they get loaded at that time. Once a dependent object is loaded, subsequent container calls to the ejbLoad() method must include those dependent objects for reload to synchronize the changes with the persistent store.

Store Optimization (Dirty Marker) Strategy

A common problem with bean-managed persistence occurs when persisting the complete object graph during an ejbStore() operation. Since the EJB Container has no way of knowing what data has changed in the entity bean and its dependent objects, the burden is on the developer to determine what data to persist, and how to persist the data.

Some EJB containers provide a feature to identify what objects in *Composite Entity*'s graph need to be stored due to a prior update. Developers can do this by implementing a special method in the dependent objects, such as isDirty(), which is called by the container to check if the object has been updated since the previous ejbStore() operation.

A generic solution is to use an interface, DirtyMarker, as shown in the class diagram in Figure 7.33.

The idea is to have dependent objects implement the DirtyMarker interface to let the caller (typically the ejbStore() method) know if the state of the dependent object has changed. This way, the caller can choose whether to obtain the data for subsequent storage.

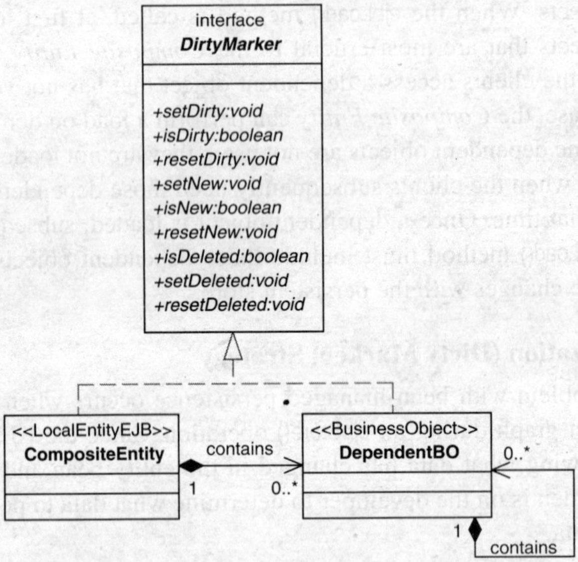

Figure 7.33 *Store Optimization* Strategy Class Diagram

Figure 7.34 on page 399 shows an example interaction for this strategy.

The client performs an update to the CompositeEntity, which results in a change to DependentObject3. DependentObject3 is accessed via its parent DependentObject2. The CompositeEntity is the parent of DependentObject2. When this update is performed, the setDirty() method is invoked in the DependentObject3. Subsequently, when the container invokes the ejbStore() method on this CompositeEntity instance, the ejbStore() method can check which dependent objects have gone dirty and selectively save those changes to the database. The dirty marks are reset once the store is successful.

The DirtyMarker interface can also include methods that can recognize other persistence status of the dependent object. For example, if a new dependent object is included into the *Composite Entity*, the ejbStore() method should be able to recognize what operation to use—in this case, the dependent object is not dirty, but is a new object. By extending the DirtyMarker interface to include a method called isNew(), the ejbStore() method can invoke an insert operation instead of an update operation. Similarly, by including a method called isDeleted(), the ejbStore() method can invoke the delete operation as required.

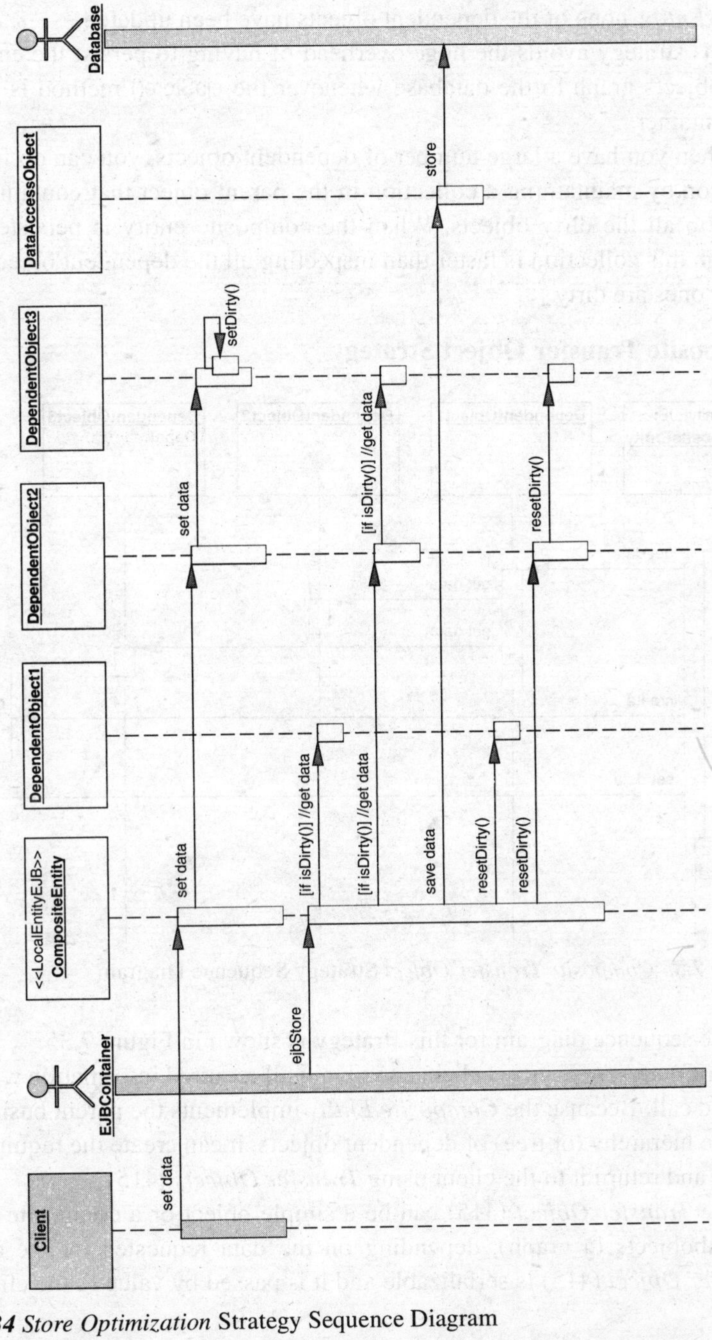

***Figure 7.34** Store Optimization* Strategy Sequence Diagram

In cases where ejbStore() is invoked with no intermediate updates to the *Composite Entity*, none of the dependent objects have been updated.

This strategy avoids the huge overhead of having to persist the entire dependent objects graph to the database whenever the ejbStore() method is invoked by the container.

When you have a large number of dependent objects, you can do further optimization by maintaining a collection in the parent object that contains the references to all the dirty objects. When the composite entity is persisted, walking through this collection is faster than inspecting all the dependent objects to check which ones are dirty.

Composite Transfer Object Strategy

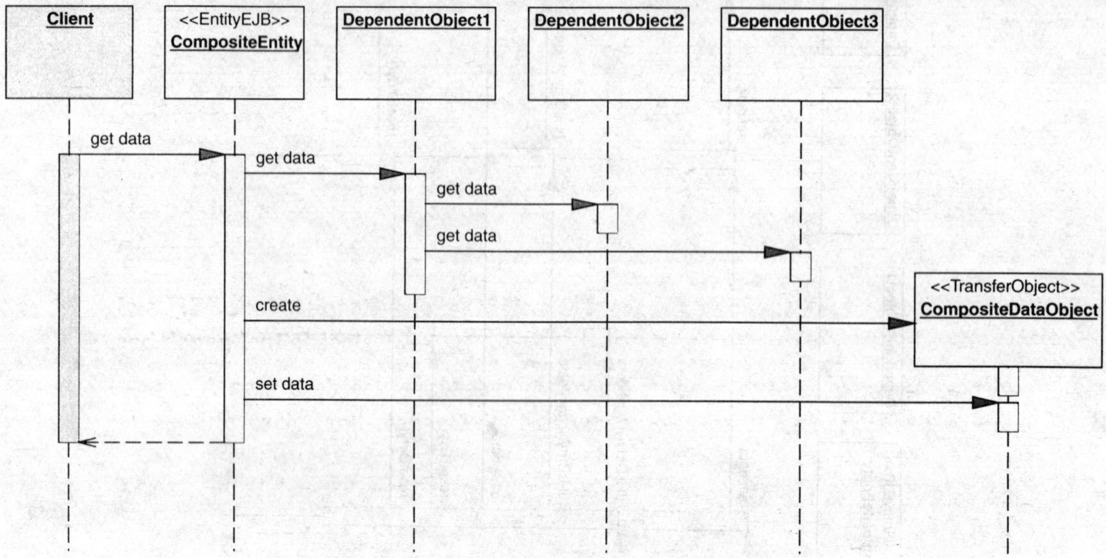

Figure 7.35 *Composite Transfer Object* Strategy Sequence Diagram

The sequence diagram for this strategy is shown in Figure 7.35.
With a *Composite Entity*, a client can obtain all required information with just one method call. Because the *Composite Entity* implements the parent business object and the hierarchy (or tree) of dependent objects, it can create the required transfer object and return it to the client using *Transfer Objects* (415).

The *Transfer Object* (415) can be a simple object or a composite object that has subobjects (a graph), depending on the data requested by the client. The *Transfer Object* (415) is serializable and it is passed by value to the client.

The preferred strategy is for the *Composite Entity* to be implemented as a local entity bean and returned values in local EJBs are passed by value. Therefore, returning a *Transfer Object* (415) protects the data from being manipulated by the client, typically a *Session Façade* (341).

Consequences

- ***Increases maintainability***
  When parents and dependent *Business Objects* (374) are implemented using *Composite Entity* with POJO dependent objects, you can reduce the number of fine-grained entity beans. When using EJB 2.x, you might want to implement the dependent objects as local entity beans and leverage other features, such as CMR and CMP. This improves the maintainability of the application.
- ***Improves network performance***
  Aggregation of the parent and dependent *Business Objects* (374) into fewer coarse-grained entity beans improves overall performance for EJB 1.1. This reduces network overhead because it eliminates inter-entity bean communication. For EJB 2.x, implementing *Business Objects* (374) as *Composite Entity* using local entity beans has the same benefit because all entity bean communications are local to the client. However, note that co-location is still less efficient than working with POJO *Business Objects* (374) due to container services for lifecycle, security, and transaction management for entity beans.
- ***Reduces database schema dependency***
  Composite Entity provides an object view of the data in the database. The database schema is hidden from the clients, since the mapping of the entity bean to the schema is internal to the *Composite Entity*. Changes to the database schema might require changes to the *Composite Entity* beans. However, the clients are not affected since the *Composite Entity* beans do not expose the schema to the external world.
- ***Increases object granularity***
  With a *Composite Entity*, the client typically looks up the parent entity bean instead of locating numerous fine-grained dependent entity beans. The parent entity bean acts as a *Facade* [GoF] to the dependent objects and hides the complexity of dependent objects by exposing a simpler interface. *Composite Entity* avoids fine-grained method invocations on the dependent objects, decreasing the network overhead.

- ***Facilitates composite transfer object creation***
  The *Composite Entity* can create a composite *Transfer Object (415)* that contains all the data from the entity bean and its dependent objects, and returns the *Transfer Object (415)* to the client in a single method call. This reduces the number of remote calls between the clients and the *Composite Entity.*

Sample Code

Consider a professional service automation application (PSA) where a Resource business object is implemented using *Composite Entity.* A Resource object represents an employee resource that is assigned to a project. Each Resource object can have different dependent objects as follows:

- BlockOutTime – Represents the time period the Resource is unavailable for reasons, such as training, vacation, timeoffs, etc. Since each resource can have multiple blocked out times, the Resource-to-BlockOutTime relationship is a one-to-many relationship.
- SkillSet – Represents the Skill that a Resource possesses. Since each resource can have multiple skills, the Resource-to-SkillSet relationship is a one-to-many relationship.

Implementing the Composite Entity Pattern

The pattern for the Resource business object is implemented as a *Composite Entity* (ResourceEntity), as shown in Example 7.23. The one-to-many relationship with its dependent objects (BlockOutTime and SkillSet objects) is implemented using collections.

Example 7.23 ResourceEntityBean.java: Composite Entity

```

package corepatterns.apps.psa.ejb;

import corepatterns.apps.psa.core.*;
import corepatterns.apps.psa.dao.*;
import java.sql.*;

import javax.sql.*;
import java.util.*;
import javax.ejb.*;
import javax.naming.*;
```

```
public class ResourceEntityBean implements EntityBean {
  public String employeeId;
  public String lastName;
  public String firstName;
  public String departmentId;
  ...

  // Collection of BlockOutTime Dependent objects
  public Collection blockoutTimes;

  // Collection of SkillSet Dependent objects
  public Collection skillSets;

  ...

  private EntityContext context;

  // Entity Bean methods implementation
  public String ejbCreate(ResourceTO resource)
  throws CreateException {
    try {
      this.employeeId = resource.employeeId;
      setResourceData(resource);
      getResourceDAO().create(resource);
    } catch (Exception ex) {
      throw new EJBException("Reason:" + ...);
    }
    return this.employeeId;
  }

  public String ejbFindByPrimaryKey(String primaryKey)
  throws FinderException {
    boolean result;
    try {
      ResourceDAO resourceDAO = getResourceDAO();
      result =  resourceDAO.findResource(primaryKey);
    } catch (Exception ex) {
      throw new EJBException("Reason:" + ...);
    }
    if (result) {
      return primaryKey;
    }
```

```
    else {
      throw new ObjectNotFoundException(...);
    }
  }

  public void ejbRemove() {
    try {
      // Remove dependent objects
      if (this.skillSets != null) {
        SkillSetDAO skillSetDAO = getSkillSetDAO();
        skillSetDAO.deleteAll(employeeId);
        skillSets = null;
      }
      if (this.blockoutTime != null) {
        BlockOutTimeDAO blockouttimeDAO =
          getBlockOutTimeDAO();
        blockouttimeDAO.deleteAll(employeeId);
        blockOutTimes = null;
      }

      // Remove the resource from the persistent store
      ResourceDAO resourceDAO = new ResourceDAO();
      resourceDAO.delete(employeeId);
    } catch (ResourceException ex) {
      throw new EJBException("Reason:"+...);
    } catch (BlockOutTimeException ex) {
      throw new EJBException("Reason:"+...);
    } catch (Exception exception) {
      ...
    }
  }

  public void setEntityContext(EntityContext context) {
    this.context = context;
  }

  public void unsetEntityContext() {
    context = null;
  }

  public void ejbActivate() {
    employeeId = (String)context.getPrimaryKey();
```

```
}

public void ejbPassivate() {
  employeeId = null;
}

public void ejbLoad() {
  try {
    // load the resource info from
    ResourceDAO resourceDAO = getResourceDAO();
    setResourceData((ResourceTO)
      resourceDAO.findResource(employeeId));

    // Load other dependent objects, if necessary
    ...
  } catch (Exception ex) {
    throw new EJBException("Reason:" + ...);
  }
}

public void ejbStore() {
  try {
    // Store resource information
    getResourceDAO().update(getResourceData());

    // Store dependent objects as needed
    ...
  } catch (SkillSetException ex) {
    throw new EJBException("Reason:" + ...);
  } catch (BlockOutTimeException ex) {
    throw new EJBException("Reason:" + ...);
  }
  ...
}

public void ejbPostCreate(ResourceTO resource) {
}

// Method to Get Resource transfer object
public ResourceTO getResourceTO() {
  // create a new Resource transfer object
  ResourceTO resourceTO = new ResourceTO(employeeId);

```

```
    // copy all values
    resourceTO.lastName = lastName;
    resourceTO.firstName = firstName;
    resourceTO.departmentId = departmentId;
    ...
    return resourceTO;
  }

  public void setResourceData(ResourceTO resourceTO) {
    // copy values from transfer object into entity bean
    employeeId = resourceTO.employeeId;
    lastName = resourceTO.lastName;
    ...
  }

  // Method to get dependent transfer objects
  public Collection getSkillSetsData() {
    // If skillSets is not loaded, load it first.
    // See Lazy Load strategy implementation.
    return skillSets;
  }
  ...

  // other get and set methods as needed
  ...

  // Entity bean business methods
  public void addBlockOutTimes(Collection moreBOTs)
  throws BlockOutTimeException {
    // Note: moreBOTs is a collection of BlockOutTimeTO
    // objects
    try {
      Iterator moreIter = moreBOTs.iterator();
      while (moreIter.hasNext()) {
        BlockOutTimeTO botTO =
          (BlockOutTimeTO) moreIter.next();
        if (! (blockOutTimeExists(botTO))) {
          // add BlockOutTimeTO to collection
          botTO.setNew();
          blockOutTime.add(botTO);
        } else {
          // BlockOutTimeTO already exists, cannot add
          throw new BlockOutTimeException(...);
```

```
        }
      }
    } catch (Exception exception) {
      throw new EJBException(...);
    }
  }

  public void addSkillSet(Collection moreSkills)
  throws SkillSetException {
    // similar to addBlockOutTime() implementation
    ...
  }

  ...

  public void updateBlockOutTime(Collection updBOTs)
  throws BlockOutTimeException {
    try {
      Iterator botIter = blockOutTimes.iterator();
      Iterator updIter = updBOTs.iterator();
      while (updIter.hasNext()) {
        BlockOutTimeTO botTO =
          (BlockOutTimeTO) updIter.next();
        while (botIter.hasNext()) {
          BlockOutTimeTO existingBOT =
            (BlockOutTimeTO) botIter.next();
          // compare key values, to locate BlockOutTime
          if (existingBOT.equals(botTO)) {
            // Found BlockOutTime in collection
            // replace old BlockOutTimeTO with new one
            botTO.setDirty(); //modified old dependent
            botTO.resetNew(); //not a new dependent
            existingBOT = botTO;
          }
        }
      }

    } catch (Exception exc) {
      throw new EJBException(...);
    }
  }

  public void updateSkillSet(Collection updSkills)
```

```
    throws CommitmentException {
      // similar to updateBlockOutTime...
      ...
    }

    ...

}
```

Implementing the Lazy Loading Strategy

Let's assume that when the *Composite Entity* is first loaded in the ejbLoad() method by the container, only the resource data is to be loaded. This includes the attributes listed in the ResourceEntity bean, excluding the dependent object collections. The dependent objects can then be loaded only if the client invokes a business method that needs these dependent objects. Subsequently, the ejbLoad() method needs to keep track of the dependent objects loaded in this manner and include them for reloading.

The relevant methods from the ResourceEntity class are shown in Example 7.24.

Example 7.24 Implementing Lazy Loading strategy

```

  ...
  public Collection getSkillSetsData() {
  throws SkillSetException {
    checkSkillSetLoad();
    return skillSets;
  }

  private void checkSkillSetLoad()
  throws SkillSetException {
    try {
      // Lazy Load strategy...Load on demand
      if (skillSets == null)
        skillSets =
          getSkillSetDAO().findAllSkills(resourceId);
    } catch (Exception exception) {
      // No skills, throw an exception
      throw new SkillSetException(...);
    }
  }

```

```
  ...

  public void ejbLoad() {
    try {
      // load the resource info from
      ResourceDAO resourceDAO = new ResourceDAO();
      setResourceData(
        resourceDAO.findResource(employeeId));

      // If the lazy loaded objects are already
      // loaded, they need to be reloaded.
      // If there are not loaded, do not load them
      // here...lazy load will load them later.
      if (skillSets != null) {
        reloadSkillSets();
      }
      if (blockOutTimes != null) {
        reloadBlockOutTimes();
      }
      ...
      throw new EJBException("Reason:"+...);
    }
  }
```

Implementing the Store Optimization (Dirty Marker) Strategy

To use the *Store Optimization* strategy, the dependent objects need to have implemented the DirtyMarker interface, as shown in Example 7.25. The ejbStore() method for storing only data that has been modified using this strategy is listed in Example 7.26.

Example 7.25 SkillSet-dependent object implements DirtyMarker interface

```

public class SkillSetTO
implements DirtyMarker, java.io.Serializable {
  private String skillName;
  private String expertiseLevel;
  private String info;
```

```
    ...

    // dirty flag
    private boolean dirty = false;

    // new flag
    private boolean isnew = true;

    // deleted flag
    private boolean deleted = false;

    public SkillSetTO(...) {
      // initialization
      ...
      // is new TO
      setNew();
    }

    // get, set and other methods for SkillSet
    // all set methods and modifier methods
    // must call setDirty()
    public setSkillName(String newSkillName) {
      skillName = newSkillName;
      setDirty();
    }
    ...

    // DirtyMarker methods
    // used for modified transfer objects only

    public void setDirty() {
      dirty = true;
    }
    public void resetDirty() {
      dirty = false;
    }
    public boolean isDirty() {
      return dirty;
    }

    // used for new transfer objects only
    public void setNew() {
      isnew = true;
```

```
    }
    public void resetNew() {
      isnew = false;
    }
    public boolean isNew() {
      return isnew;
    }

    // used for deleted objects only
    public void setDeleted() {
      deleted = true;
    }
    public boolean isDeleted() {
      return deleted;
    }
    public void resetDeleted() {
      deleted = false;
    }

}
```

Example 7.26 Implementing Store Optimization

```

    ...

    public void ejbStore() {
      try {
        // Load the mandatory data
        getResourceDAO().update(getResourceData());

        // Store optimization for dependent objects
        // check dirty and store
        // Check and store commitments
        if (skillSets != null) {
          // Get the DAO to use to store
          SkillSetDAO skillSetDAO = getSkillSetDAO();
          Iterator skillIter = skillSet.iterator();
          while (skillIter.hasNext()) {
            SkillSetTO skill =
              (SkillSetTO) skillIter.next();
            if (skill.isNew()) {
              // This is a new dependent, insert it
```

```
                skillSetDAO.create(skill);
                skill.resetNew();
                skill.resetDirty();
            }
            else if (skill.isDeleted()) {
                // delete Skill
                skillSetDAO.delete(skill);
                // Remove from dependents list
                skillSets.remove(skill);
            }
            else if (skill.isDirty()) {
                // Store Skill, it has been modified
                skillSetDAO.update(skill);
                // Saved, reset dirty.
                skill.resetDirty();
                skill.resetNew();
            }
        }
    }

    // Similarly, implement store optimization
    // for other dependent objects such as

    // BlockOutTime, ...
    ...
  } catch (SkillSetException ex) {

    throw new EJBException("Reason:"+...);
  } catch (BlockOutTimeException ex) {
    throw new EJBException("Reason:"+...);
  } catch (CommitmentException ex) {
    throw new EJBException("Reason:"+...);
  }
}

...
```

Implementing the Composite Transfer Object Strategy

Now consider the requirement that the client must obtain all the data from the ResourceEntity, and not just one part. This can be done using the *Composite Transfer Object* strategy, as shown in Example 7.27.

Example 7.27 Implementing the Composite Transfer Object

```
public class ResourceCompositeTO {
  private ResourceTO resourceData;
  private Collection skillSets;
  private Collection blockOutTimes;

  // transfer object constructors
  ...

  // get and set methods
  ...
}
```

The ResourceEntity provides a getResourceDetailsData() method to return the ResourceCompositeTO *Composite Transfer Object*, as shown in Example 7.28.

Example 7.28 Creating the Composite Transfer Object

```

...
public ResourceCompositeTO getResourceDetailsData() {
  ResourceCompositeTO compositeTO =
    new ResourceCompositeTO (getResourceData(),
        getSkillsData(), getBlockOutTimesData());
  return compositeTO;
}
...
```

Related Patterns

- ***Business Object (374)***
  The *Business Object* (374) pattern describes in general how domain model entities are implemented in J2EE applications. *Composite Entity* is one of the strategies of the *Business Object* (374) pattern for implementing the *Business Objects* (374) using entity beans.

- ***Transfer Object (415)***
  The *Composite Entity* creates a composite *Transfer Object* (415) and returns it to the client. The *Transfer Object* (415)is used to carry data from the *Composite Entity* and its dependent objects.

- ***Session Façade (341)***
  Composite Entities (391) are generally not directly exposed to the application clients. *Session Façades* (341) are used to encapsulate the entity beans, add integration and web service endpoints, and provide a simpler coarse-grained interface to clients.

- ***Transfer Object Assembler (433)***
  When it comes to obtaining a composite transfer object from the *Business Object* (374), the *Composite Entity* is similar to a *Transfer Object Assembler* (433). However, in this case, the data sources for all the *Transfer Objects* in the composite are parts of the *Composite Entity* itself, whereas for the *Transfer Object Assembler* (433), the data sources can be different entity beans, session beans, *Data Access Objects* (462), *Application Services* (357), and so on.

Transfer Object

Problem

You want to transfer multiple data elements over a tier.

J2EE applications implement server-side business components as *Session Façades* (341) and *Business Objects* (374), and some of their methods return data to the client. These components are typically implemented as remote objects, such as session beans and entity beans. When these business components expose fine-grained get and set methods, a client must invoke several getter methods to get all the attribute values it needs.

However, this can cause efficiency problems because every method call to an enterprise bean is potentially remote. Such remote calls create a network overhead, even if the client and the EJB container are both running in the same JVM, OS, or physical machine. It's extremely inefficient to use multiple calls to remote objects' getter methods when you receive only a single piece of data back each time. The more remote method calls you use, the chattier the application gets and the worse application performance can become.

Even when not accessing remote components, you still need to access components that are encapsulated in a different tier, such as a *Business Objects* (374) in the business tier or *Data Access Object* (462) in the integration tier. While these components are not remote objects, you still should access them with a coarse-grained interface to send and receive data.

Forces

- You want clients to access components in other tiers to retrieve and update data.
- You want to reduce remote requests across the network.
- You want to avoid network performance degradation caused by chattier applications that have high network traffic.

Solution

Use a *Transfer Object* to carry multiple data elements across a tier.

A Transfer Object is designed to optimize data transfer across tiers. Instead of sending or receiving individual data elements, a *Transfer Object* contains all the data elements in a single structure required by the request or response.

The *Transfer Object* is passed by value to the client. Therefore all calls to the *Transfer Object* are made on copies of the original *Transfer Object*.

Structure

Figure 7.36 shows the class diagram that represents the *Transfer Object* pattern in its simplest form.

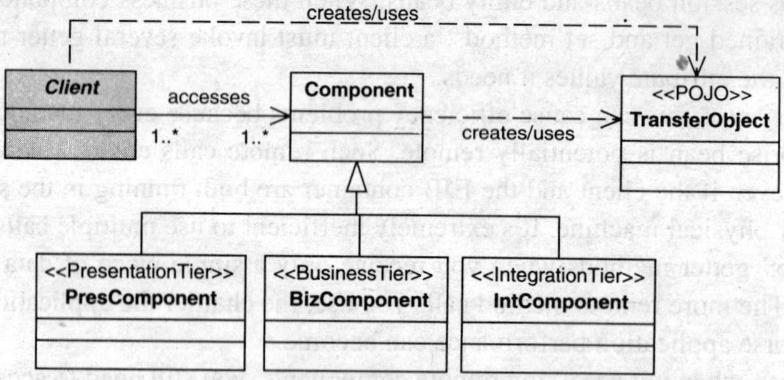

Figure 7.36 *Transfer Object* Class Diagram

As shown in this class diagram, an instance of a TransferObject is constructed on demand by the Component and returned to the client. The Component creates the TransferObject and returns it to the client upon request. When the TransferObject is serialized and sent to the Client over the network, the Client receives and uses it as its own local copy. The Client can also create its own TransferObject instances to send to the Component to perform an update.

A TransferObject class can provide a constructor that accepts all the required attributes to create an instance of TransferObject. A TransferObject can expose all its members by declaring them as public, without any getter and setter methods. If some control is necessary to manage what goes in and out of a TransferObject, then define the members as protected or private as appropriate, and provide methods to get and set the values. To protect an immutable TransferObject from modification after its creation, don't provide setter methods.

Choosing whether to make the TransferObject's attributes private and accessed by getter and setter methods, or public, is a design choice you make based on the application requirements.

Participants and Responsibilities

Figure 7.37 contains the sequence diagram that shows the interactions for the *Transfer Object* pattern.

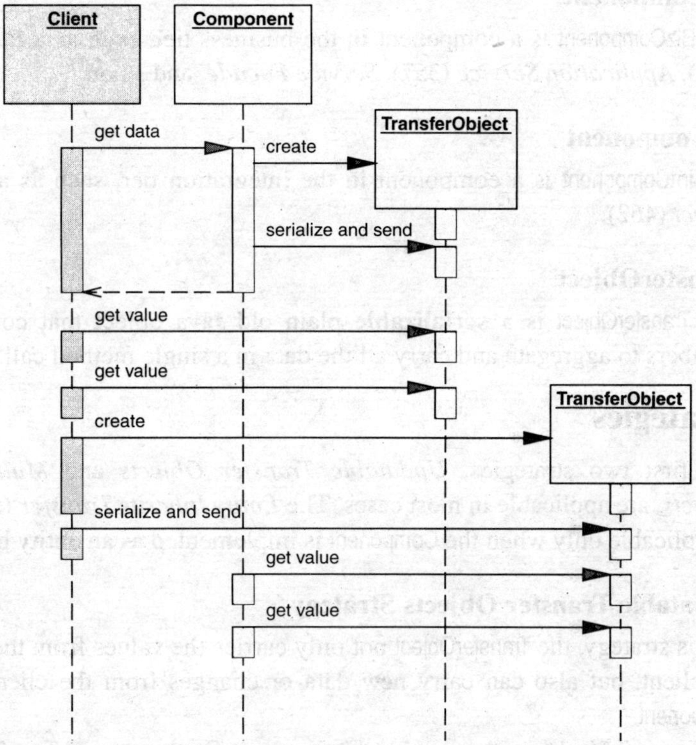

Figure 7.37 *Transfer Object* Sequence Diagram

Client

The Client needs to access a Component to send and receive data. Typically, the Client is a Component in another tier. For example, a Component in the presentation tier can act as a client of some business-tier components.

Component

The Component can be any component in another tier that the client accesses to send and receive data. The Component can be in the presentation tier (PresComponent), business tier (BizComponent) or integration tier (IntComponent).

PresComponent

The PresComponent is a component in the presentation tier, such as a helper object, an instance of a BusinessDelegate, a command object, and so on.

BizComponent

The BizComponent is a component in the business tier, such as a *Business Object* (374), *Application Service* (357), *Service Facade*, and so on.

IntComponent

The IntComponent is a component in the integration tier, such as a *Data Access Object* (462).

TransferObject

The TransferObject is a **serializable** plain old Java object that contains several members to aggregate and carry all the data in a single method call.

Strategies

The first two strategies, *Updatable Transfer Objects* and *Multiple Transfer Objects*, are applicable in most cases. The *Entity Inherits Transfer Object* strategy is applicable only when the Component is implemented as an entity bean.

Updatable Transfer Objects Strategy

In this strategy, the TransferObject not only carries the values from the Component to the client, but also can carry new data or changes from the client back to the Component.

Figure 7.38 shows the relationship between Component and TransferObject.

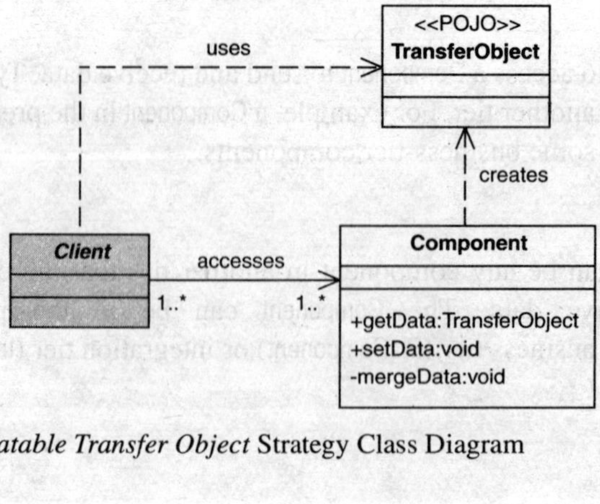

Figure 7.38 *Updatable Transfer Object* Strategy Class Diagram

The Component creates the TransferObject. Recall that a client might need to access the Component values, not only to read them, but to modify these values, so the Component must provide setter methods.

Instead of providing fine-grained set methods for each attribute, which results in network overhead, the Component can expose a coarse-grained setData() method that accepts a TransferObject as an argument. The TransferObject passed to this method holds the updated values from the client. Since the TransferObject has to be mutable, the TransferObject class has to provide setter methods for each attribute that can be modified by the client. The setter method for the TransferObject can include atomic field-level validations and integrity checks. Once the client obtains a TransferObject from the Component, the client invokes the necessary set methods locally to change the attribute values. Such local changes do not impact the Component until the setData() method is invoked.

The setData() method serializes the client's copy of the TransferObject and sends it to the Component. The Component receives the modified TransferObject from the client and merges the changes into its own attributes.

The merging operation can complicate the design of the Component and the TransferObject. One strategy to update only attributes that have changed, rather than updating all attributes. You can use a change flag in the TransferObject rather than a direct comparison to determine the attributes to update.

This *Updatable Transfer Objects* strategy makes update propagation, synchronization, and version control more complex.

Adopting the *Updatable Transfer Objects* strategy allows the client to modify the local copy of the TransferObject. However, updates made on the Component might not be propagated to the local copies of the TransferObject instances that the clients had previously obtained. This happens because the Component is unaware of any clients' local copies of TransferObject instances. This makes the original local copies potentially incorrect.

The Component must also handle the situation where two or more clients simultaneously request conflicting updates to the remote data. Allowing such synchronous updates might result in data conflicts and inconsistencies. Version control is one way of avoiding such conflict. The Component can include a version number or a last-modified time stamp. The version number or time stamp is copied over from the Component into the TransferObject. An update transaction can resolve conflicts using the time stamp or version number attribute. If a client holding a stale TransferObject tries to update the Component, the Component can detect the stale version number or time stamp in the TransferObject and inform the client of this error condition. The client then must obtain the latest TransferObject and retry the update. In extreme cases this can result in client starvation—the client might never accomplish its updates.

Figure 7.39 shows the sequence diagram for the entire update interaction

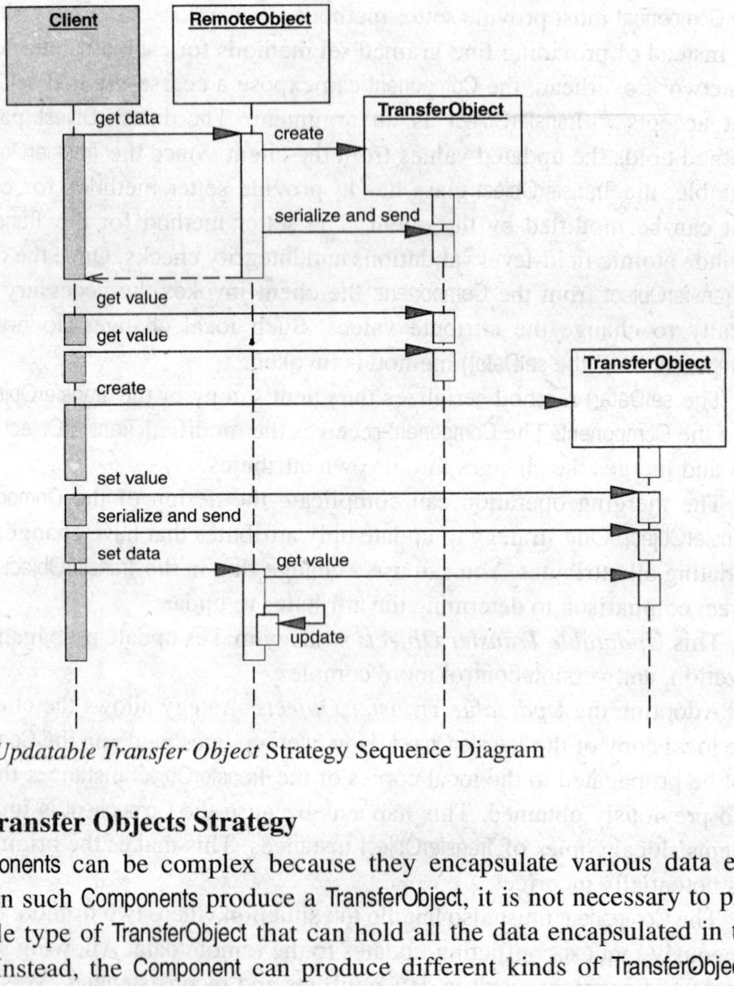

Figure 7.39 Updatable Transfer Object Strategy Sequence Diagram

Multiple Transfer Objects Strategy

Some Components can be complex because they encapsulate various data elements. When such Components produce a TransferObject, it is not necessary to produce a single type of TransferObject that can hold all the data encapsulated in the Component. Instead, the Component can produce different kinds of TransferObjects, each carrying only as much data as is needed to satisfy a kind of request or a use case.

You might do this in the following circumstances:

- When the Component is implemented as a session bean, typically as a *Session Façade* (341), the bean might interact with several other business components to provide the service. The session bean produces its TransferObject from different sources.

- Similarly, when the Component is implemented as a *Composite Entity* (391), the entity bean can encapsulate a graph of dependent objects.

In both these cases, it is good practice to produce *Transfer Objects* that represent parts of the encapsulated data.

For example, in a trading application, a *Composite Entity* (391) that implements a customer portfolio *Business Object* (374) can be a coarse-grained complex component with several dependent objects. This *Composite Entity* (391) can produce different *Transfer Objects* that provide data for parts of the Portfolio, such as CustomerInformation, StockHoldingsList, and so on.

Another example in the same application is a CustomerManager service object implementing a *Session Façade* (341). The facade provides services by interacting with a number of other Components and business components. The CustomerManager bean can produce discrete small *Transfer Objects*, such as CustomerAddress, ContactList, and so on, to represent parts of its overall model.

For both these scenarios, you can implement the Component so that it provides many getter methods to obtain different *Transfer Objects*.

The class diagram for the *Multiple Transfer Objects* strategy is shown in Figure 7.40.

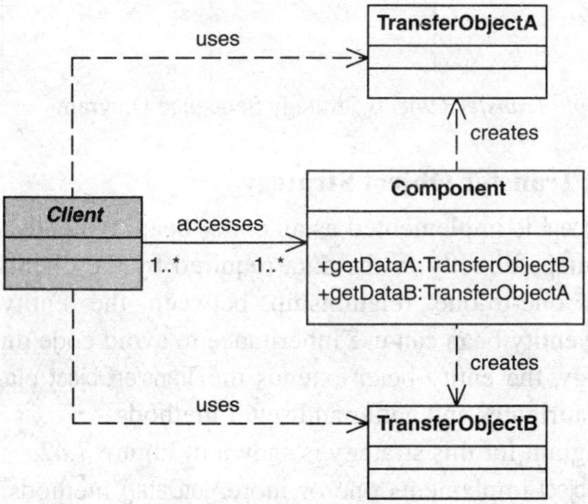

***Figure 7.40** Multiple Transfer Objects* Strategy Class Diagram

When a client needs a transfer object of type TransferObjectA, it invokes the Component's getDataA() method requesting TransferObjectA. When it needs a transfer object of type TransferObjectB, it invokes the Component's getDataB() method requesting TransferObjectB, and so on.

This is shown in the sequence diagram in Figure 7.41.

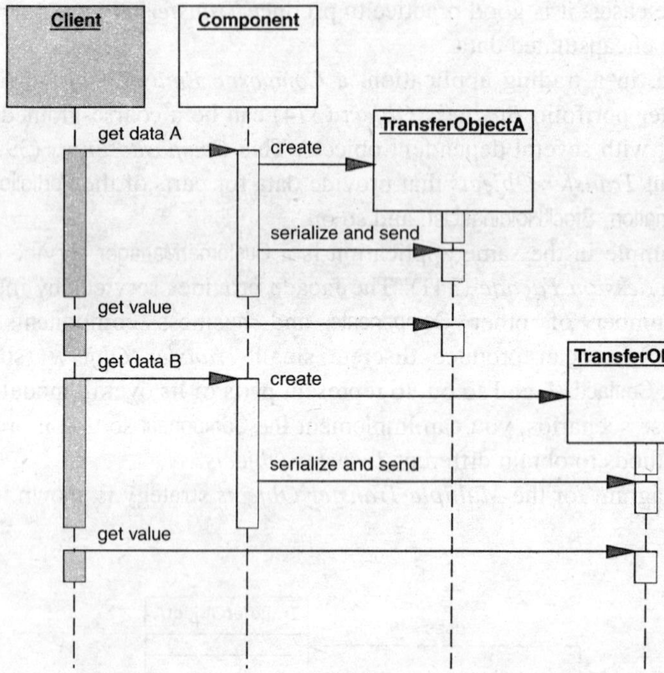

Figure 7.41 *Multiple Transfer Objects* Strategy Sequence Diagram

Entity Inherits Transfer Object Strategy

When the Component is implemented as an entity bean, typically, the data held by the component maps directly to the data required by the clients. In such cases, since there's a one-to-one relationship between the entity bean and its TransferObject, the entity bean can use inheritance to avoid code duplication.

In this strategy, the entity bean extends the TransferObject class and therefore shares the same attributes and getter and setter methods.

The class diagram for this strategy is shown in Figure 7.42.

The TransferObject implements one or more getData() methods, as described in the *Multiple Transfer Objects* strategy. When the entity inherits this TransferObject class, the client invokes an inherited getdata() method on the entity bean to obtain a TransferObject instance.

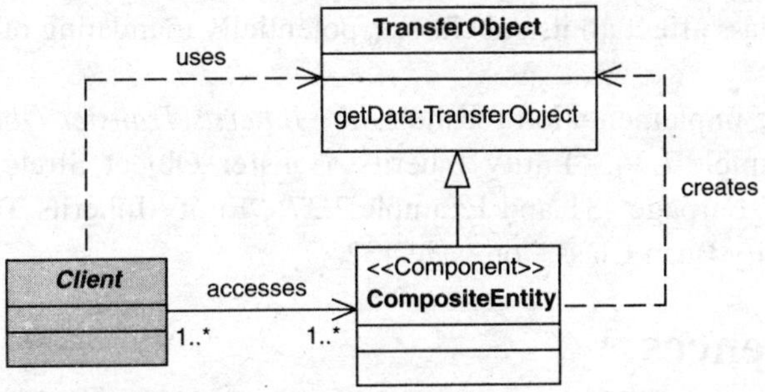

Figure 7.42 Entity Inherits Transfer Object Strategy Class Diagram

The sequence diagram in Figure 7.43 demonstrates this strategy.

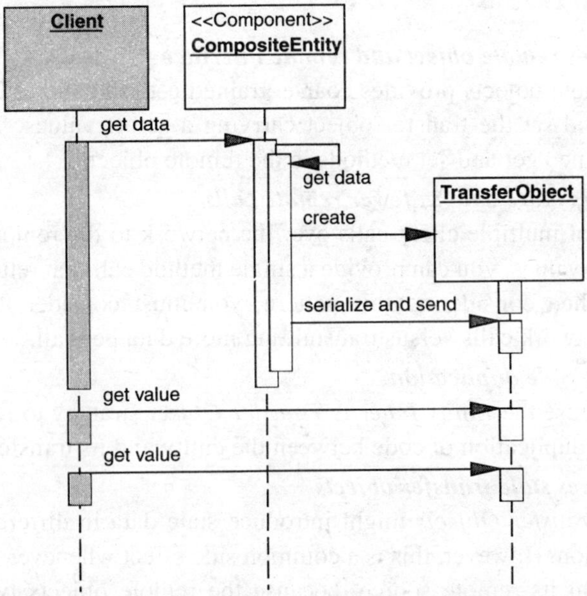

Figure 7.43 Entity Inherits Transfer Object Strategy Sequence Diagram

Thus, this strategy eliminates code duplication between the entity bean and the TransferObject. It also helps manage changes to the TransferObject requirements by isolating the change to the TransferObject class and preventing the changes from affecting the entity bean.

This strategy has a trade-off related to inheritance. Changes to this TransferObject class affect all its subclasses, potentially mandating other changes to the hierarchy.

The sample implementation for the *Entity Inherits Transfer Object* strategy is shown in Example 7.36, "Entity Inherits Transfer Object Strategy – Transfer Object Class," on page 431 and Example 7.37, "Entity Inherits Transfer Object Strategy – Entity Bean Class," on page 432.

Consequences

- ***Reduces network traffic***
  A *Transfer Object* carries a set of data values from a remote object to the client in one remote method call, thereby reducing the number of remote calls. The reduced chattiness of the application results in better network performance.
- ***Simplifies remote object and remote interface***
  The remote objects provides coarse-grained getData() and setData() methods to get and set the transfer object carrying a set of values. This eliminates fine-grained get and set methods in the remote objects.
- ***Transfers more data in fewer remote calls***
  Instead of multiple client calls over the network to the remote object to get attribute values, you can provide a single method call that returns aggregated data. When considering this pattern, you must consider the trade-off of fewer network calls versus transmitting more data per call.
- ***Reduces code duplication***
  You can use the *Entity Inherits Transfer Object* strategy to reduce or eliminate the duplication of code between the entity and its transfer object.
- ***Introduces stale transfer objects***
  Using *Transfer Objects* might introduce stale data in different parts of the application. However, this is a common side effect whenever you disconnect data from its remote source, because the remote objects typically do not keep track of all the clients that obtained the data, to propagate changes.
- ***Increases complexity due to synchronization and version control***
  When using the *Updatable Transfer Objects* strategy, you must design for concurrent access. This means that the design might get more complex due to the synchronization and version control mechanisms.

Sample Code

Implementing the Transfer Object Pattern

Consider an example where a business object called Project is modeled and implemented as an entity bean. The Project entity bean must send data to its clients in a *Transfer Object* when the client invokes its getProjectData() method. The *Transfer Object* class for this example, ProjectTO, is shown in Example 7.29.

Example 7.29 Implementing the Transfer Object Pattern – Transfer Object Class

```

// Transfer Object to hold the details for Project
public class ProjectTO implements java.io.Serializable {
    public String projectId;
    public String projectName;
    public String managerId;
    public String customerId;
    public Date startDate;
    public Date endDate;
    public boolean started;
    public boolean completed;
    public boolean accepted;
    public Date acceptedDate;
    public String projectDescription;
    public String projectStatus;

    // transfer object constructors...
}
```

The sample code for the entity bean that uses this *Transfer Object* is shown in Example 7.30.

Example 7.30 Implementing the Transfer Object Pattern – Entity Bean Class

```

...
public class ProjectEntity implements EntityBean {
    private EntityContext context;
    public String projectId;
    public String projectName;
    public String managerId;
```

```
    public String customerId;
    public Date startDate;
    public Date endDate;
    public boolean started;
    public boolean completed;
    public boolean accepted;
    public Date acceptedDate;
    public String projectDescription;
    public String projectStatus;
    private boolean closed;

    // other attributes...

    private ArrayList commitments;
    ...

    // Method to get transfer object for Project data
    public ProjectTO getProjectData() {
        ProjectTO proj = new ProjectTO();
        proj.projectId = projectId;
        proj.projectName = projectName;
        proj.managerId = managerId;
        proj.startDate = startDate;
        proj.endDate = endDate;
        proj.customerId = customerId;
        proj.projectDescription = projectDescription;
        proj.projectStatus = projectStatus;
        proj.started = started;
        proj.completed = completed;
        proj.accepted = accepted;
        proj.closed = closed;
        return proj;
    }
    ...
}
```

Implementing the Updatable Transfer Objects Strategy

You can extend Example 7.30 to implement this strategy. In this case, the entity bean provides a setProjectData() method to update the entity bean by passing a transfer object that contains the data for the update. The sample code for this strategy is shown in Example 7.31.

Example 7.31 Implementing the Updatable Transfer Object Strategy

```
...
public class ProjectEntity implements EntityBean {
  private EntityContext context;
  ...

  // attributes and other methods as in
  // Example 7.4 on page 331
  ...

  // method to set entity values with a transfer object
  public void setProjectData(ProjectTO updatedProj) {
    mergeProjectData(updatedProj);
  }

  // method to merge values from the transfer object
  // into the entity bean attributes
  private void mergeProjectData(ProjectTO updatedProj) {
    // version control check may be necessary here
    // before merging changes in order to
    // prevent losing updates by other clients
    projectId = updatedProj.projectId;
    projectName = updatedProj.projectName;
    managerId = updatedProj.managerId;
    startDate = updatedProj.startDate;
    endDate = updatedProj.endDate;
    customerId = updatedProj.customerId;
    projectDescription = updatedProj.projectDescription;
    projectStatus = updatedProj.projectStatus;
    started = updatedProj.started;
    completed = updatedProj.completed;
    accepted = updatedProj.accepted;
    closed = updatedProj.closed;
  }
  ...
}
```

Implementing the Multiple Transfer Objects Strategy

You probably don't always want to get the same type, or same amount, of information, from your data store. To accommodate this need for different types of information, you can make multiple transfer objects, each requesting a different set of information, and you use the appropriate object for each request.

Consider a professional services application example where the client wants to get different levels of detail for a resource. You might provide two *Transfer Objects*, ResourceTO and ResourceDetailsTO, that clients access to request data. ResourceTO transfers data for a small set of attributes and ResourceDetailsTO, transfers data for a larger set of attributes.

This example presents a subset/superset approach, where you have one transfer object with a large amount of data and one with a small subset of that data. You can create *Transfer Objects* for separate, non-overlapping data sets, such as a ContactInfo transfer object containing a manager's mailing address and phone numbers; and an HRInfo transfer object containing a manager's name and salary, and the name and salary of all that manager's reports.

The sample code for the two *Transfer Object*s for this example is shown in Example 7.32 and Example 7.33. The sample code for the entity bean that produces these *Transfer Object*s is shown in Example 7.34, and finally the entity bean client is shown in Example 7.35.

Example 7.32 Multiple Transfer Objects Strategy – ResourceTO

```

// ResourceTO: This class holds basic information
// about the resource
public class ResourceTO implements java.io.Serializable {
    public String resourceId;
    public String lastName;
    public String firstName;
    public String department;
    public String grade;
    ...
}
```

Example 7.33 Multiple Transfer Objects Strategy – ResourceDetailsTO

```

// ResourceDetailsTO This class holds detailed
// information about resource
public class ResourceDetailsTO
implements java.io.Serializable {
```

```
      public String resourceId;
      public String lastName;
      public String firstName;
      public String department;
      public String grade;

      // other data...
      public Collection commitments;
      public Collection blockoutTimes;
      public Collection skillSets;
}
```

Example 7.34 Multiple Transfer Objects Strategy – Resource Entity Bean

```

// imports

public class ResourceEntity implements EntityBean {
   // entity bean attributes
   ...

   // entity bean business methods
   ...

   // Multiple Transfer Object method : Get ResourceTO
   public ResourceTO getResourceData() {

      // create new ResourceTO instance and copy
      // attribute values from entity bean into TO
      ...
   }

   // Multiple Transfer Object method : Get
   // ResourceDetailsTO
   public ResourceDetailsTO getResourceDetailsData() {

      // create new ResourceDetailsTO instance and copy
      // attribute values from entity bean into TO
      ...
   }

   // other entity bean methods
   ...
}
```

Example 7.35 Multiple Transfer Objects Strategy – Entity Bean Client

```
...
private ResourceEntity resourceEntity;
private static final Class homeClazz =
  corepatterns.apps.psa.ejb.ResourceEntityHome.class;
...

try {
  ResourceEntityHome home = (ResourceEntityHome)
    ServiceLocator.getInstance().getLocalHome(
      "Resource", homeClazz);
  resourceEntity = home.findByPrimaryKey(resourceId);
} catch (ServiceLocatorException ex) {
  // Translate Service Locator exception into
  // application exception
  throw new ResourceException(...);
} catch (FinderException ex) {
  // Translate the entity bean finder exception into
  // application exception
  throw new ResourceException(...);
} catch (RemoteException ex) {
  // Translate the Remote exception into application
  // exception
  throw new ResourceException(...);
}
...

// retrieve basic Resource data
ResourceTO to = resourceEntity.getResourceData();
...

// retrieve detailed Resource data
ResourceDetailsTO dto =
  resourceEntity.getResourceDetailsData();
...
```

Implementing the Entity Inherits Transfer Object Strategy

Consider an example where an entity bean ContactEntity inherits all its properties from a *Transfer Object*'s ContactTO. Example 7.36 shows the code sample for an example *Transfer Object*'s ContactTO that illustrates this strategy.

Example 7.36 Entity Inherits Transfer Object Strategy – Transfer Object Class

```

// This is the transfer object class inherited by the
// entity bean
public class ContactTO  implements java.io.Serializable {

   // public members
   public String firstName;
   public String lastName;
   public String address;

   // default constructor
   public ContactTO() {}

   // constructor accepting all values
   public ContactTO(String firstName, String lastName,
       String address) {
     init(firstName, lastName, address);
   }

   // constructor to create a new TO based
   // using an existing TO instance
   public ContactTO(ContactTO contact) {
     init(contact.firstName, contact.lastName,
       contact.address);
   }

   // method to set all the values
   public void init(String firstName, String lastName,
       String address) {
     this.firstName = firstName;
     this.lastName = lastName;
     this.address = address;
   }

   // create a new transfer object
   public ContactTO getData() {
     return new ContactTO(this);
   }
}
```

The entity bean sample code relevant to this pattern strategy is shown in Example 7.37.

Example 7.37 Entity Inherits Transfer Object Strategy – Entity Bean Class

```

public class ContactEntity extends ContactTO
implements javax.ejb.EntityBean {
  ...
  // the client calls the getData method
  // on the ContactEntity bean instance.
  // getData() is inherited from the transfer object
  // and returns the ContactTO transfer object
  ...
}
```

Related Patterns

- ***Session Façade (341)***
  The *Session Façade* (341) frequently uses *Transfer Objects* as an exchange mechanism with participating *Business Objects* (374). When the facade acts as a proxy to the underlying business service, the *Transfer Object* obtained from the *Business Objects* (374) can be passed to the client.
- ***Transfer Object Assembler (433)***
  The *Transfer Object Assembler* (433) builds composite *Transfer Objects* from different data sources. The data sources are usually session beans or entity beans whose clients ask for data, and who would then provide their data to the *Transfer Object Assembler* (433) as *Transfer Objects* (415). These *Transfer Objects* (415) are considered to be parts of the composite object assembled by the *Transfer Object Assembler* (433).
- ***Value List Handler (444)***
  The *Value List Handler* (444) is another pattern that provides lists of dynamically constructed *Transfer Objects* by accessing the persistent store at request time.
- ***Composite Entity (391)***
  The *Transfer Object* pattern addresses transferring data across tiers. This is one aspect of the design considerations for entity beans that can use the *Transfer Object* to carry data to and from the entity beans.

Transfer Object Assembler

Problem

You want to obtain an application model that aggregates transfer objects from several business components.

Application clients frequently need to obtain business data or an **application model** from the business tier, to either display it or to perform some intermediate processing. An application model represents business data encapsulated by business components in the business tier. When the clients need the application model data, they must locate, access, and obtain different parts of the model from different sources, such as *Business Objects* (374), *Data Access Objects* (462), *Application Services* (357), and other objects in the business tier. This approach leads to several problems:

- Direct access between the clients and these components in a different tier introduces coupling between the tiers. Due to tight coupling, changes made to the business tier components cause a ripple effect throughout the clients. The client code complexity increases because the client has to interact and manage with several business components and business logic to construct the model that gets embedded in the client code.
- Furthermore, as different clients start implementing similar logic to obtain and construct model data, you get more code duplication, increasing maintenance overhead. If the business components accessed by the clients are distributed and remote, performance is reduced because the clients have to access several business components over the network layer to obtain application model data.

Forces

- You want to encapsulate business logic in a centralized manner and prevent implementing it in the client.
- You want to minimize the network calls to remote objects when building a data representation of the business-tier object model.
- You want to create a complex model to hand over to the client for presentation purposes.

- You want the clients to be independent of the complexity of model implementation, and you want to reduce coupling between the client and the business components.

Solution

Use a *Transfer Object Assembler* to build an application model as a composite *Transfer Object* (415). The *Transfer Object Assembler* aggregates multiple *Transfer Objects* (415) from various business components and services, and returns it to the client.

The *Transfer Object Assembler* retrieves *Transfer Objects (415)* from the business components. The *Transfer Objects (415)* are then processed by the *Transfer Object Assembler,* which creates and assembles a composite *Transfer Object (415)* to represent the application model data. The clients use the *Transfer Object Assembler* to obtain this application model for read-only purposes to display or to perform other intermediate processing. Clients do not change the data in the composite *Transfer Object (415)*.

A *Business Object* (374) also can produce a composite *Transfer Object (415)* by using only the data encapsulated within itself. *Transfer Object Assembler*, on the other hand, obtains data from multiple sources, such as *Business Objects* (374), *Session Façades* (341), *Application Services* (357), *Data Access Objects* (462), and other services. The *Transfer Object Assembler* can use a *Service Locator* (315) to locate a business service component, such as a *Session Façade* (341).

Structure

Figure 7.44 shows the relationships for the *Transfer Object Assembler* pattern.

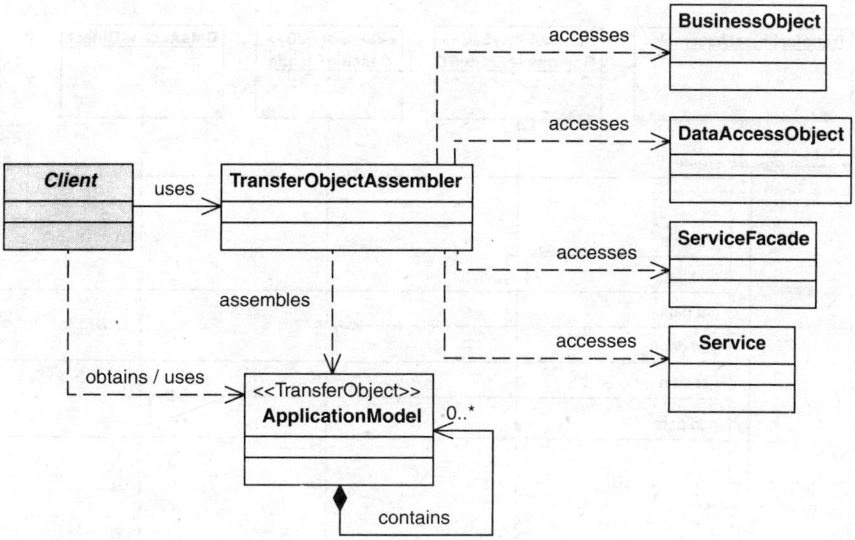

Figure 7.44 *Transfer Object Assembler* Class Diagram

Participants and Responsibilities

The sequence diagram in Figure 7.45 shows the interaction among the various participants for the *Transfer Object Assembler* pattern.

Client

Client invokes the TransferObjectAssembler to obtain the application model data. The Client can be a component in the presentation tier or can be a *Session Façade* (341) that provides the remote access layer for the clients accessing the TransferObjectAssembler. If the TransferObjectAssembler is implemented as a session bean, then the Client can be a *Session Façade* (341) or a *Business Delegate* (302).

TransferObjectAssembler

The TransferObjectAssembler is the main class of this pattern. The TransferObjectAssembler constructs a new composite transfer object based on the requirements of the application when the client requests the application model data.

ApplicationModel

The ApplicationModel object is a composite *Transfer Object (*415*)* that is constructed by the TransferObjectAssembler and returned to the Client.

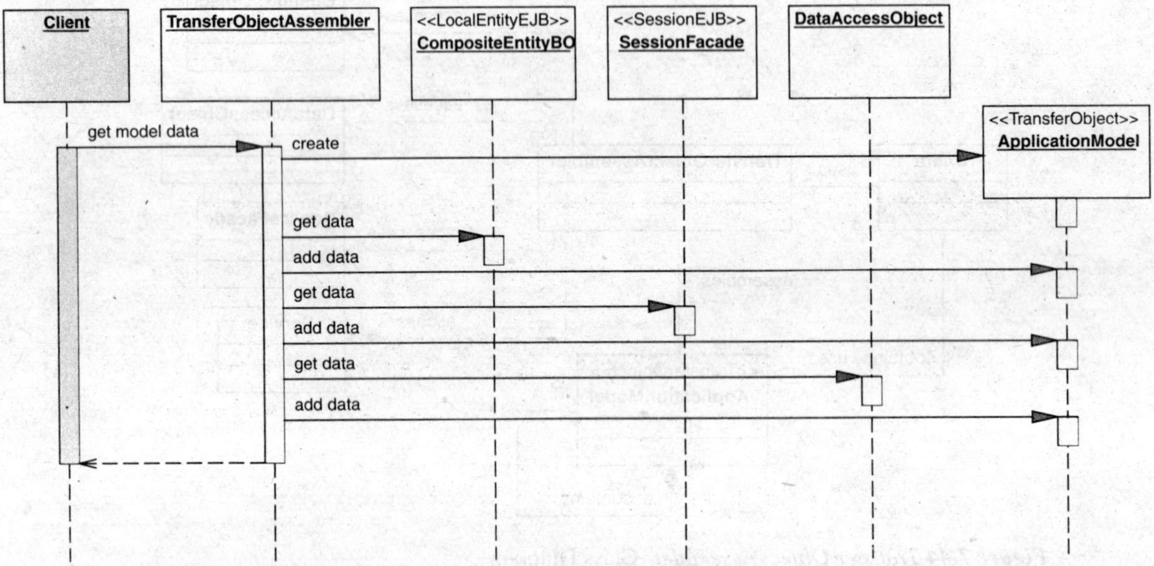

Figure 7.45 *Transfer Object Assembler* Sequence Diagram

BusinessObject

BusinessObject represents a *Business Object* (374) that provides *Transfer Objects (415)* to the TransferObjectAssembler to assemble the ApplicationModel.

SessionFacade

The SessionFacade represents a *Session Façade* (341) that provides part of the data required to construct the ApplicationModel transfer object.

DataAccessObject

DataAccessObject represents a *Data Access Object* (462), used when the TransferObjectAssembler needs to obtain data directly from the persistent store.

Service

The Service is any arbitrary service object including an *Application Service* (357) in the business tier that provides the data required to construct the ApplicationModel object.

Strategies

POJO Transfer Object Assembler Strategy

The *Transfer Object Assembler* can be an arbitrary Java object and doesn't need to be an enterprise bean. In such implementations, a session bean usually fronts the *Transfer Object Assembler.* This session bean is typically a *Session Façade* (341) that performs its other duties related to providing business services. The *Transfer Object Assembler* runs in the business tier, regardless of the implementation strategies. The motivation for this is to prevent the remote invocations, from the *Transfer Object Assembler* to the source objects, from crossing the tier.

Session Bean Transfer Object Assembler Strategy

This strategy implements the *Transfer Object Assembler* as a session bean (as shown in the class diagram). When you use a session bean implementation to provide the *Transfer Object Assembler* as a business service, you should typically use a stateless session bean. The business components that make up the application model are constantly involved in transactions with various clients. As a result, when a *Transfer Object Assembler* constructs a new composite transfer object from various business components, it produces a snapshot of the business-tier object model at the time of construction. The business-tier object model could change immediately afterwards if another client changes one or more *Business Objects* (374), effectively changing the business application model.

Therefore, implementing *Transfer Object Assembler* as a stateful session bean provides no benefits over implementing it as a stateless session bean, because preserving the state of the application model when the underlying business-tier object model is changing is futile. If the underlying object model changes, the *Transfer Object* (415) that the assembler is holding becomes stale.

The next time the *Transfer Object Assembler* is asked for the *Transfer Object (415)*, the *Transfer Object Assembler* either returns a stale state or reconstructs the *Transfer Object (415)* to obtain the most recent snapshot. Therefore, the *Transfer Object Assembler* is typically implemented as a stateless session bean.

However, if the underlying business-tier object model rarely changes, then the *Transfer Object Assembler* can be implemented as a stateful session bean and retain the newly constructed *Transfer Object (415)*. In this case, the *Transfer Object Assembler* must include mechanisms to recognize changes to the underlying business-tier model and to reconstruct the application model for the next client request.

Consequences

- ***Separates business logic, simplifies client logic***
  When the client includes logic to manage the interactions with distributed components, clearly separating business logic from the client tier becomes difficult. The *Transfer Object Assembler* contains the business logic to maintain the object relationships and to construct the composite transfer object representing the model. The client doesn't need to know how to construct the model or know about the different components that provide data to assemble the model.
- ***Reduces coupling between clients and the application model***
  The *Transfer Object Assembler* hides the complexity of the construction of model data from the clients and reduces coupling between clients and the model. With loose coupling, if the model changes, then the *Transfer Object Assembler* requires a corresponding change and insulates the clients from this change.
- ***Improves network performance***
  The *Transfer Object Assembler* (315) reduces the number of remote calls required to obtain an application model from the business tier, since typically it constructs the application model in a single method invocation. However, the composite *Transfer Object (415)* might contain a large amount of data. This means that, though using the *Transfer Object Assembler* (315) reduces the number of network calls, the amount of data transported in a single call increases. Consider this trade-off when you use this pattern.
- ***Improves client performance***
  The server-side *Transfer Object Assembler* (315) constructs the model as a composite *Transfer Object (415)* without using any client resources. The client does not spend any resources in assembling the model.
- ***Can introduce stale data***
  The *Transfer Object Assembler* (315) constructs an application model as a composite *Transfer Object* (415) on demand, as a snapshot of the current state of the business model. Once the client obtains the composite *Transfer Object (415)*, it is local to the client and is not network aware. Subsequent changes made to the business components are not propagated to the application model. Therefore, the application model can become stale after it is obtained.

Sample Code

Implementing the Transfer Object Assembler

Consider a project management application where a number of business-tier components define the complex model. Suppose a client wants to obtain the model data composed of data from various business objects, such as:

- Project information from the Project component
- Project manager information from the ProjectManager component
- List of project tasks from the Project component
- Resource information from the Resource component

A composite transfer object to contain this data can be defined as shown in Example 7.38. A *Transfer Object Assembler* (315) pattern can be implemented to assemble this composite transfer object. The *Transfer Object Assembler* (315) sample code is listed in Example 7.42.

Example 7.38 Composite Transfer Object Class

```

public class ProjectDetailsData
implements java.io.Serializable {
   public ProjectTO projectData;
   public ProjectManagerTO projectManagerData;
   public Collection listOfTasks;
   ...
}
```

The list of tasks in the ProjectDetailsData is a collection of TaskResourceTO objects. The TaskResourceTO is a combination of TaskTO and ResourceTO. These classes are shown in Example 7.39, Example 7.40, and Example 7.41.

Example 7.39 TaskResourceTO Class

```

public class TaskResourceTO implements java.io.Serializable {
   public String projectId;
   public String taskId;
   public String name;
   public String description;
   public Date startDate;
   public Date endDate;
```

```
    public ResourceTO assignedResource;
    ...

    public TaskResourceTO(String projectId, String taskId,
        String name, String description, Date startDate,
        Date endDate, ResourceTO assignedResource) {
      this.projectId = projectId;
      this.taskId = taskId;
      ...
      this.assignedResource = assignedResource;
    }
    ...
}
```

Example 7.40 TaskTO Class

```

public class TaskTO implements java.io.Serializable {
    public String projectId;
    public String taskId;
    public String name;
    public String description;
    public Date startDate;
    public Date endDate;
    public assignedResourceId;

    public TaskTO(String projectId, String taskId, String name,
        String description, Date startDate, Date endDate,
        String assignedResourceId) {
      this.projectId = projectId;
      this.taskId = taskId;
      ...
      this.assignedResource = assignedResource;
    }
    ...
}
```

Example 7.41 ResourceTO Class

```

public class ResourceTO implements java.io.Serializable {
    public String resourceId;
    public String resourceName;
    public String resourceEmail;
```

```
    ...

    public ResourceTO (String resourceId, String resourceName,
        String resourceEmail, ...) {
      this.resourceId = resourceId;
      this.resourceName = resourceName;
      this.resourceEmail = resourceEmail;
      ...
    }
}
```

The ProjectDetailsAssembler class that assembles the ProjectDetailsData object is listed in Example 7.42.

Example 7.42 Implementing the Transfer Object Assembler

```

public class ProjectDetailsAssembler
implements javax.ejb.SessionBean {

  ...

  public ProjectDetailsData getData(String projectId){

    // Construct the composite transfer object
    ProjectDetailsData pData = new
      ProjectDetailsData();

    // get the project details;
    ProjectHome projectHome =
      ServiceLocator.getInstance().getLocalHome(
        "Project", ProjectEntityHome.class);
    ProjectEntity project =
      projectHome.findByPrimaryKey(projectId);
    ProjectTO projTO = project.getData();

    // Add Project Info to ProjectDetailsData
    pData.projectData = projTO;

    //get the project manager details;
    ProjectManagerHome projectManagerHome =
      ServiceLocator.getInstance().getLocalHome(
        "ProjectManager", ProjectEntityHome.class);

```

```
    ProjectManagerEntity projectManager =
      projectManagerHome.findByPrimaryKey(
        projTO.managerId);

    ProjectManagerTO projMgrTO = projectManager.getData();

    // Add ProjectManager info to ProjectDetailsData
    pData.projectManagerData = projMgrTO;

    // Get list of TaskTOs from the Project
    Collection projTaskList = project.getTasksList();

    // construct a list of TaskResourceTOs
    ArrayList listOfTasks = new ArrayList();

    Iterator taskIter = projTaskList.iterator();
    while (taskIter.hasNext()) {
      TaskTO task = (TaskTO) taskIter.next();

      //get the Resource details;
      ResourceHome resourceHome =
          ServiceLocator.getInstance().getLocalHome(
          "Resource", ResourceEntityHome.class);

      ResourceEntity resource =
          resourceHome.findByPrimaryKey(
          task.assignedResourceId);

      ResourceTO resTO = resource.getResourceData();

      // construct a new TaskResourceTO using Task
      // and Resource data
      TaskResourceTO trTO =
          new TaskResourceTO( task.projectId, task.taskId,
          task.name, task.description, task.startDate,
          task.endDate, resTO);

      // add TaskResourceTO to the list
      listOfTasks.add(trTO);
    }

    // add list of tasks to ProjectDetailsData
    pData.listOfTasks = listOfTasks;
```

```

        // add any other data to the transfer object
        ...

        // return the composite transfer object
        return pData;

    }
    ...
}
```

Related Patterns

- ***Transfer Object (415)***
  The *Transfer Object Assembler (*315) uses *Transfer Objects* (415*)* to create and transport data to the client. The created *Transfer Objects (*415*)* carry the data representing the application model from the business tier to the clients requesting the data.
- ***Business Object (374)***
  The *Transfer Object Assembler (*315) uses the required *Business Objects* (374) to obtain data to build the required application model.
- ***Composite Entity (391)***
  Composite Entity (391) produces composite transfer objects from its own data. On the other hand, *Transfer Object Assembler (*315) constructs the application model by obtaining data from different sources, such as *Session Façades* (341), *Business Objects* (374), *Application Services*, *Data Access Objects* (462), and other services.
- ***Session Façade (341)***
  When *Transfer Object Assembler (*315) is implemented as a session bean, you could view it as a limited special application of the *Session Façade* (341). If the client needs to update the business components that supply the application model data, it accesses a *Session Façade* (341) (session bean) that provides that update service.
- ***Data Access Object (462)***
  A *Transfer Object Assembler* (**433**) can obtain certain data directly from the data store using a *Data Access Object* (462).
- ***Service Locator (315)***
  The *Transfer Object Assembler* (433) uses a *Service Locator* (315) to locate and use various business components.

Value List Handler

Problem

You have a remote client that wants to iterate over a large results list.

Many J2EE applications have clients that perform various searches. Frequently, these searches are initiated by the presentation tier, executed by the business tier and displayed in the browser.

You can fulfill these searches in various ways. If your *Business Objects* (374) are implemented as entity beans, you might use entity bean finder methods. When you are not using entity beans, you typically use a *Data Access Object* (462) to perform the search. When these searches return a small set of results, there's no problem. However, for searches that result in a large number of matching entity beans, entity bean finder methods are inefficient.

Another problem is that clients might not be capable of handling large results, and want the server to manage the results. Clients often do not use all the results from the search and discard the results set after inspecting and using a portion of it. For example, a user might use a web browser to perform a search, view the first few results, discard the rest and perform another search.

Therefore, you typically don't need to return the entire search results to the client. If the client displays the first few results and then abandons the query, the network bandwidth is not wasted, because the data can be cached on the server side and never sent to the client.

Forces

- You want to avoid the overhead of using EJB finder methods for large searches.
- You want to implement a read-only use-case that does not require a transaction.
- You want to provide the clients with an efficient search and iterate mechanism over a large results set.
- You want to maintain the search results on the server side.

Solution

Use a *Value List Handler* to search, cache the results, and allow the client to traverse and select items from the results.

The *Value List Handler* provides the search and iteration functionality. To perform a search, the *Value List Handler* uses a *Data Access Object* (462) to execute the query and retrieve the matching results from the database. This bypasses using the EJB finders for your applications where *Business Objects* (374) are implemented as entity beans.

DESIGN NOTE: DRAWBACKS OF ENTITY BEAN FINDER METHODS AND EJB SELECT METHODS

Entity bean finder methods are useful for looking up matching entities for a given criteria. However, when used to perform large searches, they have a huge performance overhead. The finder methods return a collection composed of either remote reference objects if your entity beans are remote, or a collection of local reference objects if your entity beans are local. The entity bean EJB Select methods are similar to the finder methods, but EJB Select methods are used within the entity beans and not exposed to their clients. Select methods are used by entity beans to select related entity beans using a pre-defined query specified using EJB Query Language (EJB-QL).

In the case of the remote entity bean, each call to the entity bean is a remote network call and can be very expensive. In the case of a local entity bean, though, the entity bean call is local and more efficient than a remote call. When compounded with multiple calls to get a set of values, this also becomes quite an expensive operation.

Another aspect to note is that according to the EJB specification, a container can invoke ejbActivate() methods on entities found by a finder method, which can consume considerable resources. Some container implementations might introduce additional finder method overhead by associating the entity bean instances with these EJBObject instances, to give the client access to those entity beans. However, this is a poor use of resources if the client is not interested in accessing the bean or invoking its methods.

This overhead can reduce application performance if the application includes queries that produce many matching results.

Structure

The class diagram in Figure 7.46 illustrates the *Value List Handler* pattern.

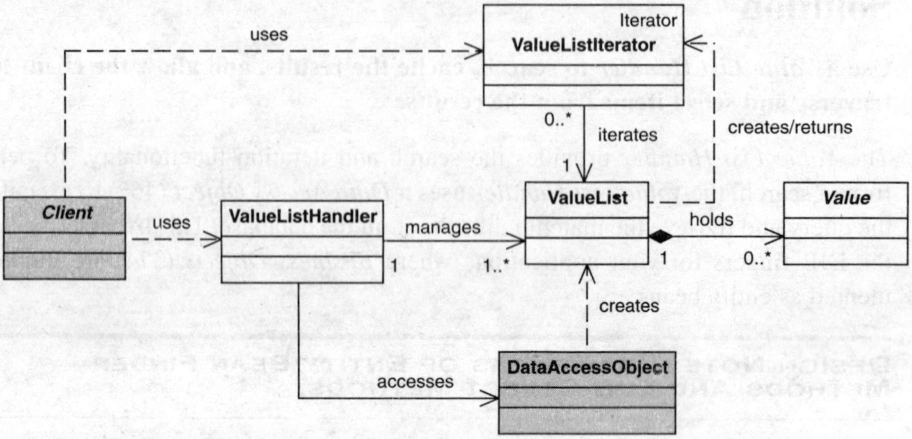

Figure 7.46 *Value List Handler* Class Diagram

Participants and Collaborations

Figure 7.47 on page 447 shows the interactions for the *Value List Handler.*

Client

A Client is any client that needs to execute a query that returns a large set of results. The client can be a presentation-tier component that wants to display search results to a user. The client can also be a session bean that encapsulates the **ValueListHandler**.

ValueListIterator

A ValueListIterator provides an iteration mechanism with the following methods to iterate over the contents of the ValueList.

ValueListHandler

The ValueListHandler executes the search and obtains the query results, which it manages in a privately held collection represented by the ValueList object. The ValueListHandler creates and manipulates the ValueList collection typically using a *Data Access Object* (462). When the client requests the results, the ValueListHandler creates a sub-list from the original ValueList and sends it to the Client. Typically, a ValueListHandler manages a single ValueList. However, ValueListHandler can manage more than one ValueList instances in case it has to combine and handle multiple search results.

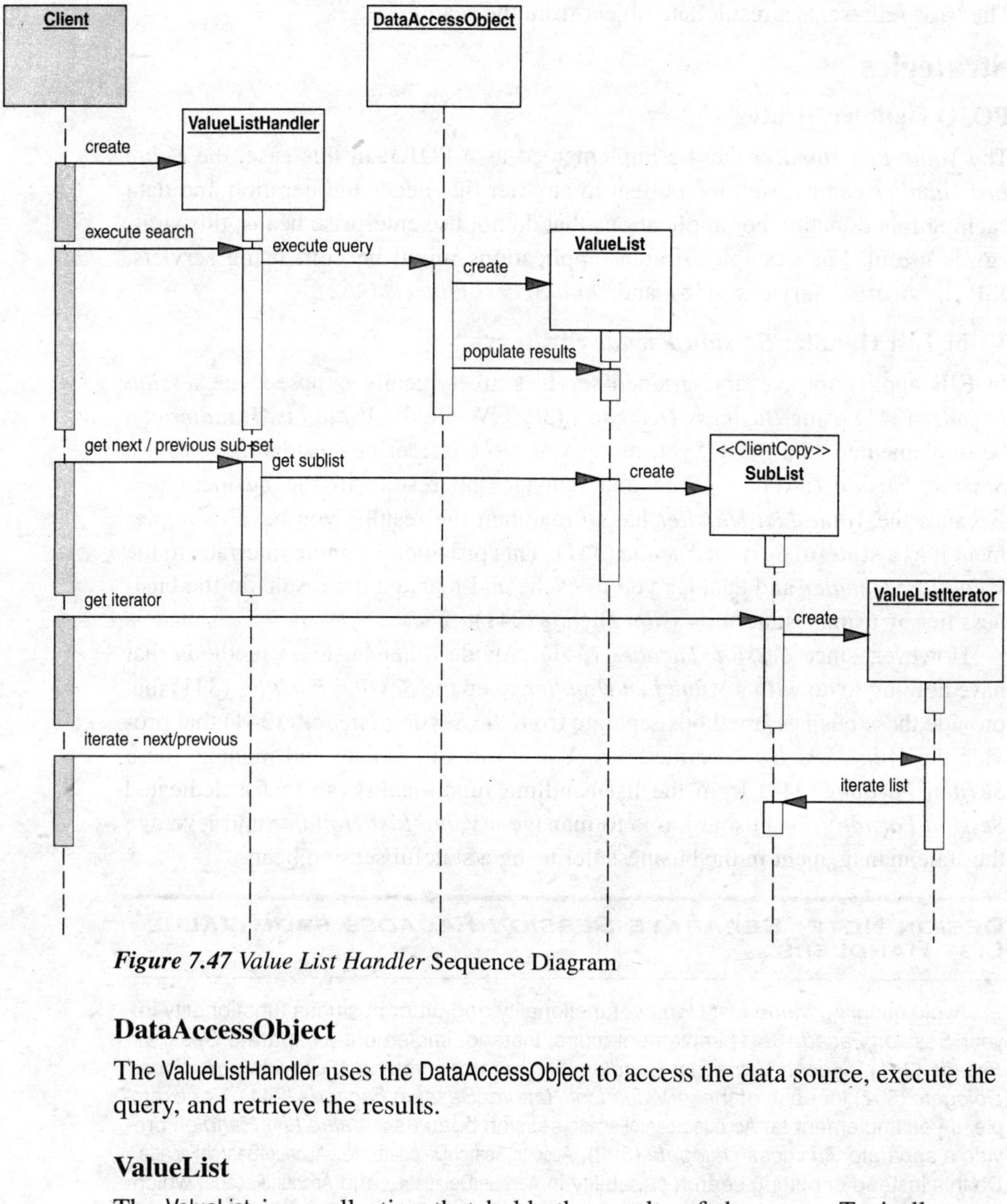

Figure 7.47 Value List Handler Sequence Diagram

DataAccessObject

The ValueListHandler uses the DataAccessObject to access the data source, execute the query, and retrieve the results.

ValueList

The ValueList is a collection that holds the results of the query. Typically, you might use a List implementation from the Java Collections API or implement your own custom List based on your needs.

Value

The Value represents a result data object from the search.

Strategies

POJO Handler Strategy

The *Value List Handler* can be implemented as a POJO. In this case, the *Value List Handler* can be used by a client in any tier that needs the iteration and data caching functionality. For applications that do not use enterprise beans, this strategy is useful. For example, simpler applications might be built using servlets, JSP, *Application Services* (458), and *Data Access Objects* (462).

Value List Handler *Session Façade* Strategy

In EJB applications, coarse-grained services are typically exposed via *Session Façades* (341) using *Business Delegates* (302). While the *Value List Handler* can be implemented as a POJO, you might want to consider encapsulating it with a *Session Façade* (341) to cache and manage the results in the business tier. Because the *Value List Handler* has to maintain the results, you have to implement it as a **stateful** *Session Façade* (341). This provides a remote interface to the *Value List Handler* and enables you to cache and manage the results in the business tier by using a stateful *Session Façade* (341).

However, since *Session Façades* (341) provide other business methods that have nothing to do with a *Value List Handler*, keep the *Session Façades* (341) that provide these business methods separate from the *Session Façades* (341) that provide the *Value List Handler* methods. You do this to isolate and manage these *Session Façades* (341) from the list handling functionality, so that a dedicated *Session Façade's* (341) sole job is to manage a *Value List Handler* and leverage the state management in the business tier using a stateful session bean.

DESIGN NOTE: SEPARATE *SESSION FAÇADES* FROM VALUE LIST HANDLERS

Avoid mingling *Value List Handler* functionality and other business functionality in your *Session Façade* (341) implementations. Instead, implement a separate *Session Façade* (341) for each *Value List Handler*. Furthermore, you must provide a *Business Delegate* (302) for each of these *Value List Handler Session Façades* (341). For example, if you implement an AccountSearchFacade session bean as a *Value List Handler*, provide a separate *Business Delegate* (302), AccountSearchDelegate, for AccountSearchFacade. Do this instead of putting search capability in AccountDelegate and AccountFacade, which provide other use case functionality. Such separation of *Session Façades* (341) encapsulates all search procedures in distinct components, and allows you to separate stateful/stateless characteristics of your *Session Façades* (341).

Value List from Data Access Object Strategy

A main participant of the *Value List Handler* is the *Value List* that it manages. The *Value List* is typically obtained from the *Data Access Object* (462) either using the *Transfer Object Collection* strategy or the *RowSet Wrapper List strategy.*

Decide which approach is best for your application. For predetermined queries that return a well-known small set of results, you might want to use the *Transfer Object Collection* strategy. When you can't predict the result size or when you execute a query that can return a large number of results, you might be better off using the *RowSet Wrapper List* strategy.

Design Note: Value List Handler: What to Get From the Data Access Object

As described in the various strategies of the *Data Access Object* (462), the *Value List Handler* can obtain the search results in different forms: JDBC ResultSet, JDBC RowSet, or Java Collection, such as a List. While the *Data Access Object* (462) can be made to return a ResultSet, you might want to think about which kind of object is appropriate to be returned by the integration tier to the business tier and beyond. It is important to note that the ResultSet is closely tied to the relational database table structure. Interacting with the ResultSet requires the business tier (clients) to be knowledgeable about table structures, column positions, and column data types.

Moreover, the ResultSet maintains the connection with the database and passing it across the integration tier might violate its encapsulation and protection and potentially introduce performance problems and abuse of connections. The RowSets provide an improved interface over the ResultSet. As described in *Data Access Object* (462), you can either implement your own RowSet or use other implementations of a disconnected RowSet, where the connection is released before the RowSet is returned by the *Data Access Object* (462).

However, the RowSet still retains the same drawbacks as the ResultSet when it comes to using RowSet in the business tier, namely knowledge of the table structures, column positions, and column data types.

Therefore, a better solution is to let the *Data Access Object* (462) encapsulate the RowSet and ResultSet interfaces and not expose anything related to the java.sql and javax.sql packages outside of the data access layer. Instead, the *Data Access Object* (462) can return a collection or list implementation that iterates over the search results and provide an object-oriented view, instead of a relational view of the data. The *Data Access Object* (462) strategies that are recommended for use in conjunction with the *Value List Handler* are *Transfer Object Collection* strategy or *RowSet Wrapper List* strategy.

Consequences

- ***Provides efficient alternative to EJB finders***
  Value List Handler provides an alternative way to perform searches, and a way to avoid using EJB finders, which are inefficient for large searches.
- ***Caches search results***
  The result set needs to be cached when a client must display the subset of the results of a large result set. The result set might be a collection of transfer objects that can be iterated over when using the DAO *Transfer Object Collection* strategy, or the results might be a special List implementation that encapsulates a JDBC RowSet when you use the DAO *RowSet Wrapper List* strategy.
- ***Provides flexible search capabilities***
  You can implement a *Value List Handler* to be flexible by providing ad-hoc search facilities, constructing runtime search arguments using template methods, and so on. In other words, a *Value List Handler* developer can implement intelligent searching and caching algorithms without being limited by the EJB finder methods.
- ***Improves network performance***
  Network performance improves because only a requested subset of the results, rather than the entire result set, is sent to the client on demand. If the client/user displays the first few results and then abandons the query, the network bandwidth is not wasted, since the data is cached on the server side and never sent to the client.

  However, if the client/user processes the entire result set, it makes multiple remote calls to the server for the result set. When the client/user knows in advance that it needs the entire result set, the handler bean can provide a method that sends the client the entire result set in one method call.
- ***Allows deferring entity bean transactions***
  Caching results on the server side and minimizing finder overhead might improve transaction management. For example, a query to display a list of books uses a *Value List Handler* to obtain the list without using the Book entity bean's finder methods. At a later point, when the user wants to modify a book in detail, the client invokes a *Session Façade* (341) that locates the required Book entity bean instance with appropriate transaction semantics as needed for this use-case.

- ***Promotes layering and separation of concerns***
  The *Value List Handler* encapsulates list management behavior in the business tier and appropriately uses *Data Access Object* (462) in the integration tier. This promotes layering in the application, and keeps business logic in the business-tier components and data access logic in *Data Access Objects* (462).
- ***Creating a large list of Transfer Object* (415) *can be expensive***
  When the *Data Access Object* (462) executes a query, and creates a collection of *Transfer Objects* (415), it can consume significant resources if the results of the query returns a large number of matching records. Instead of creating all the *Transfer Objects* (415) instances, limit the number of rows retrieved by the DAO in the query by specifying the maximum number of results the DAO fetches from the database. You might also want to use the *DAO Cached RowSet* and *RowSet Wrapper List* strategy.

DESIGN NOTE: EJB HOME BUSINESS METHODS

According to the EJB version 2.1 specification, EJB Home methods are methods that the bean provider supplies. These Home methods implement business logic that acts upon one or more entity beans in an aggregate manner. While you can use these Home methods to perform business aggregate operations, the methods do not offer the flexibility of the *Value List Handler* in terms of maintaining the cached list in the business-tier. If you have EJB Home business methods that return aggregate results, you can have the *Value List Handler* use the EJB Home business method to obtain the ValueList instead of using the *Data Access Object* (462).

However, if the EJB Home business method itself is using the same *Data Access Object* (462), then using that Home business method might introduce another layer of indirection.

Sample Code

Implementing the Value List Handler

Consider an example where a list of Project business objects is retrieved and displayed. You can use the *Value List Handler* in this case. The sample code for this implementation is listed in Example 7.43 as ProjectsListHandler, which is responsible for providing the list of Projects. This class extends the ValueListHandler base abstract class, which provides the generic implementation for a *Value List Handler.*

The ValueListHandler sample code is listed in Example 7.44. The ProjectsListIterator, shown in Example 7.47 implements the iterator interface

ValueListIterator, shown in Example 7.46. The relevant code sample from the data access object ProjectDAO, used by ValueListHandler to execute the query and obtain matching results, is shown in Example 7.48.

Note: The ProjectListHandler shows a POJO implementation of a *Value List Handler*. If you want to use the *Value List Handler Session Façade* strategy, then you can implement this ProjectListHandler as a stateful session bean.

Example 7.43 Implementing Value List Handler: ProjectListHandler

```

package com.corej2eepatterns.vlh;

// imports

public class ProjectListHandler
extends ValueListHandler {

  private ProjectDAO dao = null;
  . . .

  // Client creates a ProjectTO instance, sets the
  // values to use for search criteria and passes
  // the ProjectTO instance as projectCriteria
  // to the constructor and to setCriteria() method
  public ProjectListHandler()
  throws ProjectException, ListHandlerException {
    try {
      this.dao = PSADAOFactory.getProjectDAO();
    } catch (Exception e) {
      // Handle exception, throw ListHandlerException
    }
  }

  // executes search. Client can invoke this
  // provided that the search criteria has been
  // properly set. Used to perform search to refresh
  // the list with the latest data.
  public void executeSearch(ProjectTO projectCriteria)
  throws ListHandlerException {
    try {
      if (projectCriteria == null) {
```

```
            throw new ListHandlerException(
               "Project Criteria required...");
         }
         List resultsList =
            dao.findProjects(projectCriteria);
         setList(resultsList);
      } catch (Exception e) {
         // Handle exception, throw ListHandlerException
      }
   }
}
```

The ValueListHandler is a generic iterator class that provides the iteration functionality.

Example 7.44 Abstract ValueListHandler Base Class

```

package com.corej2eepatterns.vlh;

// imports

public abstract class ValueListHandler {

    List valueList;
    ...

    // you only need to implement this method
    public abstract void executeSearch(Object criteria);

    ...

    protected void setList(List valueList) {
        this.valueList = valueList;
    }

    public List getNextElements(
            int startPosition, int endPosition) {
        return valueList.subList(startPosition, endPosition);
    }

    public List getPreviousElements(
            int startPosition, int endPosition) {
```

```
        return valueList.subList(startPosition, endPosition);
    }

    public Object getValue(int index) {
        return valueList.get(index);
    }

    public int size() {
      return valueList.size();
    }

    // if using multiple value lists
    // provide methods that accept a list id as an argument
    // e.g. public List getPreviousElements(int listId,
    // int startPosition, int endPosition), and so on

    ...
}

```

Example 7.45 ValueList implementation: ProjectsValueList

```

package com.corej2eepatterns.vlh;

// imports

public class ProjectsList extends ArrayList {
    ...

    // implement iterator() to return your custom iterator,
    // if any
    public Iterator iterator() {
        return new ProjectsListIterator(this);
    }

    // implement iterator() to return your custom iterator,
    // if any
    public ListIterator listIterator() {
        return new ProjectsListIterator(this);
    }

    public List subList(int fromIndex, int toIndex) {
```

```
        ProjectsList subList = new ProjectsList();
        for (int index=fromIndex; index<toIndex; index++) {
            subList.add(this.get(index));
        }
        return subList;
    }

...
}

```

Example 7.46 ValueListIterator interface

```

package com.corej2eepatterns.vlh;

// imports

// sample shows extending ListItertor
public interface ValueListIterator extends ListIterator {
    // specify convenience methods here
}
```

Example 7.47 ValueListIterator implementation: ProjectsListIterator

```

package com.corej2eepatterns.vlh;

// imports

// typically, this is implemented as an inner class of the
// custom Value List you implement. In this example,
// ProjectListIterator can be implemented as an inner class of
// ProjectsList. Shown here as a separate class for example
// purposes.

public class ProjectsListIterator implements ValueListIterator
{
    private List projectsList;
    private int currentIndex = -1;
    private int size = 0;

    public ProjectsListIterator(List projectsList) {
        this.projectsList = projectsList;
```

```
            size = projectsList.size();
            currentIndex=0;
        }

        // implement other methods
        public boolean hasNext() { ... }
        public Object next() { ... }
        public boolean hasPrevious() { ... }
        public Object previous() { ... }
        public int nextIndex() { ... }
        public int previousIndex() { ... }
        public void remove() { ... }
        public void set(Object o) {...}
        public void add(Object o) { ... }
    }
```

Example 7.48 ProjectDAO Class

```

package com.corej2eepatterns.dao;

// imports

public class ProjectDAO {
    final private String tableName = "PROJECT";

    // select statement uses fields
    final private String fields = "project_id, name," +
        "project_manager_id, start_date, end_date, " +
        " started, completed, accepted, acceptedDate," +
        " customer_id, description, status";

    // the methods relevant to the ValueListHandler
    // are shown here.
    // See Data Access Object pattern for other details.
    ...
    private List findProjects(ProjectTO projCriteria)
    throws SQLException {

      Statement stmt= null;
      List list = null;
      Connection con = getConnection();
      StringBuffer selectStatement = new StringBuffer();
```

```
    selectStatement.append("SELECT " + fields + " FROM " +
      tableName + "where 1=1");

    // append additional conditions to where clause
    // depending on the values specified in
    // projCriteria

    if (projCriteria.projectId != null) {
      selectStatement.append (" AND PROJECT_ID = '" +
        projCriteria.projectId + "'");
    }
    // check and add other fields to where clause
    ...

    try {
      stmt = con.prepareStatement(selectStatement);
      stmt.setString(1, resourceID);
      ResultSet rs = stmt.executeQuery();
      list = createResultsList(rs);
      stmt.close();
    }
    finally {
      con.close();
    }
    return list;
  }

  private List createResultsList(ResultSet rs)
  throws SQLException {
    ArrayList list = new ArrayList();
    while (rs.next()) {
      int i = 1;
      ProjectTO proj = new ProjectTO(rs.getString(i++));
      proj.projectName = rs.getString(i++);
      proj.managerId = rs.getString(i++);
      proj.startDate = rs.getDate(i++);
      proj.endDate = rs.getDate(i++);
      proj.started = rs.getBoolean(i++);
      proj.completed = rs.getBoolean(i++);
      proj.accepted = rs.getBoolean(i++);
      proj.acceptedDate = rs.getDate(i++);
      proj.customerId = rs.getString(i++);
      proj.projectDescription = rs.getString(i++);
```

```
            proj.projectStatus = rs.getString(i++);
            list.add(proj);
        }
        return list;
    }
    ...
}
```

Related Patterns

- ***Iterator [GoF]***
  This *Value List Handler* uses the *Iterator* pattern, described in the GoF book, *Design Patterns: Elements of Reusable Object-Oriented Software.*

- ***Data Access Object (462)***
  This *Value List Handler* uses the *Data Access Object* (462) to perform searches using either the DAO *Transfer Object Collection* strategy to obtain a collection of transfer objects or using the DAO *RowSet Wrapper List* strategy to obtain a custom List implementation.

- ***Session Façade (341)***
  The *Value List Handler* is often implemented as a specialized version of the *Session Façade* (341) responsible for managing the search results and providing a remote interface. Some applications might have *Session Façades* (341) that expose other business methods and also include the functionality of the *Value List Handler.* However, it might be better to keep the list handling functionality of the *Value List Handler* separate from the business methods of a *Session Façade* (341). Thus, if the *Value List Handler* needs a remote interface, provide a dedicated session bean implementation that encapsulates and facades the *Value List Handler.*

Integration Tier Patterns

Topics in This Chapter

- Data Access Object
- Service Activator
- Domain Store
- Web Service Broker

Chapter 8

Data Access Object

Problem

You want to encapsulate data access and manipulation in a separate layer.

Many real-world J2EE applications implement persistent objects as *Business Object* (374), which use POJOs or entity beans. An application with simpler requirements might forego using business objects and instead use *Session Façades* (341), *Application Services* (357), or other helper objects that directly access and manipulate data in the persistent storage. Such business objects and application components require access to business data in a persistent store.

Most enterprise applications typically use relational database management systems (RDBMS) as the persistent store. However, enterprise data can reside in other types of repositories, such as mainframe or legacy systems, Lightweight Directory Access Protocol (LDAP) repositories, object-oriented databases (OODB), flat files, and so on. Another example of persistent storage is where data is provided by services in external systems, such as business-to-business (B2B) integration systems, credit card bureau services, and so on.

Access mechanisms, supported APIs, and features vary among such persistent stores. Even within a single API, the underlying implementations might provide proprietary extensions in addition to standard features.

Mingling persistence logic with application logic creates a direct dependency between the application and the persistence storage implementation. Such code dependencies in components make it difficult and tedious to migrate the application from one type of data source to another. When the data source changes, the components must be modified to handle the new type of data source.

Forces

- You want to implement data access mechanisms to access and manipulate data in a persistent storage.
- You want to decouple the persistent storage implementation from the rest of your application.
- You want to provide a uniform data access API for a persistent mechanism to various types of data sources, such as RDBMS, LDAP, OODB, XML repositories, flat files, and so on.
- You want to organize data access logic and encapsulate proprietary features to facilitate maintainability and portability.

Solution

Use a *Data Access Object* to abstract and encapsulate all access to the persistent store. The *Data Access Object* manages the connection with the data source to obtain and store data.

The *Data Access Object* (also known simply as **DAO**) implements the access mechanism required to work with the data source. Regardless of what type of data source is used, the DAO always provides a uniform API to its clients. The business component that needs data access uses the simpler interface exposed by the DAO for its clients. The DAO completely hides the data source implementation details from its clients. Because the interface exposed by the DAO to clients does not change when the underlying data source implementation changes, this allows you to change a DAO implementation without changing the DAO client's implementation. Essentially, the DAO acts as an adapter between the component and the data source.

The DAO is implemented as a stateless. It does not cache the results of any query execution, or any data that the client might need at a later point. This makes the DAOs lightweight objects and avoids potential threading and concurrency issues. The DAO encapsulates the details of the underlying persistence API. For example, when an application uses JDBC, the DAO encapsulates all the JDBC usage inside the data access layer and does not expose any exception, data structure, object, or interface that belongs to the java.sql.* or javax.sql.* packages to the clients outside the data access layer.

Structure

The diagram in Figure 8.1 shows the structure of the *Data Access Object* pattern.

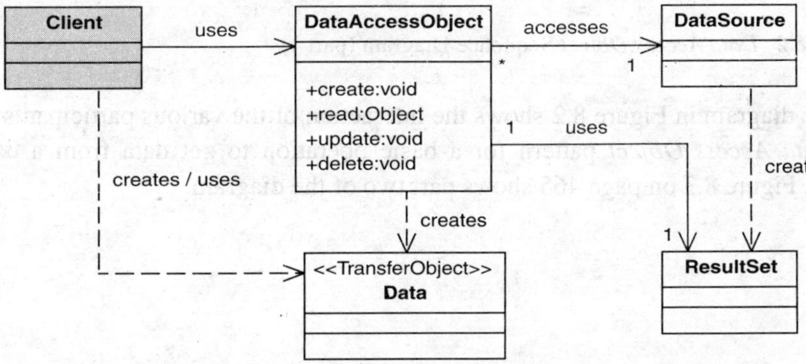

Figure 8.1 *Data Access Object* Class Diagram

Participants and Responsibilities

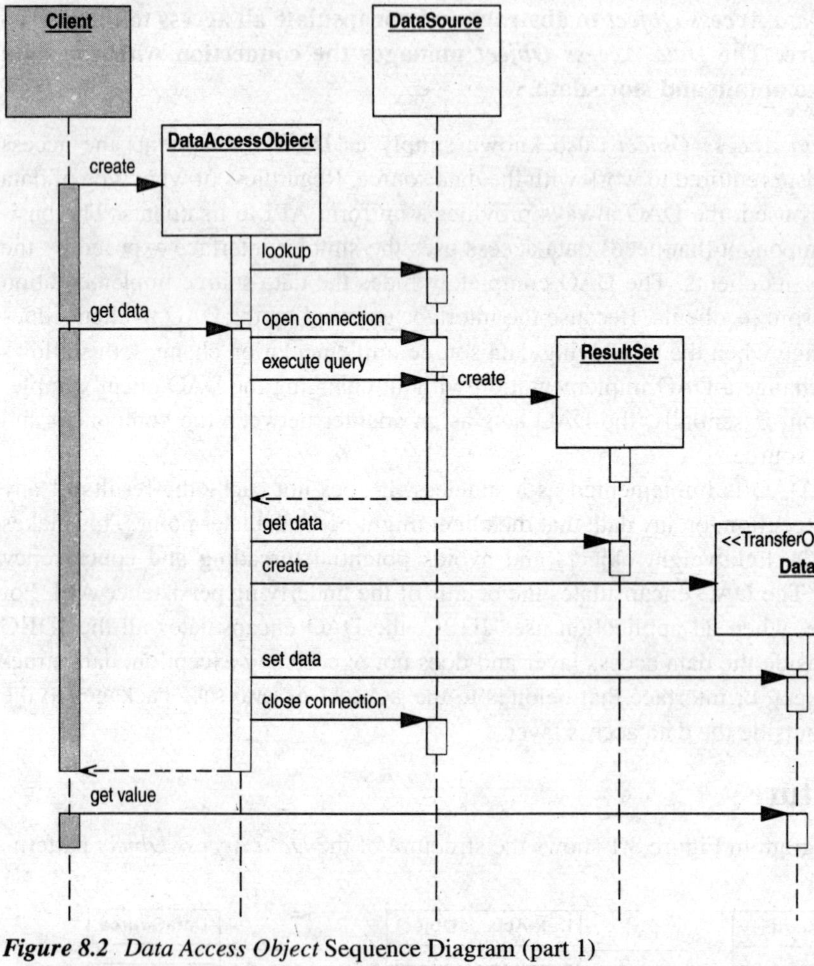

Figure 8.2 *Data Access Object* Sequence Diagram (part 1)

The diagram in Figure 8.2 shows the interaction of the various participants of the *Data Access Object* pattern for a basic operation to get data from a data source. Figure 8.3 on page 465 shows part two of the diagram.

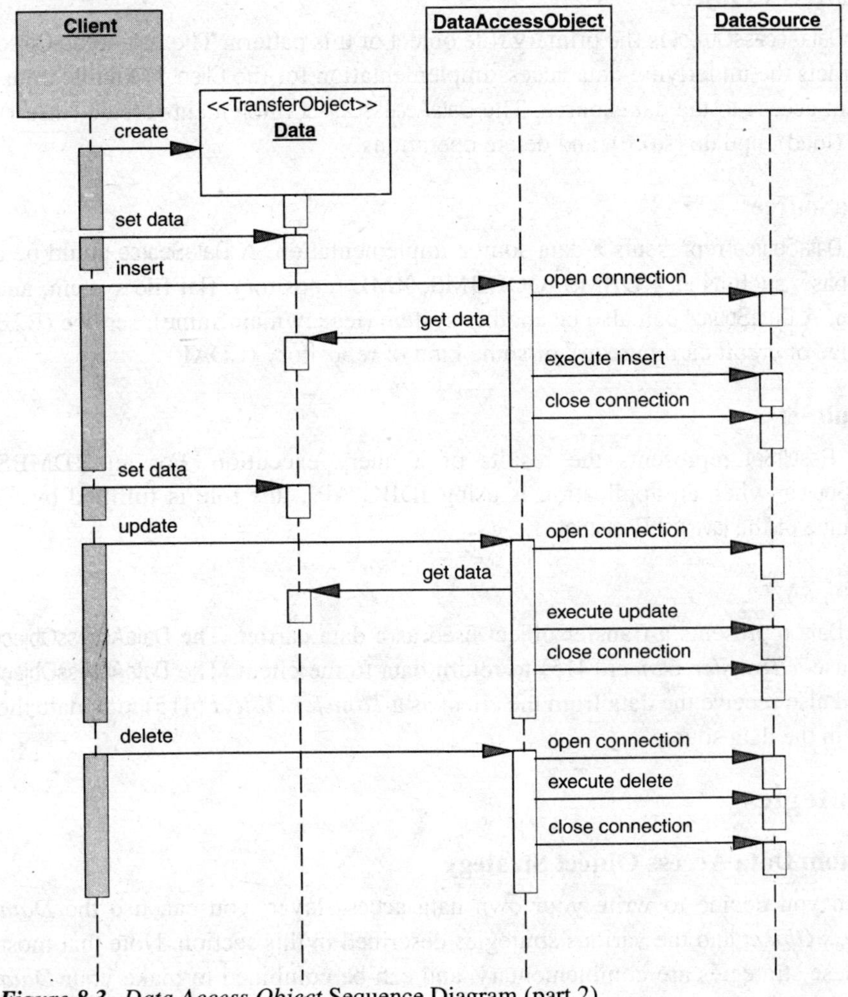

Figure 8.3 *Data Access Object* Sequence Diagram (part 2)

Client

The Client is an object that requires access to the data source to obtain and store data. The Client can be a *Business Object*, a *Session Façade*, an *Application Services* (357), a *Value List Handler* (444), a *Transfer Object Assembler* (433), or any other helper object that needs access to persistent data.

DataAccessObject

The DataAccessObject is the primary role object of this pattern. The DataAccessObject abstracts the underlying data access implementation for the Client to enable transparent access to the data source. The DataAccessObject implements create (insert), find (load), update (store), and delete operations.

DataSource

The DataSource represents a data source implementation. A DataSource could be a database, such as an RDBMS, OODBMS, XML repository, flat file system, and so on. A DataSource can also be another system (legacy/mainframe), service (B2B service or credit card bureau), or some kind of repository (LDAP).

ResultSet

The ResultSet represents the results of a query execution. For an RDMBS DataSource, when an application is using JDBC API, this role is fulfilled by an instance of the java.sql.ResultSet.

Data

The Data represents a transfer object used as a data carrier. The DataAccessObject can use a *Transfer Object* (415) to return data to the client. The DataAccessObject could also receive the data from the client as a *Transfer Object* (415) to update the data in the data source.

Strategies

Custom Data Access Object Strategy

When you decide to write your own data access layer, you can use the *Data Access Object* and the various strategies described in this section. Note that most of these strategies are complementary, and can be combined to make your *Data Access Objects* (462) more powerful and flexible. However, some of these strategies might add too much complexity to your implementation, so use them judiciously.

In its most basic form, a *Data Access Object* provides the operations to create, delete, update, and find data in a database. A sample implementation for this is shown in Example 8.2. The *Data Access Object* typically exchanges data with its clients using *Transfer Objects* (415), as shown in Example 8.1. Furthermore, a *Data Access Object* also provides other methods to find multiple results (finder methods) to return a List or other Collection objects.

The sample code in Example 8.1 shows a *Transfer Object* (415) for customer data used by the CustomerDAO. The CustomerDAO sample implementation is shown in Example 8.2 with the methods to create, update, find, and delete a customer record from the database.

Example 8.1 CustomerTO.java: Transfer Object Used by CustomerDAO and Its Clients

```
package com.corej2eepatterns.to;

public class CustomerTO implements java.io.Serializable {
  private String id;
  private String name;
  private String address;
  . . .

  public String getId(){ return id; }
  public void setId(String id){ this.id = id; }
  public String getName(){ return name; }
  public void setName(String name){ this.name = name; }
  public String getAddress(){ return address; }
  public void setAddress(String address){
    this.address = address;
  }
  // other getters and setters
  . . .
}
```

Example 8.2 CustomerDAO.java: Data Access Object

```
package com.corej2eepatterns.dao;

// imports

public class CustomerDAO {
  protected static final String FIELDS_INSERT =
       "customer_name, customer_address, " +
       "customer_contact, customer_phone, customer_email";

  protected static final String FIELDS_RETURN =
       "customer_id, " + FIELDS_INSERT;

  protected static String INSERT_SQL =
       "insert into customer ( " + FIELDS_INSERT +
```

```
        " ) " + "values ( ?, ?, ?, ?, ?)";

    protected static String SELECT_SQL = "select " +
        FIELDS_RETURN +
        " from customer where customer_id = ? ";

    protected static String UPDATE_SQL =
        "update customer set customer_name = ?, " +
        "customer_address = ?, customer_contact = ?, " +
        "customer_phone = ?, customer_email = ? " +
        "where customer_id = ? ";

    protected static String DELETE_SQL =
        "delete from Customer where customer_id = ? ";

    // the data source used to connect to the back-end database
    private DataSource datasource;

    public CustomerDAO() throws DAOException {
      try {
        // Shown here for clarity only. Typically, looking
        // up a data source is done by a Service Locator
        // and the DAO just uses the Service Locator to
        // obtain a data source.
        InitialContext initialContext =
            new InitialContext();
        datasource = (DataSource) initialContext.lookup(
            OracleDAOFactory.DATASOURCE_DB_NAME);
      } catch (NamingException e) {
        throw new DAOException (
            "Cannot locate data source at " +
            DAOFactory.DATASOURCE_DB_NAME, e);
      }
    }

    public String create(CustomerTO cust) throws DAOException {
      // initialize variables
      Connection con = getConnection();
      String customerId = null;

      PreparedStatement prepStmt = null;
      try {
        // create and setup statement
```

```
      prepStmt = con.prepareStatement(INSERT_SQL);
      int i = 1;
      prepStmt.setString(i++, cust.getName());
      prepStmt.setString(i++, cust.getAddress());
      . . .

      // execute the statement
      prepStmt.executeUpdate();

      // obtain the newly created customer id value
      . . .

    } catch (Exception e) {
      // handle exception
    } finally {
      // close connections
    }

    // return the newly created customer id value
    return customerId;
  }

  public CustomerTO find(String customerId)
    throws DAOException {
    // initialize variables
    CustomerTO cust = null;
    Connection con = getConnection();
    PreparedStatement prepStmt = null;
    ResultSet rs = null;

    try {
      // setup statement and retrieve results
      prepStmt = con.prepareStatement(SELECT_SQL);
      prepStmt.setString(1, customerId);
      rs = prepStmt.executeQuery();
      if (rs.next()) {
        //create the transfer object using data from rs
        cust = new CustomerTO();
        cust.setId(rs.getString(1));
        cust.setName(rs.getString(2));
        . . .
      }
    } catch (Exception e) {
```

```
      // handle exception
    } finally {
      // close connections
    }
    return cust;
  }

  public void update(CustomerTO cust) throws DAOException {
    Connection con = null;
    PreparedStatement prepStmt = null;
    try {
      // prepare statement
      con = getConnection();

      prepStmt = con.prepareStatement(UPDATE_SQL);
      int i = 1;

      // add fields first
      prepStmt.setString(i++, cust.getName());
      prepStmt.setString(i++, cust.getAddress());
      . . .

      // now add where parameters
      prepStmt.setString(i++, cust.getId());
      int rowCount = prepStmt.executeUpdate();
      prepStmt.close();
      if (rowCount == 0) {
        throw new DAOException(
          "Update Error:Customer Id:" + cust.getId());
      }
    } catch (Exception e) {
      // handle exception
    } finally {
      // close connections
    }
  }

  public void delete(String customerId) throws Exception {
    // setup variables
    Connection con = getConnection();
    PreparedStatement prepStmt = null;

    try {
```

```
         // execute database update
         prepStmt = con.prepareStatement(DELETE_SQL);
         prepStmt.setString(1, customerId);
         prepStmt.executeUpdate();
      } catch (Exception e) {
         // handle exception
      } finally {
         // close connections
      }
   }

   // other methods for finders, etc.
   . . .
}
```

Data Access Object Factory Strategies

You can make *Data Access Object* creation highly flexible by adopting the *Abstract Factory* [GoF] and the *Factory Method* [GoF] patterns.

When applications use a single type of persistent store (such as Oracle RDBMS), and there is no need to change the underlying storage from one implementation to another, implement the *DAO Factory Method* strategy to produce a variety of DAOs needed by the application.

Example 8.3 OracleDAOFactory.java: Data Access Object Strategy Using Factory Method [GoF]

```
package com.corej2eepatterns.dao;

// imports
public class OracleDAOFactory extends DAOFactory {

   // package level constant used look up the
   // DataSource name using JNDI
   static String DATASOURCE_DB_NAME =
         "java:comp/env/jdbc/CJPOraDB";

   public static CustomerDAO getCustomerDAO()
         throws DAOException {
      return (CustomerDAO) createDAO(CustomerDAO.class);
   }

   public static EmployeeDAO getEmployeeDAO()
         throws DAOException {
```

```
      return (EmployeeDAO) createDAO(EmployeeDAO.class);
    }

    // create other DAO instances
    . . .

    // method to create a DAO instance. Can be optimized to
    // cache the DAO Class instead of creating it everytime.
    private Object createDAO(Class classObj)
        throws DAOException {
      // create a new DAO using classObj.newInstance() or
      // obtain it from a cache and return the DAO instance
    }
}
```

While the *DAO Factory Method* strategy is most commonly used, you can further extend the flexibility of the factory implementation by adopting the *Abstract Factory* pattern. This need for further flexibility arises if you're likely to change persistent stores frequently or if you use more than one. To accomplish this, you must encapsulate multiple types of data sources, such that each *Data Access Object* factory provides the DAO pattern implementation for one type of persistent store. While most applications typically use a single type of data source (such as Oracle RDBMS), and therefore the *DAO Factory Method* strategy might be adequate, more sophisticated and commercial frameworks can benefit from the added flexibility of the *DAO Abstract Factory* strategy.

The sample code for a *DAO Abstract Factory* strategy is shown in Example 8.4.

Example 8.4 DAOFactory.java: Data Access Object Factory Strategy Using Abstract Factory [GoF]

```
package com.corej2eepatterns.dao;

// imports

// Abstract class DAO Factory
public abstract class DAOFactory {

  // List of DAO types supported by the factory
  public static final int CLOUDSCAPE = 1;
  public static final int ORACLE = 2;
  public static final int SYBASE = 3;
```

```
    . . .

    // There will be a method for each DAO that can be
    // created. The concrete factories will have to
    // implement these methods.
    public abstract CustomerDAO getCustomerDAO()
        throws DAOException;
    public abstract EmployeeDAO getEmployeeDAO()
        throws DAOException;
    . . .

    public static DAOFactory getDAOFactory(int whichFactory) {
      switch (whichFactory) {
      case CLOUDSCAPE:
        return new CloudscapeDAOFactory();
      case ORACLE:
        return new OracleDAOFactory();
      case SYBASE:
        return new SybaseDAOFactory();
      . . .
      default:
        return null;
      }
    }
}
```

Transfer Object Collection Strategy

In addition to the basic functions of create, find, update, and delete, most application clients also need a number of methods that can find multiple results based on a search criteria. The *Data Access Object* can implement a number of **finder** methods that accept a search criteria and return a specified number of rows with the results. The *Data Access Object* creates an SQL statement using the transfer object criteria, and executes a query against the data source to obtain a ResultSet. The *Data Access Object* then processes the ResultSet to retrieve as many matching result rows as requested by the calling client. For each row, the *Data Access Object* creates a *Transfer Object* (415) and adds it to a collection that is returned to the client.

This strategy is suitable when the client needs to obtain a small set of results as transfer objects. If the result set obtained from the query execution is large, then this strategy can be greatly resource intensive because it must create a transfer object instance for data in each row. If you need larger results sets, consider using strategies such as *CachedRowSet* strategy, *Read Only RowSet* strategy, or *RowSet Wrapper List* strategy.

A sample implementation of the *Transfer Object Collection* strategy is shown in Figure 8.5.

Example 8.5 CustomerDAO.java: Transfer Object Collection Strategy

```
package com.corej2eepatterns.dao;

// imports

public class CustomerDAO {
. . .

   // Create a list of Transfer Objects and return it
   public List findCustomers(CustomerTO criteria)
         throws DAOException {

      Connection con = getConnection();
      ResultSet rs = null;
      ArrayList custList = new ArrayList();
      String searchSQLString = getSearchSQLString(criteria);

      try {
         con = getConnection();
         java.sql.Statement stmt =
               con.createStatement(. . . );
         rs = stmt.executeQuery(searchSQLString);
         while(rs.next()) {
            //create the transfer object using data from rs
            cust = new CustomerTO();
            cust.setId(rs.getString(1));
            cust.setName(rs.getString(2));


            // add the TO to the list
            custList.add(cust);
         }
      } catch (Exception e) {
         // handle exception
      } finally {
         // close connections
      }
```

```
    return custList;
  }

  . . .

}
```

Cached RowSet Strategy

When performing an operation, such as a search, that returns multiple elements, the *Data Access Object* certainly has the option of creating a collection of **transfer objects** and returning it to the client. If the search operation returns a large list, this strategy can become quite expensive with all those transfer object creations. To avoid that performance overhead, you can leverage the JDBC RowSet interface by using a **disconnected, cached** row set implementation. Row sets can be used for read and updates, and you can choose from a variety of publicly available implementations. Sun's implementation is *CachedRowSet*, *JdbcRowSet* and *WebRowSet* [SUNRS]; other vendors such as Oracle provide their own *RowSet* implementations [ORARS]. You can use one of these public implementations if it meets your needs.

Exercise caution when using RowSets, connected or disconnected, with implementations that support the update functionality. If all you need is a results list that you use for read-only purposes (for instance, to display the results in a web page), a better alternative is to use the *Read Only RowSet* strategy or *RowSet Wrapper List* strategy.

Note on RowSet implementations: The JDBC team is working on providing a set of five standard RowSet implementations in an upcoming release, which will deprecate the sun.jdbc.rowset implementations [SUNRS]:

- JdbcRowSet - A connected RowSet providing JavaBean semantics.
- CachedRowSet - A disconnected RowSet, providing JavaBean semantics and robust synchronization mechanisms.
- WebRowSet - A disconnected RowSet provided synchronization mechanism that interact with XML data sources.
- FilteredRowSet - A disconnected RowSet that permits a filtered inbound and outbound view on the RowSet data.
- JoinRowSet - A disconnected RowSet that allows SQL JOIN relationships to be established between multiple CachedRowSets.

A sample DAO that uses a Cached RowSet implementation (sun.jdbc.rowset.CachedRowSet) is shown in Example 8.6.

Example 8.6 CustomerDAO.java: Cached RowSet Strategy

```
package com.corej2eepatterns.dao;

// imports

public class CustomerDAO {
 . . .

 // Create the CachedRowSet using the
 // ResultSet from query execution
  public RowSet findCustomersRS(CustomerTO criteria)
      throws DAOException {

    Connection con = getConnection();
    javax.sql.RowSet rowSet = null;
    String searchSQLString = getSearchSQLString(criteria);
    try {
      con = getConnection();
      java.sql.Statement stmt =
          con.createStatement(. . .);
      java.sql.ResultSet rs =
              stmt.executeQuery(searchSQLString);
      rowSet = new CachedRowSet();
      rowSet.populate(rs);
    } catch (SQLException anException) {
      // handle exception…
    } finally {
      con.close();
    }
    return rowSet;
  }

  . . .

}
```

Read Only RowSet Strategy

While the *Cached RowSet* strategy is useful for creating any kind of RowSet, most J2EE applications need only the read-only functionality of a RowSet. Instead of using an updateable RowSet implementation, you can implement your own RowSet that caters only to read-only functionality. This strategy provides an example of such a RowSet implementation called *Read Only RowSet*. The class diagram in Figure 8.4 shows the structure of the *Read Only RowSet* strategy.

The Client asks the DataAccessObject to perform a search. The DataAccessObject typically fulfills the role of the Client itself, as explained in the *Rowset Wrapper List* strategy.

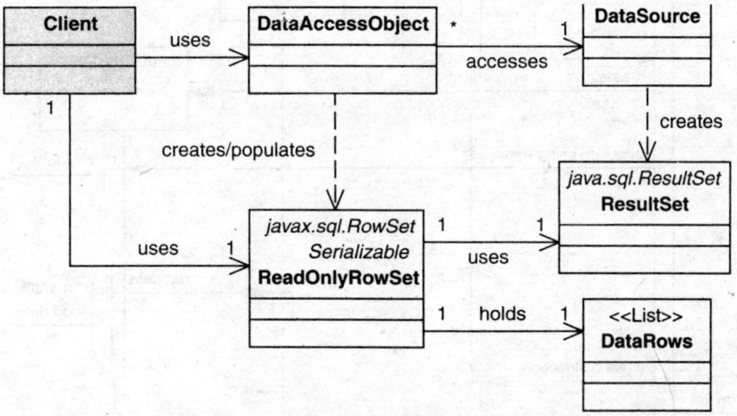

Figure 8.4 *Read Only Rowset* Strategy Class Diagram

The sequence diagram in Figure 8.5 on page 478 shows how the *Read Only RowSet* strategy works.

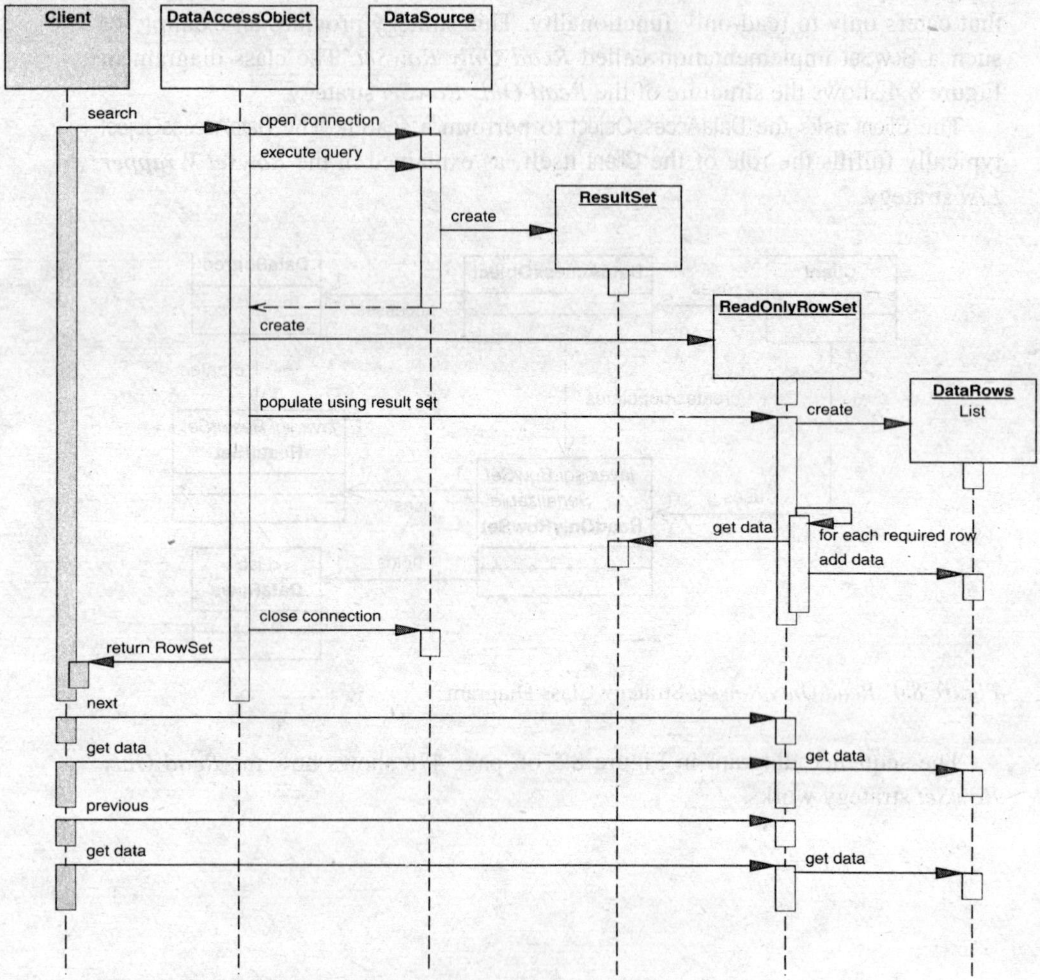

Figure 8.5 *Read Only RowSet* Strategy Sequence Diagram

The Client uses a DataAccessObject to execute a search query. The DataAccessObject executes the query and obtains a ResultSet, which it uses to create an instance of ReadOnlyRowSet. The ReadOnlyRowSet extracts values from the given ResultSet and stores them in its own array shown as DataRows.

As the DataRows list is being populated, the ReadOnlyRowSet extracts only as many rows from the ResultSet as the Client requested. Once the rows are extracted and the DataRows list is populated with the requested number of rows, the connection is closed and the ResultSet is no longer needed. Hence, the ReadOnlyRowSet described in this strategy is a **disconnected cached RowSet** implementation.

The following code example shows the implementation of the *Read Only RowSet* strategy. The sample code in Example 8.7, a *Data Access Object*, creates a ReadOnlyRowSet instance obtaining a ResultSet instance after a query execution. The client of the CustomerDAO *Data Access Object* invokes the findCustomersRORS() method and passes a CustomerTO transfer object as the search criteria, indicating the maximum number of rows to return using the howManyRows argument.

Example 8.7 CustomerDAO.java: Creating the ReadOnlyRowSet

```
package com.corej2eepatterns.dao;

// imports

public class CustomerDAO {
  . . .

  // Create the ReadOnlyRowSet using the
  // ResultSet from query execution
  public RowSet findCustomersRORS(CustomerTO criteria,
      int startAtRow, int howManyRows)
      throws DAOException {

    Connection con = getConnection();
    javax.sql.RowSet rowSet = null;
    String searchSQLString = getSearchSQLString(criteria);

    try {
      con = getConnection();
      java.sql.Statement stmt = con.createStatement(. . .);
      java.sql.ResultSet rs =
          stmt.executeQuery(searchSQLString);
      rowSet = new ReadOnlyRowSet();
      rowSet.populate(rs, startAtRow, howManyRows);
    } catch (SQLException anException) {
      // handle exception…
    } finally {
      con.close();
    }
    return rowSet;
  }

  . . .
}
```

Example 8.8 ReadOnlyRowSet.java: Populating the RowSet

```
package com.corej2eepatterns.dao.rowset;

// imports

public class ReadOnlyRowSet implements RowSet, Serializable {

  . . .

  private Object[] dataRows;

  . . .

  /** this is a read only row set */
  public boolean isReadOnly() {
    return true;
  }

  public void setReadOnly(boolean flag) throws SQLException {
    throw new SQLException(
        "ReadOnlyRowSet: Method not supported");
  }

  // Populates the rowset without the first startRow rows
  // of the ResultSet and with a maximum number
  // of rows specified by howManyRows
  public void populate(ResultSet resultSet,
      int startRow, int howManyRows)
      throws SQLException {

    // miscellaneous code not shown for brevity…

    // Create a list to hold the row values
    List dataRows = . . . ;

    // determine the number of columns from the mete data
    int numberOfColumns =
        resultSet.getMetaData().getColumnCount();

    // Discard initial rows if beginAtRow was specified
    setStartPosition(startAtRow, resultSet);

```

```
    // if number of rows is unspecified,
    // get all rows from resultset
    if (howManyRows <= 0) {
      howManyRows = Integer.MAX_VALUE;
    }
    int processedRows = 0;
    while ((resultSet.next()) &&
          (processedRows++ < howManyRows)) {
      Object[] values = new Object[numberOfColumns];

      // Read values for current row and save
      // them in the values array
      for (int i=0; i<numberOfColumns; i++) {
        Object columnValue =
            this.getColumnValue(resultSet, i);
        values[i] = columnValue;
      }

      // Add the array of values to the linked list
      dataRows.add(values);
    }

  } // end of row set constructor

. . .

  // sets the result set to start at the given row number
  private void setStartPosition(
      int startAtRow, ResultSet resultSet)
      throws SQLException {
    if (startAtRow > 0) {
      if (resultSet.getType() !=
          ResultSet.TYPE_FORWARD_ONLY) {
        // Move the cursor using JDBC 2.0 API
        if (!resultSet.absolute(startAtRow)) {
          resultSet.last();
        }
      } else {
        // If the result set does not support JDBC 2.0
        // skip the first beginAtRow rows
        for (int i=0; i< startAtRow; i++) {
          if (!resultSet.next()) {
            resultSet.last();
```

```
                    break;
                }
            }
        }
    }
}

// Reads a column value for the current row and
// create an appropriate java object to hold it.
// Return null if error reading value or for SQL null.
private Object getColumnValue(
    ResultSet resultSet, int columnIndex) {

    . . .

}

// implement the RowSet and ResultInterface methods
. . .

}
```

RowSet Wrapper List Strategy

While the *Transfer Object Collection* strategy is one way to implement your finder methods, it might prove expensive if the query returns a large set of results and you end up creating a large collection of transfer objects, which are used sparingly by the client. Clients typically search and use the first few result items and discard the rest. When an application is executing a query that returns a large set of results, the *RowSet Wrapper List* strategy might be more efficient though it requires additional work and adds more complexity.

You do not want to expose the RowSet strategies to external clients of the *Data Access Object*, regardless of what RowSet implementation you choose to use. It is better to encapsulate all usage of any objects that originate in the java.sql and javax.sql packages inside the Data Access Object. Such encapsulation ensures that the client is not dependent on low-level JDBC interfaces, such as ResultSet or RowSet interfaces. The *RowSet Wrapper List* strategy internally uses the *Read Only RowSet* strategy to obtain the query results and wraps the RowSet instance to expose the results in an object-oriented way. The wrapping is done by a custom List implementation that provides the traversal and caching functions to manipulate the RowSet in an object-oriented manner by exposing the data in the rowset as objects.

The advantage of the *RowSet Wrapper List* strategy is that you create and return *Transfer Objects* (415) only if necessary; that is, if and when the client needs it. On the other hand, for the *Transfer Object Collection* strategy, the *Data Access Object* must create all the *Transfer Objects* (415) before it returns a Collection to the client.

The class diagram in Figure 8.6 shows the interactions of the *RowSet Wrapper List* strategy.

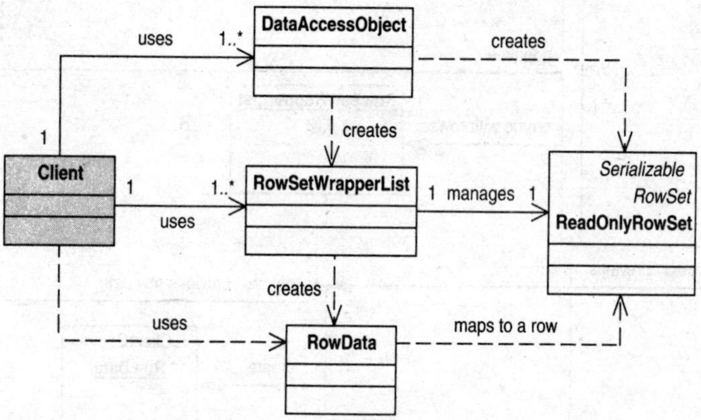

Figure 8.6 *Rowset Wrapper List* Strategy Class Diagram

The sequence diagram in Figure 8.7 shows the interactions of the *RowSet Wrapper List* strategy.

The DataAccessObject, having obtained a ReadOnlyRowSet using the *Read Only RowSet* strategy, proceeds to create a RowSetWrapperList by passing the ReadOnly-RowSet instance. The DataAccessObject returns the RowSetWrapperList to the Client, which uses that list to traverse the query results.

The RowSetWrapperList implements the List interface to provide the traversal function for the data in the ReadOnlyRowSet. The RowSetWrapperList encapsulates all data access layer functionality away from the Client, which does not have to know anything about RowSet, ResultSet, or any other classes in the java.sql or javax.sql packages. The RowSetWrapperList returns a *Transfer Object* (415) when the client wants to access the previous or next row in the results.

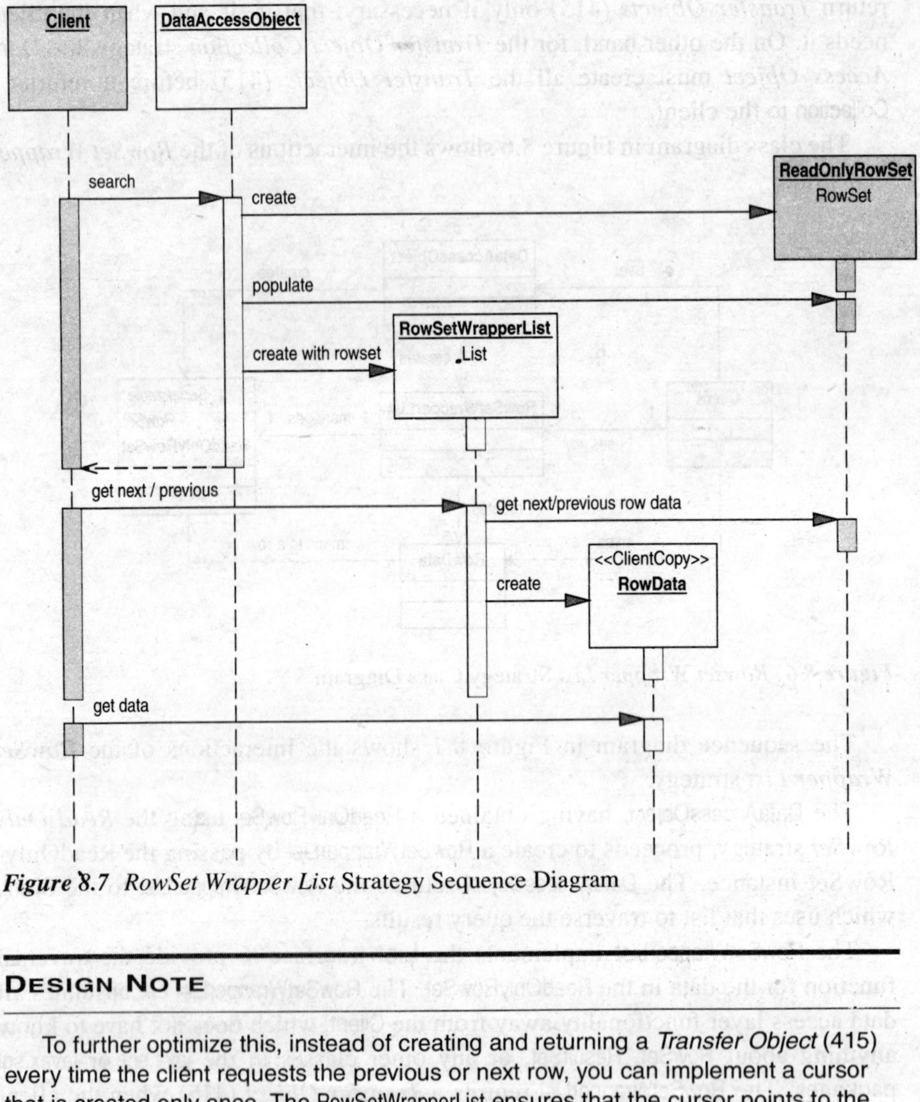

Figure 8.7 RowSet Wrapper List Strategy Sequence Diagram

DESIGN NOTE

To further optimize this, instead of creating and returning a *Transfer Object* (415) every time the client requests the previous or next row, you can implement a cursor that is created only once. The RowSetWrapperList ensures that the cursor points to the correct row before the cursor is returned to the client. For the sake of simplicity and brevity, we have opted to use the *Transfer Object* (415) instead of a cursor.

The following code examples show the implementation of the *RowSet Wrapper List* strategy. The sample code in Example 8.9 shows the CustomerDAO creating a RowSetWrapperList instance using the ReadOnlyRowSet obtained in the previous example.

A custom list iterator, DataRowListIterator, is implemented as an inner class of RowSetWrapperList, as shown in Example 8.11.

Finally, a simple DAO client CustomerDAOClient that uses CustomerDAO and the RowSetWrapperList is shown in Example 8.13.

Example 8.9 CustomerDAO.java: Creating the RowSetWrapperList

```
package com.corej2eepatterns.dao;

// imports

public class CustomerDAO {
  . . .

  public List findCustomersRL(
      CustomerTO cust, int startAtRow, int howManyRows)
      throws Exception{
    // create the search SQL string
    String searchSQLString = getSearchSQLString(cust);

    // execute the search
    return executeSearch(searchSQLString,
        StartAtRow, howManyRows);
  }

  private List executeSearch(
      String searchSQLString, int startAtRow,
      int howManyRows)
      throws Exception {

    RowSetWrapperList results = null;
    try {
      RowSet rowSet = getRORowSet(searchSQLString,
          int startAtRow,
          int howManyRows);

      results = new RowSetWrapperList (rowSet);
    } catch (Exception ex) {
      throw new Exception(ex);
    }

```

```
    return results;
  }

  private String getSearchSQLString(CustomerTO cust) {
    // convenience method to create and return
    // a "SELECT" SQL statement as a String, incorporating
    // non-null values in the supplied CustomerTO transfer
    // object into the WHERE clause
  }

  . . .

}
```

Example 8.10 RowSetWrapperList.java

```
package com.corej2eepatterns.to.list;

// imports

// Read only implementation of the List interface.
// It supports iterators and absolute positioning.

public class RowSetWrapperList
implements List, Serializable {

  // variable to hold a RowSet instance
  private RowSet rowSet;


  public RowSetWrapperList(RowSet rowSet) {
    this.rowSet = rowSet;
    . . .
  }

  // return the current row as a transfer object
  public Object get(int index) {
    try {
      rowSet.absolute(index);
    } catch (SQLException anException) {
      // handle exception
    }
    // create a new transfer object and return
```

```
    return
        TORowMapper.createCustomerTO(this);
  }
  . . .

  // Returns a Sub List of the current list.
  public List subList(int fromIndex, int toIndex) {
    // Create a new RowSet with the required rows
    ReadOnlyRowSet roRowSet = new ReadOnlyRowSet();
    roRowSet.populate(this.rowSet, fromIndex, toIndex);

    // Create a new RowSetWrapperList instance and
    // return it
    return
        new RowSetWrapperList(roRowSet);
  }

  // Returns an iterator over the elements in this list in
  // proper sequence. It is possible to define multiple
  // independent iterators for the same RowSetWrapperList
  // object.

  public Iterator iterator() {
    try {
      rowSet.beforeFirst();
    } catch (SQLException anException) {
      System.out.println(
          "Error moving RowSet before first row." +
          anException);
    }

    return this.listIterator();
  }

  // Create a List Iterator that can iterate over the
  // rowset
  public ListIterator listIterator() {
    // ListResultIterator is implemented as an inner class
    return new DataRowListIterator();
  }

  // implement the List interface methods

```

```
  . . .

}
```

Example 8.11 RowSetWrapperList.java: Inner class DataRowListIterator

```
package com.corej2eepatterns.to.lists;

// imports

public class RowSetWrapperList
implements List, Serializable {

  . . .

  private class DataRowListIterator implements ListIterator {
    int currentRow=0;
    // sets the rowset cursor to next and returns
    // the Transfer object
    public Object next() {
    // get transfer object for next row of RowSetWrapperList
    currentRow++;
    return this.get(currentRow);
  }

  public Object previous() {
    // get transfer object for previous row of
    // RowSetWrapperList
    currentRow--;
    return this.get(currentRow);

  }

  // Implement the List Iterator interface
  public boolean hasNext() {
    // Check the cursor position in the rowSet using
    // isLast, isAfterLast, isEmpty methods and
    // return true or false accordingly
  }

  public boolean hasPrevious() {
    // Check the cursor position in the rowSet using
    // isFirst, isBeforeFirst, isEmpty methods and
```

```
      // return true or false accordingly
   }

   // implement other ListIterator methods

   public int nextIndex() {
      . . .
   }

   public int previousIndex() {
      . . .
   }

   // optional methods not implemented throw
   // UnsupportedException
   public void set(Object o) {
      throw new UnsupportedOperationException();
   }

   public void add(Object o) {
      throw new UnsupportedOperationException();
   }
   . . .
}
```

Example 8.12 TORowMapper.java: A Sample Implementation

```
package com.corej2eepatterns.util;

// imports
public class TORowMapper {

   // create Customer TO
   public CustomerTO createCustomerTO(RowSet rowSet) {
      CustomerTO to = new CustomerTO();
      to.setId(getString(rowSet), 0);
      to.setName(getString(rowSet), 1);
      . . .
   }

   // create other TOs
   . . .

```

```
  // implement primitive methods used by create methods
  protected boolean wasNull(RowSet rowSet) {
    try {
      return rowSet.wasNull();
    } catch (SQLException e) {
      throw new RuntimeException(e.getMessage());
    }
  }

  protected String getString(RowSet rowSet, int columnIndex) {
    try {
      return rowSet.getString(columnIndex);
    } catch (SQLException e) {
      throw new RuntimeException(e.getMessage());
    }
  }

  protected boolean getBoolean(
      RowSet rowSet, int columnIndex) {
    try {
      return rowSet.getBoolean(columnIndex);
    } catch (SQLException e) {
      throw new RuntimeException(e.getMessage());
    }
  }

  protected java.util.Date getDate(
      RowSet rowSet, int columnIndex) {
    try {
      return rowSet.getDate(columnIndex);
    } catch (SQLException e) {
      throw new RuntimeException(e.getMessage());
    }
  }

  // Other primitive getXXX methods for all required
  // data types
  . . .

}
```

Example 8.13 A Sample DAO Client: Using the RowSetWrapperList

```
package com.corej2eepatterns.rowset;

// imports

public class CustomerDAOClient {

  ...

  public void search() {
    try {
      CustomerDAO dao = new CustomerDAO();
      CustomerTO criteria = new CustomerTO();

      criteria.setZip("94539");

      // search for all customers with Zip code 94539
      // results to contain a maximum of 1000 matching rows
      List searchResults =
          dao.findCustomersRL(criteria, 0, 999);

      int resultSize = searchResults.size();
      for (int rowNum=0; rowNum < resultSize; rowNum++) {
        CustomerTO customerTO =
            (CustomerTO)searchResults.get(rowNum);
        System.out.println("Customer Row #" +
            rowNum + " has ");
        System.out.println("Customer Id = " +
            customerTO.getId());
        System.out.println("Name = " +
            customerTO.getName());
        . . .
      }

      ...

      // get a ListIterator
      ListIterator iterator = searchResults.listIterator();

      // use the iterator to traverse to next or
      // previous row
      ...
```

```
        } catch (Exception e) {
            // handle exception
        }
    }
    . . .
}
```

Design Note: Designing a Data Access Object

As noted in various places in the *Data Access Object* section, we use *Transfer Object* (415) to pass data between a *Data Access Object* and its clients. The question arises, what object do we return to the client when executing a query?

Though the *Data Access Object* creates a ResultSet instance when the query is executed, it's best to keep the ResultSet encapsulated within the *Data Access Object* at all times. A ResultSet instance is associated with a database connection. Returning a ResultSet to a client outside the data access layer would violate encapsulation and introduce connection management problems. Another problem is that the ResultSet is a low-level interface and is tied to the relational structure of the data in an RDBMS. It is important to recall that the *Data Access Object* caters to other types of persistent stores as well, and therefore it's all the more important to avoid exposing implementation-specific data structures, such as ResultSet instances outside the data access layer. Specifically, the problems arising out of exposing such data structures to the clients are as follows:

- The clients must import and deal with interfaces and exceptions from the java.sql package.
- To extract data from the result set, a client must specify database columns or aliases. Therefore, the client is aware of details about the persistence implementation, such as relational tables and columns.
- The ResultSet carries with it any associated live database connections.
- RowSets provide a slightly higher level of abstraction than a result set and also provide additional methods that make it more convenient to use. While a RowSets instances appear to be a better way to return results from a *Data Access Object*, this approach also has other problems. The clients will have to import and deal with interfaces and exceptions from the java.sql and javax.sql packages.
- To extract data from the row set, the clients must specify database columns or aliases, making the clients aware of details about the persistence implementation, such as relational tables and columns.
- When using a connected RowSet, the database connection is still alive when the row set is returned to the clients of the *Data Access Object*.
- The RowSet is close to a ResultSet; it implements the ResultSet interface.

In spite of the issues highlighted here, you might think it appropriate to return a RowSet instance from the *Data Access Object*, depending on how you intend to use the

RowSet. Therefore, using *Transfer Object* (415) to pass data between the *Data Access Object* and its clients solves the problem of coupling the clients to the JDBC API.

Furthermore, for finder methods, using either the simpler *Transfer Object Collection* strategy or the more complex *RowSet Wrapper List* strategy is a better option for returning results to external clients of the *Data Access Objects*. These strategies use row set implementations under the covers. More importantly, these strategies provide an object-oriented access to results data and avoid dealing with data structures such as, ResultSet or RowSet from the JDBC API.

Consequences

- ***Centralizes control with loosely coupled handlers***
  Filters provide a central place for handling processing across multiple requests, as does a controller. Filters are better suited to massaging requests and responses for ultimate handling by a target resource, such as a controller. Additionally, a controller often ties together the management of numerous unrelated common services, such as authentication, logging, encryption, and so on. Filtering allows for much more loosely coupled handlers, which can be combined in various permutations.
- ***Enables transparency***
  Clients can leverage the encapsulation of data sources within the *Data Access Objects* to gain transparency to the location and implementation of the persistent storage mechanisms.
- ***Provides object-oriented view and encapsulates database schemas***
  The clients use transfer objects or data cursor objects (*RowSet Wrapper List* strategy) to exchange data with the *Data Access Objects*. Instead of depending on low-level details of database schema implementations, such as ResultSets and RowSets, where the clients must be aware of table structures, column names, and so on, the clients handle data in an object-oriented manner using the transfer objects and data cursors.
- ***Enables easier migration***
  A layer of DAOs makes it easier for an application to migrate to a different database implementation. The clients have no knowledge of the underlying data store implementation. Thus, the migration involves changes only to the DAO layer.

- ***Reduces code complexity in clients***
  Since the DAOs encapsulate all the code necessary to interact with the persistent storage, the clients can use the simpler API exposed by the data access layer. This reduces the complexity of the data access client code and improves the maintainability and development productivity.
- ***Organizes all data access code into a separate layer***
  Data access objects organize the implementation of the data access code in a separate layer. Such a layer isolates the rest of the application from the persistent store and external data sources. Because all data access operations are now delegated to the DAOs, the separate data access layer isolates the rest of the application from the data access implementation. This centralization makes the application easier to maintain and manage.
- ***Adds extra layer***
  The DAOs create an additional layer of objects between the data client and the data source that needs to be designed and implemented, to leverage the benefits of this pattern. While this layer might seem to be extra development and run-time overhead, it is typically necessary in order to decouple the data access implementation from the other parts of the application.
- ***Needs class hierarchy design***
  When you use a factory strategy, the hierarchy of concrete factories and the hierarchy of concrete products (DAOs) produced by the factories need to be designed and implemented. Consider this additional effort if you think you'll need this extra flexibility, because it increases the complexity of the design. Use the *DAO Factory Method Strategy* if that meets your needs, and use *DAO Abstract Factory Strategy* only if absolutely required.
- ***Introduces complexity to enable object-oriented design***
  While the *RowSet Wrapper List* strategy encapsulates the data access layer dependencies and JDBC APIs, and exposes an object-oriented view of the results data, it introduces considerable complexity in your implementation. You need to decide whether its benefits outweigh the drawbacks of using the JDBC RowSet API in the *Cached RowSet* strategy, or the performance drawback of using the *Transfer Object Collection* strategy.

Related Patterns

- ***Transfer Object (415)***
  Data access objects in their most basic form use transfer objects to transport data to and from their clients. *Transfer Object* (415) are used in other strategies of *Data Access Objects*. The *RowSet Wrapper List* strategy returns a list as a transfer object.
- ***Factory Method [GoF] and Abstract Factory [GoF]***
  The *Data Access Object Factory* strategies use the *Factory Method* pattern to implement the concrete factories and its products (DAOs). For added flexibility, the *Abstract Factory* pattern is used as described in the *Data Access Object Factory* strategy.
- ***Broker [POSA1]***
  The DAO pattern is related to the *Broker* pattern, which describes approaches for decoupling clients and servers in distributed systems. The DAO pattern more specifically applies this pattern to decoupling the resource tier from clients in another tier, such as the business or presentation tier.
- ***Transfer Object Assembler (433)***
  The *Transfer Object Assembler* (433) uses the *Data Access Object* to obtain data to build the composite transfer object it needs to assemble and send as the model data to the client.
- ***Value List Handler (444)***
  The value list handler needs a list of results to act upon. Such a list is often obtained using a *Data Access Object*, which can return a set of results. While the value list handler has an option of obtaining a RowSet from the *Data Access Object*, it might be better to obtain and use a *RowSet Wrapper List* instead.

Service Activator

Problem

You want to invoke services asynchronously

In enterprise applications, a majority of the processing is done in a synchronous manner. A client invokes a business service and waits until the business service returns from processing. However, the business processing in some use cases takes considerable time and resources. The business processing might even span applications, possibly integrating with applications inside and outside the enterprise. For these long-lived processes, it is not feasible for application clients to wait until the business processing completes.

Forces

- You want to invoke business services, POJOs, or EJB components in an asynchronous manner.
- You want to integrate publish/subscribe and point-to-point messaging to enable asynchronous processing services.
- You want to perform a business task that is logically composed of several business tasks.

Solution

Use a Service Activator to receive asynchronous requests and invoke one or more business services.

The *Service Activator* is implemented as a JMS Listener and delegation service that can listen to and receive JMS messages. If your application uses EJB components and your EJB container implements EJB version 2.0 or later, you can use a message-driven bean (MDB) to receive asynchronous requests. If your application does not use EJB technology, or uses a pre-EJB 2.0 compliant container, then you must implement your own custom solution using Java Message Service (JMS).

Any client that needs to asynchronously invoke a business service, such as an EJB or a POJO service, creates and sends a message to the *Service Activator*. The *Service Activator* receives the message and parses it to interpret the client request.

Once the client's request is unmarshalled, the *Service Activator* identifies and locates the correct business service component and invokes it to process the client's request asynchronously.

After the processing is completed, the client might want to receive the results. To inform the client about the outcome of the processing, the *Service Activator* can send a response to the client. This response can indicate to the client whether the processing was successful and provide the results or a handle to the results. In case of a failure in processing, the response can include the details of the failure. The details can indicate how the client can recover, whether by either resubmitting the request or by rectifying the problems causing the failure. The *Service Activator* might use a *Service Locator* (315) to locate a business component.

The client can include a unique request identifier when it submits a request. The *Service Activator* or the business service that processes the request can attach this unique identifier to the results and return it with the response.

Figure 8.8 shows the structure of the *Service Activator.*

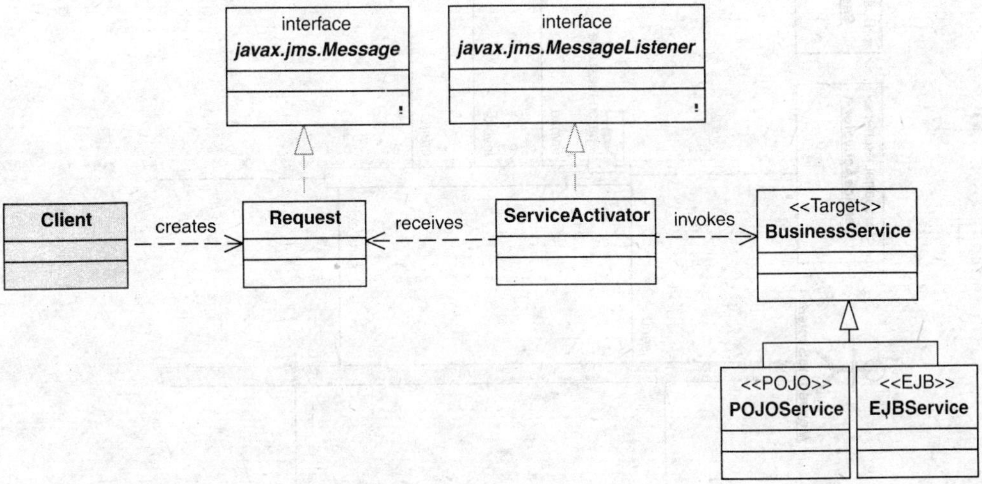

Figure 8.8 *Service Activator* Class Diagram

Participants and Responsibilities

The diagram in Figure 8.9 on page 498 shows the interaction of the various participants of the *Service Activator* pattern.

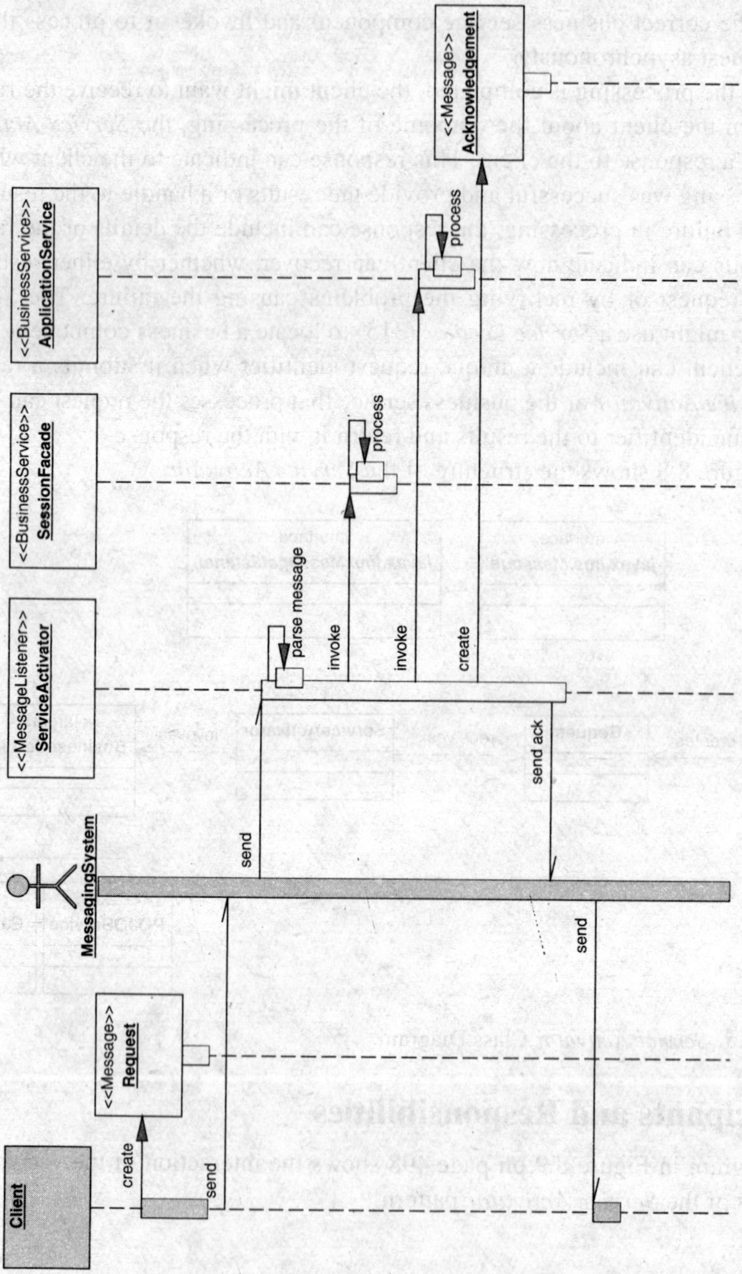

Figure 8.9 *Service Activator* Sequence Diagram

Client

The Client is any client in the application that needs to invoke a business service in an asynchronous manner. The client can be any type of application component, such as a POJO or an EJB component, that can create and send JMS messages.

The client can also be an EJB component that needs to invoke another business tier component in an asynchronous manner.

DESIGN NOTE: LEGACY APPLICATION AS A CLIENT

When integrating legacy applications with the J2EE platform, Java application clients can act as the message generators on behalf of the legacy system. The legacy system might not use Java, instead natively integrating with the message-oriented middleware to send and receive messages. In your Java application, a *Service Activator* can receive request messages from the legacy system and process them asynchronously.

Request

The Request is the message object created by the Client and sent to the ServiceActivator using the message-oriented middleware (MOM). According to the JMS specification, the Request object must implement the javax.jms.Message interface. The JMS API provides several message types, such as TextMessage, ObjectMessage, and so on, that can be used as request objects depending on what type of message you want to send.

ServiceActivator

The ServiceActivator is the main class of the pattern. It implements the javax.jms.MessageListener interface, which is defined by the JMS specification. The ServiceActivator implements an onMessage() method that is invoked when a new message arrives. The ServiceActivator parses (unmarshals) the message (request) to determine what needs to be done. The ServiceActivator might use a *Service Locator* (315) to look up or create BusinessService components.

BusinessService

The BusinessService is the target object that the client asks to do asynchronous processing. The BusinessService role is typically a *Session Façade* (341) or an *Application Services* (357). In applications with trivial business logic, the BusinessService can be a *Business Object* (374). The BusinessService can be any other service in the business tier that can process the Client's request.

DESIGN NOTE: BUSINESS SERVICE TARGETS

You can implement the role of a BusinessService using a POJO or an EJB component.

- ***Business Object*** Target – In simple applications with minimal business logic, a Business Object might be the target component processing a request.
- ***Session Façade*** Target – When you have applications with business logic involving multiple *Business Objects*, the *Service Activator* typically interacts with a *Session Façade* or an *Application Service* (357), which encapsulate business logic.
- **POJO Target** – In applications that do not use EJB components, you can implement business logic components as POJOs, such as *Application Services* (357). In this case, the *Service Activator* can invoke business methods on one or more POJOs to perform the asynchronous processing.

Response

The Response is a message object created and sent either by the ServiceActivator or a BusinessService. Response can be an acknowledgement to let the Client know that the Request was received. The Response can also be the results of the asynchronous processing.

Strategies

POJO Service Activator Strategy

The most straightforward strategy for implementing the *Service Activator* is as a standalone JMS listener that listens and processes JMS messages. This is typical in POJO applications that do not use enterprise beans. This strategy integrates using JMS into POJO applications without using a J2EE container.

If you are using an application server, then you can install and run the standalone *Service Activator* as a service of the application server. This might make it easier to manage the *Service Activator*, because it uses the application server features to monitor the *Service Activator* state and to start, restart, and stop the *Service Activator* as needed, either manually or automatically.

The sample code in Example 1.1 shows a POJO *Service Activator* implementation. Consider an order processing application where the customers shop online and the order fulfillment process happens in the background. In some cases, order fulfillment might be outsourced to a third-party warehouse. In such cases, the online store needs to invoke these fulfillment services asynchronously. This is an example that demonstrates usage of point-to-point (PTP) messaging to accomplish asynchronous processing. However, using publish/subscribe messaging would be similar, except that Topic is used instead of a Queue.

The OrderServiceActivator class can be instantiated in an application server, run in a standalone server, or registered as a startup service in your web container or EJB container.

DESIGN NOTE: WHAT TO USE, TOPIC OR QUEUE?

When your application needs to ensure that the message (request) is delivered to one and only one receiver, you use point-to-point messaging channel implemented using JMS Queues. For example, if the order processing system must ensure that the order request is delivered to one and only one order processor, and that it does not process the same order twice, you use a Queue between the sender and the order processor.

When your application needs to deliver the same message (request) to several receivers, each receiver receiving a copy of the same request, then you use a publish/subscribe-messaging channel implemented using JMS Topics. For example, in the order processing system, if you want to also deliver a copy of the order request to several other components, such as an auditor service, logging service, and so on, you use a Topic between the sender and these receivers. Each receiver that receives a copy of the request performs its own processing on the request. The order processor processes the order, the auditor service stores the request in an auditing system, the logging service logs the message to an order-received log, and so on.

The class diagram for the *POJO Service Activator* strategy is shown in Figure 8.10.

A sample *Session Façade* (341) OrderDispatcherFacade acts as a client of the *Service Activator* and dispatches Order requests to the OrderServiceActivator as shown. When the OrderDispatcherFacade's createOrder() method is invoked by a web request, the façade validates and creates a new Order. Then, it uses an OrderSenderAppService to invoké the sendOrder() method to dispatch the Order to the OrderServiceActivator. The OrderServiceActivator, on receiving an Order (request) locates and invokes back-end order fulfillment services, OrderProcessorBD and OrderProcessorFacade, to process the order.

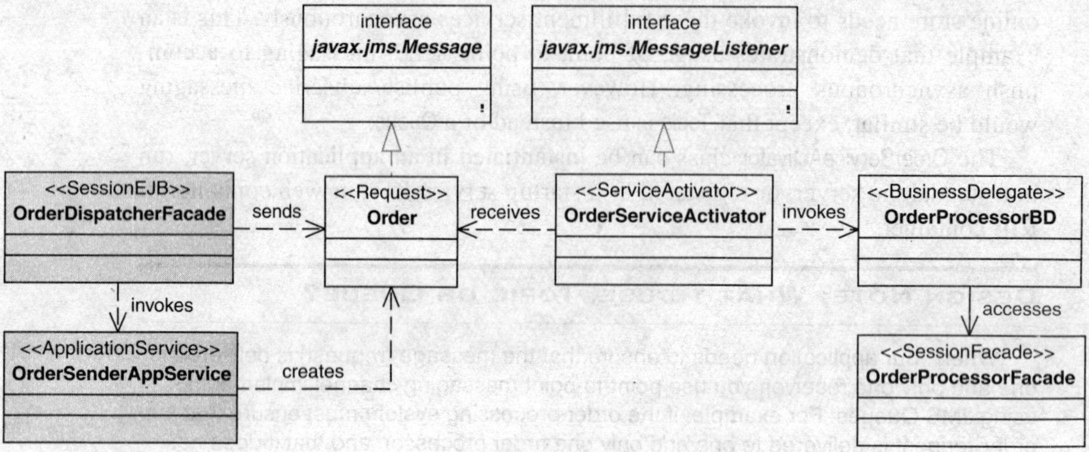

Figure 8.10 POJO Service Activator Strategy Class Diagram

Example 8.14 POJO Service Activator: OrderServiceActivator.java

```
// imports. . .

public class OrderServiceActivator implements javax.jms.MessageListener{

  // Queue session and receiver: see JMS API for details
  private QueueSession orderQueueSession;
  private QueueReceiver orderQueueReceiver;

  // Note: values should come from property files or
  // environment. Hard coded here for illustration only
   private String connectionFactoryName =
       "PendingOrdersQueueFactory";
  private String queueName = "PendingOrders";

  // use a service locator to locate administered JMS
  // components such as a Queue or a Queue Connection factory
  private ServiceLocator serviceLocator;
  private QueueConnectionFactory queueConnectionFactory;
  private QueueConnection queueConnection;

  public OrderServiceActivator(
      String connectionFactoryName, String queueName) {
    super();
    this.connectionFactoryName = connectionFactoryName;
```

```
        this.queueName = queueName;
        startListener();
    }

    private void startListener() {
        try {
            serviceLocator = ServiceLocator.getInstance();
            queueConnectionFactory =
            serviceLocator.getQueueConnectionFactory(
                    connectionFactoryName);
            queueConnection =
                    queueConnectionFactory.createQueueConnection();

            // See JMS API for method usage and arguments
            orderQueueSession =
                    queueConnection.createQueueSession (...);
            Queue ordersQueue =
                    serviceLocator.getQueue(queueName);
            orderQueueReceiver =
                    orderQueueSession.createReceiver(ordersQueue);
            orderQueueReceiver.setMessageListener(this);
        }
        catch (JMSException excp) {
            // handle error
        }
    }

    // The JMS API specifies the onMessage method in the
    // javax.jms.MessageListener interface.
    // This method is asynchronously invoked
    // when a message arrives on the Queue being
    // listened to by the ServiceActivator.
    // See JMS Specification and API for more details.
    public void onMessage(Message message) {
        try {
            // parse Message msg. See JMS API for Message.
            // Get the order object from the message
            ObjectMessage objectMessage =
                    (javax.jms.ObjectMessage) message;
            Order order = (Order) objectMessage.getObject();

            // Use the Business Delegate for Order Processor
            // Session Façade to invoke order processing
```

```
          OrderProcessorDelegate orderProcessorBD =
              new OrderProcessorDelegate();
          orderProcessorBD.processOrder(order);

          // send any response here...
        }
        catch (JMSException jmsexcp) {
          // Handle JMSExceptions, if any
          // Send error response, throw runtime exception
        }
        catch (Exception excp) {
          // Handle any other exceptions
          // Send error response, throw runtime exception
        }
      }
      public void close() {
        try {
          // cleanup before closing
          orderQueueReceiver.setMessageListener (null);
          orderQueueSession.close();
        }
        catch(Exception excp) {
          // Handle exception - Failure to close
        }
      }
    }
```

Example 8.15 Service Activator client: OrderDispatcherFacade.java

```
// imports. . .
public class OrderDispatcherFacade
  implements javax.ejb.SessionBean {
  . . .
  // business method to create new Order
  public int createOrder(...) throws OrderException {

  // create new business order entity bean
  . . .

  // successfully created Order. send Order to
  // asynchronous backend processing
  OrderSenderAppService orderSender =
      new OrderSenderAppService();
  orderSenderAppService.sendOrder(order);
```

```
     // close the sender, if done...
     orderSenderAppService.close();

     // other processing
     . . .
   }
}
```

You can put the JMS code in a separate *Application Service* (357) so that it can be reused. This JMS *Application Service* (357) OrderSenderAppService is shown in Example 8.16.

Example 8.16 Order Sender Application Service: OrderSenderAppService.java

```
// imports...

public class OrderSenderAppService {
  // Queue session and sender: see JMS API for details
  private QueueSession orderQueueSession;
  private QueueSender orderQueueSender;

  // These values could come from some property files
  private String connectionFactoryName =
       "PendingOrdersQueueFactory";
  private String queueName = "PendingOrders";

  // use a service locator to locate administered
  // JMS components such as a Queue or a Queue.
  // Connection factory
  private JMSServiceLocator serviceLocator;
  . . .
  // method to initialize and create queue sender
  private void createSender() {
    try {
      // using ServiceLocator and getting Queue
      // Connection Factory is similar to the
      // Service Activator code.
      serviceLocator = ServiceLocator.getInstance();
      queueConnectionFactory =
           serviceLocator.getQueueConnectionFactory(
           connectionFactoryName);
```

```
            queueConnection =
                queueConnectionFactory.createQueueConnection();

            // See JMS API for method usage and arguments
            orderQueueSession =
                queueConnection.createQueueSession(. . .);
            Queue ordersQueue =
                serviceLocator.getQueue(queueName);
            orderQueueSender =
                orderQueueSession.createSender(ordersQueue);
        }
        catch(Exception excp) {
            // Handle exception - Failure to create sender
        }
    }


    // method to dispatch order to fulfillment service
    // for asynchronous processing
    public void sendOrder(Order order) {
        try {
            // create a new Message to send Order object
            ObjectMessage orderObjectMessage =
                queueSession.createObjectMessage(order);

            // set object message properties and delivery
            // mode as required.
            // See JMS API for ObjectMessage

            // Set the Order into the object message
            orderObjectMessage.setObject(order);

            // send the message to the Queue
            orderQueueSender.send(orderObjectMessage);

            . . .
        } catch (Exception e) {
            // Handle exceptions
        }
        . . .
    }

    . . .
```

```
    public void close() {
        try {
            // cleanup before closing
            orderQueueReceiver.setMessageListener(null);
            orderQueueSession.close();
        }
        catch(Exception excp) {
            // Handle exception - Failure to close
        }
    }
}
```

MDB Service Activator Strategy

If you are using the EJB 2.x version specification, then you can implement the *Service Activator* as a **message driven bean** (MDB). An MDB is a special kind of stateless session bean that implements the JMS MessageListener interface, similar to the *POJO Service Activator* covered previously.

When you use an MDB, you need to provide only the implementation for the listener's onMessage() method. When you deploy an MDB in an EJB container, the EJB container uses the MDB's deployment properties to register and subscribe the MDB to the correct queue or topic, as specified in the deployment descriptor. Since the container manages MDBs, you have less work to do when implementing the *Service Activator* as an MDB, than when implementing it as a POJO. Therefore, if your container supports an MDB, use an *MDB Service Activator* instead of the *POJO Service Activator.*

Example 8.17 shows the OrderServiceActivator implemented as an MDB.

Example 8.17 MDB Service Activator, OrderServiceActivatorMDB.java

```
public class OrderServiceActivator
    implements javax.ejb.MessageDrivenBean,
    javax.jms.MessageListener {
. . .

  // The EJB container will invoke onMessage when a message
  // arrives for this Service Activator
  public void onMessage(Message message) {
    try {
      // parse Message msg. See JMS API for Message.
      // Get the order object from the message
      ObjectMessage objectMessage =
```

```
            (javax.jms.ObjectMessage) message;
        Order order = (Order)objectMessage.getObject();

        // Use the Business Delegate for Order Processor
        // Session Façade to invoke order processing
        OrderProcessorDelegate orderProcessorBD =
            new OrderProcessorDelegate();
        orderProcessorBD.processOrder(order);

        // send any response here...
      }
      catch (JMSException jmsexcp) {
        // Handle JMSExceptions, if any
        // Send error response, throw runtime exception
      }
      catch (Exception excp) {
        // Handle any other exceptions
        // Send error response, throw runtime exception
      }
    }

    // implement other methods required by the
    // Message Driven Bean
    public void setMessageDrivenContext(
        javax.ejb.MessageDrivenContext ctx)
        throws javax.ejb.EJBException { . . . }

    public void ejbCreate() { . . . }

    public void ejbRemove() { . . . }
}
```

Command Request Strategy

The Client can send a request that includes a *Command* [GoF] or a logical reference to a Command in the business tier. The *Service Activator*, upon receipt of a request, will parse it to determine the correct command, create the command instance, and execute it.

The *Command Request* strategy diagram is shown in Figure 8.11.

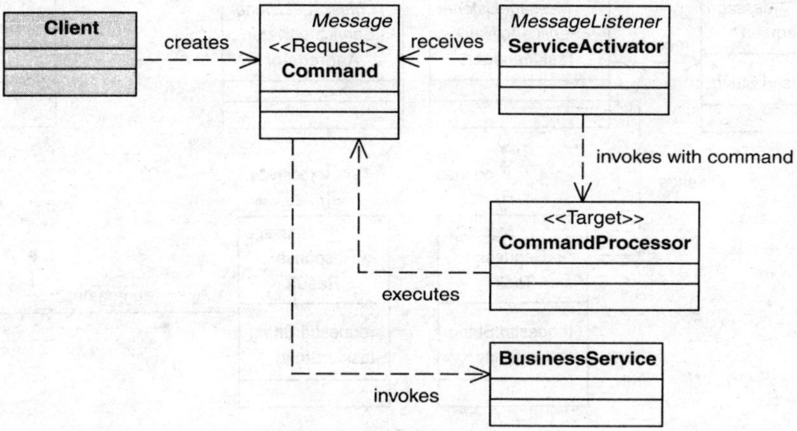

Figure 8.11 *Command Request* Strategy Class Diagram

Service Activator Aggregator Strategy

For some use cases, a business service can be logically composed of several sub-tasks, each of which can be processed asynchronously. In that case, the client can actually create several tasks and submit all of them to the *Service Activator* for asynchronous processing. Such parallel execution is useful only when each of these sub-tasks can be run independent of each other, is resource intensive, and is long-running.

For example, booking an itinerary via an online travel web site might consists of three different activities that can all be run in parallel: reserve a flight, reserve a hotel and reserve a rental car. The *Service Activator*, upon receiving each request, hands the request over to a worker object to perform the processing. The worker object is typically implemented as another *Service Activator* listening to its own queue. The problem with this approach is that the client will must aggregate all the results returned by the asynchronous workers in the *Service Activators* (496).

Alternatively, you can let the *Service Activator* deal with the aggregation. Since the *Service Activator* is a listener, this is easier when you cannot implement the listening and aggregation logic in your clients. In this strategy, several *Service Activators* (496) are used in different roles to coordinate parallel processing using multiple queues.

The *Service Activator Aggregator* is shown in Figure 8.12.

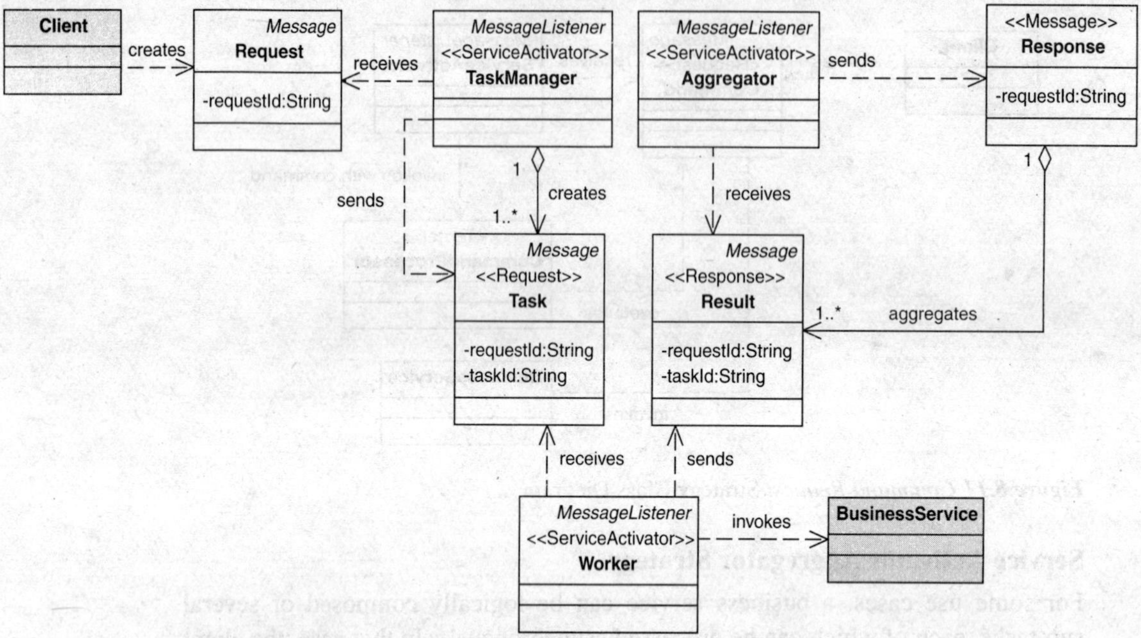

Figure 8.12 Service Activator Aggregator Strategy Class Diagram

- A **task manager** *Service Activator* that receives the initial request is responsible for dividing the service processing into a number of **tasks**, and sending each task to a particular *Service Activator* that can handle and process that task.
- The **worker** *Service Activators* (496) receiving the task requests process the task and send their results to an **aggregator** *Service Activator*, which can aggregate all the responses and send the results back to the original client. Because of the nature of the processing involved, the *Aggregator* is implemented as a stateful *Service Activator*.

A Client sends a Request with a unique request identifier. The Aggregator is a *Service Activator* that divides the Request into a number of Tasks and dispatches each Task to a Worker. Each Task is dispatched with the original unique request identifier and a task number that is unique within the tasks for that Request. A number of Workers are implemented as *Service Activators* (496), listening to different **task channels** (Queues or Topics).

When a Task arrives for a Worker, it processes the Task asynchronously and sends a Result to the Aggregator. The Aggregator receives the Result responses and, using the unique request identifier and task number, aggregates all the Result response for the original Request into a single Response and sends it back to the Client. When you implement the Aggregator, make sure it can handle Result response messages arriving out of order. For example, the Result response for Task 2 can arrive before the Result response for Task 1.

If the Aggregator is implemented as a stateless object (such as an MDB, which is a stateless session bean), it cannot hold onto the intermediate results during the aggregation process. Instead, you might have to accumulate the intermediate results in a persistent store (either a message queue or a database). The Aggregator, on receiving a Result response message, might do the following:

- Check the persistent store to get the status of tasks have been completed or still pending
- Check if the newly arrived Result completed the aggregation (i.e. if all the expected results have arrived):
  - If true, retrieve all the previously stored Results from the temporary persistent store, prepare an aggregated Response, and send it back to the client.
  - If false, store the Result to the temporary persistent store and continue waiting for other results.

Figure 8.13 through Figure 8.15 show the interaction among the roles..

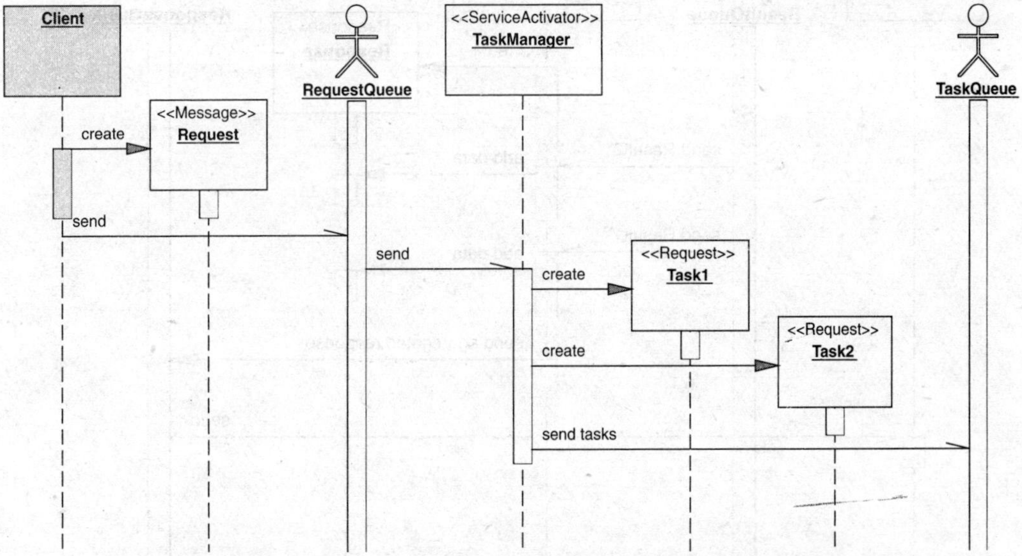

Figure 8.13 *Service Activator Aggregator* Strategy Sequence Diagram (part 1)

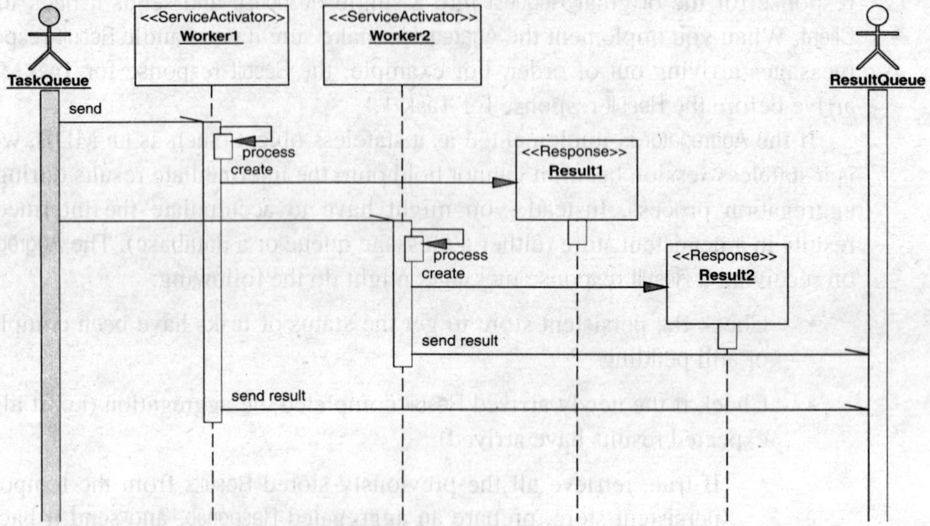

Figure 8.14 *Service Activator Aggregator* Strategy Sequence Diagram (part 2)

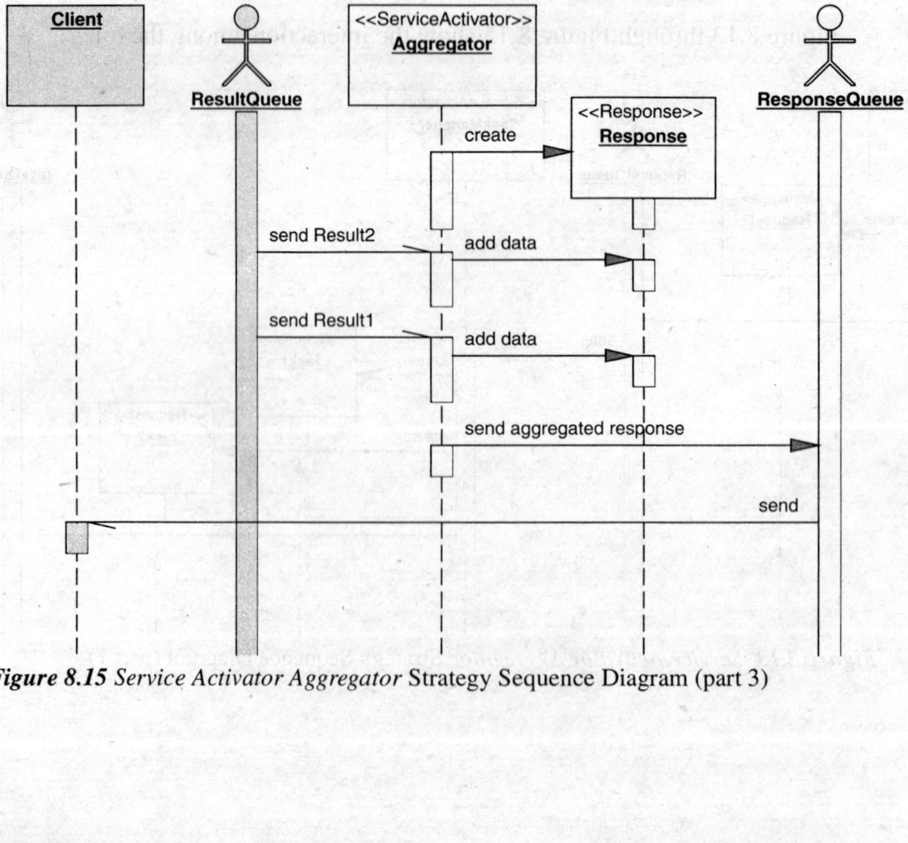

Figure 8.15 *Service Activator Aggregator* Strategy Sequence Diagram (part 3)

Response Strategies

When the *Service Activator* sends a response, you have several options for ensuring that the response gets delivered to the client that initiated the request processing.

Database Response Strategy

Poll a database – The response (with the results) can be stored in a database and the client needs to periodically poll the database using the request's unique identifier to check for the results. In most cases, polling works if you expect the results to be delivered shortly after submission. You also need decide when the client stops polling and gives up, how long you want to keep the results in the database, and when and how to purge and expire results from the database. Polling can also have a huge performance impact on your application if there are a lot of clients polling frequently.

Email Response Strategy

Send an email – In some applications, a simple way to return results asynchronously is to store them in a database, as described in the *Database Response* strategy. However, instead of having the client poll the database for the results, you can have the *Service Activator* or the business service send a status as an email to the client after the processing is completed. This might be suitable in user-interactive applications such as a Web-based e-commerce store that receives an order and sends an email to the customer later when the order is being processed in different stages: order received, order shipped, etc. In this case, the client polls the database only upon receiving such a confirmation and therefore is more scalable than periodic polling.

JMS Message Response Strategy

Send a JMS message – This is similar to sending an email. If the client is a Java application or a component, consider implementing it as another JMS listener. The *Service Activator* or the business service can send a JMS message as a response. This JMS message response can be an acknowledgement or the results data.

Consequences

- ***Integrates JMS into enterprise applications***
  The *Service Activator* enables you to leverage the power of JMS in POJO enterprise applications using the *POJO Service Activator* strategy, and in EJB enterprise applications using the *MDB Service Activator* strategy. Regardless of what platform you are running your application on, as long as you have a JMS runtime implementation, you can implement and use *Service Activator* to provide asynchronous processing capabilities in your application.
- ***Provides asynchronous processing for any business-tier component***
  Using the *Service Activator* pattern lets you provide asynchronous invocation on all types of enterprise beans, including stateless session beans, stateful session beans, and entity beans. The *Service Activator* acts as an intermediary between the client and the business service, to enable asynchronous invocation of any component that provides the business service implementation.
- ***Enables standalone JMS listener***
  The *POJO Service Activator* can be run as a standalone listener without using any container support. However, in a mission-critical application, *Service Activator* needs to be monitored to ensure availability. The additional management and maintenance of this process can add to application support overhead. An *MDB Service Activator* might be a better alternative because it will be managed and monitored by the application server.

Related Patterns

- ***Session Façade (341)***
  The *Session Façade* (341) encapsulates the complexity of the system and provides coarse-grained access to business objects. A *Service Activator* can access a *Session Façade* as a business service to invoke business processing.
- ***Application Services (357)***
  An *Application Service* (357) can also be a kind of business service that a *Service Activator* invokes to process the request.
- ***Business Delegate (302)***
  The *Service Activator* typically uses a *Business Delegate* (302) to access a *Session Façade*. This results in simpler code for the *Service Activator* and results in *Business Delegate* (302) reuse across different tiers.

- ***Service Locator (315)***
  The client can use the *Service Locator* (315) pattern to look up and create JMS-related service objects. The *Service Activator* (496) can use the *Service Locator* (315) pattern to look up and create enterprise bean components.
- ***Half-Sync/Half-Async [POSA2]***
  The *Service Activator* is related to the *Half-Sync/Half-Async* pattern. The pattern describes architectural decoupling by suggesting different layers for synchronous and asynchronous processing, and an intermediate queuing layer in between.
- ***Aggregator [EIP]***
  The *Aggregator* pattern discusses the problem of converting a request into several asynchronous tasks and aggregating the results. The *Service Activator Aggregator* strategy is based on similar concepts.

Domain Store

Problem

You want to separate persistence from your object model.

Many systems have a complex object model that requires sophisticated persistence strategies. With the addition of container-managed relationships (CMR) to EJB 2.x container managed persistence (CMP), it is much more feasible to employ CMP as a persistence strategy for complex object models (see *Composite Entity* (391). However, some developers opt to not use entity beans or run an application in a web container, and prefer to separate persistence from the object model.

Object models implemented as *Business Objects* (374) can use inheritance and have multiple levels of dependencies. The concept of **transparent persistence** (*Business Objects* that are not responsible for implementing code specific to persistence) is extremely appealing and becoming more popular as object models become more prominent in J2EE applications. When choosing to implement a persistent object model without using entity beans, you must select a persistence strategy.

Forces

- You want to avoid putting persistence details in your *Business Objects* (374).
- You do not want to use entity beans.
- Your application might be running in a web container.
- Your object model uses inheritance and complex relationships.

Solution

Use a *Domain Store* to transparently persist an object model. Unlike J2EE's container-managed persistence and bean-managed persistence, which include persistence support code in the object model, *Domain Store's* persistence mechanism is separate from the object model.

Design Note: EJB Persistence Versus Transparent Persistence

There is one key difference between using entity beans as a persistence mechanism, and using a transparent persistence mechanism. Entity beans put constraints on the object model, such as no inheritance and having EJBs programmed to support persistence. Transparent persistence keeps the persistence code out of the object model.

You can implement *Domain Store* in two ways: either write a custom persistence framework, or use a persistence product. The products are typically based on the Java Data Objects (JDO) specification or a proprietary object relational solution.

To implement *Domain Store*, you must have an object model. Many applications do not use explicit object models, but rather directly call the data resource as described in *Transaction Script* [PEAA].

Note: Many of the roles in this pattern correspond to Martin Fowler's [PEAA] object-relational patterns. For clarity, we include a <*PatternName*> [PEAA] beside the role to denote the corresponding PEAA pattern.

When using J2EE, you have persistence options, including the following:

1. No object model. Read and write data directly to the data resource for each CRUD business operation – *Transaction Script* [PEAA].
2. Use entity beans CMP
3. Use entity beans BMP – *Composite Entity* (391)
4. Code persistence into the POJO object model – *Active Record* [PEAA].
5. Separate persistence from the POJO object model.

In option 3 (entity beans BMP) and option 4 (persistence in object model) the persistence code is intermingled with the object model. In option 5(separate persistence from object model), the persistence mechanism is separated from the object model. *Domain Store* addresses option 5.

Structure

Figure 8.16 shows the class diagram for the *Domain Store* core classes.

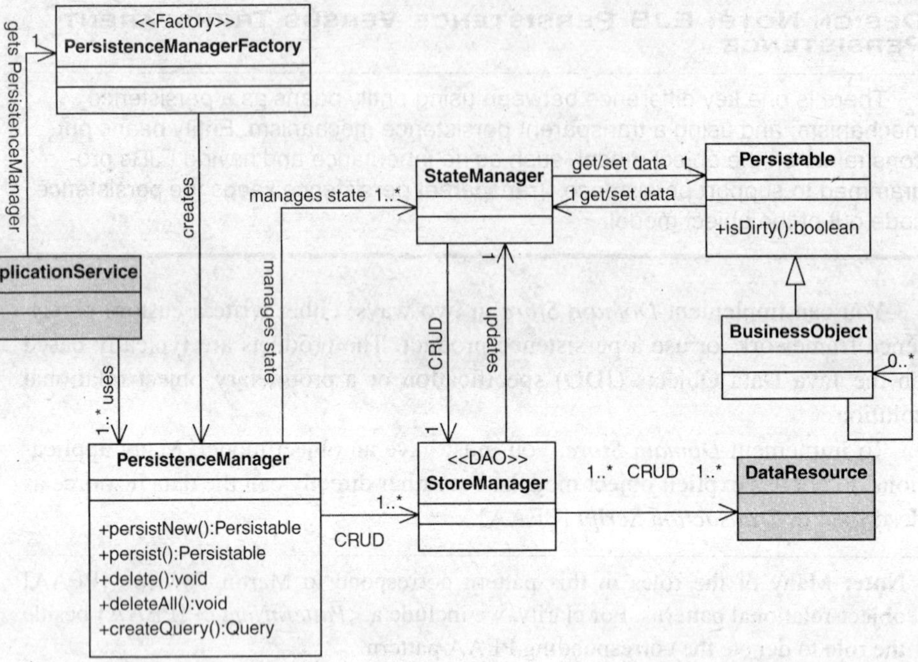

Figure 8.16 *Domain Store* Class Diagram

Figure 8.17 shows the *Domain Store* class diagram with the added participating classes.

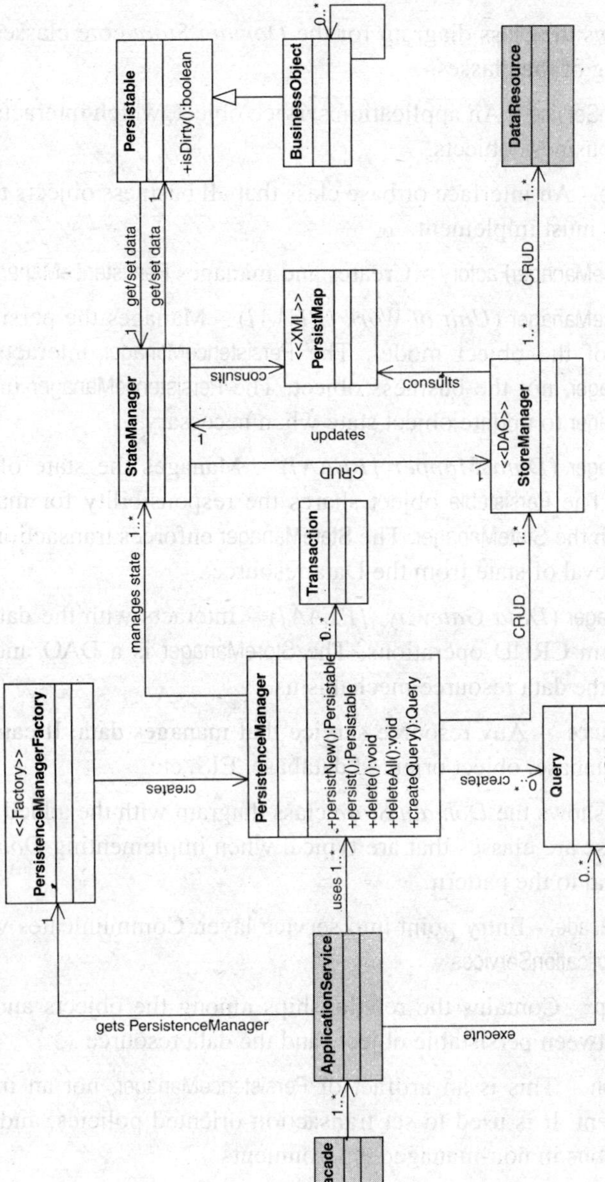

Figure 8.17 *Domain Store* Class Diagram With Participating Classes

Participants and Responsibilities

Figure 8.16 shows the class diagram for the *Domain Store* core classes. The following is a listing of the classes.

- ApplicationService – An application service object, which interacts with persistable business objects.
- Persistable – An interface or base class that all business objects that will be persisted must implement.
- PersistenceManagerFactory – Creates and manages PersistenceManagers.
- PersistenceManager (*Unit of Work [PEAA]*) – Manages the persistence and queries of the object model. The PersistenceManager interacts with the StateManager, not the business object. The PersistenceManager instructs the StateManager to update object state when necessary.
- StateManager (*Data Mapper [PEAA]*) – Manages the state of Persistable objects. The Persistable object shares the responsibility for managing its state with the StateManager. The StateManager enforces transactional storage and retrieval of state from the Data resource .
- StoreManager (*Data Gateway [PEAA]*) – Interacts with the data resource to perform CRUD operations. The StoreManager is a DAO and encapsulates all the data resource mechanisms.
- Data resource – Any resource service that manages data. It can be a relational database, object oriented database, EIS, etc.

Figure 8.17 shows the *Domain Store* class diagram with the added participating classes. These are classes that are typical when implementing *Domain Store*, but are not central to the pattern.

- SessionFacade – Entry point into service layer. Communicates with one or more ApplicationServices
- PersistMap – Contains the relationships among the objects and the mappings between persistable objects and the data resource .
- Transaction – This is an artifact of PersistenceManager, not an independent component. It is used to set transaction-oriented policies, and to delimit transactions in non-managed environments.
- Query – Encapsulates a query, typically the extent of instances to query, filtering criteria, ordering, and parameter declarations.

Figure 8.18 shows the interaction diagram for creating and persisting business objects.

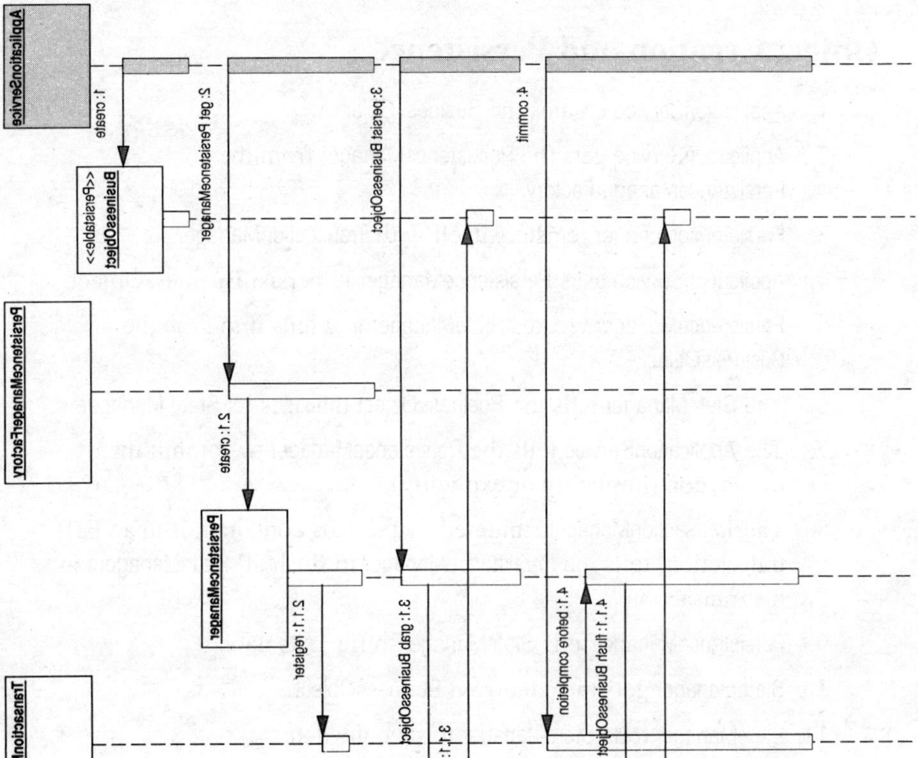

Figure 8.18 Interaction Diagram for Creating and Persisting Business Objects

The sequence is as follows:

Object Creation and Persistence

1. ApplicationService creates the BusinessObject.
2. ApplicationService gets the PersistenceManager from the PersistenceManagerFactory.
3. PersistenceManager registers itself with TransactionManager.
4. ApplicationService asks PersistenceManager to persist BusinessObject.
5. PersistenceManager creates StateManager and tells it to grab the BusinessObject.
6. The StateManager tells the BusinessObject that it is its State Manager.
7. The ApplicationService tells the PersistenceManager to commit the transaction (implicitly or explicitly).
8. The TransactionManager (initiated by the EJB container, if in an EJB transaction) tells the PersistenceManager to flush all StateManagers in the transaction.
9. PersistenceManager tells StateManager to flush its data.
10. StateManager gets the data from BusinessObject.
11. StateManager tells StoreManager to save the data.
12. Transaction commits.

Note: The previous example is just one example in which *Domain Store* objects might interact. These might be typical interactions, but are not mandatory.

Figure 8.19 shows the interaction for data retrieval. It begins with the ApplicationService getting data from the BusinessObject. The BusinessObject may check permissions on the StateManager and then get the data from the StateManager. If the StateManager does not have the data cached, it asks the StoreManager to retrieve the data. The data is cached by the StateManager and returned to the BusinessObject.

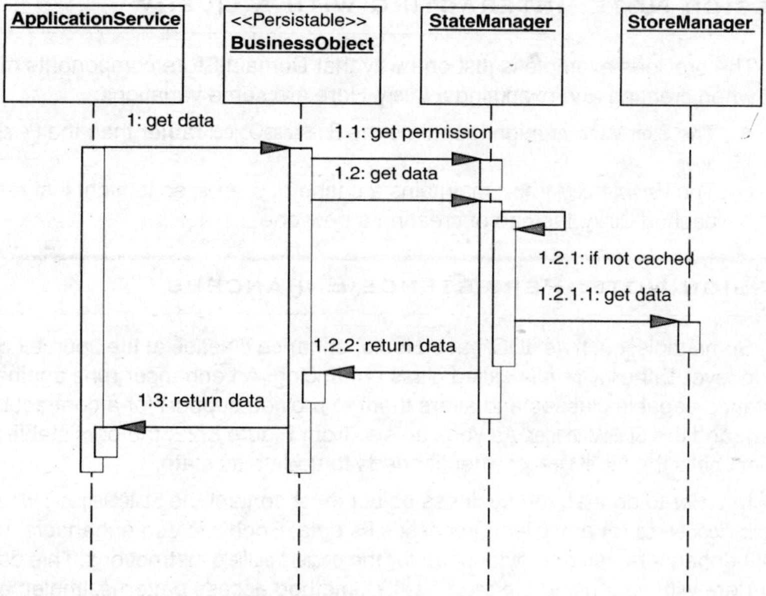

Figure 8.19 Interaction Diagram for Data Retrieval

DESIGN NOTE: STATEMANAGER

StateManager can use Identity Map [PEAA] pattern to insure that each object gets loaded only once by keeping every loaded object in a Map. Another alternative is to have the PersistenceManager maintain a list of what is cached rather than the StateManager.

Figure 8.20 on page 525 shows the sequence diagram for creating and executing a Query. It begins with the ApplicationService asking the PersistenceManager to create a Query and then run it. The Query asks the StoreManager to execute the Query. The StoreManager executes the query and returns the data to the Query. The PersistenceManager iterates over each result set row and creates a StateManager and a BusinessObject and populates them. Finally, the business objects are returned to the ApplicationService.

Design Note: Interacting with a Query

The previous example is just one way that Domain Store components might interact when creating and executing a Query. Here are some variations:

- The StoreManager might populate the BusinessObject rather than the PersistenceManager
- The PersistenceManager maintains a cache of Queries, so it might just retrieve a cached Query, instead of creating a new one

Design Note: Persistence Enhancers

Some tools, such as JDO-based tools, enhance classes at the source code or byte code level. Either way, it is called class enhancing. An enhancer runs against the persistence-capable classes and alters them to provide support for a contract between them and the StateManager. As you can see from Figure 8.22, the persistable business object calls the StateManager when it needs to update its state.

In order to do that, the business object must contact the StateManager whenever the ApplicationService (or any client) accesses its data. Sophisticated enhancers, such as JDO enhancers, replace bytecodes for the getfield/putfield instructions. This does not interfere with your using the getXXX/setXXX method access patterns. Implementing these patterns results in getfield/putfield bytecodes, which are what the enhancer deals with.

If you use a JDO product, you will use a byte code enhancer allowing you to avoid having to change your code to support persistence. However, if you are building a custom persistence framework, you will have to write your own enhancer to run against source code or byte code.

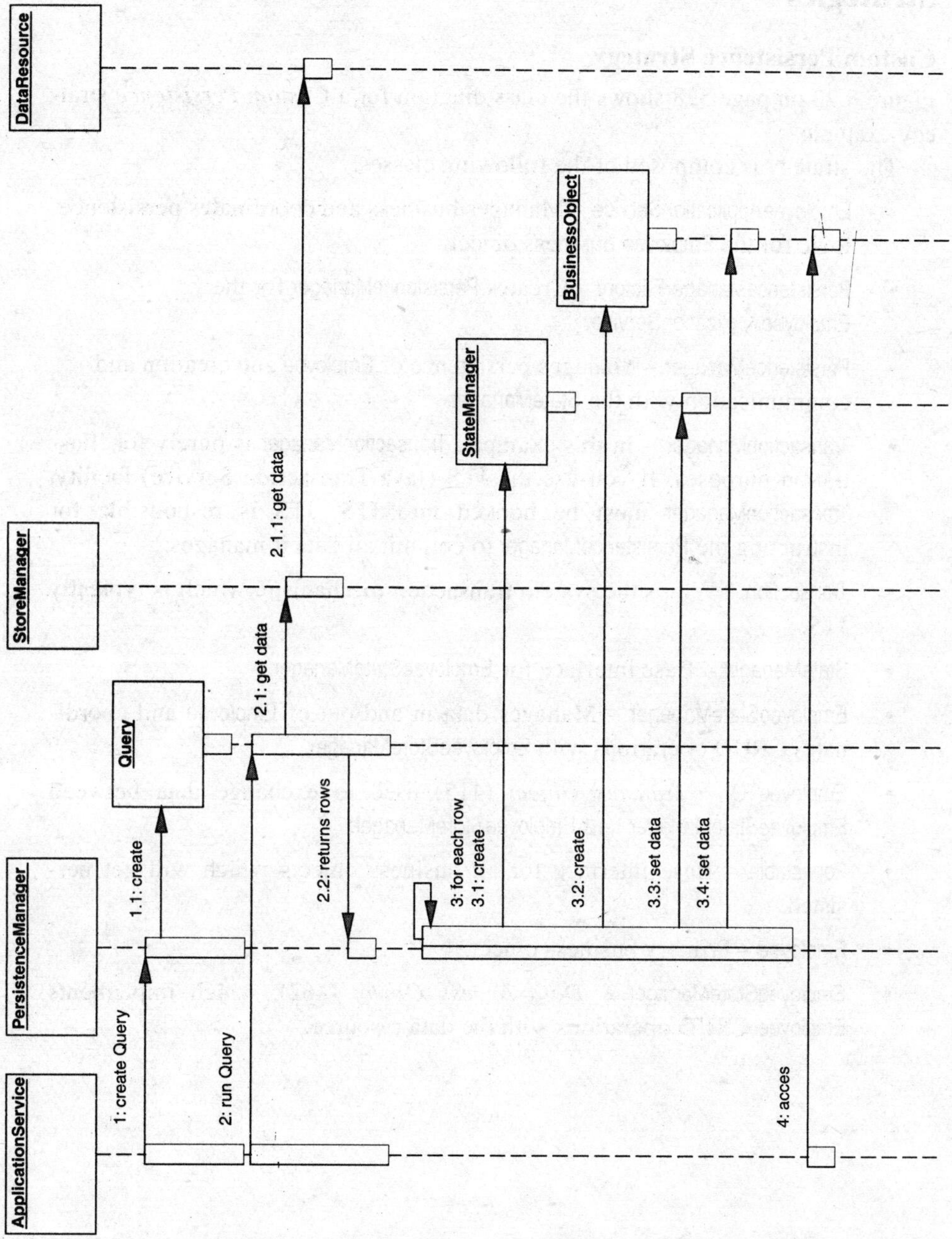

Figure 8.20 Create and Execute a Query Sequence Diagram

Strategies

Custom Persistence Strategy

Figure 8.22 on page 528 shows the class diagram for a *Custom Persistence* strategy example.

The strategy is composed of the following classes:

- EmployeeApplicationService – Manages business and coordinates persistence logic for the Employee business object.
- PersistenceManagerFactory – Creates PersistenceManager for the EmployeeApplicationService.
- PersistenceManager – Manages persistence of Employee and creation and communication with the StateManager.
- TransactionManager – In this example, TransactionManager is purely for illustration purposes. If you use the JTS (Java Transaction Service) facility, TransactionManager must be hooked into JTS. JTS is responsible for instructing the PersistenceManager to commit all data it manages.
- Transaction – Wraps the system transaction mechanism, which is typically JTS.
- StateManager – Base interface for EmployeeStateManager.
- EmployeeStateManager – Manages data in and out of Employee and coordinates CRUD operations with EmployeeStoreManager.
- EmployeeTO – *Transfer Object* (415) used to exchange data between EmployeeStateManager and EmployeeStoreManager.
- Persistable – Base interface for all business objects which will get persisted.
- Employee – Primary business object.
- EmployeeStoreManager – *Data Access Object* (462), which implements Employee CRUD operations with the data resource.

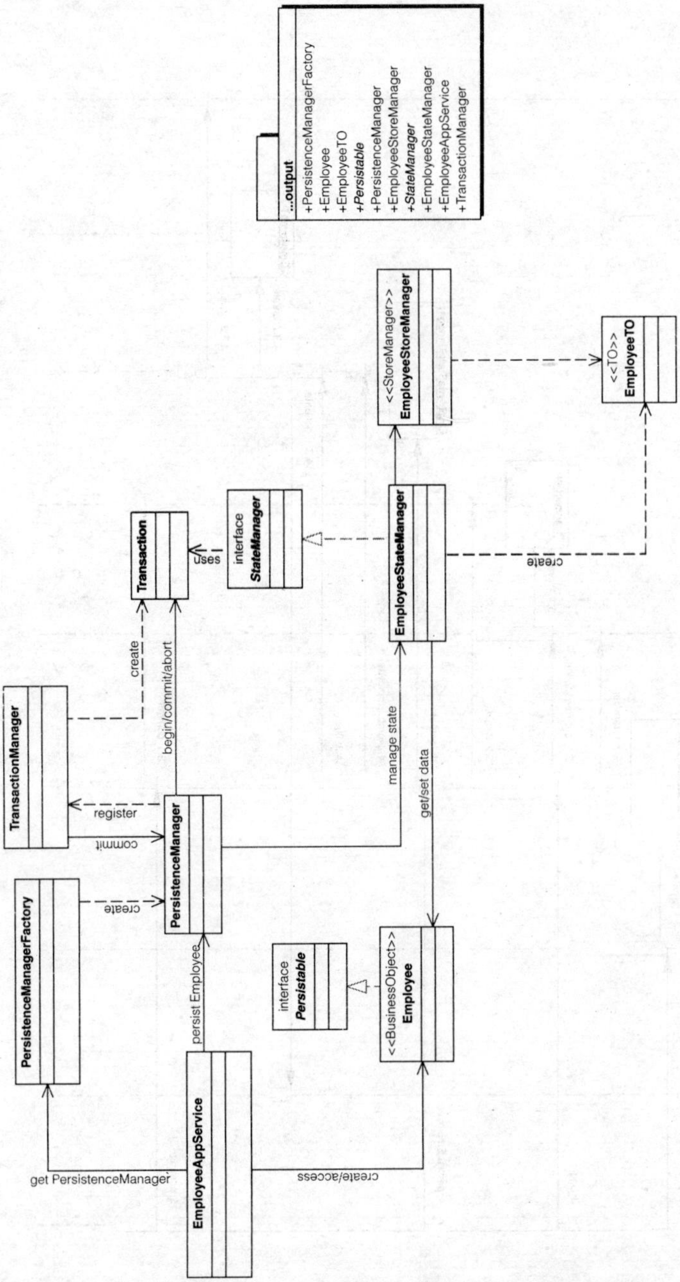

Figure 8.21 *Custom Persistence* Strategy Example Class Diagram

Figure 8.22 shows creating and persisting an Employee business object.

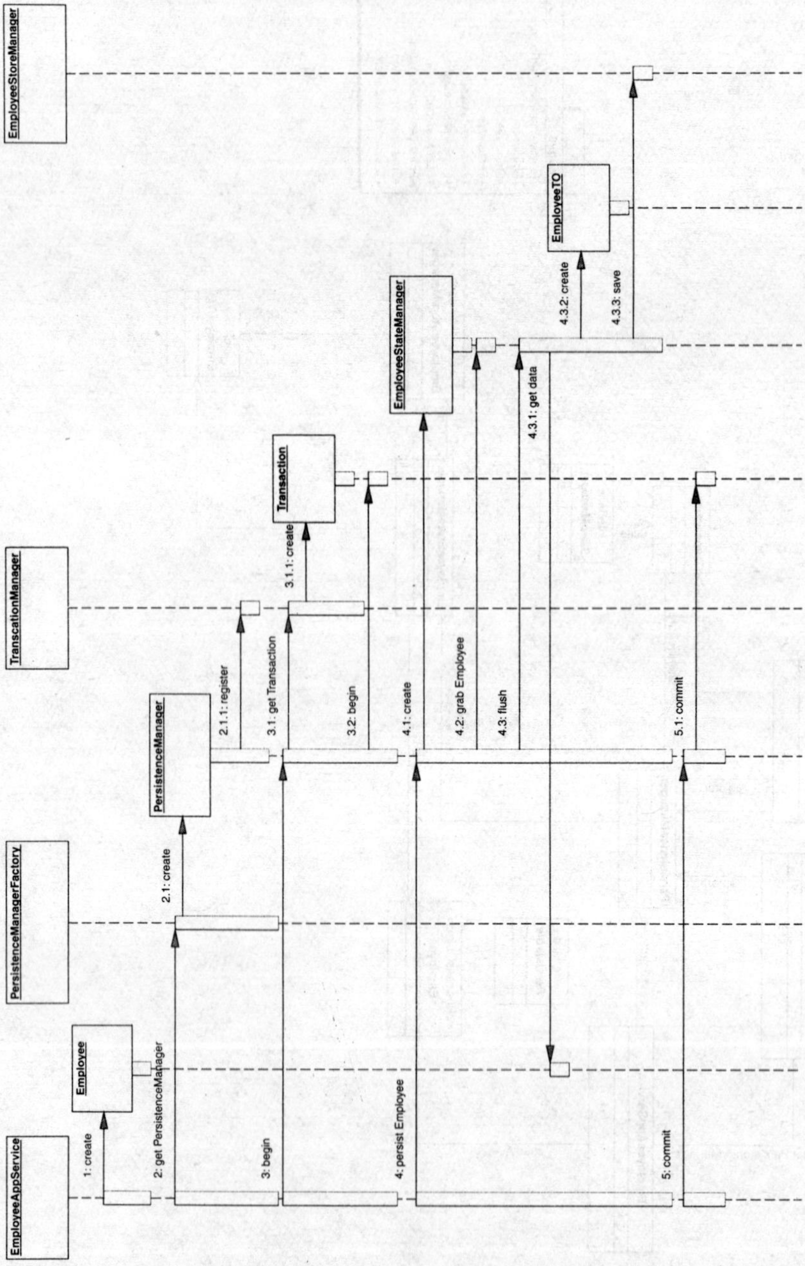

Figure 8.22 *Custom Persistence* Strategy Example Interaction Diagram

The following describes the interaction:

- EmployeeApplicationService creates Employee
- EmployeeApplicationService requests the PersistenceManager from the PersistenceManagerFactory
- PersistenceManagerFactory creates the PersistenceManager and returns it to the EmployeeApplicationService
- PersistenceManager registers itself with the TransactionManager.
- EmployeeApplicationService tells the PersistenceManager to begin the Transaction
- PersistenceManager creates a Transaction and calls begin.
- EmployeeApplicationService tells the PersistenceManager to persist the Employee
- PesistenceManager creates EmployeeStateManager and tells it to grab the Employee and flush the data
- EmployeeStateManager gets the data from Employee and creates the EmployeeTO transfer object (A *Transfer Object* (415) is used here for convenience)
- EmployeeStateManager sends the EmployeeTO to EmployeeStoreManager to save the data
- EmployeeApplicationService tells PersistenceManager to commit the transaction
- PersistenceManager calls commit on the Transaction, which causes the data to be committed in the data resource

DESIGN NOTE: STATEMANAGER CODE GENERATION

One of the most important elements in the *Custom Persistence* strategy is the State Manager shown in Example 8.21. In the case of this example, there is a tight coupling between the EmployeeStateManager and the Employee business object. Since the EmployeeStateManager is responsible for managing the state of the Employee, it must have detailed knowledge of the data in the Employee object. When you implement a custom persistence strategy, you can generate StateManagers based on the BusinesObject class.

The following code examples show the code for the *Custom Persistence* strategy example.

Example 8.18 EmployeeApplicationService Code

```
import javax.transaction.*;

public class EmployeeApplicationService {
  public String createEmployee(String lastName,
      String firstName, String ss, float salary,
      String jobClassification, String geography) {
    String id = null;
    String divisionId = null;

    // Create new id
    divisionId =
        getDivisionId(jobClassification, geography);

    // Create Employe
    Employee e = new Employee(
        id, lastName, firstName, ss, salary, divisionId);

    PersistenceManagerFactory factory =
        PersistenceManagerFactory.getInstance();
    PersistenceManager manager =
        factory.getPersistenceManager();
    try {
      manager.begin();
      e = (Employee) manager.persistNew(e);
      manager.commit();
    } catch (SystemException e1) {
    } catch (NotSupportedException e1) {
    } catch (HeuristicRollbackException e1) {
    } catch (RollbackException e1) {
    } catch (HeuristicMixedException e1) {
    }
    return id;
  }

  public void setEmployeeSalary(String id, float salary) {
    PersistenceManagerFactory factory =
        PersistenceManagerFactory.getInstance();
    PersistenceManager manager =
        factory.getPersistenceManager();
    Employee e = manager.getEmployee(id);
    if (e != null) {
```

```
            e.setSalary(salary);
        }
        try {
            manager.begin();
            e = (Employee) manager.persist(e);
            manager.commit();
        } catch (SystemException e1) {
        } catch (NotSupportedException e1) {
        } catch (HeuristicRollbackException e1) {
        } catch (RollbackException e1) {
        } catch (HeuristicMixedException e1) {
        }
    }
}
```

Example 8.19 Persistable Interface and Employee Class

```
public interface Persistable {
}

public class Employee implements Persistable {
    protected String id;
    protected String firstName;
    protected String lastName;
    protected String ss;
    protected float salary;
    protected String divisionId;

    public Employee(String id) {
        this.id = id;
    }

    public Employee(String id, String lastName,
            String firstName, String ss, float salary,
            String divisionId) {
        this.firstName = firstName;
        this.lastName = lastName;
        this.firstName = firstName;
        this.ss = ss;
        this.salary = salary;
        this.divisionId = divisionId;
    }

```

```
    public void setId(String id) {
      this.id = id;
    }

    public void setFirstName(String firstName) {
      this.firstName = firstName;
    }

    public void setLastName(String lastName) {
      this.lastName = lastName;
    }

    public void setSalary(float salary) {
      this.salary = salary;
    }

    public void setDivisionId(String divisionId) {
      this.divisionId = divisionId;
    }

    public void setSS(String ss) {
      this.ss = ss;
    }

    . . .
}
```

Example 8.20 EmployeeStateManager Class

```
public class EmployeeStateManager implements StateManager {
    private final int ROW_LEVEL_CACHING = 1;
    private final int FIELD_LEVEL_CACHING = 2;

    int cachingType = ROW_LEVEL_CACHING;
    boolean isNew;
    private Employee employee;
    private PersistenceManager pm;

    public EmployeeStateManager(PersistenceManager pm,
        Employee employee, boolean isNew ) {
      this.pm = pm;
      this.employee = employee;
      this.isNew = isNew;
```

```
}

public void flush() {
  if (pm.isDirty(employee)) {
    EmployeeTO to =
        new EmployeeTO(employee.id, employee.lastName,
            employee.firstName, employee.ss,
            employee.salary, employee.divisionId);

    EmployeeStoreManager storeManager =
        new EmployeeStoreManager();
    if (isNew) {
      storeManager.storeNew(to);
      isNew = false;
    } else {
      storeManager.update(to);
    }
    pm.resetDirty(employee);
  }
}

public void load() {
  EmployeeStoreManager storeManager =
      new EmployeeStoreManager();
  EmployeeTO to = storeManager.load(employee.id);
  updateEmployee(to);
}

public void load(int field) {
  if (fieldNeedsReloading(field)) {
    EmployeeStoreManager storeManager =
        new EmployeeStoreManager();
    if (cachingType == FIELD_LEVEL_CACHING) {
      //Object o =
      //   storeManager.loadField(employee.id, field);
      // updateEmployee( field, o );
    } else {
      EmployeeTO to = storeManager.load(employee.id);
      updateEmployee(to);
    }
  }
}
```

```
private boolean fieldNeedsReloading(int field) {
  // Caching and valid data rule apply here
  // data can be cached at the field or the row level

  switch (field) {
    case EmployeeStateDelegate.LAST_NAME:
      if (employee.lastName == null)
        return true;
      break;
    case EmployeeStateDelegate.FIRST_NAME:
      if (employee.firstName == null)
        return true;
        break;
    case EmployeeStateDelegate.DIVISION_ID:
      String did = employee.divisionId;
      if (did == null || did.indexOf("99-") == -1)
        return true;
      break;
    case EmployeeStateDelegate.SS:
      if (employee.ss == null)
        return true;
      break;
    case EmployeeStateDelegate.SALARY:
      if (employee.salary == 0.0)
        return true;
      break;
    }
  return false;
}

private void updateEmployee(EmployeeTO to) {
  employee.id = to.id;
  employee.lastName = to.lastName;
  employee.firstName = to.firstName;
  employee.ss = to.ss;
  employee.salary = to.salary;
  employee.divisionId = to.divisionId;
  isNew = false;
}

public boolean needsLoading() {
  if (pm.needLoading(employee))
     return true;
```

```
      else
        return false;
    }
}
```

Example 8.21 EmployeeTO Class and EmployeeStoreManager Class

```
public class EmployeeTO {
  public String id;
  public String lastName;
  public String firstName;
  public String ss;
  public float  salary;
  public String divisionId;

  public EmployeeTO(String id, String lastName,
      String firstName, String ss, float salary,
      String divisionId ) {
    this.id = id;
    this.lastName = lastName;
    this.firstName = firstName;
    this.ss = ss;
    this.salary = salary;
    this.divisionId = divisionId;
  }
}

public class EmployeeStoreManager {
  public void storeNew(EmployeeTO to) {
    String sql = "Insert into Employee( id, last_name," +
        " first_name, ss, salary, division_id ) " +
        " values( '?', '?', '?', '?', '?', '?' )";
    . . .
  }

  public void update(EmployeeTO to) {
    String sql = "Update Employee set last_name = '?'," +
        " first_name = '?', salary = '?'," +
        " division_id = '?' where id = '?'";
    . . .
  }

  public void delete(String empId) {
```

```
        String sql = "Delete from Employee where id = '?'";
        . . .
    }

    public EmployeeTO load(String empId) {
        . . .
    }
}
```

Example 8.22 PersistenceManagerFactory Class

```
public class PersistenceManagerFactory {
    static private PersistenceManagerFactory me = null;
    public synchronized static
        PersistenceManagerFactory getInstance() {
      if (me == null) {
        me = new PersistenceManagerFactory();
    }
    return me;
    }
    private PersistenceManagerFactory() {
    }
    public PersistenceManager getPersistenceManager() {
      return new PersistenceManager();
    }
}
```

Example 8.23 PersistenceManager Class

```
import javax.transaction.*;
import java.util.HashSet;
import java.util.Iterator;

public class PersistenceManager {
    HashSet stateManagers = new HashSet();
    TransactionManager tm;
    Transaction txn;

    public PersistenceManager() {
      tm = TransactionManager.getInstance();
      tm.register(this);
    }

    public Persistable persistNew(Persistable o) {
```

```
    if (o instanceof Employee) {
      return setupEmployee(
          new EmployeeStateDelegate((Employee)o), true);
      }
      return o;
    }

    public Persistable persist(Persistable o) {
      // Must already be an EmployeeStateDelegate
      if (o instanceof Employee) {
        EmployeeStateDelegate esd =
            (EmployeeStateDelegate) o;
        return esd;
      }
      return o;
    }

    public void commit()
        throws SystemException, NotSupportedException,
        HeuristicRollbackException, RollbackException,
        HeuristicMixedException {
      if (txn == null) {
        throw new SystemException(
            "Must call Transaction.begin() before" +
            " Transaction.commit()");
      }
      Iterator i = stateManagers.iterator();
      while (i.hasNext()) {
        Object o = i.next();
        StateManager stateManager = (StateManager) o;
        stateManager.flush();
      }
      txn.commit();
      txn = null;
    }

    public void begin()
        throws SystemException, NotSupportedException {
      txn = tm.getTransaction();
      txn.begin();
    }

    public Employee getEmployee(String employeeId) {
```

```
      EmployeeStateDelegate esd =
          new EmployeeStateDelegate(employeeId);
      setupEmployee(esd, false);
      return esd;
    }

    private EmployeeStateDelegate setupEmployee(
        EmployeeStateDelegate esd, boolean isNew) {
      EmployeeStateManager stateManager =
        new EmployeeStateManager(this, esd, isNew);
      stateManagers.add(stateManager);
      esd.setStateManager(stateManager);
      return esd;
    }

    public void setDirty(Persistable o) {
      // set dirty marker to true
    }

    public void resetDirty(Persistable o) {
      // reset dirty marker to false
    }

    public boolean isDirty(Persistable o) {
      // check if object is dirty
      return true;
    }

    public boolean needLoading(Persistable o) {
      // check if needs to be loaded
      return true;
    }
}
```

Example 8.24 TransactionManager Class

```
import javax.transaction.*;
import java.util.Iterator;
import java.util.LinkedList;

public class TransactionManager {
  static TransactionManager me = null;
```

```

  private LinkedList persistenceManagers = new LinkedList();

  class PManager {
    Thread thread;
    PersistenceManager manager;

    PManager(Thread thread, PersistenceManager manager) {
      this.thread = thread;
      this.manager = manager;
    }

    boolean equals(
        Thread thread, PersistenceManager manager) {
      if (this.thread == thread &&
          this.manager == manager) {
        return true;
      }
      return false;
    }
  }

  public synchronized static
      TransactionManager getInstance() {
    if (me == null) {
      me = new TransactionManager();
    }
    return me;
  }

  private TransactionManager() {
  }

  public Transaction getTransaction() {
    return new Transaction();
  }

  public void register(PersistenceManager manager) {
    . . .
  }

  public void notifyCommit(Thread t)
      throws SystemException, HeuristicRollbackException,
```

```
        NotSupportedException, RollbackException,
        HeuristicMixedException {
      Iterator i = persistenceManagers.iterator();
      while (i.hasNext()) {
        . . .
        pm.manager.commit();
      }
    }
}
```

Example 8.25 Transaction Class

```
import javax.ejb.SessionContext;
import javax.naming.InitialContext;
import javax.naming.NamingException;
import javax.transaction.*;

public class Transaction {
  UserTransaction txn;

  public void setSessionContext( SessionContext ctx ) {
    ctx.getUserTransaction();
  }
  public Transaction() {
    InitialContext ic = null;
    try {
      ic = new InitialContext();
      txn = (UserTransaction)ic.lookup(
          "java:comp/UserTransaction");
    } catch (NamingException e) {
    }
  }
  public void begin()
      throws SystemException, NotSupportedException {
    txn.begin();
  }

  public void commit()
      throws SystemException, HeuristicRollbackException,
      RollbackException, HeuristicMixedException {
    txn.commit();
  }

```

```
    public void rollback() throws SystemException {
      txn.rollback();
    }
}
```

On-demand State Retrieval

In the previous example, much of the emphasis is put on creating an Employee business object and persisting it. However, in other cases a business object is retrieved and then accessed. In this scenario, EmployeeStateManager might choose to populate the Employee data when the Employee object is created from the EmployeeStoreManager, or opt to get the data on demand.

Example 8.26 shows a possible implementation for state caching using a StateDelegate. The main difference is that an EmployeeStateDelegate class subclasses Employee and overrides all getter methods. When the Employee *Application Service* (357) asks the PersistenceManager for an Employee business object, it gets a EmployeeStateDelegate object, which can be treated exactly like an Employee object. When a getter method is called, the EmployeeStateDelegate checks to see if the data is already in the Employee object. If it is not, the EmployeeStateDelegate asks the EmployeeStateManager to load the data into the Employee object.

Design Note: Custom Persistence Strategy

As you can see, the custom strategy is powerful and lends itself to code generation for both the StateManager and the StateDelegate. However, as the number of classes in the object model grows in size, the number of generated classes also grows. This can easily become quite complex, so it's a good idea to use a JDO-style product to do the work for you.

Example 8.26 EmployeeStateDelegate Class

```
public class EmployeeStateDelegate extends Employee {
  static final int LAST_NAME = 1;
  static final int FIRST_NAME = 2;
  static final int SS = 3;
  static final int SALARY = 4;
  static final int DIVISION_ID = 5;

  private EmployeeStateManager stateManager;

  public EmployeeStateDelegate(String id, String lastName,
      String firstName, String ss, float salary,
      String divisionId) {
```

```
      super(id, lastName, firstName, ss, salary, divisionId);
   }

   public EmployeeStateDelegate(Employee e) {
      super(e.id, e.lastName, e.firstName,
            e.ss, e.salary, e.divisionId);
   }

   public EmployeeStateDelegate(String employeeId) {
      super(employeeId);
   }

   public EmployeeStateDelegate(String employeeId,
         EmployeeStateManager stateManager) {
      super(employeeId);
      this.stateManager = stateManager;
   }

   public void setStateManager(
         EmployeeStateManager stateManager) {
      this.stateManager = stateManager;
   }

   public String getFirstName() {
      stateManager.load(FIRST_NAME);
      return firstName;
   }

   public String getDivisionId() {
      stateManager.load(DIVISION_ID);
      return divisionId;
   }

   public String getLastName() {
      stateManager.load(LAST_NAME);
      return lastName;
   }

   public String getSS() {
      stateManager.load(SS);
      return ss;
   }

```

```
   public float getSalary() {
      stateManager.load(SALARY);
      return salary;
   }

   public EmployeeStateManager getStateManager() {
      return stateManager;
   }
}
```

JDO Strategy

Example 8.27 through Example 8.39 show the source code for the classes for an HR Service which implements *Domain Store* using JDO (Java Data Objects).

Example 8.27 shows the HRApplicationService class. It is the top-level application service, which contains the logic to create and persist the business objects. The business objects include: Employee, Department, Project, and two Employee types: FullTimeEmployee and PartTimeEmployee.

The HRApplicationService uses two helper classes, Factory and Queries. The HRApplicationService delegates all business object and query creation to the Factory, which is shown in Example 8.27 and Example 8.28. The Factory via the FactoryImpl is responsible for communication to the JDO PersistenceManager. The Queries via the QueriesImpl is responsible for executing queries. It uses the Factory to gain access to the JDO query mechanism.

As you can see, this JDO example explicitly uses some of the classes in *Domain Store*. Specifically:

- PersistenceManagerFactory – Implemented as the FactoryImpl class
- PersistenceManager – JDO PersistenceManager created by the FactoryImpl class
- Query – Implemented by the QueriesImpl class which delegates to the JDO Query class
- BusinessObjects – Interfaces Employee, Department, Project, PartTimeEmployee and FullTimeEmployee. Implemented by EmployeeImp, DepartmentImpl, ProjectImpl, PartTimeEmployeeImpl and FullTimeEmployeeImpl respectively.
- PersistMap – Not shown, but used by the JDO runtime.

JDO runtime implicitly implements the rest of the classes in *Domain Store*:

- Persistable – Not required by the JDO generator.
- Transaction – Not shown in this example.

- StateManager – Generated by the JDO generator and used by the JDO runtime.
- StoreManager – Generated by the JDO generator and used by the JDO runtime.

Example 8.27 HRApplicationService Class

```
// HRApplicationService.java

package com.corej2eepatterns.service;

import com.corej2eepatterns.business.hr.*;
import java.math.BigDecimal;

/**
 * @author  Craig Russell
 */
public class HRApplicationService {
  private Factory factory;
  private Queries queries;

  /** Creates a new instance of HRApplicationService */
  public HRApplicationService(Factory factory) {
    this.factory = factory;
    this.queries = factory.getQueries();
  }

  public Employee getEmployee(long id) {
    return queries.getEmployee(id);
  }

  public Department getDepartment(String name) {
    return queries.getDepartment(name);
  }

  public Project getProject(String name) {
    return queries.getProject(name);
  }

  public PartTimeEmployee createPartTimeEmployee(
      long id, String firstName, String lastName,
      BigDecimal wage, String departmentName) {
    PartTimeEmployee employee =
```

```
            factory.createPartTimeEmployee(
            id, firstName, lastName);
        employee.setWage(wage);
        Department department =
          queries.getDepartment(departmentName);
        employee.setDepartment(department);
        factory.persistObject(employee);
        return employee;
    }

    public FullTimeEmployee createFullTimeEmployee(
          long id, String firstName,String lastName,
          BigDecimal salary,vString departmentName) {
        FullTimeEmployee employee =
            factory.createFullTimeEmployee(
            id, firstName, lastName);
        employee.setSalary(salary);
        Department department =
            queries.getDepartment(departmentName);
        employee.setDepartment(department);
        factory.persistObject(employee);
        return employee;
    }
}
```

Example 8.28 Factory Class

```
// Factory.java

package com.corej2eepatterns.business.hr;

/**
 * @author  Craig Russell
 */
public interface Factory {

    PartTimeEmployee createPartTimeEmployee(
        long id, String firstName, String lastName);

    FullTimeEmployee createFullTimeEmployee(
        long id, String firstName, String lastName);

    Department createDepartment(String name);
```

```
  Project createProject(String name);
  Queries getQueries();
  void persistObject(Object object);
  void persistObjects(Object[] objects);
}
```

Example 8.29 FactoryImpl Class

```
// FactoryImpl.java

package com.corej2eepatterns.business.impl;

import com.corej2eepatterns.business.hr.*;
import javax.jdo.PersistenceManager;

/**
 * @author  Craig Russell
 */
public class FactoryImpl implements Factory {
  PersistenceManager pm;

  /** Creates a new instance of FactoryImpl */
  public FactoryImpl(PersistenceManager pm) {
    this.pm = pm;
  }

  PersistenceManager getPersistenceManager() {
    return pm;
  }

  public Department createDepartment(String name) {
    return new DepartmentImpl(name);
  }

  public FullTimeEmployee createFullTimeEmployee(
      long id, String firstName, String lastName) {
    return new FullTimeEmployeeImpl(
        id, firstName, lastName);
  }

  public PartTimeEmployee createPartTimeEmployee(
      long id, String firstName, String lastName) {
    return new PartTimeEmployeeImpl(
```

```
          id, firstName, lastName);
  }

  public Project createProject(String name) {
    return new ProjectImpl(name);
  }

  public Queries getQueries() {
    return new QueriesImpl(this);
  }

  public void persistObjects(Object[] objects) {
    pm.makePersistentAll(objects);
  }

  public void persistObject(Object object) {
    pm.makePersistent(object);
  }
}
```

Example 8.30 Queries Interface

```
// Queries class
package com.corej2eepatterns.business.hr;

/**
 * @author  Craig Russell
 */
public interface Queries {
  Department getDepartment(String name);
  Employee getEmployee(long id);
  Project getProject(String name);
}
```

Example 8.31 QueriesImpl Class

```
// QueryImpl.java

package com.corej2eepatterns.business.impl;

import com.corej2eepatterns.business.hr.Department;
import com.corej2eepatterns.business.hr.Employee;
import com.corej2eepatterns.business.hr.Project;
import com.corej2eepatterns.business.hr.Queries;
```

```java

import javax.jdo.Query;
import javax.jdo.PersistenceManager;
import java.util.Collection;
import java.util.Iterator;

/**
 * @author  Craig Russell
 */
public class QueriesImpl implements Queries {
  private FactoryImpl factory;

  /** Creates a new instance of QueryImpl */
  public QueriesImpl(FactoryImpl factory) {
    this.factory = factory;
  }

  public Department getDepartment(String name) {
    PersistenceManager pm =
        factory.getPersistenceManager();
    Query q = pm.newQuery(
        DepartmentImpl.class, "this.name == name");
    q.declareParameters("String name");
    Collection departments = (Collection) q.execute(name);
    Iterator iterator = departments.iterator();
    return (iterator.hasNext()) ?
        (Department) iterator.next() : null;
  }

  public Employee getEmployee(long id) {
    PersistenceManager pm =
        factory.getPersistenceManager();
    Query q = pm.newQuery(
        EmployeeImpl.class, "this.id == id");
    q.declareParameters("long id");
    Collection employees =
        (Collection) q.execute(new Long(id));
    Iterator iterator = employees.iterator();
    return (iterator.hasNext()) ?
        (Employee) iterator.next() : null;
  }

  public Project getProject(String name) {
```

```
    PersistenceManager pm =
        factory.getPersistenceManager();
    Query q = pm.newQuery(
        ProjectImpl.class, "this.name == name");
    q.declareParameters("String name");
    Collection projects = (Collection) q.execute(name);
    Iterator iterator = projects.iterator();
    return (iterator.hasNext()) ?
        (Project) iterator.next() : null;
  }
}
```

Example 8.32 Project Class

```
// Project.java

package com.corej2eepatterns.business.hr;

import java.util.Set;

/**
 * @author  Craig Russell
 */
public interface Project {
  String getName();
  Set getEmployees();
}

```

Example 8.33 ProjectImpl Class

```
// ProjectImpl.java

package com.corej2eepatterns.business.impl;

import com.corej2eepatterns.business.hr.Project;

import java.util.Collections;
import java.util.HashSet;
import java.util.Set;

public class ProjectImpl implements Project {
  String name;
  Set employees = new HashSet();
```

```

  /** Creates a new instance of ProjectImpl */
  ProjectImpl(String name) {
    this.name = name;
  }

  public Set getEmployees() {
    return Collections.unmodifiableSet(employees);
  }

  public String getName() {
    return name;
  }

  boolean addEmployee(EmployeeImpl employee) {
    return employees.add(employee);
  }

  boolean removeEmployee(EmployeeImpl employee) {
    return employees.remove(employee);
  }
}
```

Example 8.34 FullTimeEmployee Class

```
// FullTimeEmployee.java

package com.corej2eepatterns.business.hr;

import java.math.BigDecimal;

/**
 * @author  Craig Russell
 */
public interface FullTimeEmployee extends Employee {
  BigDecimal getSalary();
  void setSalary(BigDecimal salary);
}
```

Example 8.35 FullTimeEmployeeImpl class

```
//FullTimeEmployeeImpl.java

package com.corej2eepatterns.business.impl;
```

```

import com.corej2eepatterns.business.hr.FullTimeEmployee;

import java.math.BigDecimal;

/**
 * @author  Craig Russell
 */
public class FullTimeEmployeeImpl
    extends EmployeeImpl implements FullTimeEmployee {
  private BigDecimal salary;

  /** Creates a new instance of FullTimeEmployeeImpl */
  public FullTimeEmployeeImpl(
      long id, String firstName, String lastName) {
    super(id, firstName, lastName);
  }

  public BigDecimal getSalary() {
    return salary;
  }

  public void setSalary(BigDecimal salary) {
    this.salary = salary;
  }
}
```

Example 8.36 Department Class

```
// Department.java
package com.corej2eepatterns.business.hr;

import java.util.Set;

public interface Department {
  String getName();
  Set getEmployees();
}
```

Example 8.37 DepartmentImpl Class

```
// DepartmentImpl.java
package com.corej2eepatterns.business.impl;

```

```java
import com.corej2eepatterns.business.hr.Department;

import java.util.Collections;
import java.util.HashSet;
import java.util.Set;

/**
 * @author  Craig Russell
 */
public class DepartmentImpl implements Department {

  String name;
  Set employees = new HashSet();

  /** Creates a new instance of DepartmentImpl */
  DepartmentImpl(String name) {
    this.name = name;
  }

  public Set getEmployees() {
    return Collections.unmodifiableSet(employees);
  }

  boolean addEmployee(EmployeeImpl employee) {
    return employees.add(employee);
  }

  boolean removeEmployee(EmployeeImpl employee) {
    return employees.remove(employee);
  }

  public String getName() {
    return name;
  }
}
```

Example 8.38 Employee Class

```java
// Employee.java
package com.corej2eepatterns.business.hr;

import java.util.Set;

```

```
/**
 * @author  Craig Russell
 */
public interface Employee {
  long getId();
  String getFirstName();
  String getLastName();
  Department getDepartment();
  void setDepartment(Department department);
  Set getProjects();
  boolean addProject(Project project);
  boolean removeProject(Project project);
}
```

Example 8.39 EmployeeImpl Class

```
// EmployeeImpl.java

package com.corej2eepatterns.business.impl;

import com.corej2eepatterns.business.hr.Department;
import com.corej2eepatterns.business.hr.Project;
import com.corej2eepatterns.business.hr.Employee;

import java.util.Collections;
import java.util.HashSet;
import java.util.Set;

/**
 * @author  Craig Russell
 */
public class EmployeeImpl implements Employee {
  private long id;
  private String firstName;
  private String lastName;
  private DepartmentImpl department;
  private Set projects = new HashSet();

  /** Creates a new instance of EmployeeImpl */
  EmployeeImpl(long id, String firstName, String lastName) {
    this.id = id;
    this.firstName = firstName;
    this.lastName = lastName;
```

```
  }

  public boolean addProject(Project project) {
    boolean result = projects.add(project);
    if (result) {
      ((ProjectImpl) project).addEmployee(this);
    }
    return result;
  }

  public boolean removeProject(Project project) {
    boolean result = projects.remove(project);
    if (result) {
      ((ProjectImpl) project).removeEmployee(this);
    }
    return result;
  }

  public Department getDepartment() {
    return department;
  }

  public void setDepartment(Department department) {
    if (this.department != null) {
      this.department.removeEmployee(this);
    }
    this.department = (DepartmentImpl) department;
    this.department.addEmployee(this);
  }

  . . .

  public Set getProjects() {
    return Collections.unmodifiableSet(projects);
  }
}
```

Consequences

- ***Creating a custom persistence framework is a complex task***
  Implementing *Domain Store* and all the features required for transparent persistence is not a simple task due to the nature of the problem and due to complex interactions between several participants and this pattern framework. So, consider implementing your own transparent persistence framework after exhausting all other options.
- ***Multi-layer object tree loading and storing requires optimization techniques***
  Business Object hierarchy and interrelations can be quite complex. When persisting a *Business Object* and its dependents, you might only want to persist those portions of the hierarchy that has been modified. Similarly, when loading a *Business Object* hierarchy, you might want to provide different levels of lazy loading schemes to load the most used part of the hierarchy first and lazy load other parts when accessed.
- ***Improves understanding of persistence frameworks***
  If you are using a third party persistence framework, understanding *Domain Store* will greatly improve your understanding of that framework. You can compare and contrast how that framework implements transparent persistence with what has been described in *Domain Store*.
- ***A full-blown persistence framework might be overkill for a small object model***
  For simpler persistence needs where you have a simple object model and basic persistence needs, a persistence framework using *Domain Store* may be an overkill. In such cases, a basic framework using *Data Access Object* (462) might be adequately appropriate.
- ***Improves testability of your persistent object model***
  Domain Store it lets you separate the persistence logic from the persistent business objects. This greatly improves testability of your application as you can test your object model without actually enabling and performing persistence. Since persistence is transparent, you can always enable it once you finish testing your *Business Object* model and business logic.
- ***Separates business object model from persistence logic***
  Since *Domain Store* enables transparent persistence, your *Business Objects* do not need to contain any persistence related code. This frees the developer from dealing with the intricacies of implementing persistence logic for your persistent *Business Objects*.

Related Patterns

- ***Unit of Work [PEAA]***
  Maintains a list objects affected by a business transaction. *Unit of Work* closely relates to PersistenceManager.
- ***Query Object [PEAA]***
  An object that represents a database query. Relates to the Query role described in *Domain Store.*
- ***Data Mapper [PEAA]***
  A layer of Mappers that moves data between objects and database. Relates to StateManager.
- ***Table Data Gateway [PEAA]***
  An object that acts as gateway to a database table. Relates to StoreManager.
- ***Dependent Mapping [PEAA]***
  Has one class perform the database mapping for a child class. Relates to parent dependent object and PersistMap.
- ***Domain Model [PEAA]***
  An object model that has behavior and data. Relates to BusinessObject.
- ***Data Transfer Object [PEAA]***
  Same as *Transfer Object* (415).
- ***Identity Map [PEAA]***
  Ensures each object only gets loaded once. Relates to StateManager.
- ***Lazy Load [PEAA]***
  An object which contains partial data and knows how to get complete data. Relates to StateManager and StoreManager interaction for lazy loading.

Web Service Broker

Problem

You want to provide access to one or more services using XML and web protocols

J2EE applications expose coarse-grained business services using *Service Facade* (360). However, these services might be too fine grained to expose as a web service or may not be designed to be exposed outside of their application.

Another factor is that enterprise services run on various platforms and are implemented in a variety of languages. This heterogeneity often introduces incompatibilities, increasing the amount of complexity involved in seamlessly integrating these systems, such as with J2EE and .NET applications. This means that whether you have existing J2EE services, .NET services, or legacy services, you rarely wish to expose each one as a web service. Even with coarse-grained J2EE services, businesses typically want to expose only a limited set of the J2EE service methods for web service access. Additionally, systems often have a requirement to coordinate and aggregate several existing services.

Note: W3C provides this definition of a web service:

- A web service is a software system identified by a URI [RFC 2396], whose public interfaces and bindings are defined and described using XML. Its definition can be discovered by other software systems. These systems may then interact with the web service in a manner prescribed by its definition, using XML based messages conveyed by Internet protocols.
- A collection of EndPoints.
- An EndPoint is an association between a binding and a network address, specified by a URL, used to communicate with an instance of a service. A port indicates a specific location for accessing a service using a specific protocol and data format.

Forces

- You want to reuse and expose existing services to clients.
- You want to monitor and potentially limit the usage of exposed services, based on your business requirements and system resource usage.

- Your services must be exposed using open standards to enable integration of heterogeneous applications.
- You want to bridge the gap between business requirements and existing service capabilities

Solution

Use a Web Service Broker to expose and broker one or more services using XML and web protocols.

A *Web Service Broker* is a coarse-grained service exposed as a web service. It coordinates interactions among one or more services, aggregates responses and may demarcate and compensate transactions. A *Web Service Broker* is exposed either using an RPC (remote procedure call)-style interface such as WSDL, or a messaging interface. For RPC style interface, you can use a J2EE 1.4 session bean web service endpoint or a JAX-RPC implementation object as a web service endpoint. Both of these are exposed using WSDL. Figure 8.23 shows the diagram for*Web Service Broker.*

Structure

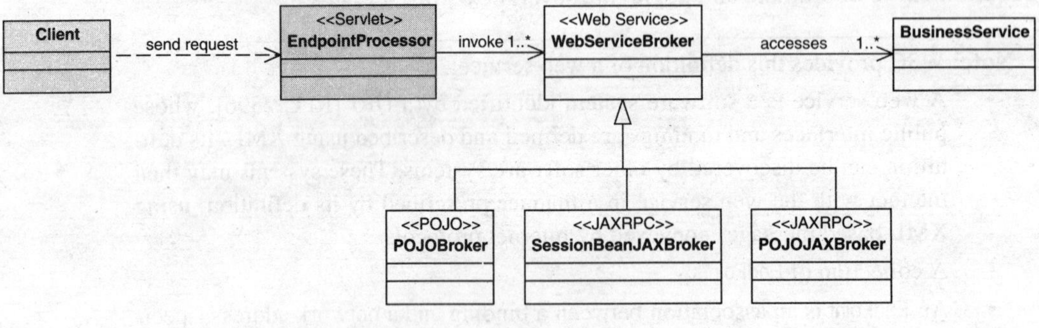

Figure 8.23 *Web Service Broker* Class Diagram

Participants and Responsibilities

The participants for Figure 8.23 are shown in this section.

Client

The Client can be anything that is capable of making a web service request.

EndpointProcessor

The EndpointProcessor is a servlet. It is the initial point of entry into the web service, and is responsible for accepting and processing a request. The request is typically based on an HTTP request, such as a SOAP request. Typically, the EndpointProcess is built-in to the runtime system, such as when using JAX-RPC. You can also build a custom EndpointProcessor.

WebServiceBroker

The WebServiceBroker is a web service that serves as a broker to one or more services. Those services can be J2EE services, such as *Session Façade* (341) and *Application Services* (357), or legacy EIS systems. The WebServiceBroker can be realized in three ways.

POJOBroker

A POJOBroker is a WebServiceBroker implemented as a POJO.

SessionBeanJAXBroker

The SessionBeanJAXBroker is a JAX-RPC based, EJB 2.1 Session Bean declared as a web service endpoint. It is implemented as a stateless session bean, and described using WSDL. A SessionBeanJAXBroker component needs to run inside an EJB 2.1 compliant EJB container.

POJOJAXBroker

The POJOJAXBroker, like the SessionBeanJAXBroker, it is based on JAX-RPC, but is not a session bean. It is a POJO and doesn't need to run in an EJB container – it can run in a web container. The POJOJAXBroker is written much like an RMI component and must use the JAX-RPC runtime to operate.

BusinessService

The BusinessService can be a J2EE *Session Façade*, an *Application Service* (357), or a *POJO Façade* to EIS.

Figure 8.24 shows the interaction diagram for the Web Service Broker. It begins with the client sending a request to the EndpointProcessor which extracts the request and invokes the WebServiceBroker which then invokes one or more BusinessServices.

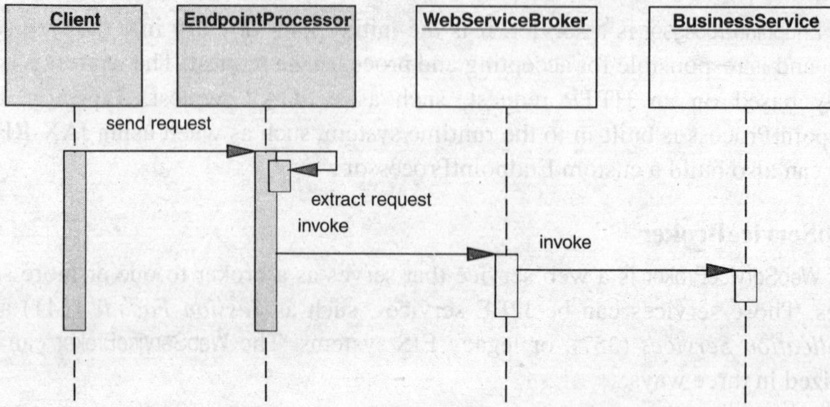

Figure 8.24 Web Service Broker Interaction Diagram

Strategies

Custom XML Messaging Strategy

The **Custom XML Messaging Strategy**, is based on sending messages to the *Web Service Broker*. The sequence diagram for the *Custom XML Messaging* strategy is shown in Figure 8.25. The object referred to as XMLDoc can be an XML document sent over HTTP or an XML document packaged in a SOAP message.

The Figure 8.25 interaction shows the Client sending the Request to the CustomProcessor servlet. After the CustomProcessor receives the Request, it extracts the XMLDoc, processes it and invokes the WebServiceBroker.

Java Binder Strategy

The *Java Binder Strategy* uses a Java binding technology, such as JAX-B, to process and generate *Transfer Objects (*415*)* from the XMLDoc. Using JAX-B is simple, but requires up front work. First the XML schema or DTD is defined, and the Java binder tool generates the necessary transfer object classes. The Java Binder runtime processes the XMLDoc and populates the transfer objects at runtime.

There are two ways to implement this strategy. The first is to send an XMLDoc to the CustomProcessor and have the CustomProcessor invoke the Java Binder mechanism. The second is to have a JAX-RPC based WebServiceBroker receive the XML document as a javax.xml.transform.Source data type, extract the XML document and send it to the Java Binder for processing.

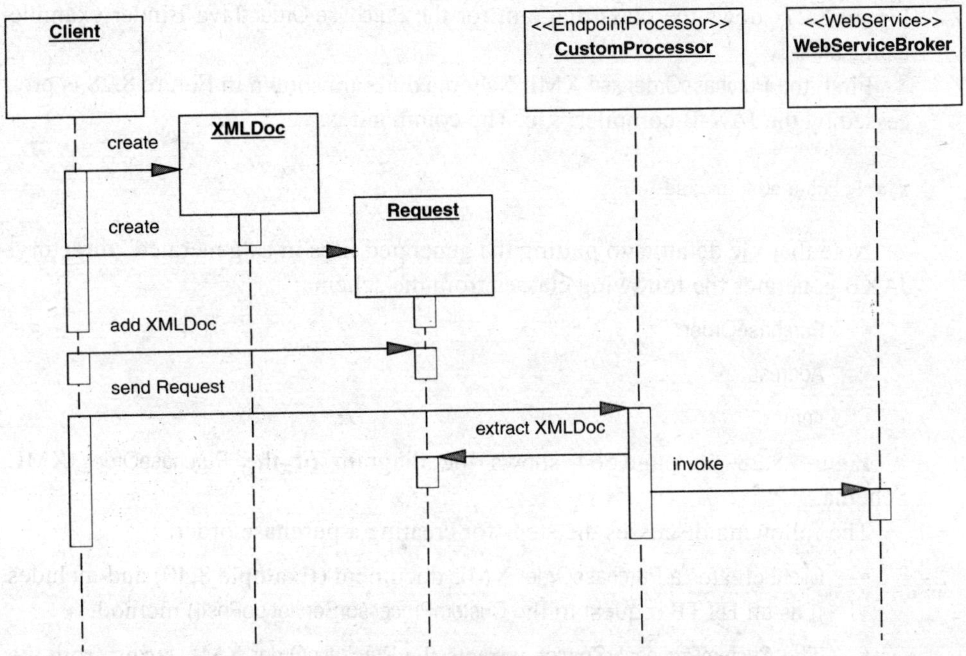

Figure 8.25 Custom Messaging Strategy Sequence Diagram

Figure 8.26 shows the class diagram for the Java Binder Strategy using the CustomProcessor.

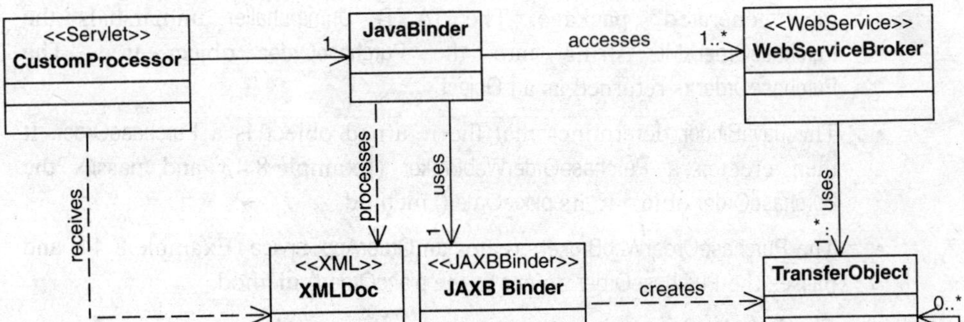

Figure 8.26 Java Binder Strategy Class Diagram

Java Binder Strategy Example

Figure 8.27 shows the class diagram for the Purchase Order Java Binder example using JAX-B.

First, the PurchaseOrder.xsd XML Schema diagram shown in Figure 8.28 is processed by the JAX-B compiler; **xjc**. The command is:

```
xjc PurchaseOrder.xsd
```

Note that **xjc** defaults to putting the generated files in a "generated" directory. JAXB generates the following classes from the schema:

- PurchaseOrder
- Address
- Item

Figure 8.28 on page 564 shows the diagram of the PurchaseOrder XML Schema.

The following discusses the steps for creating a purchase order:

- Client creates a PurchaseOrder XML document (Example 8.40) and includes it as an HTTP request to the CustomProcessorServlet doPost() method.
- The CustomProcessorServlet extracts the PurchaseOrder XML string from the HTTPRequest and sends it to JavaBinder (Example 8.42). The CustomProcessorServlet then calls its routeDocument() method, passing in the PurchaseOrder XML string.
- JavaBinder creates a JAXBContext, and tells it that the generated files are in the "generated" package. The JAXB Unmarshaller unmarshals the PurchaseOrderXML string into the PurchaseOrder object tree. The PurchaseOrder is returned as an Object.
- The JavaBinder determines that the returned object is a PurchaseOrder. It then creates a PurchaseOrderWebBroker (Example 8.43 and passes the PurchaseOrder object to its placeOrder() method.
- The PurchaseOrderWebBroker creates an OrderAppService (Example 8.44) and passes the PurchaseOrder object to the placeOrder() method.
- The OrderAppService does the appropriate logic and extracts the necessary data from the PurchaseObject tree.

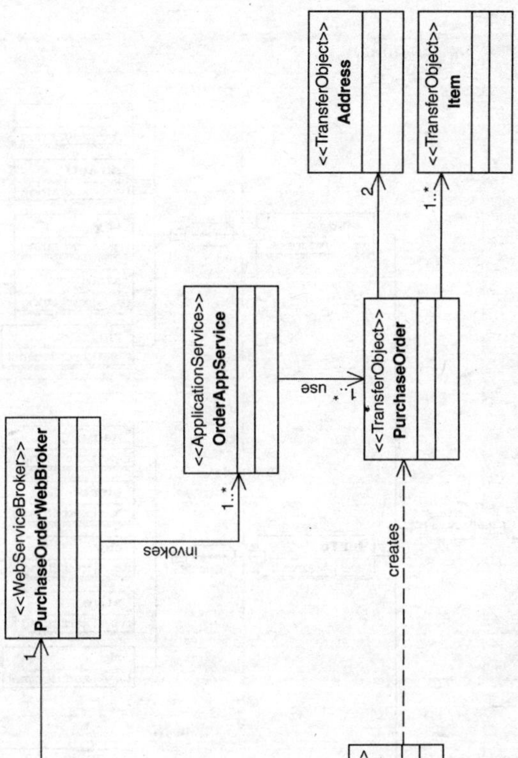

Figure 8.27 *Java Binding* Strategy Class Diagram for Purchase Order Example

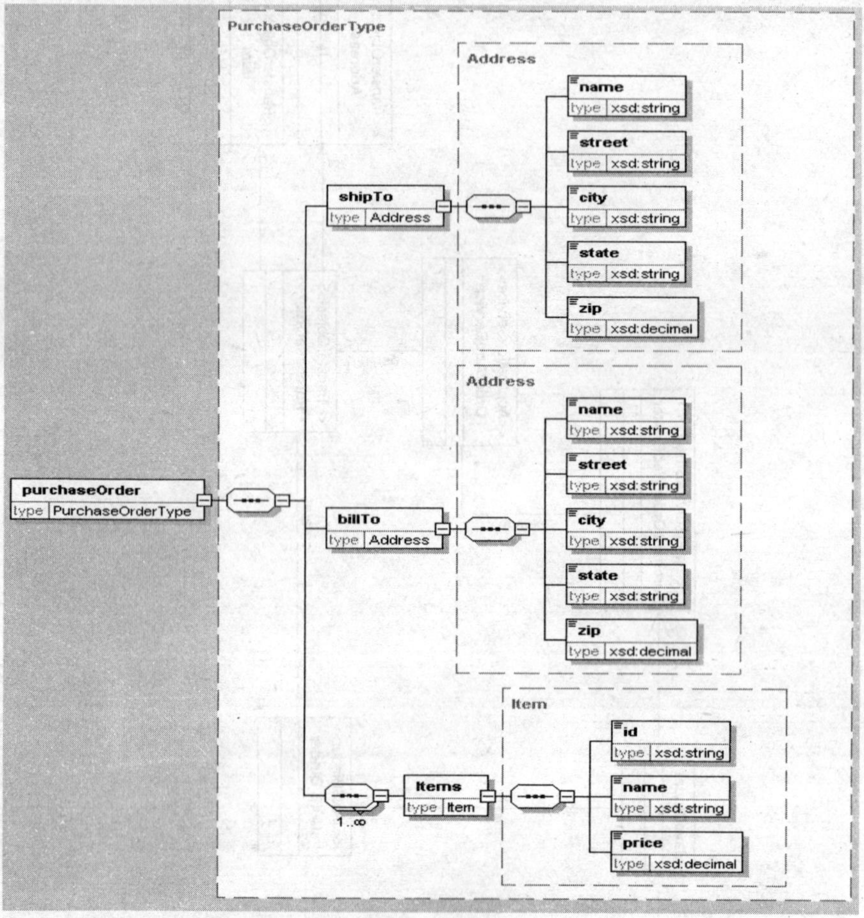

Figure 8.28 PurchaseOrder XML Schema Diagram

Example 8.40 through Example 8.44 show the XML file and classes for this example.

Example 8.40 PurchaseOrder XML File

```
<?xml version="1.0" encoding="UTF-8"?>

<purchaseOrder orderDate="2003-01-15"
xmlns:xsi="http://www.w3.org/2001/XMLSchema-instance"
xsi:noNamespaceSchemaLocation="po2.xsd">
   <shipTo>
```

```
      <name>Jo Miller</name>
      <street>Grand View Drive</street>
      <city>Bethesda</city>
      <state>MD</state>
      <zip>20816</zip>
    </shipTo>
    <billTo>
      <name>Jane Miller</name>
      <street>Grand View Drive</street>
      <city>Bethesda</city>
      <state>MD</state>
      <zip>20816</zip>
    </billTo>
    <Items>
      <id>101</id>
      <name>Core J2EE Patterns</name>
      <price>59.99</price>
    </Items>
    <Items>
      <id>102</id>
      <name>Enterprise Patterns</name>
      <price>59.99</price>
    </Items>
    <Items>
      <id>103</id>
      <name>WebService Patterns</name>
      <price>59.99</price>
    </Items>
</purchaseOrder>
```

Example 8.41 CustomProcessorServlet Class

```
import javax.servlet.RequestDispatcher;
import javax.servlet.ServletException;
import javax.servlet.http.HttpServlet;
import javax.servlet.http.HttpServletRequest;
import javax.servlet.http.HttpServletResponse;

public class CustomProcessorServlet extends HttpServlet {
  public String getServletInfo() {
    return "Servlet description";
  }

```

```
    protected void dispatch(HttpServletRequest request,
        HttpServletResponse response, String page)
        throws javax.servlet.ServletException,
        java.io.IOException {

      RequestDispatcher dispatcher =
          getServletContext().getRequestDispatcher(page);
      dispatcher.forward(request, response);
    }

    public void init() throws ServletException {
    }

    protected void doGet(HttpServletRequest request,
        HttpServletResponse response)
        throws javax.servlet.ServletException,
        java.io.IOException {
    }

    protected void doPost(HttpServletRequest request,
        HttpServletResponse response)
        throws javax.servlet.ServletException,
        java.io.IOException {
      String xmlDocument =
          request.getParameter("PurchaseOrder");
      JavaBinder binder = new JavaBinder();
      binder.routeDocument(xmlDocument);
    }
}
```

Example 8.42 JavaBinder Class

```
import generated.Item;
import generated.PurchaseOrder;

import javax.xml.bind.JAXBContext;
import javax.xml.bind.JAXBException;
import javax.xml.bind.Unmarshaller;
import javax.xml.transform.stream.StreamSource;
import java.io.StringReader;
import java.util.Iterator;
import java.util.List;

```

```
public class JavaBinder {
  public JavaBinder() {
  }

  private Object parse(String xmlDocument) {
    Object o = null;
    try {
      JAXBContext jc =
          JAXBContext.newInstance("generated");
      Unmarshaller u = jc.createUnmarshaller();
      o = u.unmarshal(new StreamSource(
          new StringReader(xmlDocument)));
    } catch (JAXBException e) {
    }
    return o;
  }

  public void routeDocument(String xmlDocument) {
    Object o = parse(xmlDocument);
    if (o instanceof PurchaseOrder) {
      PurchaseOrder po = (PurchaseOrder) o;
      printIt(po);
      PurchaseOrderWebBroker broker =
          new PurchaseOrderWebBroker();
      broker.placeOrder(po);
    }
  }

  private void printIt(PurchaseOrder po) {
    System.out.println(po.getBillTo());
    System.out.println(po.getShipTo());
    System.out.println(po.getOrderDate());
    List items = po.getItems();
    Iterator i = items.iterator();
    while (i.hasNext()) {
      Item item = (Item) i.next();
      System.out.println("Id : " + item.getId() +
          " Name : " + item.getName() +
          " Price : " + item.getPrice());
    }
  }
}
```

Example 8.43 PurchaseOrderWebBroker Class

```
import generated.PurchaseOrder;

public class PurchaseOrderWebBroker {
  public void placeOrder(PurchaseOrder po) {
    // Do security checks here, if necessary
    OrderAppService as = new OrderAppService();
    as.placeOrder(po);
  }
}
```

Example 8.44 OrderAppService Class

```
import generated.Address;
import generated.PurchaseOrder;

import java.util.List;

public class OrderAppService {
  public OrderAppService() {
  }

  public void placeOrder(PurchaseOrder purchaseOrder) {
    Address shipTo = purchaseOrder.getShipTo();
    Address billTo = purchaseOrder.getBillTo();
    List items = purchaseOrder.getItems();

    // Update data store
  }
}
```

JAX-RPC Strategy

In the JAX-RPC Strategy, the JAX-RPC mechanisms are used for communication. The WebServiceBroker is implemented as an EJB 2.1 stateless session bean, which is exposed as a web service endpoint. Note the two constraints imposed on the web service endpoint session bean.

- The web service session bean has a Remote and Implementation class.
- The web service session bean must be stateless.

Figure 8.29 shows the class diagram for this strategy. The EndpointProcessor is a JAX-RPC Endpoint-based servlet. It processes the request and forwards it to the WebServiceBroker. Note that this is built into the JAX-RPC runtime and is transparent to the developer. Also shown in the diagram is that the WebServiceBroker is described by WebServiceBrokerWSDL. WebServiceBrokerWSDL is not an object, but rather an XML-based WSDL definition of the WebServiceBroker interface.

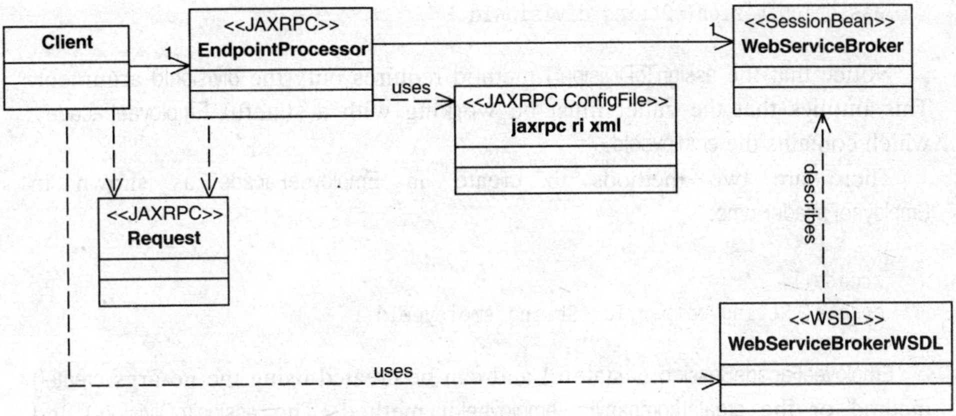

Figure 8.29 JAX-RPC Strategy Class Diagram

JAX-RPC Style Strategy Example

Figure 8.30 shows the class diagram for the classes in the **JAX-RPC Style Strategy** example. It shows the CompanyWebBrokerService, which is an EJB 2.1 stateless session bean declared as a web service endpoint. The CompanyWebBrokerService invokes the CompanyFacadeSession and the EmployeeFacadeSession; both are *Session Façades* (341).

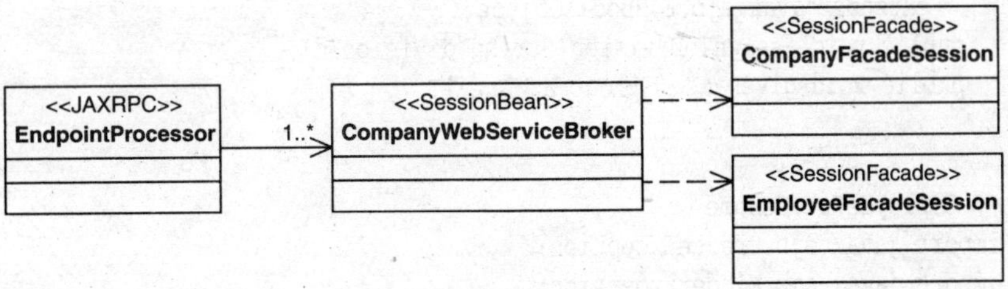

Figure 8.30 JAX-RPC Style Strategy Example

Code Example

The following code excerpt shows the code for EmployeeFacade, EmployeeFacadeHome and EmployeeFacadeSession which make up the EmployeeFacade component.

There are two business methods shown in EmployeeFacade and EmployeeFacadeSession:

```
addEmployee( String employeeId, String lastName, String firstName )
assignToDivision( String divisionId )
```

Notice that the assignToDivision() method requires only the divisionId argument. This implies that the caller must be working with a stateful EmployeeFacade, which contains the employeeId.

There are two methods to create an EmployeeFacade as shown in EmployeeFacadeHome:

```
create()
create( String companyId, String employeeId )
```

EmployeeFacadeSession is stateful and can be created using the no-args create() method or the create(companyId, employeeId) method. The assignToDivision() and giveRaise() methods subsequently make calls to the business object or DAO to persist the data.

Example 8.45 EmployeeFacade, EmployeeFacadeHome, EmployeeFacadeSession code example

```
// EmployeeFacade
import java.rmi.RemoteException;

public interface EmployeeFacade
      extends javax.ejb.EJBLocalObject {
   public void assignToDivision(String divisionId);
   public void giveRaise( float amount );
}
```

```
// EmployeeFacadeHome
import javax.ejb.CreateException;
import javax.ejb.FinderException;

public interface EmployeeFacadeHome
      extends javax.ejb.EJBLocalHome{
   public EmployeeFacade create( )
        throws CreateException;
   public EmployeeFacade create(
        String companyId, String employeeId )
```

```
        throws CreateException;
}
```

```
// EmployeeFacadeSession
import javax.ejb.SessionContext;
import javax.ejb.EJBException;
import javax.ejb.CreateException;
import javax.ejb.FinderException;

public class EmployeeFacadeSession
    implements javax.ejb.SessionBean {
  String companyId;
  String employeeId;

  public void assignToDivision(String divisionId) {
    // Call to business object or DAO to assign
    // employee to Division
  }
  public void giveRaise( float amount ) {
    // Call to business object or DAO to add
    // the new employee
  }
  public void setSessionContext(SessionContext sessionContext)
      throws EJBException {   }

  public void ejbRemove() throws EJBException {   }
  public void ejbActivate() throws EJBException {    }
  public void ejbPassivate() throws EJBException {    }
  public void ejbCreate( ) throws CreateException {    }
  public void ejbCreate( String companyId, String employeeId )
      throws CreateException {
    this.companyId = companyId;
    this.employeeId = employeeId;
  }
}
```

The following code excerpt shows the code for CompanyFacade, CompanyFacadeHome, and CompanyFacadeSession, which make up the CompanyFacade component. CompanyFacade and CompanyFacadeSession have three business methods:

```
createCompany( String companyId )
    addDivision( String divisionId, String divisionName )
    addEmployee( String employeeId, String lastName, String firstName)
```

The CompanyFacadeHome has two create methods:

```
create()
create( String companyId )
```

Example 8.46 CompanyFacade, CompanyFacadeHome, CompanyFacadeSession

```
//CompanyFacade
import java.rmi.RemoteException;

public interface CompanyFacade
     extends javax.ejb.EJBLocalObject {
  public void createCompany(
       String companyId, String companyName );
  public void addDivision(
     String divisionId, String divisionName );
  public void addEmployee(String employeeId,
       String lastName, String firstName );
}
```

```
// CompanyFacadeHome
import javax.ejb.CreateException;

public interface CompanyFacadeHome
     extends javax.ejb.EJBLocalHome {
  public CompanyFacade create( )
       throws CreateException;
  public CompanyFacade create( String companyId )
       throws CreateException;
}
```

```
// CompanyFacadeSession
import javax.ejb.SessionContext;
import javax.ejb.EJBException;
import javax.ejb.CreateException;

public class CompanyFacadeSession
     implements javax.ejb.SessionBean {
```

```
    String companyId;

    public void createCompany( String id, String name ) {
      // Create and Persist Company
      // Keep companyId for stateful conversations
      this.companyId = id;
    }

    public void addDivision(
          String divisionId, String divisionName) {
      // Call to business object or DAO to add
      // Division to Company
    }

    public void addEmployee(String employeeId,
          String lastName, String firstName) {
      // Call to business object or DAO to assign
      // employee to Division
    }

    public void setSessionContext(SessionContext sessionContext)
      throws EJBException {
    }

    public void ejbRemove() throws EJBException {    }
    public void ejbActivate() throws EJBException {    }
    public void ejbPassivate() throws EJBException {    }
    public void ejbCreate() throws CreateException {    }
    public void ejbCreate( String companyId )
          throws CreateException {
      // Lookup Company business object
      this.companyId = companyId;
    }
}
```

The following code excerpt shows the CompanyFacadeService and CompanyFacade code, which make up the WebServiceFacade component. Since the CompanyFacadeService is stateless, all the relevant information related to the operation must be passed into the method. There are four methods:

```
createCompany( String companyId, String companyName )
```

```
    addCompanyDivision( String companyId, String divisionId, String
        divisionName )
addEmployee( String companyId, String employeeId,
String lastName, String firstName )
assignEmployeeToDivision( String companyId, String employeeId, String
    divisionId )
```

Notice that each method passes in all the data required to perform the transaction. Table 8-1describes the CompanyWebServiceBroker methods and the subsequent SessionFacade methods called.

Table 8-1 CompanyWebServiceBroker, CompanyFacadeSession, **and** EmployeeFacadeSession **methods**

CompanyWebServiceBroker Method	*SessionFacade Method Called*
createCompany()	CompanyFacadeSession.createCompany()
addCompanyDivision()	CompanyFacadeSession.addDivison()
addEmployee()	CompanyFacadeSession.addEmployee()
assignEmployeeToDivision()	EmployeeFacadeSession.assignToDivision()

Example 8.47 CompanyWebService and CompanyWebServiceBroker

```
import java.rmi.RemoteException;

public interface CompanyWebService extends javax.ejb.EJBObject {
  public void createCompany(
        String companyId, String companyName )
        throws RemoteException;

  public void addCompanyDivision(String companyId,
        String divisionId, String divisionName )
        throws RemoteException;

  public void addEmployee(String companyId, String employeeId,
        String lastName, String firstName )
        throws RemoteException;

  public void assignEmployeeToDivision(String companyId,
        String divisionId, String employeeId )
            throws RemoteException;
```

```
}
```

```
// CompanyWebServiceBroker
import javax.ejb.SessionContext;
import javax.ejb.EJBException;
import javax.ejb.CreateException;

public class CompanyWebServiceBroker
    implements javax.ejb.SessionBean {
  public void setSessionContext(SessionContext sessionContext)
      throws EJBException {   }

  public void ejbRemove() throws EJBException {   }
  public void ejbActivate() throws EJBException {   }
  public void ejbPassivate() throws EJBException {   }
  public void ejbCreate() throws CreateException {   }

  private CompanyFacadeHome getCompanyHome()
      throws ServiceLocatorException {
    CompanyFacadeHome home = (CompanyFacadeHome)
        ServiceLocator.getInstance().getLocalHome(
            "CompanyFacade");
    return home;
  }

  public void createCompany(
      String companyId, String companyName ) {
    try {
      CompanyFacadeHome home = getCompanyHome();
      CompanyFacade cf = home.create();
      cf.createCompany( companyId, companyName );
    } catch (CreateException e) {
    } catch (ServiceLocatorException e) {
    }
  }

  public void addCompanyDivision(String companyId,
      String divisionId, String divisionName ) {
    try {
      CompanyFacadeHome home = getCompanyHome();
      CompanyFacade cf = home.create( companyId );
      cf.addDivision( divisionId, divisionName );
    } catch (ServiceLocatorException e) {
```

```
      } catch (CreateException e) {
      }
   }

   public void addEmployee(String companyId, String employeeId,
         String lastName, String firstName ) {
      try {
         CompanyFacadeHome home = getCompanyHome();
         CompanyFacade cf = home.create( companyId );
         cf.addEmployee(employeeId, lastName, firstName);
      } catch (ServiceLocatorException e) {
      } catch (CreateException e) {
      }
   }

   private EmployeeFacadeHome getEmployeeHome()
         throws ServiceLocatorException {
      EmployeeFacadeHome home = (EmployeeFacadeHome)
            ServiceLocator.getInstance().getLocalHome(
                  "EmployeeFacade");
      return home;
   }

   public void assignEmployeeToDivision(String companyId,
         String divisionId, String employeeId ) {
      try {
         EmployeeFacadeHome home = getEmployeeHome();
         EmployeeFacade ef =
               home.create( companyId, employeeId );
         ef.assignToDivision( divisionId );
      } catch (ServiceLocatorException e) {
      } catch (CreateException e) {
      }
   }
}
```

Example 8.48 shows the CompanyWebBroker.wsdl WSDL file. It is used by the EJB 2.1 container to describe the CompanyWebServiceBroker session bean.

Example 8.48 CompanyWebService.wsdl

```
<?xml version="1.0" encoding="UTF-8"?>
. . .

    <wsdl:message name="createCompanyRequest">
        <wsdl:part name="CompanyId" type="xsd:string"/>
        <wsdl:part name="CompanyName" type="xsd:string"/>
    </wsdl:message>
    <wsdl:message name="addEmployeeRequest">
        <wsdl:part name="CompanyId" type="xsd:string"/>
        <wsdl:part name="EmployeeId" type="xsd:string"/>
        <wsdl:part name="LastName" type="xsd:string"/>
        <wsdl:part name="FirstName" type="xsd:string"/>
    </wsdl:message>
    <wsdl:message name="addCompanyDivisionRequest">
        <wsdl:part name="CompanyId" type="xsd:string"/>
        <wsdl:part name="DivisionId" type="xsd:string"/>
        <wsdl:part name="DivisionName" type="xsd:string"/>
    </wsdl:message>
    <wsdl:message name="assignEmployeeToDivisionRequest">
          <wsdl:part name="CompanyId" type="xsd:string"/>
          <wsdl:part name="DivisionId" type="xsd:string"/>
          <wsdl:part name="EmployeeId" type="xsd:string"/>
    </wsdl:message>

    <wsdl:message name="addEmployeeResponse">
    </wsdl:message>

    <wsdl:message name="createCompanyResponse">
    </wsdl:message>

    <wsdl:message name="addCompanyDivisionResponse">
    </wsdl:message>

    <wsdl:message name="assignEmployeeToDivisionResponse">
    </wsdl:message>

    . . .

    </wsdl:portType>

    <wsdl:binding name="CompanyWebServiceSoapServiceBinding"
```

```
            type="impl:CompanyWebServiceBroker ">
        <wsdlsoap:binding style="rpc" transport=
                "http://schemas.xmlsoap.org/soap/http"/>
        <wsdl:operation name="createCompany">
            <wsdlsoap:operation soapAction=""/>
            <wsdl:input name="createCompanyRequest">
                <wsdlsoap:body use="encoded" encodingStyle=
                "http://schemas.xmlsoap.org/soap/encoding/"
                namespace="http://DefaultNamespace"/>
            </wsdl:input>
            <wsdl:output name="createCompanyResponse">
                <wsdlsoap:body use="encoded"
                   encodingStyle=
                     "http://schemas.xmlsoap.org/soap/encoding/"
                    namespace="http://DefaultNamespace"/>
            </wsdl:output>
        </wsdl:operation>

        <wsdl:operation name="addCompanyDivision">
            <wsdlsoap:operation soapAction=""/>
            <wsdl:input name="addCompanyDivisionRequest">
                <wsdlsoap:body use="encoded"
                    encodingStyle=
                      "http://schemas.xmlsoap.org/soap/encoding/"
                     namespace="http://DefaultNamespace"/>
            </wsdl:input>

        . . .

    <wsdl:service name=" CompanyWebService">
        <wsdl:port name=" CompanyWebServicePort "
                binding=
                  "impl: CompanyWebServiceBrokerSoapBinding">
            <wsdlsoap:address location=
                    "http://localhost:8080/CompanyWebService"/>
        </wsdl:port>
    </wsdl:service>

</wsdl:definitions>
```

Example 8.49 shows the client side for creating a company.

Example 8.49 JAX-RPC Web Service Client Code

```
Context ctx = new InitialContext();
CompanyWebService service = (CompanyWebService)
     ctx.lookup("java:comp/env/service/CompanyWebService");
CompanyWebServiceProvider provider =
     service.getCompanyWebServiceProviderPort();
provider.createCompany("1001", "Joes Company" );
```

Consequences

- ***Introduces a layer between client and service***
- ***Existing remote Session Façades (341) need be refactored to support local access***
- ***Network performance may be impacted due to web protocols***

Related Patterns

- ***Aggregator***
  http://www.enterpriseintegrationpatterns.com/Aggregator.html
- ***Application Service (357)***
  Application Service (357) components can be called from *Web Service Broker* components.
- ***Session Façade (341)***
  Session Façade (341) components can be called from *Web Service Broker* components.
- ***Mediator***
  Mediator is a hub for interaction like *Web Service Broker* [Frank Buschmann, et al.]
  http://www.vico.org/pages/PatronsDisseny/Pattern Broker/
- ***Message Router***
  http://www.enterpriseintegrationpatterns.com/MessageRouter.html

Epilogue

Topics in This Chapter

- Web Worker Micro-Architecture

Web Worker Micro-Architecture

This chapter discusses an advanced topic in our pattern work: **micro-architectures**. We define micro-architecture as a set of patterns used together to realize parts of a system or subsystem. We view a micro-architecture as a **building block** for piecing together well-known, cohesive portions of an overall architecture. A micro-architecture is used to solve a coarser-grained, higher-level problem that cannot be solved by a single pattern. Thus, a micro-architecture represents a higher level of abstraction than the individual patterns described in the J2EE Pattern Catalog. You can think of a micro-architecture as a prescriptive solution derived by linking a set of patterns.

Any architecture is dependent on, among other things, the external characteristics of each of the architectural sub-elements, and how these elements interact. Just as the overall architecture has a conceptual integrity, so will the individual micro-architectures.

Micro-architectures come in many forms. We've chosen to describe a **Web Worker** workflow integration micro-architecture. Web Worker is not about the patterns internal to a workflow processes, but rather how to integrate a J2EE system with a workflow system.

Workflow Mini-Primer

The Workflow Management Coalition (WfMC) definition of workflow is:

> "The automation of a business process, in whole or part, during which documents, information or tasks are passed from one participant to another for action, according to a set of procedural tasks."

Workflow systems are composed of workflow processes, which include activities, decision points, and sub-processes. Specifically, activities generate work items, which can be completed in two ways.

- In a **manual** workflow process, work items are offered to users in the appropriate roles. Users implicitly or explicitly accept (acquire) the work item and proceed to do the manual work.
- In an **automated** workflow process, work items are completed by systems, not people. Once the work item is complete, the user or system commits the work item to the workflow system.

Workflow systems are composed of various elements, which include:

- **Workflow definitions**
- **Workflow processes**
- **Activities**
- **Decision points**
- **Work-items**
- **Worklist**

Here is a simple example, of a workflow definition called **Bake-a-Cake**. Bake-a-Cake is composed of the following serial activities and a decision point. (Note that in this example each activity must complete before the next activity can begin.)

1. Start workflow process
2. Pour ingredients into a bowl – **Activity**
3. Mix ingredients to form a batter – **Activity**
4. Pour batter into a pan – **Activity**
5. Turn on oven – **Activity**
6. Bake cake in oven – **Activity**
7. Is cake done?- **Decision Point**, **True:** move to Activity 8, **False:** return to Activity 6
8. Take pan out of oven - **Activity**
9. Wait 10 minutes to allow cake to cool – **Activity**
10. Serve cake – **Activity**
11. End workflow process

The Bake-a-Cake workflow definition describes the workflow for baking a cake. It does not relate to the type of cake that is being baked. When the Bake-a-Cake workflow definition is executed, the running instance is called a workflow process. You might have three Bake-a-Cake workflow processes running at the same time, which represent:

- Baking a chocolate cake,
- Baking a pound cake, and
- Baking a cheese cake

Let's look at a more sophisticated example – hiring an employee.

The workflow definition (shown in Figure 9.1) is called "Hire Employee"

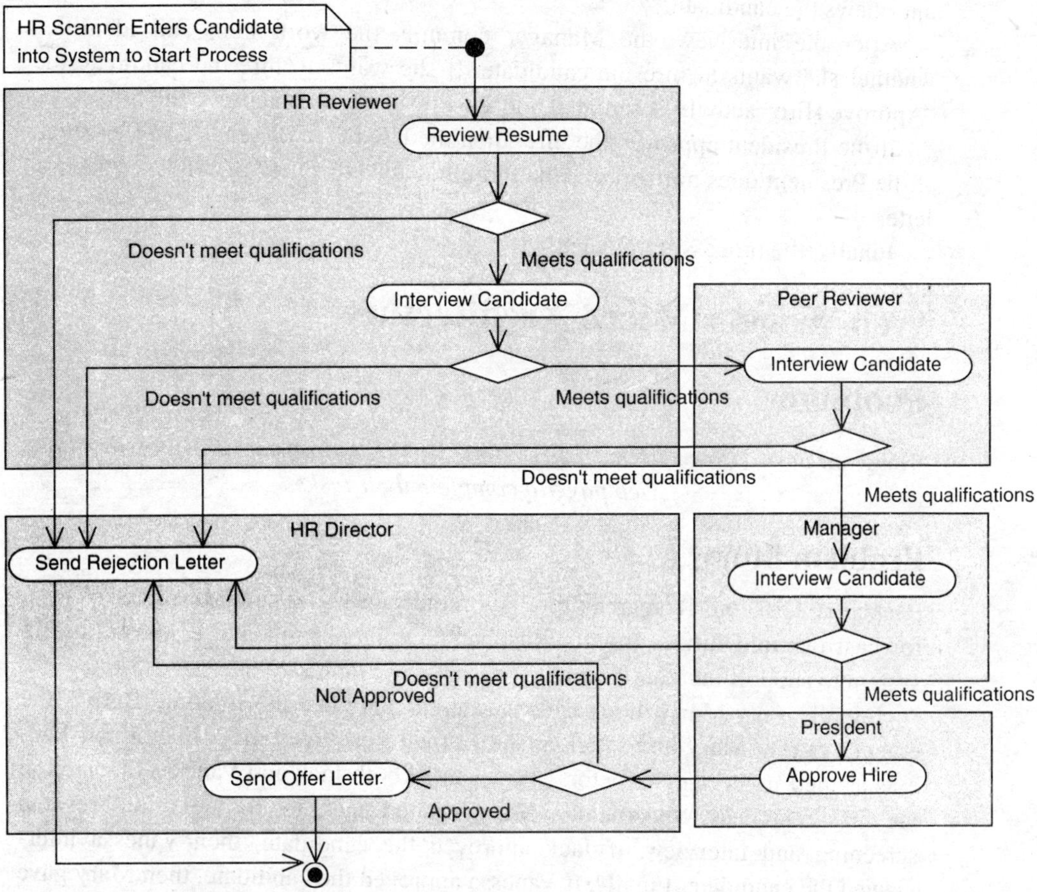

Figure 9.1 Hire Employee Workflow

The workflow process begins after the HR Screener enters the candidate into the systems. This initiates the "Review Resume" activity. An HR Reviewer reviews the resume and commits the work item identifying whether the candidate meets the qualifications.

If the candidate does not meet the qualifications, then the activity "Send Rejection Letter" starts and the process terminates. If the candidate meets the qualifications, then the "Interview Candidate" activity is initiated and a Peer Reviewer interviews the candidate.

After the interview, the Peer Reviewer commits the work item identifying whether the candidate meets the qualifications. If the candidate meets the qualifications, then the "Interview Candidate" activity is initiated and the Manager interviews the candidate.

After the interview, the Manager commits the work item and identifies whether she wants to hire the candidate. If she wants to hire the candidate the "Approve Hire" activity is initiated and the President must approve the hire.

If the President approves the hire, then the HR Director sends an offer letter. If the President does not approve the hire, then the HR Director sends a rejection letter.

Finally, the process terminates.

Web Worker Micro Architecture

Problem

You want a workflow system to direct users to the appropriate J2EE application web page to complete their tasks

Problem Story

Raspberry Offshore Resources Inc. is a rapidly growing small business. With a forecast of rapid future growth, Raspberry Offshore built a J2EE-based hiring system to support increased hiring.

Initially, only Mary, the president entered candidate information. But, as the company grew, Mary hired Jack as the Human Resource (HR) director and Vanessa as the Engineering director. Mary wanted both Jack and Vanessa involved in the hiring process. Specifically, Mary wanted Jack to do the initial resume screening and interview. If Jack approved the candidate, then Vanessa interviewed the candidate. Finally, if Vanessa approved the candidate, then Mary gave the final interview and hiring approval.

Mary wanted all the hiring information captured and automated using the hiring system. However, before this could happen, Joe, the company developer extraordinaire had to re-code the application since it was built assuming one person would enter all the information. Also, Mary wanted Vanessa and herself notified via email, with the following information:

- Time and date for the interview
- Resume in HTML
- URL to click on when the interview is complete

It wasn't too much work for Joe; he added some role checks and sent an email using the HiringAppService (*Application Service* (357)) object to Mary and

Vanessa when an interview was scheduled. Joe also had to modify some of the presentation code to extract the ID of the candidate so the JSP could be populated with the appropriate candidate information. Using popular J2EE refactoring techniques, Joe implemented the changes in only two days.

The next year, Raspberry Offshore Resources grew rapidly. Now, there were two new HR screeners and three new Engineering directors involved in the hiring process. Joe said it seemed that he was getting new hiring system requirements (who could enter what, and when) almost daily. Joe realized he had added a tremendous amount of process logic along with the business logic in the past year and the process logic had become quite complex.

Initially, the basic hiring process logic was easy:

1. If Jack approved the candidate, Vanessa interviewed the candidate.
2. If Vanessa approved the candidate, Mary interviewed the candidate.
3. If Mary approved candidate, then Jack sent an offer letter to the candidate.

However, now there are so many steps and branches as to who must participate in the interview process, the code has become unmanageable. Also, there used to only be one person per role, and now there are many.

Joe convinced Vanessa to invest in a workflow system to run the process logic. This would make Joe's life easier by putting the dynamic process logic in the workflow system and update it without touching the business logic in the hiring system.

Now Joe just had to figure out how to integrate the J2EE hiring system with the workflow system and achieve the same effect as before.

Joe familiarized himself with the interactions among user, web application, and workflow systems as shown in Figure 9.2. The steps include:

- Step #1 – **User 1** submits a web page to the web application.
- Step #2 – The **Web Application** translates the business event into a workflow command (Start Workflow) and executes it. This might include starting, pausing, or stopping a workflow process; or acquiring, releasing, or committing a work item.
- Step #3 – The **Workflow System** generates a work item.
- Steps #4 and #5 – A work-item is sent to all the users (worklists) in the appropriate role.
- Step #6 – **User 3** acquires the work item via the worklist.

- Step #7– The work item is removed from **User 2's** worklist.
- Step #8 – **User 3** is directed to a web page.
- Step #9 – **User 3** submits the web page after the work is complete.
- Step #10 – The work item is committed.

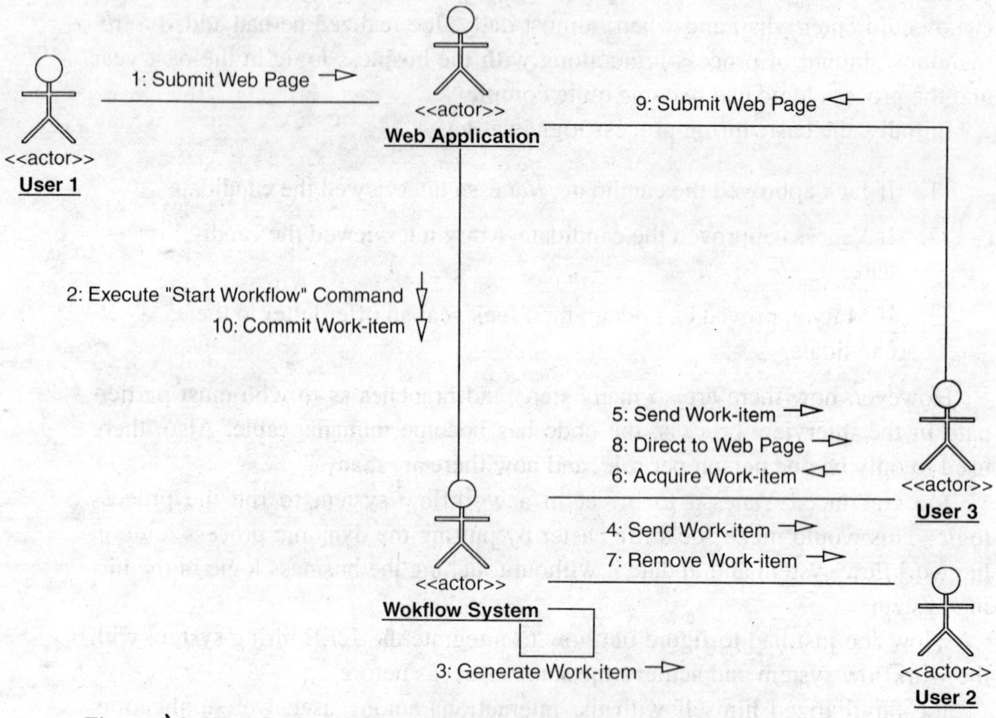

Figure 9.2 Workflow Interaction Example

In this example, there seems to be a bit of magic associated with the integration between the web application and the workflow system. Specifically:

- How does a web page submission translate into a workflow command?
- How does a workflow system direct users to the appropriate web page?
- How does a web page submission, in response to an acquired work item, get translated into a committed work item?

These are the problems *Wab Worker* addresses.

Forces

- You have business process logic that is identifiable and changing.
- You have business process logic that is sophisticated and can be executed as separate subsystem.
- You have business process work (a work item) that is user-centric.
- Your workflow definitions are represented by activities that occur in succession and/or in parallel.
- Your process logic needs to be coordinated with users.
- You want the user to acquire the work from the work list and commit the work via the web application.

Solution

Use *Web Worker* to integrate users, a web application, and a workflow system.

Web Worker focuses on two integration points: the point between the web application and workflow system, and the point between the workflow system and user. Since the workflow system is treated as a black box, integration is done between the web application and the workflow system using an inbound adapter (*Action Adapter*) and between the workflow system, user and web application using an outbound adapter (*Work Adapter*).

Note 1: The *Action Adapter* sits in the integration tier and is invoked from the business tier, not the presentation tier.

Note 2: The *Work Adapter* directs the user to the initial web page, not all the web pages to complete the task.

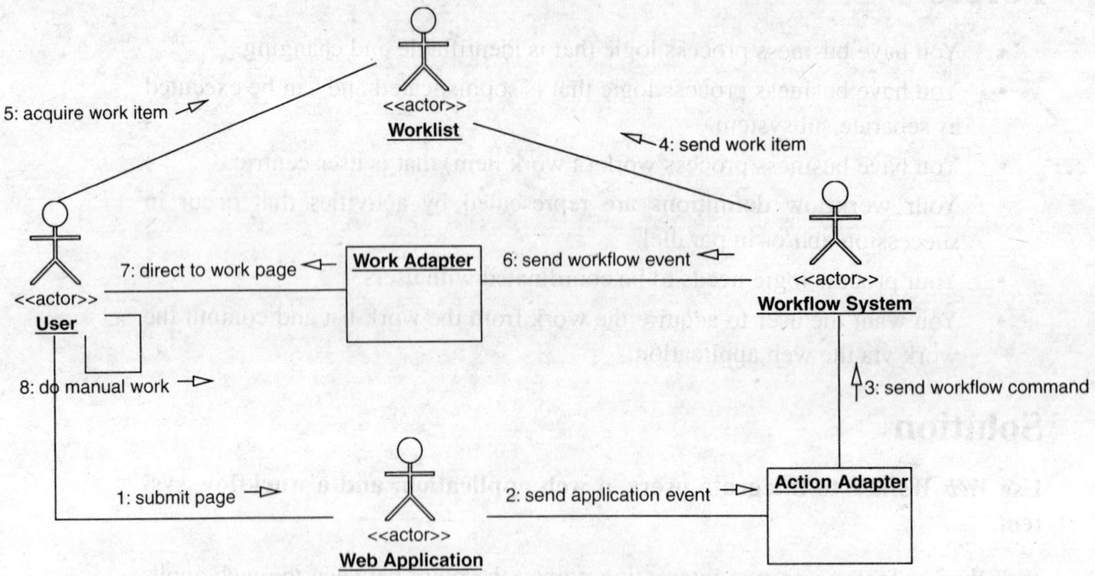

Figure 9.3 *Action Adapter* and *Work Adapter* Collaboration Diagram

Figure 9.3 shows the interactions among the systems when used with the *Action Adapter* and the *Work Adapter*. Specifically:

1. **User** submits the web page to **Web Application**
2. **Web Application** sends an application event to **Action Adapter**
3. **Action Adapter** sends a workflow command to **Workflow System**
4. **Workflow System** sends a work item to **Worklist**
5. **User** acquires the work item from **Worklist**
6. **Workflow System** sends a workflow event to **Work Adapter**
7. **Work Adapter** directs the user to the work page
8. **User** does manual work and submits the work page

After the user does the manual work and submits the work page, the process repeats. However, in this example the submitted page will eventually translate into the work item being committed.

Figure 9.4 shows the interactions applied to the Hire Employee workflow. It includes the following steps:

1. **HR Screener** adds a new candidate to the **Web Application**
2. **Web Application** sends a ***new candidate*** application event to the **Action Adapter**
3. **Action Adapter** translates the application event to a workflow command (Start Hire Employee process Command)
4. **Action Adapter** sends a ***start Hire Employee process*** command
5. **Workflow System** starts the Hire Employee workflow process
6. **Workflow System** sends a Review Candidate work item to **Worklist**
7. **HR Reviewer** acquires the work item
8. **Workflow System** sends a ***work item acquired*** event to the **Work Adapter**
9. **Work Adapter** translates the ***work item acquired*** event to the ***CandidateReviewPage***
10. **Work Adapter** directs the **HR Reviewer** to the ***CandidateReview-Page***
11. **HR Reviewer** interviews the candidate
12. **HR Reviewer** submits the ***CandidateReviewPage*** to the **Web Application**
13. **Web Application** sends a ***candidate reviewed*** event to the **Action Adapter**
14. **Action Adapter** translates application event to workflow command (Commit Review Candidate Work Item command)
15. **Action Adapter** sends a commit Review Candidate work item command to the **Workflow System**

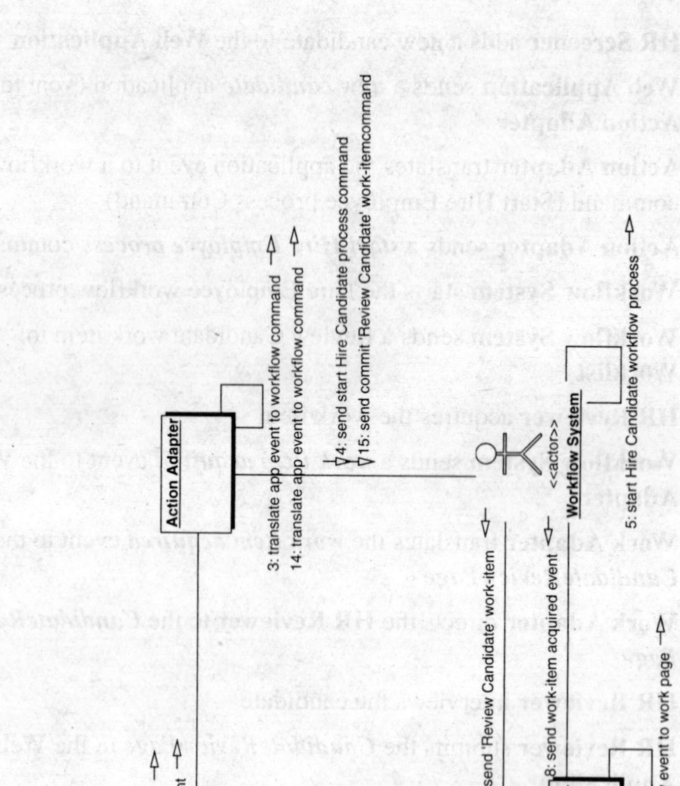

Figure 9.4 Hire Employee Workflow Interaction With Action Adapter, Work Adapter

Structure

Action Adapter

The *Action Adapter* component is composed of the following patterns and classes, as shown in Figure 9.5.

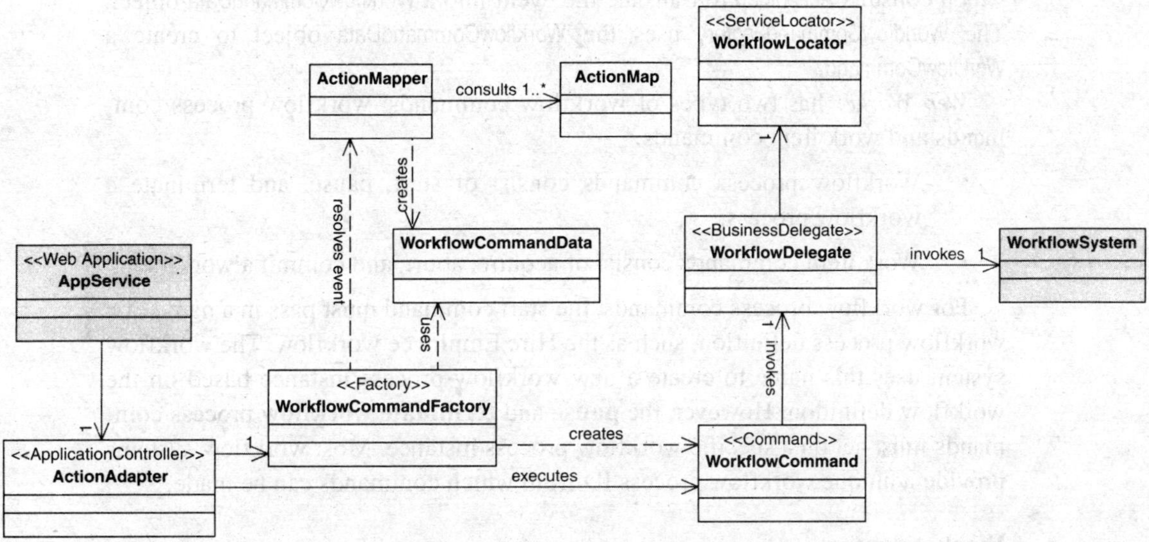

Figure 9.5 Action Adapter Class Diagram

Application Controller (205) Using Command Handler Strategy

- ActionAdapter
- ActionMapper
- ActionMap
- WorkflowCommandFactory
- WorkflowCommandData
- WorkflowCommand

Business Delegate

- WorkflowDelegate

Service Locator

- WorkflowLocator

The ActionAdapter has a business-like interface that corresponds to the AppService interface. For example, the CandidateAppService (AppService) might have an interviewApproved() method and the CandidateActionAdapter (ActionAdapter) would have a subsequent interviewApproved() method.

The ActionAdapter sends an application event to the WorkflowCommandFactory to retrieve the WorkflowCommand. The WorkflowCommandFactory uses the ActionMapper, which consults ActionMap to translate the event into a WorkflowCommandData object. The WorkflowCommandFactory uses the WorkflowCommandData object to create a WorkflowCommand.

Web Worker has two types of workflow commands: workflow process commands and work item commands.

- Workflow process commands consist of start, pause, and terminate a workflow process.
- Work item commands consist of acquire, abort, and commit a work-item.

For workflow process commands, the start command must pass in a name of a workflow process definition, such as the Hire Employee workflow. The workflow system uses this name to create a new workflow process instance based on the workflow definition. However, the **pause** and **terminate workflow** process commands must act on a specific workflow process instance. Most workflow systems provide a unique workflow process ID from which commands can be made.

Work Adapter

The *Work Adapter* component is composed of the following patterns and classes as shown in Figure 9.6.

Application Controller With Command Handler strategy

- WorkMapper
- WorkMap
- WorkPageFactory
- WorkPageRef

Service Activator

- WorkAdapter
- WorkDispatcher

The WorkAdapter receives notifications from the workflow system whenever a workflow event occurs. Note that some workflow system will asynchronously call a listener and some require that the listener poll the workflow system for events. The events specifically of interest to WorkAdapter are:

- Workflow Process Started
- Workflow Process Paused
- Workflow Process Terminated
- WorkItem Acquired
- WorkItem Aborted
- WorkItem Committed
- WorkItem TimedOut

If the workflow event is WorkItem Acquired, the WorkAdapter asks the WorkPageFactory to create a WorkPageRef. A WorkPageRef is an object that encapsulates the URL of the business web page that must be completed after the work item work is complete.

The WorkAdapter sends the work item information to the WorkMapper, which consults the WorkMap to determine the appropriate WorkPage URL. The WorkPage is a web page the user is directed to after the work is complete. This information about the web page can be given in the form of email or some other means. The WorkAdapter then uses the WorkDispatcher to notify the user of the WorkPage URL.

Figure 9.6 shows two types of typical WorkDispatchers: an EmailDispatcher and a WorkListDispatcher. The EmailDispatcher sends the user the WorkPage URL via email and the WorkListDispatcher sends the WorkPage URL to the user's WorkList.

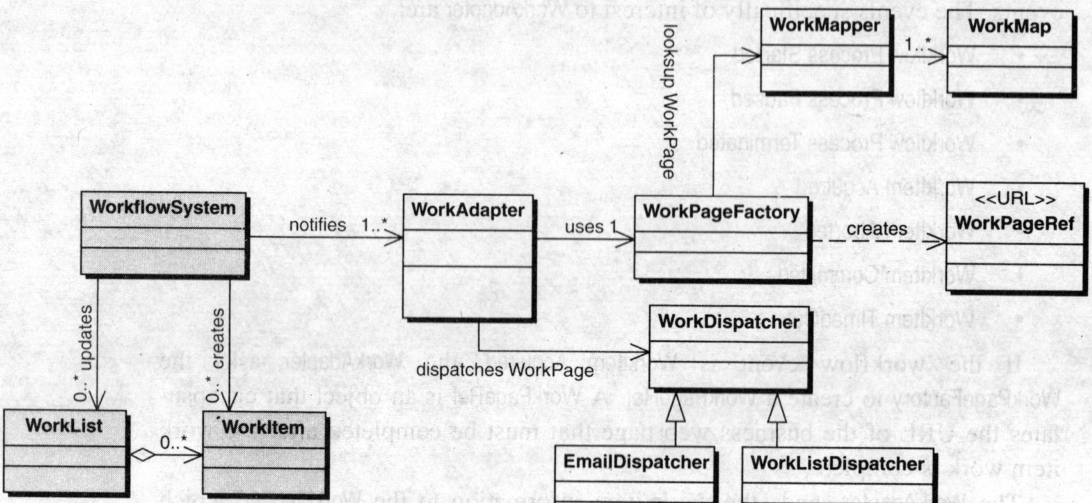

Figure 9.6 *Work Adapter* Class Diagram

Participants and Responsibilities

Action Adapter

Figure 9.7 shows the *Action Adapter* interaction. The interaction diagrams cover the first three events of the Hire Employee workflow:

- Create Candidate
- Review Candidate
- Interview Candidate

For Create Candidate, the steps are:

1. The CandidateAppService calls the HireEmployeeActionAdapter candidateCreated() method.
2. The HireEmployeeActionAdapter sends a CANDIDATE_CREATED business event to the WorkflowCommandFactory to get a WorkflowCommand.
3. The WorkflowCommandFactory asks the ActionMapper for the CommandData object.
4. The ActionMapper consults the HireEmployeeActionMap to translate the business event to a CommandType.

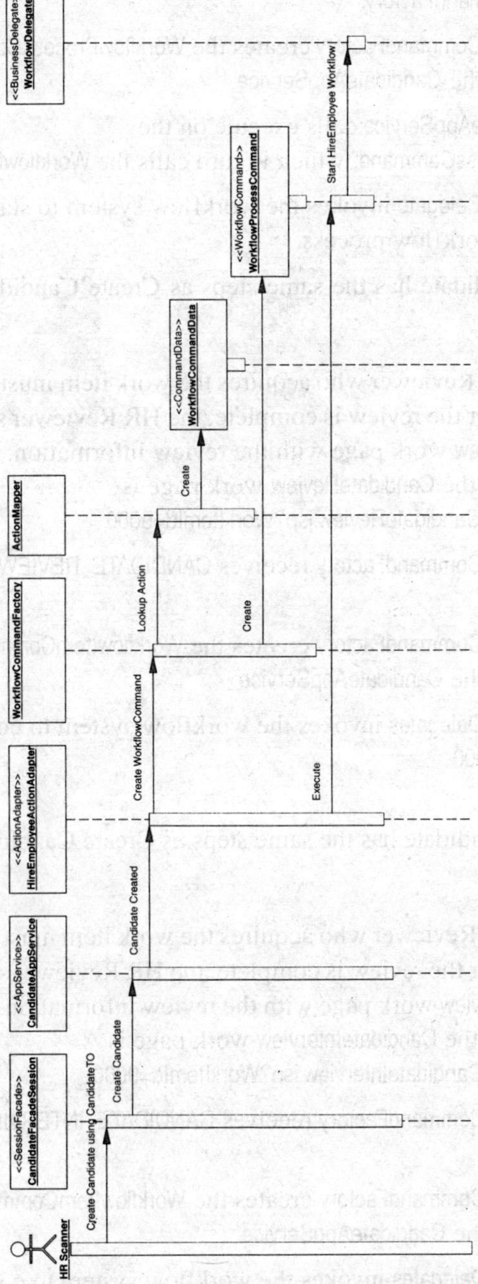

Figure 9.7 ***Action Adapter*** **Sequence for Candidate Interactions**

5. The ActionMapper returns a StartWorkflow command to the WorkflowCommandFactory.
6. The WorkflowCommandFactory creates the WorkflowProcessCommand and returns it to the CandidateAppService.
7. The CandidateAppService calls execute on the WorkflowProcessCommand, which in turn calls the WorkflowDelegate.
8. The WorkflowDelegate invokes the workflow system to start the Hire Employee workflow process.

Reviewing a candidate has the same steps as Create Candidate, with the following exceptions:

1. The first HR Reviewer who acquires the work item must review the resume. After the review is complete, the HR Reviewer submits the CandidateReview work page with the review information. Note that the URL for the CandidateReview work page is HireEmployee/CandidateReview.jsp?WorkItemId=8000
2. The WorkflowCommandFactory receives CANDIDATE_REVIEWED business event
3. The WorkflowCommandFactory creates the WorkflowItemCommand and returns it to the CandidateAppService
4. The WorkflowDelegates invokes the workflow system to commit the WorkItemId=8000

Interviewing a candidate has the same steps as Create Candidate, with the following exceptions:

1. The first HR Reviewer who acquires the work item must review the resume. After the review is complete, the HR Reviewer submits the CandidateInterview work page with the review information. Note, that the URL for the CandidateInterview work page is HireEmployee/CandidateInterview.jsp?WorkItemId=9000
2. The WorkflowCommandFactory receives CANDIDATE_INTERVIEWED business event
3. The WorkflowCommandFactory creates the WorkflowItemCommand and returns it to the CandidateAppService
4. The WorkflowDelegates invokes the workflow system to commit the WorkItemId=9000

The following lists show the CandidateAppService and CandidateAppService and HireEmployeeAA methods called for the Create, Review, and Interview Candidate interactions. Also shown are the arguments and values for each HireEmployeeAA method.

Interactions and Method Call Information

Create Candidate

- CandidateAppService method – createCandidate()
- HireEmployeeAA method – candidateCreated()
- HireEmployeeAA arguments – userId, workflowProcessId, workItemId
- HireEmployeeAA values – User-101,null, null

Review Candidate

- CandidateAppService method – submitReview()
- HireEmployeeAA method – candidateReviewed()
- HireEmployeeAA arguments – userId, workflowProcessId, workItemId
- HireEmployeeAA values – User-102, null, 8000

Interview Candidate

- CandidateAppService method – submitInterview()
- HireEmployeeAA method – candidateInterviewed()
- HireEmployeeAA arguments – – userId, workflowProcessId, workItemId
- HireEmployeeAA values – User-103, null, 9000

The list shows for each interaction, the business event passed to the ActionMapper.getCommandData() method, the command string returned from the HireEmployeeActionMap.xml file and the CommandData type returned.

Business Event, Command String, and Type Returned

Create Candidate

- Business event passed in to ActionMapper – CANDIDATE_CREATED
- Command String returned by **HireEmployeeActionMap** – StartWorkflow
- **CommandData** type returned by **ActionMapper** – WorkflowProcessData

Review Candidate

- Business event passed in to ActionMapper – CANDIDATE_REVIEWED
- Command String returned by **HireEmployeeActionMap** – CommitWorkItem
- **CommandData** type returned by **ActionMapper** – WorkItemData

Interview Candidate

- Business event passed in to ActionMapper – CANDIDATE_INTERVIEWED
- Command String returned by **HireEmployeeActionMap** – CommitWorkItem
- **CommandData** type returned by **ActionMapper** – WorkItemData

The next set of lists shows, for each interaction, the WorkflowCommand returned from the WorkflowCommandFactory, and the WorkflowDelegate method called when the WorkflowCommand.execute() method is called. It also shows the arguments and values passed to the WorkflowDelegate method.

WorkflowCommand and WorkflowDelegate Actions

Create Candidate

- WorkflowCommand returned from WorkflowCommandFactory–WorkflowProcessCommand
- WorkflowDelegate method called – start()
- Argument – WorkflowName
- Value – HireEmployee

Review Candidate

- WorkflowCommand returned from WorkflowCommandFactory – WorkItemCommand
- WorkflowDelegate method called – commitWorkItem()
- Argument – WorkItemId
- Value – 8000

Interview Candidate

- WorkflowCommand returned from WorkflowCommandFactory – WorkItemCommand
- WorkflowDelegate method called – commitWorkItem()
- Argument – WorkItemId

- Value – 9000

Example 9.1 CandidateFacadeSession Code

```
package ActionAdapter;
import javax.ejb.EJBException;
import javax.ejb.SessionContext;
import java.rmi.RemoteException;

public class CandidateFacadeSession implements
    javax.ejb.SessionBean {
  public void createCandidate(CandidateTO to)
      throws CandidateException {
    CandidateAppService as = new CandidateAppService();
    as.createCandidate(to.getId(),
    to.getLname(),
    to.getFname(),
    to.getStreet(),
    to.getCity(),
    to.getState(),
    to.getZip(),
    new WorkflowContext(
        to.getWorkflowName(), to.getWorkflowProcessId(),
        to.getWorkItemId()) );
  }

  public void submitReview(CandidateTO to,
      ReviewInfoTO rto ) {
    CandidateAppService as = new CandidateAppService();
    as.submitReview(to.getId(), rto,
    new WorkflowContext(
        to.getWorkflowName(), to.getWorkflowProcessId(),
        to.getWorkItemId() ) );
  }

  public void submitInterview(CandidateTO to,
      InterviewInfoTO ito) throws CandidateException {
    CandidateAppService as = new CandidateAppService();
    as.submitInterview(to.getId(), ito,
    new WorkflowContext(
        to.getWorkflowName(), to.getWorkflowProcessId(),
        to.getWorkItemId() ) );
  }
```

```
    public void setSessionContext(SessionContext sessionContext)
        throws EJBException, RemoteException { }

    public void ejbRemove() throws EJBException,
        RemoteException { }

    public void ejbActivate() throws EJBException,
        RemoteException { }

    public void ejbPassivate() throws EJBException,
        RemoteException { }
}
```

Example 9.2 HireEmployeAA Code

```
package ActionAdapter;

import Core.HireEmployeeConstants;

public class HireEmployeeAA {
  WorkflowCommandFactory factory;

  public HireEmployeeAA() {
    factory = WorkflowCommandFactory.getInstance();
  }

  public void candidateCreated(String userId,
      String workflowProcessId, String workItemId) {
    doCommand(userId, workflowProcessId, workItemId,
        HireEmployeeConstants.CANDIDATE_CREATED);
  }

  public void candidateInterviewed(String userId,
      String workflowProcessId, String workItemId) {
    doCommand(userId, workflowProcessId, workItemId,
        HireEmployeeConstants.CANDIDATE_INTERVIEWED);
  }

  public void candidateReviewed(String userId,
      String workflowProcessId, String workItemId) {

    doCommand(userId, workflowProcessId, workItemId,
        HireEmployeeConstants.CANDIDATE_REVIEWED);
```

```
  }

  private void doCommand(String userId,
      String workflowProcessId, String workItemId,
      String action) {
    WorkflowCommand command =
    factory.createCommand( userId, workflowProcessId,
        workItemId, action );
    command.execute();
  }
}
```

Example 9.3 HireEmployeeConstants Code

```
package Core;

public class HireEmployeeConstants {
  final public static int START_WORKFLOW_TYPE = 1;
  final public static int STOP_WORKFLOW_TYPE = 2;
  final public static int PAUSE_WORKFLOW_TYPE = 3;

  final public static int ACQUIRE_WORKITEM_TYPE = 4;
  final public static int COMMIT_WORKITEM_TYPE = 5;
  final public static int ABORT_WORKITEM_TYPE = 6;

  final public static String START_WORKFLOW = "StartWorkflow";
  final public static String STOP_WORKFLOW = "StopWorkflow";
  final public static String PAUSE_WORKFLOW = "PauseWorkflow";

  final public static String ACQUIRE_WORKITEM =
      "AcquireWorkItem";
  final public static String COMMIT_WORKITEM =
      "CommitWorkItem";
  final public static String ABORT_WORKITEM = "AbortWorkItem";
  final public static String CANDIDATE_CREATED =
      "CandidateCreated";
  final public static String CANDIDATE_REVIEWED =
      "CandidateReviewed";
  final public static String CANDIDATE_INTERVIEWED =
      "CandidateInterviewed";
}
```

Example 9.4 ActionMapper Code

```
package ActionAdapter;

import Core.HireEmployeeConstants;
import java.util.Properties;

public class ActionMapper {
  String workflowName = "HireEmployee";
  String mapFile;

  public ActionMapper(String mapFile) {
    this.mapFile = mapFile;
  }

  public CommandData getCommandData(String action,
      String workflowProcessId, String workItemId) {
    // Get real commandString from mapFile using Action
    String commandString = "";
    // Get properties from mapFile for Action
    Properties properties = null;
    CommandData data = null;
    if(commandString.equals(
        HireEmployeeConstants.START_WORKFLOW)) {
      data = new WorkflowCommandData(workflowName,
          workflowProcessId, HireEmployeeConstants.
          START_WORKFLOW_TYPE);
    } else if (commandString.equals(
        HireEmployeeConstants.STOP_WORKFLOW)) {
      data = new WorkflowCommandData(workflowName,
          workflowProcessId, HireEmployeeConstants.
          STOP_WORKFLOW_TYPE);
    } else if(commandString.equals(
        HireEmployeeConstants.PAUSE_WORKFLOW)) {
      data = new WorkflowCommandData(workflowName,
          workflowProcessId, HireEmployeeConstants.
          PAUSE_WORKFLOW_TYPE);
    } else if(commandString.equals(
        HireEmployeeConstants.ACQUIRE_WORKITEM)) {
      data = new WorkItemCommandData(workItemId,
          HireEmployeeConstants.ACQUIRE_WORKITEM_TYPE);
    } else if(commandString.equals(
        HireEmployeeConstants.ABORT_WORKITEM)) {
```

```
      data = new WorkItemCommandData(workItemId,
        HireEmployeeConstants.ABORT_WORKITEM_TYPE);
    } else {
      data = new WorkItemCommandData(workItemId,
        HireEmployeeConstants.COMMIT_WORKITEM_TYPE);
    }
      return data;
  }
}
```

Exampie 9.5 HireEmployeeActionMap.xml File

```
<ActionMap>
  <Action Name="CandidateCreated">
    <WorkerRole>HR Screener</WorkerRole>
    <WorkflowProcessCommand>StartWorkflow
    </WorkflowProcessCommand>
    <WorkflowName>HireEmployee</WorkflowName>
  </Action>
  <Action Name="ReviewResume">
    <WorkerRole>HR Reviewer</WorkerRole>
    <WorkItemCommand>CommitWorkItem</WorkItemCommand>
  </Action>
  <Action Name="CandidateInterviewed">
    <WorkerRole>HR Reviewer</WorkerRole>
    <WorkItemCommand>CommitWorkItem</WorkItemCommand>
  </Action>
</ActionMap>
```

Example 9.6 CommandData, WorkflowCommandData and WorkItemCommandData Code

```
package ActionAdapter;

abstract public class CommandData {

  protected int commandType;

  protected CommandData(int commandType) {
    this.commandType = commandType;
  }

  public int getCommandType() {
    return commandType;
```

```
    }
}
```

```
package ActionAdapter;
public class WorkflowCommandData extends CommandData {
  private String workflowName;
  private String workflowProcessId;

  public WorkflowCommandData(String workflowName,
      String workflowProcessId, int commandType) {
    super(commandType);
    this.workflowName = workflowName;
    this.workflowProcessId = workflowProcessId;
  }

  public void setWorkflowName(String workflowName) {
    this.workflowName = workflowName;
  }

  public void setWorkflowProcessid(String workflowProcessId) {
    this.workflowProcessId = workflowProcessId;
  }

  public String getWorkflowProcessId() {
    return workflowProcessId;
  }

  public String getWorkflowName() {
    return workflowName;
  }
}

```

```
package ActionAdapter;

public class WorkItemCommandData extends CommandData {
  private String workItemId;

  public WorkItemCommandData(String workItemId,
      int commandType) {
    super(commandType);
    this.workItemId = workItemId;
  }
```

```

  public String getWorkItemId() {
    return workItemId;
  }
}
```

Example 9.7 ReviewInfoTO, InterviewInfoTO and WorkflowContext Code

```
package ActionAdapter;

import java.io.Serializable;

public class ReviewInfoTO implements Serializable {
  private String notes;
  private int rating;

  public ReviewInfoTO( String notes, int rating ) {
    this.notes = notes;
    this.rating = rating;
  }
  public String getNotes() {
    return notes;
  }
  public int getRating() {
    return rating;
  }
}

```

```
package ActionAdapter;

import java.io.Serializable;

public class InterviewInfoTO implements Serializable {
  private String notes;
  private int rating;

  public InterviewInfoTO( String notes, int rating ) {
    this.notes = notes;
    this.rating = rating;
  }
  public String getNotes() {
    return notes;
```

```
  }
  public int getRating() {
    return rating;
  }
}

```

```
package ActionAdapter;

public class WorkflowContext {
  String workflowName;
  String workflowProcessId;
  String workItemId;

  public WorkflowContext(String workflowName,
      String workflowProcessId, String workItemId) {
    this.workflowName = workflowName;
    this.workflowProcessId = workflowProcessId;
    this.workItemId = workItemId;
  }

  public String getWorkflowName() {
    return workflowName;
  }
  public String getWorkflowProcessId() {
    return workflowProcessId;
  }
  public String getWorkItemId() {
    return workItemId;
  }
}
```

Example 9.8 CandidateAppService Code

```
package ActionAdapter;

public class CandidateAppService {
  public void createCandidate(String userId, String lname,
      String fname, String street, String city, String state,
      String zip, WorkflowContext context ) {
    // do logic
    // store data
    HireEmployeeAA aa = new HireEmployeeAA();
```

```
    aa.candidateCreated(userId,context.getWorkflowProcessId(),
        context.getWorkItemId() );
  }
  public void submitReview(String userId, ReviewInfoTO to,
      WorkflowContext context ) {
    // do logic
    // store data
    HireEmployeeAA aa = new HireEmployeeAA();
    aa.candidateReviewed(userId,
        context.getWorkflowProcessId(),
        context.getWorkItemId());
  }
  public void submitInterview(String userId,
      InterviewInfoTO to, WorkflowContext context)
      throws CandidateException {
    // do logic
    // store data
    HireEmployeeAA aa = new HireEmployeeAA();
    aa.candidateInterviewed(userId,
        context.getWorkflowProcessId(),
        context.getWorkItemId());
  }
}
```

Example 9.9 WorkflowCommandFactory Code

```
package ActionAdapter;

public class WorkflowCommandFactory {
  final String ACTION_MAP = "ActionMapper.xml";
  ActionMapper map;

  static private WorkflowCommandFactory me =
      new WorkflowCommandFactory();

  protected WorkflowCommandFactory() { }

  public static WorkflowCommandFactory getInstance() {
    return me;
  }

  public WorkflowCommand createCommand(String userId,
      String workflowProcessId, String workItemId,
```

```
        String action) {

      ActionMapper mapper = new ActionMapper(ACTION_MAP);

      CommandData commandData =
          mapper.getCommandData(action,
          workflowProcessId, workItemId);

      if (commandData.getClass() == WorkflowCommandData.class) {
        return new WorkflowProcessCommand(userId, commandData);
      } else if (
          commandData.getClass() == WorkItemCommandData.class) {
        return new WorkItemCommand(userId, commandData);
      }
      return null;
    }
}
```

Example 9.10 WorkflowCommand, WorkflowProcessCommand and WorkItemCommand Code

```

package ActionAdapter;

public interface WorkflowCommand {
  public void execute();
}

```

```
package ActionAdapter;

import Core.HireEmployeeConstants;

public class WorkflowProcessCommand
    implements WorkflowCommand {
  private String userId;
  private CommandData commandData;

  public WorkflowProcessCommand(String userId,
      CommandData commandData) {
    this.userId = userId;
    this.commandData = commandData;
  }
```

```
  public void execute() {
    WorkflowCommandData d = (WorkflowCommandData) commandData;
    String workflowName = d.getWorkflowName();
    String workflowProcessId = d.getWorkflowProcessId();
    WorkflowDelegate delegate = new WorkflowDelegate(userId);
    if (d.commandType ==
        HireEmployeeConstants.START_WORKFLOW_TYPE) {
      delegate.start(workflowName);
    } else if (d.commandType ==
        HireEmployeeConstants.STOP_WORKFLOW_TYPE) {
      delegate.stop(workflowProcessId);
    } else if (d.commandType ==
        HireEmployeeConstants.PAUSE_WORKFLOW_TYPE) {
      delegate.pause(workflowProcessId);
    }
  }
}
```

```
package ActionAdapter;

import Core.HireEmployeeConstants;

public class WorkItemCommand implements WorkflowCommand {
  private String userId;
  private CommandData commandData;

  public WorkItemCommand(String userId,
      CommandData commandData) {
    this.userId = userId;
    this.commandData = commandData;
  }

  public void execute() {
    WorkItemCommandData d = (WorkItemCommandData) commandData;
    String workItemId = d.getWorkItemId();
    WorkflowDelegate delegate = new WorkflowDelegate(userId);
    if (d.commandType ==
        HireEmployeeConstants.ACQUIRE_WORKITEM_TYPE) {
      delegate.acquireWorkItem(workItemId);
    } else if (d.commandType ==
        HireEmployeeConstants.COMMIT_WORKITEM_TYPE) {
      delegate.commitWorkItem(workItemId);
```

```
    } else if (d.commandType ==
        HireEmployeeConstants.ABORT_WORKITEM_TYPE) {
      delegate.abortWorkItem(workItemId);
    }
  }
}
```

Example 9.11 WorkflowDelegate Code

```
public class WorkflowDelegate {
  private String userId;

  public WorkflowDelegate(String userId) {
    this.userId = userId;
  }

  public void start(String workflowName) {
    // Proprietary call to workflow system
  }

  public void stop(String workflowProcessId) {
    // Proprietary call to workflow system
  }

  public void pause(String workflowProcessId) {
    // Proprietary call to workflow system
  }

  public void acquireWorkItem(String workflowProcessId) {
    // Proprietary call to workflow system
  }

  public void commitWorkItem(String workflowProcessId) {
    // Proprietary call to workflow system
  }

  public void abortWorkItem(String workflowProcessId) {
    // Proprietary call to workflow system
  }
}
```

Work Adapter Components

Figure 9.8 shows the Work Adapter for the Candidate interactions diagram.

Before the Work Adapter gets invoked for reviewing a candidate, the following occurs:

- The HR Screener creates a candidate, which causes the HireEmployee workflow process to begin.
- The workflow system generates a ReviewCandidate work-item (id = 8000) and sends it to all HR Reviewers worklists.
- An HR Reviewer acquires the work item and reviews the candidate.

The next steps follow:

1. The workflow system notifies the HireEmployeeWA (WorkAdapter) that the work item id = 8000 has been acquired
2. The HireEmployeeWA asks the WorkPageFactory to create a WorkPageRef
3. The WorkPageFactory in turn asks the WorkMapper, which consults the HireEmployeeWorkMap to get the WorkPage URL, and returns the WorkPageRef to the HireEmployeeAA (ActionAdapter)
4. The HireEmployeeAA extracts the work page URL, HireEmployee/CandidateReview.jsp?WorkItemId=8000 and sends the URL to the EmailDispatcher
5. The EmailDispatcher sends an email it to the HR Reviewer which contains the URL
6. Once the HR Reviewer finishes the interview, he or she submits the page, which causes the *Action Adapter* to commit the work item

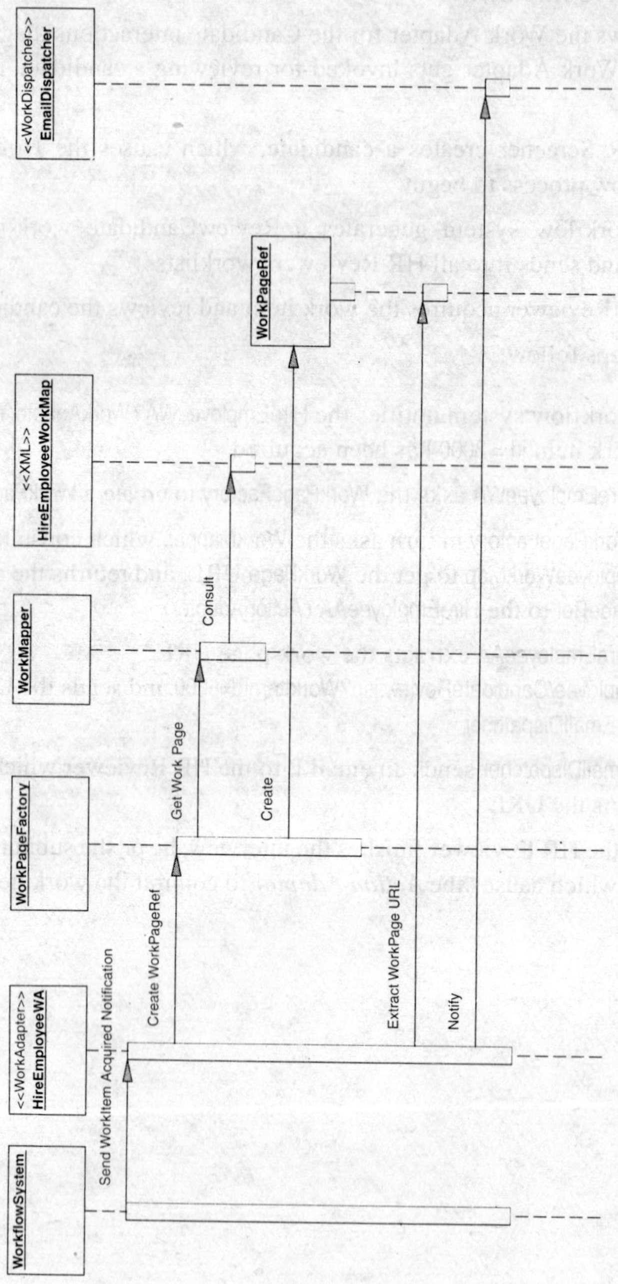

Figure 9.8 Work Adapter for the Candidate Interactions Diagram

The steps for Interviewing a Candidate are the same as the steps for Reviewing a Candidate, with the following exceptions:

1. The workflow system notifies the HireEmployeeWA (WorkAdapter) that the work item ID = 9000 has been acquired
2. The HireEmployeeAA extracts the work page URL, HireEmployee/CandidateInterview.jsp?WorkItemId=9000 and sends the URL to the EmailDispatcher. The workflow system notifies the HireEmployeeWA (WorkAdapter) that the work item id = 9000 has been acquired.
3. The HireEmployeeAA extracts the work page URL, HireEmployee/CandidateInterview.jsp?WorkItemId=9000 and sends the URL to the EmailDispatcher

Code for Work Adapter

The following list shows HireEmployeeWA.workitemAcquired() method and the arguments and values for each interaction.

Interactions and HireEmployeeWA workItemAcquired() Information

Create Candidate

- workItemAcquired() arguments – userId, userRole ,workflowName, workItemName, workItemId
- workItemAcquired() values – User-101, HRReviewer, HireEmployee, SubmitReview, 8000
- Action taken after WorkItem acquired – HR Reviewer reviews resume

Review Candidate

- workItemAcquired() arguments – userId, userRole, workflowName, workItemName, workItemId
- **workItemAcquired() values** – User-102, HRReviewer, HireEmployee, SubmitReview, 9000
- Action taken after WorkItem acquired – HR Reviewer interviews candidate

Interview Candidate

- workItemAcquired() arguments – userId, userRole, workflowName, workItemName, workItemId

- workItemAcquired() values – User-103, PeerReviewer, HireEmployee, SubmitInterview, 10000
- Action taken after WorkItem acquired – Peer interviews candidate

Then the HireEmployeeWA workItemAcquired() method calls the WorkPageFactory createWorkPageRef() method shown in Listing 9.13. In turn, that method calls the WorkMapper getWorkPageRef() shown in Listing 9.14.

The WorkMapper consults the HireEmployeeWorkMap.xml file shown in Listing 9.15 to get the actual WorkPage based on the workflow event, work item name and user role. The WorkMapper returns a WorkPageRef shown in Listing 9.16. Finally, the HireEmployeeWA sends the WorkPage URL to the EmailDispatcher shown in Listing 9.17.

Example 9.12 HireEmployeeWA Code

```
package WorkAdapter;

import Core.HireEmployeeConstants;
import Core.UtilHelper;

public class HireEmployeeWA {

  public void workflowProcessStarted(String workflowName,
      String workflowProcessId, String userId) { }

  public void workflowProcessStopped(String workflowName,
      String workflowProcessId, String userId) { }

  public void workflowProcessPaused(String workflowName,
      String workflowProcessId, String userId) { }

  public void workItemAcquired(String userId, String userRole,
      String workflowName, String workItemName,
      String workItemId) {
    WorkPageFactory f = WorkPageFactory.getInstance();
    WorkPageRef ref = f.createWorkPageRef(userId, userRole,
        HireEmployeeConstants.ACQUIRE_WORKITEM, workflowName,
        null, workItemName, workItemId);
      String email = UtilHelper.userIdToEmail(userId);
      WorkDispatcher dispatcher =
          new EmailDispatcher(workflowName, ref.getURL(),
          email);
      dispatcher.dispatch();
```

```
  }

  public void workItemAborted(String workflowName,
      String workItemId, String userId, String userRole) { }

  public void workItemCommitted(String userId,
      String userRole, String workflowName,
      String workItemId) { }
}
```

Example 9.13 WorkPageFactory Code

```
package WorkAdapter;

public class WorkPageFactory {
  final String WORK_MAP = "WorkMapper.xml";

  private static WorkPageFactory me;

  public synchronized static WorkPageFactory getInstance() {
    if (me == null) {
      me = new WorkPageFactory();
    }
    return me;
  }

  private WorkPageFactory() { }

  public WorkPageRef createWorkPageRef(String userId,
      String userRole, String workflowEvent,
      String workflowName, String workflowProcessId,
      String workItemName, String workItemId) {
    WorkMapper map = new WorkMapper(WORK_MAP);
    String ref = map.getWorkPageRef(WORK_MAP, workflowEvent,
        workflowName, workItemName, userRole);
    return new WorkPageRef(ref, userId, workflowProcessId,
        workItemId);
  }
}
```

Example 9.14 WorkMapper Code

```
package WorkAdapter;

public class WorkMapper {
  public WorkMapper(String map) { }

  public String getWorkPageRef(String workMapFile,
      String action, String workflowName, String workItemName,
      String userRole) {
    // Lookup up WorkPage in the workMapFile
    return null;
  }
}
```

Example 9.15 HireEmployeeWorkMap.xml File

```
<WorkMap>
  <WorkflowEvent Type="AcquireWorkItem">
    <WorkItem>
      <Name>SubmitReview</Name>
      <UserRole>HR Reviewer</UserRole>
      <WorkPage>HireEmployee/CandidateReview.jsp</WorkPage>
    </WorkItem>
  </WorkflowEvent>
  <WorkflowEvent Type="AcquireWorkItem">
    <WorkItem>
      <Name>SubmitInterview</Name>
      <UserRole>Peer Reviewer</UserRole>
      <WorkPage>HireEmployee/CandidateInterview.jsp</WorkPage>
    </WorkItem>
  </WorkflowEvent>
</WorkMap>
```

Example 9.16 WorkPageRef Code

```
package WorkAdapter;

public class WorkPageRef {
  String workPageRef;
  String userId;
  String workflowProcessId;
  String workItemId;

  public WorkPageRef() { }
```

```

  public WorkPageRef(String workPageRef, String userId,
      String workflowProcessId, String workItemId) {
    this.workPageRef = workPageRef;
    this.userId = userId;
    this.workflowProcessId = workflowProcessId;
    this.workItemId = workItemId;
  }

  public String getURL() {
    StringBuffer s = new StringBuffer(workPageRef);
    s.append("?UserId=");
    s.append(userId);

    if (workflowProcessId != null && workItemId != null) {
      s.append("?");
    }
    if (workflowProcessId != null) {
      s.append("&WorkflowProcesId=").
      append(workflowProcessId);
    }
    if (workItemId != null) {
      s.append("&WorkItemId=").append(workItemId);
    }
    return s.toString();
  }
}
```

Example 9.17 WorkDispatcher, EmailDispatcher and WorkListDispatcher Code

```
package WorkAdapter;

abstract public class WorkDispatcher {
  String workflowName;
  String workPageURL;
  String email;


  public WorkDispatcher(String workflowName,
      String workPageURL, String email) {
    this.workflowName = workflowName;
    this.workPageURL = workPageURL;
```

```
      this.email = email;
    }
    public abstract void dispatch();
  }

  package WorkAdapter;

  public class EmailDispatcher extends WorkDispatcher {

    public EmailDispatcher(String workflowName,
        String workPageURL, String email) {
      super( workflowName, workPageURL, email );
    }
    public void dispatch() {
      // Notify user via email
    }
  }

  package WorkAdapter;

  public class WorkListDispatcher extends WorkDispatcher {

    public WorkListDispatcher(String workflowName,
        String workPageURL, String email) {
      super(workflowName, workPageURL, email);
    }
    public void dispatch() {
      // Notify Worklist
    }
  }
```

Refactoring Required for Web Application

The goal of *Web Worker* is to integrate users, web application, and workflow system with minimal change to the existing web application. However, in order to achieve this, you need to do some refactoring:

Presentation Tier

1. If the WorkItemId and/or the WorkflowProcessId parameters are passed in from the URL, the presentation tier component must extract the parameters.
2. If the presentation-tier helper sends a *Transfer Object* (415) to the *Business Delegate* (302), then it must add the WorkItemId and WorkflowProcessId to the *Transfer Object* (415).

Business Tier

3. Add a WorkItemId and WorkflowProcessId fields to the relevant *Transfer Object* (415).
4. Have the SessionFacade or ApplicationService invoke the ActionAdapter after the transaction is completed.

The following set of lists shows the refactoring table for the web application. For each workflow command type, the table lists the data needed by the Workflow System and the refactoring needed by the presentation components, BusinessDelegate, and TransferObject.

Refactorings for Workflow Event

Start Workflow Process

- What's needed by the Workflow system – Workflow Name
- Presentation components refactoring – None
- BusinessDelegate refactoring – None
- TransferObject refactoring – None

Stop, Pause and Terminate Workflow Process

- What's needed by the Workflow system – Workflow Process Id
- Presentation components refactoring – Extract WorkflowProcessId and add it to TransferObject
- BusinessDelegate refactoring – Add set/unset WorkflowProcessId() methods and set WorkflowProcessId in TransferObject
- TransferObject refactoring – Add WorkflowProcessId field

Acquire WorkItem

- What's needed by the Workflow system – WorkItem Id
- Presentation components refactoring – None
- BusinessDelegate refactoring – None
- TransferObject refactoring – None

Commit and Abort WorkItem

- What's needed by the Workflow system – WorkItem Id
- Presentation components refactoring – Extract WorkItemId and add it to TransferObject
- BusinessDelegate refactoring – Add set/unset WorkItemId methods and set WorkItemId in TransferObject
- TransferObject refactoring – Add WorkItemId field

Consequences

- ***Separation of business logic and process logic***
- ***Provides a clean separation of concerns***
- ***Relieves business logic from having to understand process logic***
- ***Allows developer to write business logic code without being affected by changes to the business flow code***
- ***Associates role security with process logic***
- ***Creates a separation of security roles between business logic and process logic***
- ***Requires additional expertise and maintenance for workflow system***
- ***Requires workflow process definition expertise***
- ***Requires custom code to integrate with the workflow system***

The Apache Software License, Version 1.1

Redistribution and use in source and binary forms, with or without modification, are permitted provided that the following conditions are met:

1. Redistributions of source code must retain the above copyright notice, this list of conditions and the following disclaimer.

2. Redistributions in binary form must reproduce the above copyright notice, this list of conditions and the following disclaimer in the documentation and/or other materials provided with the distribution.

3. The end-user documentation included with the redistribution, if any, must include the following acknowledgement:

"This product includes software developed by the Apache Software Foundation (http://www.apache.org/)."
Alternately, this acknowlegement may appear in the software itself, if and wherever such third-party acknowlegements normally appear.

4. The names "The Jakarta Project", "Tomcat", and "Apache Software Foundation" must not be used to endorse or promote products derived from this software without prior written permission. For written permission, please contact apache@apache.org.

5. Products derived from this software may not be called "Apache" nor may "Apache" appear in their names without prior written permission of the Apache Group.

THIS SOFTWARE IS PROVIDED ``AS IS'' AND ANY EXPRESSED OR IMPLIED WARRANTIES, INCLUDING, BUT NOT LIMITED TO, THE IMPLIED WARRANTIES. OF MERCHANTABILITY AND FITNESS FOR A PARTICULAR PURPOSE ARE DISCLAIMED. IN NO EVENT SHALL THE APACHE SOFTWARE FOUNDATION OR ITS CONTRIBUTORS BE LIABLE FOR ANY DIRECT, INDIRECT, INCIDENTAL, SPECIAL, EXEMPLARY, OR CONSEQUENTIAL DAMAGES (INCLUDING, BUT NOT LIMITED TO, PROCUREMENT OF SUBSTITUTE GOODS OR SERVICES; LOSS OF USE, DATA, OR PROFITS; OR BUSINESS INTERRUPTION) HOWEVER CAUSED AND ON ANY THEORY OF LIABILITY, WHETHER IN CONTRACT, STRICT LIABILITY, OR TORT (INCLUDING NEGLIGENCE OR OTHERWISE) ARISING IN ANY WAY OUT OF THE USE OF THIS SOFTWARE, EVEN IF ADVISED OF THE POSSIBILITY OF SUCH DAMAGE.

This software consists of voluntary contributions made by many individuals on behalf of the Apache Software Foundation. For more information on the Apache Software Foundation, please see <http://www.apache.org/>.]

Index

A

G

H

I

Q

S

U

V